M000035794

OFFICE SYSTEMS AND PROCEDURES

Second Edition

ERASE EOL
PRINT
7
8
4
5
6
1
2
3
Ø
.

OFFICE SYSTEMS AND PROCEDURES

Second Edition

CHERYL M. LUKE
University of South Carolina

C. B. STIEGLER
Northern Kentucky University

GLENCOE
McGraw-Hill
New York, New York   Columbus, Ohio   Mission Hills, California   Peoria, Illinois

Cheryl M. Luke is an Associate Professor of Business Administration at the University of South Carolina. Prior to receiving her doctorate at Indiana University she taught for several years at the high school level and acquired full-time secretarial experience. She maintains her involvement with secretaries, their supervisors, and their employers through the seminars and in-house training programs she conducts for professional organizations and businesses. Dr. Luke is active in professional organizations, including the National Business Education Association, Association of Business Communications, and National Collegiate Association for Secretaries. She has been involved in researching the competencies needed for the electronic office.

C. B. Stiegler is Professor of Business at Northern Kentucky University. She has written extensively and is a frequent lecturer before teacher and business groups. In her capacity as Coordinator of Business Education Teacher Preparation Programs at Northern Kentucky, Dr. Stiegler works closely with classroom teachers. In addition, she has a private consulting firm specializing in motivational and productivity techniques for management and support personnel. Dr. Stiegler is active in professional organizations, including the Administrative Management Society, National Business Education Association, and American Vocational Association.

The authors wish to thank the many office procedures teachers around the country for their suggestions and comments, and particularly those teachers and their students who contributed to the revision process through their participation in the learner verification study.

Cover Design by Russell Brough
Cover Photograph by Malysko Photography

Imprint 1995

Printed in the United States of America.

ISBN: 0-395-38429-X
6 7 8 9 10 11 12 13 14 15 RAN/LP 00 99 98 97 96 95

C O N T E N T S

UNIT 1

UNIT 2

UNIT 3

UNIT 4

ADMINISTRATIVE SUPPORT RESPONSIBILITIES

UNIT 5

TELECOMMUNICATIONS IN THE OFFICE

UNIT 6

MAILING AND SHIPPING PROCEDURES

UNIT 7

BUSINESS CORRESPONDENCE

UNIT 8

BUSINESS REPORTS AND SPECIAL DOCUMENTS

UNIT 9

RECORDS MANAGEMENT SYSTEMS

UNIT 10

FILING SYSTEMS

UNIT 11

REPROGRAPHIC SYSTEMS

UNIT 12

INFORMATION PROCESSING SYSTEMS

UNIT 13

UNIT 14

UNIT 15

APPENDIXES

PREFACE

The character of the business office has changed considerably in recent years, and with it, the role of the office worker. One of the major influences has been the increased reliance on electronic technology. Today, computers are utilized in telecommunications, information processing, reprographics, records management, and inventory control. With the existence of computer networks, these business functions have become more interdependent, necessitating the integration of systems and procedures.

These changes in today's office have created a demand for office workers with a broader variety of skills, an awareness of the interrelatedness of office functions, and a knowledge of new procedures and terminology. In addition, today's employees are expected to demonstrate good human relations skills, exercise sound judgment, be cost conscious, and apply time management principles.

Objectives

Office Systems and Procedures, Second Edition, is designed to prepare students for employment opportunities in today's rapidly changing business environment. This new edition, which builds on the strengths of the previous edition, has been revised to help students:

1. Acquire skills and knowledge of office procedures and equipment.
2. Apply skills and knowledge gained in other business courses.
3. Utilize time management principles, cost-effective techniques, and decision-making skills in their work.
4. Develop personal characteristics, work attitudes, and communication skills essential for success on the job.
5. Understand the interrelatedness of office systems—their procedures, equipment, and workers.

Organization

Office Systems and Procedures can be used in a one- or two-semester course and in a variety of classroom settings. The textbook consists of 46 chapters divided into 15 units. Units 1–3 discuss employment skills, such as communication, human relations, and organization. In Units 4–10, a solid foundation in office skills and procedures is developed. These skills and procedures are related to major office systems, such as filing, information processing, and accounting, in Units 11–13. In Unit 14, a new unit, a model company illustrates how office systems are integrated. Unit 15, with its focus on employment, is an appropriate conclusion to this job-oriented textbook.

Features

The authors' primary goal in revising *Office Systems and Procedures* has been to present the most up-to-date information on actual office practices. Attention has been given to providing realistic office experiences through end-of-chapter activities. This attention to realism also appears in the four simulation activities, in which students not only complete tasks, but determine priorities and procedures for completing them.

Secondly, attention has been paid to the readability of the materials and to the development of a business vocabulary. A new feature of this edition is a glossary of all boldfaced terms.

In addition to realism and readability, the *Office Systems and Procedures* materials are designed to reinforce other skills, such as language arts and math. Grammar, punctuation, spelling, and math activities are included at the end of each chapter and keyed to the Appendixes.

Supporting Materials

Office Systems and Procedures is the cornerstone of a complete instructional program consisting of a workbook, tests, and a teacher's manual. The workbook, *Student Activities,* contains business stationery for end-of-chapter activities, optional proofreading activities, the four office simulation activities, and an optional information processing activity. Each four-to-five-hour simulation is designed to be used individually at the completion of specified units. The simulations can also be combined as a capstone project.

The student package is rounded out by a complete testing program. The 32-page test booklet contains unit tests, a midterm, and a final examination. The teacher's manual provides an additional testing option in the form of chapter tests on blackline masters. It also includes general methodology; course outlines for one- and two-semester courses; suggestions for tailoring the course to secretarial, clerical, and other specialized emphases; teaching suggestions and additional activities for each unit; dictation activities; and transparency masters. Answer keys are provided for all activities and tests.

Cheryl M. Luke and C. B. Stiegler

UNIT 1

THE PROFESSIONAL OFFICE WORKER

- Careers in Modern Offices
- Skills for Success
- Personal Qualifications for Success

CHAPTER 1

CAREERS IN MODERN OFFICES

You are beginning to prepare for an office career. You will be excited to know that this is an area of employment with a great demand. This demand is predicted to continue through the 1990's. If you look in the Help Wanted ads in your local newspaper, you will realize just how many job openings there are for office support workers, such as receptionists, secretaries, administrative assistants, clerk-typists, and word processing operators.

With an office career, you can work just about anywhere. Because opportunities are available in all sections of the United States, you will probably be able to find an office position wherever you live. With your office skills and knowledge you can be sure that you will be able to contribute to the success of the city, state, and country in which you live by being a productive worker.

As you study this chapter, you will find answers to the following questions:

- How does the use of automated office equipment increase the demand for office workers?
- Why are office workers often referred to as office support workers?
- Why are office careers exciting and fulfilling?
- How can you prepare for a career as an office worker?
- What do the following terms mean: **procedures, office support workers, interpersonal skill?**

THE DEMAND FOR OFFICE WORKERS

One benefit of an office career is that skilled office workers are always in demand. Automated office equipment provides information faster and in larger quantities than ever before possible. As a result, more office workers who understand new technologies are needed to help process this additional information.

The need for more office workers because of growth is only part of the demand. Office workers will also be needed to replace employees who stop working for personal reasons, retire, or die.

Opportunities for office workers exist not only in all parts of the country but in all types of businesses. Depending on your interests and training, you may work in a business office, government agency, doctor's or lawyer's office, factory, or retail store.

THE MODERN BUSINESS OFFICE

The modern business office is an exciting place to work. The technological changes that have taken place in recent years have improved the procedures for performing tasks. As a result, office workers have become more accurate and efficient.

mo·not'o·nous

ac'ti·vate

Today's office work is no longer monotonous and tedious. Tasks that were completed by hand a few years ago are now done quickly and accurately by machines. The human voice can now be used to activate a computer and produce printed copy. There are even computers that can actually talk. In

Illustration 1 – 1 Skilled office workers are needed to fill a variety of positions

many offices, text-editing equipment that can find keyboarding errors is frequently used. In many other offices, desk-top computer terminals are used. All of these improvements help make office careers exciting.

ADVANTAGES OF AN OFFICE CAREER

Office workers generally have many benefits, such as pleasant working conditions, the systematic nature of work, good salary and employee benefits, and opportunities for advancement.

Pleasant Working Conditions

tem'per·a·ture

Most offices provide an attractive and comfortable setting for office workers. Office furniture is designed to provide comfort and efficient work space. Proper lighting and attractive use of color are combined to reduce eye strain. Temperature controls provide uniform heat and cooling so that workers do not get too tired. Noise is reduced through the use of carpet, wall coverings, and even plants. Modern equipment and proper supplies help office workers to perform tasks effectively. All of these factors help produce a pleasant working environment.

The Systematic Nature of Office Work

Most office workers are responsible for certain tasks within the office. Set responsibilities enable workers to develop regular schedules or routines for

Illustration 1 – 2 Modern office equipment has increased efficiency and accuracy

Illustration 1 – 3 Many office workers enjoy comfortable, attractive surroundings

completing work. Most office tasks follow set **procedures** or guidelines so that workers can complete the tasks more efficiently. These procedures allow office workers to use their time most efficiently to complete their assigned tasks in a systematic way. Most office workers like to know exactly what is to be done and how each task is to be completed. This knowledge helps office workers gain confidence in their ability to work effectively.

sys·tem·at'ic

Salary and Employee Benefits

Salaries for office workers depend on several things, including the supply of and demand for skilled workers, the cost of living in the area, the size of the company, the nature of the job, and the skills and experience of the employee. Most full-time employees are paid by the hour and work 35 to 40 hours a week. If they must work overtime, they receive one and one-half times the regular hourly rate of pay for the additional hours.

ben'e·fits

Most companies provide a number of benefits for employees in addition to the regular pay. Employee benefits may include the following:

- paid vacation
- sick leave
- life insurance
- medical and dental insurance
- maternity leave
- free parking
- disability income
- pension plans
- stock purchase plans
- profit-sharing plans
- educational assistance plans
- accident insurance

It is expensive to provide these benefits for workers. Employee benefits can cost the company as much as 35 percent of the salaries paid to employees. For example, if a company pays a $10,000 salary to an employee, it may also provide up to $3,500 in benefits. Employees are helped by benefits because they would have to pay for these benefits themselves if the company did not provide them.

Opportunities for Advancement

op'por·tu·ni·ties

As you develop your skills and gain experience, you will find opportunities to assume more responsibility. Many companies prefer to promote their own employees to better positions rather than hire outsiders. A promotion not only means more responsibility and challenge; it usually means a higher salary as well. Your opportunities for advancement will depend on the size of the company, the needs of the individual departments, and your level of skill and ability.

Some office workers start in a position such as a receptionist. As these workers gain experience and improve their skills, they may be promoted to positions as typists or word processing operators. If these workers continue to improve their skills and increase their knowledge, they may be promoted to positions as secretaries. From there, they may move up to become executive secretaries or administrative assistants.

THE ROLE OF OFFICE WORKERS

Office workers, with their knowledge and skills, assist all levels of a business. Because office workers support the work of every department of a company,

Illustration 1 – 4
Skill and experience bring opportunities for advancement

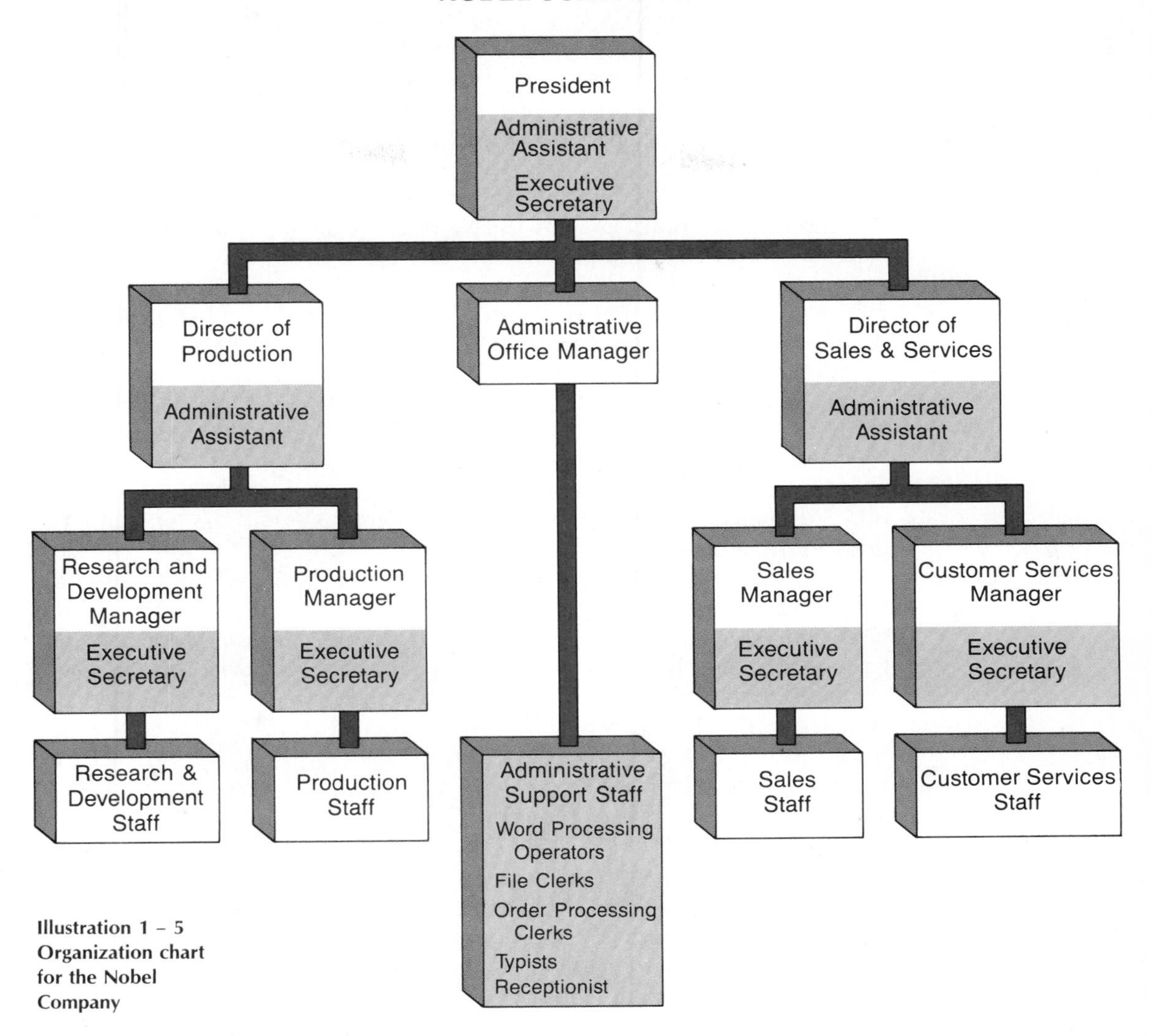

Illustration 1 – 5 Organization chart for the Nobel Company

they are also referred to as **office support workers.** Illustration 1 – 5 shows that the Nobel Company has a large office support staff. Administrative and executive secretaries report to a single executive or manager. They handle much of the daily paperwork and tasks for the executive. They also assist the executive in providing information to the employees who report to the executive, to other company employees, and to customers. The Administrative Support Staff — word processing operators, file clerks, accounting clerks, order processing clerks, typists, and the receptionist — support the work that is done in all of the departments of the company. When employees in other departments need keyboarding done or orders processed, they request help through the Administrative Office Manager.

proc'ess

Office support workers process the information and the paperwork that help businesses run smoothly. For example, in a small service business, such as a heating and air-conditioning repair company, office support workers keep records, order parts and supplies, bill customers, and handle correspondence.

cor·re·spon'dence

in'ven·to·ry

In a medium-sized retail business such as a furniture store, office workers maintain the inventory, prepare the payroll, and handle banking tasks. They also keyboard letters and prepare monthly bills for customers.

In a large manufacturing company, they are needed in every department. These workers prepare orders for the materials used in making the products. They maintain all records for the employees of the company. They handle all correspondence between the company and the customers. They complete all the forms related to the sale and delivery of the products. Without the services of skilled office workers, no business could survive.

What makes office workers so important to a company's success? The work of each department within a company depends on the work of every other department. If the employees in one department are not efficient, the work of other departments will be affected.

knowl'edge·a·ble

All departments must have office workers who are knowledgeable, skilled, and able to work together to help their companies succeed. As you help your company grow, you will be helping yourself. More positions become available within a growing company, and you will find increased opportunities for promotion to a better position.

PREPARATION FOR A CAREER AS AN OFFICE WORKER

de·vel'op

If you plan to become an efficient office worker, you should begin now to learn as much as you can about business. You should try to develop your office skills to the highest level you possibly can. You should also strive to improve your ability to get along with others.

You can learn about business in school by taking courses such as recordkeeping and accounting, general business, business law, business English, business mathematics, keyboarding, word and data processing, shorthand, business machines, and business principles. You can read about business in books, magazines, and newspapers. You can talk to people who are involved in the business world.

You can sharpen your office skills by practicing them every day. Math, keyboarding, shorthand, language, and proofreading skills can be used each day in your school work. You should become an expert in using these and other important skills.

in·ter·per'son·al

One of the most important requirements for success in the office is the ability to get along with others — called **interpersonal skill.** Many

an'a·lyz·ing

ac·quire'

employers say the reason most people are unsuccessful in the office is that they are unable to get along with coworkers and supervisors. You can improve your interpersonal skills by carefully analyzing yourself and finding ways of improving your weak areas. You can participate in school and community activities that provide opportunities for you to work with others.

The knowledge and skills you develop in school will help you find an office job. Once you begin work, you will find many opportunities to develop additional skills. Many companies encourage employees to acquire additional skills by sponsoring training programs or paying for their employees to attend school. You should take advantage of every opportunity to acquire additional knowledge and to develop new skills.

Illustration 1–6 shows the training and personal qualifications as well as job descriptions for various office support positions. This information will help you determine which type of career you want as an office worker.

Illustration 1 – 6

QUALIFICATIONS FOR OFFICE POSITIONS

Position	Training and Personal Qualifications	Work Description
Accounting Clerk	High school diploma. Business math, recordkeeping, office machines, keyboarding, and accounting are desirable. Aptitude for working with numbers is essential. Knowledge of computers is an asset. The ability to exercise good judgment is necessary.	Keeps records in journals and ledgers. Analyzes and records financial transactions. Prepares customer bills, vouchers, and invoices.
File Clerk	High school diploma preferred. Keyboarding and office procedures are desirable. Spelling and reading skills are necessary. Skill in alphabetic filing required. Must not be bored by repetitive tasks. A good sense of organization is a must.	Performs general alphabetic and numeric filing. Locates material upon request. Keeps records of file uses.
Office Machine Operator	High school diploma. Business math and office machines are a must. Good finger dexterity, eye and hand coordination, and vision required. A positive attitude and dependability a must.	Uses machines to record or reproduce information, compute bills and inventories, and perform other calculations.

(Continued)

QUALIFICATIONS FOR OFFICE POSITIONS		
Position	**Training and Personal Qualifications**	**Work Description**
(Continued)		
Receptionist	High school diploma. English, spelling, keyboarding, and office procedures are helpful. Good human relations skills are essential. A neat appearance, pleasant voice, and even disposition are important.	Receives callers, and directs them to their destination. Keyboards, files, and sorts mail, or operates the switchboard.
Secretary	High school diploma or a college degree. Keyboarding, shorthand, and office procedures are usually required. English skills, good vocabulary, poise, a pleasant personality, a professional attitude, good judgment, and initiative are important.	Schedules appointments, gives information to callers, takes and transcribes shorthand dictation, and relieves employers of office work and minor administrative tasks.
Administrative Assistant	High school diploma and experience or a college degree. Keyboarding, office procedures, and shorthand sometimes required. English skills, good vocabulary, poise, pleasant personality, professional attitude, good judgment, initiative, and ability to work without supervision are needed. Management skills are helpful.	Provides administrative support for a high-level manager or executive. May handle correspondence and reports. Supervises office workers. (Job description may vary from company to company.)
Word Processing Operator	High school diploma. Keyboarding, good knowledge of grammar, punctuation, spelling, proofreading, and formatting needed. The ability to use reference materials is important.	Processes text from keyboarded, rough draft, and handwritten materials. Processing may include inputting, editing, and printing business documents.
Typist	High school diploma preferred. Keyboarding, office procedures, and office machines are assets. English skills are essential. Must be dependable and accurate.	Keyboards letters, reports, tabulations, and other items from handwritten, printed, and recorded words. Also answers the telephone, files, and operates office machines.

REVIEWING KEY POINTS

1. Office automation has increased the demand for workers who have skills and who understand new technologies.
2. The technological changes in office equipment have made jobs more challenging.
3. Pleasant working conditions, the systematic nature of work, good salaries and benefits, and opportunities for advancement are some of the advantages of an office career.
4. Office workers support all levels of management within a company. Office workers are needed in all businesses.
5. Office workers who increase their skills and gain experience will probably find many opportunities for advancement.
6. To prepare for an office career, you should learn as much as you can about business and improve your ability to get along with others.

DEVELOPING HUMAN RELATIONS SKILLS

1. You and Sallie work in a small office after school. Your duties include making copies, filing, and preparing the mail and depositing it at the post office. Since Sallie goes by the post office on her way home, she is supposed to leave 10 minutes early to deposit the mail. A few weeks ago, Sallie started leaving a little earlier each day. She now leaves 30 minutes before you do. She has asked you not to tell anyone.

   Yesterday, your supervisor had some mail that had to go out right away. When your supervisor called for Sallie to pick up the mail, he was angry when he learned that Sallie had already left. Your supervisor asked you what has been going on.

   a. What would you tell your supervisor?

   b. What would you say to Sallie?

2. You are talking to Jim about your part-time job. When Jim learns that you operate the copy machine, he asks you to make a copy of the report he wrote for a class. Jim is a very good friend and you want to maintain your friendship.

   a. How would you handle this situation?

   b. What would you say to Jim?

IMPROVING COMMUNICATION SKILLS

1. A sentence is a group of words that has at least one subject and one verb and that expresses a complete thought. The four kinds of sentences are simple, compound, complex, and compound-complex.

   A simple sentence contains one independent clause. It can have more than one subject and more than one verb.

   Jay and Jessica interviewed the office manager.

   Jay and Jessica will write and type the report.

   A compound sentence contains two or more independent clauses that are joined by a coordinating conjunction or a semicolon.

   Marianna applied for a job as a receptionist, but she got a job as a typist.
   Jeff worked in the mail room all day; he went to school at night.

   Write, type, or keyboard the following sentences on a sheet of paper. Underline the subject(s) once and the verb(s) twice. Label each sentence *Simple* or *Compound.*

   a. Eric wants to prepare for an office career.

   b. The word processing operators will keyboard the report, and the secretaries will proofread it carefully.

   c. Steve and Theresa operate the reprographic equipment and manage the supply room.

   d. Office workers must be accurate and efficient.

   e. Betsy works quickly and accurately; she is well organized.

   f. The demand for trained office workers increased steadily.

   g. Jason passed the employment test.

   h. Find the report and take it to Mrs. Jones.

2. On a separate sheet of paper, write, type, or keyboard the following sentence beginnings. Complete each sentence by supplying your own words.

   a. Most office workers must be able to . . .

   b. A growing company will provide its workers with many opportunities for . . .

   c. The office support career that sounds most exciting to me is . . .

   d. Office careers are popular because . . .

   e. Many office workers go to school to learn about new office technology because . . .

   f. In addition to salaries, many companies provide . . .

   g. To prepare for an office career, I will . . .

   h. Office workers provide support for . . .

BUILDING PROBLEM-SOLVING SKILLS

1. Good math skills are important to all office support workers. Test your math skill by completing these problems. Write your answers on a separate sheet of paper.

a.	547 +231	**f.**	379 − 91	**k.**	29 × 8	**p.**	48 ÷ 3
b.	798 + 23	**g.**	297 − 99	**l.**	372 × 43	**q.**	189 ÷ 21
c.	1,279 + 134	**h.**	4,364 − 935	**m.**	1,209 × 246	**r.**	3828 ÷ 88
d.	12.98 + 6.32	**i.**	23.68 −19.99	**n.**	5,135 × 617	**s.**	$94.50 ÷ 3.50
e.	598.23 +120.99	**j.**	937.56 −845.63	**o.**	7,093 × 591	**t.**	$127.50 ÷ 2.50

2. Jason's company has conducted a study comparing the office positions available in 1985 to those forecast for 1990. A chart showing their findings appears below. On a separate sheet of paper, write, type, or keyboard the answers to the questions that follow the chart.

A COMPARISON OF OFFICE POSITIONS

Job Title	Positions Available 1985	Positions Forecast 1990
Accounting Clerk	1,700,000	2,116,500
Receptionist	635,000	885,825
Secretary	2,500,000	3,487,500
Stenographer	280,000	263,200
Typist	1,100,000	1,369,500

a. What job will have the most number of positions available in 1990?

b. What job has the lowest number of positions available in 1985?

c. What job will have a decrease in the number of positions in 1990?

d. What job will have the smallest increase in the number of positions between 1985 and 1990?

e. What job will have the largest increase in number of positions between 1985 and 1990?

f. What is the total number of positions available in 1985?

g. What will be the total number of positions available in 1990?

Activities 1 and 2 can be done on information processing equipment.

APPLYING OFFICE SKILLS

1. Refer to the organization chart in Illustration 1-5. Then on a separate sheet of paper, write, type, or keyboard answers to these questions.

a. Which workers report to the Adminstrative Office Manager?

b. Which two managers report to the Director of Production?

c. An employee in Customer Services receives a call from a customer asking about an order she placed. Which employee would know if the order has been processed?

d. All of the managers are preparing monthly reports and need word processing support. Which manager will decide whose report is completed first?

2. Office workers are expected to be able to understand office communications and follow directions. Read the memorandum below. Then on a separate sheet of paper, write, type, or keyboard the answers to the questions that follow the memo.

CB PRODUCTS

CB Products, Inc.
1001 Lake Avenue,
Pueblo,
Colorado
80120

MEMORANDUM

TO: All Employees

FROM: Cyndi Shoals, Personnel Manager

DATE: February 15, 19--

SUBJECT: Vacation Requests

We expect to have the summer vacation schedule completed by April 1. Vacation requests are handled according to seniority. When more than one person in a department requests the same dates for vacation, the request from the person with the most seniority will be honored.

Please complete the attached vacation request form and return it to my office by March 15. If you want to change your vacation schedule after April 1, please come to the Personnel Office. If there is no conflict, we will change the dates of your vacation.

a. Who is giving the directions for the new procedures?

b. When do employees have to return the vacation request form?

c. When will the vacation schedules be completed?

d. What should a worker do if the worker wants to request a change in the vacation schedule?

CHAPTER 2

SKILLS FOR SUCCESS

Most employers would agree that their best employees have several things in common. They have the basic skills that enable them to learn their jobs quickly and perform their duties accurately. They have the training and knowledge of office procedures and the skills needed to operate various types of office equipment. They also have the personal characteristics and work habits that make them valuable additions to their office support work teams.

As you study this chapter, you will find answers to the following questions:

- What basic skills does an employer look for in a prospective worker?
- How can good communication skills help an employee?
- What organizational skills help office employees work more effectively?
- Why do employers hire employees who demonstrate good human relations skills?
- What do the following terms mean: **flexibility, filing?**

BASIC SKILLS NEEDED BY OFFICE WORKERS

For most office jobs, employers look for workers who have basic skills in several important areas. They want to hire workers who

com·mu'ni·cate

- communicate well with others
- possess problem-solving skills
- work productively and efficiently
- produce accurate work
- are flexible
- possess good human relations skills
- have good math skills
- write legibly

Communication Skills

As an office worker, you will find that you must communicate frequently with other employees and with customers. Good communication requires good speaking, listening, reading, and writing skills.

con·cise'

When you speak, it is important that you use the right words to express your ideas. Your listener will be able to understand what you say and what you mean if you speak in clear, concise terms. Your choice of words and the way you speak will determine whether you deliver your message accurately. Your wording and tone of voice are especially important when you talk on the telephone. Because your listener cannot see your facial expressions and gestures, your voice alone must carry your message.

at·ten'tive

In order to listen carefully, you must be alert and attentive. If necessary, take notes during a conversation to help you remember what was said. Taking notes saves you from having to ask that the message be repeated later.

You will find that your job in the office also requires good reading ability. You must be able to read and understand instructions about the tasks you are assigned. You will need to read company policies that affect you and your work. You will also need to read and understand price lists, tax tables, office manuals, correspondence, and other materials in completing your tasks.

Office workers also communicate through written messages, such as letters, memorandums, informal notes, and reports. Your written messages must be clear, complete, concise, correct, and courteous. If you write in complete sentences with clear, concise words that are used correctly, your messages will be easier to understand. As you compose your message, also try to keep your reader in mind by writing in a courteous manner. People respond more favorably to messages written in a courteous tone. As you study office procedures, you will have an opportunity to review your communication skills in the Improving Communication Skills activities at the end of each chapter.

Illustration 1–7 Speaking and listening skills are equally important for office workers

Problem-Solving Skills

As an office worker, you will occasionally face problems that you must handle by yourself. When a problem occurs, you must be able to think through it in a clear and logical manner and determine the best approach for handling it. Employers expect office workers to possess good problem-solving skills. They know that the more responsibility you assume in your job, the more problems you will face. As a result, greater emphasis will be placed on your problem-solving skills.

Productivity and Efficiency

Productive and efficient workers do not waste time, energy, or materials. They complete their work on schedule so that they do not prevent other workers from completing their work. You can increase your productivity and efficiency by planning your work and organizing the materials you need.

in·ef·fi′cient

Employers are very conscious of employee productivity. They realize that slow, inefficient, and wasteful workers cost money and are a drain on the profits of the company. Unproductive workers are usually the first to lose their jobs. Productive workers, on the other hand, are usually the first to be considered for promotion.

Accuracy

To be an effective office worker, you must be accurate in your work. Errors cost money. Errors that are detected can cost the business many dollars to correct. Errors that are not detected until too late can cost the company even more through the loss of customers. You must work carefully so that errors do not creep in. And you must get in the habit of checking your completed work for errors. Effective office workers learn to locate errors, correct them, and find ways of preventing such errors in the future.

Flexibility

flex·i·bil'i·ty

Because the office is constantly changing as a result of technological advances, office workers today must demonstrate **flexibility**; that is, they must be able to adapt to change. Changes in the office may require you to learn new procedures or learn how to operate new equipment. You must be willing to accept new ways of completing tasks, even when they are not the ways you were taught in school. Flexibility is the mark of a successful office worker today.

Flexibility is even more important when you realize that some of the jobs people hold today did not even exist ten years ago. And today there is little or no demand for workers in certain occupations. For this reason, today's office worker must be willing to learn new skills. If you don't make an effort to keep current, your job skills may quickly become out of date, and you may be out of a job.

Illustration 1–8 Effective workers check the accuracy of their work

Interpersonal Skills

Regardless of the size of the company you work for, you will have frequent contact with people on the job. In order to be successful and happy in your work, you must be able to get along with coworkers, supervisors, and customers. The larger the business, the more people you are likely to be working with. Even in a small office, however, you will be working with your supervisor and coworkers.

To get along with others, you must treat them with respect and courtesy. Even in tense situations — when you're dealing with an angry customer, for example — you must remain calm and courteous. You must be willing to listen to the other person's point of view. Most of all, you must be able to put the Golden Rule into practice; that is, treat others as you would like to have them treat you.

Math Skills

Arithmetic skills are used daily by most office workers — in completing invoices, figuring discounts, adding columns of figures, and even centering tables. Even though you may have a calculator to help you perform such tasks, you need to understand the operation you are performing in order to know when to add, subtract, multiply, or divide.

es'ti·mate
ap·prox'i·mate

People who work with figures need to develop a "number sense" that helps them locate errors. For example, you can learn to estimate answers so that you know what the approximate answer to a problem is going to be. If the answer you find is not close to your estimate, you know that you need to rework the problem.

com·pu·ta'tions

Businesses sometimes use tables for frequently performed calculations. For example, a sales tax table may be used to find the amount of tax to be charged for the amount of a sale. To use the table in Illustration 1–9, for example, you find the amount you know — the sale price — and read across to find the amount you're looking for — the tax to be charged. Tables are also used for figuring payroll tax deductions, insurance rates, and interest charges. These tables save time by helping you locate correct answers quickly. They also reduce your chance of making an error in your calculation. You may find that you can develop your own tables for computations you perform frequently in your work.

Clear Handwriting

leg'i·bly

On the job, office workers frequently complete forms and write materials that must be read by someone else. Words, letters, or figures that are poorly written may be misread and cause costly errors. Because others will be reading what you write, it is important that you have a clear writing style. With practice, you can improve your handwriting so that you can write rapidly yet clearly and legibly.

SCHEDULE OF TAX COMPUTATIONS – $0.11 TO $50.00

Price Range	Tax	Price Range	Tax	Price Range	Tax
$ 0.11 - $ 0.25	$0.01	$ 16.88 - 17.12	$ 0.68	$ 33.63 - 33.87	$ 1.35
0.26 - 0.50	0.02	17.13 - 17.37	0.69	33.88 - 34.12	1.36
0.51 - 0.75	0.03	17.38 - 17.62	0.70	34.13 - 34.37	1.37
0.76 - 1.12	0.04	17.63 - 17.87	0.71	34.38 - 34.62	1.38
1.13 - 1.37	0.05	17.88 - 18.12	0.72	34.63 - 34.87	1.39
1.38 - 1.62	0.06	18.13 - 18.37	0.73	34.88 - 35.12	1.40
1.63 - 1.87	0.07	18.38 - 18.62	0.74	35.13 - 35.37	1.41
1.88 - 2.12	0.08	18.63 - 18.87	0.75	35.38 - 35.62	1.42
2.13 - 2.37	0.09	18.88 - 19.12	0.76	35.63 - 35.87	1.43
2.38 - 2.62	0.10	19.13 - 19.37	0.77	35.88 - 36.12	1.44
2.63 - 2.87	0.11	19.38 - 19.62	0.78	36.13 - 36.37	1.45
2.88 - 3.12	0.12	19.63 - 19.87	0.79	36.38 - 36.62	1.46
3.13 - 3.37	0.13	19.88 - 20.12	0.80	36.63 - 36.87	1.47
3.38 - 3.62	0.14	20.13 - 20.37	0.81	36.88 - 37.12	1.48
3.63 - 3.87	0.15	20.38 - 20.62	0.82	37.13 - 37.37	1.49
3.88 - 4.12	0.16	20.63 - 20.87	0.83	37.38 - 37.62	1.50
4.13 - 4.37	0.17	20.88 - 21.12	0.84	37.63 - 37.87	1.51
4.38 - 4.62	0.18	21.13 - 21.37	0.85	37.88 - 38.12	1.52
4.63 - 4.87	0.19	21.38 - 21.62	0.86	38.13 - 38.37	1.53
14.88 - 15.12	0.60	31.63 - 31.87	1.27	48.38 - 48.62	1.94
15.13 - 15.37	0.61	31.88 - 32.12	1.28	48.63 - 48.87	1.95
15.38 - 15.62	0.62	32.13 - 32.37	1.29	48.88 - 49.12	1.96
15.63 - 15.87	0.63	32.38 - 32.62	1.30	49.13 - 49.37	1.97
15.88 - 16.12	0.64	32.63 - 32.87	1.31	49.38 - 49.62	1.98
16.13 - 16.37	0.65	32.88 - 33.12	1.32	49.63 - 49.87	1.99
16.38 - 16.62	0.66	33.13 - 33.37	1.33	49.88 - 50.12	2.00
16.63 - 16.87	0.67	33.38 - 33.62	1.34		

Illustration 1–9
Using tables for frequently performed calculations saves time

RESPONSIBILITIES OF OFFICE WORKERS

For most office positions, employers require employees to have training or experience in several skill areas. Keyboarding ability, of course, is a requirement for many office jobs, but there are other job skills that are just as important. Depending on the type of position you apply for, you may be expected to perform the following tasks skillfully:

skill'ful·ly

- keyboarding
- filing
- using the telephone
- meeting the public
- using office machines
- handling the mail
- processing information by computer
- processing information by hand
- handling financial tasks

Keyboarding and Formatting

Most positions in the office require keyboarding skill. Positions that require a great deal of keyboarding are generally classified as typist, clerk-typist, or word processing positions. You may be required to format letters, business forms, reports, and tables. Speed and accuracy in keyboarding are important. Many companies require speeds of 50 to 60 words a minute with no more than five errors in five minutes. With correcting typewriters it is easier to

Illustration 1–10
Keyboarding skills are required for most office positions

correct errors today. However, proofreading skill, in addition to keyboarding skill, is still important.

Knowledge and skill in using a keyboard will also help you in word processing and data processing jobs. Many workers find that once they have mastered a keyboard, it is easy to learn how to operate other types of office machines with keyboards.

Filing

or'der·ly

Filing is the arranging and storing of business documents in an orderly way so that they can be found quickly and easily. The information contained in the files is often used for making important decisions. Knowing how to locate needed information quickly will make you a valuable employee. To have good filing skills, you must be able to spell correctly and write legibly. Knowledge of basic filing rules is essential, but you must also be willing to learn the filing system and procedures used by your company.

Meeting People

ver'i·fy

Many office workers assist customers and callers from outside the company. For example, a receptionist greets callers who come to the office. In a small retail business, a clerk-typist may be called upon to serve customers in rush periods. A file clerk may meet with a customer to verify or check information contained within the files. An accounting clerk may explain charges on an account to a customer. The amount of contact you will have with the public depends on the size of your company, the nature of the business, and the position you hold.

Illustration 1–11 Visitors expect to receive prompt and courteous attention

cour'te·ous·ly

Your company's reputation will be determined to a large degree by your actions and those of other employees. Whenever you meet with people from outside the company, it is important to act courteously and to provide as much service as possible. Some of the most successful employees are those who make the first impression of them and their company a favorable one.

Processing Mail

Each year American companies mail billions of pieces of business correspondence, and they rely on office workers to perform a variety of mail duties. Mailing procedures vary according to the size of the company. Preparing items for the mail usually involves collecting and sealing the mail, selecting the proper class of mail service, attaching the correct amount of postage, and depositing the mail at the post office for delivery. There are still other tasks that must be performed when mail is received by the company. To be skilled at handling the mail, you must be knowledgeable about postal regulations. You also need to be familiar with your company's employees, its products, and its operations.

Using Office Equipment

We live in an age in which there is equipment to do almost everything, and business offices are no exception. Office workers use electronic calculators, copying machines, dictating and transcribing machines, word processing equipment, and computers to complete their tasks. This equipment saves time, reduces errors, and eliminates much routine work. To enjoy these benefits, of course, you must know how to use this equipment properly. You should become skilled at operating as many pieces of office equipment as you can in order to be successful in the changing offices of today.

Using Telecommunications Equipment

Businesses today would find it very difficult to operate without the telephone. As an office worker, you must be skilled in its use. You must know how to answer the telephone properly, how to make and receive calls for your supervisor, and how to record information received over the telephone. Part of the skill of using the telephone properly is projecting a good company image through the use of your voice. Remember that when the other person hangs up, he or she is left with an impression of your voice and your willingness to be of help.

pro·ject'ing

In many offices, telephones and telephone lines are used to transmit information from text editor to text editor, from computer to computer, and from copier to copier. In offices that have equipment linked by telephones or telephone lines, office workers are expected to be able to operate the equipment to transmit messages accurately and efficiently.

trans·mit'

Processing Information by Computer

Because computers are used so widely in business today, there are very few office jobs that have not been affected by computer forms, terminology, and procedures. Office workers are frequently called upon to prepare reports or

ter·mi·nol'o·gy

Illustration 1–12
Computers have not eliminated the need for accuracy in processing information

forms to be entered into the computer. They may enter information into the computer using computer terminals. Or, they might have the task of verifying the information contained on computer print-outs. Every company has certain procedures that must be followed if the computer is to be used effectively. Every office worker needs some understanding of computers and how they are used in processing information.

Processing Information Manually

man'u·al·ly

Even though most companies rely on computers to perform many routine operations, there are still many tasks that must be performed manually. Tasks such as receiving payments, processing refunds, and taking orders usually require office workers to complete and process certain forms. You may be responsible for recording information or verifying information that appears on completed forms. Your duties may require you to use calculators and other basic office machines. For all tasks related to processing information by hand, clear handwriting and accuracy are required.

Processing Financial Transactions

Many office workers are assigned tasks involving banking and financial responsibilities. Accepting payments, giving receipts, making change, completing payrolls, and preparing bank deposits are common tasks. You might also be responsible for verifying invoices, writing checks, and handling petty cash. In a small firm, your responsibilites may include reconciling the bank statements.

To perform your financial duties successfully, you need good math skills, accuracy and attention to detail, and familiarity with the procedures and forms used by your company. Just as important, however, is a sense of responsibility about your work. A careless attitude about your financial duties can lead to errors that cost your company money.

Variations in Job Responsibilities

spe'cial·ized

The specific job competencies you need to be successful will depend upon the size of the company, the type of equipment used, and the particular position you hold. In large firms, many office positions are specialized. Specialized positions include payroll clerk, file clerk, and word processing operator. In smaller companies, workers are generally responsible for a wider range of tasks that might be performed less frequently. For example, a secretary or clerk-typist may have filing, receptionist, keyboarding, and telephone responsibilities.

You should prepare yourself to assume as many responsibilities as possible so that you will have a wider range of opportunities. Regardless of your position, all of the duties you perform on the job are important and can contribute to your success and to that of your company.

REVIEWING KEY POINTS

1. Good communication skills, which include the ability to read, write, speak, and listen, are very important skills for office support workers.
2. Employers expect office workers to possess problem-solving skills.
3. Employers look for workers who are productive, efficient, accurate and flexible.
4. Good human relation skills, that is, the ability to work with coworkers, are valuable for all employees.
5. Office skills such as keyboarding, filing, operating office equipment, and processing mail are valuable skills for a prospective office worker.
6. Office workers process information manually as well as with the use of a computer.
7. The duties and responsibilities of office workers vary according to the size and type of company they work for.

DEVELOPING HUMAN RELATIONS SKILLS

1. Office jobs provide a wide variety of duties, responsibilities, and working conditions. To be successful in any office job, you must like what you are doing. You can get an idea of the type of job and working conditions you would like most by answering the following questions. Use a separate sheet of paper.
   - **a.** Why do you want to work?
   - **b.** Why do you want to work in an office?
   - **c.** In what kind of office would you like to work?
   - **d.** How do you think your business courses will help prepare you for the kind of office job you want?
2. You work as a part-time clerk-typist for the State-Wide Real Estate Company. Tim Boyd, who works at the desk next to yours, helped you when you first started working. At your afternoon break, Tim told you that your coworkers are concerned with your work habits. Everyone takes five minutes extra at break time. And, no one worries about completing work on time. If the work is not finished on time, it can be finished later and overtime will be paid. Tim suggests you conform to the work habits of your coworkers.
   - **a.** What do you think about Tim's suggestion?
   - **b.** What would you say to Tim about his suggestion?

IMPROVING COMMUNICATION SKILLS

1. A complex sentence has an independent clause and one or more dependent clauses.

   Since office technology is changing rapidly, you will see many changes in the way office work is done.

   Write, type, or keyboard the following sentences on a separate sheet of paper. Underline each independent clause once and each dependent clause twice. Label each sentence *Simple, Compound,* or *Complex*.

   a. Although Stephanie keyboarded very rapidly, she was not very accurate.
   b. Many office positions require keyboarding speed of 60 words a minute.
   c. Kathy takes accurate notes, but she does not transcribe them accurately.
   d. While office skills help you obtain a job, good interpersonal skills are important for keeping the job.
   e. David wants a job in a small office; Ellen wants to work for a large corporation.
   f. Allison keyboarded and filed the report.
   g. Once you develop office skills, you are eligible for many office positions.
   h. Joel and Mark are the best file clerks at Apex, Inc.
   i. Taxes are easy to compute when you have a table.
   j. Diane was promoted to executive secretary; Bill was promoted to typing specialist.
   k. Efficiency and attention to detail can save your company money; carelessness can lead to costly errors.
   l. We helped distribute the reports that Elena prepared.

2. Complete each sentence in your own words. Write, type, or keyboard your sentences on a separate sheet of paper.

   a. Bill's part-time job requires keyboarding, . . . skills.
   b. Kara was nervous because . . .
   c. Dana and Kaye wanted . . .
   d. Because his handwriting was very poor, . . .
   e. Although both of Mary's parents work in offices, their jobs . . .
   f. Office workers who know about new technologies . . .
   g. Tasks formerly done by hand . . .
   h. Emma may be promoted . . .
   i. Office support workers . . . all levels in the organization.
   j. Telecommunications . . . transmit messages promptly.
   k. You can increase your productivity by . . .
   l. Tom is not a good proofreader, so . . .

BUILDING PROBLEM-SOLVING SKILLS

1. Find the following percentages. Write your answers on a separate sheet of paper.

   a. 20% of 798
   b. 60% of 350
   c. 45% of 594
   d. 85% of 500
   e. 15% of 950
   f. 33% of $6.19
   g. 12% of $9.39
   h. 29% of $1.25
   i. 97% of $8.75
   j. 50% of $4.50
   k. 2.5% of 7.70
   l. 5.5% of 10.10
   m. 9.3% of 125
   n. 25.5% of 211
   o. 33.3% of 6.65

2. Read through the inventory/price list shown here. Then write, type, or keyboard your answers to the following questions on a separate sheet of paper.

INVENTORY/PRICE LIST

Quantity in Stock	Item	Old Price	New Price
20	3-ring binders	$ 2.70	$ 3.25
18	rotary card files	19.95	21.95
7	typists copy stands	15.80	16.75
5	chained pens	3.40	3.75
3	desk file racks	18.25	18.75
5	electric pencil sharpeners	24.75	23.95
5	desk staplers	12.35	12.60
10	framed cork boards	7.45	7.75
5	adjustable desk lamps	42.50	45.00
3	stacking file trays	2.60	2.65

   a. Which item is the most expensive item in the new price list?
   b. Which item decreased in price?
   c. Which item increased the least amount in price?
   d. Which item has the largest quantity in stock?
   e. Which item has the smallest quantity in stock?
   f. Which item had the lowest percentage of increase in price?
   g. Which item had the largest percentage of increase in price?

APPLYING OFFICE SKILLS

1. On a separate sheet of paper, copy the paragraph that appears at the top of page 28, using your best handwriting. Before you start, read through the paragraph and practice doing what it suggests.

There are many documents that are still handwritten in business. Because other people may have to read your handwriting, it is important that you write legibly. You can improve your handwriting by practicing these suggestions. Practice holding your pen or pencil loosely as you write. Try to make all letters about the same size and with an even slant. As you write, imagine a line between the printed lines on the page. Use this "pictured" line to help you keep the letters the same size.

2. The chart shown here appears in your workbook. Use it to set goals for the level of skill you would like to achieve by the end of this course. First, indicate your speed and accuracy goals for keyboarding and shorthand (if applicable). Then, indicate the skills in which you would like to become competent by the end of the course by placing a check mark in the column marked *Goal.* When you feel you have developed that skill, place another check mark in the column marked *Competent.* If you do not have a workbook, prepare a copy of the chart on a separate sheet of paper.

COMPETENCIES FOR OFFICE WORKERS

Speed/Accuracy											5-Minute Goals Speed/Accuracy
Month											
Typewriting											
Shorthand											

	Goal	Competent
Filing		
Calculator Operation		
Copy Machine Operation		
Duplicating Machine Operation		
Legible Handwriting		
Using the Telephone		
Meeting the Public		
Handling the Mail		
Basic Math Computations		
Machine Transcription		
Handling Financial Tasks		

	Goal	Competent
Basic Typewriting Competencies:		
Centering		
Typing numbered lists		
Typing on lines		
Typing tables		
Typing letters		
Typing memos		
Typing from rough drafts		
Typing forms		
Typing reports		
Typing itineraries		
Typing news releases		
Typing envelopes		
Typing minutes		
Personal Goals:		

CHAPTER 3

PERSONAL QUALIFICATIONS FOR SUCCESS

You must have business skills and knowledge to qualify for an office position. Skills and knowledge, however, are only some of the qualifications you need for a career as a successful office worker. Your personality, appearance, and business behavior are also qualities that will contribute to your success in an office career.

As you study this chapter, you will find answers to the following questions:

- What personality traits does an employer look for in a prospective office worker?
- What factors contribute to developing a professional appearance?
- What is considered appropriate etiquette for a business office?
- What do the following terms mean: **interdependent, attitude, setting priorities, poise, initiative, discretion?**

PROFESSIONAL CHARACTERISTICS OF OFFICE WORKERS

Some employees stand out from the others as special. They get along with their supervisors, coworkers, and customers. They work hard and seem to enjoy their work. Their clothing and appearance make a good impression on people. They are able to handle all kinds of situations with courtesy and tact. These employees have the personality traits, personal appearance, and appropriate behavior that set them apart as "professionals."

Personality Traits

Your personality is what makes you different from other people. Certain personal characteristics make some people more pleasant to work with than others. Some personal characteristics that contribute to a good business personality include characteristics such as being cooperative, having a good attitude, being dependable, using good judgment, being confident, maintaining poise, and having initiative.

Being cooperative In most office jobs, employees have to work with other people as part of a team. The ability to work with others is a quality that most employers value in their employees. A successful team is made up of individual members who do their jobs well and who support others on the team. The team is **interdependent** — that is, the success of one team member depends in part on the success of other team members. As a member of a team, you must work cooperatively. You must be willing to assist other team members when they need help performing their work. And you must perform your job well, because it affects the work of other team members.

in·ter·de·pend′ent

co·op′er·a·tive·ly

Having a good attitude During the job interview, many employers try to determine the applicant's attitude. **Attitude** refers to a person's outlook, disposition, or normal frame of mind. A person's attitude may generally be described as positive or negative. If you have a positive attitude, you usually make a better employee.

You can determine whether you have a positive or negative attitude by asking yourself questions like these:

- Do I try not to be moody?
- Do I avoid complaining and try to accept situations that I may not like but can do little about?
- Do I try to be agreeable most of the time?
- Do I try to look for the good in people rather than dwell on the bad?
- Do I usually feel good about myself and my work?

a·gree′a·ble

If you are able to answer *yes* to these questions, the chances are good that you usually have a positive attitude.

Illustration 1–13
Work assignments must be completed accurately and on schedule

Being dependable A dependable person is one who does what is expected at the appropriate times. A dependable worker can be given a task to do and can be counted on to do it. You can demonstrate that you are dependable by arriving at work and beginning on time and by completing your work accurately and on schedule. You also show you are dependable when you continue working on a task until it is completed.

Using good judgment Employers rely on their employees to solve minor problems on their own and make decisions about their work. To find the best solution and make the best decision, you need to use good *judgment.* Good judgment requires that you think through a situation carefully, consider all of the facts, and act in the best interest of everyone concerned.

You can learn to be a good decision maker by using common sense and by following these steps:

1. Know the nature of the problem to be solved.
2. Consider the various choices available.
3. Think about the possible results of the choices you might make.
4. Remember similar decisions you have made in the past.
5. Make your decision.

Decision making is involved whenever you have to decide which of several tasks you should complete first. This process is known as **setting priorities.** In order to make the best decision, study the choices available and consider the priorities of your department and company. You will learn more about setting priorities and making decisions in Unit 3.

pri·or'i·ties

con'fi·dent

Being confident It is important to believe in yourself. If you know you have good skills and abilities, you should feel confident about your work. Many workers lack self-confidence, especially during the early weeks on the job because there are so many new things to learn. Even though the specific procedures of your job may vary somewhat from those you learned in the classroom, the basic procedures are probably very similar. By learning the specific procedures and developing the necessary skills quickly, you will soon feel confident about your work.

As you gain confidence, you will learn to work under pressure without losing self-control. Every job can be demanding at one time or another. However, you need to remain calm and work efficiently even when you are under pressure.

crit'i·cism

As you become more confident, you will also learn to accept criticism better. Your supervisors will offer constructive criticism and suggestions about your work. By following their suggestions, you can become more efficient on the job.

Maintaining poise **Poise** is the ability to appear calm, composed, and confident even though you may feel tense, nervous, or unsure of yourself. Poise is valuable in many high-pressure jobs because your poise can make the people around you feel relaxed and calm, too. By breathing deeply when you begin to feel tense, you may be able to relax somewhat and overcome your anxious feelings. Good posture will also help give you the appearance of being poised and self-confident.

anx'ious

Having initiative **Initiative** is the ability to begin or follow through with a task without being told to do so. Initiative is a very valuable asset for an office worker. An office worker frequently has to work with little or no supervision. When a supervisor is not around to direct work, an employee is expected to complete work that must be done. As you gain experience in an office position, it will become easier to use your own initiative in completing work.

Professional Appearance

Your personal appearance is important. Your appearance makes an impression on the people with whom you come in contact. It may be a favorable or an unfavorable impression. The ability to make a favorable impression is a valuable asset to you and to your company.

Appearance may also be related to other personal qualities. For example, some employers believe that people who don't seem to care about their appearance probably do not care about the quality of their work either.

Employees represent their companies to the public. Because of this, companies are concerned about the appearance of their employees. There are some aspects of your appearance that you can do very little about. However, most people can improve their appearance by paying attention to their clothes and accessories, hair, personal hygiene, and health.

Illustration 1–14
Personal appearance is important for job success

Clothing and accessories A well-dressed person is one who wears clean, neat-appearing clothes that are appropriate for the situation. Although casual clothing may be acceptable for relaxing and recreation, it is not appropriate for most offices. A business suit, on the other hand, may be appropriate to wear in the office but not for sports activities.

tran·si'tion

When you begin working in the office, you will make a transition from student to office worker. This transition will probably require you to dress quite differently. You should determine what is considered appropriate for the office so that you will feel comfortable about what you wear. How can you find out what to wear? You can ask other workers in the office what is considered appropriate. You can observe people on the job and going to and from work. You can study photographs of office workers in your area. After a few days on the job, you should have an understanding of what kind of clothing is acceptable in your particular company.

co·or'di·nat·ing

You may find that you need to purchase some new items in order to dress appropriately for work. If you are on a limited budget — as many beginning workers are — it may be a good idea to purchase coordinating pieces that allow you to mix and match items. A basic wardrobe might consist of three or four skirts or pairs of slacks, several shirts or blouses, and two or three jackets or blazers. With the proper accessories — ties, scarves, shoes, and jewelry — you can create several different outfits out of the basic pieces that you have in your wardrobe.

The key to selecting a good basic wardrobe is choosing a flattering color and style for your complexion, hair color, and body build. Many fashion experts recommend that you buy the best quality that you can afford when you buy basic wardrobe items. Quality clothes in basic styles — tailored, traditional pieces — are usually more economical in the long run. Because they generally do not go out of style quickly, you do not have to replace them often. High fashion items and clothes that are "the latest thing" may go out of style in one season.

ec·o·nom'i·cal

Your clothes should always be clean, pressed, and mended. If you are ever in doubt about whether a garment is clean enough for one more day in the office, chances are that it should be cleaned before you wear it again.

Shoes are also an important part of your overall appearance. They should be polished and kept in good repair. If your job requires a lot of standing or walking, wear comfortable shoes. There are few things that are more distracting than tired, sore feet. Like the rest of your outfit, shoes should be appropriate for the office. Most high-fashion styles and sports shoes should not be worn to work.

Many career counselors recommend that you dress for the job you hope to reach, not the position that you currently have. If you think you can wait until after you receive a promotion to dress appropriately, you may be passed over because you do not "look the part."

pro·mo'tion

Hair Well-cared-for hair is always flattering. Your hair should be neat, clean, and styled so that you do not have to fuss with it while you are working. It can be very distracting to work with people who are constantly pushing hair out of their face or playing with it. You may want to consult a hair stylist for a neat hair style that is easy to care for. Once your hair is cut and properly styled, it should be easier to manage. Wash your hair daily, if necessary, and have it trimmed frequently to keep its shape.

Personal hygiene Your daily routine should include a bath or shower. Daily use of an antiperspirant or deodorant and freshly laundered clothes are recommended. People within an office are in close contact with each other; therefore, personal cleanliness is of the utmost importance.

Clean and healthy teeth are also important to your appearance. Care should include brushing regularly after each meal. If it is impossible to brush after each meal, you should brush at least twice daily. For fresh breath during the day, you might use mouthwash or breath mints.

Women should use make-up with care. If properly applied, make-up can enhance a person's appearance; however, too much make-up detracts from your appearance.

en·hance'

Men and women alike should avoid wearing strongly scented lotions or colognes at work. Men who wear beards or mustaches should keep them neatly trimmed.

Personal health You need a well-balanced diet, regular exercise, and sufficient sleep to maintain your health. A well-balanced diet maintains your

suf·fi'cient

energy level and helps your body function efficiently. Regular exercise is important to maintain muscle tone and provide energy. You need sufficient sleep to stay alert and efficient. The amount of sleep needed varies from one person to the next person, so you should determine how much sleep is enough for you.

Not only will a well-balanced diet, regular exercise, and enough sleep make you feel better, work more efficiently, and take fewer sick days, but they will also improve your appearance.

PROFESSIONAL BEHAVIOR

Another factor that contributes to the success of an office worker is the type of business behavior demonstrated. Appropriate behavior includes using good work habits, assuming responsibility, and following good etiquette.

Using Good Work Habits

As you read in the last chapter, companies expect their employees to be productive and work efficiently. You can increase your productivity by using good work habits. There are many good work habits you can begin to develop right now. You can learn to work steadily so that you complete your work within a reasonable amount of time. You can plan your work so that you do not waste time or supplies.

stead'i·ly

On the job, plan to arrive at the office on time and ready to begin work. If the workday begins at 8:00, you should be at your desk at 8:00. Don't arrive at 8:00 and then spend 15 minutes getting coffee, combing your hair, and

Illustration 1–15
Your personal health contributes to your job success

ex·ces′sive

talking with coworkers. Even if the office atmosphere is informal, you should not waste time during the day by excessive visiting with the other people in your office. Save your personal conversations for breaks and lunch time.

Another good work habit that most companies insist on is notifying your supervisor when you will be absent or late for work. Your supervisor needs to know if you will not be at the office so that plans can be made to have someone do your work.

Assuming Responsibility

re·spon·si·bil′i·ties

Each office worker is hired to perform certain tasks. You can increase your value as a worker by assuming your responsibilities cheerfully and carrying them out efficiently. As you learn your job, you should be willing to assume responsibility for additional tasks. Accepting new responsibilities will not only increase your value to your employer, but it will make your job more interesting too.

Professional Etiquette

When you begin to work in an office, it is important that you behave in a professional manner. Behavior that is acceptable when you are with your friends may not be acceptable in an office. As circumstances arise in the office, you must adapt your behavior to fit each circumstance. Office workers are expected to use courtesy, consideration, tact, discretion, and respect with other employees and customers.

Courtesy Courtesy refers to the way you treat others in the office. For instance, using first names is usually acceptable unless visitors are present. Then it may be more appropriate to refer to the others in the office by titles such as Miss, Mr., Mrs., and their last names.

Consideration Being considerate means that you think about the needs and feelings of others. Although the atmosphere in an office may be informal, you should maintain a business-like attitude. This means that you avoid behavior such as loud talking. This behavior is not only inappropriate but is inconsiderate of others and reduces productivity.

Tact A person who has tact is sensitive to situations and acts or speaks in such a way so as not to offend anyone. For example, a worker may have to deny service to a customer whose bill is overdue. In doing so, the worker must be careful not to offend the customer. Upsetting a customer may damage the company's reputation.

Discretion An office worker demonstrates **discretion** by using good judgment in speaking and acting. For example, when your supervisor is away on business, it is not appropriate for you to tell a caller exactly where your supervisor is, even if the caller asks!

PERSONAL DEVELOPMENT FOR SUCCESS

After reading about the personal characteristics that employers value, do you feel confident about your chances for success as an office worker? Think about your strengths. Then consider your areas of weakness. Do you have a negative attitude? Do you lack self-confidence? Do your appearance or work habits need improvement? Fortunately, you can change many things about yourself.

In order to develop your strengths and overcome your weaknesses, you must want to change. Changing your behavior, appearance, and attitudes requires effort. But the results are definitely worth the effort. Most people today spend 2,000 hours a year at work. As long as your job is going to require so much of your time, you might as well be successful at it!

REVIEWING KEY POINTS

1. Personality traits distinguish one person from another and make some people more pleasant to work with than others.
2. Being cooperative, having a good attitude, being dependable, using good judgment, being confident, maintaining poise, and having initiative are personal characteristics that employers look for in prospective office workers.
3. Your professional appearance is influenced by your clothes and accessories, hair style, personal hygiene, and personal health.
4. Using good work habits means that a person works steadily in order to complete assigned tasks within a reasonable amount of time.
5. Good office etiquette requires an office worker to behave in a professional manner, show consideration and sensitivity for other workers and customers, and use discretion in all office situations.
6. You can enhance your office employment opportunities by developing professional traits, appearance, behavior, and etiquette.

DEVELOPING HUMAN RELATIONS SKILLS

1. Karla works as a receptionist in Dr. Craige's office after school. Dr. Craige has told Karla that she can do her homework when she has free time. Yesterday afternoon while Karla was trying to study for an exam, she made a sign and put it on her desk. The sign read, "Please sign in and have a seat."

a. What do you think about the way Karla handled this situation?

b. What suggestions would you make to Karla?

2. Adam, a good friend of yours, just told you that he did not get a promotion that he felt he deserved. He is upset with his supervisor because she told him that his appearance was not appropriate for his new job. Adam is angry because he has been working very hard and thought the promotion was "in the bag."

a. What would you say to Adam?

b. Does Adam have a right to be angry with his supervisor? Explain.

IMPROVING COMMUNICATION SKILLS

1. A compound-complex sentence contains two or more independent clauses and one or more dependent clauses.

Although the mail arrived at 8:30, Jamie did not sort it until 9:00, and she did not deliver it until 9:30.

Write, type, or keyboard the following sentences on a separate sheet of paper. Underline each independent clause once and each dependent clause twice. Label each sentence *Simple, Compound, Complex,* or *Compound-Complex.*

a. When information is confidential, it is filed in a secure place.

b. Place your order before April 15, and get a dozen free pens.

c. While the supervisor was sick, Jan signed the reports, and Beth approved special requests.

d. Sheila had the highest employment test score.

e. Although Tom and Shirley completed the project early, it was not submitted until the due date.

f. Nancy got a promotion; Bill only got a raise.

g. As the temperature fell, the rain turned to ice, and the ice caused power failures.

h. Young workers are often criticized for negative attitudes and unprofessional behavior.

i. Tammy's work is excellent, but her attitude is poor.

j. If a person uses proofreader's marks to edit documents, anyone can make the changes.

2. Add your own words to complete the following sentences. Write, type, or keyboard your sentences on a separate sheet of paper.

a. An efficient worker is one who . . .

b. Using good judgment means . . .

c. Beginning office workers gain self-confidence by . . .

d. . . . is called poise.
e. Personal cleanliness is important because . . .
f. A person's professional qualifications include . . .
g. A tactful person . . .
h. . . . shows consideration.
i. Professional appearance means . . .
j. . . . reflects a good attitude.

BUILDING PROBLEM-SOLVING SKILLS

1. Express each fraction as a percent. Write your answers on a separate sheet of paper.

a. 1/4	d. 3/8	g. 1/20	j. 4/5	m. 3/5
b. 2/5	e. 1/3	h. 5/8	k. 3/4	n. 2/10
c. 2/25	f. 2/3	i. 1/10	l. 7/8	o. 1/25

2. Read through the following chart, which shows employment test results. On a separate sheet of paper, write, type, or keyboard your answers to the questions that follow the chart.

TEST RESULTS

Name	Spelling	Punctuation	Math	Keyboarding (Speed/Accuracy)
B. Kirk	93	87	90	63/4
J. Lowe	99	95	94	73/2
C. Mier	87	90	85	57/7
M. Ross	79	79	84	56/7
W. Ware	84	80	85	59/5

a. Which person had the highest spelling score?
b. Which person had the lowest spelling score?
c. Which person had the highest punctuation score?
d. Which person had the lowest punctuation score?
e. Which person had the highest math score?
f. Which person had the lowest math score?
g. Which person had the highest speed and accuracy score?
h. Which person had the highest overall scores?
i. Which person had the lowest overall scores?
j. Which two people scored the same on a test? which test?

Activity 1 can be done on information processing equipment.

APPLYING OFFICE SKILLS

1. Develop a list of tips for building a good business personality. Prepare (type or keyboard) your list in an attractive format on a separate sheet of paper. Title your list "Developing a Good Business Personality."
2. On a separate sheet of paper, copy the paragraph below in your best handwriting. Correct any spelling errors that you find. Study the guide that follows and try to imitate the clear, even style.

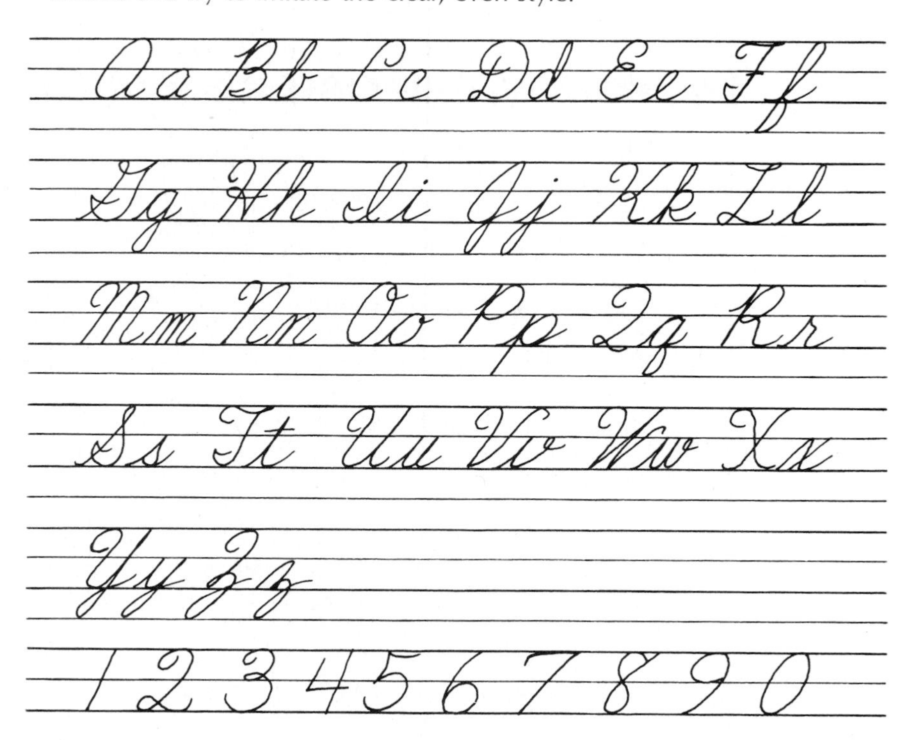

A person's qualifcations for office work does not relate to a person's age. Experence helps a person gain self-confidance. Because some young workers have negative atitudes, some experienced workers think all young workers have a negative atitude. If you do your best on all tasks assigned to you, you will gain the self-confidance that comes with experience. If you approach your job with a good atitude, your coworkers will soon accept you as a valuable member of the office team. The skills you learn in school will help you preform your assigned tasks efficiently. Your knowledge, skills, attitude, and appearance will help you gain poise. If you preform your best, no one will be able to criticize you.

Saving Time and Money

1. Keep reference materials such as telephone directories, a dictionary, a secretarial handbook, and a thesaurus handy. You should also keep references that are related to your job and your company within easy reach. Refer to Appendix D for a list of references frequently used in business offices.
2. When you have time, study your company's style guides and procedures manuals. This practice may eliminate having to refer to these sources every time you have a question about company style or policy.
3. Keep a pocket calculator handy at all times in the office — especially if you regularly work with financial matters.
4. If you have access to information processing equipment in your company, take the opportunity to learn how to use that equipment. Look for ways of using electronic equipment to make your routine office tasks easier and less time consuming.

PROFESSIONAL INSIGHTS

LIFE-LONG LEARNING

Many people think that once they have finished school and learned the skills necessary for their jobs, they need no further instruction or training. However, the skills that help office workers get and hold jobs are appropriate for only a short time. As a company buys new equipment or upgrades present equipment, new systems and procedures are put into effect. As a result, employees must be trained to use that new equipment and to follow the new procedures.

Skills required for office work are changing so rapidly that today's worker must be committed to the concept of "life-long learning" in order to survive and advance on the job. Life-long learning involves taking every opportunity to participate in company training, pursue degree or certificate programs at colleges, and attend seminars and workshops offered by professional organizations. Subscribing to professional journals is also helpful in keeping up to date in one's field.

Many companies have career centers set up in their personnel departments where employees can learn about opportunities for advancement. Such centers also provide information about training offered in and out of the company. In addition, many companies now offer tuition reimbursement for courses taken to develop and refine existing skills or to learn new skills and procedures.

1. What changes have occurred in your chosen field over the past year? What changes can you foresee in that field over the next few years?
2. Think about the skills required for most office workers today. Which of those skills will be more important in the office of the future? Which will be less important?

UNIT 2

BUSINESS COMMUNICATION SKILLS

- The Communication Process
- Written Communication Skills
- Interpersonal Communication Skills

CHAPTER 1

THE COMMUNICATION PROCESS

Communication is the exciting process of sharing information, ideas, and feelings with other people. Whether you are making a suggestion to your supervisor, helping a coworker, or dealing with a customer, you must be able to express yourself clearly and confidently. Employees with good communication skills perform their job responsibilities effectively and can do more to assist their supervisors. They get along better with their coworkers. They also make a good impression on customers. For these reasons, employees who communicate well are valued by their employers and have a better chance for success.

As you study this chapter, you will find answers to the following questions:

- What are the five elements of the communication process and how do they fit together?
- How can you improve your speaking and listening skills?
- What role does body language play in the communication process?
- What do the following terms mean: **communication, verbal, nonverbal, process, channel, decode, feedback, body language?**

BUSINESS COMMUNICATION

com·mu·ni·ca'tion

ver'bal

non·ver'bal

Communication is the exchange of information by means of speech, writing, or signals. Communication is a two-way process of sending and receiving information. It can be **verbal** (either written or spoken) or **nonverbal** (including facial expressions and gestures). Because the purpose of communication is to share information, it is important to have good communication skills. Understanding the process of communication can help you develop the necessary skills.

The Process of Communication

mes'sage

A **process** is a series of actions or operations that leads to a result. The process of communication, which is shown in Illustration 2–1, contains five elements: the sender, message, channel, receiver, and feedback. How the elements fit together can be illustrated by observing John Dennison.

John Dennison has been an accounting clerk with the Norton Corporation for six months. Before that, he worked in the accounting department of a larger company in the area. Many of the billing procedures at Norton are similar to the ones John used at his last job. Some of them, however, are different. John thinks that some of the procedures at Norton could be improved to make the accounting department more efficient. So, he decides to discuss his idea with his supervisor.

chan'nel

John is the *sender* of this communication exchange. His suggestions for improvement are his *message.* John chooses appropriate wording for his message based on his knowledge of his supervisor (the *receiver*) and his particular office setting. Next, he must decide which **channel** or method to use for sending his message. He can call his supervisor on the telephone; write her a letter, memo, or report; or talk to her face to face. The channel he chooses should be the best one for the particular message. For example, it is better to write a message containing important facts and figures than to give it over the telephone. This is because there is less chance that it will be misunderstood in written form. John decides to present his suggestions in a memo to his supervisor.

Illustration 2–1
The communication process

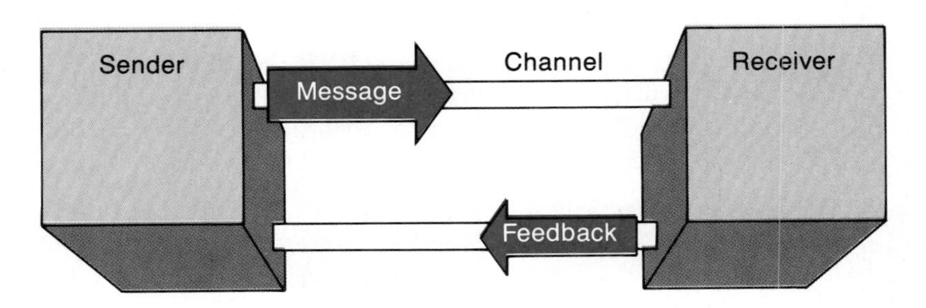

feed'back

When his supervisor receives the message, she must **decode** it, that is, determine the meaning from it. Based on her understanding of the message, she provides **feedback** to John — that is, she responds through actions or words — and the process begins all over again.

The Tools of Communication

lis'ten·ing

In order to participate in the communication process, everyone must be able to send and receive messages using the tools of communication. You send messages by speaking and writing. You receive messages by listening and reading. You send *and* receive messages through nonverbal signals. It is these five tools that allow the sender and the receiver to exchange information.

As you can see, there are many factors at work in the communication process. With so much going on you might wonder how people manage to communicate at all!

Many people don't communicate well — or not as well as they could if they really worked at it. People often spend several years preparing for their future occupations by studying, practicing, and refining their job skills. Most people, though, don't take the time to refine their communication skills. They have the necessary tools — reading, writing, speaking, and so forth — but they don't use them skillfully. Without good communication skills to accompany your job skills, you are only half prepared for your job.

Joan's situation points out how having poor communication skills can hurt you.

> *Joan is an excellent word processing operator. She can keyboard straight-copy material at 90 words a minute with very few errors, if any. Joan has not had any difficulty finding positions in the past year because she always scores high on the keyboarding employment tests.*
>
> *Once she is employed, though, Joan's problems begin. She has trouble following her supervisor's insructions for setting up letters, reports, and tables. She also has a hard time understanding written directions and finds it embarrassing to ask questions when she is unsure. Because she so often completes work without understanding exactly what is desired, she frequently has to rekeyboard her work.*
>
> *Joan's wasted time, wasted supplies, and need for close supervision make her a very costly employee. She is so expensive, in fact, that she has been fired from two jobs already!*

su·per·vi'sion

How can you develop good communication skills and avoid Joan's fate? You can do both by sharpening your communication tools and practicing effective communication techniques. In this chapter, you will focus on skills used in conversation. You will find suggestions to help you

- polish your speech image
- discipline yourself to listen more effectively
- be aware of nonverbal signals

CONVERSATION SKILLS

Conversation skills involve effective speaking, listening, and nonverbal communication. These skills are necessary in any job that brings you in contact with other people either face to face or by telephone.

Effective Speaking

Speaking is a tool that can be polished and refined to help you communicate more effectively. People judge you by the way you speak, so you want to sound like the best possible you! A good speaking image can help you get the job you want. Coupled with on-the-job performance, a good speaking image can open opportunities for advancement in your career.

per·form'ance

You do not have to be brilliant to speak well. However, you do need to be aware of the things that make your speaking ineffective and work to avoid them. Some common speaking problems that detract from your message and make a poor impression include:

de·tract'

im·pres'sion

- talking through the nose
- speaking too quietly
- mumbling or swallowing words
- talking in a monotonous tone
- speaking at a fast or slow pace
- using "fillers" such as *um, okay*
- lisping
- mispronouncing words

Using effective speaking techniques, on the other hand, helps you get your ideas across to the receiver. Speaking effectively is especially important when you use the telephone since your voice alone makes an impression on

Illustration 2–2
Make sure your voice conveys a positive image of you

the listener. Effective speech techniques include speaking clearly, varying your tone and pace, eliminating distractions, and planning your message.

Speak clearly Project your voice — that is, direct it so that it can be heard clearly — so that people don't have to strain to hear you. Not only should you speak loudly enough to be heard, but you should also pronounce each syllable distinctly. Don't be afraid to move your lips and open your mouth. Remember that mumbling is unappealing and annoying to the listener.

Vary the tone of your voice Use all the notes in your range, and vary your tone to emphasize specific words. For questions, raise your voice at the end of the sentence. Well-placed pauses draw attention to the words that follow and make your speech more interesting.

mis·pro·nounced'

Eliminate distractions from your speech Avoid using words such as *er, um, okay,* and *you know.* You may not notice these fillers, but listeners do! Listeners are also distracted by slang, shrill or nasal voices, mispronounced words, and strong regional accents.

Plan your message When you are the one who begins the conversation, know what it is you want to say and try to get to the point quickly. This is especially true in business situations. If there is a problem you need to discuss with your supervisor or coworker, for example, choose a convenient time. Then organize your thoughts. Make notes, if necessary, especially if you are speaking by telephone. Your listener will appreciate the well-organized expression of your ideas.

e·val'u·ate

If you are unaware of the speech image you project, ask one of your parents, teachers, friends, or school counselors to evaluate you. Then work on correcting the problems they identify.

Effective Listening

As Illustration 2–1 shows, successful communication depends on your ability to listen well. In fact, in terms of the amount of time devoted to it, listening is the most important communication tool you have. The average person spends more time listening each day than in any other communication activity. Despite its importance, however, many people have listening problems. Tests show that after 10 or 15 minutes, most people can remember only about half of what they have heard. After 24 hours, they remember only a fourth of the original message.

re·quire'ment

Good listening skills are a requirement for success as an office worker. Much of the information and instructions you need to do your job will be given to you in conversation. You will frequently be required to take messages over the telephone. And, if you have transcribing duties, you will be expected to keyboard dictated material from tape recordings. If you are like most people, your listening skills will need improvement.

Illustration 2–3 Transcribing is one office task that requires good listening skills

con·cen·tra′tion

Although hearing is as automatic as breathing, effective listening takes effort and concentration. It is difficult to change listening habits. To become a better listener, you first must recognize bad listening habits and then work to improve them.

Tune in to the speaker Most people respond well to what is familiar to them. When they hear a person discussing something they know little about, something they don't agree with, or something they aren't interested in, they close their ears and stop listening. Sometimes they make the mistake of assuming that they know what the speaker is going to say. For example, how many times have you asked, "How are you," and then not listened to the response? You simply assume that the answer will be "Fine, thanks." Good listeners make themselves listen to the entire message to see what they can learn from it.

dis·trac′tions

Screen out distractions Hearing and listening are two different activities. Listening requires concentration, whereas hearing is involuntary. Poor listeners allow distractions to break their concentration. They may tune in on outside disturbances, such as a conversation in the next room or a clock ticking. They may even create their own distractions, such as counting the number of times the speaker says *um* or tapping their pencils on desk tops. Although they hear the message, poor listeners do not make an effort to understand it. To improve your concentration, pay attention with each of your senses — watch the speaker with your eyes, listen with your ears, and use your hands to take notes.

Ask questions One of the common causes of a breakdown in the communication process is failure to understand the message. Either the sender or the receiver of the message may be responsible for the breakdown. As the receiver, though, it is your responsibility to make sure that you understand what is said. If you are unsure or confused, ask the speaker to clarify the message or give you more information. Don't be embarrassed or feel stupid. If you're afraid you might forget what the speaker says, write down the main points. By asking questions and taking notes, you can save time and effort.

clar'i·fy

Changing your listening habits is not easy. You need to recognize poor habits and make an effort to do something about them. Good concentration and a desire to change will make it easier. So tune in to the speaker, screen out distractions, and ask questions.

Nonverbal Communication

A skillful listener gets added information from a speaker's nonverbal message, which is called **body language**. Nonverbal communication is the process by which meanings, thoughts, and attitudes are expressed in symbols other than words. These symbols include speech patterns, posture, gestures, and facial expressions. Examples of several nonverbal messages are shown in Illustration 2–4.

ges'tures

In developing your communication skills, remember that your posture, gestures, facial expressions, and other movements should serve a purpose. When you speak, your nonverbal messages should clarify your verbal

Illustration 2–4

DICTIONARY OF BODY LANGUAGE

Body Language	Meaning
Wearing	
. . . a school letter jacket.	I'm an athlete.
. . . a diamond ring.	I'm engaged.
. . . a souvenir t-shirt.	I'm a traveler.
. . . running shoes.	I'm a jogger.
Talking	
. . . in a monotonous voice.	I'm bored.
. . . in a loud, strong voice.	I'm angry or excited.
. . . in a low, quiet voice.	This is a secret.
Standing	
. . . with arms folded in front.	Don't come too close.
. . . with hands on hips.	I'm in charge.
. . . with good posture.	I'm self-confident.
Making	
. . . a fist.	I'm angry.
. . . a pointing gesture.	Look at this one.

message for the listener. When you listen, you can give the speaker meaningful feedback through your use of body language.

You can become aware of effective body language by observing other people, especially those people who make a good impression as speakers. Watch them as they speak or listen. What gestures do they use to emphasize a point? How do they express interest in other people's ideas? Are their hands distracting, or do they clarify what is being said?

Observing other people can also make you more alert to their feelings, which they show through nonverbal signals. The skillful observer notices when nonverbal messages are different from the verbal message. For example, you might notice the look of disappointment on the face of a friend who says, "I'm so happy for you." In this situation, you need to respond to both messages. The nonverbal message says, "I'm disappointed for myself," and the verbal one says, "I'm happy for you, though, because you are a friend of mine."

dis·ap·point'ment

Through nonverbal communication, you can project your poise and self-confidence. If your gestures and posture show others that you are capable and knowledgeable about your job, they will have more confidence in you. Your poise and self-confidence will make a good impression on your supervisor, coworkers, and customers. So make sure your nonverbal message is a positive one.

REVIEWING KEY POINTS

1. Communication is defined as the two-way process of sending and receiving information.
2. Communication can be either verbal (using words) or nonverbal (using body language).
3. To communicate with others, you must select an appropriate channel through which to send your message. Types of channels include face-to-face conversations, telephone calls, letters, reports, and memos.
4. The five tools of communication are speaking, writing, listening, reading, and nonverbal signals.
5. A good speech image can help you reach your employment goals. You can make your speech work for you if you speak clearly, give variety to your voice, avoid distracting phrases and accents, and plan your message.
6. Skillful listeners tune in to the speaker, screen out distractions, and ask questions for clarification.
7. Body language and other nonverbal signals are important in clarifying your message, in understanding other speakers, and in giving feedback.

DEVELOPING HUMAN RELATIONS SKILLS

1. For clear, positive interactions, which communication channel would you use in each of the following situations?
   a. Your supervisor has left for the day. Just as you are leaving, Mr. Allen, vice president of your company, calls to say that he needs to see your supervisor first thing in the morning. What is the best way to get this message to your supervisor?
   b. Your company's annual sales meeting has been scheduled for 11 months from now. Choice of a meeting site will be based on responses to a 15-question survey. What communication channel would be best for getting responses to the survey from five hotels in your city?
   c. On Monday morning, your supervisor asks you to notify four people in your office about a meeting they must attend on Friday. Your supervisor gives you the date, time, place, and purpose of the meeting. What communication channel would you use to notify these people?
2. A coworker asks for your help in arranging a training seminar. She says to you, "We are going to have a large group in for training at the end of the month. It'll help me a lot if you will reserve a room for the seminar and make sure that the seating is properly arranged."
   a. What feedback should you give in order to best help your coworker?
   b. What additional information do you need in order to make the proper arrangements?

IMPROVING COMMUNICATION SKILLS

Refer to Appendix A 2.1–2.2.

1. On a separate sheet of paper, write, type, or keyboard the following sentences, choosing the verb that agrees with the subject in each case.
   a. A box of papers (is, are) on the desk.
   b. Each of the reports (is, are) important.
   c. Her thoughtlessness and discourtesy (annoy, annoys) me.
   d. Joyce, with her four coworkers, (is, are) in the cafeteria.
   e. Mrs. Baldwin, together with the other managers, (is, are) planning the Christmas party.
   f. The committee (has, have) the power to make a recommendation.
   g. Five minutes (is, are) a long time to wait for an answer.
   h. Lester or she (is, are) to program the computer.
   i. Zelma or I (has, have) to lead the discussion.
   j. No one (is, are) doing what was asked.

2. Read the sentences shown here. Decide how you would express the meaning of each sentence in your own words (this is known as paraphrasing). On a separate sheet of paper, write, type, or keyboard your sentences. A sample sentence that has been paraphrased is shown here.

As each of us is a person unlike any other, we cannot approach a communication situation from exactly the same point of view.

Since we are all different, we cannot see each communication situation in exactly the same way.

   a. Some people have no real interest in a particular subject or lack a desire to understand it.
   b. Our actions often contradict our words.
   c. Nonverbal communication takes place all the time.
   d. Immediate feedback contributes more to effective communication than does delayed feedback.
   e. Most people enjoy talking more than they enjoy listening.
   f. In a communication exchange, it is the speaker's responsibility to make sure that the listener understands the intended message.
   g. Little progresss can be made in communication unless the sender thinks about how much the listener already knows about the subject to be discussed.
   h. Just because a person can hear does not mean that he or she can listen effectively.

BUILDING PROBLEM-SOLVING SKILLS

1. On a separate sheet of paper, write the answers to the following problems. Refer to Appendix C if necessary.

   a. 2.50 + 30 + 0.9 =
   b. 3.3 + 1.1 + 0.6 =
   c. 5 + 15 + .47 + .028 =
   d. .4789 + 23.04 + .555 =
   e. .555 + 32 =
   f. 1.6 + 0.04 + 0.4 =
   g. 28 − 0.45 =
   h. .76 − .2 =
   i. 123.1 − 34.074 =
   j. 1.9999 − .698 =

2. Study the table shown on the top of the next page. Then, on a separate sheet of paper, answer the questions that follow.

   a. What is the total number of word processing operators in all of the departments?
   b. What is the total number of word processors in all of the departments?

Dept.	Total No. of Employees	No. of Word Processing Operators	Total No. of Word Processors
A	2540	21	20
B	8733	35	32
C	225	5	5
D	1248	12	12
E	3465	18	20
F	4037	56	49
G	2870	7	8
H	2850	22	14
I	465	11	11
J	3600	36	26

c. What fraction of the employees in Department C are word processing operators?

d. Three-fourths of the word processing operators in Department F work full time. How many operators in that department work part time?

e. Three-fifths of the employees in Department A submit work to be done on word processors. How many employees in this department do *not* submit work to be done on word processors?

Activities 2 and 3 can be done on information processing equipment.

APPLYING OFFICE SKILLS

1. Observe on television two of the following: a news commentator, a talk show host or hostess, or an actor or actress from a weekly series. Record the following information on the form provided in your workbook or on a separate sheet of paper.

   - name of person observed
   - a brief description of their typical gestures, facial expressions, speech patterns, and dress habits

   Then answer the following questions, explaining the reasons for your answers.

   a. Was the body language of the people you observed appropriate for their profession or role?

   b. Which nonverbal techniques identified with the television personalities would be appropriate for office workers?

2. Your supervisor has just returned from a workshop on communication skills in which the speaker provided the following suggestions for training coworkers. On a separate sheet of paper, prepare (type or keyboard) this list of suggestions. Center the title "Guidelines for Training Fellow Employees" in all capital letters 2 inches from the top edge. Use 1-inch left and right

margins. Begin typing or keyboarding the three side headings at the left margin. Triple space before and double space after each heading. Single space each numbered item; double space between items.

Preparation

1. Identify the task to be done.
2. Explain the importance of the activity.
3. Review similar tasks that your coworker is already familiar with.

Presentation

1. Introduce your coworker to the materials, equipment, and special terms related to the task.
2. Always begin with the simple and move gradually to the complex.
3. Demonstrate and explain each step clearly, answering all questions completely as they are raised.

Application

1. Have your coworker explain the procedure in his or her own words
2. Have your coworker perform the task with as little supervision as possible.
3. Give feedback and suggestions for improvement.

3. Interview an experienced office worker. Ask him or her to discuss an incident in the office that shows the importance of communication skills in working effectively with others. On a separate sheet of paper, prepare a short summary of this interview.

CHAPTER 2

WRITTEN COMMUNICATION SKILLS

Telephone calls and face-to-face conversations are appropriate channels to use for some types of business communication. However, written materials play an important role in the exchange of information within and between companies. Every day, millions of letters, memorandums, reports, and legal documents are written to serve a variety of purposes. They may inform company employees of a new company policy or explain to customers new procedures for billing. They may ask for information about new products or request permission to attend a conference. The purpose of all written communication, however, is simply to give or request information.

Even beginning employees need to be able to understand what other people have written. You will probably learn much about your new job by reading job descriptions, procedures manuals, and other written materials. To succeed in the business office, therefore, you need good reading and good writing skills.

As you study this chapter, you will find answers to the following questions:

- What steps can you take to improve your reading skills and comprehension?
- What are *The Five C's* of effective business writing, and how can you use them to improve your own writing?
- What do the following terms mean: **The Five C's, outline, synonyms, homonyms, positive words?**

READING COMPREHENSION

Reading is the means of obtaining information through the written or printed word. It serves as the basis for many of your decisions, ideas, and opinions. In today's world, a poor reader is at a definite disadvantage.

com·pre·hend'

So many activities require you to read and to comprehend what you have read. For example, research is required in many office jobs. You may be given a topic and asked to find information about it for your supervisor to use in a report. Your own job responsibilities may require you to look up facts for your own information. It is necessary not only to understand what you read but also to be able to evaluate and remember it. If you are not a good reader, your effectiveness as a communicator, a decision maker, and an employee will be weakened.

ef·fec'tive·ness

In school, mistakes that result from your failure to understand written instructions may mean the difference between a *B* and a *C*. On the job, these mistakes may be more serious. They may cost your company money. If you make too many mistakes, like Joan in the last chapter, you may lose your job.

Developing Reading Skills

How do you become a better reader? Here are some basic guidelines that you can follow to help improve your ability to read, comprehend, and remember. These guidelines work equally well whether applied to a chapter of this book or to an operating manual for a piece of office equipment.

Choose a good reading environment Your reading area should have quiet surroundings, adequate lighting, a comfortable temperature, and a chair that encourages good posture. Adequate lighting and good posture are necessary to help you avoid fatigue. If your job requires you to do a lot of close reading or research, you may be given a quiet work area with additional lighting. In addition, some companies also provide a library or a reading room for their employees to use.

pre·lim'i·nar·y

Make a preliminary survey Glance through the material before you start to read. Skim the introduction, headings, and summary to get a mental outline of the content and organization.

thor'ough·ness

Define your purpose Your purpose for reading will determine the thoroughness with which you read and the rate at which you read. Read slowly and carefully when you are trying to understand explanations or instructions. Read more quickly when you are reading for pleasure or looking for a particular item of information.

Concentrate on what you are reading You waste time when you don't concentrate because you have to go back over passages you have already read.

Illustration 2-5
A good environment for reading is well lighted, quiet, and comfortable

To improve your concentration, eliminate distractions — turn off the radio or close the door. Move to another location, if necessary. Try to keep your eyes and mind on the material in front of you.

Improving Comprehension

You can improve your understanding of what you read by building your vocabulary, taking notes, reviewing, and asking for feedback.

Build your vocabulary Your reading speed and comprehension increase as your vocabulary grows. When you come across an unfamiliar word in your reading, write it down. Then look it up in a dictionary as soon as possible. To help yourself remember the meaning, try to use each new word in a sentence the same day.

Take notes to help you remember After you have read an entire section, make notes or underline the main points. Usually there is one sentence in each paragraph that contains the main idea.

re·call'

Review When you finish the article or chapter, try to recall the main points. Summaries and end-of-chapter materials are designed to help you review, so use them.

sum'ma·rize

Ask for feedback It is very important that you understand what you read, especially when you are trying to follow written instructions or explanations of procedures. If you are not sure you understand something, ask your supervisor or an experienced coworker for feedback. To let them know you have read the materials and made an effort to understand them, summarize the main facts in your own words. For example, you might say, "I've read the procedures for preparing credit memos. Let me see if I've understood this correctly." By asking for feedback, you prevent errors caused by any misunderstanding.

WRITING SKILLS

Written materials play an important role in the processing of information in a business. When you first begin a job, your responsibility for the quality of written messages may be limited to keyboarding them neatly and making sure the spelling is correct. Your supervisor may ask you to make minor corrections in grammar, punctuation, capitalization, and wording in the materials you keyboard. With time, you may be given responsibility for answering business correspondence.

How can you make sure that the business messages that you keyboard and write will be understood quickly, easily, and thoroughly? Before you keyboard them in final form, check to see that they are *complete, clear, correct, concise,* and *courteous.* These qualities are frequently referred to as **The Five C's** of effective business writing.

Completeness

out'line

A complete message contains all the information that the reader needs in order to understand and respond. The easiest way to make sure that you include the necessary informaton is to *think* about your purpose and then plan what you need to say to achieve that purpose. An **outline** is a written plan of what you want to say. It is prepared before you begin writing the first sentence of your message.

Assume that you are a receiving clerk. You find a shortage in a shipment and want to inform your supervisor about it. This is your purpose. To write a complete report of the situation, you might prepare the following outline:

1. List the items that were ordered. Include the purchase order number and the name of the supplier.
2. State what items were received and the invoice number.
3. List the missing items.

log'i·cal

As you write the message in paragraph form, refer to your outline to make sure that you cover the main points. Following an outline also helps you to present the information in a logical order and helps you keep to your topic. You will read more about outlines in Unit 8.

Clear Language

Using an outline helps you organize your thoughts. But you must also understand the meaning of words and use words that say what you mean.

Use familiar language Words that are similar in meaning are called **synonyms**. Synonyms include words such as *ask* and *inquire, finish* and *complete, use* and *utilize.* Using synonyms adds variety to your writing, but it can also add confusion. Some people use long, unfamiliar words (such as *ebullient* instead of *excited*) because they think it makes them sound more important and intelligent. But, if your reader doesn't understand the words you use, you are not communicating. For this reason, it is usually a good idea to use familiar language in business writing.

spe·cif'ic

Use specific language Another way to help your reader understand your exact meaning is to avoid the use of vague words. The adjective *large* is an example of a vague word. When you write, "We will need a *large* room for the committee meeting," the reader does not receive enough information to help you. How large? Do you need a room to seat 25 people or 125? Be as specific as you can to avoid misunderstandings in written communication.

Correctness

Follow the rules of spelling, grammar, and punctuation to make sure your writing is correct and easy to understand.

no'tice·a·ble

Spelling A misspelled word is very noticeable in a keyboarded message. Spelling errors present a bad image of your company and distract the reader's attention from the message. Develop the habit of referring to a dictionary whenever you are in doubt about the spelling of a word.

Some words are so frequently misspelled that they appear in lists of commonly misspelled words. Such lists can be found in most office reference manuals. They usually contain the following words — and many others:

accommodation
acknowledgment
benefited
bookkeeper
congratulate
maintenance
occasionally
privilege

Spelling difficulties sometimes result when one word is confused with another. Words that are pronounced exactly alike but have different meanings and spellings are called **homonyms.** Homonyms can cause problems when you are taking dictation or transcribing from tapes. You need to be alert to the differences in meanings and spellings of common words such as:

their — there — they're
to — too — two
site — sight — cite
principal — principle

Illustration 2–6
Reference sources contain the basic rules of spelling, grammar, and punctuation

Another group of words confuses readers and writers because they have similar spellings, but different meanings. Examples include *advice* and *advise, affect* and *effect, formerly* and *formally, adapt* and *adopt.* A dictionary, a thesaurus, or a book on usage can help you distinguish between these words and show you when to use each one.

dis·tin'guish

Grammar and punctuation Reference guides, such as the one at the back of this book in Appendix A, contain the basic rules of grammar and punctuation. Use them. Although you study these rules in school, you forget them if you don't review them periodically and apply them in your writing.

Some people argue that using correct grammar and punctuation is unnecessary because readers can figure out what you mean even if it is incorrect. Can they? Notice how the meaning of these sentences changes when you change one word or punctuation mark.

I like Susan better than him. (*I like Susan more than I like him.*)	I like Susan better than he. (*I like Susan more than he does.*)
Bob Drew and I are on the team. (*Two people are on the team.*)	Bob, Drew, and I are on the team. (*Three people are on the team.*)

Correct grammar and punctuation are necessary not only for communicating clearly but also for making a good impression. Using incorrect grammar or punctuation causes many readers to question the knowledge of the writer. They think, "If the grammar is incorrect, what about the facts?"

Content There is one last thing that must be correct in all business writing — the content. Remember that the purpose of communication is to exchange information. Therefore, always make sure that the information you use is the most up to date. Check names, dates, and amounts with someone who is in a position to know if there have been any recent changes.

Conciseness

Being concise means that you use no more words than necessary to express your thoughts. Various surveys show that as much as 30 percent of the average business letter consists of unnecessary words. These extra words are expensive to compose, type, and read. Sometimes they get in the way, obstructing or hiding your message.

char'ac·ter·ized

Concise writing is characterized by short words and brief sentences. Notice how some commonly used phrases can be replaced with just a simple word.

Wordy	Concise
In the event that it rains . . .	*If* it rains . . .
Enclosed *please find* the report . . .	Enclosed *is* the report. . . .

re·dun'dant

Some writers use unnecessary words because they think this writing style sounds important or official. They string together redundant words (words that repeat the meaning), producing sentences that are unnecessarily long. The following expressions are redundant; only the underlined word is necessary for meaning.

first began	each and every
completely finished	past experience

Try to eliminate unnecessary words from your sentences. You'll find that what you write is easier to read and understand, as this example shows:

Due to the fact that we first began this project before the advance planning was completely finished, each and every aspect of the job had to be redone a second time.

Because we began this project before the planning was finished, each aspect of the job had to be redone.

Courteousness

Courtesy makes a good impression on people and encourages them to respond favorably. In business writing, you can show your reader courtesy by using polite phrases such as *thank you, please,* and *at your convenience.* You can avoid the overuse of self-centered pronouns, such as *I, we, my, mine, us,* or *me.* And, you can try to use positive words.

Positive words are words that suggest *good* instead of *bad, pleasant* instead of *unpleasant,* and *favorable* instead of *unfavorable.* It is not always easy to word your message positively. However, you *can* avoid using negative words such as *not, delay, fail, regret, mistake, unable,* and *impossible.* Avoid saying that it is impossible to fill a customer's order or that the order will be late. Instead, try to emphasize when the order will arrive or what you plan to do to ensure that it arrives promptly.

Courtesy and positive words can sell your company's products, services, and image. Using positive words can also sell *you* to your employer, coworkers, and customers.

REVIEWING KEY POINTS

1. Improve your reading skills by choosing a good reading environment, surveying the material, defining your purpose, and concentrating on what you read.
2. Improve your reading comprehension by building your vocabulary, taking notes, reviewing the main points, and asking for feedback when needed.
3. Every business message should be complete, clear, correct, concise, and courteous.
4. An outline is a written plan that helps a writer include the main points in an order that will be easily understood.
5. Use familiar and specific language for clear writing.
6. To make your writing easier to understand and make a good impression on the reader, use correct spelling, grammar, punctuation, and content.
7. A concise message is clear and complete and as brief as the topic allows.
8. When you write, you can show courtesy to the reader by using polite phrases, avoiding self-centered pronouns, and by using positive words.

DEVELOPING HUMAN RELATIONS SKILLS

1. In the business environment, there are many situations in which good conversation skills are necessary. On a separate sheet of paper, write, type, or keyboard three questions or comments that you would use to start a conversation in each of the following situations.
   a. Welcoming the new receptionist for your office.
   b. Visiting with your supervisor at a break in the cafeteria.
   c. Meeting for the first time a coworker from another department who has been with the company for 20 years.
   d. Being introduced to your coworker's wife as you leave for the day.
   e. Talking with a customer who is waiting to see your supervisor.
2. Recently you were assigned to work with Patricia, a new employee, on several important projects in your office. You have found out Patricia is not

well organized and often has to redo her part of an assignment. As a result of her poor work habits, you have already missed your first deadline.

a. What should you say to Patricia?

b. How would you explain this problem to your supervisor?

c. What can be done to make sure you do not miss future deadlines?

IMPROVING COMMUNICATION SKILLS

Refer to Appendix A 2.1–2.2.

1. On a separate sheet of paper, write, type, or keyboard the following sentences, choosing the verb that agrees with the subject in each case.

a. Either of the clerks (is, are) acceptable for the job.

b. Joan and Michael (need, needs) to earn money for college.

c. Sharon, with the help of the supervisors, (schedule, schedules) vacations for all office workers.

d. Neither of the drafts (is, are) accurate.

e. Four copies of the original report (was, were) mailed to him.

f. The man and his son (work, works) in the same building.

g. Many homeowners, along with the developer of the subdivision, (is, are) pleased with the landscaping work.

h. Each of the ten players on the team (is, are) to sell $50 worth of tickets.

i. Politics (is, are) not a subject that can be discussed peacefully.

j. Tanya, in addition to the other members of the committee, (plan, plans) to study the report before the staff meeting.

2. On a separate sheet of paper, paraphrase (rewrite in your own words) the following statements.

a. If you ever feel insecure, just remember that everyone is insecure to some degree.

b. If you are cold and shy with other people, they may feel uncomfortable and think you are self-centered.

c. If you monopolize a conversation more than a moment or two, you will seem to be seeking the spotlight.

d. In most cases, it is better to let your superior lead the conversation.

e. Saying *you* when you praise and not saying *you* when you criticize will help you communicate positively.

f. Cooperation is an investment that pays dividends.

g. When you can make suggestions to coworkers or your boss without offending them, you will be a real asset to your company.

h. Criticism makes it possible for you to grow professionally.

BUILDING PROBLEM-SOLVING SKILLS

1. On a separate sheet of paper, write the answers to the following problems. Refer to Appendix C if necessary.

   a. 2.4 × 3.89 =
   b. 89 × 2.1007 =
   c. .0007 × 2.860 =
   d. .568 × 1.42 =
   e. 0.6132 × 10.4 =
   f. 82.56 ÷ 24.9 =
   g. .78 ÷ 5 =
   h. 33 ÷ 6.6 =
   i. 178 ÷ 5.79 =
   j. 55.5 ÷ 30.6 =

2. One of your coworkers recently conducted a survey of the record-buying habits of the employees in your company. The table shown here lists how many records, by category, employees in various age groups purchased over the past year. Study the table, then on a separate sheet of paper answer the questions that follow.

RECORD PURCHASES BY AGE GROUP

Category	Ages 18–23	Ages 24–28	Ages 29–33	Ages 34–39	Ages 40 +
Rock	28	25	34	22	10
Country	12	10	10	15	41
Easy Listening	9	8	6	18	39
Classical	11	15	16	18	24

   a. What is the total number of records bought in all categories?
   b. What was the most popular category for each age group?
   c. What was the least popular category for each age group?
   d. What percent of the total do purchases of classical records represent?
   e. What percent of the total records purchased were bought by employees in the 18–23 age group?

APPLYING OFFICE SKILLS

Activities 1 and 2 can be done on information processing equipment.

1. You have made the following notes from an article on how to accept criticism well. Prepare (type or keyboard) a copy of your notes on a separate sheet of paper, centering the title "Coping with Criticism" in all capital letters. Use 1-inch left and right margins. Triple space after the title. Single space each numbered item and double space between the items.
   1. Be silent while hearing the complaint, but show that you are listening.
   2. Look at the person who is speaking.
   3. Under no circumstances — not a word or lifted eyebrow — find fault with the person who is criticizing.

4. Don't try to be funny.
5. Don't create the impression that you are destroyed by the criticism.
6. Don't exaggerate the complaint.
7. Don't sidestep the issue or change the subject.
8. Don't imply that the criticizer has an outside motive.
9. Make necessary changes in behavior or attitude as swiftly as possible.
10. Don't hold a grudge against the criticizer; be grateful for the information that helps you grow professionally.

2. The receptionist in your department has a difficult time keeping track of people because they work staggered hours (called *flextime*) and take their lunches at different times. Your supervisor has asked you to help the receptionist by preparing a listing of the names of the people in the department, the hours they work, and their usual lunch times. You have collected the information shown below.

Prepare this information in an attractive format. Double space between each employee's entry. Type or keyboard the names in alphabetical order by last name — last name (comma) and initial. Center the title "Flextime Schedules" in all capital letters.

Employee	Hours	Lunch
P. Finn	8:00 - 5:00	1:00 - 2:00
D. Roaden	7:30 - 4:30	12:30 - 1:30
S. Stravinski	7:30 - 4:30	12:00 - 1:00
R. Chelko	8:30 - 5:30	1:00 - 2:00
W. Chang	8:00 - 5:00	1:00 - 2:00
S. Wolnitzek	8:00 - 5:00	12:00 - 1:00
T. Voss	8:30 - 5:30	12:30 - 1:30
G. Tribor	9:00 - 6:00	1:30 - 2:30
T. Ming	8:00 - 5:00	12:30 - 1:30
S. Baldwin	8:30 - 5:30	1:00 - 2:00
O. Lassiter	8:00 - 5:00	12:00 - 1:00

CHAPTER 3

INTERPERSONAL COMMUNICATION SKILLS

In the office you have frequent opportunities to meet, work with, and build relationships with people of all ages, abilities, backgrounds, and interests. Your relationships with other people are called interpersonal relationships, meaning between persons. Because you usually do not get to choose the people you work with, not all of your interpersonal relationships at work will be warm or pleasant. But all of your work relationships should be productive. You must not allow personal feelings to prevent you or other people from doing the job you were hired to do. As an employee, you are expected to cooperate with others to achieve the company's goals.

Using your communication skills to interact with others is the process of interpersonal communication. Interpersonal communication includes face-to-face communication (such as conversations, interviews, and meetings), as well as telephone conversations. As you know, you communicate your ideas and feelings through words and body language.

There are several work situations in which good communication skills will help you build productive interpersonal relationships. They include meeting people and developing friendships, giving and receiving feedback, handling criticism, and dealing with customers.

As you study this chapter, you will find answers to the following questions:

- Why is the development of good interpersonal communication skills essential to job success?
- How can effective feedback prevent the costly mistakes that result when people do not understand one another?
- What do the following terms mean: **interpersonal communication, feedback, constructive criticism?**

BUILDING WORK RELATIONSHIPS

Beginning a new job is exciting! You have a chance to apply your knowledge and experience, to learn new skills and new ways of doing things, and to meet new people. But the first week or two can be lonely. Even though you are surrounded by people, most of them are strangers. How will you ever be able to remember their names? How will you like working with them? What if they aren't friendly?

self-con′fi·dence
in·ter·per′son·al

It is quite natural to have fears and doubts about being accepted and liked by your coworkers. Having self-confidence and a positive attitude makes it easier for you to build work relationships, but good interpersonal communication skills are necessary, too. **Interpersonal communication** involves using communication skills, both verbal and nonverbal, to interact with others. By making an effort to be friendly, considerate of others, easy to talk to, and pleasant to be around, you can encourage others who work with you to achieve your company's goals.

Getting to Know Your Coworkers

Make an effort to be friendly. Whether you are new to the company or have been transferred from another department, it is important to start out on the right foot. One way to make a good impression on people is to call them by

Illustration 2–7 Make an effort to get to know your coworkers

name. It will be easier to remember names if you follow these steps when you are introduced to coworkers:

1. Get the name clearly. If you aren't sure you heard it correctly, ask the person to repeat it.
2. Repeat the name immediately. (''It's nice to meet you, Wayne.'')
3. Associate the name with another word that reminds you of the person. (Example: *Marge* works with *Marvin.*)
4. Repeat the name several times in conversation.
5. Write the name down when you get back to your desk.

as·so'ci·ate

Respecting Your Coworkers

Show respect for other people. Respecting others means that you show them special consideration or hold them in high esteem. People are more likely to accept your ideas and cooperate with you if you satisfy their basic need for respect. In the office, there are many ways that you can show your respect.

con·sid·er·a'tion

Compliment people when they do an especially good job Praise is a form of recognition that everyone likes to receive. But praise is more meaningful when it is earned, and more useful when it is specific. Instead of giving a general compliment, such as ''You did a nice job on that report,'' pinpoint the part of the job that was done unusually well. For example, ''Good job, Jon. Double spacing this report makes it much easier to read.''

rec·og·ni'tion

Show an interest in others People like to talk about themselves, and your interest in hearing about them is a form of flattery. To build good interpersonal relationships, place emphasis on the other person, not on yourself.

flat'ter·y

Try to understand how others feel Empathy is the ability to put yourself in another person's place — to understand how they feel or why they act the way they do. You can build your understanding of others by listening to them and being sensitive to their problems.

em'pa·thy

sen'si·tive

Practice good work habits Every person in the office is a member of the team. But people lose their team spirit and their willingness to cooperate when other team members have annoying or distracting behavior. So be considerate: Arrive on time; be neat and organized; and avoid irritating habits such as tapping your pencil on your desk, talking too loudly, or whistling.

ir'ri·tat·ing

Developing Your Conversation Skills

Good conversation skills help to establish good working relationships. Through conversations, you get to know people; you learn about their likes, dislikes, interests, attitudes, and opinions. Your knowledge of others makes it easier to choose the right words and actions when communicating.

re·la'tion·ships

Illustration 2-8
Show appreciation for work well done

Many people find it difficult to begin a conversation, especially with people they don't know well. But it is really quite simple. Try starting a conversation with:

- Basic information. ("Where are you from?" "Hi, my name is . . .")
- Small talk. (Is it still raining hard?" "This elevator seems to take forever.")
- Compliments. ("Your car is in great shape." "Congratulations on your promotion.")
- Request for or offer of assistance. ("Can you tell me where the library is?" "I'm going to the cafeteria. Can I bring you something?")

con·trib'ute

A conversation is a two-way exchange. If you want a conversation to continue, you must contribute more than the opening remark. You can keep a conversation going by doing these things:

- Relate your comments to what the speaker is talking about. ("Your comment makes me think of a movie I saw recently." "I didn't know you liked science fiction. Have you read . . .?")
- Ask questions that call for more than a *yes* or *no* answer. ("What do you think she'll do now?" "What kind of stereo do you want to buy?")
- Show your interest through nonverbal symbols. (Nod your head or make eye contact.)

Being Positive in Your Comments and Attitudes

Perhaps you know someone who always sees the negative side of things or expects the worst. Do you enjoy being around that person? To get cooperation from other people and to have them enjoy working with you, you need to think, act, and speak positively. Notice the difference being positive makes.

Negative	*Positive*
● "You claim you left the report on my desk? I suppose it walked away on its own?"	● "I've misplaced that report, Ben. Will you help me find it?"

There are several things you can do to project a more positive image. First, you can avoid negative words, such as *don't, can't,* and *impossible* in your speech. Instead of saying, "I can't finish this by lunch time," say, "I'll have this ready for you at 3:00." Second, you can try to think positively. A negative person will see a bright summer sky and think, "It's too hot to do anything!" The positive thinker will say, "What a perfect day for a swim!" Third, you can use positive body language. Smile, make eye contact, nod in agreement, pick your feet up when you walk, and look energetic. You'll look and feel better, and you'll make the people around you feel better, too.

en·er·get'ic

GIVING AND GETTING FEEDBACK

To work successfully with other people, you have to be sure that your actions and words are clearly understood. You also have to be sure that you

Illustration 2–9 Pleasant work relationships make your job more enjoyable

understand what your supervisors, customers, and coworkers say, mean, and do. This understanding is reflected by the response that others give you or the response you give others.

Paying Attention to Your Listeners

Feedback is the verbal or nonverbal response that a listener gives a speaker. By observing your listener's responses, you can tell if your message has been received and understood. If feedback shows that your listeners are confused — if they look puzzled, scratch their heads, or ask questions — then you should repeat the message, using different words or adding examples.

in·ter′pret

At first, you may find it difficult to interpret feedback, especially nonverbal feedback. If you are not sure that your listeners have heard or understood you, try asking, "Is this clear?" or "Do you have any questions?" You can encourage feedback by pausing and looking directly at your listeners. This allows them to ask questions.

Being an Active Listener

You can improve your interpersonal communications by becoming a more active listener. Giving immediate feedback is one way to let people know whether you have heard and understood them. For example, a nod indicates that you understand or agree; a frown tells the speaker that you are confused or uncertain about the meaning. If the speaker doesn't notice your nonverbal signals, interrupt politely with your question at the next pause in the conversation. If you don't interrupt, the speaker will automatically assume that you understand.

in·ter·rupt′

At times, you may *think* you understand the speaker's message but feel unsure because there is more than one way to interpret it. When this happens, you should repeat the speaker's message as *you* understand it. Say, for example, "Let me see if I've got this right. First, . . ." The speaker can then correct you if you are wrong.

By being aware of the feedback you receive and giving feedback to others, you can improve the quality of your interpersonal communication. You can also prevent the costly mistakes that often result when people misunderstand each other.

HANDLING CRITICISM

Praise and criticism are special forms of feedback. Although praise is more pleasant to give and receive, criticism is just as important. When the purpose of criticism is to help another person improve or change behavior, criticism can actually strengthen a relationship.

Responding Positively to Criticism

How do you respond to criticism? Do you withdraw? Do you make excuses for your actions? Do you begin to attack or criticize the speaker?

Every office worker must face criticism at one time or another. Sometimes the criticism is deserved and intended to help. This type is called **constructive criticism**. At other times, the criticism is unfair and unjustified. In either case, there is a wrong way and a right way to respond to others' criticism.

un·just'i·fied

The wrong way to handle criticism is to withdraw or keep silent, to make excuses for the criticized behavior, or to attack the speaker. These are natural reactions to criticism — after all, your public image and self-concept have been threatened. However, such behavior is unproductive. It may anger the person giving the criticism. What began as a comment intended to help you improve may turn into an argument and create permanent hard feelings.

What is the right way to handle criticism? First, try to remain calm. Count to three or five (or any number you choose) to prevent yourself from responding angrily. Then follow these two guidelines.

Find out how you can improve Sometimes criticism is too general to be helpful; for example, "Your work is sloppy." In order to change your behavior, you need more specific information. In this situation you might ask, "Can you show me examples?" "What kind of paper would you prefer I use?" "How would you like me to do this in the future?"

Agree with the speaker No matter what a person says, you can find something to agree with. Expressing agreement with the speaker — even over a small point — adds a positive note to your interaction. It emphasizes what you have in common instead of your differences. For example, if your supervisor says, "You're late, and I cannot allow people to be late," you can respond, "Yes, I am late this morning. I'm sorry" or "I understand why you don't like us to be late."

Once you have shown that you are willing to accept the criticism, you can give an explanation for your behavior, if one is necessary. By responding positively to criticism — asking questions and agreeing with the speaker — you show that you are interested in finding a solution to the problem. It also sets the stage for resolving future conflicts that may arise as you work with other workers.

re·solv'ing

Being Considerate When You Criticize

Giving criticism is no more enjoyable than getting it. Sometimes, however, it is necessary to discuss problem behavior with others. When this situation occurs, be considerate of the other person's feelings. For example, discuss the problem in private, not in front of the entire office staff. Word your comments so it is clear that you are criticizing an action or behavior, not the person. Be specific about the problem so that the person knows exactly what behavior needs to be changed. Finally, don't criticize those things a person can't change!

un·de·sir'·a·ble

When you work with other people, your behavior cannot please everyone — nor can everyone's behavior please you. With good interpersonal communication techniques, however, you and the people you work with can change undesirable behavior. You can learn to work together to accomplish your company's goals.

DEALING WITH CUSTOMERS

dis·sat'is·fied

Customers are very important to any business organization. They are the people who buy your company's products and services. By doing so, they pay for your building, equipment, wages, and company benefits. Because customers are a company's most effective form of advertising, no company can afford to have even one dissatisfied customer.

In some ways, customers are just like the other people you work with. If you treat them fairly and courteously, most customers will be pleasant in return. But some customers — perhaps because they are paying for your service — feel that they can take up a lot of your time, ask unnecessary questions, or complain about prices, products, and service. When you meet these difficult customers, it is important to remind yourself that customers are the reason your company exists. Remember that without customers to buy your company's products and services, you would not have a job!

Illustration 2-10
Treat your customers courteously and fairly

REVIEWING KEY POINTS

1. Interpersonal communication is the process of using your communication skills to interact with others through words and body language.
2. Good interpersonal communication skills are necessary in order to build productive work relationships.
3. Your work relationships will be more pleasant if you make an effort to get to know your coworkers, show respect for them, develop your conversation skills, and be positive in your comments and attitudes.
4. Effective feedback prevents the costly mistakes that result when people do not understand one another.
5. Encourage feedback by asking questions, pausing, keeping eye contact with your listener, and asking your listener to repeat your message.
6. An active listener contributes to the communication process by giving immediate feedback.
7. The most productive way to handle criticism is to find out how you can improve and to find a point of agreement with the speaker.
8. Give criticism in private. To be helpful, criticize the act and not the person; be specific; and don't criticize those things a person can't change.
9. Building good relationships with customers is important. Customers are the reason your company exists.

DEVELOPING HUMAN RELATIONS SKILLS

1. Your company gives all employees a two-week paid vacation and five sick days each year. You have used up your vacation time, but you have not used any sick days. Your best friend just called to tell you that tickets for your favorite group are going on sale at ten the next morning. She wants you to take the day off from work to stand in line and buy tickets and then go shopping with her in the afternoon. You know the concert will be sold out by noon.
   - **a.** How do you feel about using paid sick time for personal business?
   - **b.** What problems would you cause for your coworkers if you call in sick?
2. Recall a situation in which you became irritated or annoyed at how you were treated by a salesclerk, bank teller, or other customer service employee. On a separate sheet of paper, prepare a two- or three-paragraph description of the situation. As part of your explanation, include answers to the following questions:
   - **a.** How should the situation have been handled?
   - **b.** What would you do if you were to run into this type of situation again?

IMPROVING COMMUNICATION SKILLS

Refer to Appendix A 2.1–2.2.

1. On a separate sheet of paper, write, type, or keyboard the following sentences, making any necessary corrections in subject and verb agreement that are necessary.
   - **a.** Each of the men want a copy of the refund policy.
   - **b.** Mr. Jastrow, not his assistants, proofreads all correspondence.
   - **c.** Some of the prices was increased last month.
   - **d.** Fifteen minutes are all the time you have to complete the letter.
   - **e.** The supervisor and his assistant was called to speak with the customer.
   - **f.** The vice presidents of the company are expected to attend.
   - **g.** A good knowledge of information processing procedures are essential.
   - **h.** The impact of computers are likely to be felt at all levels of business.
2. On a separate sheet of paper, paraphrase (state in your own words) the meaning of the following sentences:
   - **a.** When a customer gives you money, state the amount due and the amount of money given to you.
   - **b.** Follow store policy by calling the accounting department or computer center to get approval for charges over a certain amount.
   - **c.** Always compare a customer's signature on a card against the signature on a credit card form.
   - **d.** If a question arises about the amount of money that has changed hands, avoid arguing with the customer.
   - **e.** In telephone orders, always repeat the order to the customer for verification.
   - **f.** What is a problem to one customer may not be a problem at all to another customer.
   - **g.** When you call a customer, get all the necessary information from the files before you dial the telephone.
   - **h.** In a written complaint, underline the complaint and all key points provided.
   - **i.** Many companies operate on policies that are implied or understood by managers, but not written down.
   - **j.** A procedures manual should contain examples of all forms used in interactions with customers.

BUILDING PROBLEM-SOLVING SKILLS

1. On a separate sheet of paper, convert the fractions on page 77 to decimals. Round your answers to two decimal places. If needed, refer to Appendix C.

a. $\frac{1}{4}$ =	c. $\frac{7}{12}$ =	e. $\frac{5}{9}$ =	g. $\frac{3}{4}$ =	i. $\frac{4}{10}$ =
b. $\frac{2}{5}$ =	d. $\frac{1}{6}$ =	f. $\frac{2}{3}$ =	h. $\frac{6}{8}$ =	j. $\frac{9}{16}$ =

2. Your company is sponsoring a basketball team in the city league. Study the table listing the positions and heights of the players. Then, on a separate sheet of paper, answer the questions that follow.

Name	Position	Height
Chris Starr	Center	6′1″
Tresa Mitchell	Center	6′0″
Fran Jointer	Forward	6′0″
Andrea McFadden	Guard	5′7″
Karon O'Connor	Guard	5′6″
Pam Marr	Forward	6′0″
Molly Baroody	Guard	5′7″
Britt Gardner	Forward	6′2″
Chris Brown	Guard	5′8″
Penny Edwards	Forward	6′1″

a. What fraction of the players are 6′ or over?
b. Forwards make up what fraction of the team?
c. What fraction of the players are shorter than 6′?
d. What is the average height of the players? (Round to the nearest inch.)
e. Centers make up what fraction of the team?

Activities 1 and 2 can be done on information processing equipment.

APPLYING OFFICE SKILLS

1. Your supervisor gave you the information below and asked you to arrange it in an attractive format so that it can be posted on the bulletin board. Prepare (type or keyboard) this information on a half sheet of paper with the title "Commandments for Customer Service."

Customers are the reason for this and every other business.
Customers do not interrupt our work; they are the purpose for it.
Customers are not just a number; they have feelings and emotions.
Customers deserve courteous and attentive treatment.
Customers bring us their wants; we fill those wants.
Customers do us a favor when they call attention to our shortcomings.
Customers are always right.

2. Your company prepares a quarterly evaluation for each of its suppliers. The purpose of the evaluation is to rate the supplier performance. Referring to the chart that follows, develop a listing in which you arrange the items by actual rating from the lowest to the highest rating. When there is more than one item at a rating, arrange the items for that rating alphabetically. Prepare (type or keyboard) your listing in an attractive format. Use the title "Kramer's Products Quarterly Evaluation."

KRAMER'S PRODUCTS
Quarterly Evaluation
March 31, 19 – –

Item	Possible Rating	Actual Rating
Competitive Price	3.00	2.50
Delivery at Quoted Price	2.00	2.00
Cost Reductions	2.00	1.50
Truck Schedules Met	3.00	2.00
Communication	3.00	2.50
Emergency Service	2.00	2.00
Technical Assistance	3.00	2.50
Handling of Rejections	3.00	2.00
Promises Kept	2.00	1.50
Instructions Followed	3.00	2.50
Sample Delivery	1.00	1.00

Saving Time and Money

Many supervisors save interesting and informative articles to use in speeches or reports. You may be asked to assist by reading through magazines and newspapers to find appropriate articles. By gathering this material yourself, you save your supervisor time and your company money. All you need is a little direction.

1. Ask your supervisor to recommend magazines and newspapers for you to examine for articles. Arrange to have them routed to your desk.
2. Obtain a one-page list of general topics and key words (such as *motivation, performance reviews,* or *supervisory techniques*) that will help you to identify the kinds of articles you should save.
3. Prepare a file folder for each topic. As you find suitable articles, clip them (or reproduce them), label them by topic, and place them in the appropriate folders. (Put the most recent articles in the front of the folder.)
4. Develop a system for periodically discarding older articles. Work with your supervisor to develop an acceptable system.

UNIT 3

ORGANIZING FOR EFFICIENT WORK

- Organizing Your Work Environment
- Using Your Time Efficiently
- Developing Your Decision-Making Ability

CHAPTER 1

ORGANIZING YOUR WORK ENVIRONMENT

The environment in which you work affects the amount and quality of your work. It also affects the way you feel about your job. Suppose you have just started working in an office that does not have windows. At the end of the day, your eyes may be tired because you were working under artificial light. You may also have a headache from the lack of fresh air. After a few days, you may be displeased with your job. You may not have produced as much work as you are capable of producing. Most companies know that when employees are comfortable and feel good about their work environment, they are more productive.

As you work, you will find that your environment needs to be comfortable and well organized. It is the company's responsibility to provide a comfortable working environment. It is your responsibility to maintain a well-organized work space.

As you study this chapter, you will find answers to the following questions:

- How should you organize your work space?
- How does an organized work space help you become more productive?
- What can office workers do to maintain efficient office surroundings?
- What do the following terms mean: **desk organizer, stationery separator?**

ORGANIZING YOUR WORK SPACE

as·signed′

As an office worker, you will be assigned work space of your own. This work space will include furniture such as a desk and a chair. It will also include the office equipment and supplies needed to perform the duties required by your job. All of these items need to be arranged so that you can work efficiently.

hab′its

To determine the best arrangement for your equipment and supplies, you need to study your work style carefully. This can be done by asking yourself questions about your work habits. What equipment and supplies do you use most often? What equipment and supplies do you seldom use? What hand do you write with? Questions such as these are easy to answer and save you time in organizing your work space.

Arranging Your Desk

Once you have studied your work habits to determine your work style, you can organize your desk. Begin by placing the equipment you use most often (such as your typewriter, word processor or computer, and your telephone) in positions that are convenient. This placement should help you avoid unnecessary movements. Remember to position items so that they do not interfere with your working area. If you keyboard a great deal and are also responsible for answering the telephone, position the telephone close to the typewriter, word processor, or computer. When the telephone rings, you then have just a short reach to answer it. This saves time by reducing the movement back and forth between these two objects.

re·ceiv′er

The hand that you write with determines where you should place some equipment, such as the telephone. If you write with your right hand, you should place your telephone on the left side of your desk. This allows you to hold the receiver with your left hand while you write a message or take notes with your right hand. If you write with the left hand, place the telephone on the right side of your desk so that your left hand is free to write.

Work supplies such as pens, pencils, and note paper should be placed in containers so that they are easy to find. Position these items close to your telephone so that they are always available for message taking when you receive a call. Other items that you use frequently — stapler, tape dispensers, and paper clips — should be placed on the desk within easy reach. Items that are not used frequently, such as a ruler or a pair of scissors, can be stored so that you do not clutter your desk top.

As you arrange your office equipment and desk supplies, keep a space clear that can be used as a working area. When working on a project, try to complete one task before starting another task. As you complete each task, put equipment and unused supplies away. This will help keep your working area neat and clean.

When you must keep several projects on your desk at the same time, use a desk organizer. A **desk organizer** is a vertical or horizontal device with four

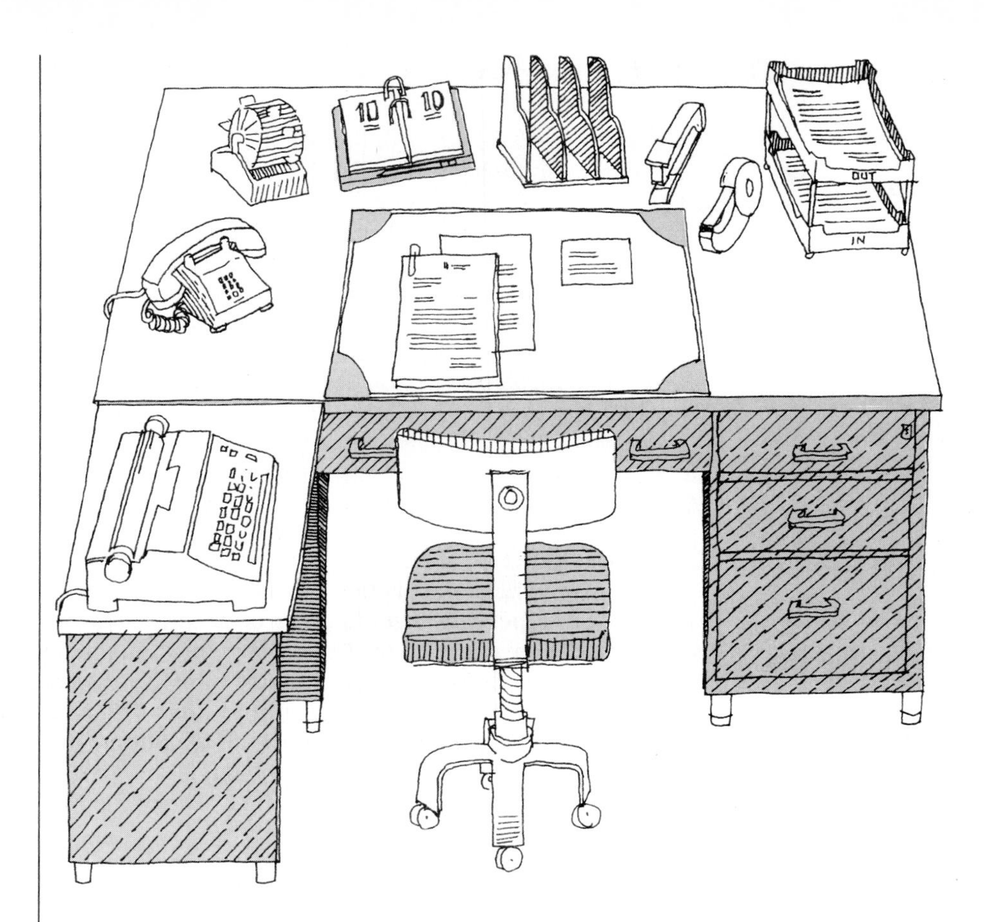

Illustration 3–1
Arrange items on your desk for efficiency

or five compartments for the storing of papers or other materials at a desk or work station. An organizer that stores work vertically is shown in Illustration 3–1. Some workers place one project on top of another on their desks. This habit is a very inefficient one that you won't want to start. Each time that you need a project you have to search through the entire stack to find the one that you need. Searching for lost projects takes time and is annoying. And, frequently, the item that you are looking for is at the bottom of the stack. With a desk organizer, however, your work is stored neatly and is easy to find when needed.

ref'er·ence

Reference books such as dictionaries, office manuals, and telephone directories should be kept handy. Those books that you use most often should be placed on your desk within easy reach. Other reference books can be kept on a nearby shelf. Appendix D contains a list of the reference sources most frequently found in business offices.

Many workers add a personal touch to their desks with a plant or a photograph of someone special. If you want to place personal items on your desk, arrange them so that they do not interfere with your work. Too many

dis·tract'

photographs or plants take up too much space and may distract other workers from their work.

By keeping your desk neat, you can work more efficiently and accurately. A neat desk also makes a favorable impression on your supervisor, coworkers, and visitors to the office. An organized desk is the sign of an organized individual who cares about his or her work and pays attention to detail.

Organizing Your Desk Drawers

sta'tion·er·y

Desk drawers are used to store those supplies that are used frequently but that do not need to be placed on the top of the desk. Supplies should be placed in the desk drawers according to the frequency of use. For example, you use stationery daily, so it makes sense to store your stationery in a side drawer. Most desks contain a stationery separator. A **stationery separator**, as shown in Illustration 3–2, is a device that allows you to store several types of stationery within the same drawer. The type of stationery that you use most often should be placed in the separator slots closest to the front of the drawer.

Extra pens, pencils, and paper clips should be stored in the center top desk drawer. Less frequently used supplies, such as weekly or monthly report forms, can be stored in a lower side drawer that is less convenient. Many office workers also keep a box of tissues, a comb or brush, mouthwash, other personal items in one of the lower side drawers. Although these items are stored separately from work supplies, they are still handy if needed.

Adjusting Your Chair

ad·just'

pos'ture

You will be seated at your desk most of the day as you work. It is important, therefore, that you adjust your chair so that you are comfortable and can work without undue strain. The seat of your chair should be low enough that your feet rest on the floor. The back of the chair should firmly support the small of your back.

Illustration 3–3 shows the correct posture for working when you are seated at your desk. Notice that the body is supported so that there is not any

Illustration 3–2 Organize your desk drawers

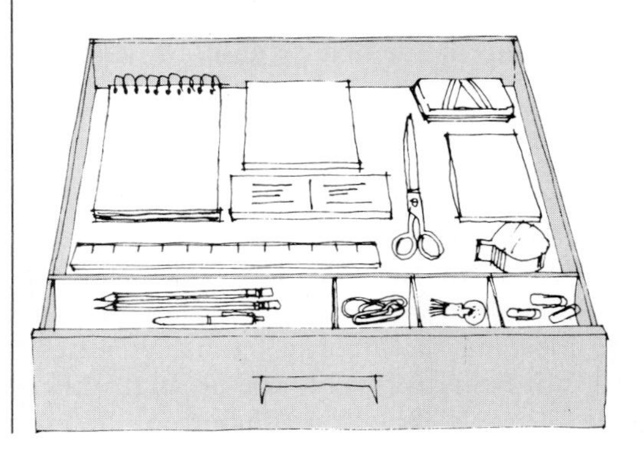

Illustration 3–3
Correct posture reduces fatigue

unnecessary strain on any part of the body. Having correct posture when you are seated is very important. If you sit on your foot or rest your feet on the chair base, your blood circulation is cut off, the muscles are strained, and fatigue sets in.

MAINTAINING AN EFFICIENT OFFICE ENVIRONMENT

One of the advantages of working in a modern business office is the pleasant work environment. It is true that it is your company's responsibility to provide a comfortable working environment. However, there are some things that you can do to help the company maintain your pleasant surroundings.

Eliminating Distracting Noise

In offices where several people work within a department, distractions are common. Noise cannot be totally avoided in an office. People must talk to one another, people move around, telephones ring, and office equipment makes noise. Too much noise, however, is very distracting.

con'cen·trate

One of the most distracting and irritating noises in the office is the human voice. It is difficult to concentrate on your work when people around you are talking. That is why it is important to eliminate unnecessary conversations within the office. When you are talking or listening to someone, you are not paying attention to your work. You are also keeping others from their work. Save social conversations for breaks. Some offices insist that workers take their breaks away from their desks, either in an employee lounge or cafeteria. This time has been set aside so that workers can get away from their desks and visit with their friends. You can help reduce office noise by eliminating all unnecessary conversations during work hours.

Using Music to Increase Efficiency

The noise of people talking, laughing, and moving around draws people's attention away from their work. In offices with many workers, background music is used to cover up such noise. Music can also be used to reduce tension and prevent boredom. It has been found that efficiency among workers can be encouraged through the use of soft background music played throughout the working day. To be effective, the music must be instrumental — not vocal — and played only as background music. Music that encourages workers to sing along should be avoided because it distracts the workers from the work that needs to be done.

sub·scrip'tion

Through paid subscription to a special music service a company can provide "piped-in" music. This is music that is broadcast to the company over a special network. Other offices use radios tuned to a local FM station. If a radio is used to provide the music, a station should be chosen that plays music most of the time and has few commercials and very little talking.

Maintaining a Comfortable Climate

im·pu'ri·ties

Indoor climate control has become a concern of many people within the last few years. Ventilating systems are used in many offices to circulate the air and filter out impurities such as smoke. Many people are allergic to smoke or find it offensive. In order to provide clean air for all employees, some businesses do not allow people to smoke at their desks. Workers who smoke may be asked to smoke only during breaks or at lunch time.

reg'u·late

Most offices regulate their thermostats according to federal government guidelines. In an attempt to conserve energy, businesses have been asked to set their thermostats at 65 degrees in the winter and 78 degrees in the summer. While you may not be accustomed to these temperatures, you can learn to plan your choice of clothing so that you are comfortable at work. Many office workers keep a sweater or a lightweight jacket in one of their desk drawers just in case one is needed. Others dress in layers. Wearing a shirt or blouse, a vest, and a jacket allows you to take off or put on layers according to the temperature of the office.

Comfortable surroundings make working more pleasant. When you feel good about what you are doing, then the quality as well as the quantity of your work increases.

REVIEWING KEY POINTS

1. A comfortable working environment enables workers to perform their duties efficiently.
2. Studying your work habits and the equipment and supplies you use most often helps you organize your work space so you can work efficiently.
3. A neat work space makes a good impression on your employer, coworkers, and visitors to the office; it tells them that you are an organized individual.
4. Your desk should contain the equipment and materials that you use frequently.
5. Your chair should be adjusted so that it provides proper back support and helps you maintain good posture while you work.
6. Office workers should try to reduce office noise because it causes distractions and makes it difficult to concentrate.
7. Background music can be used to help cover up noise, help reduce tension, and prevent boredom in the office.
8. Indoor climate control provides comfortable surroundings and makes working more pleasant.

DEVELOPING HUMAN RELATIONS SKILLS

1. Your work space is next to the copy machine. People who use the copy machine visit with each other while waiting to make their copies. Some of the people also borrow your staple remover and other desk supplies. These disturbances are distracting and cause you to make errors.
   - **a.** How can you stop these people from disturbing your work?
   - **b.** What should you do to keep others from borrowing your desk supplies?
   - **c.** How can your supervisor help?
2. Some of your assigned tasks require you to be away from your desk periodically during the day. When you are away from your desk, Jim answers your telephone. This morning while you were on an errand, your supervisor called and asked Jim to tell you to call as soon as you returned to your desk. Your supervisor has just called you again and angrily asked why you had not returned the call. This is the first you have heard about the call.
   - **a.** How should you explain to your supervisor what happened?
   - **b.** What should you say to Jim?
   - **c.** How can you prevent this situation from happening again?

IMPROVING COMMUNICATION SKILLS

Refer to Appendix A 2.3 – 2.6.

1. Review capitalization rules 1–4. On a separate sheet of paper, write or keyboard the following sentences, supplying correct capitalization.
   a. carol fisher is moving to new orleans, louisiana.
   b. i was hired last spring as a typist and promoted to secretary last month.
   c. craig wants to work in the northwest.
   d. modern office supplies, inc., has an advertisement for part-time office workers.
   e. our new office music system was installed by the music company.
   f. carl ordered seven desk organizers from carolina office equipment.
   g. left-handed people are frequently called "southpaws."
   h. office workers in large cities in the northeast frequently earn higher salaries than office workers in the south.
   i. jennifer is a senior at southside high school.
   j. paul c. edmunds was promoted to office manager of the branch office in st. louis, missouri.
2. On a separate sheet of paper, write or keyboard a sentence to answer each of the following questions. Check your sentences to make certain that the subjects and verbs agree and that words are correctly capitalized.
   a. What items will you find in your assigned work space?
   b. How will you decide where to place these items in your work space?
   c. What kinds of equipment will you have in your work space?
   d. What items will you keep on the top of your desk?
   e. What items will you keep in your desk drawers?
   f. Why are office chairs adjustable?
   g. What is one of the most distracting noises in the office?
   h. What can you do to help control distracting noises in the office?
   i. What kind of background music should be played in the office?
   j. Why do most businesses try to provide a comfortable working climate?

BUILDING PROBLEM-SOLVING SKILLS

1. On a separate sheet of paper, write the answers to the following problems.

   a. $\frac{1}{2} \times 3 =$
   b. $7 \times \frac{5}{8} =$
   c. $\frac{1}{3} \times \frac{3}{4} =$
   d. $\frac{1}{2} \times \frac{1}{5} =$
   e. $2\frac{3}{4} \times \frac{1}{3} =$
   f. $21 \div \frac{2}{3} =$
   g. $\frac{1}{2} \div \frac{1}{4} =$
   h. $34 \div \frac{3}{4} =$
   i. $21\frac{5}{6} \div \frac{2}{3} =$

2. The Write Pen Company has recently conducted a study of its working conditions. The results are shown below.

ENVIRONMENTAL STUDY

Department	Number of Employees	Space in Square Feet	Average Daily Temperature: Winter	Average Daily Temperature: Summer
Accounting	3	225	68	78
Credit	5	350	70	77
Order	10	675	68	79
Shipping	5	370	67	75

a. How much total space is occupied by these departments together?

b. Which department has the most space per employee?

c. Which department has the least space per employee?

d. Which department has the largest difference in temperatures between winter and summer?

e. Which department has the least difference in temperatures between winter and summer?

Activity 1 can be done on information processing equipment.

APPLYING OFFICE SKILLS

1. On a full size sheet of paper, prepare a table that includes the following items that are found in your work space. Arrange the items by the date of purchase, the most recent item first. Start keyboarding on line 22 from the top edge of the paper. Set the left margin at 11 (10 pitch) or 20 (12 pitch). Set a tab at 48 (10 pitch) or 57 (12 pitch). Use the title "Office Equipment" and the column headings "Equipment" and "Date of Purchase." Double space between each line of the table.

   a. computer, February 15, 1983
   b. calculator, August 3, 1982
   c. file cabinet, July 1, 1984
   d. chair, July 15, 1984
   e. electric pencil sharpener, May 2, 1983
   f. desk, June 12, 1982
   g. desk lamp, October 1, 1982
   h. telephone, September 3, 1984
   i. stapler, April 2, 1982
   j. transcribing machine, March 5, 1983

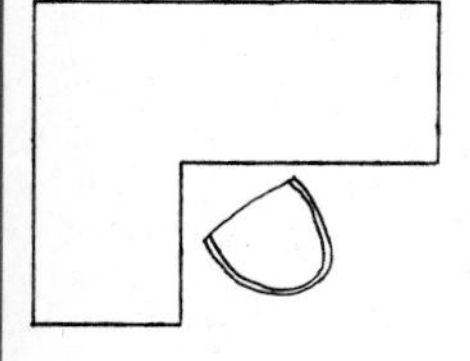

2. On a separate sheet of paper, draw the L-shaped figure shown here. This will represent the top of your desk. Using your organizational skills, show where you would place each of the following materials and equipment.

telephone	in-out baskets	message pad
desk organizer	tape dispenser	typewriter, word processor, or computer
plant	pens and pencils	

CHAPTER 2

USING YOUR TIME EFFICIENTLY

How often do you feel that you don't have enough time to do all the things that you should do? Almost everyone feels this way at one time or another. Yet, some people seem to get all of their work done and still have time to relax and enjoy life. Sometimes you think that these people don't have much to do. However, if you watch them, you may find that they get a lot more done than you do. They have learned how to organize themselves and how to manage their time.

Time is a valuable resource. If you learn to manage this resource efficiently, you will find that you can accomplish many things that you didn't think you could.

As you study this chapter, you will find answers to the following questions:

- How can I assess my use of time?
- How can I learn to set priorities?
- How can I learn to use my time efficiently?
- What do the following terms mean: **planning, setting work priorities, office interrupters?**

ASSESSING THE USE OF TIME

Before you can learn how to use your time more wisely, you must determine how you spend your time now. To determine how you are using your time, keep a time study chart similar to the one shown in Illustration 3–4. For a period of one or two weeks, record what you do during each 15-minute period of the day. Then study the chart to see how your time was spent.

As you review your chart, look for periods of wasted time. For example, did you waste time chatting with friends before starting work? Did you waste time waiting for class to end? Chatting with friends is a pleasant experience and getting ready to leave class early ensures that you are ready to leave on time. Nevertheless, you are wasting time.

Let's take a look at how one office worker analyzed her time for a week. Jane Hogan is a file clerk for Morgan Insurance Company. During the week of March 25 she kept a record of her time on the chart shown in Illustration 3–4. Notice that Jane wrote exactly what she had achieved at the end of each 15-minute period each day of the week. On Monday, Jane was late for work, talked to a coworker, took an extra 15 minutes for lunch, visited with a friend in the copy center, made a personal telephone call, and got ready to leave work 15 minutes early. It is easy to see that Jane wasted over an hour of work time. If Jane used her time wisely, she could get more work done each day.

a·chieved'

PLANNING YOUR WORK

The time study chart tells you how you presently use your time. When you know this information, you can begin **planning**. This involves setting out the details of your activities to make the most efficient use of your time.

Setting Your Work Priorities

Planning isn't easy, but it is necessary. Every job has some tasks that are more important than others. In some offices the supervisor helps employees determine which tasks are most important and must be completed first. This is called **setting work priorities**. If your supervisor does not set work priorities for you, you must evaluate your duties and responsibilities to decide which tasks are most important.

You can decide which tasks are most important by determining when each task must be completed. The task that needs to be completed first is given the highest priority. Take this example:

> *Peter arrived at work one morning to find several pieces of work on his desk. Among the work were 7 letters to be keyboarded; a 15-page report, of which 25 copies needed to be made by 10:30 A.M.; the morning mail, which needed to be sorted and delivered; and 3 requests for files. At the same time the telephone rang and a visitor walked into the office.*

Peter needs to decide what should be done first. In other words, he has to set his priorities. Obviously, Peter must answer the telephone first and then greet the visitor. These are top priorities. Next, Peter must look at the work, estimate how long each task will take to complete, and find out when each task is needed.

Let's suppose that Peter's supervisor needs the files to prepare for a 10:30 meeting, that it takes at least two hours to get the copies of the report made, and that the letters are routine and do not require immediate attention. If you were Peter, how would you arrange your work for the morning?

In this situation, Peter should begin by delivering the report to be copied to the Reprographic Center. Then he should get the files, sort and deliver the mail, and keyboard the letters.

TIME	MONDAY	TUESDAY	WEDNESDAY	THURSDAY	FRIDAY
9:00	Late/overslept	open desk, sort mail, greet	open desk, opened & sorted	opened desk, opened & sorted	opened desk, opened & sorted
9:15	opened desk, opened mail	others, made coffee	mail, greeted	mail, greeted others, made coffee	mail, made coffee
9:30	sorted mail, Greeted others	talked to supervisor about	others, made coffee	Processed	completed forms
9:45	typed report	project assigned	typed report	reports	for purchases
10:00	↓	started project	↓	↓	↓
10:15		coffee			coffee
10:30	coffee	Project	talked to supervisor	coffee	typed letters
10:45	typed report	↓	coffee	typed letters	↓
11:00	called friend about lunch	Phone call made lunch plans	completed forms		↓
11:15	talked to supervisor about report	Project	for data		made copies
			pro		
		sorted & opened		collated	
1:45	↓	afternoon mail/	typed letters	materials, prepared	↓
2:00	made copies talked with Ann	visited with Cathy	↓	materials for mail	made copies
2:15	in copy room	made copies		sorted mail by	opened & sorted
2:30	opened & sorted afternoon mail	of project		zip for mail	afternoon mail
2:45	Addressed envelopes	coffee	coffee	↓	Filed
3:00	Personal phone call	typed letters	checked supply	coffee	↓
3:15	coffee	↓	cabinet-reordered	typed reports	coffee
3:30	completed forms		Process time cards	↓	Filed
3:45	for inventory		↓		Personal telephone
4:00	control & made copies	made copies			Filed
4:15	filed	cleaned desk	↓	↓	↓
4:30	↓	Filed	File time cards	made copies of reports	Put work away,
4:45	put work away prepared to leave	↓	Prepared to leave	Prepared to leave	prepared to leave
5:00					

Illustration 3–4
Time study chart

To make these decisions, Peter has to understand the needs of his supervisor and the work being done. If he had just started by keyboarding the letters, he would not have received the copies of the report until several hours after the meeting. As you learn your job, try to determine the importance of each task. Once you know the importance of each task, you can decide what must be done first and what can be set aside until there is more time.

Making Efficient Use of Your Time

Setting priorities will help you recognize the order in which work must be completed; however, you will still find things that cause you to waste time. Let's look at some ideas for using your time more efficiently.

Organize your work by planning Take a few minutes at the beginning of each work period to plan your work. During this time, decide what items you will need to complete the task. Also estimate how much time it will take.

Learn to organize your work As you begin each task, make sure you have all the materials you need to complete the task. You may need to get information from the files or supplies from the supply room. If you get all of the materials you need before you begin, you can complete your work without interruption. If you can eliminate unnecessary steps, organizing your work means that you are working smarter, not harder. By working smarter, you will probably find that you can complete more work in less time.

Do things right the first time Many people begin work on a task before they read directions or understand what actually needs to be done. They *think* they are saving time. However, they frequently discover that they did not do what needed to be done. It is more efficient to take a few extra seconds to read and follow directions or ask questions if you do not understand what needs to be done. It makes sense to do the job correctly the first time. Finding and correcting errors takes a lot of time. When you must do a task over to correct mistakes, you have wasted all of the time you spent doing it the first time.

Complete one task before starting another Whenever possible, you should complete one task before you begin another. Each time you begin a task, you must determine what has to be done. If you stop in the middle of a task, when you return to it you have to figure out where you stopped. You also have to determine, once again, what needs to be done.

Although finishing one task before beginning another is the most efficient way to work, you must learn to be flexible. There will be times when you are working on one task and your supervisor will hand you another task that needs to be done immediately. You should be able to stop what you are doing and go to the other task without being upset by the interruption.

Avoid interrupting others unnecessarily When you must ask questions about a task, look through the entire task and write down all of the questions you want to ask. This allows you to ask all of your questions at one time, making it unnecessary to interrupt your supervisor more than once. This saves your time as well as your supervisor's time. It also shows that you are able to organize your thoughts and present them in an orderly manner.

Develop a "Do it now" attitude It is only natural for people to avoid tasks that are unpleasant or difficult. If you develop a "Do it now" attitude, you will find that you won't dread completing some tasks. Once you get unpleasant or difficult tasks out of the way, you will have a feeling of accomplishment; and the rest of your work will go quickly.

Take breaks Everyone needs to take breaks from work occasionally. When you are under pressure to complete a task, skipping a break may be the worst thing you can do. You will find that getting away from the task for a few minutes allows you to relax physically and mentally. This short break may actually enable you to finish the job faster. Of course, you must use good judgment and common sense when taking a break. If you have only a half hour to complete a task and it will take you at least twenty minutes, wait until after you have completed the task to take a break.

phys'i·cal·ly

Use slack time wisely In every job there are times when there isn't much work to be done. For example, when your supervisor is out of town, you may find that you have completed all of the required work and have nothing left to do. Special projects should be set aside for such slack times. Tasks such as

Illustration 3–5 Clean out the files when you have slack time

dead'lines

straightening the supply cabinet, cleaning files, addressing envelopes, and transferring information from one calendar to another are time-consuming tasks that usually do not have deadlines. Save these tasks for slack time.

If you find that you usually finish your daily work and have spare time, ask your supervisor to give you more responsibility or more work. Most employers look for employees who are willing to accept additional responsibility. By doing this you are letting your supervisor know you are interested in your job and your company. Employees who demonstrate that they are capable of handling more work and responsibility are the ones who are usually considered for promotions.

ca'pa·ble

Learn to make decisions Decisions are made as a matter of course in an office. From time to time, situations do arise when employees must make decisions on their own. Let's suppose that you need to have five copies of a very important report ready for your supervisor by 1:00 P.M. The company policy states that you should use the convenience copier, but it is out of order and will not be repaired until after lunch. Your supervisor must have the report, so you must decide how to get the work done. If you put the report on your supervisor's desk and say, "I'm sorry; the machine was out of order," you are not helping your supervisor. If you ask your supervisor what you should do, you are wasting your time and bothering your supervisor with minor details. The right thing to do is to find another copier and get the work done for your supervisor.

au·thor'i·ty

There are some decisions, however, that you do not have the authority to make. Let's say that your company has set the policy that no one can remove confidential records from the filing room without a signature from the supervisor. Suppose Sandra asks you for a confidential file without the required signature. In a situation like this, you do not have the authority to make the decision to give her the file. Your supervisor or the filing department manager must make this decision. You must use good judgment in determining which decisions you can and cannot make.

Avoiding Wasted Time

To manage your work time most efficiently, avoid wasting time. As you work, you may be tempted to make personal telephone calls, visit with other employees, extend breaks, and arrive late or leave early. All of these activities that disrupt the normal office schedule are referred to as **office interrupters** because they waste time. Let's take a look at ways of avoiding them within the office.

con·ven'ience

Telephone calls The telephone is a necessary convenience. However, its ringing and the distraction created by people talking disturb other employees. Many offices have policies in regard to the use of the telephone for personal calls. If you are not aware of your company's policies in regard to telephone calls, ask your supervisor.

When someone calls you and you are busy, learn to say that you have work to do. For instance, John is busy when Mark calls to get some information. John gives Mark the information he needs, and then Mark starts discussing his weekend plans. John should say, "Gee, Mark, I'd like to discuss your plans; but I have a report to prepare. Maybe we can get together after work or for lunch to discuss them." If you placed the call, you can always say, "I'm sorry I interrupted you. I'll let you get back to work."

Visits with other employees A major time waster is the visiting that takes place among employees. As one employee walks past another employee's desk, they greet each other and spend a few minutes talking. This time adds up quickly. One way to avoid being interrupted for too long is to continue working. The other employee will usually move on quickly if you are working. In other cases, it may be necessary to say very tactfully, "Can we visit later (at break or lunch); I have some work that I really need to get out."

Extended breaks Most employers give each employee a 10- to 15-minute break, one in the morning and another in the afternoon. Breaks give you a chance to get away from your work briefly. They help ease the physical and mental pressures of the job. They also help employees maintain a high level of work output. Be careful not to abuse your right to breaks by extending them. When this happens, you are not giving your company the time it is entitled to.

ex·tend'ing

Arriving late or leaving early Employees are expected to arrive at their work areas and be prepared to begin their assigned work at the scheduled beginning of each workday. They are also expected to work until the scheduled end of each workday.

Arriving late and leaving early is costly to businesses. At $4 an hour, every 5-minute period wasted costs the company approximately 33 cents. It doesn't take very long for this amount to add up.

The suggestions given here will help you in your everyday life as well as on the job. Try using these hints to organize your time while you are in school. When you begin work, you will be able to show your supervisor how efficient you really are.

REVIEWING KEY POINTS

1. You can learn to use your time efficiently by determining how you spend your time and avoiding those activities that waste time.
2. An efficient office worker knows how to set priorities to meet the requirements of the job and the requirements of the supervisor.

3. An efficient office worker plans work so that it is completed in the least amount of time using the most efficient methods.
4. It is more efficient to do a task correctly the first time than to correct errors.
5. If you develop a "Do it now" attitude for those tasks that are difficult, you will have a feeling of accomplishment when you are finished.
6. Tasks that do not have a deadline, such as cleaning files, should be done during slack periods.
7. Visiting among employees wastes time and should be avoided.
8. Arriving late for work, leaving early, and extending breaks are major time wasters in offices and should be avoided.

DEVELOPING HUMAN RELATIONS SKILLS

1. Jena is a secretary in the sales department of Winters, Inc. There are eight salespeople in the department. All give Jena work to do and expect her to complete the work right away. Jena can do all the work that is given to her; however, she can't complete all of it as soon as it is given to her.
   - **a.** How would you handle this situation?
   - **b.** What would you tell the salespeople who ask for "rush" work?
2. Greg works for the accounting firm of Link and Moses. On days when Greg is not busy, he takes a long lunch and leaves work early. Yesterday afternoon, for example, Greg left work 20 minutes early because he had finished his work and the accountants were out of the office. At 4:45 P.M., Mr. Moses returned to the office with a job that needed to go out right away. This morning Mr. Moses threatened to fire Greg because he left work early.
   - **a.** Do you think Greg deserved to be threatened? Explain.
   - **b.** What advice would you give Greg?

IMPROVING COMMUNICATION SKILLS

Refer to Appendix A 2.7 – 2.9.

1. Review capitalization rules 5–7. On a separate sheet of paper, write or keyboard the following sentences, supplying correct capitalization.
   - **a.** ellen will begin working full time on monday, june 5.
   - **b.** the staff meeting will be held in room 210.
   - **c.** the new text editor is a model d.
   - **d.** bill's mother subscribes to the local newspaper, daily news, for him.
   - **e.** since christmas is on tuesday, the office will not be open on monday.
   - **f.** jeanne will move to the southern part of california in january.

g. i've enjoyed the novel, gone with the wind, each time i've read it.
h. peggy works for the lafayette school system in lafayette, louisiana.
i. jeremy celebrated his third birthday last friday, may 13.
j. our new branch office is located in east st. louis.

2. Use the information given here to compose ten sentences. Write or keyboard your sentences on a separate sheet of paper.
   a. a meeting, Tuesday, November 9, Room 209
   b. topic of meeting, setting priorities
   c. consultant, Ms. Jan Stout
   d. avoid interrupting others, listen attentively
   e. beginning of workday, 8:30 a.m.
   f. 15-minute morning break, 10:30 a.m.
   g. 30-minute lunch period, 11:30 a.m.-1:30 p.m.
   h. 15-minute afternoon break, 2:45 p.m.
   i. end of work day, 4:30 p.m.
   j. tardiness and extended breaks not tolerated

BUILDING PROBLEM-SOLVING SKILLS

1. Find the lowest common denominator for each set of fractions. Write your answers on a separate sheet of paper. Refer to Appendix C if necessary.

   a. $\frac{1}{2}, \frac{3}{4}$ c. $\frac{2}{5}, \frac{1}{3}$ e. $\frac{1}{10}, \frac{1}{4}$ g. $\frac{1}{4}, \frac{1}{6}$ i. $\frac{1}{9}, \frac{1}{5}$
   b. $\frac{2}{3}, \frac{1}{6}$ d. $\frac{7}{8}, \frac{1}{12}$ f. $\frac{2}{3}, \frac{3}{8}$ h. $\frac{2}{7}, \frac{1}{3}$ j. $\frac{1}{20}, \frac{4}{15}$

2. The table that follows shows the hours and breaks for the employees at United Office Equipment, Inc. Answer the questions that follow the table on a separate sheet of paper.

Employee	Begin Work	A.M. Break	Lunch	P.M. Break	End Work
J. Tucci	7:45	15 min.	60 min.	10 min.	4:45
T. Beck	7:30	10 min.	50 min.	10 min.	4:40
A. Yeun	8:15	15 min.	30 min.	10 min.	5:00
M. Dunn	8:05	15 min.	30 min.	15 min.	4:45
S. Evans	8:20	15 min.	45 min.	10 min.	5:15

   a. Which worker began work at the earliest time?
   b. Which worker began work at the latest time?
   c. Which worker left work at the earliest time?

d. Which worker worked at the latest time?

e. Which worker took the longest lunch?

f. Which worker took the least amount of time for breaks and lunch?

g. Which worker took the most amount of time for breaks and lunch?

h. Which worker took the most break time during the day?

i. Which worker worked the shortest amount of time during the day?

j. Which worker worked the longest amount of time during the day?

Activities 1 and 2 can be done on information processing equipment.

APPLYING OFFICE SKILLS

1. Study the following list of tasks and determine the order in which you would perform them. Keyboard the list on a separate sheet of paper. Use the title "Work for Friday, December 5, 19 – –."

   a. Keyboard a memo that your supervisor wants to send out before lunch.

   b. Open and distribute the mail.

   c. Get the file related to your supervisor's 9:30 appointment.

   d. Complete a requisition form for stationery.

   e. Make a copy of a report to be attached to the memo in *a.*

   f. Keyboard a letter requesting information from a consultant.

   g. Call the repair service to report a broken word processor.

   h. Get information from the files for a report your supervisor will work on tomorrow.

   i. Keyboard a four-page report that is needed on December 19.

   j. File the correspondence that is on your desk.

2. The following notice is to be posted on the company bulletin board. Prepare it on a half sheet of paper. Start typing the title "Office Support Training Seminar" on line 10. Center each line horizontally. Double space between lines.

   A training seminar on work organization
   will be held in the Training Center
   Tuesday, November 15, 19 – –
   Session 1 — 9:30 to 11:30 A.M.
   Session 2 — 1:30 to 3:30 P.M.
   Call the Training Center for reservations

CHAPTER 3

DEVELOPING YOUR DECISION-MAKING ABILITY

We make decisions in almost everything we do. Some decisions are more important than others. For instance, when you decided what to wear to school today, you probably considered the weather conditions and what activities you would be involved in during the day. Then, based on that information, you chose what clothes to wear to school. That decision was important for your personal comfort. However, if you had chosen to wear different clothes, your school day and your future would probably not be greatly affected.

On the other hand, when you met with your advisor to schedule classes for this school year, you made several very important decisions. These decisions will have an impact on your future. Your choice of courses may help you decide what you will do after you finish school. A course you are taking may help you choose a career. The choices you made among courses may play an important role in your getting into college if you decide on a college education. You can see that these decisions are far more important than choosing what clothes to wear.

As you study this chapter, you will find answers to the following questions:

- How can I learn to make better decisions?
- How can I evaluate my choices?
- How do I know if my decisions are good ones?
- What do the following terms mean: **advice, intuition, implementing, predicting?**

WHO MAKES DECISIONS?

Everyone makes decisions about many things every day. In business, workers at all levels make decisions related to their jobs. Office support workers make decisions about how they will complete the tasks assigned to them. In making such decisions, these workers consider what effect their decisions will have on the organizations for which they work. Supervisors and managers make decisions about how tasks are to be assigned and completed. They also consider the effect their decisions will have on the organization. Officers of an organization make decisions that affect the future of the organization. These top management people make decisions related to what kinds of products and services the organization will provide for customers. They, too, must take into consideration the effect their decisions will have on the organization.

TYPES OF DECISIONS

mer'chan·dise

as·so·ci·a'tions

People must make decisions in all aspects of their lives. They make *personal* decisions when they choose friends, buy clothes or other merchandise, decide what to eat, and make other choices related to their everyday lives. They make *career* decisions when they make choices about their education, accept employment, or select professional associations to belong to. And, they make *social* decisions when they vote for public officials, choose a place to live, or become members of clubs or organizations.

THE DECISION-MAKING PROCESS

Some people make decisions on a whim. They do not think about what will happen as a result of their decisions. Unfortunately, these people are not good decision makers because their decisions often create problems. Good decision makers think about what will happen as a result of each choice they make, and then they select the choice that will bring about the best results. Good decision makers are not just born, they are made. Almost everyone can improve his or her decision-making skills. Illustration 3–6 shows the steps good decision makers take in making a decision.

Identifying the Problem

i·den'ti·fy·ing

The first step in becoming a good decision maker is identifying the problem. Let's look at a situation that requires a decision to be made.

> *On Wednesday evening, one of Dana's friends calls to ask her to go to the movies. Dana is tired and had planned to spend the evening at home watching television.*

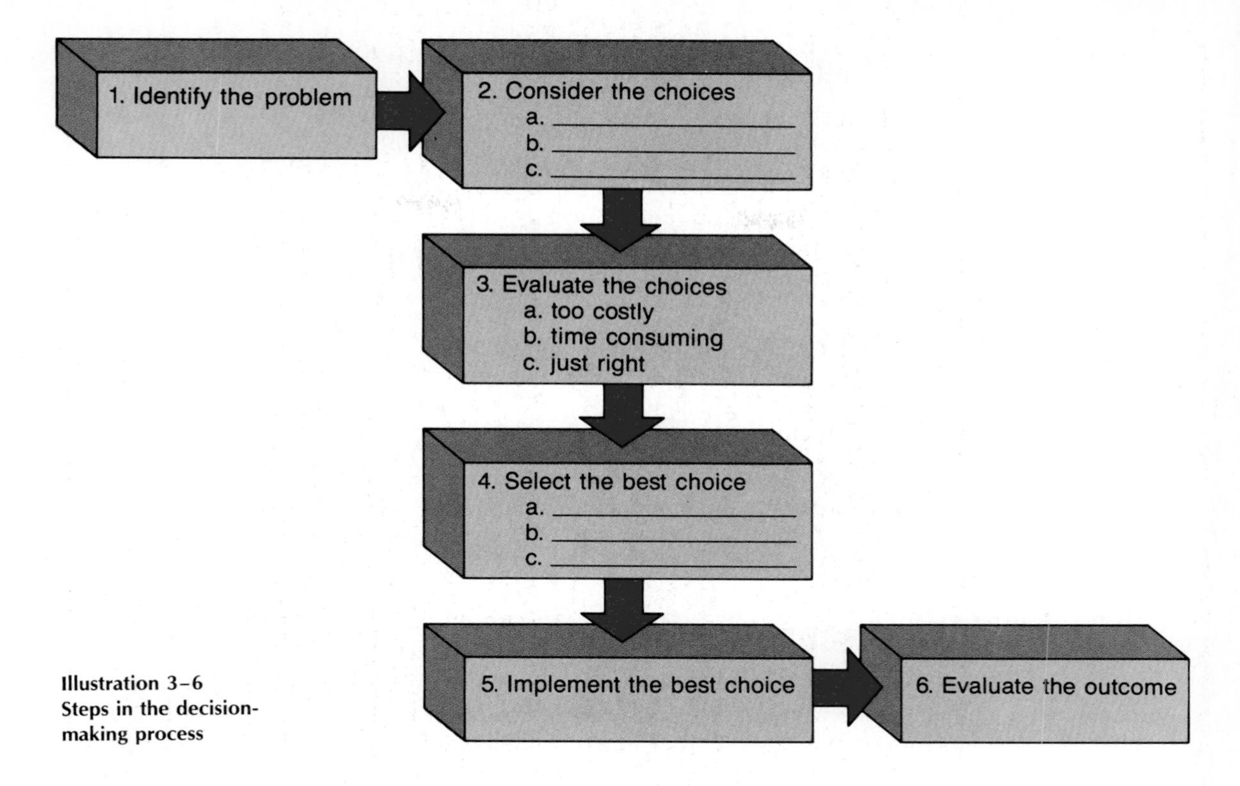

Illustration 3–6
Steps in the decision-making process

Dana's problem is easy to identify. She must decide what she wants to do. She can either go to the movies with her friend or stay at home and watch television. Often, however, our problems are more difficult to identify. Let's look at another situation in which the problem is not quite as easy to identify as it was in the earlier example.

When Marty arrived at work this morning, he found two rush jobs on his desk in addition to his regular work. One of the rush jobs is a report for Sue Mills, who leaves on a business trip at the end of the day. Sue has promised to send a copy of the report to a customer before she leaves town. The other rush job is a sales proposal from Jeff Banks. He needs the proposal for a 2 P.M. meeting.

Can you identify Marty's problem? If you said that Marty has too much work to do, you are incorrect. Marty is often given rush jobs to complete in addition to his regular work. Marty's real problem is that he doesn't know which work should be done first.

Considering the Choices

Once you have identified the problem, it's time to take a look at possible choices. The easiest way to do this is to make a list of all the possible choices.

un·ac·cept'a·ble

As each choice comes to mind, just jot it down on your list. At this point, don't take time to evaluate each choice. A choice that may seem unacceptable at first may prove to be a very good choice when you compare it to other possible choices.

Let's identify all of Marty's possible choices. Marty could

- do his regular Monday morning work
- keyboard Sue Mills's report
- keyboard Jeff Banks's proposal
- ask for help in completing the work
- ask his supervisor which work should be completed first
- explain the problem to both Sue and Jeff and ask their help in deciding which work should be completed first
- go home sick

You may be able to identify even more choices available to Marty. Notice that all choices are listed at this stage, even ones that seem unreasonable. This is done because you are identifying all of the possible choices now, not evaluating them.

Evaluating the Choices

e·val'u·at·ing

Once you have identified all of the possible choices, you are ready for the next step — evaluating the choices. At this point, you should begin by asking yourself, "What will happen if I make this choice?" Let's ask ourselves this question as we look at Marty's choices.

Illustration 3–7 After you have identified your choices, you must analyze them and select the best one

If Marty does his regular work and neglects the two rush projects, the company stands to lose the business of the customers for whom the report and proposal were being prepared. This obviously is not in the best interest of the company.

If Marty prepares only Sue's report, Jeff could lose his customer's business. In addition, Marty won't get his regular work done.

On the other hand, if Marty prepares Jeff's proposal, Sue could lose her customer. Once again, Marty won't get his regular work done.

If Marty asks for help to complete the work, his supervisor may think that he is incapable of doing his work. This might have an effect on his next work evaluation.

If Marty asks his supervisor which work should be completed first, his supervisor may think that Marty is incapable of making decisions. Once again, this might have an effect on his evaluation and any future promotion possibilities.

If Marty asks Sue and Jeff to help him decide which work should be done first, a dispute could develop between Sue and Jeff.

Notice that there is no clear-cut answer to the question, "Which work should Marty do first?" Selecting the best choice in this case requires additional thought.

Selecting the Best Choice

Once you know what the possible choices are, selecting the best choice should be easy. This selection process can be made even easier if you ask others for advice, depend on your past experiences, and rely on your own intuitions.

Asking other people for advice may help you in selecting the best choice. **Advice** is someone else's opinion of what should be done. Marty could ask one of his coworkers for advice. That person may be able to give Marty some additional ideas. However, you must remember that advice is nothing more than someone else's opinion of what should be done. Marty must still make the decision.

When faced with a decision, often you can use what you have learned from similar experiences in the past. For instance, if Marty had this problem or a similar one at another job, he could use this past experience to help him make a choice. If his supervisor has been helpful in the past, Marty would know that asking the supervisor for help would be the best solution. If Marty knew that Sue and Jeff were both very cooperative and would understand that all the work could not be accomplished, Marty would know that asking them to help him decide which work should be done first would undoubtedly be the best answer.

ac·com'plished

Intuition could also help Marty select the best choice. **Intuition** is a subconscious feeling of what should be done. Sometimes our intuition tells us that something is right or wrong. Many business people admit that they frequently use intuition when making decisions.

in·tu·i'tion

Once you have evaluated the possible choices, asked for advice, reviewed past experiences, and taken any subconscious feeling into consideration, you can select the best choice.

Implementing the Best Choice

im'ple·ment·ing

When you have selected the best choice, the next step in the decision-making process is to carry it out. This is usually called **implementing** the choice.

Let's assume Marty decides to ask his supervisor which work should be done first. When Marty asks his supervisor about the work, his supervisor may react in a number of ways. In this instance, he helps Marty develop a set of priorities so that he can handle the work that needs to be done. As you can see, Marty has implemented his choice. Now it is time for Marty to evaluate the outcome of his decision.

Evaluating the Outcome

After a choice has been made and implemented, you must evaluate the outcome of your choice. That is, you must ask yourself the question, "Did the choice I made satisfactorily solve the problem?" Sometimes, we can decide whether the right choice was made very soon after the work is completed. Other times, though, it is necessary to wait for several weeks or even months to decide whether the right choice was made. Generally, if the problem has been solved, we can assume the choice was probably a good one. However, if the problem still exists or is even worse, the choice may not have been the best choice. In this instance, you may be able to adjust your plan of action to correct the situation. However, you may have to start from the very beginning and repeat all of the steps.

Let's consider Marty's situation again. At the end of the week, he may find that the set of priorities his supervisor helped him set out allows him to complete the work on time and to everyone's satisfaction. As a result, we can say that the set of priorities is acceptable. If he was unable to complete the work, he may have to readjust his set of priorities with the help of his supervisor.

THE RISKS OF DECISION MAKING

pre·dict'ing

as·sump'tion

com·plex'

Decision making is difficult because it involves **predicting**, or forecasting, what will happen under given conditions. As you know, it is difficult to predict the future accurately. The choice you make in any given situation is based on the assumption that certain things will happen. If these things don't happen, the choice you made may not solve the problem.

The more complex the problem, the more difficult it is to make a choice and the greater the chance of making a mistake. Some people put off making decisions because they do not want to risk making a mistake. As a result, they have a difficult time completing their work. If you make a mistake, the best thing to do is admit that you made a mistake. Then, do whatever you can to correct it. After you have corrected the mistake, you should study the situation carefully. By studying the situation carefully, you can learn from your mistake and perhaps avoid making a similar mistake in the future.

REVIEWING KEY POINTS

1. People make many decisions each day. These decisions affect not only their personal lives but their social lives and careers as well.
2. When a problem must be solved, a good decision maker identifies all possible choices.
3. In order to make good decisions, you must evaluate what will happen as a result of each available choice. Then you must select the choice that will have the best results.
4. Advice, past experiences, and intuition help a person evaluate choices.
5. When we make decisions, we are trying to predict what will happen. If our predictions are not accurate, our decisions may not solve the problem.
6. Everyone who makes decisions risks making the wrong choice. We learn from mistakes and use this information for future decision-making situations.

DEVELOPING HUMAN RELATIONS SKILLS

1. Blythe's supervisor has just scolded her because she was late for work for the third time in two weeks. Each time Blythe was late, she had a good excuse. The first day she missed the bus because she had to sign some papers for her son's school work. The second day she was late because the bus was delayed at a train crossing. Today she was late because she had to stop at a grocery store to get change to ride the bus to work. Blythe's supervisor did not feel sorry for her. She warned Blythe that the next time she was late she would be issued a written warning that could cost Blythe her job.
   - **a.** What problem does Blythe have?
   - **b.** What are Blythe's choices?
   - **c.** How would you recommend that Blythe solve her problems?
2. Bev and Steve work for ten people in the same department. Bev, who started working in the department a few weeks ago, just learned that the previous secretary and Steve always brought a cake to the office whenever

someone had a birthday. Bev thinks it's a nice gesture. However, she is very busy with night classes and her family and doesn't have time to bake cakes to take to the office.

a. What choices does Bev have in this situation?

b. What do you think Bev should do?

IMPROVING COMMUNICATION SKILLS

Refer to Appendix A 2.3 – 2.9.

1. Write or keyboard the following paragraph on a separate sheet of paper, supplying all capitalization.

   shelton's insurance company is sponsoring a training seminar for its office employees. the speaker for the seminar will be angela hancock, a professor at the local university. the seminar will be held at the main office in beaumont, texas, on wednesday, november 14, in conference room 309 from 9:30 a.m. to 4:15 p.m. topics for the seminar include: setting priorities, managing time, and making decisions. employees from the branch offices in lafayette, louisiana; bryan, oklahoma; and houston, texas, are invited to participate in the seminar. employees who wish to attend the seminar should make arrangements with their supervisors before wednesday, november 7.

2. On a separate sheet of paper, write or keyboard a sentence to answer each of the following questions. Check your sentences to make certain that the subjects and verbs agree and that words are correctly capitalized.

   a. Who makes decisions?

   b. Why do people make decisions?

   c. What is the first step in making a decision?

   d. How do decision makers evaluate their choices?

   e. How can past experiences be used to evaluate a choice?

   f. What is advice?

   g. What is intuition?

   h. What happens when a choice is implemented?

   i. How is an implemented choice evaluated?

   j. What should be done if the choice made is wrong?

BUILDING PROBLEM-SOLVING SKILLS

1. On a separate sheet of paper, write the answers to the following problems.

a. $1/4 + 3/4 =$	**d.** $1/6 + 3/4 =$	**g.** $4 - 7/8 =$
b. $3/8 + 7/8 =$	**e.** $1/3 + 1/6 =$	**h.** $1/2 - 1/10 =$
c. $1/2 + 1/4 =$	**f.** $1 - 2/3 =$	**i.** $3/5 - 1/10 =$

2. State Manufacturing, Inc., has established a new vacation policy. According to this policy, each employee is entitled to ten days of vacation. After five years of service, each employee will be given an extra vacation day for each additional full year of employment. Referring to the table that follows, calculate the number of vacation days each employee will have after this new policy goes into effect. Write your answers on a separate sheet of paper.

Employee	Years Employed	Employee	Years Employed
D. Noble	3 1/2	B. Simms	10
C. Orth	7	S. Taines	8 3/4
Y. Pezold	5 1/4	B. Vincent	4
L. Quinn	17	E. Walls	6 1/2
Y. Rizzo	13 1/4	H. Yates	9

APPLYING OFFICE SKILLS

Activities 1, 2, and 3 can be done on information processing equipment.

1. You are working part time in the Masterson Company office. When you arrive at your work station on Monday morning, the following tasks and instructions are on your desk. Prepare a list showing the order in which you would complete the tasks.
   - **a.** A rough draft of a report that Ms. Jung needs Friday afternoon.
   - **b.** A letter Mr. Tyre wants to sign and mail this afternoon.
   - **c.** The summer vacation schedule on which Mr. Dess wrote, "Please keyboard when you have time."
   - **d.** A report Mr. Tyre needs for a meeting Tuesday afternoon.
   - **e.** A list of files Mr. Boyd wants prepared for Tuesday's meeting.
   - **f.** A letter welcoming a new customer on which Ms. Noel wrote, "Please give this to me by the end of the week."
   - **g.** Some invoices to be keyboarded and mailed for Ms. Jung, who wrote, "These should go out no later than Thursday afternoon."
   - **h.** A note from Ms. Noel asking you to pick up some materials from the printer a block away, "sometime today."
2. Each afternoon this term you will be working in the school office. On the next page is a list of items that you will be keyboarding. Next to each item your supervisor has indicated its priority. On a full sheet of paper, prepare a table showing the order of priority. Start keyboarding on line 22 from the top edge of the paper. Set the left margin at 12 (10 pitch) or 21 (12 pitch). Set a tab at 65 (10 pitch) or 73 (12 pitch). Center the title "Priorities for

Keyboarding." Use the column headings "Priority" and "Task." Double space between each of the lines.

Correspondence for teachers (4)
Reports for teachers (3)
Tests (1)
Class handouts (2)
Articles for the school paper (10)
Letters of recommendation for students (8)
Minutes of faculty committee meetings (5)
Correspondence for student organizations (7)
Reports for faculty committees (6)
Announcements for the parents' organization (9)

3. As you keyboard the paragraph below, make the following changes:

a. Change all dates from the informal style (8/10/--) to the more formal style (August 10, 19--).

b. Rather than keyboard the name in full, keyboard the initials and last name.

c. Spell out all abbreviations.

At the employee group meeting on 11/30--, James Edward Hunter was elected pres. He will serve until 6/30--. He was elected to replace Sue Ann Turner, who resigned when she moved away. At the same meeting Julie Carson was appointed chairperson of the committee to plan the Xmas party that will be held on 12/14--. Carol Lind passed out copies of the activity report that was dated 10/30--. Martin John Dumanoski asked for four volunteers for the Finance Com. The following people volunteered: Megan Lewis, Redmond Raux, Wendy Wong, and Jordan Marshall. Vivian Ballard, sec., expressed a desire to be considered an alternate for the Com. Martin John Dumanoski announced that the first meeting of the Com. would be held on Mon., 12/5--. At this meeting the Com. plans to review the group's budget. The meeting was adjourned at 3:30. The next meeting will be held on Mon., 12/12--.

Saving Time and Money

1. Check your supply drawer at the beginning of each day. Replenish items that are in short supply. In this way you won't need to stop to get supplies during the day.
2. To insure the safety of you and your fellow workers, do not drape electrical or telephone cords over desks or where people will be working.
3. Develop the habit of looking at the next day's schedule before you leave the office. You will be better prepared to organize your work when you arrive the next morning.
4. As soon as you are finished with the task, put all of the materials away. Return reference materials and equipment to its proper place.

PROFESSIONAL INSIGHTS

ERGONOMICS

Office automation has had some positive effects on productivity. The introduction of VDTs (video display terminals) into the work place has reduced the drudgery of many office functions. However, the impact of the VDT is not all positive.

Employers have long been aware of the advantages of a comfortable work environment. However, the introduction of new technology into the office has created a whole new set of problems.

One major difficulty is that VDTs are often used with furniture and in environments designed for other purposes. Often the work areas in traditional offices have too much light for comfortable viewing of VDT screens. The layout of the work station itself—for example, the height of the table or the angle of the screen—contributes greatly to the physical problems reported by VDT users. The type of work done at a VDT also has an impact on the employee. Highly paced work and deadlines can cause visual and muscular problems even when the work environment has been adapted to VDT use.

As the problems related to VDT use become apparent, some employers are working to make the VDT user's environment less stressful. By adapting lighting conditions and providing furniture designed specifically for use with VDTs, employers help prevent VDT use from creating physical stress.

1. Some employers believe that the problems created by VDT use are no different from those created by any type of office work. Do you agree?
2. Do the problems related to VDT use outweigh the advantages?
3. Are the problems related to VDTs serious enough to require development of federal standards to regulate their design and use?

UNIT 4

ADMINISTRATIVE SUPPORT RESPONSIBILITIES

- Meeting People
- Scheduling Appointments
- Scheduling Travel and Meetings

CHAPTER 1

MEETING PEOPLE

When you work in an office, your office support responsibilities may include some public relations duties. Meeting and greeting customers, clients, sales representatives, and applicants for employment can be interesting and rewarding work. If you are hired as a receptionist, your responsibilities will probably include greeting all visitors and directing them to the appropriate office. You may also be responsible for answering the telephones and providing general information about the company.

Even if you are not hired as a receptionist, you may have some public relations duties. You may be the person assigned to greet people who have appointments with your supervisor. Good interpersonal skills and knowledge of your company will enable you to perform your public relations duties well.

As you study this chapter, you will find answers to the following questions:

- How can I make a good impression on visitors to the office?
- What is an appropriate way to greet visitors to the office?
- What should I do when a visitor does not have an appointment?
- How do I handle difficult visitors?
- What do the following terms mean: **impression, goodwill, screening, tact?**

CREATING A PROFESSIONAL IMPRESSION

im·pres'sion

re·cep'tion

Impression refers to the image or feeling that is retained by the mind. You and your surroundings make an immediate impression on visitors to your office. The reception area, your appearance, and the way you greet visitors all play a part in creating a good impression. The impression you make can influence the visitor's opinion of your company. Thus, you play an important public relations role for the firm.

The Reception Area

The reception area should be kept neat and orderly. Although most companies have a cleaning service, the cleaning is usually done after office hours. To keep the area neat throughout the day, check to see that magazines and other reading materials are in order and that any waste paper is picked up. Your efforts will make the reception area a pleasant place for office visitors.

A neat desk helps to create an impression of an organized, efficient company. Since it is difficult to work efficiently in cluttered surroundings, keep on your desk only those items that you use frequently or that you need to perform the task at hand.

Illustration 4–1
The reception area should be a pleasant area to wait

Your Appearance

Your appearance reflects how you feel about yourself and about the company you work for. You can make a good first impression by choosing a hair style and clothing that are flattering to you. When you look your best and dress appropriately for the office, you usually feel more confident and act with more poise.

Your Behavior

ap·pro'pri·ate

Loud laughing and talking are never appropriate in the office. Naturally, there are times when funny things happen that make you laugh. However, when it sounds as if there is more laughing than work being done, you are giving visitors a bad impression of your company.

Office workers should use good judgment in discussing certain topics when visitors are present. Information about customers, new products or services, and other company employees should not be revealed to the public. For example, it is usually sufficient to tell visitors, "Ms. Scott is out of the office and won't be back until Friday." They don't need to know that Ms. Scott is in New Orleans on vacation or in Fort Wayne trying to make a sale. Although you are expected to be helpful and friendly to visitors, be careful not to reveal information that should be kept confidential.

con·fi·den'tial

Illustration 4–2
Greet visitors to the office in a helpful and courteous manner

GREETING VISITORS

cour'te·ous·ly

All office visitors should be greeted promptly and courteously. If you have a genuine interest in your company and in helping people, you will enjoy this part of your job.

When visitors walk into your office, show them that they are welcome. "Good morning (or afternoon), may I help you?" is an appropriate greeting. Most people will respond to your greeting by giving you their names, business associations or companies, and the names of the persons they would like to see. For example: "Hello, I'm Erica Boyd from City Office Suppliers. I have a 9:15 appointment with Mrs. Thomas."

ac·knowl'edge

cir'cum·stanc·es

If visitors arrive while you are talking to someone on the telephone or in person, give a friendly smile to acknowledge their arrival. Then complete or interrupt the conversation at the first convenient point and greet them. If it appears that you are going to be tied up for a while, say, "I'll be with you in a few moments. Would you like to have a seat?" Under no circumstances should personal visits and telephone calls keep you from greeting your visitors promptly and giving them the attention they deserve.

Some visitors may not know the names of the persons they should see. To help you direct visitors to the correct persons or departments, you may want to develop a reference guide. The guide should contain the names of key people within each department. It should also contain a description of the functions of each department.

Many of your visitors will be people who regularly call on your company. You should learn the names and business associations of these callers. Be prepared to greet them by name. Greeting office visitors by name helps build that feeling of friendliness or **goodwill** for your company, your supervisor, and yourself.

Screening Visitors

cli'ents

col'leagues

There will be many types of visitors who will compete for your supervisor's time and attention. Customers and clients will come to conduct business. Colleagues and other company employees will meet to discuss the operations of the company. Salespeople will call to demonstrate their products.

In some offices there may be so many visitors that it is difficult for your supervisor to get any work done. You may be asked to help by **screening** visitors. When you screen properly, you make sure that only the people who need to be seen are seen by your supervisor.

as·sis'tants

Some business people will see only those people with scheduled appointments. Others will see all visitors unless they are already meeting with someone else. Business people often have assistants who can handle callers with routine questions. No matter how busy they are, though, most people will see family members and close friends whenever they come in. You can learn your supervisor's preference for seeing visitors by asking for guidelines.

Here is an example of effective screening. The visitor does not need to see the department manager, as the receptionist discovers.

RECEPTIONIST: Good morning. May I help you?
VISITOR: Hello, my name is Brian Pantoja. I understand there is an opening for a part-time file clerk in this department. I would like to talk with the department manager about this position.
RECEPTIONIST: Our personnel department is accepting applications for that position. It is located in Room 102 on the first floor, to the left as you get off the elevator. Carla Stringer in personnel will give you an application and answer your questions. Here, let me write down her name and office number for you.
VISITOR: Thank you.
RECEPTIONIST: You're welcome. Good luck!

TURNING VISITORS AWAY

When visitors arrive without an appointment, they are often disappointed to learn that the person they want to see cannot see them. You must use **tact**; that is, you must take care in the way you explain to them that your supervisor is not available. By applying good human relations skills, you can

Illustration 4–3 Check with your supervisor before showing visitors in

say *no* and keep the goodwill of the visitor. For example, you might say, "May I schedule an appointment for you on Wednesday or Thursday? Mrs. McBride has a deadline to meet and asked that she not be disturbed today." Be careful not to give the impression that the visitor is not important. For example, don't say "Mrs. McBride can't see you" when in fact she can't see anyone.

ANNOUNCING VISITORS

When a person arrives for a scheduled appointment, inform your supervisor, either by telephone or in person. Your supervisor will tell you whether or not to show the person in. If your supervisor is ready to see the caller, show him or her to the correct office. Some business people come out to meet callers in the reception area. However, when callers are familiar with the office and know where they are going, you need only tell them that your supervisor is ready to see them: "Miss Lowell is expecting you. Would you like to go in?"

Your supervisor may count on you to help maintain the daily schedule. If an appointment is running overtime and other people are waiting, you can hand your supervisor a note that says that the person with the next appointment has arrived. You can also telephone your supervisor with a quick reminder. Your supervisor can then make the decision to continue the meeting in session or to reschedule it for another time.

re·mind'er

HANDLING DELAYS

When visitors with appointments arrive before your supervisor is ready to see them, try to make their wait pleasant. Show them where they can hang their coats, hats, or umbrellas. Offer them a seat in a comfortable chair and keep them informed about the delay. Providing magazines or other reading materials can make their wait more enjoyable.

People value their time and do not like to waste it waiting for a late appointment. If you notice early in the day that appointments are running behind schedule, there are some things that you can do. First, you can ask if your supervisor plans to get back on schedule. It may be possible to catch up by cutting each appointment a few minutes short. If it appears that it is not possible to get back on schedule, then you should contact the people with scheduled appointments and inform them of the delay so that they can plan to arrive later. You can also ask people who are in the reception area if they would like to reschedule their appointments for another day.

HANDLING DIFFICULT VISITORS

Most of the visitors to your office will be professional people who behave in a professional manner. However, there are always exceptions. Occasionally,

oc·ca'sion·al·ly

you will meet visitors who are rude or difficult to handle. For example, they may refuse to tell you their names or the nature of the visit, or they may insist on seeing your supervisor immediately. Even if the caller is rude, it is important that you remain calm and courteous. Most people respond to courtesy and will give you the information you request. If you react rudely, you may cause your company to lose a customer. You should always remember to treat all visitors to your office with the same courtesy that you would want to receive.

Notice how Duane, a receptionist in the administrative offices of a large department store, handles a difficult visitor:

DUANE: Hello. May I help you?

CALLER: I need to see Mr. Williams immediately.

DUANE: Mr. Williams has a full schedule for the day. If you let me know what you need to see him about, I'm sure I can find someone else to help you.

CALLER: I don't want to talk with someone else. I want to see Mr. Williams. Don't try to give me the run-around!

DUANE: If you don't think anyone else can help you, I can schedule you to see Mr. Williams later in the week. Would Thursday at 2:00 be convenient for you, Ms. . . . ?

CALLER: Shepherd. Mrs. Alice Shepherd. I guess Thursday will do.

DUANE: All right. And can I tell Mr. Williams the nature of your visit?

CALLER: What business is it of yours?

DUANE: Mrs. Shepherd, Mr. Williams likes to prepare for his appointments. There may be some information he would like to gather in order to be of more assistance.

CALLER: Well, then, tell him I'd like to discuss your credit policy.

DUANE: Mr. Williams will probably ask Miss Carlucci, the credit manager, to sit in on your meeting Thursday. I think she's in this morning. I can see if she's available to meet with you now. It may save you a trip on Thursday.

CALLER: Well, if you think she can help me . . .

DUANE: (Telephoning Miss Carlucci's office) Hello. This is Duane in Mr. Williams' office. I have a customer here, Mrs. Alice Shepherd, who would like to discuss the store's credit policy . . .(Duane arranges for Mrs. Shepherd to meet with Miss Carlucci). (To Mrs. Shepherd) Miss Carlucci can see you. Her office is on the fourth floor, Room 410.

CALLER: Thank you for your help.

DUANE: My pleasure.

Duane's courtesy and willingness to spend a little extra time with Mrs. Shepherd enabled him to get the information that he needed to direct her to the appropriate person in the company. By screening, Duane saved Mr. Williams' and Mrs. Shepherd's time. Duane's professional manner resulted in a satisfied customer who left with a good impression of the company.

Record of Visitors						
Date	Visitor's Name	Title	Company Name	Telephone Number	Arrival Time	Departure Time
10/29	S. Fisher	Consultant	J & B Associates	747-5395	11:00	11:55
10/29	M. Miller	Manager	Brooks, Inc.	781-1743	2:45	3:00
10/30	L. Burdin	Sales Rep.	Busy B's	776-8284	9:40	11:10
10/30	B. Downs	Attorney	State Ins.	775-0291	1:20	1:45
11/2	L. Kane	Director	Temps, Inc.	721-4395	9:05	9:30
11/2	J. Warren	Consultant	Gold Star Co.	787-1279	10:00	10:45

Illustration 4–4
Record of visitors

KEEPING A RECORD OF VISITORS

ro'ta·ry

Many companies maintain a record of all customers, clients, and regular visitors. These records may be stored in a rotary file, a card file, or in the computer. Each record usually contains the date, the visitor's name, business title, company, address, and telephone number. You can courteously ask for this information when the person telephones for an appointment or visits the office for the first time.

Such records are frequently found in the offices of dentists, lawyers, and other professional people who charge a fee for office visits. Any other information about the visitor that will help your company provide better service should also be noted. For example, you may want to record the caller's account number or home telephone number. It is wise to check this information occasionally to make sure it is up to date. If kept up to date, this information can be helpful.

LEAVING THE RECEPTION AREA

If one of your job responsibilities is to greet all visitors, then you must be near your desk at all times. When you must leave your work area — to go to lunch, to the mail room, or to the copier — you should arrange to have someone nearby watch for and greet visitors. If no one is available to cover for you, you should tell your supervisor that the desk will be unattended for a while. You might say: "Ms. Watson, I'm going to the central files to pick up the records you need. Mike Hart should be arriving within the next few minutes for his 3:00 appointment." Your supervisor will know to watch for the visitor's arrival.

REVIEWING KEY POINTS

1. As an office worker, your office support responsibilities may include receiving visitors to the office.
2. The reception area, your appearance, and the way you greet visitors influence the impression you create of your company and yourself.
3. Greet all visitors cordially as soon as they arrive. If you are busy when a visitor arrives, you can acknowledge the visitor's arrival with a smile.
4. When you greet a frequent visitor to your company by name, you build goodwill for your company.
5. By screening visitors, you can make sure that only those visitors who need to be seen are seen by the most appropriate person.
6. Being tactful is important when turning visitors away. When you use good human relations skills, you can say *no* and still maintain the goodwill of the visitor.
7. Part of your receptionist's duties includes announcing visitors and showing them to the appropriate office.
8. When your supervisor is running behind schedule, inform visitors with appointments of the delay so that they can plan to arrive later.
9. If you react in a calm and courteous manner to rude or angry visitors, the visitors will usually calm down.
10. The reception area should never be left unattended. If you must leave the reception area, ask another employee to watch the area and greet visitors.

DEVELOPING HUMAN RELATIONS SKILLS

1. A receptionist and two clerks work near the reception area in the Freeman Real Estate Office. Mack Cobb, a clerk, has been having a lot of personal problems. Serena, the receptionist, and Rick, the other clerk, have been understanding when Mack was upset. When Mack arrived on Monday morning, he spent the first hour telling Serena and Rick about his horrible weekend. While Mack was talking, several visitors arrived and were waiting in the reception area. When Serena realized that everyone was listening to Mack's personal problems, she was embarrassed.
   - **a.** What is the problem?
   - **b.** What should Serena do?
   - **c.** How can this situation be prevented from developing again?
2. Jo Anne Rosotti, receptionist, was keyboarding when a visitor walked into the office. The visitor said, "Hi! I'm Bill Busch, an old football buddy of Jim

Hold; and I'm in town for the afternoon. Can I surprise Jim?" Mr. Hold has some important clients in his office, and he has several other important appointments scheduled for the afternoon. Mr. Hold does not like to be disturbed when he is with clients.

a. How should Jo Anne handle this situation?

b. What should Jo Anne tell Mr. Busch?

IMPROVING COMMUNICATION SKILLS

Refer to Appendix A 1.1–1.5.

1. Use a period at the end of a declarative sentence that makes a statement and at the end of an imperative sentence that gives a command or makes a request. Use a question mark at the end of an interrogative sentence that asks a direct question.

   Your responsibilities include greeting visitors. (Declarative sentence)
   Greet each visitor. (Imperative sentence)
   Did you greet that visitor? (Interrogative sentence)

   Review the use of the period and the question mark by supplying each of the following sentences with the correct end punctuation. Write or keyboard your sentences on a separate sheet of paper.

   a. A courteous receptionist creates a good impression for the company

   b. Will you answer the telephone for me while I'm at lunch

   c. A receptionist should greet all visitors promptly

   d. The reception area should be kept neat and orderly

   e. Why are good public relations skills necessary for greeting visitors

   f. When you announce a visitor, give the person's full name

   g. Who shall I say is calling

   h. Why is it important to ask who is calling

   i. A record of callers is often found in dentists' offices

   j. Why should someone always be available to greet visitors

2. Paraphrase each paragraph below in your own words. Write or keyboard your paragraphs on a separate sheet of paper.

   a. The receptionist is usually the first person that a visitor sees when the visitor arrives at an office. Since the first impression is usually a lasting one, it is important that the receptionist make a good first impression on visitors. A neat and clean reception area helps to make a good impression. The appropriate appearance and behavior on the part of the receptionist also help to make a good first impression.

   b. The meeting will be held on Monday, November 29, in Room 206, the Board Room. Each manager attending the meeting should be prepared to discuss what effect the new attendance regulations will have on subordinates and the company. Managers who are unable to attend the meeting should submit a written report to Mrs. Angelle before November 25.

BUILDING PROBLEM-SOLVING SKILLS

1. Compute the costs for each of the following items. Add 5% sales tax to each total.
   - **a.** Six pens at $1.19 each
   - **b.** Five dozen "While You Were Out" pads at $1.95 per dozen
   - **c.** Three boxes of disks at $39.95 per box
   - **d.** One dozen staple removers at $1.39 each
   - **e.** Three pairs of 6" scissors at $7.98 each
2. Refer to the "Record of Visitors" chart on page 119. Then, write or keyboard your answers on a separate sheet of paper.
   - **a.** How long did L. Karre visit?
   - **b.** Which visitor stayed the longest time?
   - **c.** Which visitor stayed the shortest time?
   - **d.** How much time were visitors in the office on October 30?
   - **e.** What is the total visiting time for all three days?

APPLYING OFFICE SKILLS

Activities 1 and 2 can be done on information processing equipment.

1. Design a form that can be used to record office visitors. Your form should include the following information: date, visitor's name, company association, person referred to, time of arrival, and time of departure. When your form is completed, record in your best handwriting the information for the following visitors.
   - **a.** Jenny Cole of Computer Temps called on June 15 at 9:40 to see Ms. Vandle. She left at 10:35.
   - **b.** Elsie Ryan of City Office Equipment saw Ms. Hart on June 15 from 10:30 to 11:05.
   - **c.** Clare Drake from Office Music, Inc., called on June 15 at 1:15. She saw Mr. Walters and left at 2:05.
   - **d.** T. B. Bates of B & B Associates called on Ms. Hart on June 15 at 2:00. He left at 3:15.
   - **e.** Matt Firmin from Firmin & Sons called on Mr. Walters on June 15 at 2:30. He left at 3:25.

2. A receptionist must know where people and offices are located in order to give clear directions. The drawing here shows the floor plan of a building. Notice where the receptionist's desk is located. Write or keyboard directions to help visitors find the following locations in the building. Assume the visitor is standing at the *X* in the reception area.

   a. Room 301
   b. Stairs to fourth floor
   c. Water fountain
   d. Conference Room
   e. Restrooms
   f. Personnel Office

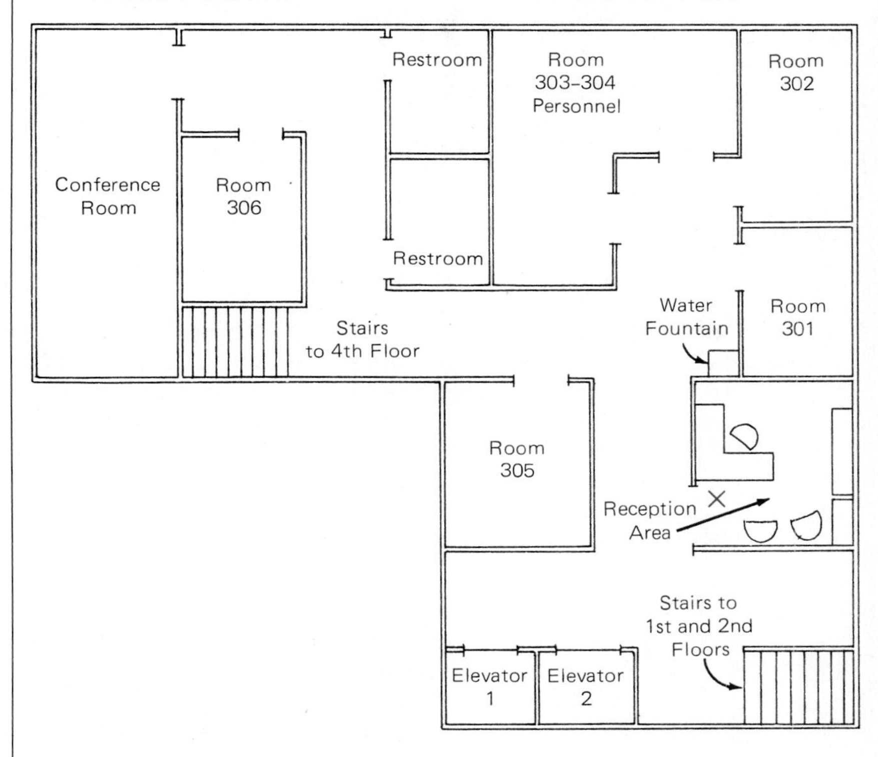

CHAPTER 2

SCHEDULING APPOINTMENTS

In the last unit you learned that time is a very valuable resource. People do not like to waste time; thus, they do not like to be kept waiting. People avoid long lines at theaters, crowded restaurants, and stores where service is slow. Most people try to reduce waiting time by making appointments to conduct their business. As an office worker, you may be responsible for scheduling appointments and helping your supervisor keep them.

As you study this chapter, you will find answers to the following questions:

- How do I schedule appointments?
- What is the most efficient way to keep records of appointments?
- How do I maintain the appointment schedule?
- How do I handle canceled appointments?
- What do the following terms mean: **preferences, appointment calendar?**

ESTABLISHING GUIDELINES

ap·point'ments
pref'er·enc·es

In order to schedule appointments for people within your organization, you must know their **preferences**. That is, you must know their choice of days and times of day for meeting with others. You must also know if they will see visitors without appointments.

Jan Evans was recently hired as a receptionist in a new department of a large firm. Mark Downs hired her to screen telephone calls and schedule appointments for the five people who work in the new department.

When Jan reported for work, she asked Mr. Downs and each of the other people for whom she would be scheduling appointments for some guidelines. Jan's questions included: "Are there any people you will see without an appointment?" "Should I keep part of the day free for uninterrupted work?" "How can I help you keep your appointments running on schedule?" Everyone in the office was pleased to see that Jan was taking her work so seriously.

Like Jan, you may have to ask for guidelines in scheduling appointments. By asking for guidelines, you can make your job easier. You can also help the people you report to work more productively.

HANDLING REQUESTS FOR APPOINTMENTS

Requests for appointments are usually made by telephone, although it is not unusual to receive a letter requesting an appointment. Occasionally someone will stop by the office to request an appointment. All requests for appointments should be given prompt attention.

When an appointment is requested, you should

ver'i·fy

1. Check the appointment calendar to verify that the day and time requested for the appointment are available. If not, suggest an available day and time.
2. Have your supervisor approve the appointment, if that is the office policy.
3. Confirm the appointment, if necessary.
4. Record the appointment on the calendar.

A telephone request could be handled like this:

RECEPTIONIST: Good morning. Belk and Jones Associates, Ken Miller speaking.
CALLER: Hello, is Sue Anders in today?
RECEPTIONIST: May I ask who's calling?
CALLER: This is John Bruner at Studio Photographics. I have some color transparencies for Sue that I'd like to drop off and discuss this afternoon.

RECEPTIONIST: Let me check her schedule and see if she'll be in. (Pause) She'll be out of the office most of the day, but it looks as if she's free after 4:00. I'll have to check with her to make sure she hasn't scheduled anything else and get back in touch with you.

CALLER: That sounds fine with me. My number is 655-7027. If I'm not in, just leave a message.

RECEPTIONIST: That's 655-7027. I'll try to let you know before noon, Mr. Bruner.

con·fir·ma'tion

After checking with Ms. Anders to make sure the appointment time is convenient, the receptionist telephones Mr. Bruner with the confirmation.

MR. BRUNER'S SECRETARY: Good afternoon. Studio Photographics, Anita Chou speaking.

RECEPTIONIST: Hello. This is Ken Miller at Belk and Jones Associates. May I speak to Mr. Bruner?

MR. BRUNER'S SECRETARY: Mr. Bruner has left for lunch. May I take a message?

RECEPTIONIST: Yes, please. Tell him that Ms. Anders will be able to see him at 4:00 today. They will meet in her office.

MR. BRUNER'S SECRETARY: That's a 4:00 meeting with Ms. Anders at Belk and Jones Associates. I'll see that Mr. Bruner gets the message. Thank you for calling.

RECEPTIONIST: Thank you. Good-bye.

Most written requests for appointments also require confirmation. If the person lives outside the local calling area, you may write a confirmation letter. Otherwise, confirmations can be made by telephone. Whether you write or call the person, be sure to mention the date, time, and meeting place when you confirm an appointment.

RECORDING THE APPOINTMENT

Once you have scheduled an appointment, you should record it on the **appointment calendar.** Appointment calendars are available in a variety of styles with several special features. In offices where scheduled appointments are rare, you might use a regular desk calendar. Some calendars have the workday broken into half-hour or 15-minute time periods. Appointment books are available that display the entire week on one page, a feature which may be useful in some offices.

When you record the appointment, be sure you have the correct information. Include the person's name and the date, time, and location of the appointment (if not in your supervisor's office). Writing down the person's business association or the purpose of the meeting helps your supervisor identify the visitor and prepare for the meeting. Listing the telephone number is useful in case it is necessary to change the appointment.

Scheduling Enough Time

You should also indicate on the calendar the amount of time needed for each appointment. This procedure prevents overlapping appointments or allowing too much time in between appointments. One method is to draw an arrow or lines through the required time period, as shown in Illustration 4–5.

Estimating the time needed for an appointment isn't easy. Some people let you know how much time is needed when they request an appointment. If the person doesn't volunteer this information, you can find out by saying something like this: "Mr. Timilty has a half-hour free this afternoon at 2:30. If you need more time, I can schedule you for 9:30 on Friday."

vol·un·teer′

As you become more familiar with the business and the regular callers, you will learn how much time to schedule for routine appointments. Until you do, you can always ask your supervisor for an estimate.

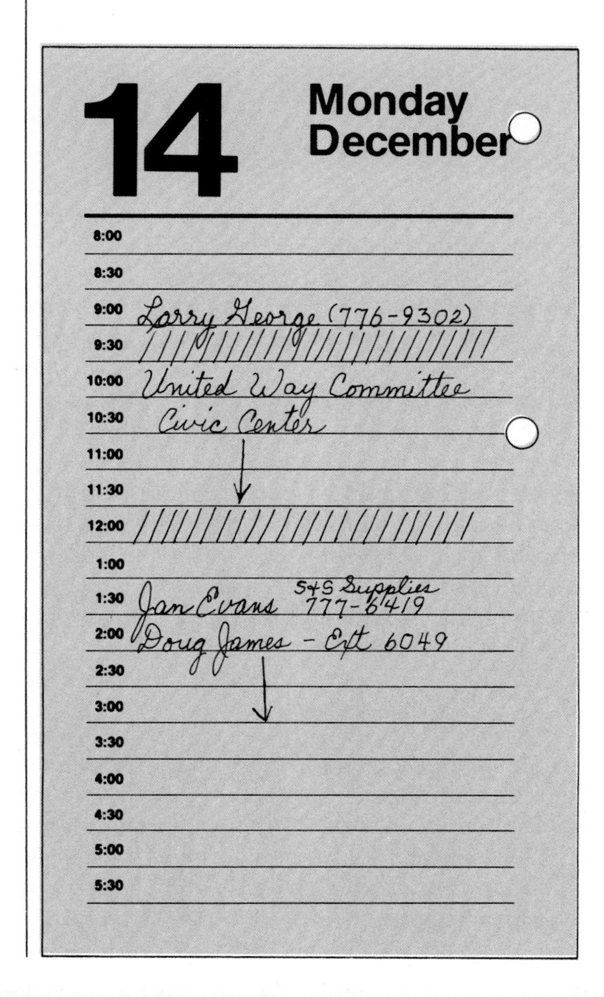

Illustration 4–5 Indicate the estimated length of each appointment

Keeping a Neat Calendar

Neatness is important when you record information on an appointment calendar. Your handwriting must be legible so your supervisor and the others you schedule appointments for can easily read it. You must write telephone numbers clearly. You may need to contact the caller to reschedule the appointment.

Keeping a neat calendar reduces your chances of making mistakes. Messy scratch outs can result in the scheduling of two appointments at the same time. Eliminate confusion by using a calendar with enough space to write in the necessary information.

MAINTAINING THE APPOINTMENT SCHEDULE

There are several ways in which you can help your supervisor stay on schedule and use time efficiently.

Planning the Day's Schedule

As the appointment calendar begins to fill up for the day, be sure to leave a few minutes of unscheduled time. Your supervisor will need some free time during the day to attend to other important activities, such as returning urgent telephone calls. In addition, you may need to set aside 10 to 15 minutes of a busy day so that you and your supervisor can discuss any office matters.

Your supervisor will appreciate a few minutes between appointments in which to prepare for the next appointment or make telephone calls. It is important to allow just the right amount of time between appointments. Too little or too much time between appointments may result in wasted time. Look at the schedule in Illustration 4–6, for example. Each appointment has been scheduled so that there is a half-hour between it and the next appointment. A half-hour is not enough time to set up, perform, and complete many tasks. A better schedule is the one in Illustration 4–7. It allows longer periods of uninterrupted work time.

un·in·ter·rupt′ed

Maintaining Several Calendars

If you schedule appointments for more than one person, you should use a separate appointment calendar for each person. Or, for convenience, you can use an appointment book that contains several columns, like the one in Illustration 4–8 on page 130. An appointment book with several columns is easier to maintain than three or four separate appointment books.

Many business people schedule their own appointments and record them on their own desks or pocket calendars. If both you and your supervisor

10 Thursday December

Time	Appointment
8:00	
8:30	
9:00	Pat Hess - Interview (256-7923)
9:30	
10:00	Andy Bozeman (256-7134)
10:30	
11:00	Clara Ames (732-0913)
11:30	
12:00	//////////////////////
1:00	Doug Smith (Comptroller's Office)
1:30	
2:00	Anna Magini - Ext. 7407
2:30	
3:00	Bill Busé - Interview (256-0319)
3:30	
4:00	Susan Farr - Interview (731-4601)
4:30	
5:00	
5:30	

Illustration 4–6
Poorly planned schedule

10 Thursday December

Time	Appointment
8:00	
8:30	
9:00	Pat Hess - Interview (256-7923)
9:30	Andy Bozeman - R - TEL (721-7137)
10:00	
10:30	
11:00	
11:30	Clara Ames (732-0913)
12:00	//////////////////////
1:00	Doug Smith (Comptroller's Office)
1:30	Anna Magini - Ext. 7407
2:00	Bill Busé - Interview (256-0319)
2:30	
3:00	
3:30	
4:00	Susan Farr - Ext 2811
4:30	
5:00	
5:30	

Illustration 4–7
Well-planned schedule

co·or'di·nate

schedule and record appointments, you need to coordinate your calendars so that they are accurate and up to date. Otherwise, you and your supervisor may schedule two appointments for the same time.

Keeping Your Supervisor Informed

ef·fec'tive·ly

re·mind'ers

Busy people need to know their schedules for the day in order to plan work effectively. If your supervisor does not keep a personal calendar of appointments, you should provide a daily schedule each morning. The schedule should include all the information contained in your appointment calendar. In addition, you may want to include reminders of special tasks that must be accomplished, such as preparing a speech or making travel arrangements.

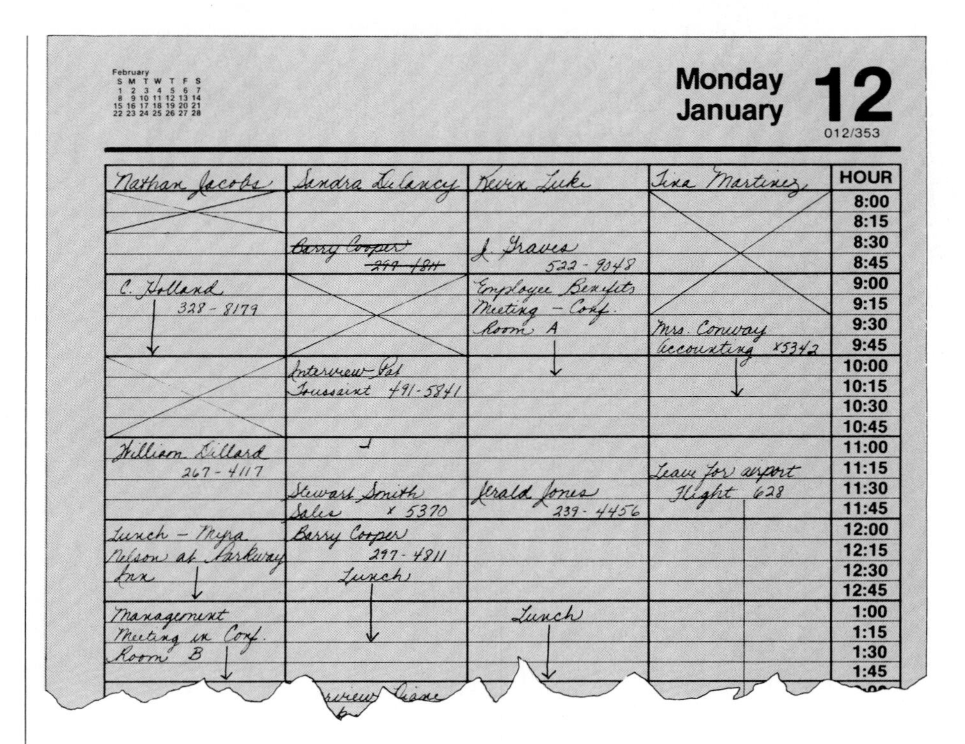

Illustration 4–8 Appointment book for scheduling appointments for several people

Illustration 4–9 shows a keyboarded daily schedule. In some companies, as you will learn in Unit 14, information about appointments is stored on an electronic calendar. Each morning a printout of the daily appointments is obtained from the computer.

SCHEDULING APPOINTMENTS WITH OTHERS

Office workers with good telephone skills are frequently asked by their supervisors to make appointments for them with other people. The first step is to ask your supervisor or check the appointment calendar for possible meeting times. Then, telephone the other person's office to request an appointment. State the purpose of the meeting, if possible. If your supervisor has a busy schedule, you should request a specific day and hour.

Such a conversation may begin: "Hello. This is Lynn Knutsen of Rosotti and Associates. Mr. Tortici would like an appointment with Mrs. Servat to discuss the Nelson contract. Would 10:30 on Tuesday morning, November 10, be convenient?" If the time is acceptable, record the time and location of the appointment on the calendar.

9 Monday February

Appointments for February 9

9:30 - 10:30	John Suire of Southern Industries (New contract)
10:30 - 11:30	Meet with sales team in Conference Room A
12:00 - 1:30	Lunch with Sara Bennett (Advertising layout)
1:30 - 2:00	Interview Gary Harris for sales position
3:30 - 4:00	Go to Personnel Department to complete forms

Reminders:

1. You have a managers meeting tomorrow at 8:30 a.m.

   A draft of your report is in the file attached.

2. Mr. Joye would like to have the reports for the accountant by tomorrow afternoon at 4:00 p.m.

Illustration 4–9 Schedule of appointments for the day

Schedule extra time between appointments for meetings held away from your office. Set aside enough time for traveling to the location of the meeting and returning to the office before the next scheduled appointment.

HANDLING CANCELLATIONS

Situations do arise that cause plans to change. Someone may call to cancel an appointment and request that it be scheduled for another time. Be sure to cross out the canceled appointment and record the new time on all calendars.

re·li′a·ble

When your supervisor must cancel an appointment, notify the other person as soon as possible. Normally it is faster and more reliable to cancel by telephone than by sending a letter. When canceling an appointment, be prepared to suggest other times when your supervisor can meet.

a·pol′o·gize

Sometimes you are unable to reach a person to cancel an appointment that has been made with your supervisor. When this happens, apologize and explain the situation when the person arrives. If there is someone else in the company who can help the caller, you should try to arrange a meeting. An acceptable explanation might go like this: "Hello, Mr. Von Berg. I'm sorry, but Ms. Grayson had an emergency and just left. I tried calling you, but you had already left your office. Would you like to see Mr. Mason? He's been assisting Ms. Grayson on your ad campaign and can show you the latest copy." If necessary, schedule another appointment with your supervisor. This appointment should be scheduled as soon as possible.

REVIEWING KEY POINTS

1. Scheduling appointments helps people use their time more efficiently because less time is spent waiting.
2. In order to schedule appointments efficiently, you must know the preferences of the people for whom you will be scheduling appointments. These preferences include who will be seen and the preferred days and times for appointments.
3. Before you schedule an appointment, check the calendar to see that the day and time are available.
4. When an appointment has been scheduled, you should record the date, time, and location; the person's telephone number; the person's business association or the purpose of the meeting; and the time required.
5. You should schedule appointments so that there is a minimum of wasted time between appointments.
6. If both you and your supervisor schedule and record appointments, coordinate the calendars so that two appointments are not scheduled for the same time.
7. When scheduling appointments for your supervisor with another person, you should check the appointment calendar for an available time, telephone or write to request an appointment, and record the appointment on the calendar.
8. When the appointment calendar is kept on your desk, provide your supervisor with a copy of the day's schedule each morning.
9. You should notify people of cancellations as soon as you find out about them in order to prevent unnecessary trips and wasted time.

DEVELOPING HUMAN RELATIONS SKILLS

1. Ray Morrison works for Toby Rogers, Mary Hamer, Bill O'Brien, and Matt Shelton. Ray's calendar for February 14 is shown on the next page. At

11:30 Dawn Kepler and Greg Brooks both arrive for appointments with Toby Rogers.

- **a.** What mistakes did Ray make in recording the appointments?
- **b.** What could Ray have done to prevent this situation from occurring?
- **c.** What should Ray say to the callers? to Mr. Rogers?

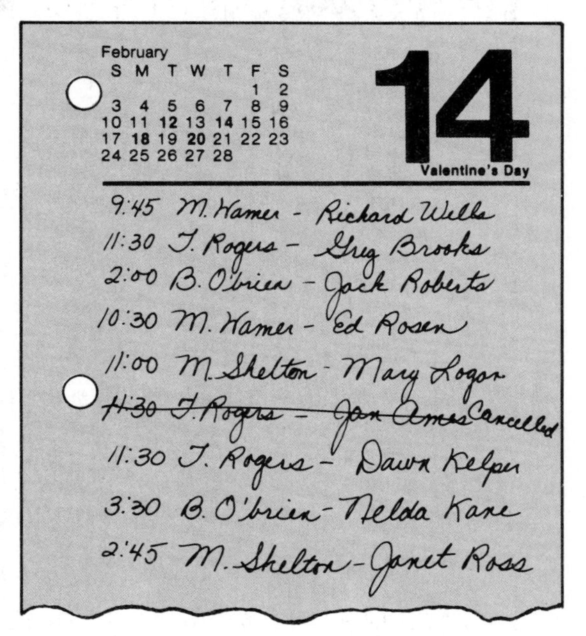

2. During the afternoon of February 14 (see calendar in activity 1), Ray asks you to greet all visitors while he is attending a training seminar. He asks you to find out the name of the caller, the person to be seen, and the reason for the visit before admitting the caller to the office. You must also obtain approval for any visitor who does not have an appointment. With these instructions in mind, how would you respond to the following visitors?
   - **a.** At 1:30 a visitor arrives and says, "I'm Shawn Welbourne. I met Mr. Rogers at a meeting in Chicago last month, and he asked me to drop by when I was in town."
   - **b.** At 2:00 another visitor comes in and says, "I don't have an appointment, but I'd like to see Bill O'Brien. My name is Alan Drury with Drury & Johnson Associates." (Note that Mr. O'Brien has a 2:00 appointment with Jack Roberts, who has not arrived yet.)
   - **c.** At 3:15 a visitor arrives and says, "I'm with Southside Office Equipment Company. I'd like to see Mr. Rogers."
   - **d.** At 4:00 a visitor comes in and says, "I'm Joan Epps with Music, Inc. I'd like to see Mary Hamer." (Ms. Hamer had a doctor's appointment and left the office early.)

IMPROVING COMMUNICATION SKILLS

Refer to Appendix A 1.6–1.7.

1. Use an exclamation mark at the end of an exclamatory sentence that expresses strong feelings or a command.

   That was a fantastic meeting! (exclamatory sentence)

   Review the use of end punctuation. On a separate sheet of paper, write or keyboard each sentence, supplying the correct end punctuation.

   a. What time is the meeting
   b. Wait I already have an appointment at 9:30
   c. Janice makes Ms. Morrison's appointments
   d. She was promoted to administrative assistant
   e. When will you complete the project
   f. Grab that phone
   g. Is he coming back to the office
   h. Mr. Jameson has an appointment at 1:30
   i. Wow What a great conference that was
   j. Ask Martin if he will work on Saturday morning

2. Here is a typical telephone conversation. On a separate sheet of paper, prepare a paragraph paraphrasing what was said.

   RECEPTIONIST: Good morning, Prestige Interior Designs, this is Jason Worth.

   CALLER: This is Steve Ames. I'd like to speak with Ms. Harter.

   RECEPTIONIST: I'm sorry, Mr. Ames; Ms. Harter is away from her desk right now. May I take a message?

   CALLER: Yes, would you tell her I called to cancel our 3:30 appointment for tomorrow. I've got to go to New York on business. I'll call her as soon as I return to set up another appointment. In the meantime, I'll drop the proposal in the mail so she can look at it. If she has any questions, have her call Diana Jakes at my office. Her number is 783-5985.

   RECEPTIONIST: Thank you, Mr. Ames; I'll give her the message.

BUILDING PROBLEM-SOLVING SKILLS

1. As receptionist for Sotheby's Law Firm, you are responsible for calculating clients' charges. The firm charges $15 for each 15-minute time period or $60 an hour. The minimum charge is $25 whether the appointment takes place in the office or over the telephone. Calculate charges for appointments on the next page. Write your answers on a separate sheet of paper.

Tuesday, December 11

9:15 – 9:35	Telephone call from Ellen Wisehunt about her automobile accident.
10:00 – 10:45	Appointment with Jim Brady regarding his will.
10:45 – 12:00	Appointment with Linda Bravo to discuss the sale of property.
1:30 – 1:40	Telephone call to Ms. Wisehunt's insurance company.
2:00 – 2:30	Appointment with Andrea Jamison in regard to the lawsuit she filed against the builders of her home.
2:45 – 3:30	Telephone call to Linda Bravo's real estate agent.
3:30 – 5:00	Dictated the documents for Andrea Jamison's lawsuit.

2. Mrs. Madison has an appointment on Friday with the regional manager in Los Angeles. Mrs. Madison is leaving on the 10:45 flight from Seattle to Los Angeles. She must be at the gate 30 minutes before the flight leaves. It will take her 1 hour to drive to the airport and park her car. The flight arrives in Los Angeles at 1:20. It will take her 1 hour and 30 minutes to claim her baggage and get to the hotel.
   a. What time must Mrs. Madison leave her home to drive to the airport?
   b. How long will the flight take?
   c. What time will she arrive at the hotel?

APPLYING OFFICE SKILLS

1. Appointment post cards are sent to remind patients of their next appointment. Using the appointment post cards in your workbook, keyboard a post card for each appointment listed below. If you do not have a workbook, use plain paper. Sign the post cards yourself.
   a. Mr. Eric Arceneaux, 5061 Avenue B, Monroe, LA 71201, Tuesday, December 4, at 10:45 A.M.
   b. Ms. Dana Boyd, 353 Fair Oaks Drive, Ruston, LA 71270, Tuesday, December 4, at 1:30 P.M.
   c. Ms. Rachel Cortez, 217 Lakeshore Drive, Monroe, LA 71201, Wednesday, December 5, at 9:00 A.M.

E. I. Walls, M.D.
P.O. Box 852
Houston, TX 77201

(Addressee)

Dear________________________

This is to remind you that it is time for your next appointment. An appointment has been scheduled for_______________________________________

________________________at_______________________.

If you cannot make this appointment, please call 748-2850. We will schedule another appointment for you.

Sincerely

2. Judith Blake schedules all of the appointments for her employer, Dr. Miles. Dr. Miles has given Judith permission to schedule appointments for her between 9:30 and 3:30. However, when Judith receives requests for appointments at other times, Dr. Miles would like to approve them. Judith receives the following requests on February 7:

a. Jerry Otis calls at 9:30 and asks for an appointment with Dr. Miles as soon as possible.

b. Emily Fox calls at 10:15 and asks for an appointment with Dr. Miles as soon as possible.

c. In the morning's mail there is a letter from Karen Wagner requesting an appointment for Thursday. She will be in town for the entire day but would like the appointment first thing in the morning.

d. Elsie Coker calls at 10:50 to cancel an appointment that she had scheduled for Friday afternoon at 3:00. She asks that the appointment be rescheduled earlier in the week — if possible, sometime in the morning.

e. At 11:30 Dr. Miles steps out of her office to tell Judith that the Hospital Advisory Board has called a special session and that she will need to be out of the office Tuesday on urgent business.

Scheduled appointments for Dr. Miles are shown on the calendar below. First, explain what steps Judith should take to handle each of the requests. Then, make the necessary schedule changes and enter them in the calendar pages provided in your workbook.

Monday — February 7	Tuesday — February 8	Wednesday — February 9
12:00-2:00 Staff luncheon in hospital cafeteria 3:00-4:00 Bob Quinn 794-3176 American Pharmaceutical Association	1:00-2:00 Prepare talk on new surgical trends for Friday staff meeting	9:00-10:30 Department head's weekly meeting – Hospital Board Room 1:00-1:30 John Marshall 794-4601 Lunch (AMA)

Thursday — February 10	Friday — February 11	Reminders
10:00-10:30 Ruth Bruner 276-9164 City General Hospital 12:00-1:30 Dr. Bell 791-1031 Hospital cafeteria	8:30-9:00 Hospital staff meeting Hospital Staff Room 3:00-3:30 Elsie Coker 776-4906 Job interview	Prepare memo about staff meeting.

CHAPTER 3

SCHEDULING TRAVEL AND MEETINGS

Today it is not unusual for a business person to fly several hundred miles — or more — to attend a meeting or visit a customer. If your supervisor has to travel to another city, you may be asked to help plan the trip and to make travel and hotel reservations. When your supervisor holds a meeting in your office, you may be asked to assist with the meeting arrangements.

As you study this chapter, you will find answers to the following questions:

- How do I make reservations for travel?
- How do I make reservations for hotel accommodations?
- What are my responsibilities when my supervisor is out of town?
- What do the following terms mean: **travel agency, first-class service, tourist-class service, travel authorization form, itinerary, gratuity?**

AIR TRAVEL

Air travel is the most popular method of transportation for business trips to destinations more than 200 miles away. Most business people prefer to fly because flying usually takes less time than any other method of travel.

Making Reservations

res·er·va'tions

Advance reservations are necessary for most airline service. You can make reservations for air travel by calling an airline or a travel agency serving your area. Before you call, find out when your supervisor must be at the desired destination. Also find out the date of return. Knowing this information, you can schedule the most convenient flights.

If you work in a city that does not have an airport or a local airline office, you can call the airline's toll-free telephone number. You can get the number for most major airlines by calling the toll-free numbers directory assistance operator at 1-800-555-1212. There is no charge for the long-distance calls or for the reservation service.

ac·com·mo·da'tions

Many people prefer to make travel arrangements through a **travel agency,** a business that arranges transportation and accommodations for travelers. Travel agencies can handle all of your travel arrangements. A reliable travel agent will help you find the best route and the most convenient flight. Travel agents can also make reservations for hotel rooms and car rentals. The agencies are paid a commission by the airlines, hotels, and car rental companies they make reservations with.

com·mis'sion

Some very large companies have their own travel departments. If this is the case in your company, simply contact the travel department; and they will make all the reservations for your supervisor.

Classes of flight Most airlines have two main classes of service, first class and tourist. Some airlines have special fare plans that allow passengers to fly at lower fares. Some companies will pay for tourist-class travel only. You should check your company's policies before calling for reservations.

First-class service entitles the passenger to the best service available: wide, comfortable seats with plenty of leg room; well-prepared meals; free beverages; and personal attention from flight attendants. First class is the most expensive class of service.

The passenger has a narrower seat, less leg room, less elaborate meals, and limited beverage service when flying **tourist-class service**. Tourist fares are more economical than first-class fares.

re·stric'tions

Many airlines have added special low-cost services such as special fares, super saver fares, unlimited mileage, and family plans. The special fares are usually limited to a few low-cost seats on each flight. In order to be eligible for these special fares, you may have to make reservations and purchase tickets several weeks in advance. There may also be restrictions on the days and time of travel and the length of stay. In order to get these or other special fares, you must request them from the airline agent or travel agency.

Sometimes airlines have special fares to certain locations or travel packages that include costs of hotel rooms as well as air fare. The locations are generally large cities, such as New York or Chicago, or vacation resorts. Check with your travel agent to see whether there are any travel packages available to the desired destination.

Methods of payment After the reservations are made, the tickets must be paid for and picked up. You or your supervisor can pick up the tickets and pay for them at the airport, an airline ticket office, or the travel agency. Airline fares can also be charged to the company or to your supervisor's credit card. If your company has credit with the airlines or travel agency, the tickets can be mailed to your office.

Suppose you are asked to make flight reservations for Alana Suarez to attend a meeting in San Antonio beginning at 8:30 A.M. on May 2. The meeting is scheduled to end at noon on May 4. Ms. Suarez wants to leave after work on May 1. She wants to charge her tickets, so she has given you her charge card number. Your conversation with the travel agent might sound something like this:

CALLER: Hello. I'd like to make a reservation for one person from Memphis to San Antonio on May 1, leaving after 5:30 P.M., tourist class or super saver. I need return reservations for May 4, leaving San Antonio after 1:00 in the afternoon.

TRAVEL AGENT: Delta has a non-stop flight leaving Memphis at 6:05 P.M. and arriving in San Antonio at . . . (the agent gives information on several flights for the dates and times requested).

CALLER: The 6:05 flight on May 1 will be fine. For the return trip I think the 2:00 Delta flight will do. Please make the reservations for Alana Suarez and charge it to American Express. Her account number is 2700-30518-98827.

TRAVEL AGENT: All right. That's a reservation for Ms. Suarez on May 1, Delta flight 311 leaving Memphis at 6:05 P.M. and arriving in San Antonio at . . . (The agent repeats the flight information, then asks) Would you like me to mail the tickets to Ms. Suarez or will someone be by to pick them up?

CALLER: Please send them to Perez Associates, P.O. Box 307, Memphis, TN 38111. Thank you.

If your supervisor travels, be sure you are familiar with your company's procedure for payment. Some companies require that all airline tickets be charged to the company account. Other companies prefer to have employees pay for their own tickets. When they return from their trips, employees submit travel expense reports of all the payments they have made for airline tickets, hotels, meals, and taxis. The company *reimburses* or repays employees for these expenses.

time'ta·ble

de·par'ture

Flight information If your supervisor is a frequent traveler, you may find it convenient to keep an up-to-date timetable of the airlines serving your area. Then, before calling to make reservations, you can check the scheduled flights and find out your supervisor's preference for arrival and departure times. If you don't have copies of the airline timetable, you can get the flight information when you call the airline or travel agent. A sample page from an airline timetable is shown in Illustration 4–10.

Another useful source of information is the *Official Airline Guide.* This guide, which contains flight schedules for all the airlines, is revised periodically during the year. Your company library or travel department may have a copy of this publication.

Illustration 4–10
Airline timetable

Lv	Ar	Flt No	Stops or Via	Mls	Rmks
From **JACKSONVILLE, FL** (cont'd)					
To **HOUSTON, TX**					
Houston Intercontinental Airport					
Airport H-Hobby					
7 15a	10 00a H	**49**/1245	**ATL**	S	
9 35a	12 20p	238/423	ATL	L	
12 30p	3 30p H	**859**/1109	**ATL**	S	
12 30p	4 55p	**859**/307	**ATL**	S/	
3 50p	6 40p	**55**/821	**ATL**	D	
5 48p	8 30p H	**146**/1041	**ATL**	S	
5 48p	9 55p	**146**/223	**ATL**		
10 30p	1 05a	390/1423	ATL		★
To **HUNTSVILLE, AL**					
7 15a	8 55a	**49**/1689	**ATL**	S	▲
9 35a	11 25a	238/1690	ATL		▲
5 48p	7 20p	**146**/1692	**ATL**		▲
To **INDIANAPOLIS, IN**					
9 35a	11 50a	238/1482	ATL	S	
12 30p	4 30p	**859**/1446	**ATL**	S	
5 48p	7 55p	**146**/1496	**ATL**		
10 30p	12 25a	390/398	ATL		★
To **JACKSON, MS**					
7 15a	9 10a	**49**/621	**ATL**	S	
9 35a	12 10p	238/549	ATL	S	
12 30p	3 17p	**859**/457	**ATL**		
3 50p	6 34p	**55**/347	**ATL**		
5 48p	7 28p	**146**/667	**ATL**	S	
10 30p	12 52a	390/575	ATL		★
To **KANSAS CITY, MO**					
9 35a	12 30p	238/1225	ATL	L	
12 30p	3 40p	**859**/1115	**ATL**	S	
3 50p	6 35p	**55**/1149	**ATL**	D	
5 48p	10 20p	**146**/1129	**ATL**		
10 30p	1 39a	390/1185	ATL		★
To **KILLEEN, TX**					
9 50a	12 55p	1085/1944	DFW	B	X7 ▲
3 40p	6 30p	477/1917	DFW	ℛS	X6 ▲
To **KNOXVILLE, TN**					
9 35a	12 10p	238/638	ATL		
12 30p	3 02p	**859**/982	**ATL**		
To **LOUISVILLE, KY**					
7 15a	11 00a	**49**/540	**ATL**	S	
9 35a	12 33p	238/1428	ATL	S	
12 30p	3 23p	**859**/1440	**ATL**		
3 50p	6 40p	**55**/1240	**ATL**	S	
5 48p	10 12p	**146**/556	**ATL**		
10 30p	1 05a	390/1413	ATL		★
To **LUBBOCK, TX**					
9 50a	12 55p	1085/1108	DFW	B	X7
3 40p	6 35p	477/1067	DFW	ℛS	
To **MACON, GA**					
7 15a	9 35a	**49**/1479	**ATL**	S	
9 35a	12 30p	238/1698	ATL		▲
12 30p	3 05p	**859**/1699	**ATL**		▲
3 50p	6 15p	**55**/1700	**ATL**		▲
5 48p	8 05p	**146**/1701	**ATL**		X6 ▲
5 48p	10 05p	**146**/1702	**ATL**		▲
10 30p	12 45a	390/1703	ATL		X6 ▲
To **MEMPHIS, TN**					
7 15a	9 30a	**49**/947	**ATL**	S	
9 35a	12 00n	238/288	ATL	S	
12 30p	2 50p	**859**/977	**ATL**		
3 50p	5 41p	**55**/990	**ATL**	S	
5 48p	7 33p	**146**/483	**ATL**	S	
10 30p	12 10a	390/1185	ATL		★
To **MINNEAPOLIS/ST. PAUL, MN**					
7 15a	10 50a	**49**/214	**ATL**	S	
12 30p	5 20p	**859**/300	**ATL**	ℛS	
5 48p	10 25p	**146**/216	**ATL**		
To **MOBILE, AL/ PASCAGOULA, MS**					
7 15a	9 25a	**49**/1437	**ATL**	S	
12 30p	2 15p	**859**/1441	**ATL**		X6
3 50p	5 45p	**55**/1255	**ATL**		
5 48p	9 15p	**146**/1439	**ATL**		X6
To **MONROE, LA**					
9 35a	1 04p	238/549	ATL	S	
3 50p	6 12p	**55**/1103	**ATL**	S	
To **MONTGOMERY, AL**					
7 15a	9 25a	**49**/1704	**ATL**	S	▲
9 35a	11 10a	238/453	ATL		
To **NEW YORK, NY/ NEWARK, NJ** (cont'd)					
12 30p	5 50p J	**859**/512	**ATL**	S	
3 50p	7 50p E	**55**/988	**ATL**	ℛS	
3 50p	**7 57p** L	**55/822**	**ATL**	ℛS	
4 20p	7 06p L	424	1	D	X6
5 48p	9 30p L	**146**/494	**ATL**	ℛS	
5 48p	**11 25p** E	**146/194**	**ATL**		
10 30p	**1 59a** J	390/**80**	**ATL**		★
To **NORFOLK/VIRGINIA BEACH/ WILLIAMSBURG, VA**					
7 15a	10 45a	**49**/1244	**ATL**	S	
9 35a	1 05p	238/1018	ATL	L	
12 30p	3 40p	**859**/1429	**ATL**		
3 50p	8 30p	**55**/422	**ATL**	D	
To **OKLAHOMA CITY, OK**					
7 15a	10 40a	**49**/1421	**ATL**	B	
9 50a	1 35p	1085/1430	DFW	B	X7
12 30p	5 05p	**859**/1253	**ATL**		
3 50p	6 45p	**55**/1471	**ATL**	D	
To **ONTARIO, CA**					
9 50a	12 41p	1085/621	DFW	ℛS	X7
12 30p	**3 35p**	**859/885**	**ATL**	S	
3 40p	**6 40p**	477/**859**	**DFW**	ℛS	
To **PANAMA CITY, FL**					
9 35a	12 10p	238/1714	ATL		▲
12 30p	2 35p	**859**/1715	**ATL**		▲
5 48p	7 50p	**146**/1717	**ATL**		▲
To **PENSACOLA, FL**					
7 15a	10 20a	**49**/1415	**ATL**	S	X6
12 30p	2 15p	**859**/1459	**ATL**		
3 50p	5 40p	**55**/1405	**ATL**		
5 48p	9 00p	**146**/1445	**ATL**		
To **PHILADELPHIA, PA**					
7 15a	10 50a	**49**/208	**ATL**	S	
9 35a	1 25p	238/670	ATL	L	
12 30p	4 00p	**859**/448	**ATL**		
3 50p	**7 40p**	**55/872**	**ATL**	D	
5 48p	11 05p	**146**/998	**ATL**		
10 30p	1 50a	390/280	ATL		★ X6

Cancellations If your supervisor's travel plans change, all you need to do is call the travel agent or airline. They will be happy to change or cancel your reservations. By canceling, you make space available for other travelers. If the ticket has been paid for, a full refund will be made when you return the ticket to the travel agent or airline.

Getting to and from the Airport

When leaving on short business trips, many people drive their own cars to the airport. Then, when they return, their cars are waiting for them. Most airports have long-term parking lots where fees are charged by the day instead of by the hour. These parking lots usually offer some protection from theft or vandalism.

van'dal·ism

lim·ou·sine'

Limousine service is frequently available between the downtown business district and the airport. Several passengers going to different locations share the limousine, so there may be several stops. For this reason, limousine service is usually slower and less expensive than taxi service. Limousine companies are listed in the Yellow Pages of the telephone directory.

Taxi service is available in all cities. Taxi service is generally fast because the passenger is taken to the destination by the fastest or most direct route. You can find the telephone numbers of local taxi companies listed under *Taxicabs* in the Yellow Pages.

Some hotels and motels have courtesy cars that pick up guests at the airport and take them back to the airport when they check out of the hotel. There is no charge for this service. You can check to see if a courtesy car is available when you make hotel reservations.

Renting a Car

If your supervisor is traveling by air and needs a car at the destination, you can arrange to have a rental car waiting at the airport. Having a rental car enables the traveler to travel at his or her convenience without depending on public transportation or taxis.

trans·por·ta'tion

You can rent a car by calling a rental company's toll-free number. Your travel agent can also reserve a car for you. Either your company must have an account with the car rental company, or your supervisor must have a major charge card.

TRAVELING BY CAR

For shorter trips or trips to areas that are difficult to reach by air, your supervisor may prefer to drive. If your company provides a car for employees traveling on business, you should call ahead of time to reserve the car.

When a personal car is used for business purposes, you or your employer may have to complete a **travel authorization form.** This form usually calls for the name and social security number of the driver, the destination, the purpose of the trip, the dates and times for departure and return, and an estimate of the round-trip mileage. The travel authorization form must be submitted so that the driver can receive payment for car expenses.

FOREIGN TRAVEL

The number of companies conducting business in foreign countries continues to increase. As a result, it is becoming more common for executives to travel to foreign countries on business.

Foreign travel requires careful planning because of differences in time zones, currency, and customs. For this reason, you will probably find the services of a reliable travel agent very helpful. Besides making all of the travel and hotel reservations, the travel agent can tell you what special travel documents (such as visas, travel permits, and passports) your supervisor needs and where to obtain them.

You can help your supervisor prepare for foreign travel by obtaining currency for the countries being visited. Large banks in major cities keep foreign currencies and will exchange them for dollars. Your employer may also appreciate any information you can provide on language, customs, and business dealings in the countries being visited. Such information can be obtained at the public library or from your travel agent.

HOTEL RESERVATIONS

When business travel requires your supervisor to stay overnight, you may be asked to make hotel or motel reservations. Travelers who are familiar with a city may be able to tell you which hotel or motel they prefer. However, when traveling to an unfamiliar city, they may not know the best place to stay. You can find such information in *The Hotel and Motel Red Book.* This guide gives names, addresses, telephone numbers, room rates, and other information for hotels and motels in all cities in the United States. A page from *The Hotel and Motel Red Book* is shown in Illustration 4–11. If your company does not have a copy of *The Hotel and Motel Red Book,* you can usually find one in the reference section of your public library.

Hotel reservations can be made through a travel agent or by calling or writing the hotel. Most major hotels have toll-free numbers. When making reservations, give the expected date and time of arrival and departure, and specify the type of accommodation. If the person traveling plans to arrive after 6:00 P.M., you may be asked to guarantee payment. The payment can be charged to the traveler's credit card or billed to the company. By guaranteeing payment, the traveler is assured of a room no matter what the time of arrival is.

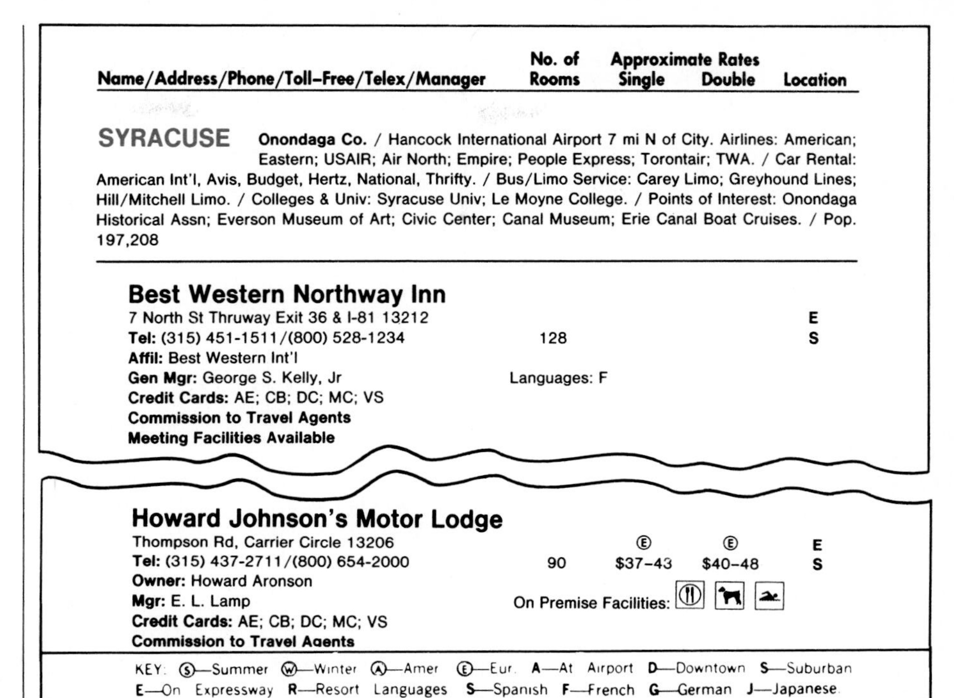

Name/Address/Phone/Toll-Free/Telex/Manager	No. of Rooms	Approximate Rates Single	Double	Location

SYRACUSE **Onondaga Co.** / Hancock International Airport 7 mi N of City. Airlines: American; Eastern; USAIR; Air North; Empire; People Express; Torontair; TWA. / Car Rental: American Int'l, Avis, Budget, Hertz, National, Thrifty. / Bus/Limo Service: Carey Limo; Greyhound Lines; Hill/Mitchell Limo. / Colleges & Univ: Syracuse Univ; Le Moyne College. / Points of Interest: Onondaga Historical Assn; Everson Museum of Art; Civic Center; Canal Museum; Erie Canal Boat Cruises. / Pop. 197,208

Name/Address/Phone/Toll-Free/Telex/Manager	No. of Rooms	Single	Double	Location
Best Western Northway Inn				
7 North St Thruway Exit 36 & I-81 13212				E
Tel: (315) 451-1511/(800) 528-1234	128			S
Affil: Best Western Int'l				
Gen Mgr: George S. Kelly, Jr	Languages: F			
Credit Cards: AE; CB; DC; MC; VS				
Commission to Travel Agents				
Meeting Facilities Available				
Howard Johnson's Motor Lodge				
Thompson Rd, Carrier Circle 13206		Ⓔ	Ⓔ	E
Tel: (315) 437-2711/(800) 654-2000	90	$37–43	$40–48	S
Owner: Howard Aronson				
Mgr: E. L. Lamp	On Premise Facilities:			
Credit Cards: AE; CB; DC; MC; VS				
Commission to Travel Agents				

KEY: Ⓢ—Summer Ⓦ—Winter Ⓐ—Amer Ⓔ—Eur. A—At Airport D—Downtown S—Suburban
E—On Expressway R—Resort Languages S—Spanish F—French G—German J—Japanese

Illustration 4–11
The Hotel and Motel Red Book

THE ITINERARY

i·tin'er·ar·y

When all travel arrangements are made, prepare a travel **itinerary** for your supervisor. An itinerary includes all plans for the trip. As Illustration 4–12 shows, an itinerary contains the following:

- date, time, airline, and flight number(s) for all transportation
- name, address, telephone number, and confirmation number for all hotel reservations
- date, time, and location of meetings and the names of people with whom meetings are scheduled.

You should prepare several copies of the itinerary. Make one copy for your supervisor to carry, one to put in the suitcase or briefcase, one for your employer's family, and one for you.

RESPONSIBILITIES IN YOUR SUPERVISOR'S ABSENCE

While your supervisor is out of town, you will be responsible for keeping the office running smoothly. You should take special care in performing your regular duties. If something happens that you cannot handle, check to see if

Illustration 4–12
Travel itinerary

ITINERARY OF FELICIA HUDSON

July 14-15, 19--

Boston, Massachusetts

Monday, July 14

7:30 a.m.	Leave Charleston International Airport, Delta Flight 923; breakfast served on flight.
8:32 a.m.	Arrive at Hartsfield Atlanta International Airport.
9:51 a.m.	Leave Hartsfield Atlanta International Airport, Delta Flight 612.
12:01 p.m.	Arrive in Boston, Logan International Airport.
1:30 p.m.	Meet with Mr. Ray David, Boston Branch Manager, Suite 2800, Beacon Trust Building, 31 Milk Street.
3:30 p.m.	Meet with Ms. Martha Haynes, Sales Representative, Suite 2800, Beacon Trust Building.
7:00 p.m.	Dinner with Mr. Davis and Mr. Foley. They will meet you at the Parker House; Tremont and School Streets.
	Overnight accommodations at Parker House, confirmation No. 127 342 769. Telephone: (617) 227-8600.

Tuesday, July 15

8:30 a.m.	Breakfast meeting at Parker House with Mr. Mark Pratt, Sales Manager.
10:00 a.m.	Meet with regional sales staff to present new products; Suite 2800, Beacon Trust Building.
12:00 p.m.	Lunch meeting at Parker House with Ms. Joan Burns, prospective accountant.
2:00 p.m.	Leave for Logan International Airport.
3:40 p.m.	Leave Boston, Delta Flight 129; dinner served on flight.
6:17 p.m.	Arrive at Hartsfield Atlanta International Airport.
7:01 p.m.	Leave Atlanta, Delta Flight 330.
7:55 p.m.	Arrive Charleston

someone else in the company can help you. If not, it may be necessary to call your supervisor to discuss the matter. If you have carefully prepared an itinerary and kept a copy, you will know when and where your supervisor can be reached.

It is usually a good idea to find out before your supervisor leaves town whether there is any routine business you can handle. Good planning and judgment can prevent problems that otherwise may occur while your supervisor is away on business.

MEETING ARRANGEMENTS

In addition to attending out-of-town meetings, your supervisor may occasionally sponsor meetings. You may be asked to help by reserving a meeting room; setting up the room; and preparing materials such as handouts, folders, and name tags. There may be meals or refreshments to plan or hotel rooms to reserve for out-of-town participants. You may also be asked to help greet the participants and assist at the meeting.

Illustration 4–13
The company conference room may be suitable for small groups

The Meeting Room

A conference room is usually necessary when more than three or four people meet to discuss business. Find out the approximate number of people expected to attend so that you can reserve a room large enough to seat the group comfortably.

Some companies have conference rooms available within the building for meetings. If your company has a suitable room, check to see if it is available for the date and time the meeting is scheduled. If so, you will need to reserve the room for your group. Be sure to set aside enough time not only for the meeting itself, but for setting up and cleaning up the room.

If a meeting room is not available in your office, you may have to reserve a meeting room at a local hotel. Most large hotels and motels have meeting rooms you can rent for a few hours or a few days. You will need to tell the hotel the number of people attending and how the chairs in the room should be arranged.

Arrangements for Food

For the comfort of the meeting participants, and particularly the speakers, you should have glasses and pitchers of water available during the meeting. For meetings that last several hours, a refreshment break may be scheduled. If the meeting is in your building, you may have to set up the refreshments

Illustration 4–14
Checklist for planning a meeting

CHECKLIST

Regional Sales Conference

Meeting Room	Townhouse Hotel, 9:00 a.m. to 4:30 p.m.
	Seating: Classroom style for 120
	Head table: Seating for____ Podium with microphone____ Overhead projector and screen____ Chalkboard (chalk and erasers)____ Water and glasses____
Refreshments	Serve at 10:15 a.m. and 3:00 p.m.
Lunch	Townhouse Hotel, 12:00 p.m. Guarantee 120
Take to Townhouse	Name tags____ Folders with papers____ New sales catalogues____
Meet at Airport	(Assigned to Allen Rabon) Mr. Henry Little - Eastern Flight 913 at 8:05 Ms. Bobby Downing - United Flight 1172 at 8:30

yourself. Plan to have everything ready at least ten minutes before the scheduled breaks. When the meeting is held in a hotel, make arrangements for refreshments with the catering manager.

ca'ter·ing

If the meeting plans include lunch or dinner, select a location that is convenient to the meeting room. Choose a nearby restaurant if the meeting is in your building. If the meeting is in a hotel, contact the catering manager about meal service. Find out from your supervisor how much to spend on each person's meal. The catering manager can then show you two or three menus in your price range. Remember that tax and tip, called **gratuity,** are added to the cost of the meals. If you select a lunch that costs $6.95 per person, the charge will probably be about $8.50 when the tax and gratuity are added.

gra·tu'i·ty

Final Preparations

Whether the meeting is in your office building or at a hotel, plan to check the meeting room before participants start arriving. Carefully inspect the audio-visual equipment to be sure it works. For example, a blackboard without chalk and an eraser is useless. Your help with these details is important for the success of the meeting. A good way to remember such details is to make a checklist similar to the one in Illustration 4–14.

If you are asked to greet participants at the meeting, remember that you will be projecting an image of your company. Take special care to dress appropriately and neatly. Greet each person in a friendly manner and let them know that you will be happy to help if they have any problems.

REVIEWING KEY POINTS

1. Most business people travel by air because it is fast and convenient.
2. Flight reservations can be made by calling the airline or a travel agent.
3. Airlines offer first-class, tourist-class, and special-fare services. Special fares usually have restrictions, such as making reservations several days in advance or flying only on certain days or times.
4. Limousines, taxis, and personal cars are used for transportation to and from the airport. Rental cars provide travelers with a convenient method of transportation once they reach their destinations.
5. Two other common methods of business travel include company or personal cars.
6. When arranging travel to foreign countries, use the services of a reliable travel agent.
7. *The Hotel and Motel Red Book* contains information about hotels and motels in cities in the United States.
8. An itinerary lists the details of a trip such as travel arrangements; names and addresses of hotels; and dates, times, and locations of appointments.
9. Before your supervisor leaves on a business trip, you should find out how emergencies should be handled while he or she is out of the office.
10. Details you may handle when making arrangements for a meeting include reserving the room, planning the refreshment breaks, checking the audio-visual equipment, and greeting the participants.

DEVELOPING HUMAN RELATIONS SKILLS

1. All of the supervisors have been out of town on business this past week. On Friday morning, you and the two other office workers have completed all of the work that has been assigned. One of the other office workers suggests that you close the office at noon so everyone can start the weekend early.
   a. What problems could result if you follow this suggestion?
   b. What would you say to the other workers?
2. Burt and Ellen have been helping Mrs. Palmisano, the district manager, plan a meeting for the branch managers. Mrs. Palmisano has just told Burt and Ellen that she wants them to make arrangements for refreshments for the breaks. When Mrs. Palmisano walked out, Burt told Ellen that she would have to make the arrangements for the refreshments because that was women's work.
   a. What do you think about Burt's comment?
   b. What should Ellen do?

IMPROVING COMMUNICATION SKILLS

Refer to Appendix A 1.1-1.7.

1. Review the use of end punctuation. On a separate sheet of paper, write or keyboard each sentence, supplying the correct end punctuation.
   - a. Will you ask Whit to meet with me on Monday at 2:30
   - b. Hold that plane I must catch that flight
   - c. Marie asked if I would keyboard the name tags for the meeting
   - d. Wow That's not the right flight
   - e. What time does Mr. Greene leave for Washington
   - f. The conference will be held in New York
   - g. Did you type the itinerary yet
   - h. Wait Your hotel reservations have not been made
   - i. Mr. Johnston always uses a travel agent
   - j. Ms. Keltner will attend the National Office conference
2. On a separate sheet of paper, paraphrase the following paragraph.

   Tyler is helping make the arrangements for a staff get-together. He must plan all of the details of the gathering. Once he selects a date, there are still many things he must do. Tyler must set the time, reserve a room, send out invitations, choose the caterer, select the refreshments, assign a committee to decorate and to clean up after the gathering. First, though, Tyler must establish a budget and submit it to Mrs. Lake, the department manager, for approval.

BUILDING PROBLEM-SOLVING SKILLS

1. Using the timetable in Illustration 4–10, answer the following questions:
   - a. How many flights leave Jacksonville after 8:00 A.M. and arrive in Indianapolis before 4:00 P.M.?
   - b. Which flights leave Jacksonville after noon and arrive in Indianapolis before 6:00 P.M.?
   - c. How long does it take to fly from Jacksonville to Memphis on the flight that leaves at 9:35 A.M.?
   - d. Claire Adams wants to work as late as she possibly can at her office in Jacksonville and then fly to Louisville in order to make a 7:30 P.M. meeting. Which flight should she take?
2. On the next page is the order form from Continental Caterers. Tyler has made his selections for the staff gathering mentioned in Improving, Activity 2, above. Calculate the total cost of the refreshments. Add 5 percent tax and $10 delivery fee. Write your answer on separate sheet of paper. Show all of your calculations on your paper.

CONTINENTAL CATERERS
488 Broadway Avenue
Dallas, TX 28030

Food and Beverage Order Form

Item	Price	Quantity	Amount	
Fried Chicken Drumettes	$20.00 (100 pieces)	2		
Assorted Finger Sandwiches	25.00 (100 pieces)			
Deli-Trays—Assorted Meats	19.95 (serves 20)			
	38.00 (serves 40)			
Deli-Trays—Assorted Meats and Cheeses	18.00 (serves 20)			
	35.00 (serves 40)	1		
Fresh Vegetables and dips	12.00 (serves 20)			
	21.00 (serves 40)	1		
Fruit Punch	7.50 (per gal.)	3		
Ice Tea	5.00 (per gal.)	2		
Coffee	6.00 (per gal.)	5		
		Item Total		
		Tax		
		Delivery Fee		
		TOTAL		

3. Cindy Denton is making arrangements for a reception to be held on January 14 at the National Business Leaders' Seminar. She has asked Continental Caterers to cater the reception.

Using the Continental Caterers' form above, figure the cost of the refreshments. Add 5 percent tax and $10 delivery fee. Write your answer on a separate sheet of paper. Include your calculations.

Her order for the reception includes the following items:

a. 3 trays of assorted finger sandwiches

b. 9 trays of deli-trays—assorted meats

c. 8 trays of fresh vegetables and dips

d. 8 gallons of coffee

Activities 1 and 2 can be done on information processing equipment.

APPLYING OFFICE SKILLS

1. Keyboard a corrected copy of the following itinerary for June Helms's trip to El Paso, Texas, on April 3–5.

Itinerary for June Helms

April 3, 19--
El Paso, Texas

April 3, 19--

10:40 a.m. –Leave Boston Logan International Airport, American Airlines Flight 421.

1:20 p.m. –Arrive at Dallas/Ft. Worth Regional Airport.

2:20 p.m. –Leave Dallas/Ft. Worth Regional Airport, American Airlines Flight 281.

2:46 p.m. –Arrive in El Paso. Overnight accommodations at the Hilton Hotel, Confirmation No. 27934622.

April 4, 19--

8:30 a.m. – 5:00 p.m. –Management Training Seminar.

April 5, 19--

7:30 a.m. –Leave for El Paso Airport.

8:45 a.m. –Leave El Paso Airport, Continental Airlines Flight 24.

10:20 a.m. –Arrive at Denver Stapleton International Airport.

11:20 a.m. –Leave Denver, United Airlines Flight 154.

5:00 p.m. –Arrive at Boston Logan International Airport.

2. Sara Little, your supervisor, is planning a meeting for the sales staff. She wants you to keyboard a schedule of activities planned for the sales staff. Keyboard the schedule below in an attractive format, making the corrections shown.

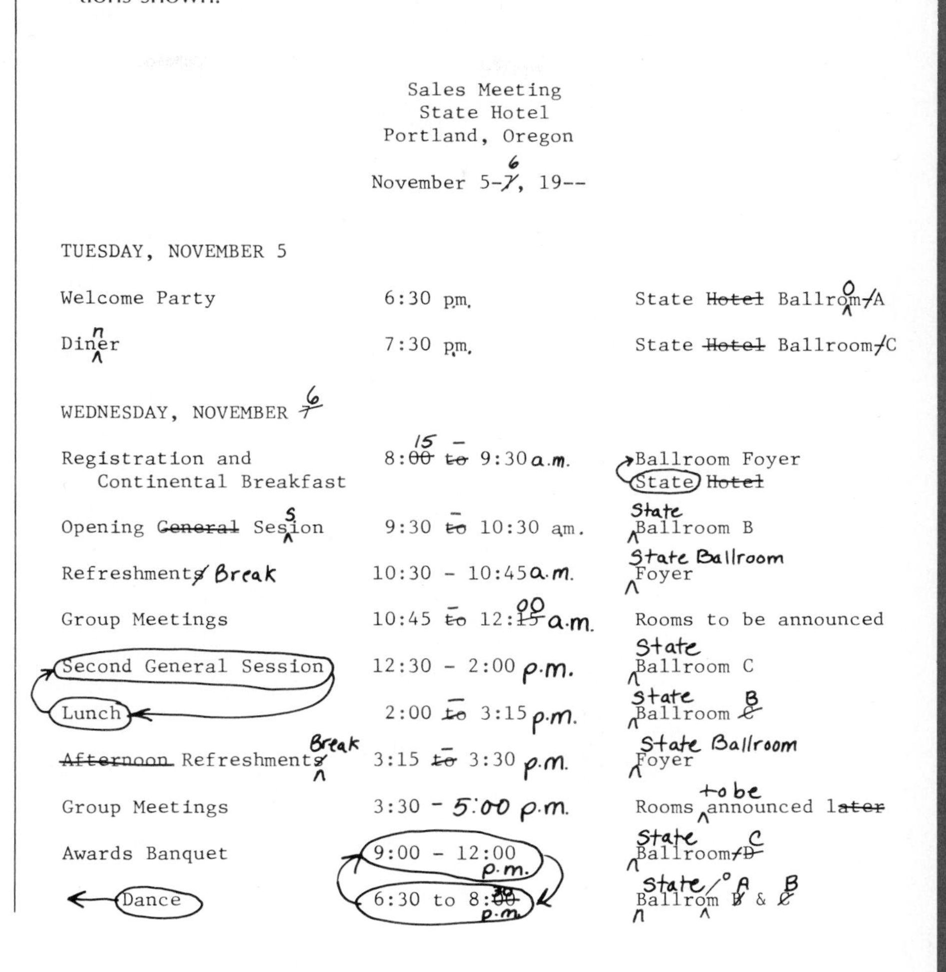

Sales Meeting
State Hotel
Portland, Oregon

November 5-7, 19--

TUESDAY, NOVEMBER 5

Welcome Party	6:30 p.m.	State Hotel Ballrm A
Dier	7:30 p.m.	State Hotel Ballroom C

WEDNESDAY, NOVEMBER 7

Registration and Continental Breakfast	8:00 to 9:30	Ballroom Foyer State Hotel
Opening General Seson	9:30 to 10:30 a.m.	Ballroom B
Refreshments	10:30 - 10:45	Foyer
Group Meetings	10:45 to 12:15	Rooms to be announced
Second General Session	12:30 - 2:00	Ballroom C
Lunch	2:00 to 3:15	Ballroom C
Afternoon Refreshments	3:15 to 3:30	Foyer
Group Meetings	3:30	Rooms announced later
Awards Banquet	9:00 - 12:00	Ballroom D
Dance	6:30 to 8:00	Ballrm B & C

Saving Time and Money

Travel may be an important part of your supervisor's regular job responsibilities. If so, here are some things that you can do to help make the travel easier.

1. Make reservations through a reputable travel agent or your corporate travel department. These people are professionals at making arrangements.
2. Make arrangements as soon as possible. Most airlines require that you book 14 to 30 days in advance to be eligible for discount fares.
3. Keep your supervisor's credit card number on file so that it will be handy when you make travel arrangements.
4. Keep a travel notebook in which you record the dates, flight numbers, and times of your supervisor's flights.
5. Ask for written confirmation of hotel reservations. If the reservation is made by telephone, record the name of the person with whom you make the reservation.
6. Ask for the daily rental and mileage rates when making car rental reservations. Insist on a confirmation number. Also ask about discounts and drop charges.
7. Prepare luggage identification tags from your supervisor's business cards. Do this by inserting cards into the identification holders.
8. Make an additional copy of your supervisor's itinerary for the supervisor's family.
9. Prepare a travel pack for your supervisor. In this pack, include a 3- x 5-inch card containing the names and home telephone numbers of workers in the office. While out of the office, your supervisor may need to contact a worker at home in regard to work.
10. Include in this pack maps and any other instructions that might be helpful to your supervisor.

UNIT 5

TELECOMMUNICATIONS IN THE OFFICE

- Telephone Procedures
- Long-Distance Telephone Service
- Telephone Equipment and Special Services
- Telecommunication Services

CHAPTER 1

TELEPHONE PROCEDURES

Approximately 90 percent of all business transactions that take place in the United States involve at least one telephone call. People call to ask the price of a product, to find out if an item is available, or to ask someone to do business for them. Each of these calls is part of a business transaction.

The telephone is a very convenient means of communicating for business people and customers because it saves time. You can obtain information by telephone much more quickly than you can by writing a letter and waiting for a response by mail. In your office, you can speak with a coworker by telephone without ever having to leave your desk.

Although the telephone can be a time saver, it can also be very annoying because telephone calls interrupt your work. When used properly, though, the telephone can help you and the people you work with do a better job.

As you study this chapter, you will find answers to the following questions:

- How can I project a good telephone image?
- What is the most courteous and efficient way to answer telephone calls in the office?
- What are the correct procedures for taking telephone messages and assisting callers?
- What are the three types of directories for finding telephone numbers, and how are they used?
- What do the following terms mean: **visualize, screen, confidential, message form, hold button?**

PROJECTING A GOOD PHONE IMAGE

fa·mil'iar

An effective office worker must have good telephone skills. Because the telephone is such a familiar item in homes and offices, many people take for granted that they know how to use it properly. However, just like other job skills, telephone skills must be developed.

The impression employees make over the telephone can be as important as the impression they make in person. Therefore, in many businesses, applicants are asked about their telephone skills during the job interview. With practice, you can develop good telephone skills that will help you make a good impression over the phone.

Speaking Clearly

dis·tinct'ly

mes'sage

When talking on the telephone, speak distinctly so that the person on the other end of the line can hear and understand you. Remember that the listener cannot see you, so your voice alone must carry your message. Pronounce each word clearly and correctly. Be careful that you don't mumble or swallow syllables. For example, avoid saying "dunno" when you mean "don't know" or "talkin" when you mean "talking."

You should also avoid talking on the telephone when you have something in your mouth. You cannot speak clearly if you are biting your fingernail, chewing gum, or holding a pencil between your teeth.

Illustration 5–1
Your voice and manner should make a good impression on callers

The pace or speed at which you speak is also important. Most people prefer a moderate pace to one that is too slow or too fast. However, you should slow down when you dictate a message so that the listener has time to write it. When spelling your name or giving your telephone number, say each letter or number distinctly.

Finally, talk into the receiver. The receiver is the part of the telephone that transmits your voice. If you move the receiver around as you talk, your voice will fade in and out; and the listener will have trouble hearing you. You may want to rest the receiver on your shoulder to free your hands for note taking. If you do so, make sure to hold the receiver firmly in place and directly in front of your mouth.

Being Courteous

Phrases such as "please," "thank you," "how are you?" and "thank you for calling" are always pleasant to hear. Such courteous phrases convey a feeling of friendliness and interest. They leave the caller with a good feeling and build a favorable image for your company. You can also show courtesy by listening attentively to your callers and making an effort to help them.

at·ten'tive·ly

Using a Friendly Voice

Your voice is a reflection of you and of your company. Your voice actually reveals much more about you than most people imagine. For example, a quiet or timid voice can convey a lack of confidence. Your voice can also reveal your irritation or annoyance. The caller who hears irritation in your voice may decide to do business with another company next time.

ir·ri·ta'tion

On the other hand, callers react favorably to a voice that is friendly and sincere. Speak in your normal talking voice, as if you were talking face to face. It may help to **visualize** (or picture) your listener so that you can relate what you are saying to the listener's point of view. You should try to react in ways that show that you understand and are interested in what the listener is saying to you.

vi'su·al·ize

ANSWERING THE TELEPHONE

As an office worker, you will probably find that part of your office duties includes answering the telephone. You may answer the phone for everyone in your office or department, or just for yourself and your supervisor. When coworkers are away from their desks, you may be expected to answer their telephones as well.

Whenever the telephone rings, answer it promptly. During business hours, callers expect the telephone to be answered within the first or second ring. Keep a message pad and pen or pencil handy in case you need to take a message while you are talking on the phone.

Identifying Yourself

When you answer the telephone, begin your conversation with a pleasant greeting. Then identify your company and yourself. For instance, "Good morning (or Good afternoon), Central Office Supply, Aimee Downs speaking." If your company has a switchboard operator, you may not have to identify your company. In this case, simply identify your supervisor and yourself. For example, "Mrs. Donnelly's office, Aimee Downs speaking."

op'er·a·tor

Identifying the Caller

Listen carefully as the caller gives his or her name. You will want to give this information to the person being called. When telling someone a call is waiting, you should identify the caller. For example, "Mrs. Donnelly, Mr. Greenberg is on the telephone." If the caller does not give a name, politely ask, "May I tell her who is calling?" or "Who shall I say is calling?"

At times your supervisor may be involved in important work or in a meeting and may not wish to be disturbed. In such cases, you may be asked to hold all calls or to let only certain calls through. Thus, you will need to **screen** incoming calls — that is, decide which ones to put through — just as you sometimes have to screen visitors. With tact, you can identify the caller and the reason for the call in such a way that the caller is not aware that you are screening the call. For example:

OFFICE WORKER: Good afternoon, Mr. Warren's office, Austin Cameron speaking.
CALLER: I would like to speak with Mr. Warren, please.
OFFICE WORKER: May I ask who is calling?
CALLER: My name is Louise Willis at Modern Equipment.
OFFICE WORKER: I am sorry, Ms. Willis, Mr. Warren is in conference. May I take your number and have him call you?
CALLER: Yes, my telephone number is 787-4213.
OFFICE WORKER: Thank you, Ms. Willis. I'll have Mr. Warren call you as soon as possible. That number was 787-4213.
CALLER: Yes, thank you.

Notice that Austin found out who was calling without giving the impression that Mr. Warren was in. If he had said, "May I tell Mr. Warren who is calling?" then Ms. Willis would have assumed that Mr. Warren was available. After identifying herself, Ms. Willis would have been offended to hear that Mr. Warren wasn't available after all — at least not to speak to her. You can see how important it is to be careful about what you say.

as·sumed'

There will be times when your supervisor is not available. If you are unable to assist the caller, take a message. Most callers will identify themselves, but there are some people who won't give their names or reasons for calling. A tactful way to get the information you need is to say, "Mrs. Johnson is out of the office, but maybe I can help you."

Providing Assistance

trans·fer'ring

There are other ways to assist callers when your supervisor is not available. Make an effort to be helpful by providing information or transferring the call to someone who can help the caller.

Giving information Although you should always try to assist callers, be careful about the type of information you give out. Some information is **confidential**; that is, it is told to you with the belief that you will not repeat it to anyone else. Other information is not intended for public knowledge. Providing too much information might give a competing company an advantage or give the wrong impression about your company.

For example, suppose that your supervisor is not in and won't be available until after lunch. If you say, "He's in conference with the Accounting Manager," callers may interpret this information to mean that your company is having financial problems. It is better to say, "He's in a meeting and I don't expect him to return until 1:30." This information is helpful for callers. It tells them when to call back or when to expect your supervisor to call them.

Transferring calls If you receive a telephone call that you or your supervisor cannot handle, transfer the call to someone who can help the caller. Suppose the caller says, "I'm calling about your new line of computers." You might respond by saying, "Miss Harden in our marketing department should be able to help you. Let me connect you with her."

The procedure for transferring calls within your office depends on the type of telephone equipment you have. Someone within your office can show you this procedure. By transferring the call, you are helping the caller and at the same time creating a good impression — one of your willingness to help.

TAKING TELEPHONE MESSAGES

An office worker should always be prepared to take telephone messages for other people in the office. When you answer the telephone, be sure that you have a message pad and pen or pencil handy. If the person being called is not in, offer to take a message. Listen carefully and record the message completely and accurately. Ask the caller to repeat or spell out words or names that you do not understand. Repeat any numbers the caller gives you to be sure you have written them correctly. Numbers such as *13* and *30, 15* and *50,* and *17* and *70* sound alike and are easily confused.

A complete telephone message includes the following information:

1. the name of the person being called
2. the date and time of the call
3. the name and the company of the caller
4. the telephone number of the caller
5. the message
6. the name or initials of the person taking the message

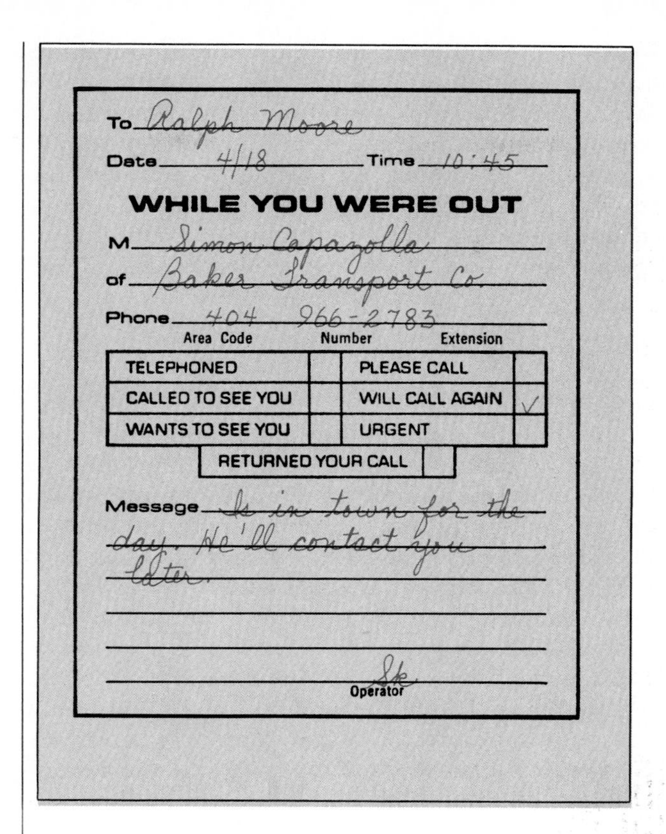

To Ralph Moore

Date 4/18 Time 10:45

WHILE YOU WERE OUT

M Simon Capazolla

of Baker Transport Co.

Phone 404 966-2783

Area Code Number Extension

TELEPHONED		PLEASE CALL	
CALLED TO SEE YOU		WILL CALL AGAIN	✓
WANTS TO SEE YOU		URGENT	
RETURNED YOUR CALL			

Message Is in town for the day. He'll contact you later.

Sk

Operator

Illustration 5–2 Record messages completely and accurately

Using message forms like the one in Illustration 5–2 saves you time in recording messages. A **message form** is a printed form used to record information about telephone calls when you take phone messages for others. All you have to do is fill in the blank spaces with the appropriate information about each call. Generally, these forms are printed on colored paper so the message is more noticeable when placed on your supervisor's desk.

When writing the message on the form, make sure the details are correct and complete. Begin by filling in the caller's name, company, and telephone number as you are talking to the caller. Remember that your supervisor may know more than one Robert Smith. Without the company name and telephone number, there is no way of knowing which Robert Smith called. Verify the telephone number (including the area code if the call is long distance) by reading it back to the caller. Recording the telephone number will save your supervisor the time it would take to look the number up.

ver'i·fy

Most message pads contain printed messages, such as *Please call* and *Returned your call,* that you can check off to save time. These are usually followed by a space for a written message. After you record the message, repeat it to the caller to be sure it is correct.

Always fill in the name of the person for whom the message is intended. This practice is especially important if you answer the telephone for more than one person. A message form without a name might be difficult to deliver. Be sure to record the date and time of the call. Sometimes there is a period of several hours to several days before the message can be delivered. It is possible that your supervisor may have spoken with the caller by the time the message is delivered. By having the date and time of the call, your supervisor knows whether or not the call has been attended to already. Complete the telephone message form by writing your initials at the bottom of the message. Your initials help to identify you in case your supervisor has any questions about the message.

INTERRUPTING AND TERMINATING CALLS

Most business phones have more than one line; that is, several calls can come in on the same piece of equipment. If you are on one line and another line rings, politely excuse yourself and answer the other call. You might say, "There is another telephone ringing, may I put you on hold?" Then press the hold button and answer the other call. If this call can be completed rather quickly, complete it. If not, explain to the second caller that you are on another line and that you will be back in just a moment.

Remember to press the **hold button** to put the caller on *hold* whenever you leave the telephone during a call. When you press the hold button, the caller is still connected but cannot overhear conversations and background sounds in your office. Be sure to return to the line every 30 to 45 seconds to let the caller know that you have not forgotten about the call. For instance, if a caller is waiting for your supervisor, you might say, "Mrs. Drucker is still on the telephone. Do you want to hold, or may I have her call you?" If the caller has been on hold while you look up some information, you might say, "Thank you for waiting. I have the information for you now."

When terminating, or ending, a call, say good-bye in a pleasant way. Saying good-bye pleasantly leaves the caller with a good impression. Some phrases that are helpful include "thank you for calling," "I'm glad I was able to help you," or "you're welcome, Mr. Benze." To be certain that all questions have been answered and that the call has been completed, let the caller hang up first.

USING TELEPHONE DIRECTORIES

In most offices, the telephone is an important tool for performing your job. You will place calls to get information, make reservations, schedule appointments, and order supplies. With the number of calls you will be making, you can't be expected to remember all of the telephone numbers you use. However, knowing where to obtain a telephone number quickly when it is needed will make you a more valuable employee.

Using City Telephone Directories

di·rec'to·ry

Check your city telephone directory to find the number of a local business or individual. The telephone company publishes the White and Yellow Pages for your area. They are usually bound in one book. In some very large cities, however, the Yellow Pages may be printed as a separate directory. Keep a copy of your city directory handy at your work space at all times. Directories for other frequently called cities can be obtained from the telephone company.

sub·scribe'

White Pages The White Pages directory is an alphabetic listing of the names and telephone numbers of individuals and businesses that subscribe to, or purchase, telephone service. In order to find numbers quickly in the telephone directory, you must know the correct spelling of the person's or company's name. If you aren't sure of the spelling, look it up in your correspondence file.

Many large organizations, such as the company in Illustration 5–3, list numbers for various departments and branch offices. This listing also gives the number of the company operator. Dial this number when you need general information or when you don't know which department can handle your telephone call. The company operator will connect you with someone in the company who can help you.

a'gen·cy

At one time or another most people need to contact a government agency, such as the Internal Revenue Service or the Driver License Bureau.

Illustration 5–3
Many companies list the number of their central switchboard

Olsen Manufacturing Co
638 Frontage Rd
For Faster Service Look Below For
The Correct Telephone Number Of
The Person Or Department You
Wish To Call

If The Number Is Not Shown Dial . .	657-5500
Employ-Pers.	657-5700
Accts Pay.	657-5680
Advg & Mktg	657-5753
Cash Control	657-5685
Customer Service	
New England-New York Areas. . . .	657-5931
Mid-Atlantic Areas.	657-5800
Mid-West-West Coast Areas	657-5860
Matrls Mat Div	657-5610
Merchandising.	657-5570
Planning & Info Svcs	657-5590
Pres	657-5592
Exec V P	657-5531
V P Mktg.	657-5548

Telephone numbers for government agencies are listed under the appropriate level of government. For example, federal government telephone numbers are listed under *United States Government.* Telephone numbers for state agencies are listed under the state name, as in *Texas, State of.* County government and city government telephone numbers are listed under the appropriate county or city name, as in *King, County of* and *Boston, City of.*

If you are unable to locate a telephone number in your city telephone directory, dial directory assistance. In most cities, the telephone company charges for local directory assistance after the first several requests per month. To save time and money, record the telephone numbers in your directory for future reference.

Yellow Pages The Yellow Pages contain an alphabetic listing of businesses arranged according to product or service provided. Refer to the Yellow Pages when you want to find products or services quickly but don't know the name of a particular business. For example, the names and telephone numbers of businesses that sell office equipment are listed under *Office equipment.* These businesses may also be listed under specialized areas, such as *Computers, Calculators,* and *Dictation equipment.*

Using Personal Directories

If you have a telephone on your desk at work, you probably should keep a personal telephone directory. Using a personal directory saves time, since you do not have to look through the larger city directory. Your personal

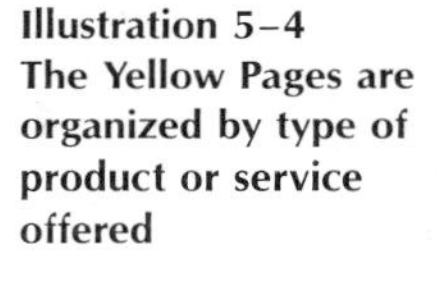

Illustration 5–4
The Yellow Pages are organized by type of product or service offered

e·mer'gen·cies

directory should contain the names and telephone numbers of those people and businesses that you call frequently. It should also include emergency numbers, such as the fire department, police, and ambulance service. When emergencies occur in or near the office, you need to report them to the proper authorities without delay.

Your personal directory can be a keyboarded list posted on your wall or taped next to your telephone. As your list grows, you may find an alphabetic card file more convenient. A card file is easier to correct and maintain in alphabetical order than a list.

Using Company Directories

Many large companies publish their own telephone directories. In a company directory, company employees and departments are listed alphabetically with their telephone extensions. Use this directory when you have to call or transfer a call to another company employee. If your company does not have a directory of its own, keep a listing of frequently called company numbers within your personal directory.

MAKING TELEPHONE CALLS

When calling someone in your city or local dialing area, first look up the correct telephone number in the directory. Don't trust your memory if the number is one you have not called recently. Then pick up the receiver, listen for the dial tone, and dial the number carefully. When the call is answered, identify yourself and your company. Then give the name of the person with whom you would like to speak. You might begin by saying, "Hello, I'm Shawn Roberts with the Office Service Company. I'd like to speak with Jackie LeBlanc."

If you do not know the name of a particular person to ask for, give the title or briefly explain the information you want. For example, "This is Kim Wong with First City Bank. I'd like some information about ordering carbonless forms." In this way, you make it easier for the person who answers to connect you with the appropriate person.

Most businesses have a policy regarding personal telephone calls. Some firms discourage all personal calls because these calls tie up the telephones and interfere with business. Other firms permit some brief telephone calls. Usually, though, important or urgent calls are permitted. For instance, if you are working late, your supervisor will understand that you have to notify the people you ride with that you won't be ready at the usual time.

in·ter·fere'

Long and unnecessary personal calls are the ones that most businesses frown on. When you make personal calls during business hours, you not only tie up the telephone line, but you are visiting instead of working. If your friends call you at the office to chat, explain to them that you would rather talk with them after working hours when you have more time.

REVIEWING KEY POINTS

1. Telephones are vital to the business world. Ninety percent of all business transactions involve at least one telephone call.
2. A clear, distinct, and friendly voice is an asset to an office worker.
3. Answer telephone calls promptly and politely; identify your company and yourself.
4. Have a message pad and pen or pencil handy in case you need to take a message. Record the message accurately and completely.
5. When screening calls, use tact so that callers are not offended.
6. When you or your supervisor cannot help a caller, transfer the call to someone who can.
7. To find the telephone number of a individual or local business, consult the White Pages or Yellow Pages of your city telephone directory.
8. Keep a personal telephone directory of frequently called numbers and emergency services.
9. Some companies provide telephone directories that list employees and departments and their telephone numbers.

DEVELOPING HUMAN RELATIONS SKILLS

1. You work for a small real estate agency that has three incoming telephone lines. While you are on break, the file clerk answers the telephones for you. This afternoon when you returned from your break, all of the telephone lines were on hold. The file clerk explained that every time she left the desk to get files, the phones started ringing again. So she put all the phones on hold so she could get her work done.
   a. What problems does this action create?
   b. What would you say to the file clerk?
   c. What would you do to prevent this from happening again?
2. Your supervisor, Ms. Scott, asked you to place a call for her to a client, Mr. Peters. By the time you have Mr. Peters on the line, Ms. Scott is talking to someone on another line. Mr. Peters says, "Tell Ms. Scott that if she wants to talk to me to be ready when you reach me. I don't have time to waste waiting for her." You are embarrassed because you know this has happened before with Mr. Peters and with several other clients.
   a. What should you say to Mr. Peters?
   b. What suggestions, if any, would you make to Ms. Scott to prevent this problem from happening again?

IMPROVING COMMUNICATION SKILLS

Refer to Appendix A 1.8-1.18.

1. On a separate sheet of paper, write or keyboard these sentences, adding any necessary commas.
   a. Beth answered the telephones and Whit distributed the mail.
   b. Joanne has a quiet efficient way of handling telephone messages.
   c. The new receptionist will begin work on Monday December 10.
   d. The order included message pads pens pencils and envelopes.
   e. Our new mailing address is 103 Breckenridge Court Lafayette Louisiana 70506.
   f. Our office has three personal computers two electronic typewriters one 10-key calculator and a postage meter.
   g. I hope Jason that you will be able to complete the project.
   h. Marie will keyboard the introduction Sue will keyboard the body and I will keyboard the tables for the report.
   i. Katherine will you be able to work late today?
   j. The report will be finished by noon but the copies won't be run until 3:30 p.m.
2. On a separate sheet of paper, write or keyboard these paragraphs. Add two or three sentences to complete each paragraph.
   a. Many customers make their first contact with an organization over the telephone. This contact forms a first impression. Here are some suggestions to help you make a good first impression when you answer the telephone.
   b. Telephone directories are used to find telephone numbers of people and businesses. The White Pages contain an alphabetical listing of the names and the telephone numbers of individuals and businesses. When using the White Pages, follow this advice.

BUILDING PROBLEM-SOLVING SKILLS

1. On a separate sheet of paper, calculate the average number of telephone calls handled by each of the employees listed in the following table.

	Mon.	Tues.	Wed.	Thurs.	Fri.
A. Bixby	7	12	10	13	6
C. Doyle	11	17	8	9	10
E. Franz	15	12	12	10	9
G. Hanks	14	10	9	12	11
I. Joseph	10	10	9	8	7
K. Luke	6	9	13	7	12
M. Noble	8	15	9	7	10
G. Peters	11	13	7	6	9

2. Refer to the table on the preceding page. Then answer the following questions on a separate sheet of paper. Show your work.
   - **a.** Which employee handled the most calls for the entire week?
   - **b.** On which day were the most calls handled?
   - **c.** Which employee handled the fewest calls for the entire week?
   - **d.** On which day were the fewest calls handled?

APPLYING OFFICE SKILLS

1. Using the White and Yellow Pages of your local telephone directory, find a telephone number for each of the following places. Indicate whether you found the telephone number in the White or Yellow Pages. Include the telephone number and tell how the number was listed.

   Example: Local police — White Pages, 911 (listed as an emergency telephone number).

   - **a.** a computer store
   - **b.** a hospital
   - **c.** the post office nearest your home
   - **d.** a physical fitness center
   - **e.** a television repair service
   - **f.** your school

2. You work in an office with several employees. Take down messages for each of the following calls. Use the telephone message forms in your workbook or a plain sheet of paper to record the messages.
   - **a.** "This is Marty Young at the Byte Shop. Please have Claire Mackey call me. I have some software she may be interested in. My telephone number is 788-2424."
   - **b.** "This is Ken Cort with State Office Equipment. Would you tell Mr. Martin that the furniture has arrived. He can call me to set up an appointment to deliver the furniture. My number is 756-5632."
   - **c.** "This is Austin Scott, Mr. Simon's secretary. Would you tell Ms. Mackey that Mr. Simon has been called out of town on an emergency. He will not be able to meet with Ms. Mackey at lunch tomorrow. Mr. Simon will call for another appointment as soon as he returns."
   - **d.** "This is Jeff Kister with A–1 Office Workers. Would you ask Mr. Martin to call me after 3:30 P.M. today. My number is 788-0530."

CHAPTER 2

LONG-DISTANCE TELEPHONE SERVICE

If you had to do business with someone located a great distance away, what would be the best way to communicate? You could send a letter. However, you would have to wait several days for a reply. In addition, the costs of producing a business letter are constantly increasing. Telephone service, on the other hand, makes voice communication convenient, immediate, and relatively inexpensive — even when the people talking are thousands of miles apart. The improved long-distance service now available makes long-distance telephone calls even more attractive for business.

Long-distance telephone calls are those calls that are made to telephone numbers outside your local dialing area. Not only can you place long-distance calls to any telephone in any city in the United States, but you can also call practically every telephone in every city in the world! Because long-distance service is provided in addition to your local dialing service, there is an extra charge for it. So that you can control the costs of long-distance service, you need to know what types of long-distance service are available.

As you study this chapter, you will find answers to the following questions:

- What companies provide long-distance service?
- What types of long-distance service are available through AT&T?
- What other types of long-distance service are available?
- How are charges for long-distance calls calculated?
- What do the following terms mean: **Local Access and Transport Areas (LATAs), common carriers, dial-direct service, station-to-station calls, operator-assisted calls, WATS line?**

TYPES OF LONG-DISTANCE SERVICE

di·vest'ed

When American Telephone and Telegraph (AT&T) divested itself of — that is, it separated itself from — the regional Bell telephone companies in January, 1984, many changes were made in the way long-distance service is handled. Each of the regional Bell telephone companies has divided its service area into **Local Access and Transport Areas** or **LATAs**. For instance, South Carolina is divided into four LATAs. Long distance calls within a LATA are handled by the regional telephone company serving that area. AT&T still handles long-distance calls between LATAs. With the breakup of AT&T, other **common carriers** — companies that offer services for a fee — such as Sprint or MCI can also provide long-distance service. Individuals and businesses are permitted to choose which company they want to use for long-distance calls. However, in order to use one of the common carriers, an individual or business must subscribe to the service.

sub·scribe'

Dial-Direct/No-Operator-Assistance Calls

You can place long-distance calls yourself, without operator assistance, in most sections of the country. These calls are referred to as dial-direct or no-operator-assistance calls. To use **dial-direct service**, you must know the three-digit area code and the number of the party you are calling. If you do not know the area code for a particular city or town, check the listing in the reference section of your local telephone directory.

When placing a long-distance call through AT&T, dial 1, the area code (if different from your own), and the number you want to reach. For example, to call a number in Seattle, Washington, you would dial 1-206 plus the correct telephone number.

Most common carriers offer only dial-direct service, which means the customer must place calls without the help of an operator. When placing a long-distance call through a common carrier, you may have to dial a local telephone number (seven digits), an authorization or identification number, the area code, plus the telephone number desired. For example, to call the same number in Seattle, Washington, you might have to dial the local telephone number of the common carrier, an authorization number, the area code, plus the correct telephone number.

au·thor·i·za'tion

Dial-direct calls are sometimes called **station-to-station calls.** Charges on these calls begin as soon as someone answers the telephone and continue until the receiver is replaced on the telephone. In other words, you are charged for the call even if the person you want to speak with is unavailable. For this reason, you should use dial-direct service only when you are reasonably sure that the person you are calling is in. You should also use dial-direct service when it is likely that anyone who answers the telephone will be able to help you. Some companies use dial-direct service for all long-distance calls. In many cases, it is cheaper to place two dial-direct calls — one to find out when the person will be in and one when the person is in — than to place one call through the operator. Be sure to find out your company's policy on placing long-distance telephone calls.

Operator-Assisted Calls

Both AT&T and the regional Bell telephone companies offer operator-assisted calls. **Operator-assisted calls** are any long-distance calls that an operator helps you complete. These include person-to-person calls, collect calls, calling-card calls, and calls with special billing instructions. Long-distance calls placed from pay telephones and hotels are also considered to be operator-assisted calls. You can place station-to-station calls through the operator, too; but this is unnecessarily expensive. Operator-assisted calls are more expensive than dial-direct calls because they require the assistance of an operator.

To place an operator-assisted call, dial "0," the area code (if different from your own), and the telephone number. Dialing "0" signals the telephone company's computers that an operator-assisted call is being placed. An operator intercepts the call before it is completed and asks you what special services you want. When the operator answers, give the special instructions. The operator then records the type of call for billing purposes and lets the call go through.

in·ter·cepts'

There may be a few towns in the United States where the operator must place all long-distance calls. To make a long-distance call from these areas,

Illustration 5–5 Operator assistance is required for certain types of long-distance calls

you dial "0" for operator, explain what type of long-distance service you want, and give the telephone number you are calling. Check the reference section of your local telephone directory to see if this procedure must be followed for long-distance calls.

Person-to-person calls When you want to speak with a particular individual, a person-to-person call may be the most appropriate long-distance service to use. Place this call following the instructions for operator-assisted calls in your area. When the operator answers, tell the operator that you want to place a person-to-person call and give the name of the person with whom you want to speak; for example, "I'd like to place a person-to-person call to Dr. Douglas Taylor." The operator completes the call and gets Dr. Taylor on the phone for you. Charges for person-to-person calls begin when the person you request answers the phone. If the person is not in when you call, there is no charge for the call.

Collect calls A collect call is a long-distance call for which the receiver agrees to pay the charges. To place a collect call, follow the instructions for operator-assisted calls in your area. When the operator answers, say that you want to place a collect call and give your name and company. The operator will complete the call and ask the person who answers if she or he will accept the charges for the call.

In business, collect calls are frequently made by employees who travel. When they have to call the office, they call collect and have the charges billed to the company.

Calling-card calls Business people who travel regularly, such as executives and salespeople, may apply for telephone calling cards. These cards are very convenient for people who frequently place long-distance calls while away from their regular telephones. With the calling card, they can bill phone calls directly to their office phone numbers. Thus, they don't have to call collect or carry change for pay phones.

You may be asked to place calling-card calls for visitors to your office. Simply tell the operator, "This is a calling-card call," and be prepared to read the calling-card number when the operator asks for it.

Bill-to-third-number calls On occasion, you may also be asked to place a phone call for someone in your office and have the call billed to another number. For example, suppose that your supervisor needs to make a personal long-distance call from the office. If you dial direct, your supervisor's personal call will be charged to the company. Instead, you can request that the call be billed to your supervisor's home telephone number. Follow the instructions for operator-assisted calls in your area. When the operator answers, say that you would like to charge the call to a third number and give the operator the area code and telephone number. The operator will check with someone at the third number to have the billing approved.

Time-and-charge calls In some businesses, customers and clients are charged for long-distance calls made in their behalf. You can find out the charges for a call by requesting this service when you place the call. Dial the call as you would any operator-assisted call. When the operator answers, explain that you would like time and charges. Then stay near the phone after you complete the call. The operator will call you with this information.

International Calls

in·ter·na'tion·al

o·ver·seas'

International dial-direct service is available to over 105 foreign countries. These calls, which you dial yourself, are less expensive than calls that are placed through the overseas operator. To place a dial-direct call to a foreign country, dial the international access code (011), the country code, the city routing code, and the telephone number. For example, to call London, you would dial 011-44-1 and the local telephone number.

You can also place international calls that are person to person, collect, charged to a third number, and so forth. The international access code for these calls is 01. An operator will come on the line to find out what special services you desire. Instructions for placing international dial-direct calls are provided in the reference section of your local telephone directory. You can also find the country codes and routing codes for major cities listed there.

rout'ing

Dial-direct service is not available in all areas. If international dial-direct service is not available in your area, you can place overseas telephone calls by dialing the operator and giving the country, name, and telephone number of the party you are calling.

CHARGES FOR LONG-DISTANCE CALLS

in'flu·enced

The cost of long-distance telephone calls is influenced by factors other than the type of service. The time of day, the distance from the point called, and the length of the phone call also affect the cost.

Rates for Dial-Direct Calls

During regular business hours — from 8:00 A.M. to 5:00 P.M. — charges for dial-direct calls are the most expensive. The rates are lower after 5:00 P.M. The lowest rates are charged between 11:00 P.M. and 8:00 A.M. Lower rates also apply on weekends and holidays.

For dial-direct calls, you pay only for the minutes you talk. Usually, you are charged one rate for the first minute and a lower rate for each additional minute of conversation.

Rates for Operator-Assisted Calls

A separate charge is added to the dial-direct rates for all operator-assisted calls. The rate charged for operator assistance depends on the type of assistance. For instance, the charge for an operator-assisted station-to-station call from Boston is about $.44 while the charge for an operator-assisted person-to-person call is about $1.79. Check the reference section of your local telephone directory to see what rates apply in your area. As mentioned earlier in this chapter, rates for operator-assisted calls are always higher because they require the assistance of an operator.

TIME ZONE DIFFERENCES

con·ti·nen'tal

You need to be familiar with time zone differences when placing long-distance calls. The continental United States and parts of Canada are divided into four time zones: Eastern, Central, Mountain, and Pacific. As you move west, each time zone is one hour earlier. When it is 12:00 noon in the Eastern time zone, it is 11:00 A.M. in the Central time zone; 10:00 A.M. in the Mountain zone; and 9:00 A.M. in the Pacific time zone. In Alaska and Hawaii, it is 7:00 A.M. So, if you are in Washington, D.C. (Eastern time zone), and want to telephone San Francisco (Pacific time zone), you must consider the three-hour time difference. If you place a call at 9:00 A.M., you probably will not get an answer. Why? Because it is only 6:00 A.M. in San Francisco and there probably are few offices open.

Illustration 5–6
Time zone map with area codes

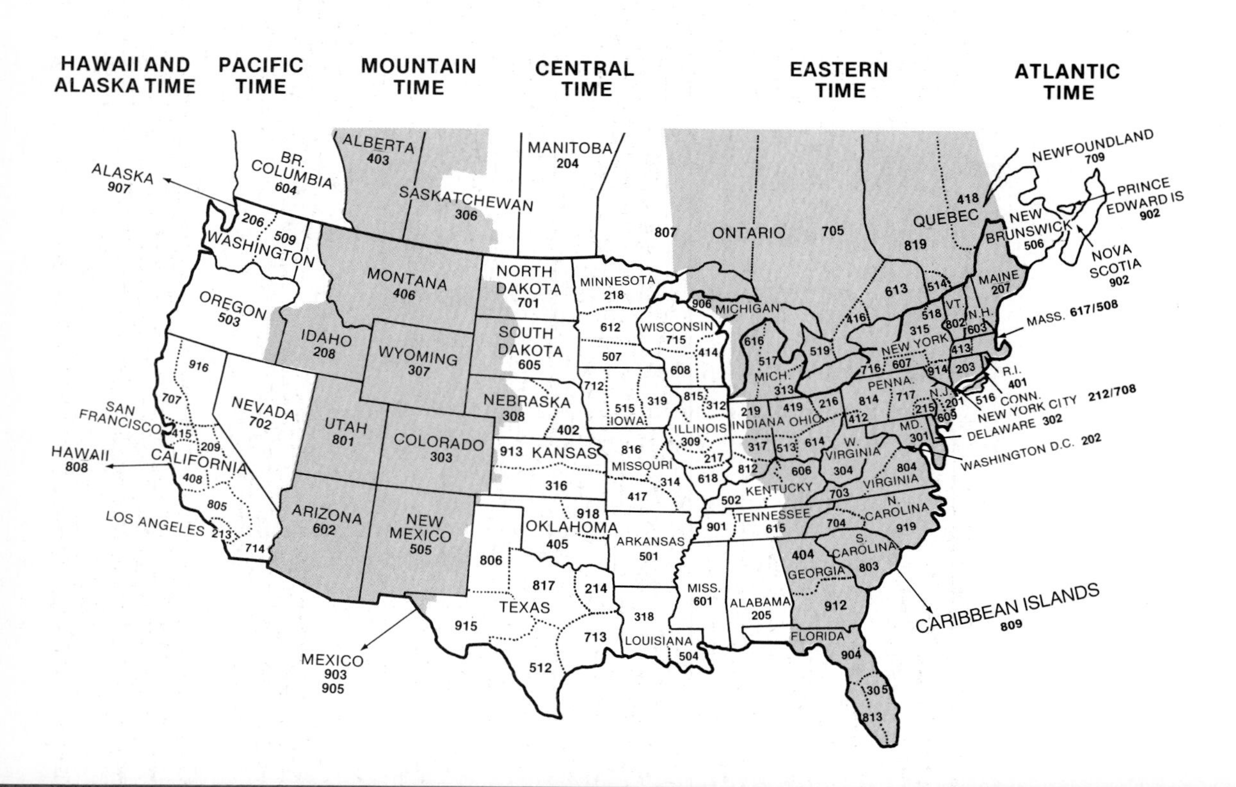

Time zone differences become even more important when you are placing calls overseas. When it is 7:00 P.M. Monday in Chicago, it is already 9:00 A.M. Tuesday in Japan.

In addition to time zone differences, you must consider daylight savings time when you place long-distance calls. States that observe daylight savings time all change on the same dates. Clocks are set one hour ahead on the last Sunday in April and one hour back on the last Sunday in October.

Most telephone directories have a time zone map similar to the one shown in Illustration 5–6. This map can help you plan your telephone calls. Remember that the rates charged for long-distance calls are determined by the time of day in the city where the call is placed.

LONG-DISTANCE DIRECTORY ASSISTANCE

If you do not know the telephone number for a long-distance call, you can get it by calling long-distance directory assistance. Dial 1, the area code (if different from your own), and 555-1212. When the directory assistance operator answers, give the name of the city and the name of the person or company you want to call. A charge may apply for these calls. Record the name and telephone number in your personal directory for future use.

A listing of area codes can be found in the reference section of your local telephone directory.

WIDE AREA TELECOMMUNICATIONS SERVICE (WATS)

A **WATS line** permits long-distance calling within a selected area for a set monthly rate. The monthly rate depends on the size of the area and the number of hours the WATS line is available. For instance, a company may pay for 25 hours of WATS service per month to telephones within a three-state area. If the company uses more than 25 hours of WATS service, it pays additional charges. Regular long-distance rates apply to calls made outside the WATS area.

Some companies — such as hotels, motels, and other businesses that operate nationwide — have an inward WATS line. Station-to-station long-distance calls can be made to these companies without charge to the caller. The company paying for the inward WATS chooses the area to be served and the number of hours of service to be provided.

All inward WATS numbers have an 800 area code. To reach these numbers, dial 1-800 and the telephone number. Many 800 numbers are listed in your telephone directory. If you cannot find a number, you can get it by calling the directory assistance operator for 800 numbers. Simply dial 1-800-555-1212.

REVIEWING KEY POINTS

1. Long-distance service is provided by AT&T, regional Bell telephone companies, and common carriers.
2. Dial-direct service is the least expensive method of placing a long-distance call.
3. An operator-assisted call is any long-distance call that requires the services of an operator to complete.
4. Person-to-person calls, collect calls, and calling-card calls are examples of operator-assisted calls.
5. International direct-dial service is available for telephone calls to foreign countries.
6. Charges for long-distance calls are based on the type of service, the time of day, the distance, and the length of the call.
7. Dial-direct rates for interstate calls are highest between 8:00 A.M. and 5:00 P.M.
8. Knowledge of time zones and daylight savings time helps you place calls efficiently.
9. Calls placed to 800 numbers are free to the caller.

DEVELOPING HUMAN RELATIONS SKILLS

1. You work for Bruce Miller at the Miller Insurance Company. Explain how you would handle the following situations:
   a. You answer the telephone and it is a person-to-person telephone call for Mr. Miller. Mr. Miller has some important clients in his office and has asked you not to disturb him. How would you handle this situation?
   b. While you are giving a client some information over the phone, another telephone rings. What would you do?
   c. While you are working alone in the office, the telephone rings. It is the operator with a collect call. How would you handle this situation?
   d. Mr. Miller has asked not to be disturbed. A telephone call from Mr. Miller's wife comes in. What would you do?
   e. Mr. Miller has been trying to place a long-distance call to Ms. Janie Evans, but her line has been busy. He asks you to continue trying to get Ms. Evans. What would you say to Ms. Evans when she answers the telephone?
2. There is a 24-hour-a-day WATS line in your office. The company allows employees to make personal calls before 8:00 A.M. and after 5:00 P.M. One

of your friends asks you if she can come to your office after work to call her sister, who lives in the next state.

a. What would you do?
b. What suggestions could you make to avoid this situation in the future?

IMPROVING COMMUNICATION SKILLS

Refer to Appendix A 1.8-1.18.

1. On a separate sheet of paper, write or keyboard the following sentences, inserting commas as needed.
   a. Mrs. Jones I'm calling for Ms. Dawes from the Independence Insurance Agency.
   b. The telephone bill that we received on January 18 19-- contained three long-distance calls to Sulphur Louisiana.
   c. I took a message for Ms. Adams but she is not in to return the call.
   d. Long-distance telephone calls can be made using AT&T the regional Bell company and other common carriers.
   e. Diana I hope you will use dial-direct long-distance service.
   f. Our records indicate Mr. Ellis that we called you on December 18 19--; January 4 19--; January 30 19--; and February 12 19--.
   g. We have branch offices in Indianapolis Bloomington Fort Wayne Lafayette and Gary.
   h. Jane works in Fresno Jill works in Spokane and I work in Olympia.
   i. Mr. Goodson called Ms. Aude in New Mexico and Ms. Fisher called Dr. Ladson in Colorado.
   j. Bob has a courteous professional voice over the telephone.
2. On a separate sheet of paper, write or keyboard the following paragraphs. Add three or four sentences to complete each paragraph.
   a. When placing long-distance calls, you must consider the type of service needed. Operator-assisted calls are more expensive than dial-direct calls. You can also save time and money by planning your calls.
   b. When placing long-distance calls, you should be familiar with the differences in time zones. The continental United States is divided into four time zones.

BUILDING PROBLEM-SOLVING SKILLS

1. Refer to the chart of telephone charges for the weeks beginning November 5 and 12 that appears at the top of the next page. Then on a separate sheet

of paper, compute the amounts that are asked for.

a. the average length of calls for each week

b. the average cost of calls for each week

c. the average length of calls for the two-week period

d. the average cost of calls for the two-week period

TELEPHONE CHARGES FOR WEEK OF NOVEMBER 5

DATE	PLACE CALLED	TELEPHONE NO.	TIME	MIN	AMT
1105	INDIANAPOLIS IN	317 924-3490	5:19A	19	4.66
1106	GREENVILLE SC	803 297-1246	11:06A	1	.26
1106	ORLANDO FL	305 334-3806	10:58A	15	6.47
1107	HUNTSVILLE TX	409 294-1285	3:06P	20	8.79
1109	COLUMBIA TN	616 388-0210	4:51P	17	5.96
1109	ORLANDO FL	305 334-2449	2:10P	3	1.43

TELEPHONE CHARGES FOR WEEK OF NOVEMBER 12

DATE	PLACE CALLED	TELEPHONE NO.	TIME	MIN	AMT
1112	HENDERSON TN	901 989-7014	5:51P	6	1.66
1113	AUBURN AL	205 826-5545	3:25P	2	.97
1115	JACKSON MS	601 968-2541	10:55A	6	2.77
1115	ORLANDO FL	305 332-2449	10:41A	12	5.21
1116	BOSTON MA	617 725-5333	4:19P	13	4.58
1116	INDIANAPOLIS IN	317 924-3490	5:09P	19	4.66

2. Again refer to the chart of telephone charges that appears above. Then answer these questions on a separate sheet of paper.

a. Which call was the shortest?

b. Which call was the longest?

c. What are the total charges for all calls to Indianapolis?

d. How many calls were made to Orlando? On what dates?

e. How many different states were called during the two-week period?

APPLYING OFFICE SKILLS

Activity 2 can be done on information processing equipment.

1. At 8:30 A.M. on Wednesday your supervisor, Mrs. Dioski, asks you to place the following long-distance calls for her during the day. She will be at her desk from 9:00 to 10:00 and from 2:30 to 3:30, so you must place the calls during those times. Your office is in St. Louis (Central time zone). At what time would you place each call? What kind of service would you use for each call?

a. Brandon Hall, branch manager of the New Orleans office, who is usually in the office all day.

b. Mark Tyson, a sales representative in San Diego, who travels frequently.

c. Kathy Anderson, the manager of computer services in the Buffalo office, who usually works in the office.

d. Bonnie Wills, branch manager of the Albuquerque office, who frequently works in the field with sales representatives.

e. Nell Walters, a sales representative in Miami, who uses Tuesdays and Thursdays for all work away from the office.

2. Use the memo form in your workbook to keyboard the following memo. Set the left margin 2 spaces after the guide word *SUBJECT*. Set the right margin equal to the left margin. Leave 2 spaces between the guide words and the keyboard information. Triple space after the heading lines. Single space the memo, leaving a double space between paragraphs. If you do not have a workbook, use plain paper.

TO: Ms. Jane Anders
FROM: Susy Hess
DATE: (Today's)
SUBJECT: Telephone Seminar

I would like to attend the Telephone Seminar, "Effective Use of Your Telephone," on Wednesday, April 3, from 2:30–4:30 p.m. Since you are going to be out of town on that date, do you think it is possible for me to attend? (P)I will be happy to make arrangements to have the telephones answered. I will also come back to the office after the seminar to make sure that all urgent work is completed. (P)Ms. Anders, I think that learning to handle the telephones more effectively will be helpful to the operation of your office. I will be happy to discuss this with you at your convenience.

CHAPTER 3

TELEPHONE EQUIPMENT AND SPECIAL SERVICES

You may have seen some of the new telephone equipment in offices, in advertisements, or even in homes. Today there is a wide variety of telephone equipment and services available. Such new equipment and systems have made voice communications easier and more convenient for business.

With such a wide variety of equipment and services available, some businesses need assistance in deciding which equipment and services best fit their needs. Most telephone companies that supply telephone service also provide consultants who study the company's communication activities, then recommend the type of equipment and services that best fit the company's needs.

The telephone companies also help businesses by providing training seminars to teach employees how to use the telephone effectively and how to project a good image. The training seminars are especially important when a company has special features built into the telephone system. Employees must understand the purpose of these features so that they can use them efficiently.

As you study this chapter, you will find answers to the following questions:

- What kinds of telephone equipment do businesses use?
- What special telephone services are available?
- How can businesses control the costs of telephone services?
- What do the following terms mean: **Touch-Tone telephone, Key Telephone System, hold key, Call Director, Private Business Exchange (PBX) System, switchboard operator, Centrex Telephone Systems, Speakerphone, Picturephone meeting service, Bank-By-Phone service, Data-phone?**

TELEPHONE EQUIPMENT

rec·om·men·da'tions

It is important for office support workers to be familiar with the various types of telephone equipment. Although you may never be responsible for selecting the type of telephone equipment to be purchased for your company, you may be asked to provide your supervisor with recommendations when new telephone equipment is being purchased.

In most offices, there is a telephone at each work space. These telephones are one of two types of equipment — rotary-dial or Touch-Tone.

Rotary-Dial Telephone Equipment

Many of you are familiar with the traditional rotary-dial telephone equipment. With a rotary-dial telephone, you dial the desired telephone number using a dial that rotates as you enter each number. Many companies still use rotary-dial telephones. Although rotary-dial telephones are not as expensive to purchase and use as the push-button telephones, they are slower to use and do not permit the user to take advantage of the many special features available for telephones.

Touch-Tone Telephone Equipment

The **Touch-Tone telephone**, sometimes called a push-button telephone, has twelve buttons instead of a rotary dial. One reason that Touch-Tone phones are so popular is that they can be used to communicate with computers. For instance, in some areas of the country, you can use a Touch-Tone phone to communicate with a bank's computers to pay your bills by telephone.

TELEPHONE SYSTEMS

Many large companies need special telephone systems that have the capacity for providing several telephone lines. These companies may use Key Telephone Systems, Private Business Exchange Systems, or Centrex Systems to handle telephone calls. Most new telephone systems being installed are electronic systems.

Key Telephone Systems

A **Key Telephone System** is installed when more than one telephone line and number are needed by a company or a busy executive. There is a key, or button, for each line. The equipment in this system comes in a variety of sizes. The smallest is a 6-key telephone the size of a regular telephone. The largest, a desk-size phone, has as many as 18 keys. Key equipment is available with either rotary or Touch-Tone dialing.

Illustration 5–7
Touch-Tone Telephone

Illustration 5–8
Key Telephone System

On all key equipment there is a **hold key**, or button, which is usually red. You use this button when you have to leave the line to answer another telephone call or to find information for the caller. This key keeps the call connected, but the caller cannot hear what you are saying or doing. Be sure to press the hold key before depressing one of the other keys; otherwise, you will disconnect the call. The hold key returns to the *up* position when you release it. If you should accidentally press one of the other buttons before you depress the hold button, depress the original key to see if the call is still connected.

dis·con·nect′
ac·ci·den′tal·ly

When an incoming call is received on key equipment, the telephone rings and a light in the button flashes. This light tells you which telephone line to answer.

Six-key telephone On a six-key telephone, the hold key is at the left; the keys in the second, third, fourth, and fifth positions are used to make and receive calls. These are individual lines that you use by depressing the appropriate key. The sixth key, which is at the far right, is sometimes used as another incoming line. However, frequently it is used as an *intercom (intercommunications) line.* When you depress this button and dial an intercom signal, you can speak on this line to another person in your office. For instance, when two buttons are lit, you may use the intercom to tell your supervisor which line to pick up for a call. The intercom line makes it convenient to speak with other people in the office without leaving your desk or tying up an outside line.

in′ter·com

Call director A **Call Director** is a small desk-size unit that permits as many as 30 lines to be answered from one location. The Call Director is operated just like a six-key phone; the only difference is in the number of lines connected to the telephone. Because a receptionist's duties frequently include handling calls as well as greeting visitors, in many offices you are likely to see a Call Director being used at the receptionist's desk.

Private Business Exchange Systems

switch'board

With a **Private Business Exchange (PBX) System,** outgoing calls can be dialed directly from any extension. Incoming calls can be directed either to extensions or to the switchboard — a business can choose the service it prefers.

Some companies choose to have all incoming calls answered by one employee, called a **switchboard operator.** Since all incoming calls must be answered at the switchboard, it must be staffed at all times during business hours. If the operator must leave the switchboard for any reason, another employee may have to take over.

Centrex Telephone Systems

Other companies prefer a switchboard service that allows incoming calls to be answered either at the extension dialed or at the switchboard. Many large organizations have **Centrex Telephone Systems,** which are also known as direct inward dialing systems. A Centrex Telephone System does not require

Illustration 5-9
A modern telephone switchboard

a switchboard operator to answer calls. Each telephone has a seven-digit number, and all incoming calls go directly to the numbers dialed.

A business with a Centrex System usually has a general number listed in the telephone directory. A switchboard operator answers calls placed to the general number. The operator then transfers each call to the proper extension or provides the caller with the telephone number of the appropriate person or department. With this system, someone must still be available to answer the general line at all times. However, other responsibilities can be assigned to this employee because most incoming calls can be answered at the extensions dialed.

ex·ten′sion

Centrex Systems allow telephone communications after regular hours because incoming calls are automatically directed to the extensions dialed. Each extension in a Centrex System operates like a private telephone line — you dial your own calls and answer incoming calls.

The electronic systems that most companies now use have features that are not available on standard phone systems. As you use business telephones, you may not actually see any difference between electronic equipment and other telephone equipment. The major difference is in the features or services available only with electronic equipment.

The number of outside lines and features available varies from one telephone system to another. As an office worker, you should take advantage of the special telephone training most companies provide so that you will better understand how to use these telephone systems efficiently.

SPECIAL EQUIPMENT

There is a variety of special telephone equipment designed to make voice communications more convenient. This equipment includes Speakerphones, mobile phones, Touch-A-Matic telephones, automatic answering machines, and personal paging equipment.

Speakerphone

A **Speakerphone** allows you to talk and listen to telephone conversations without picking up the receiver. When a call comes in, you press a button and talk from anywhere in the room. The caller's voice is amplified through a small loudspeaker. You can adjust the volume of the loudspeaker so that everyone in the room can hear the caller. A microphone in the Speakerphone picks up conversation in the room so that the person on the other end can hear everything that is said. This service is very helpful when a group of people needs to hear both sides of a conversation.

loud′speak·er

Mobile Phone

Busy executives who are out of the office and traveling by car, truck, boat, or airplane can keep in touch with their offices through the use of mobile

mo′bile

Illustration 5-10
Several people can participate in a conference call when a Speakerphone is used

telephones. A construction supervisor, for example, may need to visit several construction sites. Because buildings under construction generally do not have telephones, having a phone in the car allows the supervisor to communicate with the office. In some areas you can dial your own mobile calls. In other areas, you must call the operator, who connects you with the number you are calling. In some sections of the country, cellular phone service is available. This service provides better reception over an expanded area. Long-distance as well as local calls can be made from mobile telephones.

Touch-A-Matic Phone

On a Touch-A-Matic telephone, you can store up to 32 local or long-distance telephone numbers. There are places on the Touch-A-Matic where you can write the names of the person or company whose number is stored. When you want to call one of these telephone numbers, you simply press the button next to the name.

Automatic Answering Machines

Many businesses use telephone answering machines to give information to customers who call. Banks, government offices, and gas and electric companies frequently use answering machines to answer telephone calls after business hours or on holidays. The message may say something like "Standard Savings and Loan closed at 4:30. Please call again between 8:30 A.M. and 4:30 P.M., Monday through Friday."

Other businesses, such as small insurance agencies or law offices, may have answering machines that play a message and then record messages from callers. These recorded messages can help you keep in touch with customers even if you cannot be in the office during business hours.

Personal Paging Equipment

Personal paging systems are very helpful to people who must stay in touch with their offices while they move around the building or city. Service representatives who repair office equipment frequently carry receivers ("beepers") so that they can be contacted wherever they are. When a repair call comes in, the switchboard operator takes the message and sends a signal to the service representative's beeper. The representative then calls the office for the message.

rep·re·sen'ta·tive

Some personal paging systems allow one-way voice communication. With these systems, the person in the office can send a voice message; but the person receiving the signal cannot answer through the system.

SPECIAL TELEPHONE SERVICES

Many services that make voice communications more efficient are available to telephone subscribers. Some of these services are available only in certain sections of the country or only with Touch-Tone telephones. Check with your local telephone company to learn if these services are available in your area.

Conference Calling

Through conference calling, three or more people can participate in the same telephone call. For instance, your supervisor may need to discuss a project with four supervisors in the branch offices. Instead of placing four separate telephone calls, all five people can participate in one call. Conference calls are especially convenient because people in several different locations can share ideas without having to travel or even leave their desks.

Conference calls can be placed using all types of equipment with the help of a telephone operator. On electronic telephones, these calls can be placed without operator assistance.

Picturephone Meeting Service

Picturephone meeting service, which provides visual as well as voice communication, is now available in some major cities. Companies that frequently hold Picturephone meetings may lease or purchase the equipment and set up a special conference room, as in Illustration 5–11. With Picturephone service, callers can see the people to whom they are speaking. Therefore, visual aids, such as charts and graphs, can be used to illustrate points — just as they might be if everyone were in the same room.

Illustration 5–11 Picturephones transmit sights as well as sounds

Speed Calling

Speed Calling is available in some areas of the country. You can store up to 30 telephone numbers on a magnetic memory device in Touch-Tone telephones. To call the numbers stored, you simply dial a one-, two-, or three-digit code instead of seven or eleven digits for local or long-distance calls.

Call Forwarding

for'ward·ing

Call forwarding is a very helpful feature for small and large businesses alike. If you have to leave your work space or the office, you can forward, or transfer, your incoming calls to another telephone where they will be answered. Before forwarding your calls, be sure to tell the person who will be answering your calls where you can be reached or when you plan to return. Call forwarding helps a business serve the public better because all calls are answered promptly.

In most offices there are certain numbers that are dialed frequently. Telephones equipped with an *automatic dialing* feature enable you to dial these numbers more quickly and with less chance of getting a wrong number.

Call Waiting

Call waiting is a feature that tells you when another call is on the line. If another call comes in while you are using the phone, you hear a tone. You

Illustration 5–12
Automatic dialing equipment

can then put the person you are speaking to on hold and answer the second call. With call waiting, you do not miss any calls because your phone is busy. Call waiting is available only on Touch-Tone telephones.

COST CONTROL FEATURES

Because companies must pay an additional charge for most special telephone services, they may restrict the use of some services to certain employees or telephone stations.

Station Restriction

Telephones can be installed so that they can be used only for certain kinds of calls. For instance, when an employee does not have to place calls outside the company, telephone service may be restricted so that only *interoffice* calls (calls within the office) can be made. Or, service may be restricted so that no long-distance calls can be placed from selected telephones. Station restriction saves money for the company because fewer outside lines are needed. This feature also keeps employees from making personal calls during office hours.

Locks

un·au'thor·ized

Locks prevent unauthorized use of phones. On phones with a rotary dial, a lock can be inserted in the first hole of the dial so that no numbers can be dialed. Calls can be answered, but none can be placed. Other locks are available that hold the switch down when the receiver is removed. On a phone with one of these locks, you can neither answer nor place calls without unlocking the phone.

Call Accounting Systems

Many businesses charge customers for all calls made in their behalf. Other businesses charge calls to departments. In both cases, the business must keep records of calls made on all telephones. A computerized call accounting system provides a printout of the numbers dialed and the length of each call. The company can use these records to determine its telephone needs as well as to charge calls to the proper accounts.

TELEPHONE TRENDS

In recent years, many other uses for telephones — besides voice communications — have developed. Individuals and companies can now use Touch-Tone phones to pay bills and communicate with computers.

Banks in many cities offer Bank-By-Phone service. **Bank-By-Phone service** is a convenient way to conduct banking transactions using Touch-Tone telephones. To make a transaction, you dial the Bank-By-Phone system. When your call is answered, you simply enter your account number and press the code number for the type of transaction. If you are paying a bill, press the code number for the company you want to pay and enter the amount of the payment. If you should make an error, there is a code that cancels the transaction. The bank charges a small fee for each transaction, but the fee is usually less than the cost of the stamp for mailing your check.

Telephones are also being used to connect various pieces of office equipment so that information can be sent and received at different locations. A **Data-phone** is a piece of equipment that links computers so that stored information can be sent directly from one computer to another at a different location. A Data-phone is used only to link computers; it cannot be used for voice communications.

Computer terminals are often linked to a main computer through telephone lines. This system enables people to have access to information in the central computer, which may be miles away. For example, a company in Omaha may have a terminal that is linked by telephone lines to the main computer in Denver. This arrangement allows employees to enter and receive information in Omaha. The actual processing is done on the computer in Denver.

With this new equipment, an executive can work anywhere there is a computer terminal. Some business executives have terminals in their homes. Because of these and other improvements in electronic telephone equipment, in the future more people will be able to work without having to commute to the office!

REVIEWING KEY POINTS

1. Telephone consultants help businesses analyze their needs so that they can choose appropriate equipment and services to fit those needs.
2. Many businesses use Touch-Tone telephones rather than rotary-dial phones because Touch-Tone phones are faster and can be used to communicate with computers.
3. The intercom key on the six-button phones and Call Directors is used to speak with other people in the same office.
4. Centrex telephone equipment allows direct inward dialing so that switchboard operators do not have to answer most incoming calls.
5. With a Speakerphone, everyone in the room can hear both sides of a telephone conversation.
6. People who are frequently out of the office use mobile telephones so that they can be reached by phone or place calls while traveling.
7. Conference calls are used when three or more people in different locations want to participate in one conversation.
8. Call forwarding service transfers incoming telephone calls to another phone.
9. Automatic dialing equipment is used by companies in which the same numbers are called frequently.
10. Many companies use station restriction devices and locks to prevent unauthorized use of telephones and to control costs.

DEVELOPING HUMAN RELATIONS SKILLS

1. Your company has just installed a new telephone system. All employees are supposed to attend a seminar to learn how to use the new equipment. There are three seminars scheduled so that each employee can choose a time that is convenient. Helen Ames, your coworker, says she is too busy to attend the seminar. "I have work to do," she tells you, "and that meeting will just be a waste of time — I already know how to dial a phone!"
   - **a.** Make a short list of the things you might learn at the seminar that will be helpful to you.
   - **b.** What problems might Helen create by not attending?
2. As a receptionist for a doctor, you greet all patients and answer all telephone calls. One of the patients, who is waiting to see the doctor, tells you that he has several calls to make. Since he has to wait, he wants to use your phone to make the calls.
   - **a.** What problems might arise if you let the patient use your phone?
   - **b.** What suggestion could you make to the patient?

IMPROVING COMMUNICATION SKILLS

Refer to Appendix A 1.8-1.18.

1. On a separate sheet of paper, write or keyboard the following paragraphs, inserting the necessary commas.
   a. We are happy to announce that our new telephone system which has automatic call waiting and conference calling features will be installed next week. We will be having two training seminars and you should plan to attend one of them. The first seminar will be held on Tuesday January 21 at 9:30 a.m. The second seminar will be held on Thursday January 23 at 2:30 p.m. Call Sandra Yates at Ext. 6214 to register for one of these seminars that will help you develop an efficient professional telephone personality.
   b. I was sitting in my car waiting for a traffic light to turn green and the man in the car next to me was talking on the telephone. I noticed it because I heard someone say "Yes Andy I'll go to the office supply store to pick up the envelopes on my way back to the office." I thought he was talking to me since my name is Andy. I think the man was making effective efficient use of his time.
2. On a separate sheet of paper, write or keyboard the following paragraphs. Add two or three sentences to complete each paragraph.
   a. Communicating by telephone is fast and efficient. People can get the information they need without leaving their homes or offices. I use telephones daily.
   b. Many accessories are available to make telephone communications more efficient. But, you must know how to use the accessories to get the most benefits.

BUILDING PROBLEM-SOLVING SKILLS

1. The consultant you work for charges $40 an hour for calls made for her clients. On a separate sheet of paper, figure the charge to the client for each of the following weekly call totals (for partial hours, round to the nearest quarter hour):
   a. Don Alston, 47 mins.
   b. Cyndi Bates, 38 mins.
   c. Doug Carter, 1 hr. 35 mins.
   d. Tony D'Angelo, 2 hrs. 22 mins.
2. Belk Carpet Cleaning Service is running a telephone campaign to get new customers. The receptionist is calling residents and offering to clean three rooms of carpeting for a low price of $59.95. Mr. Belk would like to know

whether the telephone campaign is working. Study the table listing the calls made during various hours of the day, then answer the questions that follow.

	8:30 – 1:00			1:00 – 5:30		
Day	**Yes**	**No**	**No Answer At Number**	**Yes**	**No**	**No Answer At Number**
Monday	7	10	12	6	12	17
Tuesday	9	11	9	10	7	11
Wednesday	13	8	10	10	9	16
Thursday	6	12	12	11	12	19
Friday	15	7	15	8	7	17

a. What is the total number of calls made for each of the two time periods?

b. Total the number of *yes* answers for the morning hours. What percent is this amount of the total calls for that time period?

c. Total the number of *yes* answers for the afternoon hours. What percent is this amount of the total calls for that time period?

d. What period had the greater number of *no* answers?

Activities 1 and 2 can be done on information processing equipment.

APPLYING OFFICE SKILLS

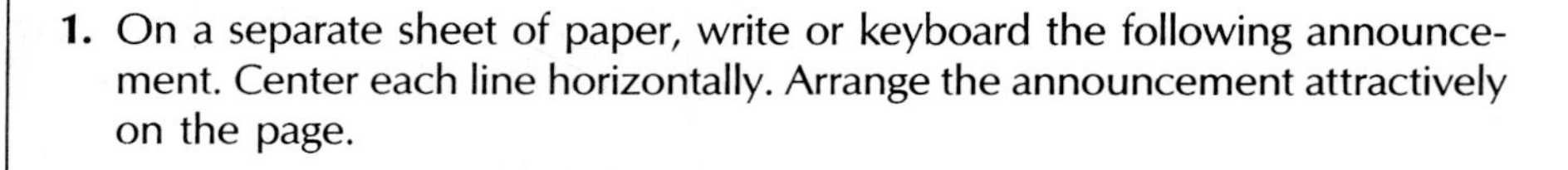

1. On a separate sheet of paper, write or keyboard the following announcement. Center each line horizontally. Arrange the announcement attractively on the page.

   You are invited to attend a
   Seminar on
   Effective Use of Your Telephone
   on Wednesday, April 3, 19 – –
   2:30 to 4:30 p.m.
   in
   The Board Room
   RSVP — 725-8248

2. Design a form that can be used to keep a record of calls made to customers. The form should contain space to record the date, the time the call is placed, the customer's name, the phone number, and the length of the call. Prepare the form on plain or ruled paper.

CHAPTER 4

TELECOMMUNICATION SERVICES

The term *telecommunication* refers to any communication — voice, written, data, or visual — sent by telephone, telegraph, radio, or satellite. In the previous chapters of this unit, you read how the telephone can be a useful and convenient device for voice communication. However, there are times that written messages must be sent or received quickly. In these situations, the telephone alone cannot do the job. Today, communications of any type — voice, written, data, or visual — can be sent very quickly (sometimes in a matter of minutes) by telephone, telegraph, radio, or satellite.

As you study this chapter, you will find answers to the following questions:

- What services are available for sending written messages?
- What are the procedures for preparing and sending written messages?
- What factors must be considered when determining the most economical service for sending written messages?
- What do the following terms mean: **full-rate telegram, overnight telegram, mailgram, cable, electronic mail, TWX and Telex, facsimile, text editor, communication satellites?**

TELEGRAMS

You can send written messages quickly to any location in the world through the services of Western Union. Western Union sends messages over telephone lines to the Western Union office nearest the receiver. Messages are usually delivered by telephone, or, for an extra fee, by messenger. Telegrams are used when it is important that a written message be received quickly.

de·liv'ered

Types of Telegrams

There are two types of regular telegrams that can be sent within the United States: the full-rate telegram and the overnight telegram. The type of telegram used will depend on the speed with which the telegram needs to be delivered. If the message is lengthy and does not need to be delivered until the next day, it is more economical to send a mailgram. To transmit a message to a foreign country, an international telegram can be sent.

Full-rate telegrams The **full-rate telegram** is the faster of the two classes of service. A full-rate telegram message is delivered by telephone within two hours (or by messenger within five hours) of its arrival at the Western Union office nearest the receiver. Telegrams sent to businesses are usually delivered during normal business hours. The charge for a full-rate telegram is based on a message of 10 words or less. An extra charge is made for each additional word. Rates are based on the number of words in the message. Words in the address and signature are transmitted free.

trans·mit'ted

Illustration 5–13
Telegram

western union — Telegram

MSG. NO	NO. WDS. CL. OF SVC.	PD.—COLL.	CASH NO.	ACCOUNTING INFORMATION	DATE	FILING TIME	SENT TIME
					May 3, 19--	A.M. P.M.	A.M. P.M.

Send the following message, subject to the terms on back hereof, which are hereby agreed to.

☐ OVERNIGHT TELEGRAM
UNLESS BOX ABOVE IS CHECKED THIS MESSAGE WILL BE SENT AS A TELEGRAM

CARE OF OR APT. NO.

TO Ms. Beverly Watson
ADDRESS & TELEPHONE NO. 207 Halsey Drive (504) 835-2789
CITY — STATE & ZIP CODE New Orleans, LA 71201

Proposal approved for $15,000. Begin immediately.
Call if information needed.

SENDER'S TEL. NO. (803) 976-6074 NAME & ADDRESS Marie Tyson, 219 Lake Drive, Columbia, SC 29209

OFFICE USE ONLY
EOM ((BILL TO) / (ADDRESS) / (CITY - STATE - ZIP) / (CHG. METH.) /
(CHG.#) / (OPR.#) / (HF) / (PC CODE) / (PC AMT.) / (GIFT AMT.) / (TAX) / (AGT. I.D.) / (SG)). X-OFF

W.U. 5210 (6/77)

Overnight telegrams Anytime before midnight, you can request that a message be sent by an **overnight telegram**. The message is transmitted during the night and delivered before 2:00 P.M. the next day. Because the message is sent during a slack period rather than immediately, the overnight telegram is less expensive than a full-rate telegram. The charge for an overnight telegram is based on a message of 10 words or less. There is an extra charge for each additional word. As with the full-rate telegram, the address and signature are transmitted free.

When selecting the type of service for a telegraphic message, you should consider time zone differences. If sent full-rate, a message sent at 5:00 P.M. from New York to California should arrive before businesses close for the day. However, a message sent from Los Angeles at 5:00 P.M. would reach New York after business hours. In the first case it would be wise to use a full-rate telegram; in the last case, it would be efficient to send an overnight telegram.

Mailgrams Many business messages cannot be condensed, or shortened, into the 10-word minimum of a full-rate or overnight telegram. You can use a

Illustration 5-14
Mailgram

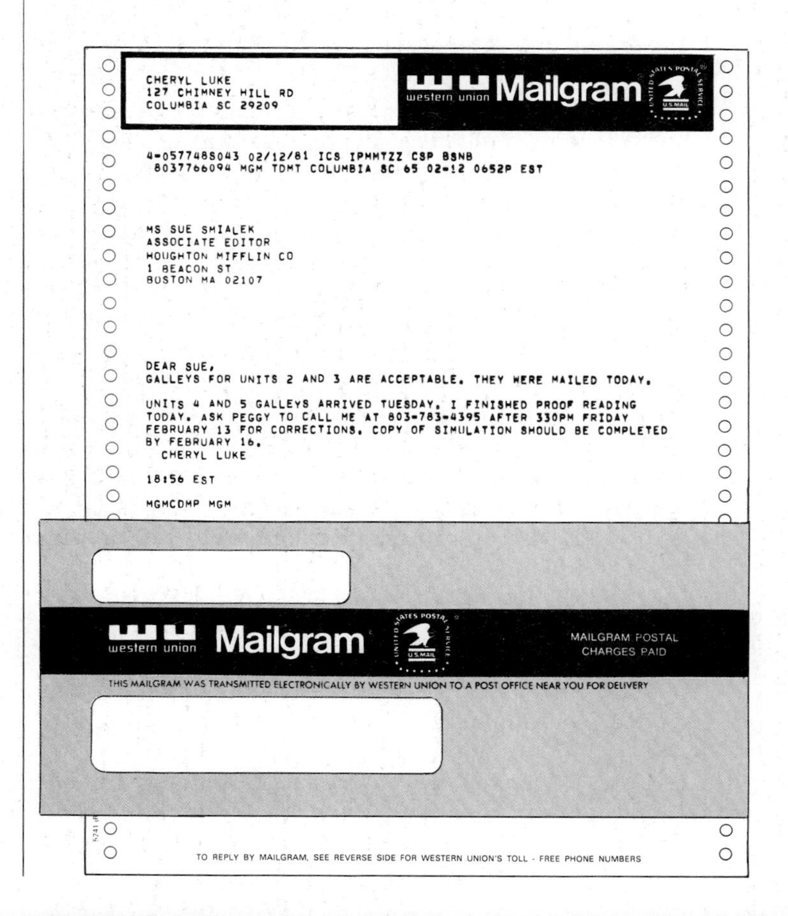
CHERYL LUKE
127 CHIMNEY HILL RD
COLUMBIA SC 29209

western union Mailgram

4-0577485043 02/12/81 ICS IPMMTZZ CSP BSNB
8037766094 MGM TDMT COLUMBIA SC 65 02-12 0652P EST

MS SUE SMIALEK
ASSOCIATE EDITOR
HOUGHTON MIFFLIN CO
1 BEACON ST
BOSTON MA 02107

DEAR SUE,
GALLEYS FOR UNITS 2 AND 3 ARE ACCEPTABLE. THEY WERE MAILED TODAY.

UNITS 4 AND 5 GALLEYS ARRIVED TUESDAY. I FINISHED PROOF READING TODAY. ASK PEGGY TO CALL ME AT 803-783-4395 AFTER 330PM FRIDAY FEBRUARY 13 FOR CORRECTIONS. COPY OF SIMULATION SHOULD BE COMPLETED BY FEBRUARY 16.
CHERYL LUKE

18:56 EST

MGMCOMP MGM

western union Mailgram

MAILGRAM POSTAL CHARGES PAID

THIS MAILGRAM WAS TRANSMITTED ELECTRONICALLY BY WESTERN UNION TO A POST OFFICE NEAR YOU FOR DELIVERY

TO REPLY BY MAILGRAM, SEE REVERSE SIDE FOR WESTERN UNION'S TOLL - FREE PHONE NUMBERS

mailgram to send these longer messages. Mailgram charges are based on groups of 50 words. There is one rate for the first 50 words and an extra charge for each additional group of 50 words or less.

A mailgram combines the features of a letter and a telegram. The message is transmitted by Western Union to the post office. Throughout the day, postal employees insert the mailgrams in envelopes and deliver them with the regular mail. Mailgrams are guaranteed delivery the following day within the continental United States.

Mailgrams are popular because they are faster than the postal service for ordinary letters, yet they are less expensive than telegrams. For example, the charge for the first 50 words is $8.75, but it only costs $2.75 for each additional group of 50 words. So, you can use a more conversational tone in messages sent by mailgram. Mailgrams can be paid for just like telegrams. And, like telegrams, mailgrams can be sent by phone. Just have the operator read the message back to you to be sure it is correct.

Many companies send form letters by mailgram. You simply give the Western Union operator the message you want sent to various people and provide their names and addresses. Western Union stores the message in its computers. Your company's mailing list can also be stored for repeated use.

ca'ble·gram

International telegrams Many companies in the United States conduct business with companies in foreign countries. Messages in any language or in code can be sent to foreign countries by cablegram. A **cable** is accepted for immediate transmission. The rate is based on a word count with a minimum charge for 7 words or less. There is an extra charge for each additional word. If you send many international messages, you should have a chart of time zones for the world so that you can choose the most appropriate service.

sig'na·ture

Because international telegrams are more expensive than domestic telegrams, many companies send messages in code. One code word may replace a common phrase that would ordinarily take several words. In such a coded message, five strokes equal one word. Punctuation marks and symbols are counted as one word. In international telegrams, each word in the address and signature is also counted. For this reason, many large companies have a one-word cable address, which you may have seen included on company letterheads. As you can see, it is important to word international telegrams very carefully to save money.

Sending Telegrams and Cables

When you send a message by telegraphic service, you must select the type of service. You should also consider the length of the message.

tel·e·graph'ic

Preparing the message Telegraphic charges are based on a minimum number of words, with an extra charge for each additional word. Thus, you want the message to be brief. You also want to word the message carefully so that it is clearly understood by the receiver.

Ted Able's supervisor was in Germany for a week-long international sales conference. He had left instructions for Ted to send 1,000 copies of the latest sales brochures by air express as soon as they came back from the printer on Tuesday. However, because of bad weather, the flight was canceled. Ted wanted to let his supervisor know the brochures would arrive a day late so that the sales presentation could be rescheduled. He sent the following message, choosing his words carefully: "Flight canceled. Brochures arrive Wednesday same time."

Keyboarding the telegram If you send telegrams frequently, you should obtain from any Western Union office a pad of telegram blanks like the one shown in Illustration 5–13. Telegram forms are also available in continuous sheets for use on information processing equipment. When keyboarding a telegraphic message, prepare an original and two copies. Send the original to the Western Union office and one copy to the addressee (the person receiving the telegram) so that the message can be verified. Keep one copy for your files. Double space the message and avoid dividing words at the end of lines.

Indicate the method of payment at the top of the form. Also indicate the type of service you want — either full-rate or overnight. The message will be sent full-rate unless you put an *X* in the box indicating overnight telegram. Other necessary information includes the date and the addressee's name, complete address, and telephone number. For delivery, the address should be the number and street address — not a post office box. Finally, include your name (or your company's name) and telephone number. Telegrams can also be prepared on plain paper. Use the telegram form as a guide.

Filing the telegram Delivering a message to Western Union is usually referred to as *filing* a telegram. Telegrams can be filed in person or by telephone. When filing a telegram in person at the Western Union office, complete a telegram form and give it to the operator. If you file a telegram by telephone, you should also complete a form first. You then have all the necessary information when the Western Union operator asks for it. You also have a copy for your files. If you do not have a local Western Union office, find the toll-free number in the White Pages of your telephone directory under *Western Union.*

If your company sends telegrams frequently, you may use a tie line. A tie line is a telephone that is connected directly to Western Union. Some companies are connected to Western Union by teletypewriter. This special machine, which is similar to a typewriter, is used to send telegraphic messages. As the message is keyboarded, it is recorded at Western Union on its teletypewriter.

Methods of Payment

You can pay for telegraphic services in several ways. Businesses that send telegrams frequently may have a charge account with Western Union. At the

Illustration 5–15
Telegrams can be filed by telephone

end of the month, they receive a bill for all the telegrams sent. Telegraphic charges can also be billed to your monthly telephone bill. Of course, you can pay cash for telegrams when you file them in person at the Western Union office. Telegrams can also be sent collect — just like telephone calls.

Optional Services

Western Union provides special services to its customers to ensure accuracy and to provide evidence that messages are received. You must indicate the special service you want on the telegram form and pay an additional charge.

Repeat back For an additional charge, your message will be sent back to you from the receiving Western Union office so that you can verify that the information is correct. If you should find an error, it can be corrected before the message is delivered to the addressee.

Report delivery Sometimes you need to know when a message is received. For instance, if there is a deadline on a contract offer, your company may want to know whether the message was received before the deadline. If you select report delivery service, Western Union will report to you when the message is delivered.

Alternate delivery Western Union will accept an alternate address for delivery of a telegram. For example, if you send a telegram to Mrs. Stephens at her office and she has already left for the day, the telegram will be delivered to her home.

Western Union Money Orders

re·cip'i·ent

One of the fastest and safest methods of sending money is by telegraphic money order. To send money through Western Union, deliver the money with the name and address of the recipient to the Western Union office. There is one charge for the money order and an additional charge for any message sent with it.

ELECTRONIC MAIL

Telegrams are one method of sending information quickly. But some types of information cannot be sent efficiently by telegram. Companies that need to send and receive information more quickly than is possible through the U.S. Postal Service are now using electronic mail. **Electronic mail** includes messages sent by TWX/Telex, facsimile, communicating text editors, and communication satellite networks.

TWX/Telex

TWX (pronounced *Twix*) **and Telex** are teletypewriter exchange services offered by Western Union. A company that subscribes to TWX/Telex is

Illustration 5–16 Mailgrams and telegrams can be sent using TWX/Telex equipment

provided with a teletypewriter for the office. A teletypewriter has a typewriter-like keyboard with a telephone dial built into the machine. Messages keyboarded on one teletypewriter can be sent to other TWX/Telex subscribers. Just as each telephone has a number of its own, each TWX and Telex location has a number.

To send a message, the TWX/Telex operator signals the Western Union equipment, gives the number of the destination TWX/Telex equipment, and keyboards the message. Both mailgrams and telegrams can be sent from TWX/Telex equipment. Rates are lower when TWX or Telex equipment is used because the subscriber, not Western Union, keyboards the message.

TWX equipment differs from Telex equipment in how it is operated and what it can do. However, as an office worker, you will probably not be called upon to operate this equipment. Your responsibility for telecommunication services will probably be to prepare messages for transmission. Make certain that the message is accurate before giving it to the TWX/Telex operator in your company.

Facsimile

fac·sim'i·le

Facsimile equipment is used to send and receive exact reproductions of pages. Facsimile has been in use for many years to send photographs, graphs, and charts to distant locations. The only equipment a company needs to send facsimile copies is the facsimile machine, a telephone, and an electrical outlet. When a page is inserted into the equipment, a special light transforms the visual image into electronic impulses. These impulses travel through regular telephone lines to the receiving equipment, where they are transformed back into visual images and printed on paper. This process takes less than a minute on the most sophisticated equipment.

so·phis'ti·cat·ed

port'a·ble

Portable facsimile equipment is available so that a person who travels regularly can send information to the office very quickly. The portable unit can be connected to a regular telephone and an electrical outlet anywhere.

Communicating Text Editors

A **text editor** is a typewriter that can store information as it is keyboarded. The stored information is then used to print error-free copies at very high speeds. Text editors can be connected through telephone lines so that information stored in one location can be printed out on a text editor at another location. The cost of sending the message is about the same as for a long-distance telephone call. You will read more about text editors as they relate to information processing systems in Unit 12.

Communication Satellites

sat'el·lites

You have probably seen many television programs that were televised from a foreign country. **Communication satellites** are used to relay programs to your area. Just as television signals can be relayed by satellite, it is now possible to relay keyboarded information to distant locations using these satellites. This form of electronic mail is currently more expensive than other methods.

More companies are beginning to use electronic mail because it is economical, fast, and reliable. Electronic mail also saves a lot of time for busy executives because they do not have to wait for important information.

REVIEWING KEY POINTS

1. Telegrams are used when written messages must be received very quickly.
2. Western Union service includes full-rate telegrams, overnight telegrams, and mailgrams for messages sent within the United States. Messages in any language or in code can be sent to foreign countries by cablegram.
3. A mailgram combines the services of Western Union and the U.S. Postal Service.
4. The cost of messages sent by Western Union is based on the number of words in the message. There is usually a base charge for a minimum number of words.
5. Optional services offered by Western Union include repeat back, report delivery, and alternate delivery.
6. Money can be sent quickly and safely by telegraphic money orders.
7. Electronic mail includes the transmission of messages by TWX/Telex, facsimile, communicating text editor, and communication satellite networks.
8. A teletypewriter is a machine similar to a typewriter that sends and receives messages through telephone lines.

DEVELOPING HUMAN RELATIONS SKILLS

1. When you arrived at your desk this morning, you found an important telegram waiting for your supervisor. The message states that your supervisor should respond before noon. Your supervisor is attending a conference at a local hotel and will not return to the office until after lunch.
   - **a.** What are the possible ways of getting this message to your supervisor?
   - **b.** Which method of contacting your supervisor would be best? Why?
2. Before your supervisor left on vacation on Friday, she gave you two important messages to send right away on the company's Telex equipment.

When you got ready to give the messages to the Telex operator, you found that the equipment was out of order and would not be fixed until Monday.

a. What should you do?

b. What other method of transmitting these messages might you use?

IMPROVING COMMUNICATION SKILLS

Refer to Appendix A 1.8-1.18.

1. On a separate sheet of paper, write or keyboard the body of this letter, adding commas where necessary.

   Thank you Mrs. Cassidy for your letter about the excellent service our service representatives Ms. Sallie Rider Ms. Shannon Lamb and Mr. Terry Verner provided. A copy of the letter has been placed in each of their folders and it will be helpful during their annual performance appraisals.

   On Tuesday June 3 we will begin our new telecommunications training program for office employees. These training programs are designed to acquaint employees with the efficient effective use of the new telecommunications technology. The training programs will be offered at our training center at 1318 Shamrock Street Tallahassee Florida. The enclosed brochure contains more information about the topics covered the length of the program and the costs for participants. We are also planning some innovative programs for the fall and we will be announcing these program topics shortly.

   If I can help you with your telecommunications systems Mrs. Cassidy please call me at 767-0649.

2. On a separate sheet of paper, write or keyboard the following topic sentences. Add a few sentences to each to develop two paragraphs.
   a. Electronic mail is a relatively new method of transmitting information.
   b. Western Union offers some optional services to ensure that messages are transmitted accurately and are received.

BUILDING PROBLEM-SOLVING SKILLS

1. Using the information in the chart below, compute the charges for sending the messages listed at the top of the next page.

Full-Rate Telegram	$8.75	for the first 10 words
	.45	for each additional word
Overnight Telegram	7.95	for the first 10 words
	.30	for each additional word
Mailgram	8.75	for the first 50 words
	2.75	for each additional group of 50 words or less

a. a full-rate telegram containing 18 words
b. an overnight telegram containing 73 words
c. a full-rate telegram containing 9 words
d. a mailgram containing 162 words
e. an overnight telegram containing 87 words
f. a mailgram containing 73 words

2. You work for Harris & Son, a marketing research firm, in St. Louis, Missouri. Your supervisor asks you to answer several questions by analyzing the chart of messages and replies that is shown below. Refer to the map of time zones that appears in Illustration 5-6 if necessary. Write your answers on a separate sheet of paper.
   a. How long did it take each message to reach each area office?
   b. How long did it take for each reply to reach St. Louis?
   c. Which area office recorded the shortest time between receiving a message and sending a reply?
   d. Which area office recorded the longest time between receiving a message and sending a reply?

MESSAGE				REPLY		
Date	Time Sent	Time Received	Area Office	Date	Time Sent	Time Received
3/12	9:45	11:05	Princeton, NJ	3/12	1:20	12:45
3/12	9:50	10:10	New Orleans, LA	3/12	2:30	2:46
3/12	2:15	12:30	San Jose, CA	3/12	2:10	4:45
3/12	2:45	2:00	Denver, CO	3/12	2:30	3:50
3/13	1:50	2:05	Houston, TX	3/14	8:45	9:07
3/13	8:30	10:05	Boston, MA	3/13	1:30	12:45
3/13	4:40	3:10	Sacramento, CA	3/15	8:45	10:58

Activities 1 and 2 can be done on information processing equipment.

APPLYING OFFICE SKILLS

1. Your supervisor, Helen Gibbs, asks you to type or keyboard the following messages. Use the telegram forms provided in your workbook or plain paper. Your office telephone number is (408) 442-3756. The address is 260 Kern Street, Salinas, CA 93903.
   a. Send an overnight telegram to: Dr. J. B. Shelton, 209 Main Street, Dixon, TN 37055, (615) 446-6477. The contract for the equipment was accepted. You must now send a certified check for $50,000 before the 15th. Delivery of the equipment is guaranteed by January 30. If you have any questions, call Liz Bee in San Jose, California, at (408) 287-4135.

b. Send a full-rate telegram immediately to: Ms. Liza Waller, Western Business Products, 2150 Menland, NE, Albuquerque, NM 87107, (505) 345-9155. Please plan to attend important conference at Omaha branch office next Thursday at 10 a.m.

2. Your supervisor, Carl Ellsworth, asked you to send the following message as a mailgram to the two people shown. Write or keyboard the message on plain paper for the Telex operator to send. Also copy the names and addresses for the messages.

Dear ____________,

Please plan to be in your office for a conference call at 3 p.m. (CST) on Wednesday, October 1. Be prepared to discuss the proposed advertising campaign.

If you cannot be in your office, send me the telephone number where you can be reached at that time.

Sincerely, CE

Mrs. Joanne Trotter, Suite 301, Colorado Building, 407 N. Main, Pueblo, CO 81003

Mr. Amos Belk, P. O. Box 372, Jefferson City, MO 65101

3. Your employer, Joanne Trotter, asks you to send an answer to Carl Ellsworth in reply to his mailgram in Activity 2. She wants you to tell Carl that she will not be in her office for his conference call at 3:00 P.M. (CST) on Wednesday, October 1. Her plans for that afternoon have changed. She must attend a meeting out of town. Joanne tells you that she will not be available for another conference call until the following Wednesday, October 8, at 2:30 p.m. (MST). She wants you to ask Carl if this date and time will be all right for him. On a plain sheet of paper, keyboard a rough draft of your answer to Carl.

Saving Time and Money

1. Put tabs on the pages of the telephone directory where the alphabet changes. For example, where the *A* section begins, put a tab marked *A*; where *B* begins, put a *B* tab; and so on through the alphabet. If you arrange the tabs so that they are spread out from the top to the bottom of the page, you will be able to find numbers much more quickly.
2. Make a list of those telephone numbers that you use frequently and tape it to the pull-out shelf on your desk.
3. When referring to your supervisor and other superiors within the company, be sure to use the correct personal title. It makes a better impression on the caller to say "Mr. Tesone is on another line" instead of "Paul is on another line."
4. Always put telephone messages in the same place so that people know where to look for them. If you answer the phone for several people, use a small desk organizer with slots labeled for each person.
5. When you have numerous telephone messages for the same person — for example, if your supervisor has been out of the office for a few days — keyboard all the messages on one sheet and include a summary of how you handled each call.
6. In some offices duplicate copies of telephone messages are kept. You can place a sheet of carbon paper in your telephone message pad or purchase message pads that come with carbon paper.
7. If your supervisor frequently has urgent calls, develop a special code signal on your intercom for emergency calls.
8. When placing telephone calls, plan what you want to say ahead of time. It will save you time and make your call much more efficient.
9. If you have a bad connection or reach the wrong number on a long-distance call, report it to the operator immediately. The charges for the call will be removed from your bill.

ENERGETICS, INC.

As you study *Office Systems and Procedures,* you will complete four office simulations. These simulations will allow you to experience office employment by placing you in a realistic office situation for a brief period of time. In these simulations you will be employed as a temporary office worker for Energetics, Inc., a physical fitness center, located in Lafayette, Louisiana. Office Simulation No. 1 has five jobs that simulate actual jobs performed in an office. An introduction to Office Simulation No. 1 follows.

Office Simulation No. 1

A few weeks ago you answered an ad posted on the school bulletin board for a temporary office worker. The ad was placed by Energetics, Inc., a physical fitness center. Late Friday afternoon the office manager, Kathleen Clay, called to tell you the job was yours.

Energetics, Inc., has a full-time staff of 31 people. On occasion, however, there is need for additional help on a temporary basis. As a temporary worker, you will be called whenever there is a backlog of work or when employees will be out of the office for a few days. Your work schedule will be flexible so that you do not miss school. Ms. Clay told you on Friday that she would probably need you to work during the Christmas and spring vacations. For the time being, you'll be helping out after school.

At this time of year, the company is preparing for the annual Branch Managers' Meeting. There is an increase in the number of telephone orders to be processed, and there are instructor training sessions to be planned. You will be helping by answering the telephone, greeting visitors, scheduling a business trip, and doing routine keyboarding.

When Ms. Clay interviewed you, she told you that she was looking to hire someone who could work independently, use good judgment, and set priorities. "We are still a fairly small company," she said, "and we count on all our employees — even temporary ones — to be able to pitch in and do whatever work needs to be done. I think you'll find temporary work at Energetics, Inc., interesting and challenging."

Turn to pages 115–126 in your *Student Activities* to learn more about the company policies and see what assignments await you your first week at Energetics, Inc.

UNIT 6

MAILING AND SHIPPING PROCEDURES

- Using Postal and Shipping Services
- Processing Incoming Mail
- Processing Outgoing Mail

CHAPTER 1

USING POSTAL AND SHIPPING SERVICES

You may not realize how much you depend on the U.S. Postal Service. Even if you do not send out much mail yourself, you probably take for granted the regular delivery of letters, magazines, bills, checks, or packages to your home or place of work. Prompt, reliable maii service is important to people — especially business people — all over the world.

The U.S. Postal Service is one of the most efficiently operated mail services in the world. The cost of mail service in the United States is lower than that of most other industrialized nations, and the accuracy rate for delivery is one of the highest. In 1970 the Postal Reorganization Act allowed the U.S. Postal service to reorganize in order to improve service, reduce costs, and increase efficiency. Although we may sometimes complain about postal service, we can usually count on prompt delivery of our letters at a reasonable cost.

Since 1970 there have been many changes in postal rates and in the types of services offered. If you handle mail in your job, you will have to keep informed about postal rates and services to ensure prompt delivery of correspondence at the lowest cost.

As you study this chapter, you will find answers to the following questions:

- What mail services does the U.S. Postal Service provide?
- What methods are available to send written messages and to ship goods?
- What do the following terms mean: **domestic mail, first-class mail, second-class mail, third-class mail, fourth-class mail** or **parcel post, priority mail, express mail, special delivery, COD, INTELPOST?**

DOMESTIC MAIL

do·mes'tic

Domestic mail includes all mail sent to addresses within the United States, its territories, and its possessions (such as Puerto Rico); to military post offices (APO and FPO); and to the United Nations.

Classes of Mail

Depending on its content, domestic mail may be classified as first class, second class, third class, or fourth class. The *air mail* classification is no longer used for domestic mail, because all first-class mail that travels more than a few hundred miles is automatically sent by air. The mailing classification of an item determines the cost of sending it and the type of handling it receives.

The rates, or costs, of the various mail classes change periodically. Your local post office can give you a list of the current rates. Generally, first-class rates are the most expensive per ounce.

First-class mail **First-class mail** includes letters, post cards, greeting cards, checks, and bills. There is a minimum charge for all first-class mail weighing up to one ounce. There is an additional charge for each additional ounce or fraction of an ounce. All mail sent first class must weigh less than 12 ounces.

frac'tion

Second-class mail **Second-class mail** includes newspapers, magazines, and other periodicals published regularly. To qualify for second-class rates, newspaper and periodical publishers must file special forms provided by the post office and pay the necessary fees. Items mailed second class must have the notation *Second class* printed on each copy and must be sorted and mailed in bulk lots — that is, in large quantities.

pe·ri·od'i·cals

When a single copy of a newspaper or periodical is mailed by anyone other than the publisher, there is a single-piece rate.

Third-class mail **Third-class mail** includes any item not classified as first-class or second-class mail and weighing less than 16 ounces. (Items weighing 16 ounces or more are sent fourth class.) This mail classification is used for advertising circulars, books, catalogues, seeds, and sample products sent by manufacturers.

Items mailed third class must be marked *Third class.* This notation may be keyboarded, stamped, or written on the front of the envelope or package. Unsealed items do not have to be marked.

The maximum size restrictions for third-class mail weighing less than two ounces are the same restrictions that apply to first-class mail. For nonstandard envelopes (larger than $6\frac{1}{8}$ by $11\frac{1}{2}$ inches) that weigh less than two ounces, there is a surcharge.

re·stric'tions

sur'charge

Fourth-class mail **Fourth-class mail** is also called **parcel post.** It includes all mail that is not covered by first-, second-, or third-class rates. Items sent

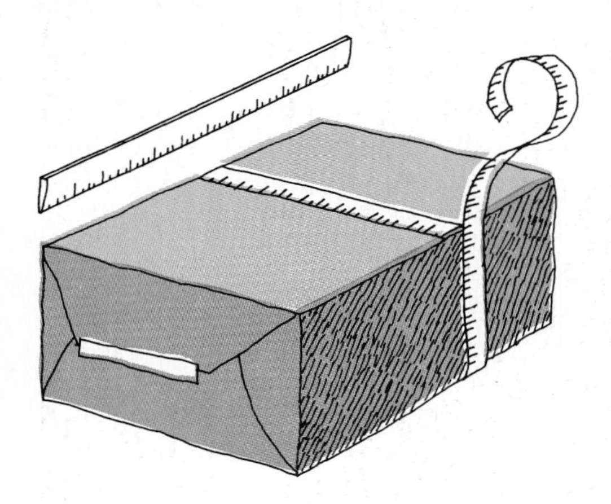

Illustration 6–1
Items sent fourth class cannot exceed 108 inches overall

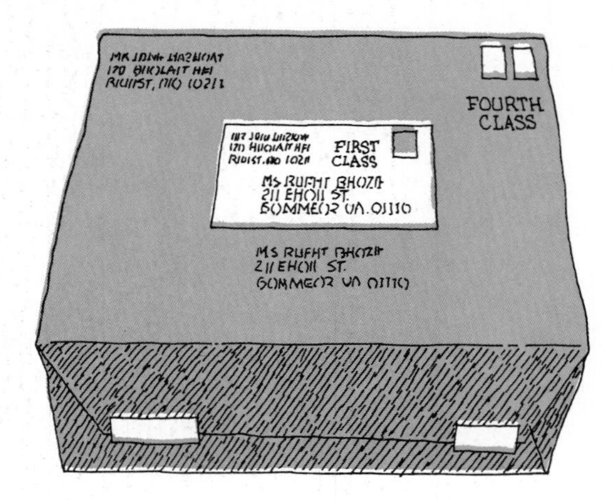

Illustration 6–2
Mailing notation indicates that first-class material is attached

fourth class must weigh between 16 ounces and 70 pounds. There are also size restrictions. Items sent fourth class cannot be larger than 108 inches overall. The size is determined by adding the length to the measurement around the package at its thickest point, as shown in Illustration 6–1.

The post office has standards for packaging fourth-class mail. The item must be packed securely, and the package must be sealed with reinforced tape. Masking tape and cellophane tape are not acceptable for sealing. Packages should *not* be tied with twine or string. These standards were developed to reduce the chances of damage to the content of packages.

When mailing items third or fourth class, you may need to attach or enclose an invoice, letter, or other first-class item. In this case, attach separate postage for the first-class item. Add a mailing notation to the front of the package indicating that first-class material is enclosed or attached.

Rates for fourth-class mail depend on the weight of the item and the distance it is transported. A special fourth-class rate is available for books. *Book rate* is cheaper than regular fourth class, but service is slower.

Special Classifications

The U.S. Postal Service offers other special mailing rates for certain types of mail. These special classifications include priority mail and express mail, which are faster than first-class mail. Reduced rates are available for library materials and materials for the blind.

li'brar·y

Priority mail Any first-class piece of mail that weighs more than 12 ounces is sent **priority mail.** Rates for priority mail are based on the weight of the item and the distance sent. Items marked priority mail are given special handling. This service is faster than regular first class.

guar·an·teed′

Express mail Items sent **express mail** are guaranteed next-day delivery. This special mail service is available only between major cities in the United States. To be sent express mail, items must be received by a post office offering this service by 5:00 P.M. The items will then be delivered by 3:00 P.M. the next day, or they can be picked up at the post office as early as 10 A.M. the next business day. If the item is not delivered on time, the sender receives a refund. Express mail has a basic fee for items weighing up to two pounds. This basic fee includes insurance. For items over two pounds, there are additional charges based on the weight of the package and the distance it is being sent.

de·liv′er·y

Other companies also provide guaranteed overnight delivery service similar to the U.S. Postal Service's Express Mail. Many businesses use these overnight express services to transmit mail that must reach its destination quickly. Most express companies charge a basic fee for items weighing up to two pounds. Additional fees may be charged for items weighing more than two pounds.

Library rate Certain materials sent to or from libraries, schools, and certain nonprofit organizations can be mailed library rate. This lower rate is based on weight. It can be used for books, periodicals, theses, microfilms, music, sound recordings, films, and other library materials.

el′i·gi·ble

Even if you don't work for a library or school, you can use library rate when you send these materials to organizations that are eligible to use the rate. Check with your local post office to see whether this rate applies to an item you are mailing. If the rate applies, seal the item securely and mark it *Library rate.*

Mail for the blind Books of Braille, sound recordings, and related items mailed to or from a blind person may be sent free or at reduced rates. Consult your local post office for more information about this and other special mail classifications.

Special Mail Services

The U.S. Postal Service provides many special services. You should be familiar with these services and know that an additional fee must be paid for each special service requested. Generally, you must go to the post office to purchase these services and fill out the necessary forms.

reg′is·tered

re·ceipt′

Registered mail First-class and priority mail can be registered for maximum security and protection. You must declare the value of the item being registered, because the fee is based on the stated value. Items that should be sent by registered mail include stock certificates, bonds, money, contracts, wills, leases, and valuable business records. The fee for registered mail includes insurance and a receipt for the sender. An item can usually be insured for up to $25,000.

dam′age

Insured mail Items sent first, third, or fourth class can be insured against damage or loss for up to $400. When you insure an item, you are given a receipt. Keep this receipt; you will need it if the item is damaged or lost. In the event of damage or loss, the post office will pay you the value of the item or the amount for which it is insured, whichever is less. For example, if you insure a watch for $75, but it is worth only $50, the post office will pay only $50 if the watch is lost in the mail.

Proof of mailing or delivery There are many situations in which the sender either wants or needs to prove that an item has been mailed. At other times, the sender may need to know whether the addressee has received the item. For example, some legal documents must be mailed or received by a certain date in order to be valid. The post office offers special services at various costs to take care of these situations.

Important items that do not have a dollar value (such as mortgage records) are frequently sent by *certified mail.* Certified mail is not insured, but the sender gets a receipt and the post office keeps a record of delivery.

Illustration 6–3
Certified mail receipt

P 518 498 455

RECEIPT FOR CERTIFIED MAIL

NO INSURANCE COVERAGE PROVIDED—
NOT FOR INTERNATIONAL MAIL

(See Reverse)

Sent to Mr. John T. Hay	
Street and No. 291 Washington St.	
P.O., State and ZIP Code Boston, Ma. 02108	
Postage	$ .15
Certified Fee	.80¢
Special Delivery Fee	
Restricted Delivery Fee	
Return Receipt Showing to whom and Date Delivered	.45¢
Return Receipt Showing to whom, Date, and Address of Delivery	
TOTAL Postage and Fees	$ 1.25
Postmark or Date	APR 23 1985 USPO

PS Form 3800, Feb. 1982

cer·tif'i·cate

A certificate of mailing simply shows that the item was accepted by the post office for mailing. It does not provide proof of delivery.

If it is important to know that the item has been delivered, the sender can request a return receipt. This card is attached to the envelope or package. When the item is delivered, the person accepting it signs the card. The mail carrier then removes the card and mails it to the sender. Return receipts are often used with registered mail, certified mail, or mail insured for more than $15.

Special delivery and special handling **Special delivery** service is available for all classes of mail. Items sent special delivery are given special handling at the destination post office to ensure prompt delivery, even on Sundays and holidays. To be sent special delivery, an item must be mailed to an address within one mile of any post office. The fee for this service is based on weight. When mailing items third or fourth class, you can obtain special handling for an additional charge. Items marked *Special handling* are sent and delivered with the first-class mail.

hol'i·days

COD **COD**, meaning collect on delivery, is used to send merchandise to a purchaser. The purchaser must pay the mail carrier the cost of the merchandise in order to receive it. When sending items COD, you pay a fee in addition to the regular postage. COD and postage fees can be paid by the sender when the item is mailed, or they can be included in the amount to be collected from the purchaser. COD can be used only if the amount due is less than $400. The fee varies with the weight, distance transported, and the amount owed.

INTERNATIONAL MAIL

Today, many companies have offices in foreign countries or do business with foreign companies. If you are responsible for preparing international mail, you should consult your local post office for information about rates, regulations, and types of service.

Rates for mail sent to Canada and Mexico are the same as those for mail sent within the United States. Rates for mail sent to other countries are higher and there are weight limits. Although air mail is no longer a classification for domestic mail service, you can request air mail service for international mail. There is a higher rate for air mail service.

ELECTRONIC MAIL

More and more businesses are using electronic equipment to send letters and other business documents. A message can be sent electronically to another location thousands of miles away in a matter of seconds. For companies that do not have the equipment to transmit messages by electronic mail, some private carriers provide electronic mail service. Western Union's Easy-Link, Federal Express's ZAPMail, and MCI's MCIMail are examples of such service. Mailgram, TWX/Telex, facsimile, communicating text editor, and INTELPOST are all considered methods of sending mail electronically.

INTELPOST

des·ti·na'tion

The U.S. Postal Service, in connection with several foreign countries, offers **INTELPOST** (International Electronic Post). Documents no larger than 8 $\frac{1}{2}$ by 14 inches are delivered to the nearest INTELPOST Service Center. There they are read by facsimile equipment and transmitted via ground lines and international satellite to the destination INTELPOST Service Center. Within a matter of seconds, an image of the document is printed by facsimile at the foreign post office. The document is then placed in an envelope and made available for counter pickup, delivered by Special Delivery, or delivered by regular mail service.

The cost of INTELPOST service is $5.00 per page.

SHIPPING SERVICES

com·bi·na'tion

Businesses rely on shipping services to deliver their products to customers. Railways, trucks, buses, planes, and ships — or a combination of these methods — are used to ship items almost anywhere in the world. Large companies usually have shipping departments that arrange shipping services. On occasion, however, you may have to ship items such as lengthy reports, computer tapes or disks, or visual aids for a sales conference. When you are selecting a method of shipping, consider the speed of delivery, convenience, and cost.

United Parcel Service

United Parcel Service (UPS) transports packages weighing up to 70 pounds and measuring up to 108 inches overall to locations within the United States. The size is measured as for parcel post. UPS rates are based on the weight of the package and the distance sent; rates include insurance up to $100. UPS is very competitive with parcel post in terms of delivery speed and cost. UPS also provides pickup service for an additional fee. For companies that have frequent shipments, this pickup fee can be very reasonable. UPS also provides "next-day air service," which guarantees delivery before 3 P.M. the next day. Rates for this service depend on the weight of the package and the distance it is being sent.

Freight Service

Freight service is used to transport heavy, bulky items in large quantities. Items can be shipped by train, truck, plane, or ship. Freight service is generally less expensive than other methods of shipping. Frequently, two or more types of freight service are combined to provide more efficient and less expensive shipping. For example, trains may transport the items to a river or seaport, where they are transferred to a ship or barge.

Express Service

Express service is used instead of freight service to ship small items. For example, heavy machines are usually shipped by freight service, whereas the parts to repair the machines are shipped by express service.

Express service is also used when items must be delivered promptly. It is faster, more direct, and more expensive than freight service. Express service is available on airlines, bus lines, and railroads.

Air express is one of the fastest methods of transporting packages. In most cases, packages are delivered the next day. When the package you are sending must reach its destination quickly, check with the air express companies as well as with the regular airlines to see what service is available. Rates for air express service vary. Usually, pickup and delivery are provided at no extra cost.

Railway express can be used to ship packages between cities that are served by railroads.

Most bus lines also offer express service. Bus express is used for fast delivery to small towns and areas not served by airports. Because there are frequent and direct bus routes between cities, and because bus terminals are frequently located in business districts, bus express is sometimes faster than air express. Pickup and delivery are usually not available.

When selecting a method of shipping, be sure to compare the parcel post rates. Consider both the cost and the speed of delivery of any service. If prompt delivery is not important, choose a less expensive shipping method.

REVIEWING KEY POINTS

1. Domestic mail includes mail sent to addresses within the United States, to its territories and possessions, to U.S. military post offices, and to the United Nations.
2. There are several classes of mail. Most business correspondence — including letters, magazines, and packages — is sent first, second, third, or fourth class.

3. There are special rates for priority mail, library materials, and materials for the blind.
4. Mail that requires extra protection can be sent registered mail or insured mail.
5. Certified mail service, certificates of mailing, and return receipts are available when proof of mailing or delivery is needed.
6. For faster delivery, items can be sent special delivery. Special handling can be requested for third- and fourth-class mail.
7. When items are sent COD, the addressee must pay for the item when it is delivered.
8. Mail sent to foreign countries is classified as international mail.
9. Electronic mail is becoming more popular because of the speed of delivery. An exact copy of a document can be transmitted thousands of miles in less than a minute.
10. Items can be shipped by railroad, truck, bus, plane, or ship to almost anywhere in the world. Express service is available from most cities.

DEVELOPING HUMAN RELATIONS SKILLS

1. As you are transcribing the morning dictation, you come across a special instruction from your supervisor. She says, "Please send this letter priority mail. It *must* reach our Chicago office tomorrow." You know that sending an item priority mail does not guarantee delivery.
   a. What would you do in this situation?
   b. What steps should you take to ensure that the letter arrives on time?
2. As part of your job, you pick up the mail from the post office in the morning and at lunch. The trip to the post office in the morning requires you to go 2 miles out of your way. At lunch, you must drive $1\frac{1}{2}$ miles round trip. The company pays you for your time, but you are not paid for the use of your car. You think that your company should pay some of the cost of operating the car while you are on business since the cost of gasoline has increased.
   a. When and how would you bring up the subject for discussion with your supervisor?
   b. What would you say?

IMPROVING COMMUNICATION SKILLS

Refer to Appendix A 1.8-1.18.

1. On a separate sheet of paper, write or keyboard the following sentences, inserting commas where needed.
   a. The office manager Janie Hudson began working for the company as a clerk-typist when she was in high school.

b. Improved procedures for example help reduce costs.
c. Today's mail which I put in the basket did not go out.
d. After I finish sorting the incoming mail I will process the outgoing mail.
e. Ms. Jamison clearly stated "Send this Express Mail."
f. "Take it to the post office before 4:30 p.m." she said.
g. Although it was mailed January 3 we did not receive it until January 16.
h. Mail the package which is on my desk before noon.
i. Doug Harrel the company courier delivers the mail at 9:15 a.m.
j. The packages on the other hand are not opened immediately.
k. Electronic mail which is easy to use can save you time and money.
l. Before we could mail the letter several corrections had to be made.
m. The responses that we received yesterday have all been recorded.

2. On a separate sheet of paper, write or keyboard a brief paragraph describing the differences between electronic mail and overnight delivery services such as Express Mail. Discuss differences in delivery and response times, cost, and types of items that can be sent.

BUILDING PROBLEM-SOLVING SKILLS

1. Based on the information in Developing Human Relations, Activity 2, compute the following on a separate sheet of paper. The company agrees to pay you 22 cents per mile. Assume that you work a five-day week, and ignore holidays and vacation time.
   a. How many miles do you travel each day for the company?
   b. How many miles do you travel each year for the company?
   c. How much will the company repay you for one day's travel?
   d. How much will the company repay you for one week's travel?
   e. How much will the company repay you for one month's travel?
2. Your supervisor has asked you to help prepare figures for a proposal to purchase new electronic scales for weighing small packages. Because the scales now being used are not accurate, 10 percent of the packages mailed have postage for one ounce more than they actually weigh. On a separate sheet of paper, answer the following questions.
   a. If the company ships 500 packages a month, how many ounces over the actual weight is the company paying for?
   b. If postage is 12 cents per ounce, how much extra is the company paying for postage each month?
   c. How much money would the company save on postage in one year by having an accurate scale?

Activity 2 can be done on information processing equipment.

APPLYING OFFICE SKILLS

1. Select the most efficient class or service of mail to use for each of the following items. Write or keyboard your answers on a separate sheet of paper.
   - **a.** monthly bills to customers
   - **b.** a two-page letter
   - **c.** a box of books mailed to one of your sales representatives
   - **d.** a pair of glasses worth $95
   - **e.** sales catalogues weighing 2.3 ounces each
   - **f.** stock certificates worth $8,000
2. Your supervisor, Marcia Glenn, gives you the following memo. Correct the errors and check the postal information. Keyboard a copy using the memo form in your workbook or plain paper. Set the left margin 2 spaces after the guide word *SUBJECT*. Set the right margin equal to the left margin. Leave 2 spaces between the guide words and the keyboarded information. Triple space after the heading lines. Single space the memo, leaving a double space between the numbered items.

```
To:        All Office Workers

From:      Marcia Glenn

Date:      (Today's)

Subject:   Postal Regulations
```

New guidelines have been developed to transmit company mail efficiently and reduce costs.

(Original typed text before handwritten corrections: "These guidelines will help to transmit our company mail in the most efficient manner and reduce the costs significantly.")

1. Use regular no. 10 envelops whenever possible.

2. Use Express Mail only for urgent company business. Remember that it must reach the post office before 3:00 p.m. if it is to be delivered the next day.

3. Please check the attached mail schedual. The truck leaves for the post office at the times indicated. A messenger will pick up the mail at each department approximately one hour before the truck leaves the office.

4. Please consult the Mial Supervisor, Terry Kinder for help when preparing volume mail.

CHAPTER 2

PROCESSING INCOMING MAIL

If you are waiting for an important document and it does not arrive when you expect it, you may be annoyed and a little inconvenienced. In many businesses, however, delays in the delivery and distribution of mail can hold up the work of many employees and cause deadlines to be missed. For many companies, the morning mail delivery determines the work that will be done that day. Letters may need replies, purchase orders need to be processed, and payments need to be recorded and deposited in the bank.

Efficient procedures for handling incoming mail help all employees in a company do their jobs effectively. The procedures followed vary from one company to another. For instance, if you work for a small company, you may handle the incoming mail as part of your daily tasks. In a large company, on the other hand, all incoming mail may be delivered to the mailroom, where it is opened, sorted, and distributed to the departments. When the mail is delivered to your department, you may be responsible for sorting and screening it for your supervisor. Whatever your responsibilities may be, you need to become familiar with the most efficient ways to handle incoming mail.

As you study this chapter, you will find answers to the following questions:

- What procedures should you follow for handling incoming mail?
- What records should you keep of incoming mail?
- How can you assist your supervisor with incoming mail?
- What do the following terms mean: **routing slips, special services register, screen?**

PERFORMING MAILROOM DUTIES

cor·re·spon′dence

Even in small cities, post offices normally receive mail shipments several times a day. When a shipment arrives, postal employees sort the mail and deliver it to the street addresses shown. Correspondence addressed to a company's post office box is deposited there; it is not delivered to the street address. In this case, the company arranges to have an employee pick up the mail at the post office.

A company that regularly receives a large volume of mail may also send employees to the post office. Usually, there is more than one scheduled pickup daily — first thing in the morning and once or twice later in the day. If only one mail pickup is made, the mail arriving in later shipments just sits at the post office. It is much more efficient to make an extra trip to the post office so that mail can be handled the same day it arrives.

dis·trib′ut·ed

Once the mail arrives — whether delivered or picked up — it is sorted, opened, and distributed. Whether you work in a large or a small company, the mailroom procedures are basically the same.

Initial Sorting

Before opening a single envelope, you should check for items delivered to the wrong address. These items should be returned to the post office promptly.

You should also quickly look for items that require special handling. Mailgrams, certified mail, registered mail, and items sent special delivery should be delivered to the addresses immediately. Mail addressed to a department or an individual is put aside, unopened, for delivery. Mail that should not be opened includes any item marked *personal* or *confidential.*

Opening the Mail

Much of the mail that companies receive is addressed to the company, not to a particular individual or department. In order to deliver such correspondence to the proper person, you must open the letter and read it.

You can easily open letters by hand using a letter opener. Insert the letter opener under the flap and quickly slice through the top fold of the envelope. It is usually faster if you take several envelopes in your hand at once and open them one after another.

Opening envelopes is even easier with an electric mail opener. The mail opener cuts a very narrow strip off the edge of the envelope. With some models, you must feed the envelopes in by hand, one at a time. Other models are automatic, so you simply place a stack of unopened envelopes in the bin and they are fed in automatically.

When opening mail, either by hand or with an electric letter opener, you can reduce the chance of damage to the contents by rapping the bottom edge of the envelopes on your desk. The contents will drop to the bottom of the

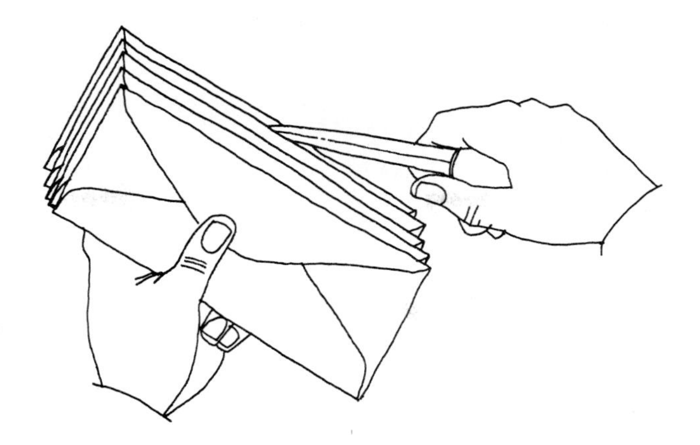

Illustration 6–4
Opening several letters at once

envelope and away from the cutting edge of the letter opener. If you do happen to slice through a letter or enclosure, tape it together neatly with cellophane tape.

Checking for Missing Information

After you have opened all the envelopes addressed to the company, remove the contents and examine them. If there is an enclosure notation on a letter, make sure that the enclosures are there and attach them to the letter. If an enclosure is missing, write a note in the margin of the letter, as shown in Illustration 6–5 on page 220.

If cash, checks, or money orders are received, check to see that the amount enclosed agrees with the amount mentioned in the letter or invoice. Each company has a procedure for handling money received in the mail. You may be asked to write in the margin the amount and date received. In some companies, all checks and money orders are turned over to the cashier or accounting office. In others, you may simply attach the check or money order to the letter or invoice.

Do not throw any envelopes away until you have checked each letter for a signature and return address. If a letter does not contain a signature or a return address, attach the envelope. The return address on the envelope will be needed if the letter requires a response.

post'mark

Finally, check the date on the letter. Generally, you should attach the envelope to the letter if the letter was dated more than two weeks ago. The postmark on the envelope will help the addressee determine whether the letter was delayed by the post office or by the sender. Knowing who caused the delay may be important if legal matters are involved.

Dating and Sorting the Mail

In many companies, incoming mail is stamped with the date and time it is received. This stamp provides a reference in case questions arise later. The

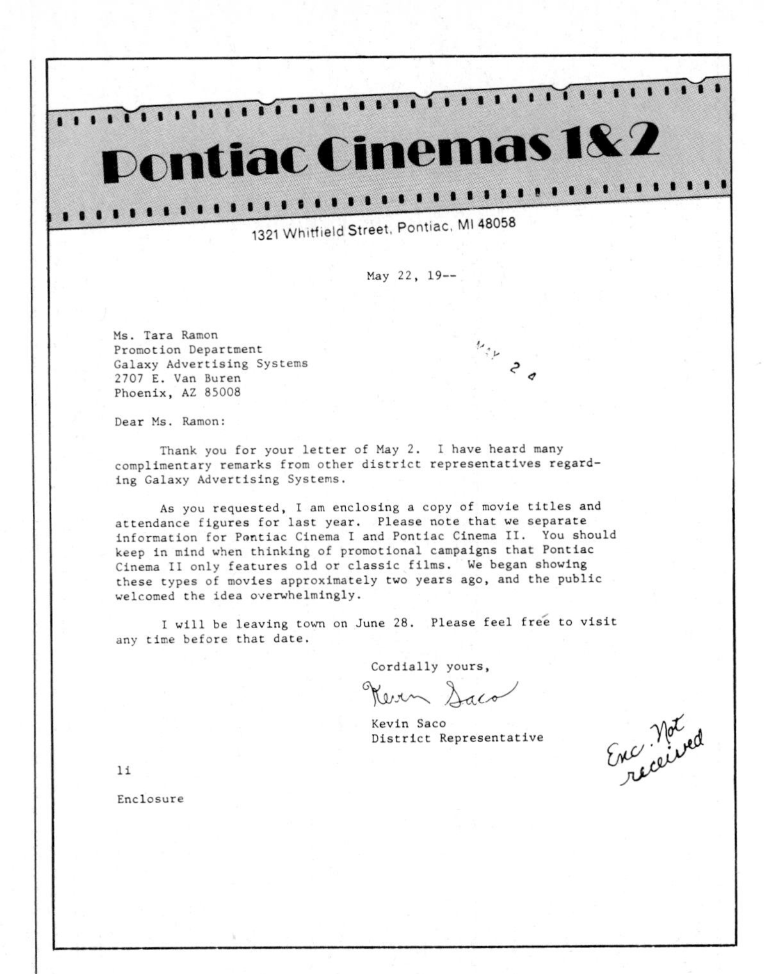

Pontiac Cinemas 1&2

1321 Whitfield Street, Pontiac, MI 48058

May 22, 19--

Ms. Tara Ramon
Promotion Department
Galaxy Advertising Systems
2707 E. Van Buren
Phoenix, AZ 85008

MAY 24

Dear Ms. Ramon:

Thank you for your letter of May 2. I have heard many complimentary remarks from other district representatives regarding Galaxy Advertising Systems.

As you requested, I am enclosing a copy of movie titles and attendance figures for last year. Please note that we separate information for Pontiac Cinema I and Pontiac Cinema II. You should keep in mind when thinking of promotional campaigns that Pontiac Cinema II only features old or classic films. We began showing these types of movies approximately two years ago, and the public welcomed the idea overwhelmingly.

I will be leaving town on June 28. Please feel free to visit any time before that date.

Cordially yours,

Kevin Saco

Kevin Saco
District Representative

Enc. Not received

li

Enclosure

Illustration 6–5
Missing enclosures should be noted in the margin

date and time received may be important if the correspondence relates to financial matters, contracts, or insurance. For example, in some businesses, buyers invite suppliers to submit bids for the services or products the buyer wants to purchase. The bid is an offer to provide the service or product at a stated price. Bids must be received by a set date in order to be considered.

After you have opened the mail and stamped it with the date, you must sort it. Group all the mail for a person or department — including the unopened envelopes addressed to particular employees — in batches. Sorting trays, bins, or racks help you sort mail efficiently. In order to sort the mail, you must determine which employee or department in the company should see each item. For this reason, if you work in the mailroom, you need to know the type of work performed by each department. You also need to be informed of specific job responsibilities of employees. For example, a book publishing company may assign one employee to process all orders for college textbooks, another employee for high school textbooks, and so forth.

By informing the mailroom of these responsibilities, the order department can spend more time filling orders and less time sorting its own mail.

Routing the Mail

As you sort the mail for distribution, you may find an item — such as a letter, magazine, or report — that should be seen by more than one person in the company. For example, a high school student might write to a local community college and request the following: (1) information on admission and an admission form, (2) financial aid information, and (3) a copy of the college catalogue. This letter would need to be routed to the Admissions Office, the Financial Aid Office, and to the Public Information Office.

com·mu'ni·ty

There are at least two ways that a situation like this can be handled in the mailroom. Some companies have **routing slips** with the names (or initials) of employees or departments. (Companies with very few employees may use a rubber stamp for this purpose.) This routing slip is attached to the letter; then, a check mark is written next to the name of each person to whom the item should be routed. When one person finishes with the item, it is sent to the next name on the list.

In other companies, mailroom employees make photocopies of items that may be of interest to more than one person or department. A copy is distributed to each of those people or departments. Although it is more expensive to make photocopies, some companies prefer this method of routing mail because it provides faster delivery.

Illustration 6–6
Routing slip

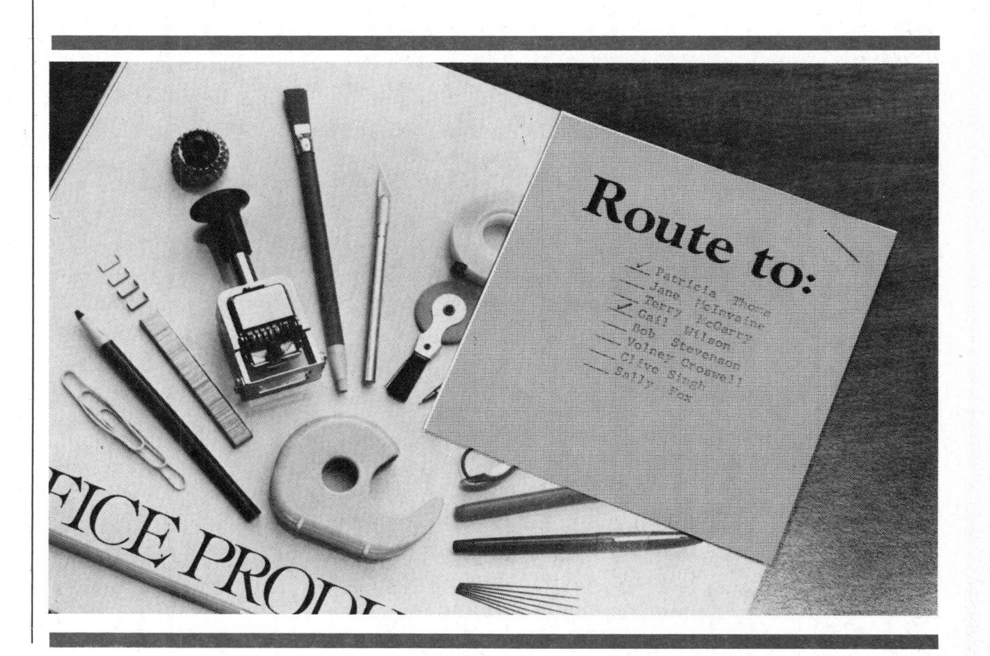

To prevent double copying, indicate on the original and each copy of a letter the names of people and departments receiving copies. This notation reduces confusion and answers questions such as, "I wonder if the accounting department has seen a copy of this letter?"

Distributing the Mail

If your responsibilities include distributing the mail, you should plan your route through the office and arrange the mail in the order of your stops. When you have more than a few items to deliver, use a pouch, basket, or cart to carry them. Wrap a rubber band around each bundle to keep the mail for the various departments separate as you make your rounds.

A recent development in mail distribution is the automatic delivery cart found in some new office buildings. This robot-like cart is designed to follow a chemical trail in the floor. It can be programmed to stop at certain locations so employees can pick up mail being delivered and deposit outgoing mail. Companies using this equipment find that it reduces costs and improves the efficiency of mail handling.

chem'i·cal

Mail delivered by special couriers, such as Federal Express or Express Mail, or by electronic methods such as TWX/Telex should be distributed promptly, just as you would distribute special delivery or registered mail. If you operate the equipment on which electronic mail is received, you must route messages promptly to the appropriate persons or departments. With some of the most sophisticated electronic mail equipment, messages may be directed to individual *electronic mailboxes* and viewed by the receiver on a computer terminal. There is no need for anyone to handle or screen such messages, since they are transmitted directly to the receivers.

KEEPING RECORDS OF INCOMING MAIL

Businesses keep records of incoming mail for later reference. There are several types of records that may be kept, depending on the business. For example, when mail with receipts attached (such as registered mail) is received, the receipt may be removed and filed. Some companies simply record incoming mail with special services (including certified, insured, and special delivery mail) in a mail register. When items requiring special handling are received, they are entered in the **special services register** before being delivered to the addressee.

Another type of register is used to keep a record of expected mail. As you are sorting the mail, you may come across a sentence or comment that indicates other materials are being mailed separately. For example, a first-class letter may arrive telling you that the merchandise you ordered is being shipped parcel post. To help you keep track of the order, you record information about it in the register. When you receive the merchandise, you

Entry Date	Sender	For	Expected Mail		Special Services	
			Sent	Rec'd	Type	Time
10/2	Belmont Studies	Art Dept.	10/3	10/5		
10/8	Council & Craft Assoc.	P. Sagan	10/6	10/9		
10/8	Sarah Foster	B. Dellovo			Express Mail	10:15
10/21	Marker Systems	Production Dept.	10/19	10/22		
11/4	Ralph Holmes	Research Dept.	11/2			
11/5	Colorfax Studios	Art Dept.	11/2	11/6		
11/8	Bender Corp.	Legal Dept.			Registered	2:30
11/9	Marker Systems	Production Dept.	11/8		Express Mail	2:30

Illustration 6–7
Mailroom register for recording incoming mail

record the date. If any items on the register are not received within a reasonable time, you can follow up on them by contacting the sender. These two registers may be combined, as shown in Illustration 6–7.

ASSISTING YOUR SUPERVISOR WITH INCOMING MAIL

Your training in office procedures prepares you for a variety of positions in a business office. Although you may work in mail distribution and perform the duties just described, it is just as likely that handling mail will be only one of the many tasks you perform each day. If this is the case, there are many things you can do to help your supervisor or department attend to incoming mail promptly.

Typically, the mail for your supervisor or department will be delivered to your desk two or more times a day. If your company has only a few mailroom employees, you may have to pick up the sorted mail from the mailroom at specified times.

Opening and Sorting the Mail

When you receive the mail, some of the items will have been opened by mailroom employees during the sorting process. The items addressed to your supervisor or department should still be sealed, however. After checking to be sure that they are not marked *Personal* or *Confidential,* open the envelopes carefully. If by chance you open a piece of personal or confidential mail, seal it with cellophane tape. Then write "Opened by mistake" on the front of the

Illustration 6–8
Sort and process incoming mail promptly

envelope and sign your name. To avoid this mistake, develop the habit of checking each envelope for these special notations. Usually, the word *Personal* or *Confidential* appears below the return address on the envelope.

As you remove the contents from each envelope, check for enclosures and missing information. Attach the enclosures and the envelope, if necessary. You will also need to write or stamp the date on each item. These are the same steps that are performed when items are opened in the mailroom.

Screening the Mail

If you work in an office that receives large volumes of mail, you may be asked to **screen** the mail — that is, to determine quickly the purpose and importance of each item. Your supervisor may not have time to handle each piece of incoming mail personally. By screening, you bring only the most important items to your supervisor's attention. If you find correspondence that can be handled by someone else in the company, you route it to that person. And if you come across items that *you* can take care of, you handle them yourself.

For example, suppose one of the items addressed to your supervisor is a request for information about the company's return policy. If this is a frequent request, you may have developed a form reply, which you can prepare and mail yourself. If you find a request for merchandise display information, you can route the request directly to the marketing department. Suppose, however, that you come across a letter inviting your supervisor to

cal'en·dar

speak at a local Chamber of Commerce meeting. Only your supervisor can handle the response to this letter. You can assist, though, by first checking the calendar to see whether your supervisor is free at that time. You might circle the meeting date and time on the letter and then, in the margin, write, "No appointments scheduled" or "Calendar clear for this date."

Another way to assist with the mail is to underline or highlight parts of letters that require your supervisor to respond or take action. Or, when you think your supervisor may need additional information in order to take action on a letter, you can attach related correspondence or other needed information from the files. Most business people will appreciate your helping them use their time more efficiently.

Identifying Priorities

After you have screened the mail, you will have a good idea about the importance of various items. Before giving the mail to your supervisor or placing it in the *in* basket, arrange it in order of importance. Items marked *Personal* or *Confidential* should be placed at the top of the stack, unopened. Next, place any items that require your supervisor's immediate or personal attention. Place less important items — such as newspapers, magazines, and advertising materials — at the bottom of the stack. By arranging the mail in the order of priority, you ensure that your supervisor sees the most important items even on particularly busy days.

If your supervisor likes to keep informed about day-to-day operations, you may want to prepare a folder of the incoming mail that you or other employees have handled. On each item, write what action has been taken: "Copy sent to M. Wyckoff" or "Brochure mailed 6/17." To find out other ways in which you can assist your supervisor with the incoming mail, ask. Your supervisor will appreciate your interest in using time more effectively.

REVIEWING KEY POINTS

1. Before opening the mail, check for mailing notations that indicate that an item needs special attention.
2. Mailgrams, certified mail, registered mail, and items sent special delivery should be delivered to the addresses immediately.
3. Envelopes marked *Personal* or *Confidential* should never be opened by anyone other than the addressee.
4. It is usually faster to open all envelopes at once. As you remove the contents of the envelope, check for enclosures, the signature, the return address, and the date.

5. Incoming mail should be dated when it is received as a reference for the addressee.
6. When two or more people in the company need to see a particular item, attach a routing slip or stamp.
7. Electronic mail or mail received by special carrier should be routed promptly to the appropriate persons or departments.
8. A mail register may be used to record incoming mail that is sent under special services or in a separate package.
9. If you sort the incoming mail for your supervisor or department, arrange the items in order of priority, with the most important items on top.

DEVELOPING HUMAN RELATIONS SKILLS

1. You and two other employees are responsible for sorting and distributing the mail in your office. One of these employees usually disappears from the mailroom when the mail arrives. Several people have complained to your supervisor that it is taking too long for the mail to be delivered. Your supervisor tells you that the situation must improve.
   a. What would you do?
   b. What, if anything, would you say to the employees and your supervisor?
2. As you are sorting your supervisor's mail, you find an item marked *Personal*. Someone in the mailroom has opened it and removed it from the envelope. This has happened several times in the past few weeks.
   a. How would you explain the open letter to your supervisor?
   b. In your opinion, who should contact the mailroom supervisor about this problem — you or your supervisor? Explain your answer.

IMPROVING COMMUNICATION SKILLS

Refer to Appendix A 1.8-1.18.

1. On a separate sheet of paper, write or keyboard the following sentences, inserting commas where necessary.
   a. Although the mail is delivered to the company by 7:30 a.m. the mail does not reach my desk until 9:15.
   b. Ms. Kelly my supervisor allows me to answer routine requests for information.
   c. This assignment much to my surprise makes my job more interesting.
   d. Most of the checks which we receive in the mail are for the correct amount.
   e. Ms. Kelly politely said "You will relieve me of a lot of work by handling the routine requests."
   f. This morning's mail which is in the folder has two mailgrams.

g. Some of the requests I handle for example are for company brochures.
h. Before I answer some requests I ask Ms. Kelly to approve my response.
i. Sally another office worker is going to ask her supervisor to let her handle routine requests.
j. While I am reading the mail for Ms. Kelly I make notations on my calendar so that all deadlines are met.

2. In this morning's mail, you received a request for a brochure about your company's line of computer accessories. The brochure has just been revised, and copies will be delivered to you by the printer next month. On a separate sheet of paper, write or keyboard the first paragraph of a letter responding to this request. In this paragraph, explain that you have received the request and will send a copy of the brochure when it is available.

BUILDING PROBLEM-SOLVING SKILLS

1. On a separate sheet of paper, compute the amount of postage needed to send each of the following items first class. First-class rates are 22 cents for the first ounce and 17 cents for each additional ounce or fraction of an ounce.
   a. a letter weighing 1.75 ounces
   b. a bill weighing .5 ounce
   c. a document weighing 5.5 ounces
   d. a letter weighing 2.3 ounces
   e. a document weighing 10.1 ounces
   f. a greeting card weighing 1 ounce
   g. a letter weighing 3 ounces
   h. a bill weighing .75 ounce
   i. a document weighing 11 ounces
   j. a greeting card weighing 1.8 ounces
2. The private carrier that your company uses is 3 miles from your office. The private carrier charges $3.50 a week for picking up packages from your office. If an employee takes packages to the private carrier's office, the company pays 20 cents a mile for car expenses. A round trip to the private carrier takes 20 minutes. The employee earns $4.50 an hour. On a separate sheet of paper, compute the following:
   a. What are the travel costs to the company each time an employee takes a package to the private carrier?
   b. What is the wage cost to the company each time an employee delivers a package to the private carrier?

c. What is the total cost to the company each time an employee takes a package to the private carrier?

d. If your company uses the private carrier only one day a week, what is the difference in cost between having an employee deliver the packages and having the private carrier pick them up?

e. If the company uses the private carrier two days a week, what is the difference in cost?

Activity 2 can be done on information processing equipment.

APPLYING OFFICE SKILLS

1. Complete the mail register in your workbook for the following pieces of mail. If you do not have a workbook, make your own form.
   a. At 10:30 A.M., April 25, a letter arrived from Ms. Jan Hasden marked *Registered Mail, Return Receipt Requested.* It was addressed to Mr. Roland Johns.
   b. A package insured for $100 addressed to Customer Services from Ann Graves was delivered on April 26 at 4:15 P.M.
   c. A certified letter from Miss Ellen Akin addressed to the Personnel Department was received at 9:30 A.M., April 27.
   d. An express mail letter from Mr. Luke Sharpe addressed to Mrs. Susan Dowis was received on April 27 at 11:45 A.M. It notified Mrs. Dowis that a report was mailed separately on April 26.
   e. A special delivery letter to Ms. Pam Bailey from Riaz Khan was delivered at 9:15 A.M. on April 28.
   f. At 4:45, April 28, a registered letter arrived from Mr. Steve Neel addressed to Mrs. Jerry Sellers.
   g. A letter received April 29 from Mike Sanchez notified Mr. John Robins that a parcel was mailed to him April 25.
   h. A package insured for $75 to Customer Services from Fuji Makoto was received at 11:30 on April 29.
   i. At 3:30, April 29, a certified letter arrived marked *Return Receipt Requested.* It was addressed to Personnel from Bill Taylor.
   j. An insured package addressed to Sam Downing from Debbie Brown was received on April 30 at 8:15 A.M.
2. Prepare a copy of the memorandum that appears on the top of the next page. Keyboard your memorandum on the memo form in your workbook. If you do not have a workbook, use plain paper. To keyboard your memo, set your left margin 2 spaces after the guide word *SUBJECT*. Set your right margin equal to your left margin. Leave 2 spaces between the guide words and the information you are keyboarding. Triple space after the heading

lines. Then single space your memorandum, leaving a double space between the paragraphs.

To:	All Employees
From:	~~Larry~~ *Bruce* Powell, Mail Department Supervisor
Date:	(today's)
Subject:	Personal Mail

It has been called to my attention that some employees receive all of ~~there~~ *their* person~~ne~~*a*l mail at the office. ~~To~~ handl~~e~~*ing* the extra volume of mail requires several hours of work ~~by an employee~~ in the mail department each day. On some days, it means employees must be paid over time.

~~Since~~ *Because* there ~~has been~~ *is* a freeze on hiring new employees, we are looking for ways to reduce costs and still provide prompt, efficient ~~mail~~ *delivery* service for all company mail. In order to do this, we are asking *that* all employees recieve only ~~company~~ business mail at the office.

Your cooperation will enable us to continue to rpovide the same excellent service in the future that has been provided in the ~~passed~~ *past*. We appreciate your help and regret any inconvenience this change may cause you. Change of address post cards have been printed and ~~will be provided~~ *are available* for you in the Mail Department. Please make all *necessary* changes before July 1.

3. After receiving the memo in Activity 2, Dana Boyd and Tim Clay had to send change of address notices to some of their correspondents. Complete the address cards in your workbook with the information given below. If you do not have a workbook, write or keyboard the information on plain paper cut to $5\frac{1}{2} \times 3\frac{1}{4}$ inches. A sample card appears on page 230.
   a. Dana Boyd's home address is 219 Orleans Boulevard, New Orleans, LA 70121. She needs to change her mailing address with each of the following companies:
      - The Gas and Electric Company, P.O. Box 7431, New Orleans, LA 70174
      - Style Magazine, P.O. Box 1394, Cleveland, OH 44120
   b. Tim Clay's home address is 299 Halsey Drive, New Orleans, LA 70123. He needs to notify the following companies of his new mailing address:
      - The Sports Shop, 719 St. Charles Avenue, New Orleans, LA 70130
      - Hinkley's Service Center, 4103 Williams Boulevard, Kenner, LA 70662

Notice of Address Change

Please change my address in your records from:

A & S Associates, Inc.
P. O. Box 10217
New Orleans, LA 70181

to my new address:

Sincerely,

Postage

CHAPTER 3

PROCESSING OUTGOING MAIL

Imagine that you and your coworkers have spent a lot of time and effort preparing a report for an upcoming regional meeting in another city. Then imagine that the report ends up sitting on someone's desk overnight because the proper mailing label wasn't prepared or the report wasn't delivered to the mailroom on time. If the report doesn't arrive at its destination in time for the meeting, then all of your time and work would have been for nothing. No matter how well written or well prepared the report may be, it is of no value if it's not mailed promptly.

Businesses spend millions of dollars each year preparing and processing information. As you can see, the efficient processing of information may be a waste of time if that information does not reach its destination on time. Following efficient procedures for preparing outgoing mail can help ensure that the work you put into preparing letters and reports is not wasted. Even if you are not responsible for mailing documents, you are likely to be involved in at least some of the stages of preparing materials for the mail.

As you study this chapter, you will find answers to the following questions:

- How do you prepare correspondence for the mail?
- How do you process volume mail?
- How can you prepare and maintain mailing lists?
- What do the following terms mean: **Optical Character Recognition (OCR), postage meter, presort first-class mail, bulk mail?**

PREPARING BUSINESS DOCUMENTS FOR THE MAIL

In most offices, the employee who keyboards correspondence is also responsible for having it signed, attaching necessary enclosures, and inserting the items in an envelope for mailing.

Selecting an Envelope

Business envelopes are available in various sizes for almost every need. Most companies use the large (No. 10) envelope for an item that contains five or fewer pages. When mailing items of more than five pages, most companies use a larger envelope — for example, a $6\frac{1}{2}$-by-$9\frac{1}{2}$ manila envelope.

Addressing Mail

op'ti·cal

The use of **Optical Character Recognition (OCR)** equipment — electronic equipment that scans the address on a properly prepared envelope — for sorting enables the post office to process mail almost eight times faster than sorting by hand. In order for OCR equipment to work, however, you must follow the size guidelines for first-class mail discussed earlier in this unit. You must also keyboard the address so that the OCR equipment can read it.

OCR equipment can read information printed within a certain area of an envelope. The rectangular space that OCR equipment can read falls within

Illustration 6–9 Envelopes correctly addressed for OCR sorting

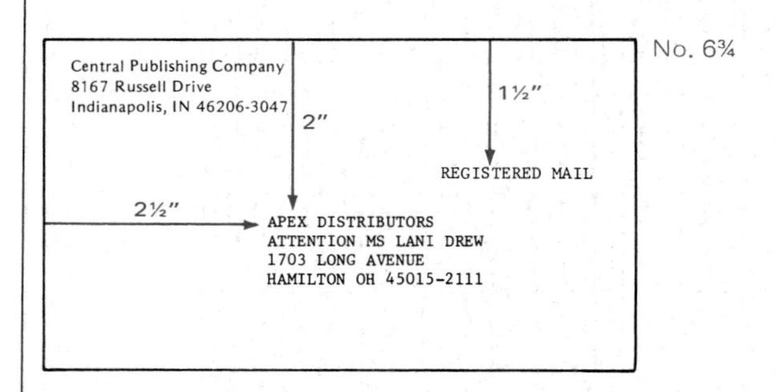

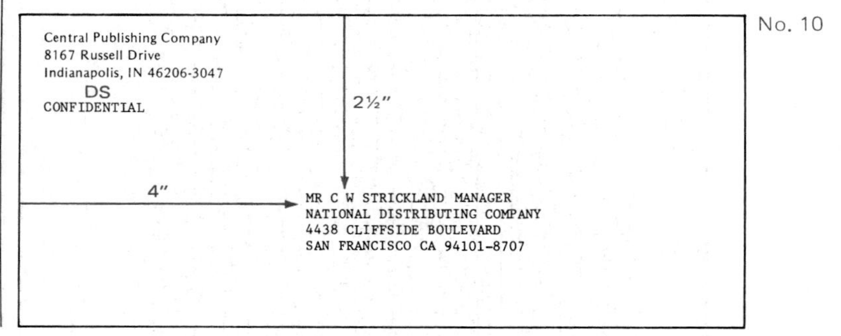

the following boundaries: sides, 1 inch from left and right edges; top, $1\frac{7}{8}$ inches from top edge of envelope; bottom, $\frac{5}{8}$ inch from bottom edge. On a No. 10 envelope, if you begin the address about $2\frac{1}{2}$ inches from the top edge and 4 inches from the left edge, the address will be well balanced in the space that OCR equipment can read. On a No. $6\frac{3}{4}$ envelope, begin about 2 inches from the top edge and $2\frac{1}{2}$ inches from the left edge.

Keyboard the address in all caps without punctuation marks. The last line of the address should contain the city, two-letter state abbreviation, and ZIP Code. Do not put anything below this last line of the address.

Folding Correspondence

After addressing the envelope, fold the correspondence neatly and place it in the envelope.

No. 10 envelope To fold and insert a letter in a No. 10 envelope, follow these steps:

1. Place the letter on the desk face up.
2. Fold the bottom of the letter up about one third of the way.
3. Fold the top of the letter down to within $\frac{1}{2}$ inch of the crease.
4. Put the letter in the envelope, inserting the last crease first.

Illustration 6–10 Folding and inserting a letter in a No. 10 envelope

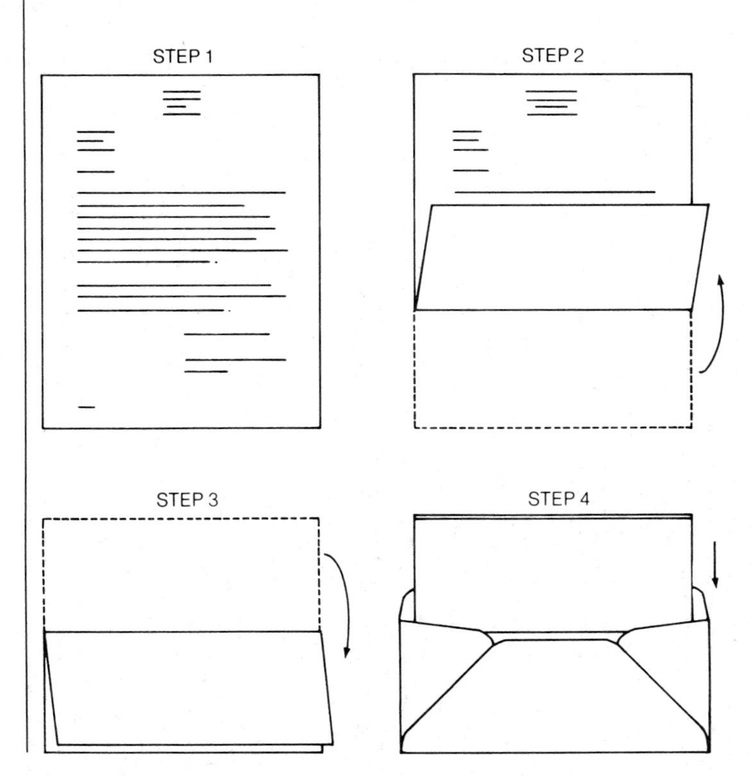

No. $6\frac{3}{4}$ envelope When using a No. $6\frac{3}{4}$ envelope, follow these steps:

1. Place the letter on the desk face up.
2. Fold the bottom of the letter up to within $\frac{1}{2}$ inch of the top edge.
3. Fold from right to left about one third of the way.
4. Fold from left to right to within $\frac{1}{2}$ inch of the right crease.
5. Put the letter in the envelope, inserting the last crease first.

Window envelopes To fold and insert a letter in a window envelope, follow these steps:

1. Place the letter on the desk face down, with the letterhead toward you.
2. Fold the edge away from you down about one third of the way.
3. Fold the edge closest to you up, making sure the address is visible.
4. Put the letter in the envelope, inserting the last crease first.
5. Before sealing the envelope, check to be sure the address is visible in the window.

Enclosures When mailing enclosures, you can either fold them with the letter or insert them into the fold so that they are pulled from the envelope with the letter. Attach small enclosures to the front of the letter. Attach larger enclosures behind the letter.

As you prepare to fold and insert mail in an envelope, check the following:

1. Does the name and address on the envelope match the name and address on the letter?

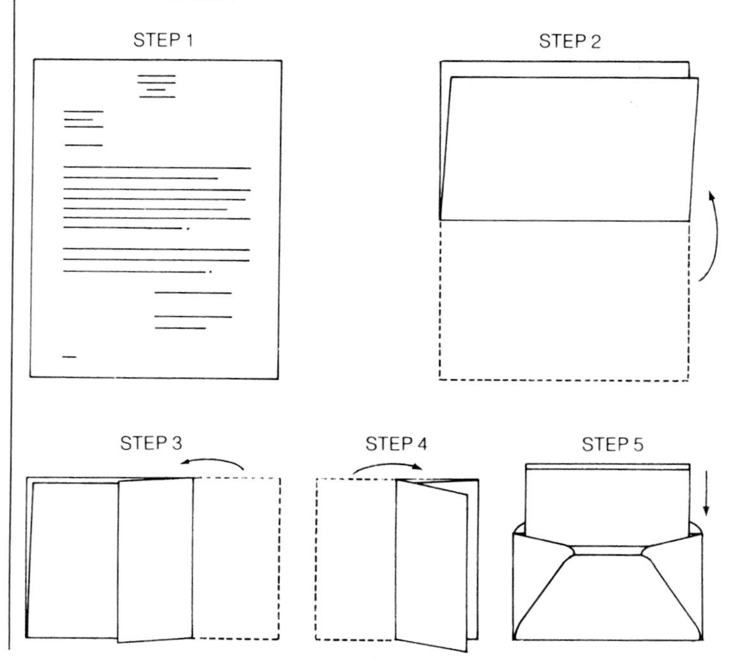

Illustration 6–11 Folding and inserting letter in a No. $6\frac{3}{4}$ envelope

2. If there is an enclosure notation on the bottom of the letter, have the enclosures been prepared?
3. Do special mailing notations appear on both the letter and the envelope?
4. Are special handling instructions such as *Personal* or *Confidential* included below the return address on the envelope?
5. Have envelopes been prepared for people receiving carbon copies of the correspondence?
6. Have envelopes or labels been prepared for any items that are being mailed separately?

Sealing the Mail

pri′va·cy

Mail marked *Personal* or *Confidential* should be sealed as soon as it is inserted in the envelope to ensure its privacy. Other items can be sealed in batches to save time.

mois′ten·er

Some companies use postage meters that seal envelopes and attach postage at the same time. If your company does not have a postage meter, you will have to seal the envelopes by hand. Open the flap on eight to ten envelopes and spread them apart as you can see shown in Illustration 6–13 on the top of the next page. Using a damp sponge or moistener, wet the

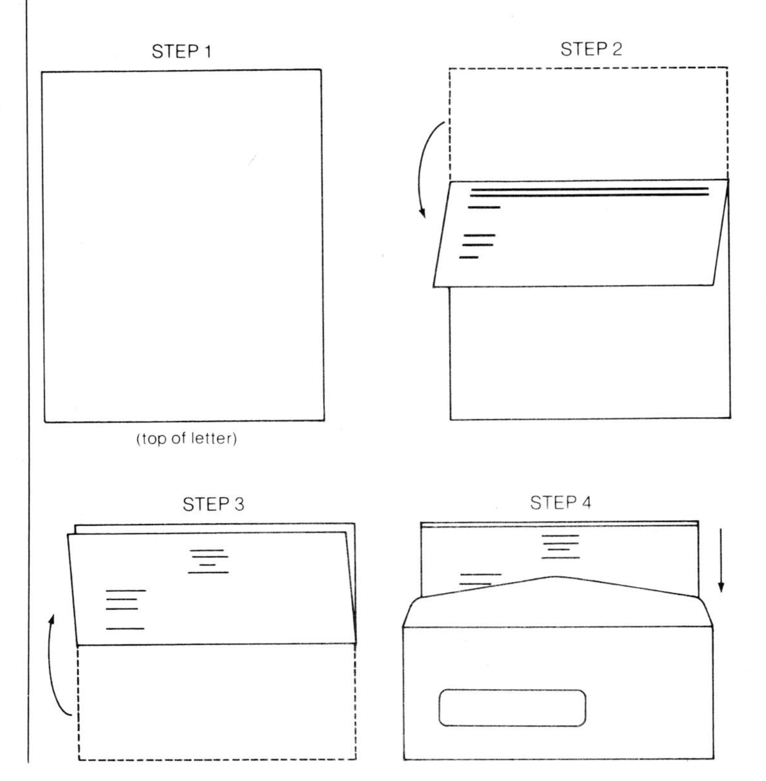

Illustration 6–12 Folding and inserting a letter in a window envelope

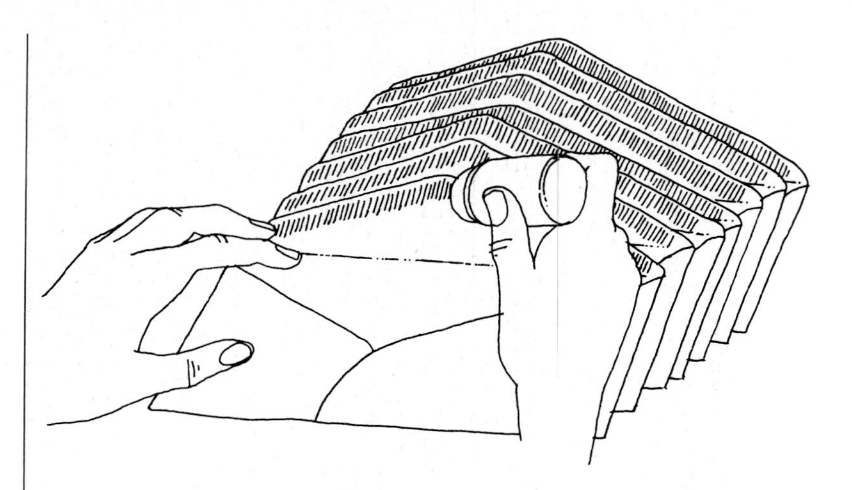

Illustration 6–13
Using a moistener to seal envelopes

gummed edge. Then quickly fold the flap down on each envelope, starting with the envelope closest to you.

Selecting the Class of Service

As you prepare correspondence and other items for the mail, you must select the class of service that is best suited for the contents being mailed. Using the wrong class of service can result in mailing delays or in wasted postage. For this reason, you must be thoroughly familiar with postal rates, services, and regulations.

thor'ough·ly

Unless you mark them for another class, items mailed in No. 10 or No. $6\frac{3}{4}$ envelopes are sent first class. If you want to send an item registered, certified, or priority mail, or with any other special service, you must keyboard a mailing notation on the envelope below the space reserved for the postage. On packages, keyboard or stamp the class of service desired on the label or where it can be seen easily.

re·served'

Weighing the Mail

Because the cost of mailing an item depends on its weight, you should have a postage scale to help you determine how much postage is needed. The scale shows the weight in ounces. Some scales also indicate the amount of postage needed for the weight of the item and class of service. Before weighing the mail, be sure that all enclosures have been inserted. It is also a good idea to have your scale checked periodically to make sure that it is accurate.

Applying Postage

The amount of postage required to mail an item depends on the weight of the item and the class of service desired. You can attach the correct postage with stamps or with an automatic postage meter.

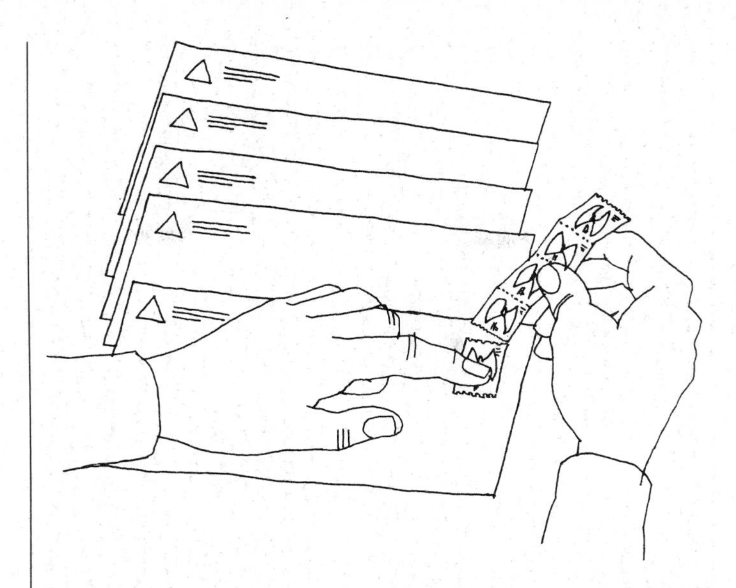

Illustration 6–14 Attaching postage stamps manually

de·nom·i·na'tions

dis·pens'ers

Stamps, envelopes, and post cards The post office sells stamps in books, sheets, or coils. The denominations, or amounts, range from one cent to five dollars. Many office workers prefer to purchase coils of stamps because they can be put in dispensers that moisten the stamps as they are removed.

When you are preparing several items for mailing, you can save time by attaching the stamps to all the envelopes at one time. Arrange eight to ten envelopes with the upper right corners showing, as in Illustration 6–14. Then moisten a strip of the same number of stamps with a damp sponge or moistener. Use one hand to press the stamp to the envelope while you tear the stamp from the strip with the other hand.

The post office also sells envelopes and post cards that are printed with first-class postage. When you purchase these envelopes or post cards in large quantities, the post office will have the company's return address printed on them for a small fee. These envelopes help you get the mail out more quickly.

can'celed

Postage meters Using a postage meter is the most efficient way to put postage on outgoing mail. A **postage meter** prints the postmark and the amount of postage selected on each piece of mail. Because it already has a postmark, metered mail does not have to be canceled once it reaches the post office. Therefore, metered mail is processed more quickly than stamped mail.

Most postage meters seal the envelopes as the postmark is printed. Some postage meters also print an advertising slogan next to the postmark. For large envelopes and packages, the postage is printed on a moistened label, ready to be applied.

Companies purchase postage meters from office supply stores. However, the postage itself is purchased from the post office. The meter is taken to the post office and set for the amount of postage purchased. As each piece of mail is put through the meter, the meter automatically records the amount of

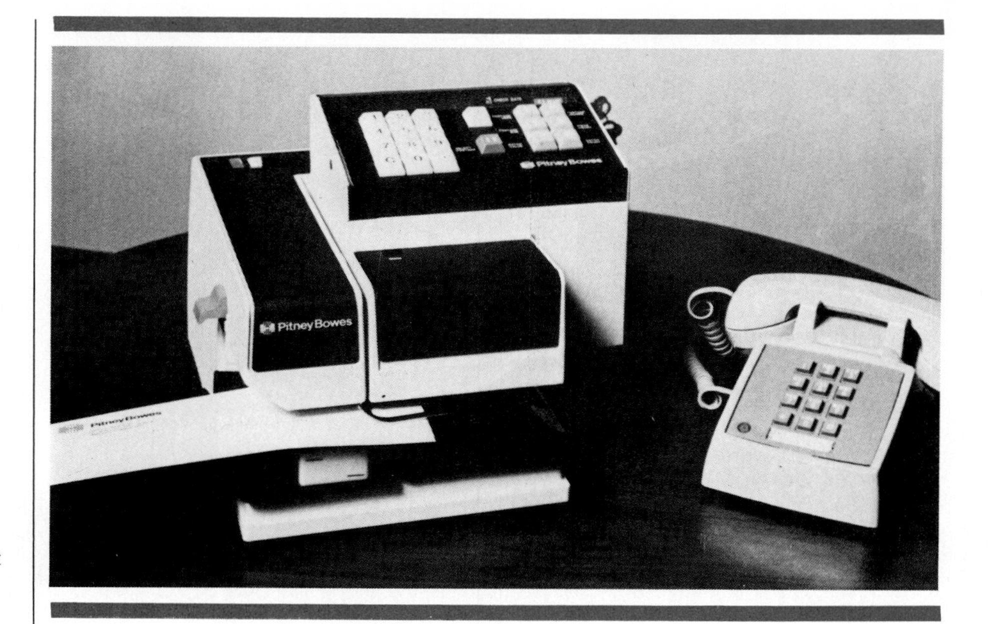

Illustration 6–15
Postage meters print the postmark and postage

postage used, the amount of postage remaining, and the number of pieces processed. When the postage paid for has been used, the meter locks. You return it to the post office to purchase more postage and to have it reset. On a regular basis, check the amount of postage left on the meter. When there is only enough postage for two or three days' mail, have the meter reset to avoid running out of postage at an inconvenient time.

Like many other office functions, this process has been automated. Many companies now use postage-by-phone meters. Through a telephone link with the post office, postage is available on such meters as it is needed. The meter does not have to be returned to the post office to be reset. The postage-by-phone system also provides an accurate record of meter use that allows a company to have better control over postage costs.

PROCESSING VOLUME MAIL

i·den'ti·cal

Many businesses periodically prepare hundreds or thousands of identical pieces of mail to send in a single mailing. For example, a company may send advertisements or merchandise catalogues to its current customers at the beginning of each season. Each month, it will prepare and send bills to its charge account customers. Special mailing lists are often maintained for different types of mailings. Many retail stores, for example, have lists of preferred customers to whom they send notices of special sales. To reduce unnecessary postage and printing expense, these mailing lists must be kept up to date.

Maintaining Mailing Lists

A mailing list contains the names and addresses of people and companies that a business sends information to regularly. Some companies actually have several mailing lists, with addresses divided into categories. For example, a company that sells copiers and duplicating equipment may divide its mailing list into schools, business offices, retail stores, and so forth. The mailing list may be kept on file cards, on address plates for an addressing machine, on address labels, or stored in computer memory.

You may be responsible for keeping your company's mailing list up to date. Customers may move, and you will have to change their addresses or delete their names from the list. New names will be added. The post office will help you maintain an up-to-date mailing list by sending you address corrections for people and companies no longer at the addresses shown on envelopes. To get this service, you must pay a small fee and have *Address correction requested* printed on each item. Also, the post office will supply you with correct ZIP Codes for each address on your mailing list. There is a fee for this service.

Addressing Envelopes

The techniques used for addressing envelopes depend primarily on the way the mailing list is kept.

File cards When the mailing list is kept on file cards, it is easy to add or remove names and keep the list in alphabetical or ZIP Code order. However, you must copy the name and address from each card and keyboard it on an envelope. If you have a fairly small mailing list and only a few mailings a year, you may keyboard each envelope individually.

Keyboarding addresses on long strips of gummed labels is faster. Even though the labels have to be attached to the envelopes by hand, they are easier and faster to prepare than envelopes.

prac'ti·cal

Addressing machines Preparing envelopes or address labels individually is not practical or efficient in many businesses. When there are frequent mailings to a large list of names, it is much faster and more accurate to use an addressing machine. As names are added to the list, a metal or stencil plate is prepared. The plates can be filed in any order and stored in special drawer files. When envelopes are needed, the plates and envelopes are loaded into the addressing machine. It is possible to code the plates so that the machine selects and prints certain categories of plates automatically.

Mailing labels When the names and addresses on a mailing list seldom change, the list can be keyboarded once, then reproduced on a copier each time labels are needed. On some machines, the labels must be cut apart and glued on envelopes. Other machines print on gummed labels.

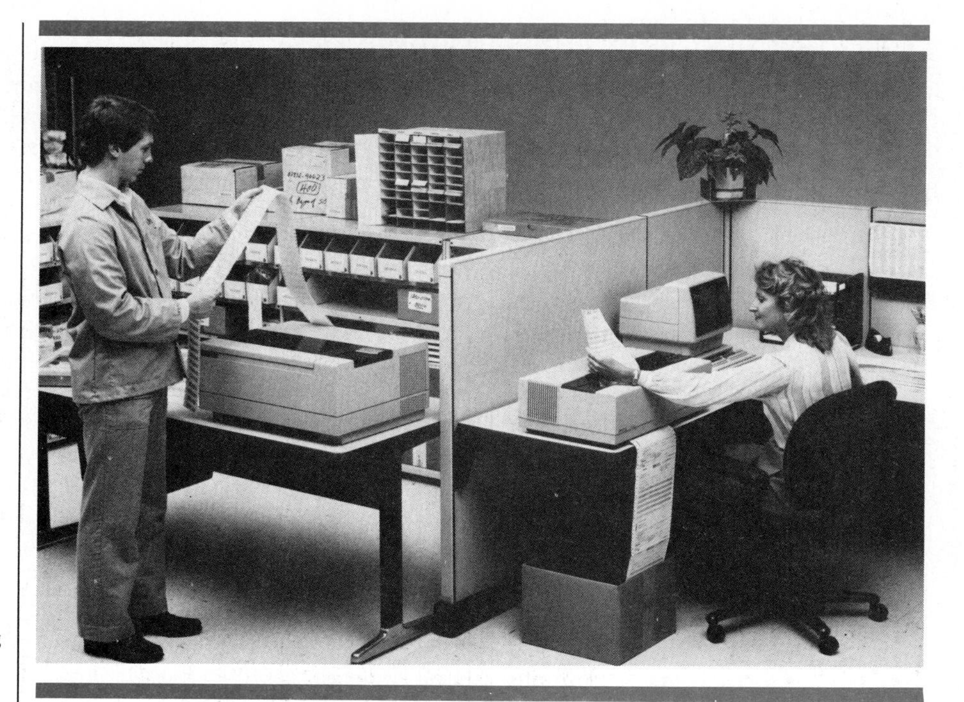

Illustration 6–16 Computerized mailing lists can be updated as needed

Computer mailing lists When names and addresses are stored in a computer, the mailing list can be updated quickly and easily. The computer can print addresses directly on envelopes, as shown in Illustration 6–17, or on address labels. The gummed labels are removed by hand and placed on the envelopes.

Sorting Volume Mail

Businesses that sort their outgoing mail by ZIP Code are eligible for lower postage rates. And, delivery is faster because the post office doesn't have to sort the mail.

pre′sort

Presort first class To be eligible for special rates for **presort first-class mail,** a company must have at least 500 pieces for each mailing and must pay an annual fee. As it is sorted by ZIP Codes, the mail is bundled or placed into trays supplied by the post office. A code sticker is attached to each bundle or tray to identify the destination of the contents. The mail must be delivered to the post office during the hours assigned by the postmaster. For specific information on procedures and regulations for presorted first-class mail, check with your local post office.

Bulk mail When there is a large volume of mail it may be sent as **bulk mail.** For mail to be eligible for bulk rates, you must sort and bundle the

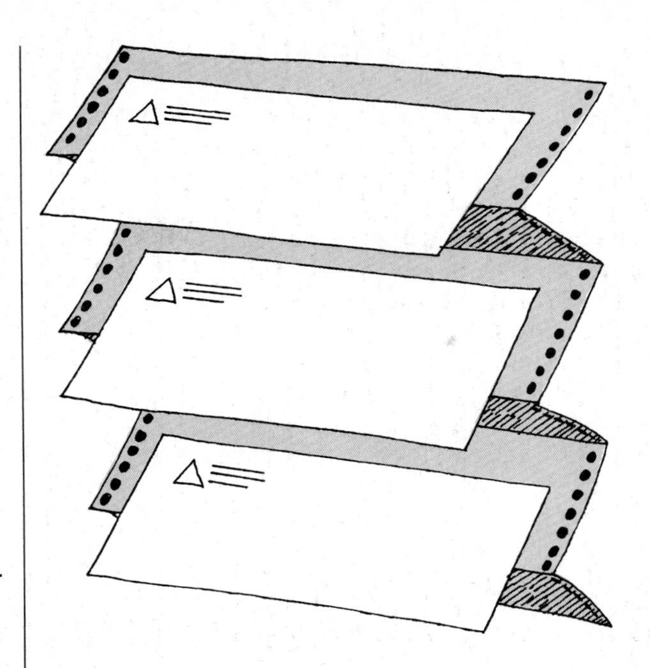

Illustration 6–17 Fanfold envelopes for use with computer mailing lists

envelopes by ZIP Codes. Each bundle must contain a minimum of ten pieces. The bundles are held together by rubber bands provided by the post office.

To save sorting time, permanent mailing lists should be arranged and printed in ZIP Code order. If your envelopes are printed in ZIP Code order — either using an addressing machine or a computer — be careful to keep them sorted as you insert the mail. If you are using address labels, fill the envelopes before attaching the labels. As you attach the labels, bundle the items into ZIP Code groups.

Using Nine-Digit ZIP Codes

Since 1981, some businesses have been using nine-digit ZIP Codes on bulk mail in order to qualify for reduced postal rates. The nine-digit ZIP Codes identify the exact block within a city to which the mail should be delivered. Use of the nine-digit ZIP Codes is voluntary. However, all business and personal correspondence should contain either the five-digit or nine-digit ZIP Code. The correct ZIP Code is necessary for prompt mail delivery. Every office should have a current ZIP Code Directory. These directories are available through the post office and at office supply stores.

vol'un·tar·y

DEPOSITING MAIL AT THE POST OFFICE

Just as the morning delivery of incoming mail is usually the heaviest of the day, so also is the afternoon pickup of outgoing mail. To avoid the delay caused by processing large volumes of mail at the post office, try to mail early in the day.

In most offices, mail is picked up several times during the day and taken to the post office. If mail is not picked up in your office, try to deposit items throughout the day in a nearby mail box. Check the times mail is collected from the box so you can time your deposits with the scheduled collections.

col·lec'tions

When you deposit mail directly at the post office, it is usually handled more quickly. While you are dropping items off at the post office, you can also purchase special services and sign for items requiring a signature. Use your time efficiently by performing several post office errands in one visit. And don't waste time getting to the post office. Remember that many people in your company and other businesses are counting on prompt delivery of letters, checks, and packages.

REVIEWING KEY POINTS

1. To prepare correspondence for the mail, you must have it signed, attach enclosures, fold the correspondence, and insert it in the envelope.
2. The address on an envelope or mailing label should be keyboarded in all capital letters without punctuation marks. The last line of the address should contain the city, two-letter state abbreviation, and the ZIP Code.
3. The class of mail, desired special services, and special handling notations should be indicated clearly on outgoing mail.
4. A postage meter is more efficient than stamps when postage is being applied to a large number of pieces of outgoing mail.
5. Mailing lists should be kept up to date. Mailing lists can be stored on file cards, address plates, mailing labels, or in computer memory.
6. When addresses are keyboarded individually for mailing, keyboarding addresses on strips of gummed labels may be faster than keyboarding each envelope individually.
7. Addressing machines are sometimes used to address large quantities of envelopes quickly and accurately.
8. When mailing lists are stored on a computer, they can be updated easily. Computers can print out the addresses in ZIP Code order or alphabetical order on envelopes or on labels.
9. Special postal rates are available to companies that use the nine-digit ZIP Code.
10. For faster processing, mail should be deposited at the post office or in a mail deposit box periodically throughout the day.

DEVELOPING HUMAN RELATIONS SKILLS

1. While processing the outgoing mail, you notice that an employee has deposited some personal letters and bills in the mail to be metered.
   a. What would you do with the mail?
   b. Would you say something to the supervisor or to the person? What would you say?
2. You are responsible each day for taking the departmental mail to the mail room in time for the last delivery to the post office. For the last two weeks Eric, one of your coworkers, has not had his mail ready for you. Today Eric had so much mail that you would have missed the delivery to the post office if you had waited for his mail. Eric is angry at you because you did not wait for his mail.
   a. What could you do to prevent this problem from happening again?
   b. What would you say to Eric?
   c. How would you explain this problem to your supervisor?

IMPROVING COMMUNICATION SKILLS

Refer to Appendix A 1.8–1.18.

1. On a separate sheet of paper, write or keyboard the following paragraph, inserting commas where necessary.

   The supervisor said "When you have some spare time I'd like all of you to discuss how we can improve our procedures." So after all of the office workers had completed their work Wednesday they held a meeting to discuss mail procedures. Marcie Hoke who had the most experience led the discussion; and Jason Cates who had been working only one week served as recorder of the discussion. The workers decided that beginning Monday December 2 all first-class fourth-class and Express mail would be delivered to the mail room at 11:15 a.m. and 4:30 each day. Any items to be transmitted by electronic methods would be delivered as soon as they were completed. When the supervisor read the notes of the discussion he told Marcie "Marcie you and all of the office workers developed some effective efficient procedures." All of the workers were happy to help because they knew that working efficiently helps their department as well as their company.
2. Suppose your supervisor learned of the problem described in Developing Human Relations Skills, Activity 2. The supervisor asked you to prepare a description of what happened so that the events could be reviewed. On a separate sheet of paper, write or keyboard a paragraph describing the problem and how you would handle it.

BUILDING PROBLEM-SOLVING SKILLS

1. Using the chart shown here, compute the cost of postage for each of the packages listed. Write your answers on a separate sheet of paper.

	Weight in Ounces			
ZONE	Up to 32	33–64	65–96	97–128
1	1.95	3.15	4.35	5.55
2	2.45	3.80	5.15	6.50
3	2.95	4.45	5.95	7.45
4	3.45	5.10	6.75	8.40
5	3.95	5.75	7.55	9.35

   a. a package weighing $2\frac{1}{2}$ pounds going to Zone 3
   b. a package weighing 4 pounds going to Zone 5
   c. a package weighing 7 pounds going to Zone 1
   d. a package weighing $5\frac{1}{4}$ pounds going to Zone 2
   e. a package weighing 1 pound going to Zone 4

2. Your company is considering using regional distribution centers from which to ship orders. Operating costs will be the same, so the main benefits will be reduced shipping costs and faster service to customers. Your supervisor has asked you to find out how much can be saved by using the new regional shipping system. On a separate sheet of paper, compute the savings in each of the following cases.
   a. You currently ship 425 packages to Zone 2 at an average cost of $3.80 per package. When the same shipments are made from the regional shipping center, the average cost per package will be $3.15.
   b. There are 290 packages shipped to Zone 3 at an average cost of $5.95. The average cost from the regional center will be $4.35.
   c. There are 350 packages shipped to Zone 4 at an average cost of $5.10. The average cost from the regional center will be $3.15.
   d. There are 500 packages shipped to Zone 5 at an average cost of $7.55. The average cost from the regional center will be $4.35.

APPLYING OFFICE SKILLS

Activity 2 can be done on information processing equipment.

1. Using OCR format, keyboard these addresses on No. 10 envelopes or on paper cut to $9\frac{1}{2}$ x $4\frac{1}{8}$ inches. Use the correct two-letter state abbreviations.
   a. Drummond and Associates, P.O. Box 11012, Columbia, SC 29201
   b. Davies Insurance Company, 3214 University Avenue, Lafayette, LA 70506

c. Ms. Felicia Hudson, Administrative Assistant, Western Industries, Flagstaff, AZ 86001, Personal

d. Mr. A. L. Grannit, Grannit Office Supplies, P.O. Box 2394, Los Angeles, CA 90053

e. Professional Career Counseling, Attention Ms. Barbara Newsome, P.O. Box 229, Lynden, WA 98036

2. The office manager, Maribeth Cooper, gives you the following draft of a letter. She asks you to correct any errors. Using the arrangement shown here and $1\frac{1}{4}$-inch margins (a 6-inch line), keyboard a final draft of the letter on the letterhead stationery provided in your workbook or on plain paper. When you have completed the letter, fold it for mailing in a No. 10 envelope.

lappin and kubic, inc.

637 Washington Street
Edina, MN 55431

March 21, 19-- ↓ line 16

↓ QS

Jackson Office Equipement, Inc.
P. o. Box 1073
Moutain Home, ID 83648 DS

Ladies and Gentleman DS

On March 10, I ordered a postage metter, model No. 37103A. The price quoted was 125. A postage meter was delivered on March 23, but it was not the model I ordered. (P) When I called your office on March 2 4, I was fold to return the incorrect model via UPS, which I did. The nect day, the correct model was delivered. DS

Today, I received your Invoice No. 2127 for the postage meter. The price listed is $137. Please check your records to see wheather I have been billed for the wrong model. If the invoice is correct, would you send an explaination of the difference between the price quoted on March 10 and your invoice prise of March 30. DS

Sincerely

↓ QS

Maribeth Coper
Office manager

Saving Time and Money

Here are some suggestions that will help you work more efficiently as you are processing the mail.

1. When affixing stamps by hand, fan-fold the stamps at the perforations so that they will tear easily.
2. Hold the envelopes up to the light to make certain that all contents have been removed.
3. Use perforated or hole-punched envelopes for interoffice mail. Then you can see easily that all contents have been removed.
4. To test the accuracy of your postal scale, place nine pennies on it. They should weigh exactly one ounce.
5. When postal rates change, purchase a new rate chart for your scale from an office supply store.
6. Many companies use only one size envelope (No. 10) for all mail.
7. When you have spare time, you can address envelopes or prepare mailing labels for people or companies that you correspond with regularly.
8. When preparing packages for mail, use lightweight filler to cushion the contents. Less weight means lower mailing costs.
9. Do not use special delivery for mail sent to a post office box or a military installation. The mail will not be delivered any sooner and you will be wasting postage.
10. When preparing lengthy reports for mailing, print on both sides of the paper to save on postage.

UNIT 7

BUSINESS CORRESPONDENCE

- Parts and Formats for Correspondence
- Correspondence Writing
- Correspondence Supplies

CHAPTER 1

PARTS AND FORMATS FOR CORRESPONDENCE

Before you even read a letter, you can learn something about the person or company that sent it. The general appearance of the envelope and letter gives you clues about the sender. A well-prepared, smudge-free envelope reveals that the sender is concerned about details and neatness. Good paper quality indicates that the company wants to project a positive image. Proper letter format shows that the sender has taken the time to learn the correct procedures for preparing business correspondence. Attention to such details is a compliment to the reader.

How a letter looks gives the reader the first impression of the sender. When a letter is neatly and correctly prepared, it makes a good impression. In this chapter you will read about the procedures for preparing attractive business documents — letters, envelopes, and memorandums — that the reader will want to read.

As you study this chapter, you will find answers to the following questions:

- What are the parts of a business letter and how are those parts arranged?
- What are the three basic formats used for business letters?
- How do you prepare an envelope using OCR format?
- What is the streamlined format used for written messages sent between employees of the same company?
- What do the following terms mean: **addressee, mixed punctuation, open punctuation, continuation sheets, originator, format, vertical placement, horizontal placement, block format, modified-block format, AMS-Simplified format, OCR format, interoffice memorandum?**

BUSINESS LETTERS

A business letter has many parts, each serving a particular purpose. Each part is keyboarded according to generally accepted rules to save time both in preparing and in reading the letter. Without a widely used method for presenting information, you would have to decide where to put the various parts every time you prepared a letter. And every time you received a letter, you would have to figure out where to begin.

Letter Parts

pro·ce'dure

The parts of a typical business letter are shown in Illustration 7–1. The purpose of each part and the procedure for keyboarding it are discussed in the following pages. Although every business letter does not contain every letter part, it is still important to know when and how to include each part.

Letterhead

sta'tion·er·y

Business letters are usually prepared on letterhead stationery. The letterhead contains the name of the company and the mailing address. It may also include the telephone number, business slogan or logo (a symbol or graphic figure), or the name and title of the sender. The letterhead serves two purposes: (1) it identifies the sender's company, and (2) it tells the reader where to address any replies to the letter.

Business letters prepared on plain paper must include a return address. The return address contains the street address or post office and the city, state, and ZIP Code of the sender.

Date

ref'er·ence

The date serves as a point of reference for the sender and the reader. It tells when the letter was prepared. Placement of the date varies, depending on the the length of the letter and the letter format being used. A chart showing date positions for letters of various lengths is shown in Illustration 7–3. When using plain paper, keyboard the date on the first line immediately below the return address.

Mailing Notation

no·ta'tion

When a special mailing service such as special delivery or registered mail is used, a mailing notation identifying the service is placed in all capital letters a double space below the date. Other notations, such as PERSONAL, CONFIDENTIAL, or PLEASE FORWARD, are sometimes included as a record of special instructions.

Inside Address

ad·dress·ee'

The inside address gives the name and the business title of the **addressee** (the person to whom the letter is being sent); the department name, if appropriate; the company name; the mailing address; and the city, state, and ZIP Code.

An inside address is placed four lines below the date at the left margin. For a pleasing appearance, the lines should be balanced — that is, they should be approximately the same length. To balance the lines of the inside address, you can place the person's name and title on the same line (separated by a comma) or on separate lines.

Mr. Ken Bralley, President
First Westside National Bank
515 Central Avenue West
Great Falls, MI 59401-6632

Miss April Visnic
Personnel Director
Nolte Machine Co.
1001 Camino Avenue
Albuquerque, NM 87107

cour'te·sy

Name and title The first line of the inside address contains the addressee's name and a courtesy or professional title. The most commonly used courtesy titles and correct abbreviations are:

For individuals	Mr. Miss (single) Mrs. (married) Ms. (single or married)
For a physician	Dr.
For a professor	Professor
For the clergy	The Reverend Sister
For a judge, lawyer, or government official	The Honorable

Always use the title that the addressee prefers. This is especially true with *Miss, Mrs., and Ms.* Look at the way a woman has signed her name in previous correspondence with your company to find which title to use. If a woman's title preference is not known, use *Ms.,* which is the acceptable form for a single or a married woman.

Be sure to spell the addressee's name correctly. If you cannot find the correct spelling in your correspondence file, call the person's company to get the correct spelling.

To show courtesy and respect and to speed the delivery of the letter in a company, use the earned titles (such as Vice President or Director) in the inside address. The title may be placed either on the same line as the name (separated by a comma) or on the second line of the inside address.

am'per·sand

Company name The company name is keyboarded in the form preferred by the company. Copy the name exactly as it appears in the company letterhead. If the company uses an ampersand (&) instead of *and* or uses abbreviations for *company* or *corporation,* then you should use them in preparing the inside address (for example, P & W Tool Co. or Audio Electronics Corp.).

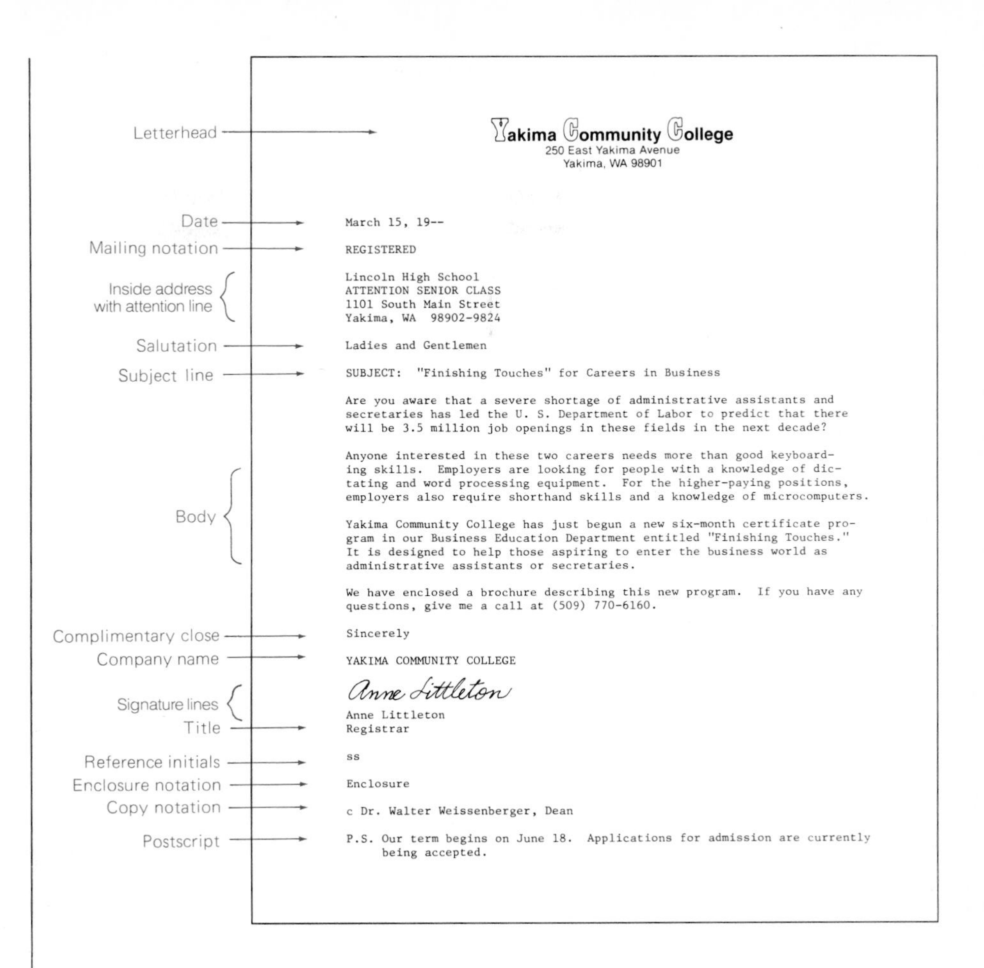

Yakima Community College
250 East Yakima Avenue
Yakima, WA 98901

March 15, 19--

REGISTERED

Lincoln High School
ATTENTION SENIOR CLASS
1101 South Main Street
Yakima, WA 98902-9824

Ladies and Gentlemen

SUBJECT: "Finishing Touches" for Careers in Business

Are you aware that a severe shortage of administrative assistants and secretaries has led the U. S. Department of Labor to predict that there will be 3.5 million job openings in these fields in the next decade?

Anyone interested in these two careers needs more than good keyboarding skills. Employers are looking for people with a knowledge of dictating and word processing equipment. For the higher-paying positions, employers also require shorthand skills and a knowledge of microcomputers.

Yakima Community College has just begun a new six-month certificate program in our Business Education Department entitled "Finishing Touches." It is designed to help those aspiring to enter the business world as administrative assistants or secretaries.

We have enclosed a brochure describing this new program. If you have any questions, give me a call at (509) 770-6160.

Sincerely

YAKIMA COMMUNITY COLLEGE

Anne Littleton

Anne Littleton
Registrar

ss

Enclosure

c Dr. Walter Weissenberger, Dean

P.S. Our term begins on June 18. Applications for admission are currently being accepted.

Illustration 7–1
Parts of a business letter

Mailing address The second line from the bottom of the inside address identifies the location to which the mail is delivered, usually the number and street or the post office box. Other address information — such as room number or building name — is placed after the company name, before the last two lines of the inside address. If an apartment, room, or suite number is part of the address, place it right after the street address, on the same line.

In business letters, spell out words that refer to compass points *(north, south, east, west)* when they are part of the street name (West 42nd Street). Compass points are usually abbreviated when they follow the street address (1141 Amity Avenue, N.W.). Also spell out words such as *Avenue, Boulevard, Street,* and *Lane.* Use figures for numbers that are part of the address, with two exceptions:

1. Spell out the number *one* when it refers to the house or building number.
   7 Poplar Street
   but One Beacon Street

2. Spell out and use the form *first, second,* and so forth for street names numbered through ten.
   1561 North 18th Street
   but 105 West Fourth Street

City, state, and ZIP Code The last line of the inside address contains the city, the two-letter state abbreviation, and the ZIP Code. A list of abbreviations for the United States and Canada is on the last page of this book. Leave two spaces between the state abbreviation and the ZIP Code. When using the 9-digit ZIP-Plus, do not space before or after the hyphen. These guidelines for the inside address also apply to the return address and the envelope address.

Attention Line

An attention line is sometimes used to direct correspondence to a particular person or department within a company. When an attention line is used, the letter is addressed to the company — not to the person or department named in the attention line.

The attention line includes the word *Attention* and the name of the person or department to whom the letter is directed. The attention line is keyboarded in all caps as the second line of the inside or mailing address. Only one space is left between the word *Attention* and the name.

Salutation

cour'te·ous

The salutation is a courteous greeting to the person or persons receiving the letter. It is placed a double space below the inside address. If **mixed punctuation** style is used, the salutation is followed by a colon. If **open punctuation** style is used, there is no punctuation mark.

for·mal'i·ty

The formality of a salutation depends on the relationship between the originator (the person sending the letter) and the reader and on the purpose of the letter. The following salutations are considered acceptable, in order of formal to informal.

Sir	Madam
Dear Sir	Dear Madam
Dear Mr. Garrison	Dear Ms. Egolf
Dear Thomas	Dear Lynn

spe·cif'ic

In writing to a company when you don't know the name of a specific individual, accepted salutations are *Ladies and Gentlemen* and *Dear Sir or Madam.* It is also acceptable to use the department name or person's title in the salutation when you do not know the name of an individual; for example: *Dear Credit Department* or *Dear Credit Manager.*

Use of an attention line does not affect the salutation. The salutation must relate to the first line of the inside address. For example, if the letter is addressed to "The Ace Company" and there is an attention line that reads "ATTENTION MR. ABBOTT," the salutation is not "Dear Mr. Abbott" but "Ladies and Gentlemen."

Subject Line

A subject line identifies the main topic of discussion in the letter. It is used because it (1) helps the writer focus on the main point of the message; (2) alerts the reader to the topic to be discussed; and (3) assists the record clerk in filing the letter.

The subject line is placed a double space below the salutation. The word *subject* is keyboarded in all capital letters, followed by a colon (:) and a short identifying phrase. Each important word in the identification phrase is also capitalized.

Body

The body of the letter is the message. It begins a double space below the salutation or the subject line. Generally, the body is single spaced with double spacing between paragraphs. However, if the message is really short (five lines or less), it can be double spaced. When double spacing is used for the body, you should use a letter format with paragraph indentions, as discussed later in this chapter.

The bodies of some business letters are very long and require an additional page or pages. Even on letters of average length, you may need to use a second page if the letter contains mailing notations, attention lines, and other optional parts. In preparing a letter of more than one page

con·tin·u·a′tion

1. Leave a one-inch margin (six lines) at the bottom of the first page.
2. Use plain bond stationery (called **continuation sheets**) for the second and all other additional pages.
3. If you must divide a paragraph at the end of a page, leave at least two lines of the paragraph at the bottom of that page and carry at least two lines over to the continuation page.
4. Identify the second and other additional pages by keyboarding the name of the addressee, the page number, and the date one inch from the top of each continuation sheet. Use either the spread or the block style shown in Illustration 7–2.
5. Triple space after the heading and continue keyboarding the body of the letter.

Illustration 7–2
Second-page headings

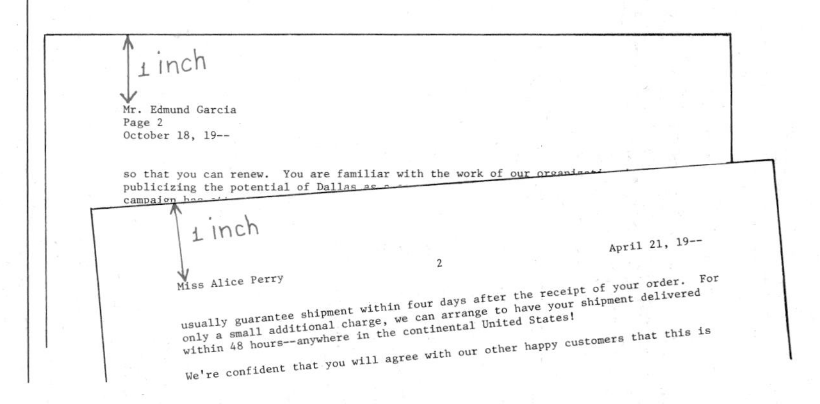

Mr. Edmund Garcia
Page 2
October 18, 19--

so that you can renew. You are familiar with the work of our
publicizing the potential of Dallas

April 21, 19--

2

Miss Alice Perry

usually guarantee shipment within four days after the receipt of your order. For only a small additional charge, we can arrange to have your shipment delivered within 48 hours--anywhere in the continental United States!

We're confident that you will agree with our other happy customers that this is

com·pli·men'ta·ry

Complimentary Close

The complimentary close is a courteous way to end the letter. The complimentary close should match the salutation in tone and formality.

The complimentary close is keyboarded a double space below the body, even with the date. Only the first word is capitalized. In mixed punctuation style, a comma follows the close. In open punctuation, no punctuation mark is used. Some frequently used complimentary closes, arranged from formal to informal, include:

Yours truly
Sincerely yours
Sincerely
Cordially yours

Company Name

Since the company name is usually printed in the letterhead, most companies do not find it necessary to repeat it at the close of a letter. However, some companies do include their names keyboarded in all caps a double space below and even with the closing. Sometimes, the company name is added to a short letter to help create a more balanced appearance on the page.

o·rig'i·na·tor

Signature Lines and Title

The signature in a business letter identifies the **originator** of the letter — the person who wrote it. It is made up of three parts: the written signature, the keyboarded signature, and the keyboarded title.

To allow room for the written signature, the keyboarded signature is placed four or five lines below and even with the complimentary close. The originator's title may be placed on the same line as the keyboarded signature, separated by a comma. Or, it may be placed on the line beneath to achieve balance. Placement of the title depends on the lengths of the items making up the complimentary close and signature. For example:

Sincerely yours

Maury Gormley

Maury Gormley
General Manager

Cordially yours,

Ray Evans

Ray Evans, Manager

mar'i·tal

The personal title of a man (Mr.) or the professional title of a man or woman (Dr., Rev.) does not appear before the keyboarded signature. However, a woman *may* identify her marital status or preference for form of address in either the written or keyboarded signature:

Sincerely yours

Patricia Gagins

Mrs. Patricia Gagins
Accountant

Yours truly

C.B. Cousineau

C.B. Cousineau
President

Every letter must have a written signature. Sometimes the originator has to leave the office before the letter is ready to be signed. In this case, you may be asked to sign the letter. Sign the originator's name in your own handwriting and write your initials next to the signature.

Sincerely

Lorraine Dwyer/hak

Lorraine Dwyer
Administrative Manager

Reference Initials
The person who keyboards the letter places his or her reference initials a double space below the originator's signature and title at the left margin.

Reference initials are usually lower-case letters. You may sometimes see two sets of initials at the bottom of a letter, such as LBJ/jbs or MAS:kh. The first set, usually in all caps and followed by a colon or diagonal, belongs to the originator; the keyboarder's initials follow in lower-case letters.

Enclosure Notation
When an item or items are being enclosed with the letter, an enclosure notation is used. This notation is a reminder to enclose the items before sealing the envelope or sending it to the mailroom. It also alerts the reader to the fact that there are other items enclosed in the envelope.

The enclosure notation is placed a double space below the reference initials at the left margin. There are several accepted forms for enclosure notations; for example:

Enc.

Enclosure

Enclosures 2

Enclosures: Check
Income Statement

Notice when the enclosed items are identified, they are listed in a vertical form. When this form is used, the items can easily be checked off as they are enclosed. The reader can also quickly check to see that the items have been received.

Copy Notation
Most offices keep a copy of each letter in the office files as a record of the correspondence. At times, copies are also sent to people in addition to the addressee. If so, the originator may want the addressee to know the names of the other people receiving copies of the letter. This information is contained in the copy notation. It is placed at the left margin a double space below the enclosure notation or the reference initials. Examples of various copy notations appear at the top of page 256.

c Dr. Beryl Swango	For either a carbon copy or a photocopy
Copy to Miss Ruth Klein	For either a carbon copy or a photocopy
cc Mr. Arnold Forman	For a carbon copy
pc Miss Ruth Klein	For a photocopy

When more than one person is sent copies, it is a good practice to list the names vertically. This vertical form reduces the chance of overlooking a person's name when you mail the copies.

If the originator does not want the addressee to know that a copy of the letter is being sent to another person, a blind copy notation, such as *bc Mr. Webster,* is used. The blind copy notation appears only on the copies of the letter, not on the original. When making a carbon copy, place a small slip of paper in front of the original before keyboarding the notation. The notation must be keyboarded separately on photocopies.

Postscript

Sometimes a postscript is used to add a comment after the letter has been keyboarded or to give special emphasis to a particular point stated in the body. The postscript is placed a double space below the enclosure or copy notation. Keyboard *P.S.* in all caps at the left margin. Do not space between the period and the *S.* However, leave one space between the *S* and the message. Align the second and any other lines of the message beneath the first word of the message.

Letter Appearance

ar·range'ment

The letter's appearance is determined by how long the letter is and how the letter parts are arranged on the page. The arrangement of letter parts according to accepted procedures is called the letter **format**.

When companies select a letter format, they must make decisions about the spacing between letter parts, the placement of the letter on the page, and indentions. The goal is to select a format that will produce a letter that is pleasing to the eye.

Balance

The parts of a business letter should be arranged so that the letter looks as if it has been framed. The length of a business letter determines **vertical placement** — how far down on the page you place certain letter parts. The margins you set determine the **horizontal placement.** Vertical and horizontal placement methods are usually combined for the most pleasing letter appearance.

The length of a letter can be estimated. As you become more experienced, you will be able to estimate the length just by looking at the rough draft or your shorthand notes. Until you develop this ability, however, you should actually count the number of words in the body. (A quick method for estimating is to figure the average number of words per line and multiply it by the number of lines in the body.)

If you know approximately how many words are in a letter, you can use a letter placement chart, as shown in Illustration 7–3, to frame or balance the letter on a page.

Illustration 7–3

LETTER PLACEMENT CHART

Length	Number of Words	Margin Width	10-Pitch Settings	10-Pitch Date Line	12-Pitch Settings	12-Pitch Date Line
Short	Under 100	1 1/4″	12-73	20	15-87	20
Medium	101–200	1 1/4″	12-73	16-14	15-87	18-16
Long	201–300	1 1/4″	12-73	12-10	15-87	14-12

Today, many companies use a standard 6-inch line for all letters. With a standard line length, side margins are the same for all letters, regardless of their length. A balanced appearance is achieved by varying the placement of the date. You can place the date lower on the page for short letters than you do for long letters. Spacing between all other letter parts should not vary.

Letter Formats

Letter format refers to the use of one of several acceptable designs for business letters. There are three basic letter formats used by most businesses: block, modified block, and AMS-Simplified.

Block format In the **block format**, shown in Illustration 7–4 on the next page, all letter parts begin at the left margin. Using the block format saves time because it requires no tabular stops.

Modified-block format In the **modified-block format**, shown in Illustration 7–5, the return address (if letterhead stationery is not used), the date, the complimentary close, and the signature and title lines are keyboarded beginning at the center of the page. (The center of the page is at space 51 for 12-pitch typewriters and space 42 for 10-pitch typewriters. On electronic equipment, center depends on the line length you have set.) All other letter parts begin at the left margin. If you prefer, you can indent the first line of each paragraph five spaces.

AMS-Simplified format The **AMS-Simplified format** was developed by the Administrative Management Society (AMS). This letter format is shown in Illustration 7–6 on page 260.

In the AMS-Simplified format, as in the block format, all letter parts begin at the left margin. However, the salutation and complimentary close

Baron & Dubois

1901 PARADISE ROAD, LAS VEGAS, NEVADA 89104

March 13, 19--

Mr. Joseph E. Rhile
Administrative Assistant
Rowe Medical Center
411 Manchester Avenue
Leesburg, FL 32748-1693

Dear Mr. Rhile:

SUBJECT: Block Format Letter

The block letter format is frequently used in business correspondence.

This format is recommended because all letter parts begin at the left margin. The machine adjustments, then, are simple, saving the keyboard operator's time.

If you compare the cost of the modified block format letter with the cost of the block format, you will find that the block format is less expensive. For that reason, we encourage our keyboard operators who have a choice between these two letter formats--block or modified block--to use the block format.

Thank you for your inquiry.

Sincerely yours,

Marion Ackman

Marion Ackman
Consultant

jks

Illustration 7–4
Block format

are eliminated to reduce keyboarding and proofreading time. Also, the AMS-Simplified format always contains a subject line. The subject line is keyboarded in all caps, with a triple space above and below. The word *subject* is not used in simplified format.

Letter formats compared Each of these formats has qualities that make it popular. Many companies prefer the time-saving features of the block style. Others use the modified-block format because of its attractive appearance. Still others prefer the AMS-Simplified format because it has the advantage of being the least expensive format. It also contains a subject line, a feature that a great many business people like.

The format that you use depends on your company's policy or supervisor's preference. When you begin a new job, be sure you find out and use the preferred format. Always check the company's procedures manual or correspondence files and study the examples you find there.

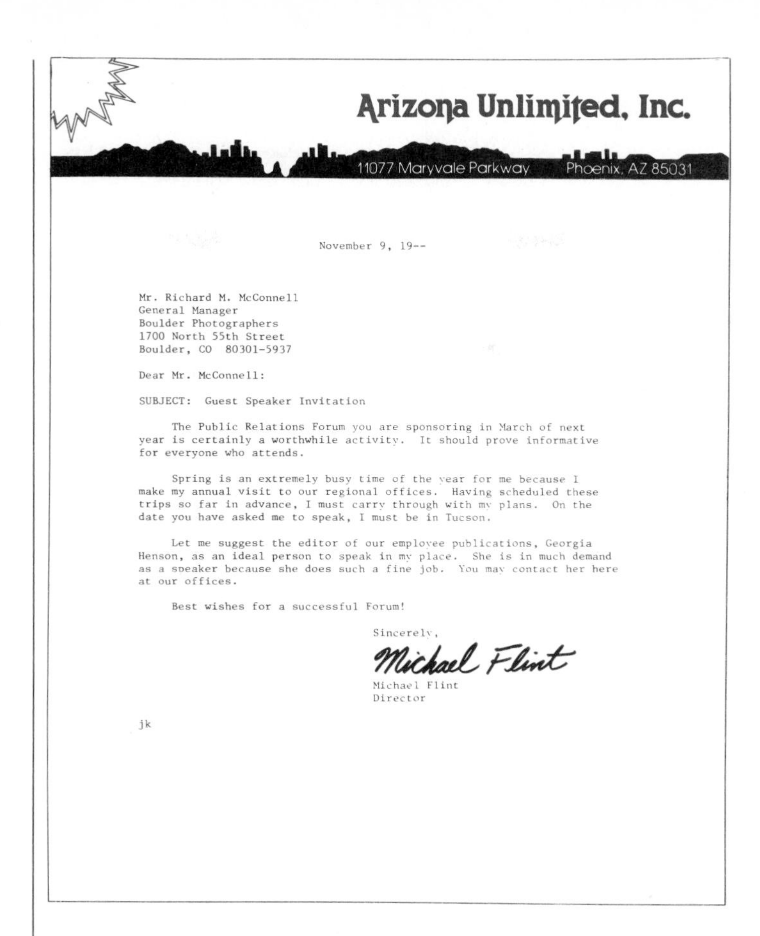

Arizona Unlimited, Inc.

11077 Maryvale Parkway Phoenix, AZ 85031

November 9, 19--

Mr. Richard M. McConnell
General Manager
Boulder Photographers
1700 North 55th Street
Boulder, CO 80301-5937

Dear Mr. McConnell:

SUBJECT: Guest Speaker Invitation

The Public Relations Forum you are sponsoring in March of next year is certainly a worthwhile activity. It should prove informative for everyone who attends.

Spring is an extremely busy time of the year for me because I make my annual visit to our regional offices. Having scheduled these trips so far in advance, I must carry through with my plans. On the date you have asked me to speak, I must be in Tucson.

Let me suggest the editor of our employee publications, Georgia Henson, as an ideal person to speak in my place. She is in much demand as a speaker because she does such a fine job. You may contact her here at our offices.

Best wishes for a successful Forum!

Sincerely,

Michael Flint

Michael Flint
Director

jk

Illustration 7-5
Modified-block format

ENVELOPES

As you read in Unit 6, correctly addressed envelopes are necessary for prompt delivery of the mail. The United States Postal Service has established formats for preparing envelopes so that they can be processed quickly using Optical Character Recognition (OCR) equipment. Because this equipment reads and sorts mail almost eight times faster than a human, correspondence reaches its destination more quickly.

Placement

In order for OCR and other postal equipment to work, envelopes must meet certain size requirements and must be addressed properly. The placement of the addressee's name and address on the envelope is especially important, because OCR equipment can only read information printed within its field of

8215 South Monroe Street, Fayetteville, NC 28302

February 14, 19--

Mrs. Marie Rodriquez
Vice President
First National Bank
5 Main Street
Red Springs, NC 28377

AMS LETTER FORMAT

The AMS style letter is the least expensive letter style for business correspondence. It is a time-saving, simplified style that was developed and is recommended by the Administrative Management Society.

To type an AMS style letter, follow these guidelines:

1. Begin all lines at the left margin.
2. Omit a salutation and a complimentary close.
3. Type the subject line in capital letters a triple space after the inside address. Omit the word Subject.
4. Triple space after the subject line and type the body.
5. Type the sender's name and title in capital letters four to six lines below the last line of the body.

This letter style has a pleasing appearance and saves time by eliminating unnecessary letter parts.

Your company correspondents will like this simplified letter format. If they have any questions, just have them call me.

Leslie Sartin

LESLIE SARTIN, CONSULTANT

dks

Illustration 7–6 AMS-Simplified format

vision. When addressing an envelope, set the tabulator stop for the left margin at 4 inches for a No. 10 (long) envelope and at $2\frac{1}{2}$ inches for a No. $6\frac{3}{4}$ (short) envelope. On a No. 10 envelope, begin the address 15 lines ($2\frac{1}{2}$ inches) from the top edge. On a No. $6\frac{3}{4}$ envelope, come down 12 lines (2 inches) from the top edge as shown in Illustration 7–7.

Address Procedures

In order for the address lines to be read by the OCR scanner, they must be single spaced. For best results, the Postal Service suggests using **OCR format**. That is, all address information should be in all caps, without punctuation. The most important delivery information is always placed in the last two lines of the address. Remember to use the two-letter state abbreviation and leave two spaces before the ZIP Code.

ab·bre·vi·a'tion

Return Address

Every envelope should have the sender's address clearly printed or keyboarded in the upper left corner. Without a return address, the letter could not be returned to the sender if it had an incorrect or incomplete mailing address.

Most companies that use letterhead stationery have matching envelopes printed with the return address. If you use a plain envelope, however, keyboard your company's complete name and address a double space from the top edge of the envelope and three spaces in from the left edge.

Mailing Notations

Notations that affect the cost of mailing, such as *special delivery* and *registered mail,* are placed in all caps below the stamp or postage area, as shown in Illustration 7–7. Notations that do not affect the cost of mailing, such as *personal* or *hold for arrival,* are placed in all caps a double space below the return address. An attention line is placed on the envelope immediately below the company name in the mailing address.

Illustration 7–7 Envelopes with mailing notations

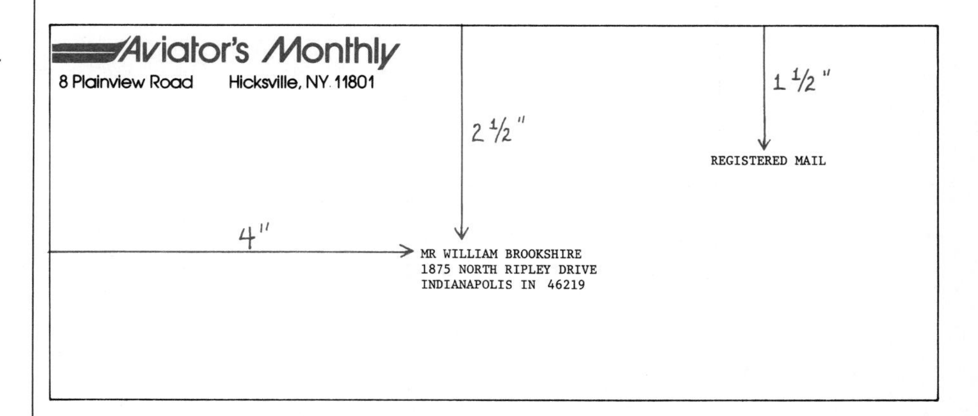

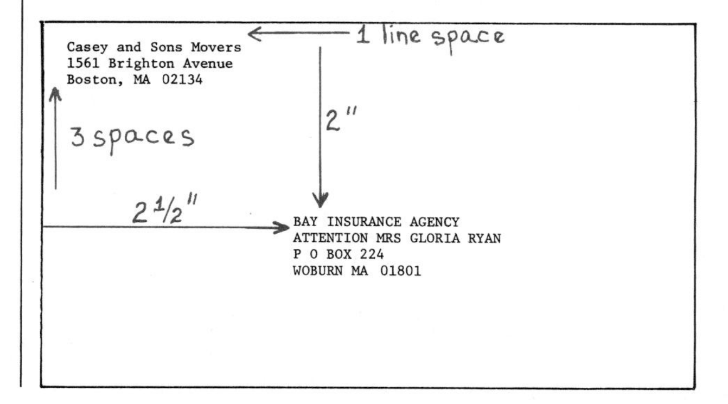

INTEROFFICE MEMORANDUMS

Much business correspondence never leaves the company. This correspondence, which is sent from one employee of the company to another, is called an **interoffice memorandum** (memo, for short).

mem·o·ran′dum

Memos are streamlined messages containing a few necessary parts: a heading, body, reference initials, and perhaps a copy or enclosure notation.

Heading

The heading usually contains the name of the person receiving the memo, the originator's name, the date, and the subject. Business titles, such as *Vice President,* are not used in the heading. Because of the volume of interoffice correspondence, most companies use memo forms printed with the necessary heading information: *To, From, Date,* and *Subject* (or *Re*).

A well-designed memo form allows for double spacing of heading lines and does not require tabulation. A block heading, shown in Illustration 7–8, thus saves preparation time. To save space, however, many printed memo forms use a horizontal format as shown in Illustration 7–9. If your company does not use printed forms, use a plain paper and keyboard the headings in caps in block format.

Illustration 7–8 Memorandum with block heading

COMPUTER DYNAMICS
Interoffice Memorandum

TO: Maria Valdez, C. W. Willard, Jan Reubew

FROM: Jon Richards

DATE: May 16, 19--

SUBJECT: Production Schedule

Because of the Memorial Day holiday, it will be necessary to prepare

Illustration 7–9 Memorandum with horizontal heading

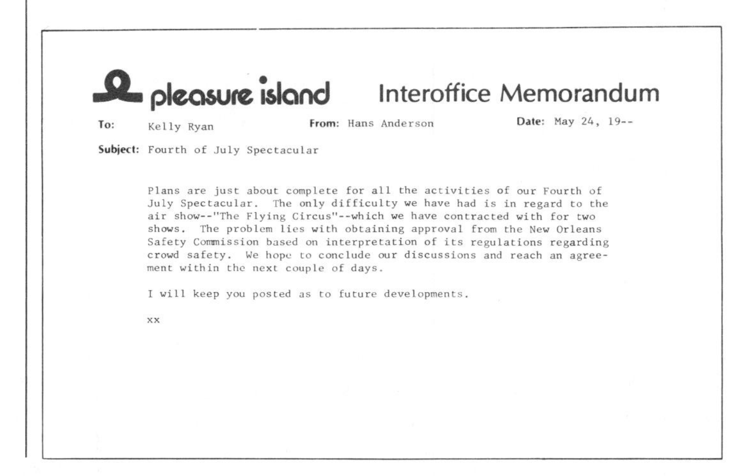

pleasure island Interoffice Memorandum

To: Kelly Ryan **From:** Hans Anderson **Date:** May 24, 19--

Subject: Fourth of July Spectacular

Plans are just about complete for all the activities of our Fourth of July Spectacular. The only difficulty we have had is in regard to the air show--"The Flying Circus"--which we have contracted with for two shows. The problem lies with obtaining approval from the New Orleans Safety Commission based on interpretation of its regulations regarding crowd safety. We hope to conclude our discussions and reach an agreement within the next couple of days.

I will keep you posted as to future developments.

xx

Body and Notations

The body of a memo begins a triple space after the heading. To save time, all lines in the body are usually blocked at the left margin and single spaced, with a double space between paragraphs. If the body is short (five lines or less), it can be double spaced. The reference initials are keyboarded at the left margin a double space below the last line in the body. Any additional notations (such as *attachment, copy,* or *postscript)* are keyboarded according to the format used in business letters.

Although there is no signature line in an interoffice memo, the originator may initial his or her name in the heading as a signature.

REVIEWING KEY POINTS

1. Standard placement of letter parts saves time in preparing and reading a letter.
2. A business letter may have as many as fifteen different parts. Each part serves a specific purpose.
3. Letter format is the arrangement of letter parts on a page according to accepted procedures.
4. The three most frequently used letter formats are block, modified block, and AMS Simplified.
5. In block and AMS-Simplified format, all letter parts are keyboarded beginning at the left margin. In modified-block format, the date and closing lines are keyboarded beginning at center.
6. The AMS-Simplified format always includes a subject line but omits the salutation and complimentary close.
7. Punctuation after the salutation and complimentary close in a business letter is optional. In open punctuation style, no punctuation is used. In mixed style, there is a colon after the salutation and a comma after the complimentary close.
8. An envelope address is prepared in OCR format by keyboarding all lines single spaced in caps with no punctuation.
9. An interoffice memorandum is a streamlined message that is sent from one employee to another within the same company.

DEVELOPING HUMAN RELATIONS SKILLS

1. As a new employee of the Barrett Company, you are responsible for preparing all correspondence for mailing. On your first day, you prepare

several letters and envelopes and take them to your supervisor for her signature. She signs the letters but objects to the format you used for the envelopes. Although she is familiar with OCR format, she prefers that it not be used.

a. How would you handle this situation?

b. What should you do if she insists on using the old format?

c. How could this situation have been prevented?

2. Thomas Tengen, a co-op student from the local high school, is starting his first day of work as a typist in your office. You have been assigned to work with him this first week. He has prepared the following letter and asks you to look at it.

a. What problems do you see in the format of the letter?

b. How would you get Thomas to correct his errors?

AAA Market Research

2700 Main Street

Bridgeport, CA 93517

April 27, 19--

Mr. John Daniels
Galaxy Advertising Systems
2707 E. Van Buren
Phoenix, AZ 85008

Dear Mr. Daniels

Enclosed is our monthly marketing report on consumer demands in the West and Southwest. As you will see, dramatic changes have occurred in certain customer preferences, particularly in the sports clothing line. The trend seems to indicate clearly a growing acceptance of physical fitness, as shown by the increased demand for recreational clothing and accessories.

Should you have any questions, we encourage you to call one of our marketing analysts. They will be happy to assist you in any way.

Sincerly,

Martha Brady, Marketing Analysis Sypervisor

MB/jw

IMPROVING COMMUNICATION SKILLS

Refer to Appendix A 1.19-1.21/1.25-1.27.

1. On a separate sheet of paper, keyboard these sentences, inserting any necessary colons and semicolons.
   a. The following letter formats are popular in business block, modified block, and AMS Simplified.
   b. I don't like to keyboard modified-block letters they require extra machine manipulations.
   c. All outgoing mail must be in the mailroom by 415 p.m.
   d. The new guidelines for preparing letters were sent to the offices in Akron, Ohio Dubuque, Iowa and York, Maine.
   e. A colon is normally used in the subject line following the word subject for example SUBJECT STOCK #321.
   f. The letter must be keyboarded by 1030 a.m.
   g. Most companies use the block format its streamlined format saves time and effort.
   h. The correspondence secretaries always proofread for these errors spelling, format, punctuation, and grammar.
2. Recall a conversation that you have had today with a friend. Using plain paper, double spacing, and one-inch margins, keyboard a short summary of that conversation. Once the information is keyboarded, edit it for correct grammar, punctuation, and spelling.

BUILDING PROBLEM-SOLVING SKILLS

1. Determine whether the letters shown in the chart below are short, medium, or long by estimating the number of words in the body of each. Copy the chart that follows on a separate sheet of paper and fill in the missing information.

No. of Words in First 3 Lines	Average No. of Words per Line	No. of Lines	Estimated No. of Words in Body	Letter Length
a. 25		10		
b. 30		15		
c. 14		25		
d. 23		9		
e. 16		32		
f. 20		43		

2. The graphs on page 266 show the percentage of time home computer users in two age groups spend on various types of activities. Review these graphs. Then on a separate sheet of paper, answer the questions that follow.

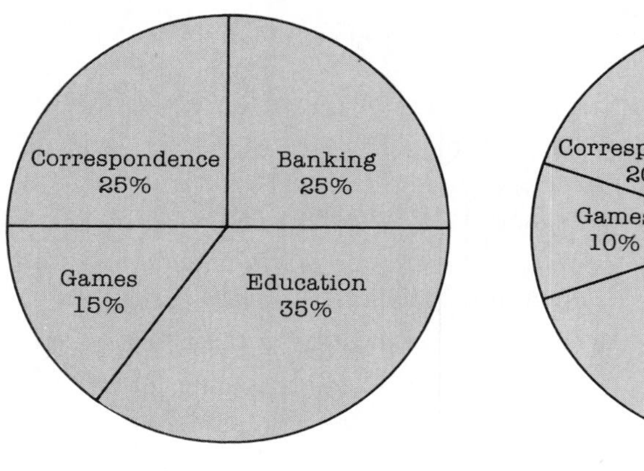

a. What activity consumes the most time in each age group?

b. What activity consumes the least time in each age group?

c. Which age group is more interested in playing computer games?

d. If those in the 26–40 age group use their computers an average of 12 hours a week, how many hours do they spend on each of the four activities?

e. If those in the 15–25 age group use their computers an average of 20 hours a week, how many hours do they spend on each of the four activities?

Activities 1 and 2 can be done on information processing equipment.

APPLYING OFFICE SKILLS

1. Prepare the following letter in modified-block format with indented paragraphs for Kenneth Houck, the training manager. Use the letterhead stationery in your workbook or plain paper. Prepare an envelope in OCR format. An envelope form is provided on the back of the letterhead in your workbook.

   Ms. Wanda Saunders/ Manager/ Henkle-Schueler Associates/ 180 East Kellog Boulevard/ St. Paul MN 55101-0021/ Dear Ms. Saunders/ Subject: Writing Training (P) For many years you have been using EFFECTIVE WRITING to train your managers and support workers. This program consists of a 40-hour classroom workshop for writers in addition to two 8-hour modules for managers. (P) In addition to EFFECTIVE WRITING, you might be interested in a supplementary program titled PUT IT IN WRITING. A copy of the brochure for this program is attached. As you will notice, this program goes beyond grammar, focusing on clarity and organization in writing. It consists of six lessons lasting two to three hours each. The materials include a slide/tape for each session and do not require a specialized instructor. (P) To conduct this program within your company, just fill out the enclosed order form and return it in the stamped, addressed envelope. We are sure that you will be pleased with the quality of this program material./ Sincerely,

2. Keyboard the following memorandums on the forms provided in your workbook or plain paper.
   a. To: Division Managers/ From: D. P. Zimmerman/ Date: (Today's)/ Subject: Sales Conference Plans/ (P) This year's sales conference will be held here at our home office on June 5–8. (P) In preparation for this conference, we need your suggestions for topics of discussion in the afternoon sessions. Please list your proposed topics on a sheet and return it to me by the end of February. (P) There are some exciting events being planned for our conference. With your input and cooperation, we feel sure that this will be a worthwhile meeting for all.
   b. To: Paul O'Brien/ From: Jan Estep/ Date: (Today's)/ Subject: Vacation Request/ (P) As you requested in your memo of January 7, 19 – –, I am putting in writing my plans for vacation this year. (P) Unless there is a scheduling problem, I would like to take the week of May 14–18 and the week of September 15–19 as my vacation time. If there are any reasons why I shouldn't take these two weeks, please let me know before April 1. (P) Thank you.

CHAPTER 2

CORRESPONDENCE WRITING

A typical job description for an office position might include phrases such as "keyboards documents," "keeps files," and "handles telephone calls." Because "writes letters and memorandums" is seldom listed, many new office workers are surprised to find that writing skills are needed.

Even beginning employees regularly write memos to their supervisors and to other company employees. For example, your supervisor may ask you to prepare a weekly progress report.

After you have been on the job a while, you may be given additional responsibility for preparing routine business documents. For example, you may be asked to make hotel reservations for out-of-town meetings. You may handle simple requests about your company's services or products.

Whether you are writing to coworkers or to customers, your messages must be written well. You should always use courteous language. Most important, your messages should contain the information your readers want or need.

As you study this chapter, you will find answers to the following questions:

- What qualities make business letters easy to understand?
- How can anticipating the reader's response help you write effective letters?
- How are form paragraphs and boilerplate copy used in business correspondence?
- How has information processing equipment changed the way business correspondence is prepared?
- What do the following terms mean: **form letters, variable, form paragraph/boilerplate copy?**

WRITING EFFECTIVE BUSINESS LETTERS

ac·com′plish

When writing for business or personal reasons, good writers follow the rules of grammar and punctuation and use clear, lively language. As you read in Unit 2, good writers apply the Five C's to ensure that their writing is complete, clear, correct, concise, and courteous. To be an *effective* writer, you must do all these things, *plus* you must plan your message to accomplish a particular purpose.

When you write a business letter, you should ask yourself: What do I hope to accomplish? First, of course, you want to give or request information; this is the purpose of all types of communication. Second, you want to create a good impression of your company. Third, you want to gain the reader's acceptance. In other words, you want the reader to believe and agree with your message. If your letter or memo does these three things, then you have communicated effectively. This chapter contains suggestions to help you choose your words for an effective business message.

Anticipating the Reader's Response

re·ac′tion

fa′vor·a·bly

Before you can write an effective letter or memo, you need to consider the reader's reaction to your message. If you begin a letter with "You have just won $2,000," you expect the reader to react favorably. If a person has requested information about a conference and you write, "The business session will begin at 9:15 A.M. on May 23," you expect the person to be interested. But if your letter begins, "You will not get a salary increase this year," you might expect the reader to be disappointed and maybe even angry.

Almost every business message will cause one of these three reader reactions: pleasure, interest, or displeasure. If you can predict how your

Illustration 7–10 Typical reactions to information

Pleasure

People react favorably when their requests are granted, when deadlines are met, or when their work is complimented.

```
in today's mail.  Ms. Eckstein likes your proposal and wants to
discuss it with you.  Please telephone her secretary to set up
```

Displeasure

People are disappointed and sometimes act unfavorably when their requests are refused, when deadlines are not met, or when their work is criticized.

```
cannot offer credit to you at this time.  Our suggestion is
that we do business on a cash basis until your company fulfills
```

Interest

Some written messages cause neither pleasure nor displeasure. The information simply satisfies the reader's interest.

```
     Here are the catalogues and price lists that you requested.
As you will notice on pages 19-22, we have introduced a complete
```

reader is likely to respond, you can plan your message. Your purpose is to word and organize it so that it gets the best reaction.

prin'ci·ples

There are three simple principles that you should keep in mind as you plan your message.

1. People respond favorably to positive and courteous words.
2. People accept good news and avoid bad news.
3. People like to know "why."

These principles, which describe people's response to information, apply to every kind of interpersonal communication. How you apply them in your writing depends on the response you expect the reader to have.

The Good News Message

A business message that carries good news or needed information usually creates a favorable response: pleasure or interest. When people request information, they are pleased to get a prompt and helpful response. Telling good news is easy, therefore, because you know the reader will accept the message and react positively.

pos'i·tive·ly

The recommended outline for a "good news" message is

1. State the good news or desired information.
2. Give the necessary details and explanations.
3. Close courteously.

This three-point outline shows the order in which you present the information. The memo in Illustration 7–11 follows this outline. Notice that it has three paragraphs, each containing one main point. In some situations more paragraphs may be necessary to give all the details of the message.

Illustration 7–11
Message following "good news" outline

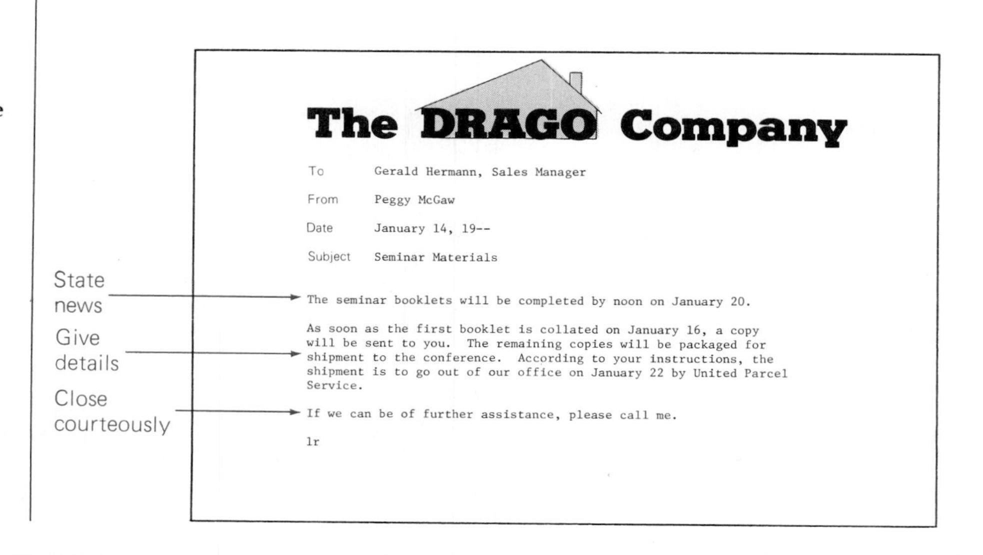

The DRAGO Company

To Gerald Hermann, Sales Manager

From Peggy McGaw

Date January 14, 19--

Subject Seminar Materials

The seminar booklets will be completed by noon on January 20.

As soon as the first booklet is collated on January 16, a copy will be sent to you. The remaining copies will be packaged for shipment to the conference. According to your instructions, the shipment is to go out of our office on January 22 by United Parcel Service.

If we can be of further assistance, please call me.

lr

This outline is recommended because it takes into account the way people respond to information. For example, you announce the good news in the first sentence where the reader is sure to see it. Because people like to receive good news, they immediately respond favorably to you and your message.

In the second paragraph, you give any additional information the reader needs to understand and to act on the message. This satisfies the reader's desire to know "why," "when," and "how much." Finally, by using courteous language throughout your message, and especially in the closing, you leave the reader with a good feeling about you and your company.

This basic outline can also be used for simple requests, especially when you expect a positive response, as in Illustration 7–12. The request is stated in the first paragraph, followed by any additional information needed to fill the request. The closing usually includes a "thank you" or a polite request for prompt service.

Illustration 7–12
A simple request for information

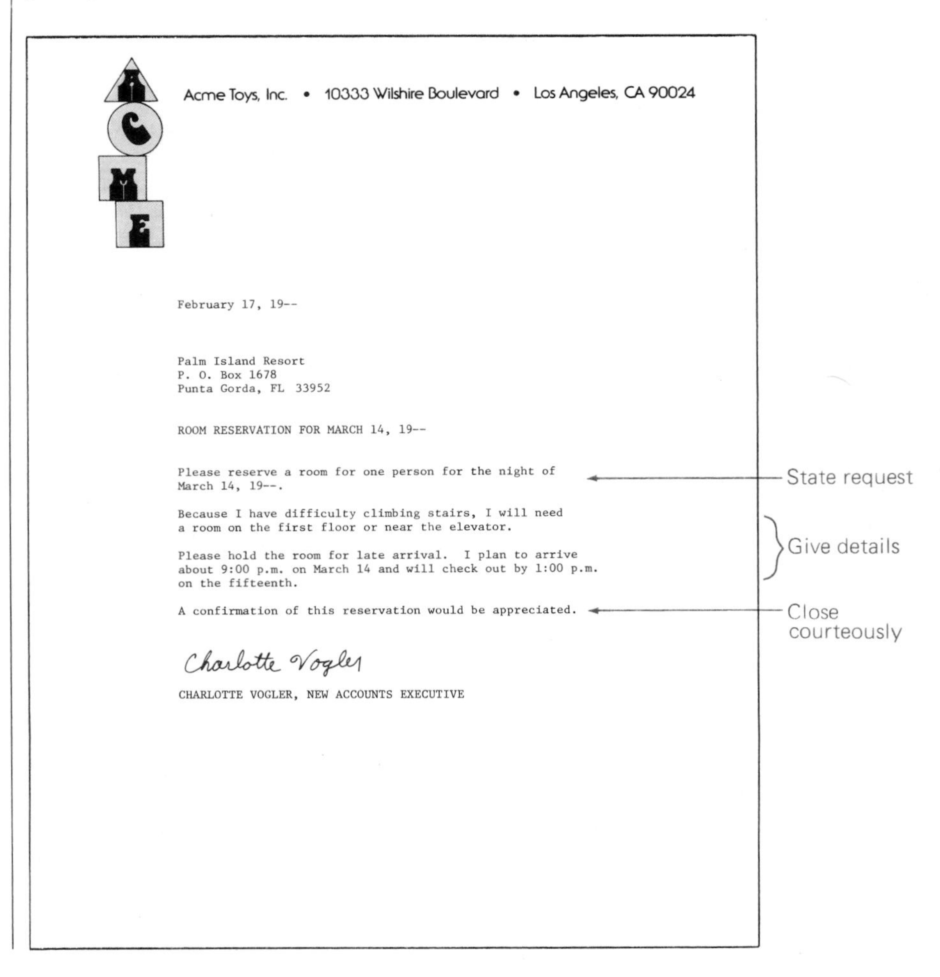

Acme Toys, Inc. • 10333 Wilshire Boulevard • Los Angeles, CA 90024

February 17, 19--

Palm Island Resort
P. O. Box 1678
Punta Gorda, FL 33952

ROOM RESERVATION FOR MARCH 14, 19--

Please reserve a room for one person for the night of March 14, 19--.

Because I have difficulty climbing stairs, I will need a room on the first floor or near the elevator.

Please hold the room for late arrival. I plan to arrive about 9:00 p.m. on March 14 and will check out by 1:00 p.m. on the fifteenth.

A confirmation of this reservation would be appreciated.

Charlotte Vogler

CHARLOTTE VOGLER, NEW ACCOUNTS EXECUTIVE

The Bad News Message

Delivering unpleasant news is never an easy task. Most people know how it feels to be disappointed or hurt, so they try to avoid disappointing others whenever possible. Unfortunately, however, writing "bad news" letters is an unavoidable part of doing business.

un·a·void'a·ble

Identify with your reader Letters and memos that might cause the reader to react unfavorably have to be carefully written. You should plan your message so that the reader

1. Reads the entire message.
2. Understands the reasons for the situation.
3. Accepts the situation.
4. Believes that the writer is interested and sincere.

In planning your message, put yourself in the reader's place. How would you react if you received a letter that began, "Your request for promotion to word processing supervisor has been refused"? If the promotion was something you wanted very badly, you would definitely be disappointed. Depending on your personality, you might get angry. Some people would stop reading and throw the letter away. These are natural reactions, because people try to avoid bad news. So the first thing to remember when writing a message containing unfavorable information is: Don't begin on a negative note! If you do, your message may not be read.

un·fa'vor·a·ble

Illustration 7–13 Memorandum following "bad news" outline

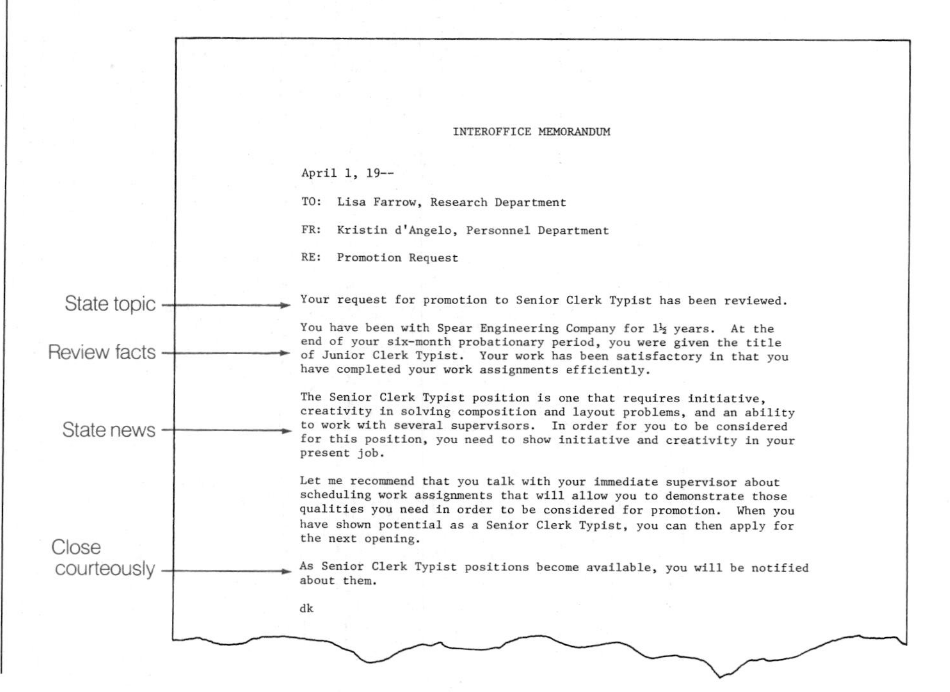

INTEROFFICE MEMORANDUM

April 1, 19--

TO: Lisa Farrow, Research Department

FR: Kristin d'Angelo, Personnel Department

RE: Promotion Request

Your request for promotion to Senior Clerk Typist has been reviewed.

You have been with Spear Engineering Company for 1½ years. At the end of your six-month probationary period, you were given the title of Junior Clerk Typist. Your work has been satisfactory in that you have completed your work assignments efficiently.

The Senior Clerk Typist position is one that requires initiative, creativity in solving composition and layout problems, and an ability to work with several supervisors. In order for you to be considered for this position, you need to show initiative and creativity in your present job.

Let me recommend that you talk with your immediate supervisor about scheduling work assignments that will allow you to demonstrate those qualities you need in order to be considered for promotion. When you have shown potential as a Senior Clerk Typist, you can then apply for the next opening.

As Senior Clerk Typist positions become available, you will be notified about them.

dk

de·pend'a·ble

Organize your message A dependable outline to use when writing messages that contain unpleasant information is

1. State the topic to be discussed.
2. Review the facts of the situation.
3. State the unpleasant information in positive words.
4. Close with a polite but neutral statement.

Beginning your message with a statement of the topic arouses the reader's interest. Your statement should be neither positive nor negative; it should simply present the subject of the message. The first paragraph in Illustration 7–13 contains an appropriate statement of the topic.

Next, by reviewing the related facts, you tell the reader what caused the situation or what factors were considered in arriving at the decision. This explanation should satisfy the reader's desire to know *why.* Present the facts in positive language and in a logical order so that the reader can clearly understand the reasons behind the decision. A statement of the unfavorable news naturally follows this explanation.

There are two advantages to presenting the explanation *before* stating the unpleasant news. First, you increase the chance that the reader will read the entire message, including the explanation. Second, you reduce the chance that the reader will respond negatively. By the time the explanation is read, the reader understands the situation and may even agree with you — even if your news is unpleasant.

neu'tral

Finally, end the message with a neutral but courteous closing statement. You might suggest what the reader can do to change or improve the situation, as the fourth paragraph in the example illustrates. Your suggestion shows that you are sincerely interested in the reader's problems and feelings.

This four-point outline can be used when you write short, informal notes to your coworkers (as in Illustration 7–14) or formal business letters to customers and suppliers. Following this outline can make unpleasant news a little easier to deliver — and easier to accept, as well.

Illustration 7–14
An informal note containing "bad news"

11/14/--

Nell

I just received your request for typing assistance this Saturday.

Three weeks ago, I agreed to a weekend trip which begins Friday after work. Since I am responsible for providing the car for this trip, I feel that I have to keep that commitment. Therefore, you will have to make other arrangements for typing assistance for this Saturday.

Let me know if you plan to work next weekend. I'd be happy to earn the overtime pay!

Emma

FORM LETTERS

Outlines, such as the ones suggested for favorable and unfavorable news, simplify letter writing. Form letters are another way to reduce the time spent on routine business correspondence. **Form letters** are standardized responses that can be used to answer a variety of similar requests. Often they contain blanks where variables can be filled in. A **variable** is an element such as a name, amount, or invoice number that varies, or changes, from one letter to the next.

Writing Form Letters

Form letters can be individually prepared as complete messages, or they can be duplicated, with space allowed to insert the date, inside address, or other variable information. When a prompt response is required, a form letter may contain a checklist. The writer fills in the date and addressee's name and places a checkmark (√) next to the appropriate comments. The reader is expected to ignore the paragraphs not checked.

When writing a form letter, use the appropriate outline for the reader's expected response to the message. You can get an idea of the best wording and the content to include from your correspondence file. Look at copies of letters dealing with the same or a similar situation to see how other people have handled it. By modifying and combining the content of the letters in your files, you can produce a useful and informative form letter. Illustration 7–15 shows the text of a simple form letter.

mod'i·fy·ing

If a greater variety of responses is desired, you may find the **form paragraph** or **boilerplate copy** approach very useful. Instead of preparing a standard letter, you write (or select from your correspondence files) several standard paragraphs. You might prepare a file of two or three opening paragraphs, three or four second paragraphs, and several closing paragraphs. From these, you select appropriate paragraphs, combine them, and create a unique letter for each situation. Like form letters, boilerplates save writing time; but they also allow for a more specific response to a request.

Using Information Processing Equipment

Information processing equipment is ideal for preparing form letters and boilerplate copy. As you will read in Unit 12, each letter or paragraph is keyboarded once, stored on a disk or in other form, and given a document number. To produce a copy of the stored content, you keyboard the appropriate document number. The equipment then automatically prints out the desired letter or paragraph. On electronic typewriters and some word processors, if addresses, dates, amounts, and other unique information need to be inserted, the machine stops at the appropriate spot. Then you keyboard the information to be inserted, and the equipment continues printing out the

au·to·mat'i·cal·ly

Wells Department Store

Anderson and Maple Streets
Seven Corners, VA 22044
226-7904

(Today's Date)

(Name)
(Street)
(City, State, Zip Code)

Dear (Name) :

We are pleased to inform you, (Name) , that your application for a Wells Department Store Credit Card has been approved. Your credit limit has been set at (Amount).

In welcoming you as a new credit customer at our store, we would like to remind you that we offer a special "Value of the Month" in each department. You indicated on your application that you are especially interested in our (Department) . So that you will be kept informed of any special sales or new products in this department, we will be sending you our regular monthly advertising circular.

The next advertising circular will be mailed on (Date) . Thank you for joining our growing family of customers.

Sincerely,

Andy Bressler, Manager

Illustration 7–15
Form letter showing locations of variables to be inserted

stored information. The result of this process is correspondence that looks like an original — individually keyboarded and error free. Time and money are saved since the information processing equipment produces accurate, keyboarded copy at a faster rate than is possible with a typewriter.

REVIEWING KEY POINTS

1. Business messages are easier to understand when they are complete, clear, correct, concise, and courteous.
2. Message outlines help a writer include the main points and arrange them in a clear and logical order.

3. Almost every business message will cause one of the following reader reactions: pleasure, displeasure, or interest.
4. Good news messages always begin with the "good news" statement.
5. Bad news messages always begin with an identification of the topic to be discussed — an information statement or subject line.
6. A form letter is a standard response that can be used to answer a variety of similar requests.
7. Boilerplate copy is a collection of form paragraphs that are coded so that they can be selected in various combinations to produce complete business letters that are unique for each situation.
8. Form letters and boilerplates produced with information processing equipment save time and money because of the speed and accuracy of the equipment.

DEVELOPING HUMAN RELATIONS SKILLS

1. Steve Delgetti, a new employee who works near you, often interrupts you to ask questions about the formats to use for letters and memos. Sometimes he simply checks over your shoulder to see how you are setting up a document. Although you didn't mind for the first few weeks while he was still new to the job, this practice is starting to annoy you. Some of the information you work with is confidential.
   a. Should you discuss this problem with your supervisor? Explain.
   b. What suggestions could you give Steve so that he would not have to keep checking with you?
2. From time to time, your coworker, Beth Ashley, has been asked by her supervisor to do personal keyboarding for him and his family. Recently, while Beth's supervisor was away on business, his wife came into the office and asked Beth to keyboard a ten-page paper for her daughter's literature class. Although she did the job, Beth politely suggested that in the future her daughter should find someone else to keyboard her papers. When Beth's supervisor returned to the office, he told her he was disappointed by her comments to his wife.
   a. How should Beth have handled this situation?
   b. What would you do if your supervisor repeatedly asked to you do personal keyboarding for him?

IMPROVING COMMUNICATION SKILLS

Refer to Appendix A 1.19-1.21/1.25-1.27.

1. On a separate sheet of paper, keyboard these sentences, adding any necessary colons or semicolons.
   a. The branch offices are located in the downtown areas of Phoenix, Arizona Dallas, Texas and Tulsa, Oklahoma.

b. We sent you a copy of our new catalogue you may use the order blanks included with it.

c. He usually works in the only quiet places in the office the library and the conference room.

d. The letter served its purpose it explained the account.

e. Please sign the enclosed card there is no cost to you.

f. Two people are absent today namely, Jim Lee and Jo Aker.

g. We begin the meeting at 1 20 p.m. you must be there then.

h. You can go to the conference however, I must stay here.

i. There are two types of messages good news and bad news.

j. Jessica will keyboard the letters Jason will keyboard the envelopes.

2. Recall a telephone conversation that you have had recently. Using plain paper, keyboard a short summary of the conversation. Try to compose the summary so that a reader will be interested in it. Be sure to use correct grammar, punctuation, and spelling.

BUILDING PROBLEM-SOLVING SKILLS

1. In your office, you use different paper sizes depending upon the type of document. On a separate sheet of paper, figure the total number of vertical lines available for formatting information on the following paper sizes (width x length). Use the standard that six vertical lines equal one inch.

a. $8\frac{1}{2} \times 11$	c. $12 \times 8\frac{1}{2}$	e. $8\frac{1}{2} \times 13$
b. $8\frac{1}{2} \times 14$	d. $5\frac{1}{2} \times 8\frac{1}{2}$	f. $7\frac{1}{4} \times 10\frac{1}{2}$

2. Your office has recently figured the cost of producing a business letter. The results are shown here. On a separate sheet of paper, answer the questions that follow.

Dictator's Time (8 minutes)	$2.72
Secretary's Time (10.7 minutes)	1.82
Nonproductive Labor	.68
Fixed Charges (nonlabor)	2.25
Materials	.58
Mailing	.48
Total	$8.53

a. What is the most expensive factor in producing a letter?

b. What is the total labor cost of producing a letter?

c. What is the cost per minute for the dictator's time?

d. What is the combined cost of the three factors other than labor?

e. Add the dictating and secretarial time. What percentage of the total is this combined cost?

Activities 1 and 2 can be done on information processing equipment.

APPLYING OFFICE SKILLS

1. Assume that you work in the Credit Department of your company. You have been asked to prepare a form letter in block format that could be sent to customers with overdue accounts. On a separate sheet of paper, prepare a rough draft of the form letter that includes the following:
   - **a.** Request payment of the overdue account.
   - **b.** Leave blanks for the insertion of the date, invoice number, description of product, and amount due.
   - **c.** State that payment must be made within 15 days of the date of this letter in order to avoid late penalties.
   - **d.** Refer to a stamped envelope enclosed for mailing the payment.
2. Using the letterhead stationery in your workbook or plain paper, prepare letters in modified-block format to be sent to the people listed here. Use the form letter you composed in the previous activity, inserting the invoice date, invoice number, description of product, and amount due for each. (If you use information processing equipment, prepare separate files for the letter and the variable information so that the two can be merged.)
   - **a.** Philip Kalbaugh, 2 Ainahau Apartments, Seaside Avenue, Honolulu, HI 96815-0999 (Two months ago today, he was sent Invoice No. 113 for a cabinet and keyboard shelf; amount due is $200.)
   - **b.** Alfred Meurer, P.O. Box 7499, Aina Haina Station, Honolulu, HI 96821-0001 (Four months ago today, he was sent Invoice No. 60 for a steel wardrobe cabinet; amount due is $163.88.)
   - **c.** Katherine Hager, 630 South Beretania Street, Honolulu, HI 96813-0024 (Three months ago today, she was sent Invoice No. 83 for a steel contemporary bookcase; amount due is $264.)

CHAPTER 3

CORRESPONDENCE SUPPLIES

The quality and kind of supplies used for business correspondence can affect the reader's first impression of a business. If the appearance of a business document makes a good impression, the reader is more likely to read it and react favorably to its message.

Businesses that recognize the importance of presenting a good image usually invest in quality paper products and good information processing equipment. *Invest* is the correct word to use, too, because quality products generally cost more. A conscientious employee uses the most expensive products only when making a good impression is important. For example, a letter being sent to your company's major customer should be prepared on your best office stationery. However, a first draft of a speech, which only your supervisor will see, can be prepared on a cheaper grade of paper.

As you study this chapter, you will find answers to the following questions:

- What are the six factors that determine the quality and cost of paper?
- What sizes of paper are used for business correspondence?
- In what three styles are printed memorandum forms available?
- What correction products can be used to ensure that business correspondence has a neat appearance?
- What do the following terms mean: **baronial, executive, government, legal, bond, kraft envelopes?**

PAPER

Many different types of paper are available for business correspondence. The quality and the cost of the paper is determined by six factors: content, weight, size, finish, type, and color.

Factors in Paper Quality

Content Paper can be made from cotton (or "rag") fibers, chemical fibers, or a combination of the two. Paper made entirely of cotton fiber (called 100 percent rag content) is strong, long-lasting, and superior in appearance and erasability. Paper with 75, 50, and 25 percent rag content also has these qualities, but to a lesser degree.

e·ras·a·bil′i·ty

Chemical fiber papers are less expensive than rag content papers and of lower quality. For their letterhead stationery, most companies choose a combination rag and chemical fiber paper.

Weight The weight of paper determines its body, stiffness, and bulk. Weight, which is measured in pounds, refers to the weight of 500 sheets of 17- by 22-inch paper. (Each sheet of this paper is large enough to be cut into 4 letter-size sheets.) The most popular papers for office use range from 9 to 24 pounds, with 20-pound paper frequently used for letterhead stationery. In general, the higher the weight, the more expensive the paper.

Size Standard letter-size paper, measuring $8\frac{1}{2}$ x 11 inches, is the most frequently used size for business correspondence. Other sizes found in business offices include:

$5\frac{1}{2}$ x $8\frac{1}{2}$ inches Baronial or half-sized
$7\frac{1}{4}$ x $10\frac{1}{2}$ inches Executive or monarch
8 x $10\frac{1}{2}$ inches Government
$8\frac{1}{2}$ x 13 inches Legal

Baronial paper is used primarily for very short messages. The **executive** size is used most often by business executives or professionals for their personal and business correspondence. **Government**-size stationery, used in the past by some federal agencies, is being replaced by the standard letter size because it costs less. **Legal**-size paper, though seldom used for business correspondence, is useful for keyboarding large charts, legal documents, and newsletters.

Finish Finish refers to the texture or coating of the paper. A smooth finish is the one most popular for general office use. Onionskins, used for carbon copies, and some fine writing papers have a ripply surface known as *cockle finish.* Other papers have a coating that makes them erasable. This coating prevents the ink from penetrating the fibers. When the ink is fresh, the type can be erased with an ordinary pencil eraser; but once the ink dries, the type is fairly permanent. Because it smudges easily, erasable paper is not recommended for work that will be handled a lot.

pen′e·trat·ing

re·pro·duc′tions

Type Some papers are produced for specific purposes. For example, letter-quality papers, also called **bond** paper, are chosen for strength, whiteness, and crispness. They have a dull, smooth finish that quickly soaks up ink so it doesn't smear. Paper used for carbon copies — also called second sheets — is lightweight and inexpensive. Mimeograph paper, photocopy paper, and other papers used in reprographic equipment have special finishes so they make good reproductions and feed easily through these machines without jamming.

Color White is the standard color for office stationery, but buff tones and pastel colors are being used more frequently. Memos, reports, and carbon copies are often prepared on color-coded paper. Color coding makes these items easier to identify and helps clerks file and locate them quickly.

Letterhead Stationery

Letterhead stationery is expensive because it is specially designed and printed. In addition, letterhead paper is usually of average or higher quality. Why do companies spend this extra money?

rep·u·ta′tion

The main reason companies use letterhead stationery is that it projects a professional image. The design of the letterhead — the arrangement of company name, address, telephone number, business slogan, or logo — reflects the reputation and personality of the company. A sporting goods store, for example, may have a colorful and bold letterhead that projects activity and energy. For a bank, the letterhead may be simple but formal, suggesting a conservative, detail-oriented organization.

Continuation sheets, the blank sheets used for additional pages of long letters, should be of the same size, color, quality, and finish as the letterhead sheets. For the closest match, letterheads, continuation sheets, and envelopes should be ordered from the same company and in similar quantities.

Today, letterhead stationery is often purchased in cartons of continuous-form paper for use with information processing equipment. This paper comes in a connected, continuous strip of sheets folded at perforations. Using continuous-form paper eliminates single feeding each sheet of paper. The same quality paper available for single-sheet letterheads is available for letterheads in continuous form. It is also possible for businesses to match the continuous-form letterhead paper with continuous-form continuation sheets and envelopes.

Carbon Paper

A copy of every letter and memo prepared in an office is usually kept as a record of the correspondence. Copies are also sent to persons who are affected by or interested in the contents of the letter. Many companies, whether typewriters or information processing equipment is used, have workers make carbon copies for these purposes because they cost less to make than photocopies.

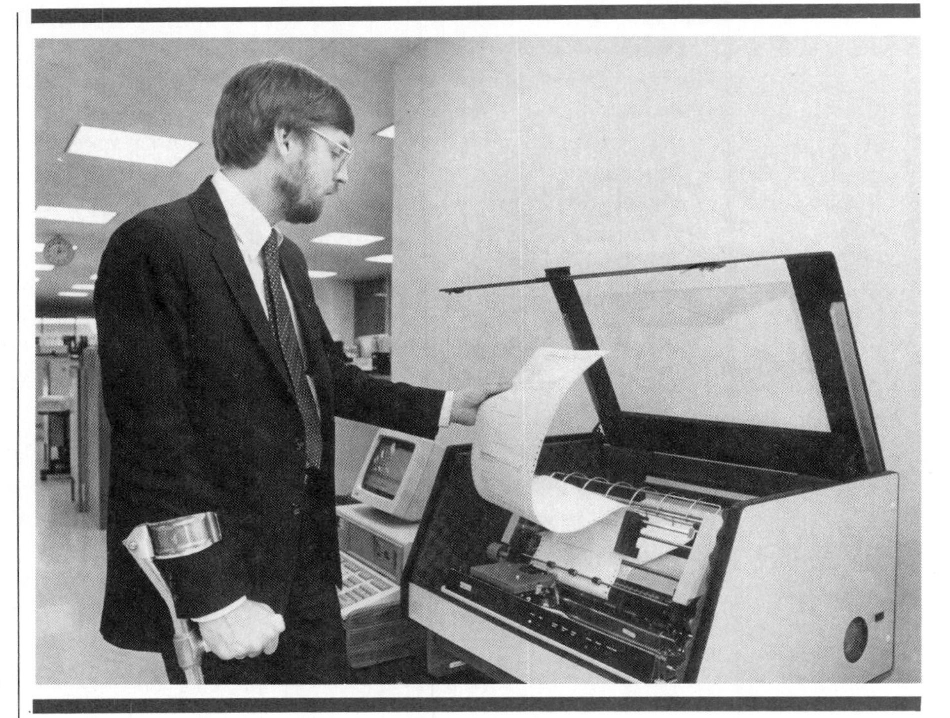

Illustration 7–16 Continuous-form paper for information processing printer

ex·pen′sive

Carbon paper comes in a variety of colors, sizes, weights, and finishes. There are carbon papers especially designed for use with typewriters or information processing equipment and with pencils or pens, as well as general-purpose carbon papers. The most expensive and long-lasting carbon paper is the solvent carbon with plastic film backing. You can keyboard as many as ten copies at a time with this paper. Standard carbon paper produces up to five copies at a time.

Most carbon papers can be used again and again; the number of times depends on the kind of paper and its quality. When the copies appear light or blurred, it's time to use a new sheet.

Most carbon papers have features that make them easy to use and handle. For example, the carbon paper you use may have two cut corners or an extended edge to make it easy to separate the carbon from the original and second sheet.

Carbon packs When preparing carbon copies, you can save time by assembling a carbon pack. A carbon pack consists of an original (the letterhead, for example), a sheet of carbon paper, and a second sheet. There are several methods for assembling a carbon pack; however, the machine method is one of the most cost effective.

You can use the *drawer method* if your desk drawer contains dividers for your stationery. Starting from the front, fill one divider with second sheets, the next with carbon paper, and the third with letterhead. To assemble the carbon pack, pull a second sheet toward you. Next, lift up a piece of carbon paper and then a sheet of the letterhead, as shown in Illustration 7–17. (You may want to use two hands at first.) Grasp the three sheets between your thumb and fingers as you remove the assembled pack from the drawer. Tap the pack lightly on your desk (with top edges down) to get the edges even. Then insert the carbon pack into the typewriter or printer and roll it into keyboarding position.

Inserting several sheets of paper into the typewriter or printer at the same time can be difficult. When you have several copies to make, you may find it easier to assemble a carbon pack using the *machine method* shown in Illustration 7–18.

1. Gather the letterhead and the necessary number of second sheets in a stack. Insert the stack in the typewriter or printer as usual, but just to the point where the papers are held in place by the platen.
2. Starting at the back, place a sheet of carbon paper (carbon side toward you) between every two sheets of paper. Flip each sheet back after you insert the carbon.
3. Roll the carbon pack into keyboarding position. (Notice that the carbon paper doesn't come all the way to the top edge of the letterhead and second sheets.)

Illustration 7–17 Assembling a carbon pack using the drawer method

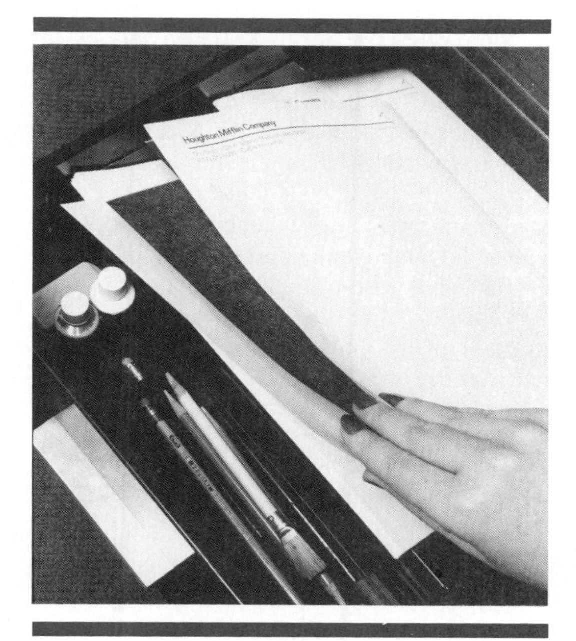

Illustration 7–18 Assembling a carbon pack using the machine method

dis·pos'a·ble

Carbon sets A carbon set is a one-time (disposable) package of carbon paper arranged between second sheets, all of which are attached at the top. A carbon set saves time in assembling carbon packs and keeps your hands clean, since you do not have to touch the carbon backing.

ENVELOPES

Most business letters are mailed in bond envelopes, often printed with a return address. Although these envelopes are usually white, they can be ordered in any color to match the company letterhead. They usually come in boxes of 500 or in continuous-form cartons of one thousand. Bond envelopes come in several standard sizes. The most common sizes used for business correspondence are:

$3\frac{1}{2}$ x 6 inches	No. $6\frac{1}{4}$ Commercial
$3\frac{5}{8}$ x $6\frac{1}{2}$ inches	No. $6\frac{3}{4}$ Commercial
$3\frac{7}{8}$ x $8\frac{7}{8}$ inches	No. 9 Official
$4\frac{1}{8}$ x $9\frac{1}{2}$ inches	No. 10 Official

Kraft envelopes are light brown mailing envelopes made from strong, unbleached paper. Although kraft envelopes are available in a wide range of styles and sizes, one of the most popular sizes is is 9 x 12 inches. This size is useful for mailing reports that are too thick to fold. When addressing a kraft envelope, prepare a gummed mailing label and attach it to the envelope.

To conserve supplies, many companies use large kraft envelopes for interoffice mail. Interoffice envelopes are printed with two to four columns of lines on which you print or keyboard the addressee's name and department or office number. These envelopes can be used again and again; just cross out the last name on the form and write the name of the addressee on the next available line.

Many companies use window envelopes to save keyboarding time in addressing correspondence. The window envelope, shown in Illustration 7–19, has a see-through panel on the front where the address appears. The correspondence is prepared and folded so that the inside address shows through the envelope window. Any enclosures must be inserted carefully so that they do not obstruct, or hide, the address information, which must show in the envelope window.

ob·struct'

INTEROFFICE MEMORANDUM FORMS

Interoffice memorandums are usually printed on inexpensive paper. Whether specially ordered or purchased off the shelf in office supply stores, memorandum forms are usually available in single sheets (full or half page)

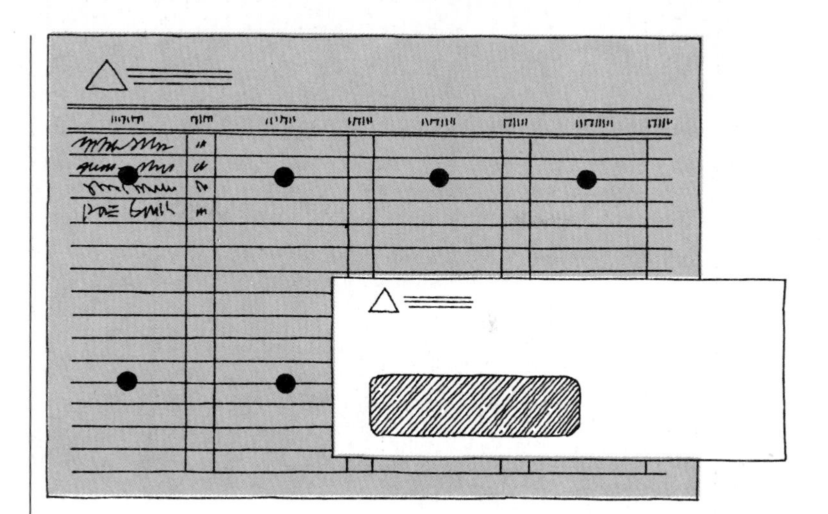

Illustration 7–19
Interoffice mail and window envelopes

or in three other styles: padded forms, snap-apart carbon sets, and carbonless forms.

Padded forms are single printed sheets attached at the top edge to a cardboard pad. You simply tear off the number of sheets you need. Carbon paper can be inserted between sheets if copies are desired.

Snap-apart carbon sets contain an original memorandum form, a one-time carbon, and a second sheet. These sets save time because they are already assembled and attached for perfect alignment. To separate the sheets after keyboarding the memorandum, hold the stub with one hand and the opposite edge of the form with the other. Since the carbon is shorter than the original and second sheets, a simple downward pull removes the keyboarded pages from the stub and carbon sheets.

a·lign′ment

Carbonless forms are made of paper coated with a chemical that makes an image under impact or pressure without carbon paper. NCR is the trade name for one kind of carbonless paper.

In addition to the standard memorandum forms, you can also purchase forms that provide space at the bottom or side of the memorandum for a reply. The forms are sold under several trade names, including Speed Letters, Rapid Letters, and Message-Reply Memos. The advantage of these forms is that they save time and paper.

CORRECTION PRODUCTS

Messy corrections can mar the appearance of any document. If you leave out a line or make several errors on a page, it is usually best to redo the entire page. Today's information processing equipment makes it easy to reprint a page after corrections have been made. However, for simple corrections on a typewriter, there are several products you can use.

Erasers

e·ra'sure

To make a clean erasure, you need an erasing guide (a card with various sizes and shapes of openings), an erasing shield (a curved metal plate or an index card), and an eraser. Use an ink or typing eraser for originals and a soft eraser for carbon copies. The erasing guide protects the correctly keyboarded characters as you erase. For carbon copies, insert the erasing shield in front of the second sheet as you erase each page separately. Then remove the shield and check for proper alignment before keyboarding the correction.

Correction Liquids

spar'ing·ly

Correction liquids are used to paint over errors and provide a new surface for corrections. Shake the liquid before using, apply it sparingly, and allow it to dry completely before keyboarding over the correction. Correction liquids are most useful for corrections in material that will be photocopied. Liquids are available in white and several colors. They can also be specially ordered to match the stationery being used.

Correction Papers

Film-base correction paper (called typewriter opaquing film), available in sheets or rolls, can be used to make corrections on originals and copies. To

Illustration 7–20
Applying correction fluids

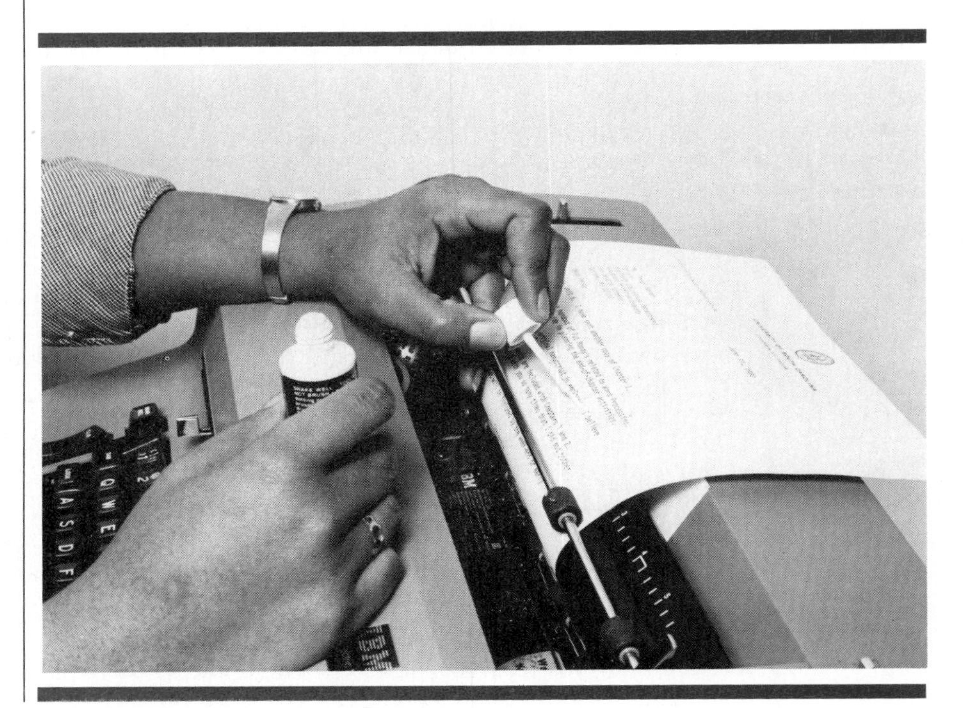

make a correction, backspace to the error. Place the correction paper, coated side down, between the typewriter ribbon and the paper. Keyboard the *incorrect* letter, covering it with the correction coating. Then remove the correction paper, backspace, and keyboard the correct letter. Although quick to make, corrections made with correction paper are usually easy to see. In addition, the covering can rub off, revealing the error.

Correction Tape

Correction tape is self-sticking paper available in strips or sheets. The tape is cut to size to cover the error (a word, a paragraph, or a line) and placed over it. Corrections are then keyboarded directly on the tape. Because corrections made with correction tape are very noticeable, use it only when the original is going to be photocopied.

no'tice·a·ble

Correcting Typewriters

Several electric typewriter models have special ribbons or cartridges that contain correction materials. On some models, the correction ribbons have a coating similar to the one found on correction papers. Other models use a sticky-backed ribbon that actually lifts the incorrect letter off the page. The quality of the correction depends on the typewriter model.

SUPPLY NEEDS

Employers expect *all* of their employees to use good judgment in selecting and using office supplies.

Selection of Supplies

Most of the basic office supplies you need will be waiting at your work space when you begin a new job. Your supervisor will usually tell you where and how to obtain any other supplies you may need. Normally, there will be a supply cabinet or supply room containing the most frequently used supplies. Supplies kept in stock include stationery, printed forms, correction materials, typewriter and printer ribbons, file folders, and pens and pencils. In some offices, you can take what you need from the supply cabinet. In others, you must fill out a requisition or order and give it to the supplies clerk, who will get the item for you. The supplies clerk is responsible for keeping a count of supplies on hand and ordering items when the stock is low.

req·ui·si'tion

Organization of Supplies

The supply room or supply cabinet must be kept neat and organized so that needed supplies can be found quickly. Frequently used supplies should be located so that coworkers do not have to bend or reach to get them. If you are responsible for keeping the supply area in order, follow these guidelines:

1. Label the shelves to help coworkers locate supplies.
2. Arrange numbered forms in numerical order.
3. Avoid filling shelves so full that supplies are difficult to remove.
4. Open the top box or package of a particular item so that the contents are ready to be used. Place additional, unopened packages beneath the opened one.
5. Keep a reorder form or pad in the supply area so that people can let you know what items are needed.
6. Discuss with your supervisor the procedures for ordering and obtaining supplies. Then, follow through by having these procedures put in the office procedures manual or distributed to every worker.

REVIEWING KEY POINTS

1. Quality supplies for business correspondence make a good impression on a reader.
2. Six factors that determine the quality and cost of paper are content, weight, size, finish, type, and color.
3. The most popular paper size for business letters is $8\frac{1}{2}$ by 11 inches.
4. Continuation sheets are blank pages of the same size, color, and finish as the letterhead paper.
5. A carbon pack consists of an original, a carbon, and a second sheet.
6. The machine method is a cost-effective way to assemble a carbon pack.
7. The most common envelope sizes used for business letters are the No. 10 and No. $6\frac{3}{4}$.
8. Interoffice memorandum forms may be purchased in padded forms, snap-apart sets, or carbonless forms.
9. Quality correction products and expert correction methods ensure a neat appearance for business messages.
10. Time and effort can be saved when office supplies are organized and systematically used.

DEVELOPING HUMAN RELATIONS SKILLS

1. Hana can't take it anymore! In addition to her many other job responsibilities, she is in charge of ordering office supplies. Because no standard procedure for requesting supplies has been established, she has been

having trouble keeping track of the supply requests. Hana receives some requests over the phone, some on written notes, and even a few that are casually mentioned in the course of conversation. In addition, she often receives requests a day or two after she has sent the order to the supplier. Obviously, this method of requesting supplies is not working.

   a. What suggestions can you give Hana for improving the procedure for supply requests?

   b. What would be the best way for Hana to introduce these changes to her coworkers?

2. Ben Angelo and Miriam Lopez work in the Customer Service Department, preparing correspondence for customer accounts. When preparing letters with carbon copies, Ben corrects only the original. Therefore, his copies have strike overs where errors have been made.

While Ben is at lunch, Miriam handles a call from a customer who questions the figures stated in a recent letter. Miriam gets the carbon copy of the letter from the files. Because of strike overs, though, she cannot read all of the figures. The reference initials show that Ben prepared the letter. Miriam tells the customer that she will call back with the correct information because she needs to locate the correct figures.

   a. What should Miriam say to Ben?

   b. Are there any advantages to Ben's correction methods?

   c. How can this situation be prevented from happening again?

IMPROVING COMMUNICATION SKILLS

Refer to Appendix A 1.19-1.21/1.25-1.27.

1. On a separate sheet of paper, keyboard these sentences, inserting colons and semicolons when necessary.

   a. Your note reached me this morning I ordered the legal-size pads this afternoon.

   b. Yes, I can have the supplies shelved today but I'll have to organize them in the morning.

   c. The head of purchasing was very clear in her directions she said the order should include these items legal pads, shorthand pads, and letter-size file folders.

   d. Remember what Mr. Harris said about the storage area "Organization is the key to doing anything well."

   e. Send four boxes of letterheads to Jane Pierce, Purchasing two boxes to William Reed, Marketing and five boxes to Cleo Recker, Accounting.

   f. An invoice usually shows what is delivered however, you must compare what you received to what you ordered.

g. The shipment is correct it included these items correctable lift-off ribbons, film ribbons for electronic typewriters, and ribbons for electronic printing calculators.

h. The paper is yellow, and the correction liquid is white therefore, the corrections will be noticeable.

2. Keyboard a summary of the following conversation. Henry Brougham is a new office worker; he's been with the company for 6 months. John Sykes is an experienced office worker who has been with the company for 15 years.

Henry: That meeting on procedures for requesting and using office supplies was a waste of time! Doesn't the company have more important things to worry about? I could have been working instead of sitting in that meeting.

John: I can understand your concern about getting your work done. But misuse of supplies can cost the company a lot of money.

Henry: Like when workers take pens and notepads home?

John: That's not really what I had in mind. I'm thinking of the problems workers cause when they keep large quantities of supplies at their work spaces. As a result, the supplies may become outdated, or the stockroom may run out of an item when someone urgently needs it. We can keep supplies fresh and keep costs down by ordering only those supplies that are needed. You can also help the stockroom run efficiently by returning equipment or supplies that you've stopped using — someone else may need them.

BUILDING PROBLEM-SOLVING SKILLS

1. On a separate sheet of paper, calculate the cost of the following supplies. Add 5% sales tax to each item.

Item	Price	Order
Carbon Paper	$ 8.15/100	250
20-lb. Bond Paper	8.95/Ream	3 Reams
25% Cotton Fiber Paper	4.25/80 Sheets	240 Sheets
9-lb. Second Sheets	9.98/Ream	$1\frac{1}{2}$ Reams
Interoffice Envelopes	24.83/100	350

2. Your company has calculated the average cost of producing a business letter for each of the last ten years. Based on the figures shown in the graph on the next page, answer the following questions.

a. How much more does it cost to produce a letter today than it did at the end of year 1?

b. Between which two years did the cost of producing a letter increase exactly 50¢?

c. Between which two years did the cost of the letter increase most?

d. What is the percentage of increase between year 1 and now?

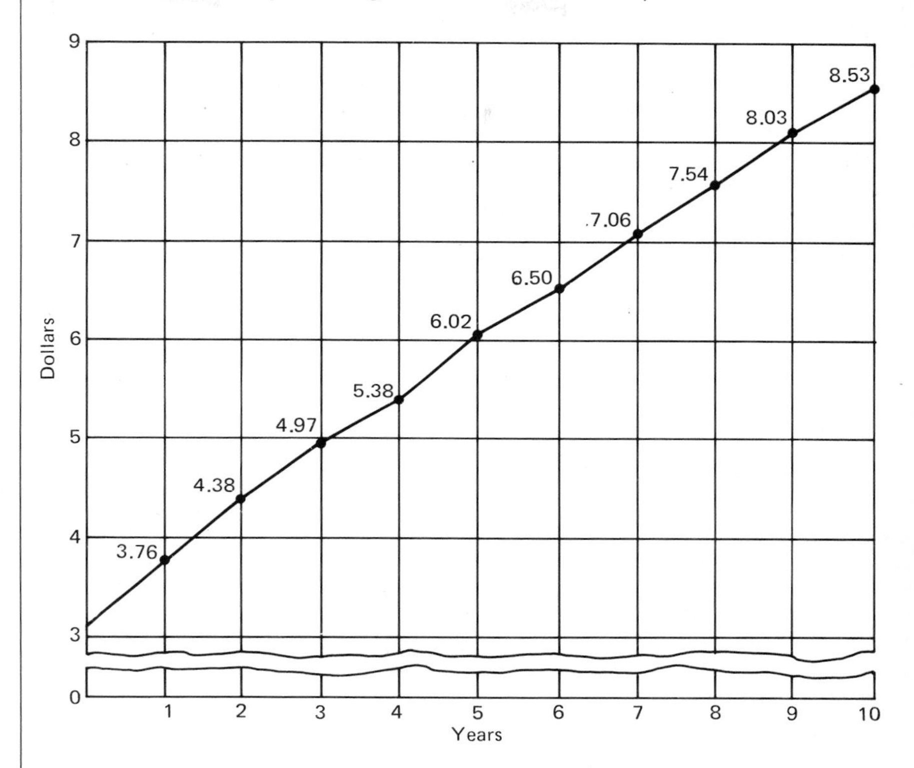

Activities 1 and 2 can be done on information processing equipment.

APPLYING OFFICE SKILLS

1. Compose and keyboard a letter to Moore Supply Company, P.O. Box 20, Wheeling, IL 60090-0102. Request that the following items be sent to you: 8 Diskette Labels #L59386 at $4.95 each; 2000 Mini-Printer Labels #L29264 at $5 for 1000; 2000 Address Labels #L24034 at $23.50 for 500. These items should be sent by UPS. Ask Moore Supply Company to bill you for the total amount. Remind them that under the usual credit terms, you will receive a 2 percent discount if you pay the amount within ten days.

   Use the letterhead in your workbook or plain paper. Format the letter according to the directions given in Chapter 1. Make a carbon copy for Andrew Grove, Purchasing Department. Prepare an envelope in OCR format.

2. Your supervisor has asked you to take inventory of the correction supplies that you have in stock. You make a list of the following items:

13 pencil erasers	6 wheel erasers
25 eraser shields	6 circular typewriter erasers
5 bottles correction liquid	5 correction fluid pens
2 packs correction sheets	24 lift-off correction typewriter ribbons
5 Taperaser dispensers	12 cover-up typewriter ribbons

Write a memo to your supervisor, Thelma Wiggins, listing the supplies you have on hand. Offer to answer any questions she may have about this inventory list. Prepare the memo in correct format on the memorandum form in your workbook or a plain sheet of paper.

Saving Time and Money

Saving Time and Money

What do you do if, after keyboarding the body of a letter, you realize it appears too high or too low on the page? Do you start over? Not necessarily. To save keyboarding time and office supplies, try making these adjustments.

To add length to a letter:

1. Repeat the company name in capital letters a double space below the complimentary close.
2. Leave four or five blank lines for the handwritten signature.
3. Keyboard the reference initials three to six lines below the keyboarded business title.

To shorten a letter:

1. Leave only two blank lines for the handwritten signature.
2. If you are using modified-block format, keyboard the reference intitials on the same line as the keyboarded business title.
3. Single space between the reference initials, the enclosure and copy notations, and the postscript.

UNIT 8

BUSINESS REPORTS AND SPECIAL DOCUMENTS

- Preparing Business Reports
- Keyboarding Business Reports
- Keyboarding Special Business Documents

CHAPTER 1

PREPARING BUSINESS REPORTS

Business reports give information about a decision, a plan, a proposal, or a situation. Reports can be long or short, formal or informal. Whatever the content, all reports have a common purpose — to present information in a form that is easy to read and easy to use.

There are generally three stages in the preparation of a business report. First, the writer prepares an outline of the major points to be discussed. Second, the writer prepares a rough draft of the report. After the rough draft is keyboarded, the writer edits the report — that is, makes necessary changes and corrections. This stage continues until the writer is satisfied that the draft is clear, complete, concise, and correct. Third, a final draft of the report is prepared in one of three formats.

As you study this chapter, you will find answers to the following questions:

- What are the two most common outline forms, and how are they organized?
- What is the best way to prepare a rough draft?
- How are proofreader's symbols used to mark changes in copy?
- What are the three formats that can be used to prepare final draft reports?
- What do the following terms mean: **outline, topic outline, sentence outline, proofreader's symbols, letter format, memorandum format, manuscript format?**

OUTLINES

To plan the content of a report, the writer prepares an outline. It is the skeleton, or bare bones, of the report. The **outline** lists the main ideas in the order in which they will be discussed. Since the outline is for the writer's personal use, it may be handwritten or keyboarded. When the report is completed, a copy of the outline may be used as the table of contents.

di·vi'sions

in'di·cat·ed

The writer uses a system of numbering to help organize information in the outline. Each level of numbers and letters indicates the relative importance of the information. As Illustration 8–1 shows, major divisions of the outline are identified by Roman numerals. Secondary, or less important, topics are identified by capital letters; major points are indicated by Arabic numerals. Minor points are identified by lower-case letters, and supporting information by Arabic numerals enclosed in parentheses.

en'tries

As you can see in the example, there must be at least two entries at each level of the outline. For example, if there is a *I*, there must be a *II*. If there is an *A*, there must be a *B*; and so on.

Illustration 8–1
Topic outline

BUSINESS REPORTS

TS
I. Introduction
DS
II. Outlines
DS
  A. Purpose
  B. Types
    1. Topic
    2. Sentence
  C. Structure
    1. Parallel
    2. Nonparallel
DS
III. Rough Drafts
DS
  A. Purpose
  B. Guidelines for Typing
    1. Paper
    2. Margins
    3. Page Numbers
DS
IV. Final Draft
DS
  A. Form
    1. Letter format
      a. Styles
      b. Special features
    2. Memorandum format
    3. Manuscript format
      a. Introductory pages
        (1) Cover
        (2) Title page
        (3) Letter of authorization
        (4) Preface
        (5) Table of contents
        (6) List of tables and charts
        (7) Summary
      b. Body
        (1) Introduction
        (2) Text
        (3) Conclusions
      c. Supplementary pages
        (1) Appendix
        (2) Bibliography
        (3) Index
  B. Proofreading
DS
V. Summary

Outlines are usually written in either topic or sentence form. In a **topic outline,** a word or short phrase identifies the content to be discussed in each section of the report. A **sentence outline** uses complete sentences to describe the content. The two forms should not be mixed. Use either phrases or complete sentences — but not both — within a single outline.

par'al·lel

In a topic outline, the phrases at each level should be parallel in structure. That is, if one entry begins with a verb, all other entries at that level should begin with verbs. If one entry contains a noun phrase, all related entries should also contain noun phrases.

Parallel Structure (Verb Phrases)	**Nonparallel Structure**
I. Listen Actively	I. Listen Actively
A. Discipline Yourself	A. Discipline Yourself
1. Reserve Judgment	1. Reserve Judgment
2. Listen Selectively	2. Selective Listening
3. Summarize Mentally	3. Mental Summaries
4. Give Feedback	4. Feedback
B. Avoid Half-Listening	B. Half-Listening
II. Be Smart	II. Listening Smarter

pre'vi·ous

When keyboarding outlines, you can save time by setting the tab stops so that the number or letter of each new level of phrases or sentences begins under the first word of the previous entry. Periods should be aligned vertically at each level and followed by two blank spaces.

ROUGH DRAFTS

The content of a report is usually keyboarded one or more times in a rough draft form. A rough draft is keyboarded accurately, but with little attention to layout or appearance. The purpose of a rough draft is to get the writer's thoughts on paper. The writer can then work on improving the organization, wording, style, and content of the report.

When preparing a rough draft, follow these general guidelines:

1. Use inexpensive letter-size paper. Colored paper is often used so that the draft copy stands out among the papers on the desk, making it easy to find and keep pages of the draft together.
2. Prepare only one copy unless directed otherwise.
3. Use wide margins and double or triple spacing. This extra space allows for writing in corrections that are easy to read.
4. Number each page with the draft number and page number. For example, page 8 in the second draft would be labeled 2–8.
5. On electric typewriters, strike over and X-out errors to save time. On information processing equipment, you can either correct errors as you keyboard or go back and make corrections after you have completed keyboarding the entire document.

Draft 2-10

Outlook

Considered by some to be mature the metal container business is oneof significant potential as new markets open up world wide. New technology have met changing demands of growing market segments. Metal container usage continues to increase.

In the decade ahead, more than sixty per cent of the can vlume in the world will be made and used outside the U. S.

Continental Can Company has a leadership position in many of these world markets, where the long term gorwth potential is good. CCC wants to become the least-cost producer. Continental will be in place as demand increases and have the capacity to meet that demand.

Illustration 8–2
Rough draft of a report

6. Save all drafts until the final report is completed and presented. (The writer may decide to add sections that were deleted from an earlier draft of the report.)

As report writers work with the content in the rough draft, they may use **proofreader's symbols** to mark changes and corrections. These symbols are a kind of shorthand with generally recognized meanings. In order to follow the writer's instructions, you need to understand what these symbols mean. Frequently used proofreader's marks and their meanings are shown in Illustration 8–3 on page 298. A rough draft of a report with proofreader's symbols is shown in Illustration 8–2.

FINAL DRAFTS

fi'nal·ized

Once the content of the rough draft has been finalized — corrected and changed for the last time — it is prepared in final report form. The content of the report may be presented in letter, memorandum, or manuscript format.

Letter Format

Reports that are prepared in **letter format** use standard letter parts. Margins and spacing are the same as those of a regular business letter. Because a letter report is usually longer than a regular business letter, it may contain headings and other features to make it easier to read and understand. Tables may be used to present financial information, as shown in the report in Illustration 8–4 on page 299.

Symbol	Meaning	Example	Corrected Copy
℘	delete, take out	manusscript	manuscript
CAPS or ≡	use capital letter	john C. Donaldson	John C. Donaldson
lc or /	use lowercase letter	Susan D. DoNaldson	Susan D. Donaldson
∧	insert here	license aplication	license application
∧	insert comma	Tom, Dick and Harry	Tom, Dick, and Harry
∨	insert apostrophe	Palomas paintings	Paloma's paintings
∨	use quotation marks	She set the quota''	She set the ''quota''
⊙	use period	Grandberg Corp	Grandberg Corp.
(:)	use colon	it was 7 35 p.m.	it was 7:35 p.m.
(;)	use semicolon	It rained we fled.	It rained; we fled.
⁀	close up	Once up on a time	Once upon a time
#	insert space	intwo colors	in two colors
¶	indent for paragraph	¶ Kay was slow in her work.	Kay was slow in her work.
no ¶	no paragraph	no ¶ They applauded	They applauded and
∿	transpose	clohting	clothing
[	move to left	[steady stream of	steady stream of
]	move to right	] liquid form	liquid form
(sp)	spell out in full	ACME Moving (Co)	ACME Moving Company
stet	let stand as is	I am, however, glad	I am, however, glad

Illustration 8–3
Common proofreading symbols

Letter format is generally used for shorter, less formal reports. If the report runs more than one page, each continuation sheet must carry an appropriate heading. Such a heading is the same as that used on the second and following pages of a regular business letter (see Unit 7).

Memorandum Format

Short, informal reports can also be prepared in **memorandum format,** as shown in Illustration 8–5 on page 300. The format, margins, and spacing of the memorandum report are the same as those used in any other interoffice memorandum. Like letter reports, memorandum reports may also include headings and tables.

Mr. Robert E. Flowers
Page 3
January 15, 19--

projection of additio
reevaluate our divide

Should you have any q
the Pueblo office (30

Sincerely

Marta Sepulveda

Marta Sepulveda
Controller

dd

CB PRODUCTS

CB Products, Inc.
1001 Lake Avenue,
Pueblo,
Colorado
80120

January 15, 19--

Mr. Robert E. Flowers
Chief Executive Officer
CB Products, Inc.
900 Southwest Fifth Avenue
Portland, OR 97204

Dear Mr. Flowers

After completing the analysis of our financial status here in the Colorado office, I am prepared to bring you up to date on the financial position of CB Products.

Progress Report on the Five-Year Plan

With the completion of the second year of the current five-year plan, all phases of the growth plan are ahead of schedule. Our sales target for 1984 were set at $5.25 billion and earnings were targeted to reach $430 million, doubling the 1979 earnings level. In 1980, the corporation achieved sales of $4.4 billion, which is 84% of the goal, and earnings reached $302 million, or 70% of the 1984 objective.

Capital expenditures for new capacity in the building products area amounted to $95 billion. Major completed projects included two new Southern pine plywood plants, a new roofing plant, seven new distribution centers, and a number of expansion projects.

Table I

CAPITAL EXPENDITURES*

CB Products, Inc.

	1980	1981
Property, Plant, and Equipment		
Building Products	$ 70	$ 95
Pulp and Paper	75	45
Chemicals	90	90
Natural Resources		
Timber	75	95
Natural Gas	10	20
Total Capital Expenditures	$450	$480

*Figures in millions to nearest 5 million.

Illustration 8–4
Letter report

Manuscript Format

man'u·script

Lengthy, formal reports are usually prepared in manuscript format. The **manuscript format** consists of paragraphs with headings that divide the paragraphs into sections. Procedures for keyboarding a report in manuscript format are discussed in the next chapter.

Formal reports are usually longer and have more complex content than reports prepared as letters and memorandums. To save the reader time and effort in reading and understanding the report, headings are used to identify the topic of each section. In addition, the writer may include additional parts as an aid to the reader. For example, there may be a summary, which briefly describes the content of the report. Special report parts that may be included in formal reports are discussed in the following section.

INTEROFFICE MEMORANDUM

TO J. W. Wilcox
FROM Elaine Wilson
DATE February 15, 19--
SUBJECT Pinnacle Consultants Study

We have received the report of the study conducted by Pinnacle Consultants, Inc., to determine the degree of receptivity to our recent advertising campaign. The following points were made.

Extent of the Study

The survey staff of Pinnacle sampled some 245 households within the county. Those surveyed subscribed to the Toledo Gazette and had at least one television set in the household. As you recall, the Gazette was used extensively to advertise our products, and television station WQVO carried four spots daily for five weeks.

Results of the Study

As reported by Pinnacle, a large percentage of those surveyed (42 percent) could readily identify the slogan selected for the campaign, "Be sure it's a Devlin." Some 27 percent of the households reported that they had at least one Devlin product on the premises.

Conclusions and Recommendations

Pinnacle concluded that the recent advertising campaign was very effective based on the high degree of recognition. They recommended that the present level of advertising be continued and, if possible, that it be extended to the adjacent counties.

The report is available for review by you and your staff. If you feel it necessary to act on the report in the immediate future, perhaps a meeting of the Executive Council should be called.

jh

Illustration 8–5
Memorandum report

PARTS OF A FORMAL BUSINESS REPORT

in·tro·duc′to·ry

sup·ple·men′ta·ry

The parts of a formal report prepared in manuscript format can be grouped according to the purposes they serve: introductory pages, the body, and supplementary pages. The *introductory pages* (cover, title page, letter of authorization, letter of transmittal, preface, table of contents, list of tables and graphs, and summary) prepare the reader to read and understand the body of the report. The *body* of the report (introduction, text, and conclusions) contains the information that the writer wishes to give the reader. The *supplementary pages* (notes, appendix, bibliography, and index) provide extra information that may interest the reader. Not every formal report contains all the parts described in this section. The writer must decide which parts of those discussed in this unit will best help the reader understand the report. Once the parts are prepared, keyboarded, and proofread, they are arranged in the order in which they are presented on pages 301–304.

REPORT ON THE RECEPTIVITY
OF THE DEVLIN PRODUCTS ADVERTISING CAMPAIGN

by

Elizabeth McRae
General Consultant
Pinnacle Consultants, Inc.

February 12, 19--

Illustration 8–6
Title page

Introductory Pages

The types of information included in the *introductory pages* of the report depend on the kinds and number of people it is written for, how complex the content is, and how long the report is. A lengthy, formal report prepared for a large audience of readers may have several pages of introductory material. A short report with a smaller audience may contain only a title page and letter of transmittal.

trans·mit'tal

Cover The cover shows the title of the report centered attractively in all capital letters. The paper used for the cover should be of the same quality as that used for the rest of the report.

Title page The title page contains the report title; the writer's name, title, and, sometimes, company; and the date. This information should be attractively arranged on the page.

CONTENTS

Illustration 8–7
Table of contents

Letter of authorization The writer may choose to include a copy of the letter of authorization in the introductory pages of the report. This is the letter written to the report writer to request that the report be prepared. A standard business letter format is used.

Letter of transmittal The letter of transmittal is a personal message from the writer to the readers of the report. Prepared in business letter format, it states the purpose of the report, includes helpful comments about using the information, and closes with a message of goodwill.

Preface The preface may be used in place of an introduction. It presents the purpose, scope, general findings, and conclusions of the report.

Table of contents The table of contents is an outline of the report showing the page on which each section begins. It saves the reader time in locating specific information.

TABLES AND GRAPHS

Illustration 8–8 List of tables and graphs

List of tables and graphs Used when a report contains many tables and graphs, the list is prepared in the same format as the table of contents, with appropriate page numbers.

Summary The summary contains the important points of the report. It saves time for those who cannot read the whole report and may also serve as a preview to the report. It is prepared in standard manuscript format.

Body

The most important pages of the report make up the body. It contains all of the information the writer wants the reader to have concerning the topic of the report. The body may be divided into three sections: introduction, text, and conclusions.

Introduction The introduction gives the reader a brief preview of the report. It explains why the report was prepared, what the subject matter is, what information was used and how it was collected, and how all of the information is being presented.

Text of the report The text consists of the facts and findings that make up the main body of the report. This is usually the longest section of the report.

Conclusions Some reports must do more than just present information. The writer may analyze the information and reach a conclusion or make a recommendation. Such information is usually presented in a list, but it may also be in paragraph form.

rec·om·men·da'tion

Supplementary Pages

Supplementary pages are pages that "add to" the content of the report. They save the reader time in using the report information or give the reader additional information relating to the report. For example, a copy of a questionnaire used in gathering information for the report might be presented in the supplementary pages.

The following supplementary parts might be used when the report is very long or technical.

Notes Many reports contain a listing of notes or footnotes arranged in numerical order. Notes identify the sources of quotes or references presented in the body of the report. A "Notes" section may be used if the sources are not identified in footnotes at the bottom of the text pages on which they are cited. The format for keyboarding notes is presented in the next chapter.

Appendix The appendix contains additional information that is related to the report content, but which does not logically fit in the body of the report. For example, questionnaires, graphs or summary tables, additional references, and other reports may be included in an appendix.

bib·li·og'ra·phy

Bibliography If a report contains information quoted or paraphrased from sources, those sources are included in the bibliography at the end of the report. The bibliography is an alphabetical listing of all sources referred to or used by the writer in preparing the report.

Index The index is an alphabetical guide to the content of the report. Although not a part of most business reports, an index can greatly aid a reader in finding specific information in the body of the report. The index consists of key words or phrases that describe the content and shows the page numbers on which these words and phrases appear.

PROOFREADING

A report must be proofread, or examined closely, at every stage of preparation to be sure that errors are corrected and that content is not left out. The final draft of the report represents the company, the writer, and those who assisted in preparing the report, so it is important that it be complete and correct.

The writer proofreads the report before it is prepared in final form. Then, before even one page of the final manuscript is keyboarded, the report must be read carefully to make sure that there are no questions about or problems with the format or content. Both the person who keyboards the report and the report writer proofread the complete report again after it is prepared in final form.

If you are preparing final draft manuscript, check it for grammar, punctuation, and format *before* you begin keyboarding it. You should be able to answer *yes* to the following questions:

1. Is every sentence in the report a complete sentence?
2. Are all words spelled correctly?
3. Are all figures, amounts, and percentages accurate?
4. Are the headings parallel in structure?
5. Are the graphs and tables titled and clearly labeled?
6. Do all reference sources contain complete information?
7. Are the sections of the report arranged in the correct order?
8. Is the report complete?

Before returning the final draft of the report to the writer, read it through two or more times. On the first reading, read for meaning. Ask yourself, "Does this make sense? Is each sentence clear, or have words been added, changed, or left out?" The second and third times through, read slowly and look carefully for keyboarding errors and for incorrect spelling, capitalization, and punctuation. Ask yourself, "Have I made all the changes marked on the rough draft? Are the corrections neat? Is this perfect?" When you are certain the report is complete and correct, arrange the pages in order and return it to the writer for approval.

REVIEWING KEY POINTS

1. Business reports give information about a decision, a plan, a proposal, or a situation.
2. The three stages of report preparation are: (1) developing an outline, (2) writing and keyboarding the rough draft, and (3) preparing the final draft.
3. An outline helps the writer organize information for the report. A numbering system — which consists of Roman numerals, capital letters, and Arabic numerals — indicates the importance of and relationship between topics in the outline.

4. An outline may be written in topic or in sentence form, but these two forms should never be mixed in one outline.
5. A rough draft is prepared so the writer can improve the wording, writing style, and content of the report. Use double or triple spacing and leave wide margins for the writer's corrections and changes.
6. Final drafts of reports may be prepared in letter, memo, or manuscript format, depending on their length and formality and the writer's preference.
7. A formal report in manuscript format may contain introductory and supplementary parts in addition to the body.
8. The person who keyboards the report is responsible for proofreading it at each stage of preparation. The grammar, punctuation, and format must be correct and the report complete.
9. If you are preparing final draft manuscript, you should read through the final draft several times before returning the document to the writer. Read for meaning, keyboarding errors, incorrect spelling, and punctuation.

DEVELOPING HUMAN RELATIONS SKILLS

1. Matthew Kirk is a correspondence specialist for an insurance company. Recently he was assigned to keyboard a 45-page sales report. He prepared a rough draft of the report and checked all the figures in the sales summary tables. After making corrections and proofreading the report, Matthew gave copies to the word processing supervisor and to the report writer.

   After three revisions, a final draft of the report was keyboarded and printed. Matthew, his supervisor, and the report writer divided up the final draft for proofreading. A week after copies of the report were sent to the regional offices, Matthew received an irate memo from the report writer. She had discovered several calculation errors in the tables. When he checked the final copy against his rough draft, Matthew saw that the errors were not his. His original figures were correct.

   a. How should Matthew explain this problem to his supervisor?

   b. How do you think the final copy of the report ended up with errors in it?

2. Janice Harrington has just been hired as a clerical worker; this is her first full-time job. Her supervisor has given her a rough draft of a report and asked her to prepare a final draft. He told her that he had carefully edited the report for format and content.

   As Janice reads through the report, she discovers that it has some punctuation errors and that three of the headings are not parallel with the rest of the headings. She decides to make the corrections without saying anything to her supervisor.

   a. What problems could result from Janice's decision?

   b. How could Janice have handled this situation better?

IMPROVING COMMUNICATION SKILLS

Refer to Appendix A 1.22-1.24.

1. On a separate sheet of paper, keyboard these sentences, inserting apostrophes where needed.
   a. Hal left the report on his supervisors desk.
   b. Pauls letter asked when payment could be expected.
   c. As a result of todays technology, the term "technostress" has been coined.
   d. The article "Managing Computer Anxiety" was published in Mays issue of Technology Update.
   e. Lynns new suit is perfect for this cool weather.
   f. The managers meeting is scheduled for Monday morning.
   g. Nancys and Harolds terminals are "down" today.
   h. The report on childrens education was completed on time.
   i. Chris outline was not ready by 4 p.m.
2. On Friday afternoon, your supervisor gives you a three-part, 55-page marketing report to keyboard in final draft format. The report must be at sales headquarters by Monday morning. If you and two of your coworkers work on the report Friday afternoon and Saturday morning, you could get it in the mail by noon on Saturday. On a separate sheet of paper, compose a memo to two coworkers (use the names of two classmates) asking for their help in putting this report together. Explain the situation. Then tell them that you need their help in this emergency and that you would appreciate a positive reply. Format the memo as you learned in Unit 7.

BUILDING PROBLEM-SOLVING SKILLS

1. Refer to the chart listing the number of report pages keyboarded each month in your information processing department. Then on a separate sheet of paper answer the questions that follow.

Month	Pages	Month	Pages
January	444	July	365
February	456	August	448
March	307	September	401
April	240	October	329
May	295	November	380
June	323	December	415

   a. What is the monthly average of report pages keyboarded?
   b. At a cost of $3.05 a page, what is the total yearly cost of keyboarding report pages?
   c. What is the average cost per month of keyboarding report pages?

2. Using the sample document library shown here, see how quickly and accurately you can locate the correct answers to these questions. Place your answers on a separate sheet of paper.
   a. How many memos are stored in the library?
   b. Which author has stored the most documents?
   c. Which operator has keyboarded the most documents?
   d. How many documents are permanently stored?
   e. On which date will most of the documents be deleted?
   f. How many documents were created on April 5?
   g. On which diskette are two of the documents stored?
   h. What is the range of the diskette numbers?
   i. On which date were the most documents created?
   j. How many different documents were created on that date?
   k. Which operator keyboarded the most documents that day?
   l. What documents did that operator keyboard?
   m. Which one of those documents will be retained the longest?

SAMPLE DOCUMENT LIBRARY

No.	Date Created	Document Name	Document Type/ Retention Date	Author/ Operator
1261A	04/03/--	OMI Equipment	Memo 6/30	Atkins, J. Rowthe, A.
1262A	04/03/--	Teaching Hospital	Report 6/30	Thiem, P. Dragul, S.
1263A	04/04/--	VRDB for Issuers	Memo 6/30	McLaughlin, D. Lowe, E.
1264A	04/04/--	Woodham	Report 6/30	Atkins, J. Dragul, S.
1265A	04/05/--	Financing Schedule	Other 6/30	Keene, L. Rowthe, A.
1266A	04/05/--	New Business	Report 12/31	Atkins, J. McCoy, W.
1267A	04/05/--	Inventory	Letter Permanent	Zwerin, S. Agosto, D.
1268A	04/05/--	VRDB Market	Report Permanent	McLaughlin, D. Dragul, S.
1269A	04/05/--	Indiana Growth	Chart 6/30	Gold, T. Dragul, S.
1270A	04/09/--	Non-Callable Bonds	Letter 6/30	McLaughlin, D. Lowe, E.

Activities 1 and 2 can be done on information processing equipment.

APPLYING OFFICE SKILLS

1. Select a current magazine article about office equipment or procedures. On a separate sheet of paper, keyboard an outline, in either topic or sentence form, on the article's content.
2. John Sullivan, a Certified Public Accountant, wants the following letter report sent to the Board of Directors, B. B. Brooks, Inc., 3830 Kelley Avenue, Cleveland, OH 44114. Using the letterhead stationery in your workbook, keyboard the report in a modified-block format.

Ladies and Gentlemen:
Subject: Auditor's Report

¶ We have examined the balance sheets of B. B. Brooks, Incorporated, and its subsidiary companies as of April 29, 19--, and the related consolidated statements of operations, retained earnings, and changes in financial position for the year. The examinations were made in accordance with generally accepted auditing standards. Included in such examinations were tests of the accounting records and such other auditing procedures as we considered necessary.

¶ In our opinion, the aforementioned consolidated financial statements present fairly the financial position of B. B. Brooks, Incorporated, and subsidiary companies as of April 29, 19--. The statements are in conformity with generally accepted accounting principles consistently applied during the period examined.

CHAPTER 2

KEYBOARDING BUSINESS REPORTS

As with business letters, the appearance as well as the content of a business report is very important. Using standard procedures for formatting and keyboarding reports helps you create a professional-looking product.

Features such as wide margins, double spacing, and headings make reports easy to read and understand. Tables, charts, and graphs can be used to present financial or statistical information clearly and concisely. If you assist in preparing reports, you should do your best to ensure that the final copies are attractive, accurate, and readable.

As you study this chapter, you will find answers to the following questions:

- How do the three methods for binding reports differ?
- What formatting guidelines are followed for each type of binding?
- How are the three levels of headings in reports formatted?
- How are tables and graphs prepared and used in reports?
- How are notes and bibliograhic references formatted and keyboarded?
- What do the following terms mean: **key line, graphs, endnotes, footnotes, bibliography, move, cut-and-paste function, header and footer instructions, automatic pagination?**

FORMATTING BUSINESS REPORTS

Formal reports are formatted (laid out on paper) according to standard guidelines set up for the type of binding, spacing, and heading being used.

Binding

A formal report may be bound, or fastened together, at the top *(topbound)* or at the left edge *(leftbound)*. A report may also be *unbound* and simply placed in a folder or large envelope. The choice of binding method determines the margin settings and the placement of page numbers for the report.

Margins

Illustration 8–9 Margins used in formal reports

As a general rule, top, left, right, and bottom margins should be about equal. For an unbound report, a standard one-inch margin is used on all pages of the body except the first, as shown in Illustration 8–9. Keep the right margin fairly straight by using correct end-of-line word divisions when necessary.

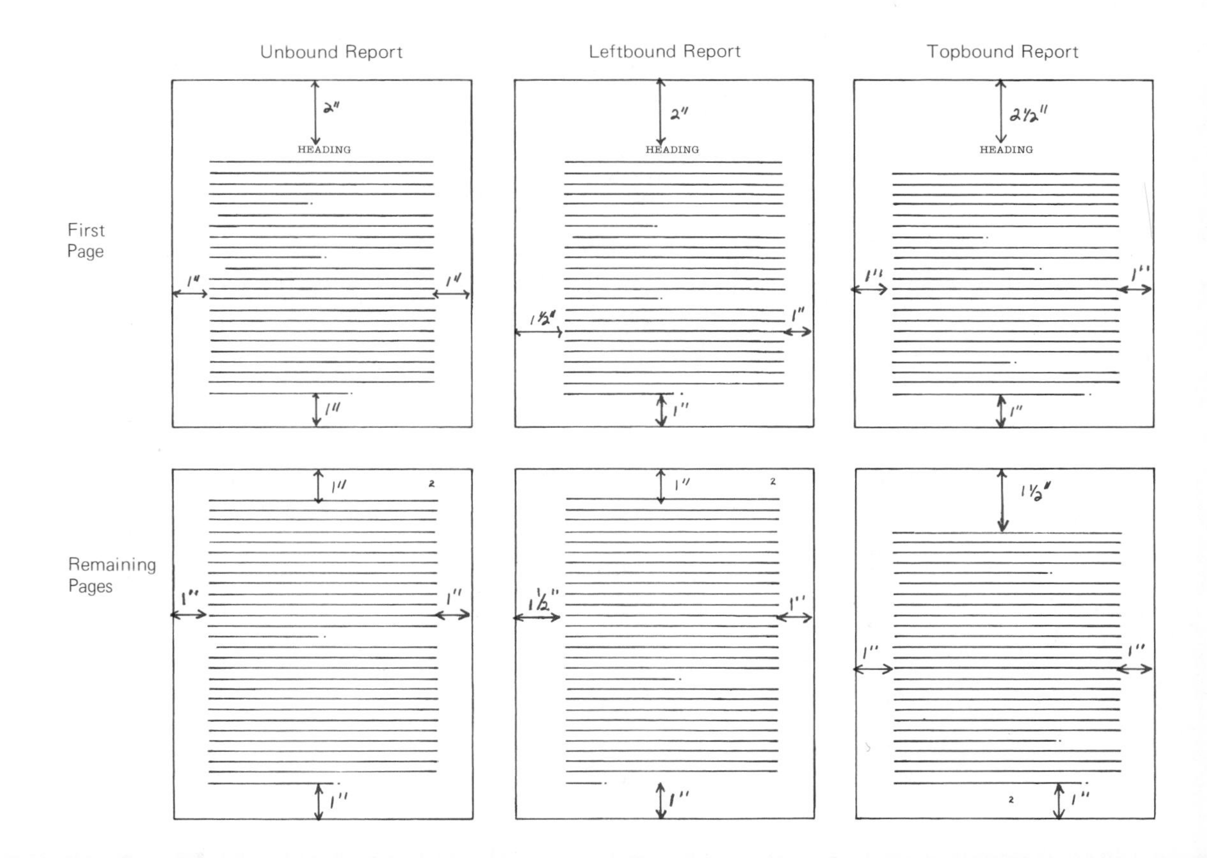

Generally speaking, however, it is not practical to use end-of-line divisions when you are keyboarding on information processing equipment.

To achieve a one-inch margin all around on bound reports, allow extra spacing where the binding is placed. Add an extra half inch to the left margin of a leftbound report and to the top margin of a topbound report. Once the report is bound, the binding will conceal the extra half inch.

Certain parts of the report have individual page layouts, so their margins will be different from the text pages. For example, title page information is usually centered vertically and horizontally. A letter of transmittal included with the report may be set up in block-letter format.

Paging

Two types of numerals are used in numbering report pages. Introductory pages — including the title page, table of contents, and so forth — are usually numbered with small Roman numerals. The title page does not carry a number, but it is understood that it is numbered "i." The remaining introductory pages are numbered beginning with the small Roman numeral "ii," centered one-half inch (three lines) from the bottom of each page.

ex·cep′tions

With certain exceptions, all pages in the body and supplementary parts of the report are numbered with Arabic numerals. If the report is *leftbound* or *unbound,* the page number is centered one-half inch from the bottom of the first page. On the remaining pages of the report, the page numbers are placed even with the right margin, one-half inch from the top of the page. For *topbound* reports all page numbers are centered one-half inch from the bottom of the page.

Often the page number on the first page of the report is omitted because it is clear by layout and content that it is page 1. Many people think the first page is more attractive without the number. If you choose to omit it, begin numbering the pages of the report with page 2.

Spacing

It is standard practice to double space the body of the report and to indent paragraphs five spaces. The main exceptions are long quotations and numbered lists.

quo·ta′tion

Quotations Quoted material is text that is copied word for word from a source such as a book, magazine, or speech. When a short quotation — three lines or less — is used in a report, it is enclosed in quotation marks within the double-spaced body of the report. If the quoted material is four or more lines, the following guidelines are used:

1. Single space the quotation.
2. Indent the entire quotation five spaces from both the left and right margins of the report.

The Bureau of Labor Statistics projects just over five million new jobs for blue-collar workers by 1990. More jobs will become available for office workers than for all categories of blue-collar employment.

> Nearly 5 million new clerical positions will become available in the next decade, with another 12 million openings due to attrition. Employment opportunities will grow most rapidly for secretaries, bank clerks, cashiers, and teachers' aides--areas with anticipated growth of about 3.5 percent annually during the decade.[4]

During the same period, office workers will be exposed to technological changes that will drastically alter their work environment. Experts predict that "vocational retraining will be required every five to seven years as job skills become obsolete."[5] An increasing number of companies will inaugurate tuition reimbursement plans for job-related courses.

Illustration 8–10 Spacing used for quoted material

3. Indent the first line of each paragraph of the quotation an additional five spaces so that it is clearly marked as a paragraph.
4. Omit the opening and closing quotation marks.

Examples of correctly spaced quoted material are shown in Illustration 8–10.

Lists If numbered or lettered items appear in the report, they are single spaced with a double space separating the items. Indent the number or letter of each item five spaces. When an item in a list takes more than one line, the additional lines are indented to align with the first word in the first line.

Headings

read·a·bil′i·ty

Headings improve the readability of reports. The reader can glance through a report, read only the headings, and get an overview of the main points discussed. Headings also act as a flag, alerting the reader to a new topic.

The most important heading in a report is the title. It is usually placed two inches (12 lines) from the top of the first page of the body. Because it is so important, it is centered in all caps. For a leftbound report, be sure to adjust the center point of the page to allow for the wider left margin.

Section headings are less important than the title. There are three standard positions for these headings. They may be centered, blocked at the left margin, or indented and run in with the first line of a paragraph. The position of a heading indicates its importance. Centered headings are more important than side headings, and side headings are more important than paragraph headings. Illustration 8–11 on page 314 shows these headings.

If a centered heading immediately follows the report title, place the heading a double space below the title. If there is not a centered heading after the title, then triple space and begin the text of the report. On information processing equipment, it is usually more efficient to quadruple space (two returns in double spacing) rather than triple space.

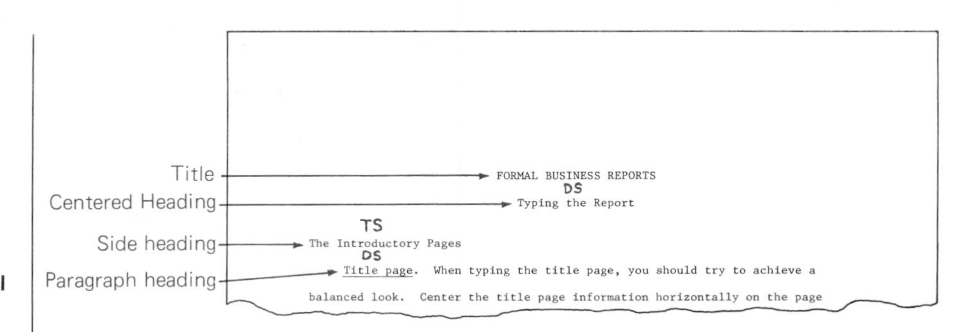

Illustration 8–11
Headings in a formal report

Centered headings Centered headings usually correspond to the major divisions of the report outline. You may keyboard these headings either in all caps or with initial caps — that is, with only the first letter of key words capitalized. If you use initial caps, you may choose to underline the heading. Unless it immediately follows the report title, triple space (or on information processing equipment, quadruple space) before a centered heading and double space after it.

sec′on·dar·y

Side headings Side headings, sometimes known as secondary headings, usually relate to the outline items identified by capital letters. These headings are blocked at the left margin and keyboarded with initial caps. Leave a triple space (or quadruple space) before them and a double space after them. You may choose to underline side headings.

Paragraph headings These headings correspond to those outline items that are labeled with Arabic numerals. Paragraph headings are indented, underlined, and followed by a period. Capitalize only the first letter of the first word. Leave two spaces after the period and begin the paragraph text on the same line with the heading. Since this heading is part of the paragraph itself, leave no extra space above or below a paragraph heading.

PREPARING TABLES AND GRAPHS

sum′ma·rize

Tables and graphs are used to present large amounts of information in a small space. They may summarize or illustrate information discussed in the report. These items are usually placed within the body, or they may be included in an appendix. If a table or graph is too large to fit on the same page with the content that refers to it, place it on the next page. So that the reader will know where to locate the table or graph, include a reference stating that it appears on the next page. Whenever possible, though, try to present the table or graph on the same page as the related content. Double space after the line of text in which the table or graph is mentioned, then begin keyboarding the table or graph. You will find specific instructions for formatting and keyboarding tables and graphs on pages 315–319.

Tables

Most tables have a major heading (or title) and column headings, and many have subheadings as well. The title tells the reader what information the table contains. The title is keyboarded in all caps, centered horizontally, and single spaced if it is more than one line long. The subheading, if one is used, is keyboarded with initial caps. It is centered a double space below the title. Column headings are keyboarded a triple space below the subheading or title. They can be centered over the column or blocked with the beginning of each column. If they are long, break them into more than one line. Column headings are keyboarded with initial caps. Underline the column headings to set them off from the table content. Double space after the headings to the body of the table.

Vertical placement The body of a table can be single or double spaced. If the table is placed in the text of the report, the vertical spacing is very often determined by the length of the table and the amount of space left on the page.

If the table is placed on a page by itself, it should be centered vertically. Follow these steps to determine the number of blank lines to leave at the top of the page:

1. Count the number of keyboarded and blank lines in the table. Include all of the lines in the table heading and body.
2. Subtract the number of lines in Step 1 from 66, the number of lines on letter-size paper.
3. Divide the difference found in Step 2 by 2. The answer is the number of *blank* lines to be left at the top and bottom of the page. If the answer is 16, for example, begin keyboarding the title of the table on line 17.
4. If you want to allow more blank space at the bottom than at the top of the page (commonly called "reading position"), subtract 3 lines from the answer you arrived at in Step 3.
5. On some information processing equipment, top and bottom margins are print settings. You can use the same method for determining vertical spacing, but you must set these margins when you print the document rather than before you begin keyboarding.

Horizontal placement All tables, whether placed within the body of the report or on a page by themselves, must be centered horizontally. One method for determining the horizontal placement of table material is the key line method, shown in Illustration 8–12 on the top of page 316. This method involves the following steps:

1. Remove all margin settings and all tab stops. On information processing equipment, it is not necessary to change the margin settings.
2. Select the longest item or heading in each column and decide the number of spaces to be left between columns — usually an even

INFORMATION PROCESSING EQUIPMENT

Percentage of Use

Jobs	Detroit	Denver	Dallas
Secretary	18.1%	25.2%	33.3%
Administrative Secretary	15.7%	14.3%	27.7%
Executive Secretary	12.3%	19.4%	26.4%
Administrative Assistant	11.4%	18.4%	15.9%
Secretary/Receptionist	12.1%	13.6%	21.1%

Key Line

Administrative Secretary123456Detroit123456Denver123456Dallas

Illustration 8–12
Key line method of horizontal centering

number between 4 and 10. Keyboard the longest item in column 1 (Administrative Secretary). Space (4 times) and keyboard the longest item in column 2 (the heading, Detroit), and so forth. This combination of the longest items from all columns and the spaces to be left between columns is called the **key line**.

3. Determine the beginning position for column 1.
   a. On a typewriter, move the carriage or carrier (typing element) to the center point of the page and backspace once for every two characters (letters, numbers, punctuation marks, and spaces) in the key line. Set the left margin at this point; column 1 will begin here. (On a leftbound report, remember to adjust the center point to provide for a $1\frac{1}{2}$-inch left margin.)
   b. On information processing equipment, use the automatic centering function to center the key line. Set a tab stop at the position where the centered key line begins; column 1 will begin here.
4. From the position where column 1 will begin, space forward once for each character in the first column of the key line (including the spaces to be left between column 1 and column 2). Set a tab stop here; this is where column 2 begins.
5. From the tab stop for column 2, space forward once for every character in the second column of the key line (including the spaces to be left between columns). Set a tab stop here; this is where column 3 will start.
6. Continue with this procedure until you have set a tab stop for each column. On information processing equipment, remember to delete the key line after setting tabs.

Table content A few general rules guide you in keyboarding the table content. In the body of a table, word columns are aligned on the left; figures are aligned on the right or aligned at the decimal points. If a dollar sign is used, it is placed on the line with the first dollar amount, but one space to the left of the longest number in that column. If the column headings contain dates or time periods, they should be arranged in order so that the most recent appears in the right column. Commas should be used to separate millions from thousands and thousands from hundreds. Totals are usually placed at the bottom of the table, with the word *Total* indented a double space below the last line of the table.

Graphs

vis'u·al

Graphs are visual aids that replace numbers or quantities with lines, bars, or sections of circles. Their purpose is to present information in a form that is easy to "see" and understand.

The three most common types of graphs used in business reports are the *line, bar,* and *circle graph.* They are shown in Illustration 8–13. Many computers and microcomputers have software that allows you to create and print line, bar, and circle graphs, often in two or more colors. If you work in a company that has such equipment, find out what graphics are available and how they are produced. Using a computer to create graphic aids can save time and money.

Illustration 8–13a
Line graph

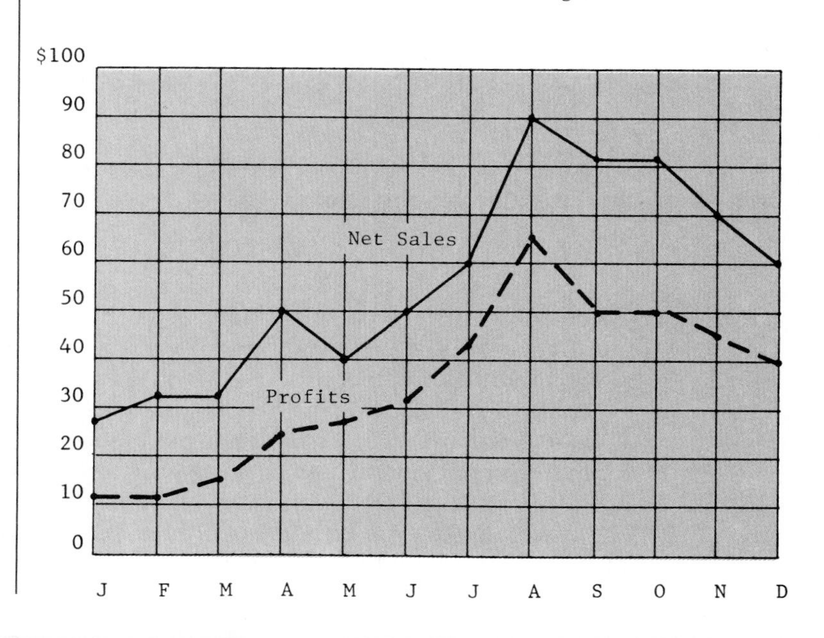

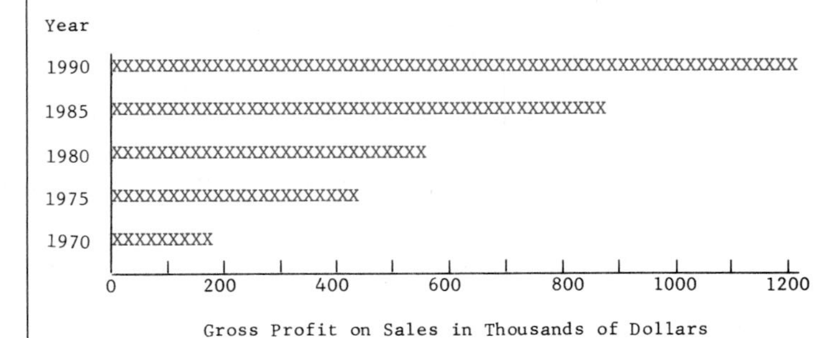

Illustration 8–13b
Bar graph

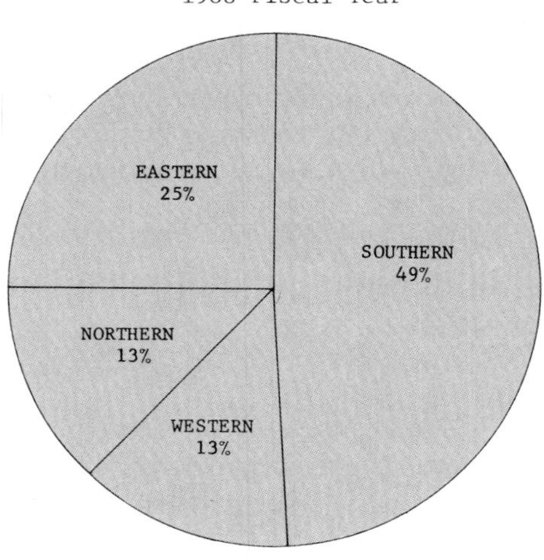

Illustration 8–13c
Circle graph

If you are asked to keyboard or assist in the preparation of a report, you will find these guidelines helpful.

Line Graph

1. Use graph paper to make a working copy.
2. Place periods of time on the horizontal scale across the bottom.
3. Place amounts and quantities on the vertical scale along the left side. Always show a zero quantity.
4. Make the width of the graph about $1\frac{1}{2}$ times the height.
5. Place all words and abbreviations horizontally so that the reader does not have to turn the page sideways to read the information.
6. If the graph contains more than one line, draw each line using a different color or type of line (solid, broken, or dotted). Explain what each color or type of line represents in a key or legend at the bottom of the graph.

Bar Graph

1. Make all bars the same width.
2. Leave a half to a whole bar width between bars.
3. Arrange bars in chronological order or in order of size.
4. Keyboard all words horizontally.

Circle Graph

To draw a circle graph, you need to use a compass and a protractor. Use the compass to make a perfect circle. Use the protractor to figure the size of each pie-shaped section.

cir·cum'fer·ence

1. Change amounts to percentages. The circumference of the circle (360°) represents 100 percent.
2. Arrange the sections of the graph so that the graph is easy to read and understand.
3. Place all words horizontally either inside the sections or outside with lines drawn to the sections.
4. Include the exact percentage that each section represents.

Every graph must be clearly titled. The current trend is to center the title above the graph, capitalizing the key words.

PREPARING NOTES

Notes give a reader two types of information. First, they explain or provide additional information about items discussed in the text of the report. Second, they identify the sources of quotations or facts used in the report. The reader is directed to the notes by raised numbers (called superior or superscript numbers) or sometimes by an asterisk (*) or other symbol. The number or symbol is placed in the text at the end of the quoted material and raised one-half line. Proper placement of superior numbers is shown in Illustration 8–10 on page 313.

as'ter·isk

Note Style

There are standard guidelines for formatting notes that contain references to particular kinds of sources, such as books, magazine articles, speeches, newspapers, or personal interviews. Note style — which includes order, punctuation, and capitalization — varies slightly depending on what reference guide you use. In general, a note contains the author's name; the title of the author's work; publication information, including the date; and the page number on which the quoted material appears. Commas are used to separate most items in a note. You can see examples of approved note style presented in Illustration 8–14 on the next page.

pub·li·ca'tion

The content of a note may be shortened if it contains a reference to a source mentioned in an earlier note. For example, some style books suggest

Illustration 8–14
Footnotes

interruptions throughout the day.[4] Many executives simply fail to instruct their secretaries to screen visitors, and frequently secretaries do not recognize that

---

[1]R. Alec Mackenzie, The Time Trap (New York: McGraw-Hill Book Company, 1975), p. 51.

[2]Alan Lakein, How to Get Control of Your Time and Your Life (New York: New American Library, 1973), p. 71.

[3]Mackenzie, p. 58.

[4]"Tomorrow, Let's Get Organized," Nations Business, March 1980, p. 81.

sub′se·quent

including only the author's name and the page number in subsequent notes. Notice footnote number 3 in the example. It contains a reference to the source in footnote 1. Check the preferred style for notes in your company's procedures manual or in a reference guide approved by the report writer.

Endnotes

Some report writers prefer to have all notes presented at the end of a report on a separate page or pages. **Endnotes,** as these are called, are very easy to set up. If you choose to place all notes at the end of the report, center the title "Notes" or "Endnotes" in all caps two inches from the top of the page. Triple space (on information processing equipment, quadruple space) after the title and keyboard the notes in numerical order. Single space the content of each note, but double space between notes.

Footnotes

In some cases, report writers may prefer to use **footnotes** — notes placed at the foot, or bottom, of the page. To keyboard footnotes at the bottom of text pages, follow these steps:

1. Single space after the last line of text.
2. Use the underscore to make a $1\frac{1}{2}$-inch line (15 spaces, 10-pitch; 18 spaces, 12-pitch) to separate the text from the footnotes, as shown in Illustration 8–14.
3. Double space and indent five spaces.
4. On a typewriter, locate the line finder. Pull the lever forward. Turn the platen knob toward you a half-line space and type the superior figure. On most information processing equipment, you can use the *superscript* function to raise the number or symbol one-half line.
5. Return the line finder to the locked position. Return the platen to the original line space.
6. Single space the content of each footnote, but double space between footnotes.
7. Leave at least a one-inch margin at the bottom of the page.

KEYBOARDING THE BIBLIOGRAPHY

The **bibliography** is an alphabetical listing of all sources used by the writer in preparing the report. It is prepared as a separate page of a report. The bibliography, like notes, contains the author's name, the title of the work, and publication information. However, this information is presented in a different format.

The title "Bibliography" is centered in all caps two inches (12 lines) from the top of the page. Triple space and begin the information for the first bibliographic reference. Start the first line at the left margin, but indent the second and remaining lines five spaces. Single space the lines of each entry; double space between entries.

Because bibliographic references are arranged in alphabetical order, the authors' names are keyboarded last name first. Periods are used to separate the three parts of a bibliographic reference: author's name, title of work, publication information. Page numbers for books are usually omitted.

o·mit'ted

Compare the format of the bibliographic references in Illustration 8–15 with the footnotes in Illustration 8–14.

Before you begin keyboarding a report, find out the writer's preference for note and bibliographic style and placement of notes. If the writer has no preference, follow the guidelines in your office procedures manual or in the reference guide used by your company. These guides usually contain examples of the various types of references that may cause you problems on the job.

Illustration 8–15
Bibliography

BIBLIOGRAPHY

Bliss, Edwin C. Getting Things Done: The ABC's of Time Management. New York: Charles Scribner & Sons, 1976.

Ferner, Jack D. Successful Time Management: The Quick Easy Way. New York: John Wiley & Sons, 1980.

Goldfein, Donna. Everywoman's Guide to Time Management. California: Les Femmes Publishing Company, 1977.

Kleiner, B. H. "Productivity Challenge: Managing Yourself." Management World, February 1980, pp. 17-23.

Lakein, Alan. How to Get Control of Your Time and Your Life. New York: New American Library, 1973.

Mackenzie, R. Alec. The Time Trap. New York: McGraw-Hill Book Company, 1975.

"Tomorrow, Let's Get Organized." Nations Business, March 1980, p. 79-81.

USING INFORMATION PROCESSING FOR REPORTS

When revising a report, a report writer may add, delete, or change text and move around paragraphs or even entire pages. If a report is prepared on a typewriter, minor changes can be time consuming. Often a change requires several pages of text to be retyped. Also, many of the features found in reports — such as footnotes or tables — take extra time and effort to set up on a typewriter.

Information processing equipment, on the other hand, is designed to make setting up and revising documents such as reports easier and faster. For example, most information processing equipment has a **move** or **cut and paste function** that allows the operator to move sections of text without having to rekeyboard them. **Header and footer instructions** print headings, page numbers, or other standard information at the top or bottom of each page. **Automatic pagination** divides a document into pages of a selected number of lines. Other functions useful for report preparation include decimal alignment (for columns of figures) and automatic centering and underlining. These and other information processing terms are defined in the Glossary. How you perform these and other functions depends on the information processing equipment you are using. You will read more about information processing in Unit 12.

REVIEWING KEY POINTS

1. Reports are set up according to how they are to be bound: topbound, leftbound, or unbound.
2. Introductory report pages are numbered with Roman numerals; Arabic numerals are used for the body and supplementary pages.
3. Most pages in a manuscript report are double spaced. Quoted material of four lines or more is indented and single spaced; listed items are single spaced with double spacing between items.
4. The title is centered and keyboarded in all caps. Section headings are centered, blocked at the left margin, or positioned in the first line of a paragraph.
5. Tables and graphs present large amounts of information in picture form and very little space.
6. The three most common types of graphs are line, bar, and circle graphs. Graph parts should be clearly labeled.

7. Notes provide additional information or reference sources for the reader. Popular note formats include *endnotes* and *footnotes.*
8. A bibliography is an alphabetical listing of all sources.
9. Today's information processing equipment can save keyboarding and formatting time and effort.

DEVELOPING HUMAN RELATIONS SKILLS

1. One afternoon recently you finished keyboarding a long report. Your supervisor asked you to make ten copies and collate and staple them. The copies had to be ready for an 8 A.M. meeting the next day. You asked Mary Lou, a coworker, to stay a few extra minutes to help you collate and staple. You made the copies as Mary Lou collated, and then you stapled them. You were able to complete the job in less than 30 minutes.

   After the meeting the next morning, your supervisor brought all of the reports back to you to be re-collated and stapled. Every copy had pages out of order. Needless to say, your supervisor was embarrassed and irritated.

   a. How should you explain this error to your supervisor?

   b. What should you say to Mary Lou?

   c. How could you prevent this problem in the future?

2. Wesley, a correspondence specialist, recently keyboarded a long report for the manager of the Trust Department. He had to call the manager several times to ask about unclear editing instructions. The report draft was so heavily edited that it was hard to tell what was being added, deleted, and changed. The manager became irritated at being interrupted, so Wesley finally just guessed at many of the changes.

   a. How could Wesley have handled this situation better?

   b. What could Wesley and the manager have done to prevent this problem from happening?

IMPROVING COMMUNICATION SKILLS

Refer to Appendix A 1.22-1.24.

1. Keyboard these sentences on a separate sheet of paper, inserting apostrophes where needed.

   a. She said that she wants James progress report by three o'clock.

   b. Mark wants the financial reports outline by three o'clock.

   c. The report stated that Wilmingtons potential for our franchise is as great as Raleighs.

   d. He said he cant pay the full amount; this surprised all of us.

   e. Are you suggesting that wed forget the report?

   f. Its not the right outline.

g. We do not have anyone to keyboard Mollys report.
h. Didnt he ask whether we should increase our prices?
i. Five students earned As on the exam.
j. This outline took two hours work.

2. Estelle Pace, your supervisor at the department store where you work, is preparing a report on the shopping practices of teenagers. She has asked for your views on this topic. Compose a one-page memo to Ms. Pace in which you answer these questions: What are the top five types of items that teenagers purchase? How do they pay for them — cash or charge? Where do they get money for their purchases? Use the memo form in your workbook or plain paper.

BUILDING PROBLEM-SOLVING SKILLS

1. In order to make a circle graph, you must be able to figure percentages. The following factors add up to the cost of writing, keyboarding, and mailing a business letter. For each factor, compute the percent of the total cost as shown. Round your answers to the nearest hundredth of a percent. Then find the number of degrees in a circle that are needed to represent that amount. The answers for the first one are provided.

Letter Cost Factors		Percentage	Degrees of Circle
Dictating time	$2.54	$2.54 ÷ $8.00 = 31.75%	.3175 × 360° = 114.3°
Secretarial time	2.72	= .3175	
Fixed charges	1.72		
Non-productive time	.50		
Mailing costs	.32		
Materials	.20		
Total	$8.00		

2. Customer service workers have to be very good at analyzing situations in order to get the facts and solve the problems. Copy the squares below on a separate sheet of paper. Then test your problem-solving skills in the situations at the top of the next page.

a.
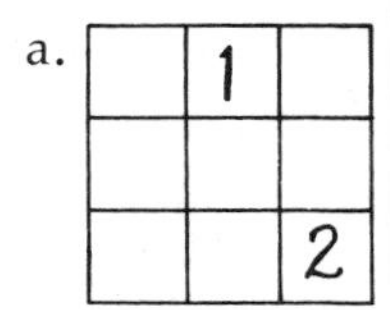

b.
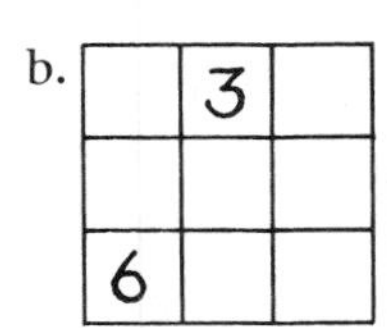

c.
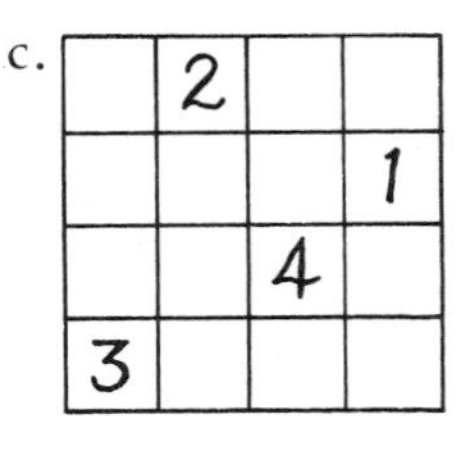

a. Place the numbers 1 through 9 in the squares (one number in each square) so that each column and each row adds up to 15.

b. Place the numbers 4, 5, 7, 8, 9, 10, and 11 in the squares so that each column and each row add up to 21.

c. Place the numbers 1, 2, 3, and 4 in the boxes so that each column contains all four numbers.

Activities 1 and 2 can be done on information processing equipment.

APPLYING OFFICE SKILLS

1. Your supervisor has asked you to prepare a bar graph on letter-size paper. The graph is to be as large as you can make it. The title is "Distribution of Staff Activities." The subtitle is "Provident National Bank, 19 – –." The information you will need for the graph follows.

   Paper Work = 22%

   Client Services = 40%

   Committee Work = 28%

   All Other = 10%

2. Keyboard the following leftbound report on plain paper. Prepare a title page that gives this information: (a) a title, "Happy Hang-ups"; (b) department identificaton, "Marketing Department, Delmar Corporation"; (c) identification of writer, "Prepared by Hester Webster, Customer Service"; and (d) current date. Keyboard all headings as side headings. Prepare a separate page of endnotes.

   Happy Hang-Ups

   (P) If you sometimes think of the phone as a modern inconvenience, you should be especially careful to avoid hasty hang-ups that offend your callers. To help you keep calls brief, not blunt, we have researched "the last word" in keeping telephone calls short but effective. (P) Eliminate Small Talk (P) Without appearing rude, you should eliminate the pleasantries that often open a business call. In fact, Alexander Stewart says, "It's bad business procedure, not just a time waster, to ask about the family or the fishing trip. It's charm school talk that's no longer charming."[1] On the other hand, most of us want to hear something warmer than a brisk, "What can I do for you?" (P) The telephone can make you sound more abrupt than you really are. Therefore, you need to adopt a one-liner to start things off. If you're worried about using "How are you?" as an opening line for fear you'll find out more than you want or need to know, try something like, "Good morning, Francis," in a friendly, leading tone; then wait. You've thrown the ball back to your caller, who has no choice but to get down to business. (P) Keep It Moving (P) If conversations drag or the point is a long time coming, Debbie Faux advises you to seek clarification.[2] To do that, simply state something like, "Sorry, Jill, I'm lost. Can you go over that again?" (P) Another easy way to keep things on a faster track is to begin by announcing that you have only so many minutes to talk; and then, as the call proceeds, make subtle references to the passage of that allotted time. (P) Cut It Short (P) If you need to bail out in mid-conversation, it's okay to interrupt — unless you are talking to your supervisor. (P) If a caller doesn't offer to call back, ask when you might return the call. This practice is not only polite, but it also gives you more control. (P) Stewart says that using a harmless white lie to get off the phone in a hurry is okay.[3] Pretend your hot line to headquarters is ringing, your overseas call is about to come through, or your next appointment has just arrived. (P) If you really can't talk, say so. Ballou cautions don't cut callers off before they've had a chance to take a breath.[4] It is a good idea to allow your callers about 45 seconds to state their business. You won't lose much time, and you will avoid upsetting people. (P) Pass It On (P) As long as you make some initial verbal contact, you can turn a call over to your secretary for an exchange of data or to schedule an appointment. There is, however, a right and a wrong way to do this. First, ask the person's permission. Then make sure that you don't hang up until you've introduced your secretary to the other party. If it's impossible for you to come to the phone or at least to say hello, your secretary should make a point of explaining your unavailability. (P) Wrap It Up (P) Some people just hate to hang up. To prepare them for the inevitable sign off, you might rustle papers in the background. Be sure to summarize what you have gotten out of the conversation, and say good-bye. (P) Endnotes (1) Alexander Stewart, Telephone Communications (New York: Wilson Publishing Company, 1986), p. 15. (2) Debbie Faux, "Etiquette in the Office," The Professional Office (January, 1986), p. 23. (3) Stewart, *Ibid.*, p. 20. (4) S. V. Ballou, "Telephone Strategies," The Professional Office (May, 1985), pp. 38–39.

CHAPTER 3

KEYBOARDING SPECIAL BUSINESS DOCUMENTS

In addition to letters, memos, and informal business reports, there are other business documents that provide information to people within and outside the company. As an office support worker, you may be called on to prepare announcements, agenda, minutes of meetings, financial statements, and legal materials. Whether you prepare these documents as a regular part of your job, or only as an occasional duty, you will be expected to follow standard guidelines for keyboarding them.

As you study this chapter, you will find answers to the following questions:

- How are special business documents prepared?
- What procedure is followed in proofreading keyboarded financial statements?
- What is the correct procedure for making corrections on legal documents?
- How has the use of information processing equipment made the preparation of legal documents more efficient?
- What do the following terms mean: **announcement, agenda, minutes, financial statements, Balance Sheet, assets, liabilities, owner's equity, Profit and Loss Statement, transposition error, legal document, backing sheet, endorsement?**

SPECIAL BUSINESS REPORTS

Most people who work in business, government, and education attend meetings as a regular part of their jobs. Many meetings are informal discussions of two or three people in one of their offices. Larger, more formal meetings may involve many participants and require careful planning. Meeting announcements, agenda, minutes, and financial statements are necessary to keep participants in these meetings informed, to help them fulfill their responsibilities in the group, and to provide a record of the group's progress in accomplishing its purpose.

par·ti′ci·pants

Meeting Announcements

When meetings are scheduled, the participants who are expected to attend are often notified by means of a keyboarded **announcement**. The announcement or notice may be in the form of a memo or a letter that is sent to each participant, or in the form of a note that is posted on the bulletin board. As the example in Illustration 8–16 shows, every notice for a meeting should make clear *who* is expected to attend, *where* and *when* they will meet, and for *what* purpose.

no′ti·fied

Meeting announcements are set up so that the reader can quickly read and understand the details. The facts about the meeting should be clearly spelled out, one fact (such as place or time) per line.

an·nounce′ments

Announcements may be prepared so that each participant receives a keyboarded original or a reprographic copy of the announcement. In a small office, the original copy of the announcement may be routed to all participants or posted on a bulletin board where it will be seen by each participant.

rout′ed

Illustration 8–16 Meeting announcement

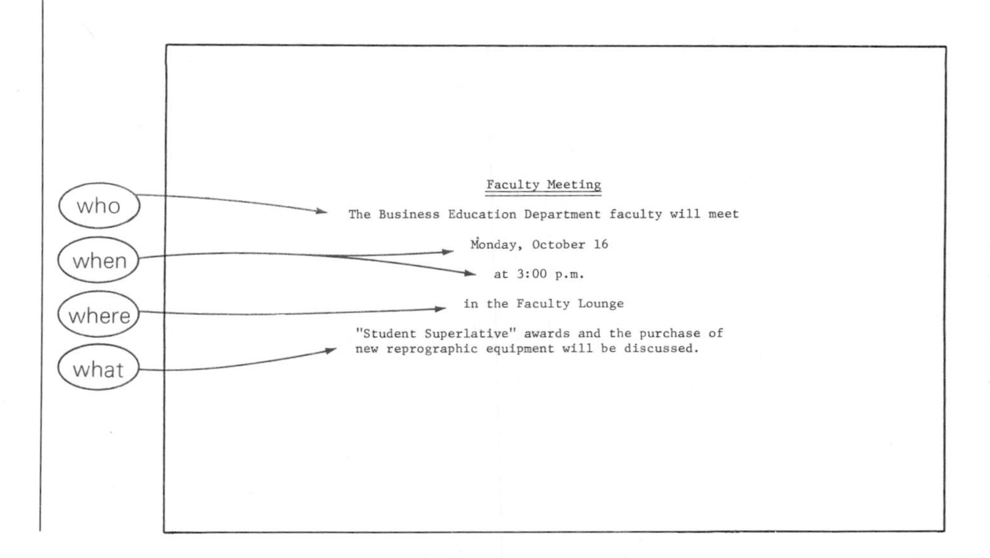

Faculty Meeting

The Business Education Department faculty will meet

Monday, October 16

at 3:00 p.m.

in the Faculty Lounge

"Student Superlative" awards and the purchase of new reprographic equipment will be discussed.

Meeting Agenda

a·gen'da

par·ti'ci·pate

The person who calls the meeting prepares an agenda to be sent out to the participants before the meeting takes place. An **agenda** is simply a plan or list of things to be done during the meeting. Knowing in advance the purpose of the meeting and the topics to be discussed makes it possible for group members to come prepared to participate.

The notice of the meeting may contain the agenda, or the notice and the agenda can be prepared and sent separately. When keyboarding an agenda, be sure that the items are listed in the exact order specified by the meeting leader. Since an agenda is prepared in outline form, the general guidelines for keyboarding outlines discussed in Chapter 1 of this Unit apply. Use wide margins and leave two or three blank lines between items so that participants can make notes on their copies during the meeting. A sample agenda is shown in Illustration 8–17.

Illustration 8–17
Meeting announcement with agenda

BRANDON COMMUNITY COLLEGE

4701 East Cliff Street, St. Joseph, Missouri 64504 (816) 565-1111

MEMORANDUM

To: All Faculty

From: Janet Miller, Faculty Senate Secretary

Date: October 5, 19--

Re: FACULTY SENATE MEETING

The next Faculty Senate meeting will be held at 3:00 p.m. on Monday, October 16, in Bethune Hall.

AGENDA

I. President's Report

II. Old Business

A. Allocation of Library Funds
B. Review of Credit Hour Audit

III. Committee Reports

A. Faculty Benefits
B. Professional Concerns
C. Budget
D. Curriculum

IV. New Business

Minutes of Meetings

of·fi'cial

After the meeting has been held, you may be asked to keyboard the minutes of the meeting. **Minutes** are the official record of what took place at a meeting. Usually, the secretary of the group is responsible for taking notes at the meeting and writing them in minutes format.

Formats for minutes Minutes are prepared according to guidelines established by the organization, group, or company. The minutes of a very formal group will contain all or most of the following:

group name	old or unfinished business
time, date, place of meeting	new business
presiding officer	next meeting date
persons attending	adjournment
approval of previous minutes	secretary's name
committee reports	

Illustration 8–18
Minutes of meeting

DPA BOARD MEETING

GROUP NAME — Cincinnati Chapter, Data Processing Association

TIME/DATE/PLACE — 4:00 p.m., July 25, 19--
Quality Inn Riverview, Covington, KY

PRESIDING OFFICER — Ms. Eileen Erwin

ATTENDANCE — D. Sweet, A. Cornet, R. Schultz, D. Pickering, L. Ivey, D. Scott, A. Banister, L. Perry, M. Keen

APPROVAL OF MINUTES — Correction to minutes made by A. Banister as follows:

Item #4, Paragraph 2, Sentence 3. Change word "appointed" to "elected."

Minutes approved as corrected.

COMMITTEE REPORTS — Treasurer's Report

No formal report given.

Membership

Dave Scott proposed Cyndia Lewis for membership. Lea Ivey seconded. Motion carried.

We have seven membership prospects.

Program

Program committee met July 12, 19--. Revised schedule of programs presented and approved.

OLD BUSINESS — Area Conference

Area conference held in Evansville, Indiana, on June 22-24. Six people attended. Next area meeting to be held in Pittsburgh in late October.

NEXT MEETING — There will be no August meeting due to vacation schedules. The next meeting will be held September 22. Members will be notified of the location.

ADJOURNMENT — The meeting adjourned at 5:15 p.m.

tab'u·lat·ed

The minutes should be organized for easy reading and reference. Notice the tabulated form of the minutes in Illustration 8–18. Side headings not only improve the appearance but also help the reader find necessary information quickly. Leave three to five spaces between the longest side heading and the text of the minutes. Either single or double spacing may be used, but double spacing is usually preferred. If the original copy of the minutes is to be filed in a three-ring binder, adjust the left margin as you would for a leftbound report.

dis·trib'ut·ed

Distribution of minutes Generally, the minutes of a meeting are prepared in a rough draft form so that they can be read and corrected by the person who prepared them. Then the final draft is keyboarded and distributed. The final draft may be photocopied. In some groups, only an original is keyboarded. It is read to the group members at the next meeting and then kept in the group's permanent records.

FINANCIAL STATEMENTS

Financial statements are summaries of accounting information. Basically, they tell the owners and managers how well the company is doing. The two most common financial statements are the Balance Sheet and the Profit and Loss Statement.

Illustration 8–19 Balance Sheet keyboarded in vertical format

Clairborne Life Insurance Company
Balance Sheet
September 30, 19--

Assets	
Investments	
Bonds and Notes	$ 524,500
Marketable Equity Securities	130,400
Real Estate, net	21,700
Policy Loans	60,800
Other	200
Cash and Receivables	22,700
Deferred Policy Acquisition Costs	23,800
Property and Equipment, net	4,700
Other Assets	4,700
Separate Accounts	55,500
Total	$ 849,000
Liabilities and Equity	
Future Policy Benefits	
Life and Annuity	$ 480,400
Accident, Health, and Other	34,500
Policy and Contract Claims	19,800
Other Policyowners' Funds	68,000
Other Liabilities	30,400
Company's Equity	215,900
Total	$ 849,000

McCarr Industrial Supply Company
Balance Sheet
March 31, 19--

Assets		Liabilities		
Cash	$ 1,800.50	Notes Payable	$ 12,600.50	
Accounts Receivable	14,600.70	Accounts Payable	13,900.40	
Inventory	46,000.00	Total Liabilities		$ 26,500.90
Office Supplies	1,610.20			
Building	58,000.00	Owner's Equity		
Delivery Equipment	3,000.00			
Furniture	8,200.00	Capital	$ 100,000.00	
Warehouse Equipment	4,800.80	Net Income	11,511.30	
Total	$138,012.20	Total Equity		111,511.30
		Total		$138,012.20

Illustration 8–20 Balance Sheet keyboarded in horizontal format

li·a·bil'i·ties

The **Balance Sheet** is prepared at regularly scheduled times during the year to show the balanced condition of the company. It may be prepared monthly, quarterly, or annually, depending on the needs of the company. The Balance Sheet shows the company's assets, liabilities, and owner's equity as of the day it is prepared. **Assets** are all the property owned by the business. **Liabilities** are debts owed by the business. And, **owner's equity** is the amount of money invested by the owners. For the financial condition of the company to be balanced, assets = liabilities plus owner's equity.

Balance Sheet information is arranged in either vertical or horizontal format. In the vertical format, assets, liabilities, and owner's equity are listed in a single column. In the horizontal format, assets are shown on the left side; liabilities and owner's equity are listed on the right side.

Besides knowing the financial condition of the business as of a particular date, the company's managers want to know how much money the business has earned or lost during a particular period. The period may be a month, a quarter, or a year. If income is greater than expenses during the period, then the company makes a profit. If expenses are greater than income, then the company loses money. The financial statement that presents the company's income and expenses for a particular period is the **Profit and Loss Statement**. Illustration 8–21 shows an example of a Profit and Loss Statement.

PREPARATION OF FINANCIAL STATEMENTS

The purpose of processing data is to give information for decision making. To be used efficiently, the information has to be organized in a form that is easy to understand. In addition, the information must be accurate. Whether the financial statement is keyboarded on a typewriter or on a computer, organization and accuracy are the goals.

or·gan·i·za'tion

Twinkle Bakery Profit and Loss Statement Year Ended December 31, 19--		
Sales		$840,000
Cost of Goods Sold		490,000
Gross Profit on Sales		$350,000
Expenses:		
Selling	$210,000	
Administrative	70,000	280,000
Net Profit from Operations		$ 70,000

Illustration 8–21 Profit and Loss Statement for a retail business

Keyboarded Statements

Financial statements are frequently prepared in a keyboarded format, especially when copies are to be distributed to individuals within and outside the company. Guidelines for preparing these statements may be contained in the company's procedures manual. If your company does not have written guidelines, you can use file copies of past statements as a guide for the format. Office style manuals, accounting books, and typewriting books also contain guidelines for keyboarding financial statements.

Most financial statements are keyboarded so that there is at least a one-inch margin on all sides. Each line of the heading is centered on a line by itself. The heading may be single or double spaced, and it is usually keyboarded with the first letter of key words capitalized. The heading is followed by a triple space.

Headings are used to organize the account titles in the body of the statement. Double spacing is normally used before headings; however, to try to keep the financial statement to one page, avoid blank spaces after major headings. Keyboard the headings and account titles in capital and lower-case letters, capitalizing only the key words. If an account title takes more than one line, indent the second line two or three spaces to show that it is a continuation of the previous line.

In a keyboarded statement, money figures are usually presented with a dollar sign. The dollar sign is used only with the first figure in a column and in totals. When keyboarding a column of figures in a statement, align the decimal points. Use commas to separate groups of three digits (going from right to left).

Examples of a keyboarded Balance Sheet and Profit and Loss Statement were shown earlier in this chapter. Notice the spacing in the statements and the careful alignment of figures. To avoid confusing the reader of the statement, be sure to use consistent capitalization, spacing, and indentions when you keyboard.

con·sis'tent

Computer-Produced Statements

Many companies store accounting information in a computer. The computer can be programmed to print financial statements and other accounting reports. On occasion, you may be asked to prepare a handwritten or keyboarded statement of selected information from the printout. Simply copy the account titles and amounts from the printout and arrange them in the format preferred by your employer.

oc·ca'sion

PROOFREADING FINANCIAL STATEMENTS

Accuracy in financial statements is essential. After keyboarding the statement, check to be sure that you have recorded the information correctly. For accuracy, try the following methods.

1. Proofread slowly and check for transpositions. It is easy to write or keyboard 123,679 instead of 123,769. The switching of the 6 and 7 is a **transposition error**.
2. Check punctuation, capitalization, and spacing of words and figures.
3. Proofread figures with another person if at all possible. Read the numbers aloud in groups to make it easier for the other person to follow along with what is said. The number $2,345,769 would be read "Two million dollars, three forty-five, seven sixty-nine."
4. Add the figures on the final copy to check the totals. Use a calculator if one is available. If the totals agree with the draft, your figures are probably correct.

LEGAL DOCUMENTS

A **legal document** is a keyboarded or printed record, usually drawn up by a lawyer, that contains details agreed to by the individuals who sign it. Legal documents that you may already be familiar with include wills, leases, sales agreements, and contracts. They are usually keyboarded, and generally they follow a standard format. The procedures for preparing legal documents vary from state to state; therefore, be sure that you follow the guidelines and use the correct forms for your state. You can usually find the procedures for

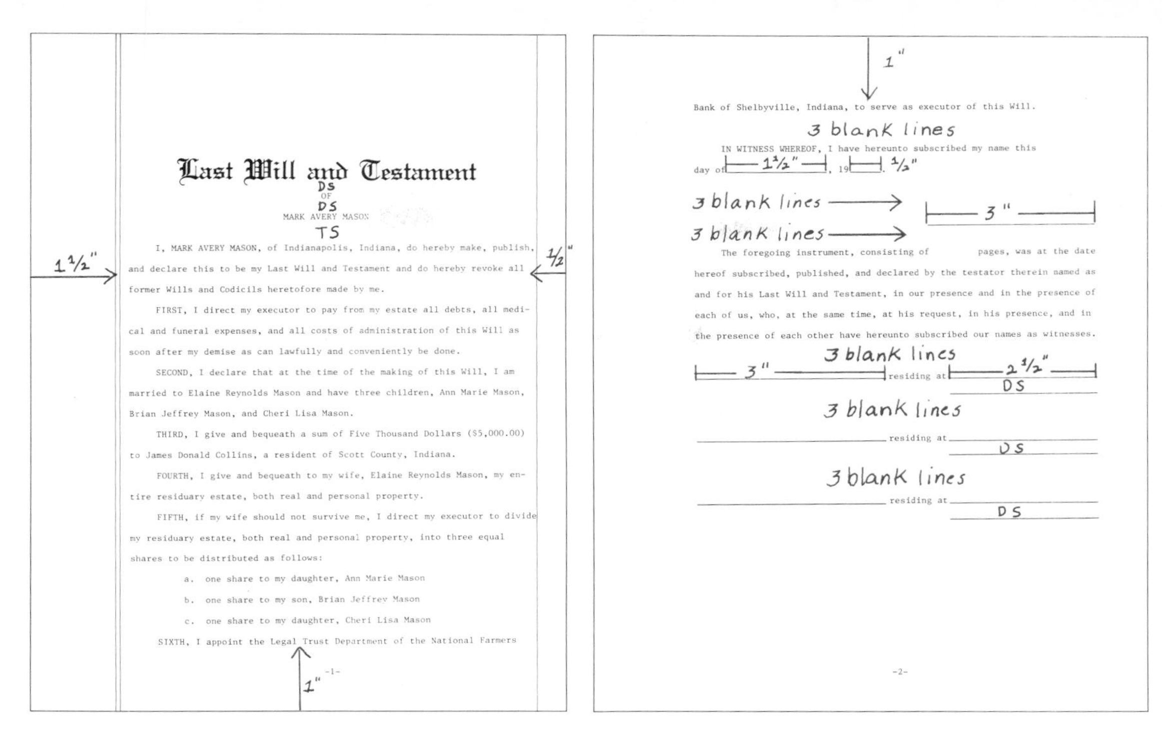

Last Will and Testament

OF

MARK AVERY MASON

I, MARK AVERY MASON, of Indianapolis, Indiana, do hereby make, publish, and declare this to be my Last Will and Testament and do hereby revoke all former Wills and Codicils heretofore made by me.

FIRST, I direct my executor to pay from my estate all debts, all medical and funeral expenses, and all costs of administration of this Will as soon after my demise as can lawfully and conveniently be done.

SECOND, I declare that at the time of the making of this Will, I am married to Elaine Reynolds Mason and have three children, Ann Marie Mason, Brian Jeffrey Mason, and Cheri Lisa Mason.

THIRD, I give and bequeath a sum of Five Thousand Dollars ($5,000.00) to James Donald Collins, a resident of Scott County, Indiana.

FOURTH, I give and bequeath to my wife, Elaine Reynolds Mason, my entire residuary estate, both real and personal property.

FIFTH, if my wife should not survive me, I direct my executor to divide my residuary estate, both real and personal property, into three equal shares to be distributed as follows:

a. one share to my daughter, Ann Marie Mason

b. one share to my son, Brian Jeffrey Mason

c. one share to my daughter, Cheri Lisa Mason

SIXTH, I appoint the Legal Trust Department of the National Farmers

-1-

Bank of Shelbyville, Indiana, to serve as executor of this Will.

IN WITNESS WHEREOF, I have hereunto subscribed my name this ____ day of ________, 19__.

____

The foregoing instrument, consisting of ____ pages, was at the date hereof subscribed, published, and declared by the testator therein named as and for his Last Will and Testament, in our presence and in the presence of each of us, who, at the same time, at his request, in his presence, and in the presence of each other have hereunto subscribed our names as witnesses.

____________ residing at ____________

____________ residing at ____________

____________ residing at ____________

-2-

Illustration 8–22
Printed legal form

preparing various legal documents in office procedures manuals. If you work in a company that does not have an office procedures manual, check the files for copies of previously keyboarded legal documents to use as guides. Legal documents may also be prepared according to the style specified in a reference guide for legal keyboarding.

Keyboarding Legal Documents

Just as there are form letters for frequently written correspondence, so too are there printed forms for frequently prepared legal documents. These forms, called legal blanks in some areas, contain lines or spaces in which the necessary information can be inserted. Most companies use legal forms when they are available because they save keyboarding time and reduce the chance of error.

Legal documents may also be prepared on legal paper. Legal-size paper ($8\frac{1}{2}$ x 13 or 14 inches) is printed with double vertical ruled lines. These lines indicate the side margins: $1\frac{1}{2}$ inches for the left margin and $\frac{1}{2}$ inch for the right margin. If neither forms nor legal paper is available, use $8\frac{1}{2}$- x 13-inch bond paper. For some legal documents, letter-size paper may be used.

Format When keyboarding legal information on a printed form, follow the guidelines given on page 336.

AFFIDAVIT FOR SALE OF REAL ESTATE

STATE OF INDIANA, Marion ________ County, ss:

Brad Allen and Janice Coombs Rutledge ________ being duly sworn, on their oath s say ____ that ____

XXXX they, X, are this day conveying by general Warranty Deed, the following described real estate in Marion County and State of Indiana, to wit:

DS

Lot numbered eighty-two (82) in Rosewood Estates, Third Section, Warren Township, Marion County, Indiana, as recorded in Plot Book 14, page 56, of the records of the Recorder's Office, Marion County, Indiana,

to Carlos and Rosa Mateos ________ and furnishing with the said Warranty Deed an Abstract of Title to said real estate continued to date of May 30 ________, 19--, by Cooper Abstract and Title Company ________ that the said Abstract of Title contains the true source from which the se affiant s obtained the title in and to the said real estate; that affiant s ha ve an indefeasible estate in fee simple in and to the said real estate and that there are no unsatisfied mortgages, judgments, liens or incumbrances of any kind thereon, except

DS

First mortgage, Farmers National Bank, Shelbyville, Indiana, September, 1976,

that affiant s ha ve not XXXXXXXXXX themselves, or by others made any conveyance of or placed any incumbrances upon said real estate or made any contract for the sale of all or any part of the said real estate, nor ha ve affiant s ordered or caused any labor or materials or both to be furnished on said real estate whereby a lien may hereafter be asserted against the same.

That there are no judgments in any of the County or United States Courts of Indiana, that is or may become a lien upon said real estate.

That the affiant s X, are not now a party to any litigation now pending in any court in Indiana, nor X, are affiant s now surety on any bond payable to the State of Indiana whereby a lien may hereafter attach to said real estate; that affiant s X, are XXXXXXXXX husband and wife Brad Allen and Janice Coombs Rutledge and of lawful age to sell said real estate, and make ____ all the above statements as representations to induce Carlos and Rosa Mateos ________ to buy said real estate.

Brad Allen Rutledge

Janice Coombs Rutledge

Subscribed and sworn to before me this ________ day of ________, 19 ____.

My Commission expires ________

________ Notary Public

THIS DOCUMENT PREPARED BY QUIMBY, SANTOS & LOUIS

Align margins

Choose correct pronoun and verb

Word choice must agree in number

X-out incorrect words

Illustration 8–23 Keyboarded legal document

1. Set the left and right margins to align with the information printed on the form.
2. Align every letter and number horizontally with the printed material.
3. On forms with blanks indicated by printed lines, place the information even with or slightly above the printed lines so that the keyboarded information rests on the line. The line should not cut through the keyboarded information.
4. X-out printed words, phrases, or sentences that do not apply. For example, cross through the inappropriate word in phrases such as *my/our* or *is/are*.
5. Keyboard the necessary word completions. For example, add *-y* or *-ies* to the word *part* in a document to form the singular or plural (*party* or *parties*) as needed, depending on the document.

com·ple'tions

pre·vent′

di·ag′o·nal

6. When keyboarding a complete word or name on a blank line, leave one or two horizontal spaces between the last printed word and the keyboarded word.
7. Numbers and amounts should be placed at the beginning of the blank lines, and the unused space should be filled with hyphens or a solid line to prevent anyone from changing the amount.
8. Add any additional wording to the printed form by keyboarding a diagonal (/) between the printed words where the insertion is to be made. Then, place the additional wording on the line directly above the diagonal.

A completed legal form is shown in Illustration 8–23.

Ruled legal paper is often used for preparation of legal reports. The vertically ruled paper has an official look and saves you time in formatting. Use the following techniques when keyboarding on legal paper:

1. Set margins one space on the inside of each ruled line.
2. Leave a two-inch top margin on all pages. (Leave one inch if letter-size paper is used.)
3. Center the title within the ruled lines. (Remember that if the left margin is larger than the right margin, the center for the page must be adjusted a few spaces to the right.) Triple space after the title.
4. Indent paragraphs five spaces.
5. Double space the content. The most common exceptions are land descriptions and quoted material, which are single spaced.
6. Leave a one-inch bottom margin on all pages.
7. Do not number the first page (except on a will), but number the remaining pages by centering the number on the fourth line from the bottom of the paper. Place a hyphen before and after the page number:

   -2-

   In some legal documents, the number of pages is stated in the page number for each page:

   Page 1 of 2

8. Allow at least three blank lines for signatures. Signature lines should be three inches long (about 30 spaces 10-pitch or 36 spaces 12-pitch).
9. Signature lines for witnesses are blocked at the left margin. Signature lines for makers of the document are keyboarded so that the lines end even with the right margin.
10. Block the appropriate keyboarded signature at the beginning of the signature line a single space below it.

When unruled paper is used for a legal document, allow $1\frac{1}{2}$ inches for the left margin and $\frac{1}{2}$ inch for the right margin. The same techniques for preparing legal documents on ruled legal paper apply when keyboarding on unruled paper.

Content Names of people in legal documents are presented without courtesy titles; however, the marital status is sometimes shown after the names. For example, the name *Mrs. Paula Chellgres* would be keyboarded as *Paula Chellgres, married.* Names of a married couple are keyboarded as separate, complete names: *James D. Raef and Ann C. Raef, husband and wife.*

Generally, when keyboarding money amounts, spell out the amount in words first; then keyboard the amount in figures in parentheses: *twenty-five thousand (25,000) dollars.* When dates are keyboarded in the legal document, they are either spelled out in words or written in figures. Use one method consistently throughout the document. For example, May 21 can be written *twenty-first day of May* or *21st day of May.* As you can see, the month and day are often transposed in legal documents.

trans·posed′

Correcting Legal Documents

Corrections in legal documents have to be made so that no question can arise as to the content agreed upon by the makers of the document. For example, say that you make a mistake keyboarding the amount of money in a legal contract and corrected the error. The parties signed the document without noticing the correction. Later, though, one of the parties might claim that the change was made *after* the contract was signed, and therefore refuse to pay the amount.

How can you be sure that your keyboarding corrections will not cause such problems? Usually, you can correct content other than sums of money, dates, or names by using standard correction procedures and products. Just be sure that all changes are clearly marked on all copies of the document. Corrections in sums of money, dates, or names may be made three ways:

1. List each correction on a sheet and attach it to the original document. This list is signed or initialed by all parties whose signatures appear on the document. The corrections are identified by page number, paragraph number, and line number, along with the appropriate change that would be made in the content.
2. X-out errors and keyboard the correct information immediately following the Xed-out material. Then all parties simply initial each correction when they sign the document.
3. Use a correction fluid/tape/ribbon to cover the incorrect information and keyboard over it with the correct information. All parties signing the document initial each correction. The only time this correction procedure cannot be used is when you are keyboarding a will.

crit′i·cal

As you can see by the care with which corrections are made in legal documents, proofreading is critical. To be sure of the content in a legal document, proofread each paragraph as you keyboard it. You should also proofread each page before you remove it from the typewriter or printer. If possible, when you finish keyboarding it, proofread the entire document aloud, spelling out names, addresses, and unfamiliar words.

Illustration 8–24 Folding a backing sheet

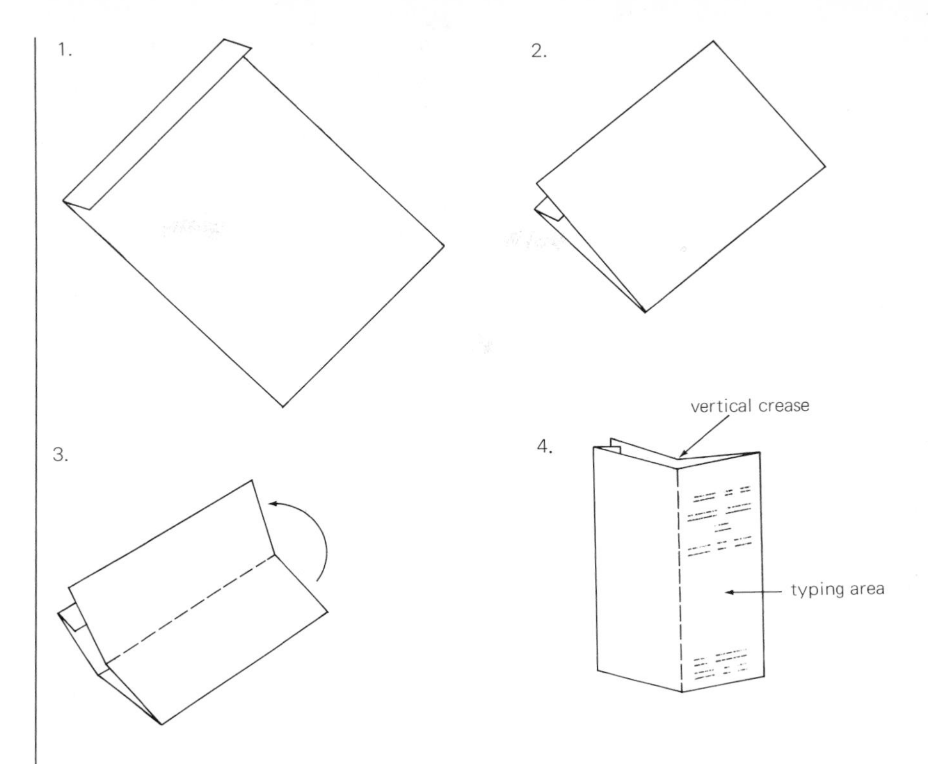

Preparing Backing Sheets

Many legal documents are bound in what is known as a **backing sheet** shown in Illustration 8–24. A backing sheet is simply a keyboarded cover for a legal document. The information that appears on this cover is called an **endorsement** or backing.

en·dorse′ment

Backing sheets are made of heavier paper than that used for the pages of the legal document. This heavier paper provides protection for the document, which may be filed and handled over a period of time. The backing sheet is about 1 inch wider and $1\frac{1}{2}$ inches longer than the legal paper. This added width and length make it possible to bind the backing sheet to the document and to fold it so that the backing sheet fully covers the pages.

pro·tec′tion

To fold, keyboard, and bind a backing sheet to a legal document, follow these steps:

1. Fold down about 1 inch of the top edge of the backing sheet.
2. Fold the bottom edge of the sheet up and even with the folded top edge.
3. Take the new bottom edge (the edge formed by the last crease) and fold it up even with the top edge. Crease the folds.
4. Unfold the last crease that was made and insert the backing sheet into your typewriter. The 1-inch fold should be at the left margin. There will be a vertical crease in the center of the backing sheet.

5. Keyboard the endorsement by centering each line horizontally in the panel to the right of the crease. Place the title of the document, the makers' names, and date in the top portion; put the company name and address in the bottom portion.
6. Remove the backing sheet from the typewriter.
7. Place the document inside the sheet so that the one-inch top folds over the top edge of the doucument. Staple the document.
8. Fold the document, using the creases made in the backing sheet as a guide.

Preparing Documents Using Information Processing

If information processing equipment is used to prepare legal documents, then corrections are not a problem, as the information can be easily accessed, corrected, and printed. Corrections, insertions, or deletions are made by rekeying words or using appropriate function keys (insert, delete, cut, paste). If the paging of the corrected legal document is the same as it was originally, only corrected pages need to be printed and inserted in the original. If the corrections make it necessary to repage the document, then the whole document is reprinted. Pages that show requested corrections are usually maintained in the files until the document is signed.

REVIEWING KEY POINTS

1. A meeting announcement may be a memo or letter that answers the questions of who, where, when, and what.
2. An agenda lists the things to be done in a meeting.
3. The official record of a meeting is the minutes.
4. Minutes are usually keyboarded first in rough draft form for editing by the person who originated them.
5. Financial statements are summaries of accounting information that tell how well a company is doing.
6. A Balance Sheet lists what is owned, what is owed, and how much the owners have invested in the company. A Profit and Loss Statement shows a business's income and expenses for a certain period of time.
7. Financial statements may be keyboarded on a typewriter or on a computer.
8. Legal blanks are printed legal forms of frequently used legal documents.
9. Legal documents may be keyboarded on legal blanks, legal-sized ruled paper, or plain $8\frac{1}{2}$- by 13-inch bond paper.
10. Corrections on legal documents have to be made so that no questions are raised concerning what was agreed upon.

DEVELOPING HUMAN RELATIONS SKILLS

1. Arnold Ventre is a new secretary in a large transportation company. As part of his duties, he is to prepare meeting reminders, agenda, and minutes for the monthly managers' meetings. He had no problems in preparing the reminder and agenda for the first monthly meeting. However, when he sat in on the meeting and started recording the minutes, he was not able to keep up with his note-taking. The discussion was rapid and more technical than Arnold had expected. He did his best in getting the information recorded. When he gave his supervisor a draft of the minutes, his supervisor got rather irritated at the lack of information and the inaccuracy in what was recorded.

   Arnold became defensive. He said that everyone talked too fast, and it was unrealistic for his supervisor to expect him to know technical information since he was new to the job.

   a. Was Arnold's supervisor unrealistic in his expectations of Arnold? Why or why not?

   b. What was Arnold's major mistake?

   c. How could Arnold have been more prepared for this meeting?

2. Arlis Webster and Myra Sawyer are secretaries in a small legal firm. Arlis is preparing three long legal documents for her supervisor; Myra offers to help her. Even though Myra is not as neat and accurate as Arlis, Arlis decides quickly to accept Myra's offer. Arlis says to Myra, "I can really use the help. I'm almost through the first document. If you could do this third document, I'll be able to complete the second one. With both of us working on them, we should be through by 5 P.M." Arlis hands Myra the information and adds the comment "And, Myra, since these documents were assigned to me, please be more conscious of your accuracy and neatness than you are usually. There is no way I can proof and rekey your mistakes." Myra wishes she had not offered to help Arlis!

   a. Should Arlis have accepted Myra's offer to help? Explain.

   b. Should Myra's feelings have been hurt as a result of Arlis's comments? Why or why not?

   c. How could Arlis have accepted the offer for help and cautioned Myra to be neat and accurate in a positive way?

IMPROVING COMMUNICATION SKILLS

Refer to Appendix A 1.22-1.24.

1. Determine where apostrophes should be placed in the following sentences. Keyboard the corrected sentences on a plain sheet of paper.

   a. The computer movement of the 80s has taken business by surprise.

   b. The meeting was held at Nora and Nicholas request.

c. Sues and Johns reports were completed on time.

d. Most employees have their B.A.s.

e. This process wont save me time.

f. The title of the article is "Stress Management in Todays High Tech Office."

g. The terminal was moved to the new employees desk.

h. Louis Computaparts repairs computers and electronic typewriters.

2. Your supervisor, Myron Crownstein, is planning to hold a meeting concerning the importance of being courteous and helpful to customers. Mr. Crownstein likes the way you deal with customers and the public. He asks you to write a memo to him giving him some of your thoughts about the importance of keeping customers and ways in which you can be polite and helpful to them. Using the memo in your workbook or plain paper, compose a memo giving this information.

BUILDING PROBLEM-SOLVING SKILLS

1. In many legal offices, clients are charged by the hour for the amount of time the lawyer spends working on their cases. Figure out the number of hours, to the nearest quarter of an hour, for which the client below should be charged.

Date	Description	Time
July 6	Telephone conversation with D. Keltner	9:15-9:35
July 8	Office conference with D. Keltner	2:45-3:25
July 9	Preparation and drafting of contract; correspondence to D. Keltner	8:30-10:10
July 12	Conference with D. Keltner and L. Sullivan at Union Trust Company	11:00-11:40
July 21	Telephone conversation with D. Keltner	4:55-5:05
July 22	Court appearance	1:30-1:55
July 27	Office conference with D. Keltner	10:45-11:15

2. Referring to the information given in Activity 1, answer these questions on a separate sheet of paper.

a. If D. Keltner is charged at the rate of $90 an hour, how much does D. Keltner owe?

b. What percentage of the total time was spent in telephone conferences?

c. What percentage of total time was spent in office conferences?

d. What percentage of the total time did the lawyer spend in court?

e. How much is D. Keltner being charged for the time the lawyer spent in court?

f. What percentage of work was done in the morning?

Activities 1 and 2 can be done on information processing equipment.

APPLYING OFFICE SKILLS

1. The notes shown here are the minutes for a meeting in your office. Prepare a rough draft of these minutes in an appropriate format on plain paper.

Summary of Managers' Meeting

Time and Place — The monthly Departmental Managers' meeting was held on Thursday, October 24, 19--, in the data processing conference room. Marc Howsom presided.

Attendance — Those in attendance were Myra Ames, Richard Bruner, Bill Guttentag, Nancy Phelps, Frank Riessman, and Lionel Tiger.

Discussion — Mr. Bruner briefly summarized the status of work on the advertising brochures for the toy show. There are no anticipated delays.

Mrs. Phelps reported the progress that has been made on the compilation of an up-to-date word processing manual for office employees. Samples of forms are now being prepared. The manual is to be completed by the end of the year. Mrs. Phelps stated that there has been a delay in the preparation of catalogue copy for next year's catalogue. The problem centers on getting product descriptions from the copy writers in the design department. Mr. Riessman will follow up on the situation in the design department to push them to meet their deadlines.

Next Meeting — The date for the next managers' meeting will be Thursday, November 20, in the conference room adjacent to the accounting department.

Adjournment — The meeting was adjourned at 11:30 a.m.

Harry Dolive
Recorder

2. Keyboard the following meeting announcement on a half sheet of paper. It will be posted on the office bulletin board. Make the corrections indicated and center the announcement horizontally and vertically on the page. Double or triple space between each item to improve the readability and appearance.

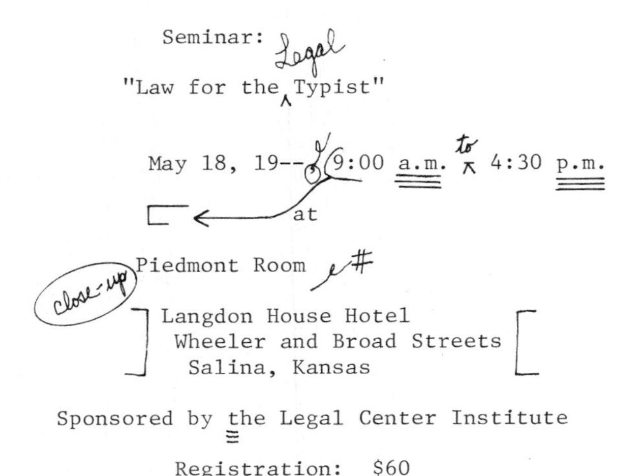

Seminar: Legal

"Law for the Typist"

May 18, 19-- 9:00 a.m. to 4:30 p.m.

at

close-up Piedmont Room #

Langdon House Hotel
Wheeler and Broad Streets
Salina, Kansas

Sponsored by the Legal Center Institute

Registration: $60

For information call 761-7061

3. **(Optional)** There are two lease forms in your workbook. One is blank and the other is filled in by hand. Keyboard a completed lease form using the handwritten copy as your guide.

Saving Time and Money

As a participant in meetings, you may be assigned the responsibility for taking minutes. Whether you write your notes in shorthand or longhand, you may want to design a form for use in organizing your notes. Your form might include these headings: attendance, purpose, topics discussed, decisions reached, and assigned responsibilities. Leave space after each heading where the appropriate information can be inserted. Copy this form and keep the copies handy. Before you prepare your minutes complete one of these forms. Then, when you keyboard the minutes, refer to this form. It will help you prepare them more quickly.

UNIT 9

RECORDS MANAGEMENT SYSTEMS

Managing Office Records •

Filing Supplies and Equipment •

CHAPTER 1

MANAGING OFFICE RECORDS

The typical office worker spends the greater part of the workday preparing and handling records of various business activities. Letters, memorandums, and reports record ideas and suggestions. Invoices record the sale of products. Sales receipts record the payment of money. Minutes record the action taken at a meeting. Often this information is prepared and handled on information processing equipment and stored electronically. All kinds of information — whether printed on paper or stored on electronic media — are stored as part of the records of the company.

As you study this chapter, you will find answers to the following questions:

- Why do businesses keep records?
- What is records management?
- What are the five different filing systems?
- What do the following terms mean: **records management, vital records, nonessential records, filing, filing system, alphabetic, numeric, chronological, decentralized files, centralized files, retrieve, essential records, retention schedule, active files, inactive files?**

WHY RECORDS ARE KEPT

his·tor'i·cal

Records are important because they provide the company's managers and owners with information on which to base their decisions. Records also provide a history of the company's activities. Business records of a historical nature are frequently used in the following ways:

doc·u·men·ta'tion

- Records provide documentation, or proof, that an action has taken place. For example, a sales receipt marked "paid" provides proof that payment was made.
- Sales records can show during which months sales are the highest.
- Minutes of a meeting provide a record, or history, of what actions were taken at the meeting.
- Records are used as a basis for decisions relating to charge accounts, sales promotions, and employee raises and promotions.

Business records are used for decision making in the following ways:

- Customer payment records show which customers pay their bills on time. Management uses these records to decide which customers can be allowed to charge future purchases.
- Sales records show which products are selling and which products are not. This information helps a manager decide whether to run a "special" on products that are not selling.
- Employee performance records help managers decide about promotions or raises.

ac·ces'si·ble

For records to fulfill these purposes, they must be accessible; that is, they must be easy to locate. The activities involved in organizing, storing, and protecting company records are known as **records management.**

RECORDS MANAGEMENT

All important records must be stored so that they can be located quickly when they are needed. Delays in finding records are not only annoying to the person who needs the record, but they can cost your company money. Take this example:

Georgia Louis tore up her credit card from Upton's Department Store last month after a bad experience with the credit department. She had written the store twice to clear up a problem with her monthly bill, but hadn't received a reply. So she finally decided to telephone the store long distance. Georgia explained the problem to Maurice King, the accounts representative. He put her on "hold" while he got her file. When Maurice returned to the telephone several minutes later, it was to tell Georgia that he couldn't find her file and would have to call her back.

Georgia was fuming! That phone call was going to cost her plenty. It was going to cost Upton's, too — Georgia would not shop at Upton's again.

To prevent delays and keep track of important records, most companies set up records management policies and procedures. Records management is concerned with these four activities:

1. developing a system of storing records and identifying which records will be kept
2. arranging records in an organized manner so they can be found quickly
3. protecting records from damage or loss
4. determining how long records should be stored

These records management activities are the subject of this chapter.

Classification of Records

In a given day's mail, you or your family may receive an advertising brochure addressed to "Occupant" and a letter from a relative or friend. There may also be a bill or two and a bank statement with canceled checks enclosed. You do not treat all of these things the same way. Some of them are more important than the others and require special attention. Some you will read and throw away; others you will file away as records. The same is true of business correspondence and other company records. Records can be classified according to their importance and usefulness to a company.

clas'si·fied

Business records are usually classified into four categories: vital, important, useful, and nonessential. The way a record is classified by a particular business determines whether it will be stored, how long it will be stored, and how it will be stored.

non·es·sen'tial

Vital records are those items that are so important that the company cannot operate without them. They include legal documents, tax records, financial records, and secret formulas. Because these records cannot be replaced, they must be stored where they are safe from theft, fire, and other damage. Many companies make copies of their vital records and store them in a separate location for safekeeping.

Important records are also necessary for the continued operation of the business. Unlike vital records, important records can be replaced. Replacing them can be difficult and expensive, however. Important records include payroll records, sales records, and personnel records.

Useful records are those items that are necessary for the smooth operation of a company. Although these records can be replaced, their loss would cause inconvenience. Copies of customer purchase orders, correspondence, reports, and catalogues are considered useful records.

Items classified as **nonessential records** may provide useful information, but they are not of a lasting interest to the company. Items such as meeting notices, news releases, and requests for information are frequently disposed of once they have served their purpose.

dis·posed'

Filing Systems

Once a company identifies which documents should be kept, it must select a system for storing them. **Filing** is a method of arranging and storing records so that they can be located quickly and easily when people in the company need them. A **filing system** consists of rules that determine how records will be organized. Records that are related to the same person, company, or topic are usually grouped together in the files. For example, correspondence with or about a particular individual may be kept in a single file folder labeled with that person's name.

se′quen·ces

chron·o·log′i·cal

Records can be arranged in one of three basic orders or sequences: alphabetic, numeric, or chronological. **Alphabetic** sequence is *A*-to-*Z* order. **Numeric** sequence is 1-2-3 order. **Chronological** sequence is arrangement according to day, month, or year.

The sequence a company chooses for its files depends on the kinds of records that are kept and the way they are requested. Suppose you wanted to see the file copy of the letter in Illustration 9–1. There are several ways you could identify that record. You could ask to see a copy of the letter sent to the Henderson Packing Company. You might refer to it as the letter about shipping delays or about Shipping Order 9231. Or, you might be interested in seeing copies of all letters sent to customers in the Midwest recently. The way records are requested affects the choice of filing systems.

Illustration 9–1
File copy of outgoing letter

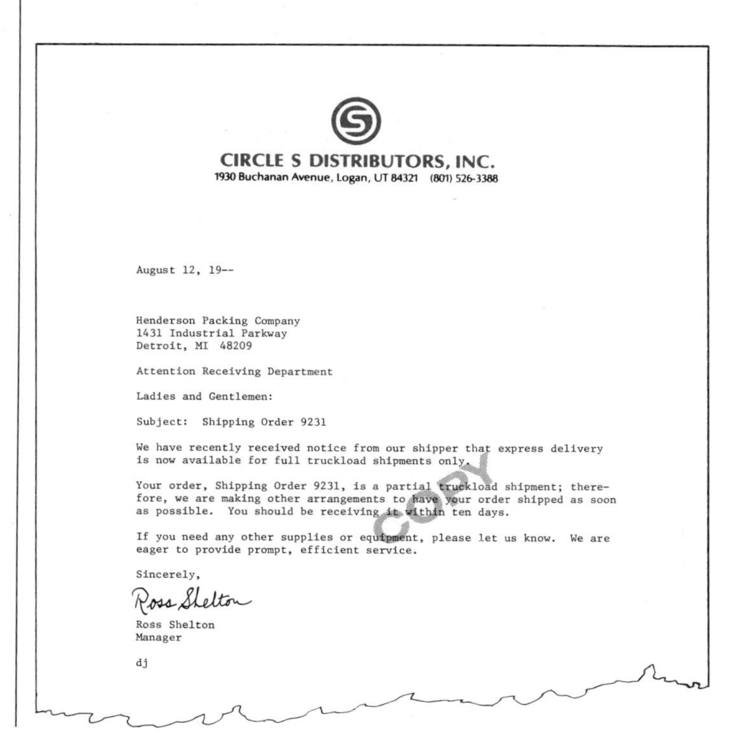

CIRCLE S DISTRIBUTORS, INC.
1930 Buchanan Avenue, Logan, UT 84321 (801) 526-3388

August 12, 19--

Henderson Packing Company
1431 Industrial Parkway
Detroit, MI 48209

Attention Receiving Department

Ladies and Gentlemen:

Subject: Shipping Order 9231

We have recently received notice from our shipper that express delivery is now available for full truckload shipments only.

Your order, Shipping Order 9231, is a partial truckload shipment; therefore, we are making other arrangements to have your order shipped as soon as possible. You should be receiving it within ten days.

If you need any other supplies or equipment, please let us know. We are eager to provide prompt, efficient service.

Sincerely,

Ross Shelton

Ross Shelton
Manager

dj

COPY

There are five main systems of filing: alphabetic, subject, geographic, numeric, and chronological.

The alphabetic name system The alphabetic name system is the most commonly used method of filing. In this system, records are arranged in alphabetical order by name of the individual or company they relate to.

The subject system Some companies group records by the subject or topic that they relate to. For example, a computer store may arrange its records in alphabetical order using subject captions such as *Cables, Modems, Monitors, Printers, and Software.*

cap'tions

The geographic system In geographic filing, records are grouped and arranged in alphabetic order by geographic location. If a company does business nationwide, the records may be grouped by state. If a company conducts business internationally, the records may be grouped by country.

in·ter·na'tion·al·ly

The numeric system In numeric filing, related records are arranged in numeric order according to the number assigned to or appearing on them. A telecommunications company, for example, may arrange customer records in numeric order by telephone number. Bank records are filed by account number. Some government records are filed by Social Security number.

The chronological system The chronological system is used to arrange records in order by date. Newspapers and magazines are examples of businesses that use this system. Their subscription records are stored according to date of expiration so that they know when to stop delivery or send renewal notices.

ex·pi·ra'tion
re·new'al

Once a filing system is selected, everyone with filing responsibilities must learn to use the same procedures and rules. You will learn more about filing systems and procedures in Unit 10.

Location of Records

A company or department must decide on the best place to store records. Convenience is one factor that determines where records are stored within a company. For many people, the most convenient storage locations are desk drawers or file cabinets near their work stations. When records are stored in many locations throughout the company, the company is said to have **decentralized files**. Decentralized files are convenient when only a few people need to work with the information stored in the files. When people throughout the company must work with the same information, it is frequently more convenient to store all records in **centralized files** — that is, files located in one place.

de·cen'tral·ized

Security must also be considered in making decisions about where records are stored. To protect records from theft, loss, fire — and even from un·au'thor·ized

unauthorized eyes — many companies find that it is better to store the records in centralized files. It is easier to provide fireproof storage, locking doors, and limited access when all records are stored in one location.

There are advantages and disadvantages to both of these kinds of storage arrangements that can be used.

Decentralized files Decentralized files are used chiefly to store personal records and records related to an individual's job responsibilities. Personal records include salary, vacation, and leave records; files related to committee assignments, civic groups, and professional associations; and confidential records. These files may be stored with business records that are used in the course of the workday. Most office desks — for secretaries and executive alike — are equipped with file drawers for these frequently used files.

When employees use the same records on a regular basis, they must either borrow them from one.another or make copies for their own files. So, although they are convenient, decentralized files are not always efficient.

Centralized files Records that are used by many people in an office are more accessible when they are stored in a central filing location. Employees do not have to make and keep copies of a document in their files. The document is available to all employees in a central file. Because the same records are available to many people, centralized files eliminate much duplication of equipment and records.

Illustration 9–2
Centralized files for records used by the entire department

re·trieve'

In a small department or office, employees may **retrieve** — that is, find and remove — the records they need themselves. When files contain records for the entire company, however, there are usually file clerks who are responsible for filing and retrieving records.

mis·filed'

con·fi·den·ti·al'i·ty

Many businesses find that centralized filing is very efficient for their purposes. Because filing employees are trained in correct filing procedures, fewer records are lost or misfiled. In addition, records can be better protected from fire, smoke, water damage, or theft in centralized files. For example, records can be stored in locked cabinets in a fireproof vault. The privacy and confidentiality of the records can also be protected by allowing only authorized employees to enter the filing area.

Centralized files have some disadvantages. The centralized files may be some distance away for your work station. The record may not be available when you need it. Another employee may be using the record, and you may have to wait until it is returned to centralized files. Many companies establish policies that state when records must be returned and where the records may be used. These policies are especially important for the efficient operation of a centralized filing system.

If you work for a company that has a centralized filing department, you may still have personal files to keep for your supervisor. So you may have to learn two sets of filing procedures: one for the personal files and one for the centralized files. You should ask your supervisor for guidelines to help you determine the kinds of records that should be kept in the personal files. You will also be expected to follow your company's procedures for using the centralized files.

Records Retention and Transfer

Every day businesses add records to their files. Large companies may add hundreds — or even thousands — of records a week. Where do they store them? Because storage space and equipment are expensive, companies look for ways to control the quantity of records they retain.

es·sen'tial

re·ten'tion

per'ma·nent·ly

One solution to the storage problem is to file only **essential records** — those classified as vital, important, or useful. Another solution is to clean the files on a regular basis, disposing of records that are no longer needed. This is usually done according to a retention schedule. A company's **retention schedule** tells how long each type of record should be kept and how records are to be disposed of.

Typically, vital and important records are stored permanently; they are never destroyed. Useful records, on the other hand, may be destroyed when they are no longer needed. The annual price list for word processing supplies, for example, may be thrown away as soon as the next year's price list is available. Correspondence may be stored for up to seven years, then destroyed. Each company should develop a retention schedule based on the types of records kept and how they are used. The federal government also has laws that provide guidelines for developing a records retention schedule.

Illustration 9–3

GUIDELINES FOR RECORDS RETENTION

Records to Be Filed Permanently
Accounting ledgers
Deeds and mortgages
Annual reports
Incorporation records
Copyrights, patents, and trademarks
Tax returns and records
Pension records
Wage and tax statements

Records to Be Retained According to The Statutes of Limitations
Contracts
Open accounts
Accident reports
Bills of lading
Freight bills and claims
Canceled payroll checks
Invoices
Time cards and tickets

Records to Be Retained until Obsolete
Publications
Price lists and catalogues
Job descriptions
Mailing lists and directories
Rates and tariffs

Records to Be Retained for 1–2 Years
Work sheets for financial statements
Internal reports and supporting data
Inventory records

Records to Be Retained for 3 Months
Incoming/outgoing correspondence
Stenographer's notebooks
Purchase requisitions
Bank statements

Records to Be Destroyed Immediately after Use
Routine memos
Telephone messages
Incoming mail with no long-term value

in·ac'tive

For storage purposes, records are often divided into active and inactive files. Frequently used records are stored in the **active files,** which are easy to get to. When they are no longer used on a regular basis, records may be transferred to the **inactive files**. Inactive files are usually stored in central filing areas, where they are protected but out of the way. The transfer schedule may be different for different items. Some records may be moved to inactive files after six months; others, after three years.

REVIEWING KEY POINTS

1. Records provide information that is necessary for decision making. In addition, they provide a history of the business activities.
2. Records management includes classifying records, managing the filing system, protecting records, and disposing of records.
3. Records are classified according to their importance and usefulness. The classifications in their order of importance are: vital, important, useful, and nonessential. The way a record is classified determines whether it is retained, how long it is kept, and where it is stored.

4. Filing is the process of arranging and storing records so that they can be found quickly when requested.
5. There are five basic systems of filing: alphabetic name filing, subject, geographic, numeric, and chronological.
6. In a decentralized filing system, records are stored in various locations throughout a company.
7. In a centralized filing system, company or department records are stored in a central location for greater access. Centralized files often reduce the duplication of records and equipment.
8. You may keep personal files for your supervisor even though there is a centralized filing system in your company.
9. Records that are used frequently are stored in active files where they are easily accessible. When they are no longer used on a regular basis, these records are moved to inactive files. In some cases, these records may even be destroyed.

DEVELOPING HUMAN RELATIONS SKILLS

1. The computer store where you work accepts no merchandise for warranty repairs unless the merchandise is accompanied by the sales receipt. This morning a customer brought in a printer that is not working properly and wants it repaired under the warranty. The warranty period for the printer is 90 days. You know the customer purchased the printer not too long ago, but you do not know the exact date. When you asked the customer for the sales receipt, the customer said it had been thrown away.
   - **a.** What would you say to the customer?
   - **b.** Can you find out when the printer was purchased? where?
2. You have been working in the filing department for nearly a year. The company has a retention policy that states how long each record should be kept. When you noticed that many outdated records were still in the active files, you asked your supervisor if you could throw the records away. Your supervisor said, "No, as long as I am supervisor, we won't throw any records away. You can't tell when someone will ask for those records."
   - **a.** What do you think of your supervisor's comments?
   - **b.** What problems is your supervisor causing by ignoring the company's retention policy?

IMPROVING COMMUNICATION SKILLS

Refer to Appendix A 1.28–1.32.

1. On a separate sheet of paper, keyboard the sentences at the top of the next page, supplying the necessary hyphens.

a. The records retention policy will be updated soon.
b. There are twenty three office employees in the company.
c. Over one half of the employees have terminals on their desks.
d. My boss is a self made person.
e. The new time saving equipment was installed; however, the employees have not been trained to use it.
f. There will be three half day training sessions for the employees.
g. My supervisor is a former all American football player.
h. The company has some good employee benefits; its matched saving program is one of the best I've seen.
i. Filing takes three fourths of my time.
j. I cleaned thirty seven files this morning.

2. On a separate sheet of paper, compose a letter that could be sent to a company to learn more about its records management program. Specifically, you want to know:
   a. Do they have a records retention program?
   b. Are their files stored in centralized or decentralized files?
   c. Do they have a training program for new filing employees?

BUILDING PROBLEM-SOLVING SKILLS

1. In your office, records of items purchased and their purchase dates are kept in active files during their warranty periods. The records are then transferred to the inactive files. Your supervisor has asked you to determine the dates for transferring the following records to the inactive files. The warranty periods are listed here:
   Printers — 90 days
   Calculators — 6 months
   Modems — 45 days
   Video terminals — 1 year
   a. Printer, January 15
   b. Modem, January 21
   c. Video terminal, January 25
   d. Printer, February 1
   e. Calculator, February 5
   f. Modem, Feburary 28
   g. Video terminal, February 28
   h. Printer, March 1
   i. Modem, March 2
   j. Calculator, March 3

2. Your company is trying to decide whether its retention and transfer policy is adequate. To provide the necessary information for this decision, the filing department manager has asked each file clerk to keep a count of the types of records filed during a one-week period. You used the chart shown on the top of page 356 to keep track of your work. Using the information contained

in this chart, answer the questions following the chart. Write your answers on a separate sheet of paper.

	Mon.	Tues.	Wed.	Thurs.	Fri.
VITAL	||||	卌	卌 |	||	卌 |||
IMPORTANT	卌 ||||	卌 卌	卌 卌	卌 ||	卌 卌 |||
USEFUL	卌 卌 |||	卌 ||||	卌 卌 卌 ||	卌 卌 卌 卌 |	卌 卌 卌 ||
NONESSENTIAL	卌	卌 |	|||	卌 卌 |	卌 ||||

a. On what day of the week did you file the most records?
b. On what day of the week did you file the least records?
c. How many records did you file during the week?
d. Did you file more vital records or nonessential records?
e. How many vital records did you file?
f. How many nonessential records did you file?
g. Did you file more important records than useful records?
h. How many important records did you file?
i. How many useful records did you file?
j. What percentage of the records that you filed during the week were useful?
k. What percentage of the records filed were vital?
l. What percentage of the records filed were nonessential?

APPLYING OFFICE SKILLS

Activities 1 and 2 can be done on information processing equipment.

1. On a separate sheet of paper, keyboard the following filing work standards in an attractive format. Use the title "Average Filing Work Standards."

Task	Peices Per Hour
File cards alpabetically	300
Sorts and files letters in an alphabetic file	175
File papers in analphabetic file	275
File papers in a geoegraphic file	340
File papers in subject file	150
File papers in numeric file	375

2. Using the memorandum form in your workbook or plain paper, prepare a corrected copy of the following memorandum.

To: All Employees

From: LynAnne Knudsen

Date: (current)

Subject: Records Department Conversion

As you all know, we have been planning to convert all of our records from paper docment storage to electronic storage. Our data-entry clerks have now completed the conversion. We will make the change during the last weekend of this month. To help you adjust to the new records storage system, we have prepared the enclosed manual. The manual explains how the system works and gives the list of codes you will need to operate the system. We have also planned some training programs for all employees. The programs will be offered several times so that all employees can attend. Please work out a schedule for all employees to atthed one of the training sessions. Teresa Anderson has been assigned to accept the responsibility of providing additional help for employees. If you encounter a problem when working on the new system, Teresa will be able to help identify and correct problems. She will also be able to help you plan programs for analyzing data stored in the system. We know that the system will be a major change. We think that you will agree that once we have all adjusted to the new system, we will be able to accomplish more with less time and effort.

CHAPTER 2

FILING SUPPLIES AND EQUIPMENT

Developing a records management program requires careful planning. The time spent in setting up an efficient filing system will save a company time in filing and finding its records. An efficient filing system saves money as well. For a system to be efficient, however, proper supplies and equipment must be used to store, organize, identify, and protect files.

Proper supplies and equipment make it easier for you to file and find business records quickly. It is much easier for you to locate the most recent letter from Arthur Peal when it has been filed properly.

Good filing supplies and equipment are also necessary to protect business records against loss or damage. The loss of just one record as the result of fire or careless handling can be costly to a business.

In some offices, you will find that all the necessary filing supplies and equipment have already been purchased. In other offices, additional supplies and equipment may be needed. You may be asked to order the necessary supplies. Knowing the kinds and quantities of records kept in your office and the types of supplies and equipment available can make this task easier.

As you study this chapter, you will find answers to the following questions:

- What supplies are used in filing?
- What types of equipment are used in filing?
- How does the use of proper supplies and equipment help when filing a company's records?
- What do the following terms mean: **file folders, cut, position, labels, caption, guides, cross-reference sheet, requisition form, out forms, vertical files, lateral files, file sorters?**

SUPPLIES FOR FILING

Filing supplies are those materials that help identify and organize business records. As an office worker, you need to understand how these supplies are used to help you file and retrieve office records.

File Folders

re·lat'ed

File folders allow you to group correspondence and other documents that are related to each other. For example, all the information about a particular client may be stored in a single folder. Folders are used to hold, identify, and protect records.

Folders are available in various sizes. Standard-sized folders are used for letter-sized correspondence, while legal-sized folders are used for legal documents and records. Special folders are also available for oversized materials such as computer printouts and blueprints.

Manila folders are the most common, but folders are available in other weights and colors. Color coding of files is found in many offices. For example, red folders may be used for customers' records and blue folders for suppliers' records.

Some of the special features of file folders are shown in Illustration 9–4. They include tabs, scoring, fasteners, pockets, and hangers.

Illustration 9–4
Useful features on file folders include tabs, scoring, fasteners, pockets, and hangers

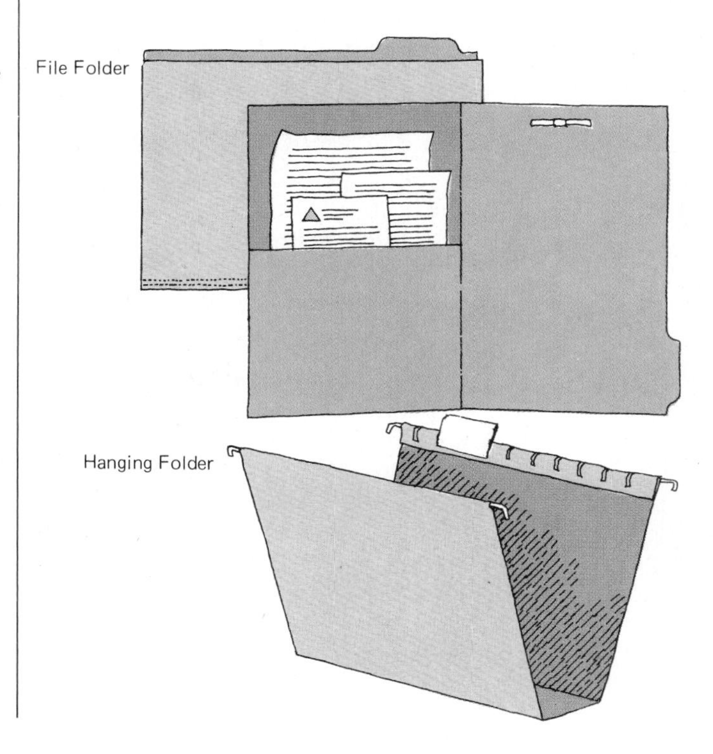

Tabs The tab holds the caption that identifies the contents of the folder. Tabs are positioned across the top edges of folders so that they can be seen easily in the files. The width of the tab is called its **cut**; the location is its **position.** The cut and position may vary. For example, a one-third cut tab is one-third the width of the folder. A tab may be positioned on the far left or right of the folder's top edge, or in the middle. Folders also come with straight-cut, one-half cut, and fifth-cut tabs, as shown in Illustration 9–5.

scor'ing

Scoring The creases at the bottom of the front of a folder are known as scoring. A folder is creased along the score lines to form a flat edge for the contents of the folder. By creasing the folder along the various scored lines, you can increase the number of records that can be neatly stored in the folder.

fas'ten·ers

Fasteners Fasteners are built into some folders to provide added protection for records. The records can be hole-punched and attached securely to the folder with the fastener. These folders are often used in medical offices where the patient's medical history is of vital importance.

Pockets Pockets are used for holding materials that are of an unusual size and may be lost. When brochures or index cards must be stored with correspondence, for example, folders with pockets are used.

Illustration 9–5
Tab positions and cuts

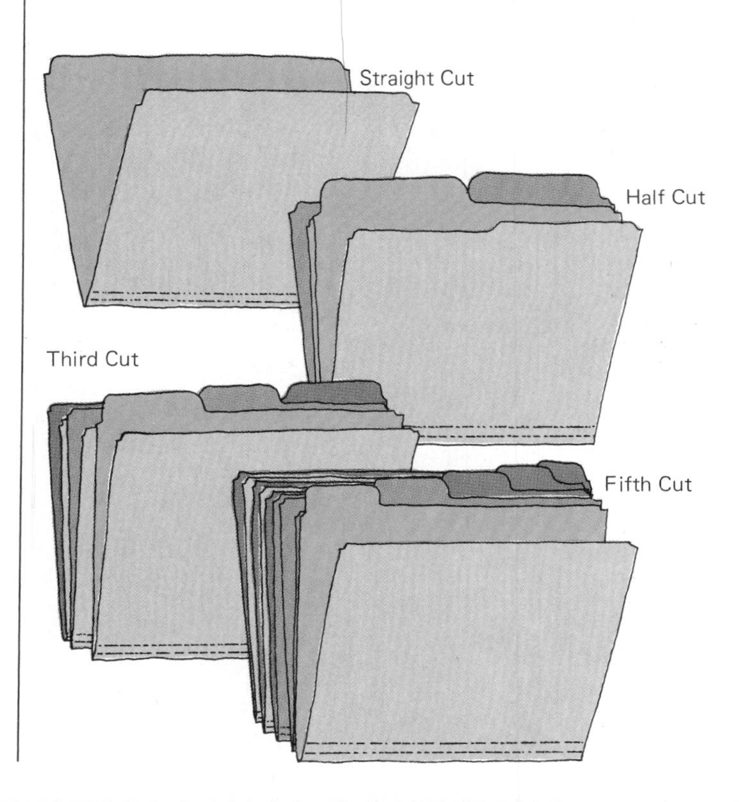

Hangers As shown in Illustration 9–4 on page 359, some folders have hangers that extend to the right and left from the top edge of the folder. These hangers hook onto rails that run down the sides of the file drawer. Hangers keep the folders in an upright position and prevent them from slipping down into the drawer.

Labels

Labels provide a convenient means for marking the captions on folders and file drawers.

Folder labels A folder label is attached to the tab of each file folder. The information provided on each label is known as a **caption**. The caption is a name, number, or short phrase that identifies the records stored within the file folder.

ad·he'sive

Folder labels come in long sheets or rolls for ease of keyboarding. They are attached to the folder with a gummed or adhesive backing. Labels come in white as well as a variety of colors so that folders can be color-coded. Color coding increases accuracy and speeds the storing and retrieving process. When files are color-coded, a misfiled folder stands out because of the difference in color.

The following are suggestions for keyboarding captions on folder labels:

1. Begin the caption two or three spaces from the left edge on the first available line. On folded gummed labels, make certain the caption begins on the first line below the fold mark.
2. Keyboard the caption using capital and lower-case letters, which are easier to read than all capitals. If the caption is too long for one line, continue it on the next line, indenting two or three spaces.
3. Place secondary references such as the address on the next line, aligned with the first line.
4. Spell out all abbreviations of words considered in filing.
5. Place labels in the same position on each folder tab. This makes the caption easier to find and read when the folders are placed in the file cabinet's drawer.

Drawer labels File drawers should be labeled to show their contents. Most file drawers have a metal frame into which a label can be inserted. The drawer label indicates that material within a given alphabetic or numeric range is located within that drawer. For example, the label for a drawer containing correspondence from William *Aaron* through Fred *Bixby* would appear as follows:

A–Bi

Labels should be consistent in style, easy to read, and easy to understand. They should be neatly keyboarded. As the contents of the drawers change due to the addition of new records, new labels must be prepared.

Guides

File **guides** are rigid pieces of cardboard that divide the file drawer into sections, serve as markers to help locate records quickly, and provide support for the folders.

Guides are available in the same sizes as folders. Like folders, guides have a tab at the top for a caption. The caption identifies the material that is filed in folders placed behind the guide. Guides can be purchased with printed captions or blank tabs. File guides with blank tabs allow companies to add their own desired captions.

Most guides have an eyelet on the bottom through which a file rod can be inserted. The file rod holds the guides in place in the drawer and prevents folders from slipping down in the drawer.

pri'ma·ry

sec'on·dar·y

Guides are classified as either primary or secondary. *Primary guides* mark the major divisions in the filing system such as *A, B, C,* and other letters of the alphabet. *Secondary guides* are used to subdivide the primary sections into smaller groups of folders. As Illustration 9–6 shows, the secondary guides in the *A* section of the files may contain the first name used in the captions of individual folders behind it.

Guides should be placed so that they mark sections of approximately 10 to 15 folders. The more guides that are used, the easier records are to find. If the guides are properly spaced, you can quickly and easily find the approximate location of the file you are looking for.

Illustration 9–6
Primary and secondary file guides

Illustration 9-7
Cross-reference sheet

CROSS-REFERENCE SHEET

Name or Subject Holmes-Simons Management Consultants

Date of Item March 30, 19--

Regarding Beacon Project

SEE

Name or Subject Simons-Holmes Management Consultant

Authorized by JM Date April 4, 19--

Cross-Reference Sheets and Guides

cross'-ref'er·ence

As you saw in the last chapter, there may be more than one name or caption by which a record may be requested. When this is the case, the record is filed in the most obvious place. Then, a **cross-reference sheet** is filed in the other possible file locations. The sheet contains the name or subject of the record, the date of the record, a brief description of the record, and the location of the record. The sheet may be prepared on colored paper so that it is easily recognized in the folder, although white paper can be used. The size of the sheet used will depend on the size of the other records kept in the file.

If you look at Illustration 9-7, you will see a cross-reference sheet that has been prepared for one of the Simons-Holmes Management Consultant's records. Because this record may be requested using the caption *Holmes-Simons Management Consultants,* this record is cross referenced under the caption *Holmes-Simons Management Consultants.* The record is filed in the Simons-Holmes Management Consultants' folder. The cross-reference sheet, is filed in the Holmes-Simons Management Consultants' folder.

Sometimes the contents of an entire folder may be requested by two or more captions. A company may change its name from National Communication Systems to International Communication Systems, for example. In this case, the entire folder would be filed under the new name; a cross-reference guide would be filed under the old name. The caption on the cross-reference might read:

National Communication Systems
SEE International Communication Systems
(name changed 12/1/82)

with·stand'

Cross-reference guides are made of sturdy cardboard to withstand the wear and tear of daily handling. They are usually the same size as the file guides.

Requisition Forms and Cards

req·ui·si'tion

Large companies with centralized filing departments usually require people requesting a record or file to complete a **requisition form** or card. As you can see in Illustration 9–8, this form describes for the file clerk the desired record or file by name or subject and date. The form also contains spaces in which the file clerk can record the date the record is taken from the files and the date it is due.

Illustration 9–8 Requisition form for record

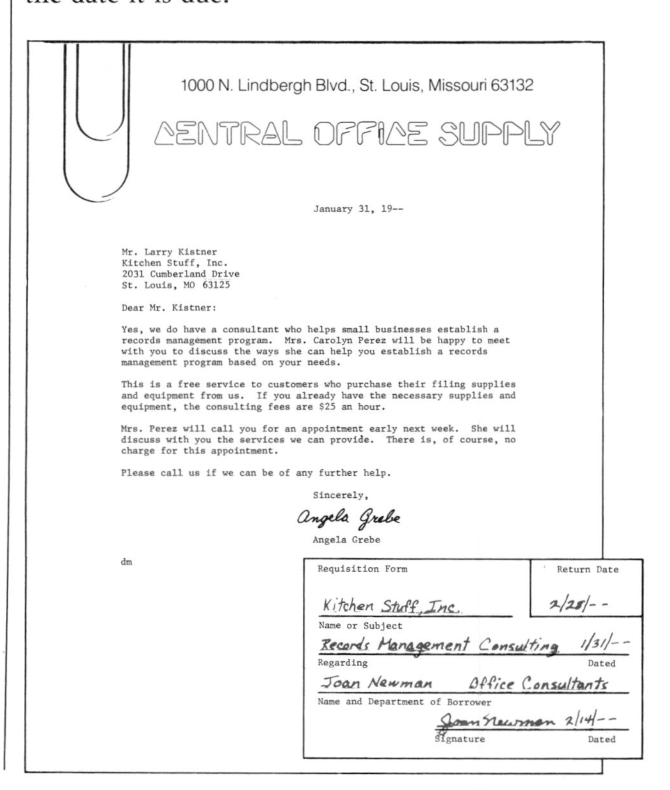

1000 N. Lindbergh Blvd., St. Louis, Missouri 63132

CENTRAL OFFICE SUPPLY

January 31, 19--

Mr. Larry Kistner
Kitchen Stuff, Inc.
2031 Cumberland Drive
St. Louis, MO 63125

Dear Mr. Kistner:

Yes, we do have a consultant who helps small businesses establish a records management program. Mrs. Carolyn Perez will be happy to meet with you to discuss the ways she can help you establish a records management program based on your needs.

This is a free service to customers who purchase their filing supplies and equipment from us. If you already have the necessary supplies and equipment, the consulting fees are $25 an hour.

Mrs. Perez will call you for an appointment early next week. She will discuss with you the services we can provide. There is, of course, no charge for this appointment.

Please call us if we can be of any further help.

Sincerely,

Angela Grebe

Angela Grebe

dm

Requisition Form — Return Date: 2/28/--

Kitchen Stuff, Inc.
Name or Subject

Records Management Consulting — 1/31/--
Regarding — Dated

Joan Newman — Office Consultants
Name and Department of Borrower

Joan Newman — 2/14/--
Signature — Dated

Out Forms

bor'row·ing

Out forms identify and hold the place of records that have been removed from the files. These forms are placed in the same position in the file as the record that has been removed. They provide spaces for entering the name and date of the record, the name of the person borrowing the record, and the date the record was checked out. Using out forms saves you time in both locating and returning records. Let's say you're looking for a record and don't find it in the files. If you find an out form in its place, you know it has been borrowed — not filed in the wrong place. When out forms are used, you save time that would otherwise be spent hunting through the files. Out forms, by marking the place where the record is to be returned, save you time when you replace the record.

The out form may be a sheet, a folder, or a guide. An out sheet is a piece of paper that replaces a single record that has been removed from a folder. Out guides and out folders are used when a complete folder is borrowed from the file. The guide is a single piece of cardboard similar to a file guide. The out folder provides a storage place for incoming records that are received while the file is out. An out form is shown in Illustration 9–9.

Illustration 9–9
Out guide

OUT

Name, Subject, or Number	Date	Issued to	Date Issued
American Hobbies	4/12	N. Lowe	6/15/--
Baker Assoc.	5/20	J. Goldman	7/14/--

EQUIPMENT FOR FILING

rec·om·men·da'tions

In some offices, you may be asked to make recommendations for new or additional filing equipment. In order to make sound recommendations for new equipment, you need to be familiar with the types of equipment available as well as with your office's filing needs.

fac'tors
cab'i·nets

You must consider a number of factors when making recommendations. One important factor is the size of the records to be stored. Filing cabinets come in many sizes. The two most common sizes are the letter size and the legal size. Cabinets are also available in other sizes. There are very small cabinets designed for index cards and disks and large cabinets for blueprints and computer printouts.

You must also consider how many records are to be stored. For instance, if only a few hundred index cards need to be stored, you would probably choose a single file box. For a much larger number of index cards, you would probably choose a cabinet with file drawers designed especially for index cards.

Often the basis for deciding on the size and type of filing equipment is the amount of space available for storage and the cost of space. Since rent is usually based on the number of square feet, many companies try to keep their storage needs to a minimum. Space-saving filing equipment is thus becoming very popular.

Vertical Files

Vertical files are the standard file cabinets found in most offices. File folders are stored on the scored edges and arranged from front to back in long drawers. To reach the last folder in a drawer, you must pull the drawer all the way out. Vertical files require extra floor space for access. Because they require extra floor space, they may not be suitable in offices where space is limited.

ac'cess

Vertical files are popular as a convenient method of storing a small number of records within a decentralized system. Their totally enclosed cabinets provide protection for records. Two-drawer cabinets are frequently used beside a desk to store the most active records and provide additional work space. Three-drawer cabinets are often used to form a counter between working areas. Four- and five-drawer cabinets are frequently used as room dividers.

ac'tive

Lateral Files

lat'er·al

The use of **lateral files** in offices is growing in popularity. In lateral cabinets, file folders are arranged from side to side. Because the drawers pull out only the width of the file folder, less aisle space is needed to provide access to the files.

Often serving as room dividers, lateral files come in two styles. Cabinets with fixed drawer fronts provide access to folders from the top of the drawer only. Cabinets with drawer fronts that lift open provide easy access from the side of the drawer as well as from the top.

Illustration 9–10 compares the space occupied by a vertical file to the space occupied by a lateral file. Notice that the open drawer of the lateral file at the left in the illustration occupies less aisle space than the open drawer of the vertical file at the right.

Illustration 9–10
Lateral files use less aisle space than vertical files

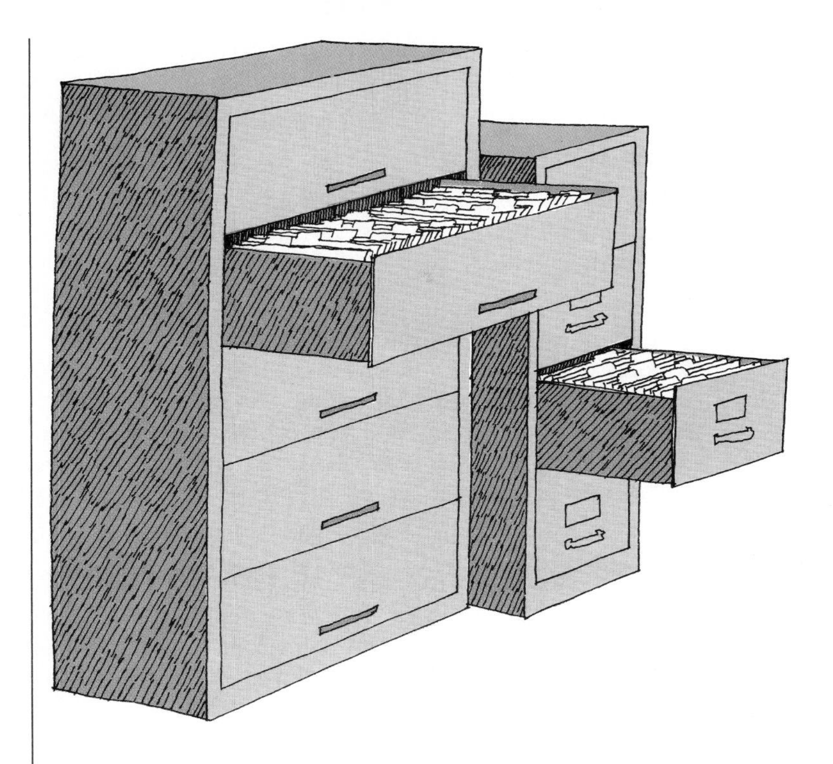

Shelf Files

In shelf filing, folders are stored in an upright position on shelves similar to those found in a library. Shelf files are frequently used for manuals, books, computer disks, and oversized documents. Shelf filing provides for direct access to records. Valuable floor space is saved because additional aisle space is not needed to accommodate an open file drawer.

ac·com'mo·date

The most common type of shelf filing is the open-shelf system, with shelves that extend from floor to ceiling. The higher the filing shelves, the more efficient the use of space. However, it is important to remember that shelves above normal reach should be used only for inactive records.

Several variations of this system are available, including movable and conveyor units. Movable open-shelf files consist of units of shelves that are mounted on rollers or tracks on the floor. When not in use, the units can be pushed together, one in front of the other or side by side. Space is saved because no aisle is left between the units. The units can then be moved manually or mechanically to provide access to the records needed.

mech'a·nized

In conveyor files, shelves are attached to a mechanized conveyor that moves them into position. (The conveyor is similar to the conveyor used at a dry cleaner's to store clothes that are waiting for customer pickup.) Usually, only one shelf is accessible at a time. When a record is needed, the file clerk dials the shelf location of the folder. The conveyor begins to turn and stops automatically when the shelf containing the folder reaches the desk.

Special Features

Filing accessories and equipment with special features can be purchased to provide added convenience or protection. Some of these features and accessories include:

- cabinets with built-in wheels that make it easier to move them from one location to another
- drawers that pull out one at a time to prevent cabinets from tipping
- combination or key locks that provide security for confidential records
- fireproof construction that provides protection from fire
- portable filing shelves or baskets that attach to the outside of a file drawer, giving you a place to put your work while you file

SPECIAL FILING EQUIPMENT

Special filing equipment is available for records that cannot be conveniently stored in standard filing equipment. Some records — such as index cards or disks — are small and compact. Records such as computer printouts and blueprints, on the other hand, are large and bulky. These records are as vital to the company as correspondence or legal records and must be stored for future reference.

Illustration 9–11
Special equipment for large and small records

Undersized Files

Card files Card files can be found in most businesses. The most common sizes of cards include 3 x 5 inches, 4 x 6 inches, and 5 x 8 inches.

in'ven·to·ry

ro'ta·ry

A variety of equipment for storing cards is available. If a few cards are used for the inventory of equipment within the office, a single file box is usually adequate. In the library, book titles, authors' names, and subjects are listed on cards in the card catalogue. File cabinets with drawers the size of the cards are used to store this larger volume of cards. Small rotary card files like the one shown in Illustration 9–11 are often seen on desks. These files provide quick access to the addresses and telephone numbers of people you frequently write or call.

Disk Files Disks for computers and text editors need special care when they are filed. Desk-top file boxes and cases are available to protect disks from dust and contaminants in the office environment. There are also specially designed file folders and binders that can be used to store disks. The folders fit into a file drawer or binder. All of these storage items come in various sizes to fit different sized disks.

mi'cro·rec·ord

Microrecord files Card files are also used to store microrecords such as microfiche and aperture cards. The use and storage of microrecords are discussed in the next unit.

Oversized Files

Oversized records such as computer printouts and blueprints require special filing equipment so that they can be stored without having to be folded. Computer printouts, for example, are often bound in binders with built-in hangers and stored upright in drawers. They may also be hung in special folders from rods in open-shelf units. Blueprints and maps are often assigned a number and stored flat in units of stacked shallow drawers. Like computer printouts, blueprints and maps may also be hung within an open shelf unit.

Sorters

File sorters are used to arrange records in filing order before they are filed. This procedure allows you to save time and unnecessary movement from one section of the file to another. File sorters come in a variety of styles and generally provide for several means of classification, including alphabetic and numeric. The most commonly used desk-top sorter, shown in Illustration 9–12, contains tabbed dividers with alphabetic and numeric captions. As you sort, you place records behind the appropriate captions. You can then arrange the records in filing order at your desk section by section.

Illustration 9–12
Desk-top sorter

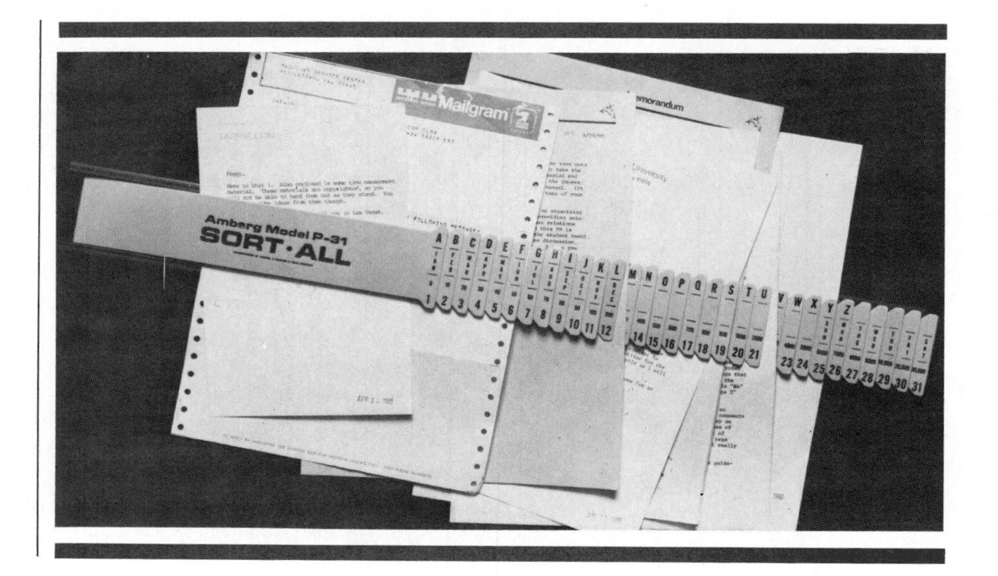

REVIEWING KEY POINTS

1. An efficient filing system requires proper supplies and equipment to hold, protect, identify, and organize your files.
2. File folders are used to group and identify records.
3. Folder labels provide a convenient means of identifying the contents of folders. Attached to the folder tab, labels should be uniform in style and placement.
4. Guides are used to divide drawers into sections, serve as markers to aid in the quick location of records, and provide support for the folders.
5. Out forms identify and hold the place of records that have been removed from the files.
6. Filing equipment should be selected according to the size of the records, the number of records to be stored, and the space available.
7. The three main types of filing equipment include vertical, lateral, and shelf.
8. Special equipment is available for records such as microfiche, disks, computers printouts, and blueprints that cannot be stored in standard filing equipment.
9. Locks, fireproof construction, portable shelves, and sorters are examples of special filing features and accessories.

DEVELOPING HUMAN RELATIONS SKILLS

1. José works at the desk next to yours. You have just heard your supervisor reprimanding José because he cannot find a folder of important papers. José has a big stack of folders on his desk, but he has to go through each folder to find out what it contains. After the supervisor leaves, José tells you, "I know those papers are in one of these folders. I just need some time to go through them to find the papers."
   a. What is wrong with José's method of filing?
   b. How can José improve his filing system?
2. You have just received a message from Sam, who works in the centralized filing department. He asks you to return a file that you checked out a week ago for your supervisor. Another supervisor needs some information from the file immediately. Your supervisor is working at home today and has taken the file home. Although it is not a policy, the managers frown on taking any company files out of the office.
   a. What would you do?
   b. What would you say to Sam?

IMPROVING COMMUNICATION SKILLS

Refer to Appendix A 1.28–1.32.

1. On a separate sheet of paper, keyboard the following sentences, supplying dashes where needed.
   a. Order 5 dozen no make that 10 dozen $5\frac{3}{4}$-inch disks.
   b. A problem is a chance for you to do your best Duke Ellington.
   c. Maria Scott a very intelligent woman is the new director.
   d. Perhaps imagination is only intelligence having fun George Scialabba.
   e. Make the reservation for 6:30 no 7:00 p.m.
   f. Rumor travels faster, but it don't stay put as long as truth Will Rogers.
   g. Our company softball team won all its games a championship season.
   h. Ask Jamie Anders no Jamie Carroll to help you.
   i. The company policy limits access to files and prohibits removal of files from the center a very strict policy.
   j. Last year's accuracy ratio for the filing department was 99.85 percent the best ever!
2. Locate the name of an office supply company in your local telephone directory. Then compose a letter to this company inquirying about desk-top file boxes for the storage of your text editor's disks. In your letter, ask about the sizes of files that are available and their capacities. Also inquire about any special features, such as tinted covers, and costs.

BUILDING PROBLEM-SOLVING SKILLS

1. Steve's department is setting up centralized files and needs to order equipment and supplies.
   a. His supervisor estimates that they will need five 4-drawer vertical file cabinets. If each cabinet costs $169.50, how much will five cost?
   b. For filing efficiency, his supervisor wants to use about 25 file guides in each drawer. How many file guides should Steve order?
   c. Steve's supervisor wants to have approximately 475 file folders on hand for setting up new files. If they come packaged in boxes of 50 folders each, how many boxes will Steve need to order?
2. In order to establish some performance standards, all employees in the filing department have been keeping records of the work they complete. Study the performance records form shown. Then, answer the questions.

CARD FILING
PERFORMANCE RECORDS

Name	Alphabetic Number of Cards Filed	Alphabetic Time in Minutes	Numeric Number of Cards Filed	Numeric Time in Minutes
J. Gainey	285	60	385	57
L. Grant	310	61	390	60
A. Herlong	295	62	410	66
J. Hope	335	65	405	65
T. Vahle	275	55	370	55

   a. Which employee has the highest rate per minute for filing cards alphabetically?
   b. Which employee has the highest rate per minute for filing cards numerically?
   c. Which employee has the lowest rate per minute for filing cards alphabetically?
   d. Which employee has the lowest rate per minute for filing cards numerically?

APPLYING OFFICE SKILLS

Activity 2 can be done on information processing equipment.

1. The following files were requested by telephone. Complete the requisition forms in your workbook with the information provided. Be careful to write clearly so that the file clerk can read the form.
   a. Kay Austin in Accounting wants the file for the Mexican Curio Shop.
   b. Paul Cortese in the Legal Department asked for the contract signed on

April 10 with the Cookie Factory for refreshments supplied the company snack bar.

c. Julie Anderson in the Credit Department wants the file for Kim Tuten.

d. Riley Downs in the Legal Department asked for the letter she wrote on June 30 to Cindy Oxford.

e. Melanie Mize in Accounting wants the file for Oil City Real Estate.

f. Joe Melke in the Credit Department asked for the file for Herdson & Son.

2. Using the memorandum form in your workbook or plain paper, prepare the following memorandum to be distributed to all department managers.

To: Department Managers/ From: Anne Rosati/ Date: (Today's) Subject: Storing Disks (P) Last week during a very busy time, we experienced some problems retrieving data from some disks. When we called a consultant for advice, the first question asked was, "Where were the disks stored?" It seems that fingerprints, dust, and other contaminants in the office atmosphere will affect the storage capability of disks. When we checked with the operators who prepared the disks, we found that many of the disks were stored without jackets in desk drawers or regular file folders. (P) In order to prevent future problems of this nature, we are in the process of ordering special disk files. The files can be obtained for $3\frac{1}{2}$-, $5\frac{1}{4}$-, or 8-inch disks and can store 20, 50, or 100 disks. The files have tabbed dividers that will help operators store and retrieve disks efficiently. (P) Each operator who prepares disks should have a file for current disks. Please study the needs of your department and let me know by Friday how many files you need of each size and capacity. (P) The files should be delivered within a week to ten days. In the meantime, please ask your operators to store the disks according to the directions provided on the box.

Saving Time and Money

1. Always keyboard the captions for folders. Keyboarded captions are easier to read.
2. Keep a small supply of out guides in the front or back of each file drawer so that they will be readily available when materials are removed from the file drawer.
3. During slack periods, clear the files of all unnecessary items according to your company's retention schedule.
4. Open only one file drawer at a time and close the drawer when you are finished. An open file drawer may cause accidents. For example, the file cabinet may tip over, or another worker may walk into the drawer or bump into it as he or she is filing nearby.
5. Develop a retention schedule for the records kept in your office if none is available. Ask your supervisor to help by telling you the length of time the different types of records are needed.
6. Use the most convenient filing space for your active files. The inactive files can be stored in a less accessible area, such as the top and bottom drawers of the file cabinet or file cabinets in a storage area.

UNIT 10

FILING SYSTEMS

Alphabetic Indexing for Personal Names •

Alphabetic Indexing for Business and Other Organizations •

Document Filing in an Alphabetic System •

Specialized Filing Methods •

CHAPTER 1

ALPHABETIC INDEXING FOR PERSONAL NAMES

Many people are surprised to learn that there are rules for filing records in alphabetical order. After all, what could be simpler than arranging things in order from *A* to *Z*? Everyone knows that cash comes before *d*ata, and *em*ployer before *ex*ecutive. In fact, alphabetizing single letters or words *is* an easy task.

In business, though, you are seldom asked to alphabetize a list of words. More often, you are dealing with the names of people and companies. For example, you may be asked to prepare personnel folders for employee records and arrange them in alphabetical order by employee name. Whose folder would you place first in the files: Andrew White's, Phyllis Bickley's, or Beverly Morelli's? If you placed Andrew White's folder first, then you would be alphabetizing by first name. If you chose Phyllis Bickley's, you would be alphabetizing by last name. Imagine the confusion in an office if some of the employees used the first method, while the other employees used the second. Because it is so important that a company's files be complete, there are standard procedures for alphabetizing. For filing efficiency, all employees must observe these procedures.

As you study this chapter, you will find answers to the following questions:

- What are the three steps involved in arranging names in alphabetical order?
- What are the rules for indexing and alphabetizing individual names?
- What are some of the common variations in indexing and alphabetizing individual names?
- What do the following terms mean: **indexing, filing units, alphabetize?**

STEPS IN ALPHABETIZING

al·pha·bet'i·cal

To arrange words or names in correct alphabetical order, you must perform three steps: indexing, dividing into filing units, and alphabetizing.

Indexing

in'dex·ing

trans·posed'

You have probably used the telephone directory many times. If you know how to find names in the White Pages of the telephone directory, then you are already familiar with a basic step in alphabetizing, called indexing. **Indexing** is the arrangement of the parts of a name in order so that the name can be alphabetized. In office files, as in a telephone directory, names of individuals are arranged — indexed — with the person's last name first. In other words, the first and last name must be transposed (reversed) before a name can be arranged in alphabetical order. Thus, if you want to find *Joanne Sciandra* in the files — or in the telephone directory — you look under *Sciandra, Joanne.*

Identifying Filing Units

u'nits

The second step in alphabetizing is to divide the name into **filing units**. The general rule is that each word, initial, or abbreviation in a name is a separate filing unit. *Joanne Sciandra* contains two separate filing units. *Mary Beth White* and *Comer D. Curry* each contain three filing units. The indexing tables used in this chapter and the next one will help you identify the filing units in a name and place the units in correct indexing order.

	INDEXING ORDER		
Name	Unit 1	Unit 2	Unit 3
Joanne Sciandra	Sciandra	Joanne	
Mary Beth White	White	Mary	Beth
Comer D. Curry	Curry	Comer	D.

Alphabetizing

Once names are indexed and divided into filing units, you can **alphabetize** them — that is, arrange the names in order from *A* to *Z*. To alphabetize, compare the names unit by unit, letter by letter. If you have personnel folders for Andrew White, Phyllis Bickley, and Beverly Morelli, for example, you would index them and arrange them in the following alphabetical order, placing B before M and M before W:

Bickley, Phyllis
Morelli, Beverly
White, Andrew

What would happen if your company hired Mary Beth White? Where would you put her folder — in front of Andrew White's folder, or behind it? When the first filing units are the same, you need to compare the second units. Because *A* comes before *M* in the alphabet, you would file Andrew's folder in front of Mary Beth's. (You apply this rule when you look up names in the telephone directory. If you find several listings for *White,* you know to look at the first names, which are arranged in alphabetical order.)

If the second filing units are also the same, arrange the names in alphabetical order according to the third filing units — and so on.

Name	INDEXING ORDER		
	Unit 1	Unit 2	Unit 3
Andrew White	White	Andrew	
Mary Beth White	White	Mary	Beth
Mary Anne White	White	Mary	Anne

The personnel folders are now arranged from front to back in this order:

Bickley, Phyllis
Morelli, Beverly
White, Andrew
White, Mary Anne
White, Mary Beth

Notice that the letter in each name that determines the alphabetical order is underlined for emphasis.

A helpful rule to remember when you are alphabetizing is that "nothing comes before something." For example, if you added Andrew J. White to the group of names above, his name would follow Andrew White's. Look at the indexing table to see why. When you compare the third filing units, you are comparing *nothing* with *something* (the initial *J*).

in·i'tial

The "nothing before something" rule also applies to initials and full names. A last name with a first initial only is filed ahead of the same last name that has a full first name beginning with the same lettter. For example, *A. White* would be filed ahead of *Andrew White.* Names with middle initials are handled the same way. Thus, the name *Mary A. White* would be filed ahead of the name *Mary Anne White.*

Name	INDEXING ORDER		
	Unit 1	Unit 2	Unit 3
Andrew J. White	White	Andrew	J.
Andrew White	White	Andrew	
Mary Anne White	White	Mary	Anne
Mary A. White	White	Mary	A.
Mary Beth White	White	Mary	Beth

Now your personnel folders are arranged in this order:

Bickley, Phyllis
Morelli, Beverly
White, A.
White, Andrew
White, Andrew J.
White, Mary A.
White, Mary Anne
White, Mary Beth

INDEXING RULES FOR INDIVIDUAL NAMES

Indexing rules tell you: (1) how to arrange the parts of a name and (2) what words (or parts of names) should be counted as separate filing units. In addition, indexing rules tell you when to use cross-reference forms to increase filing efficiency.

Each of the indexing rules presented in this chapter and the next is followed by a table containing several examples. *Please note that the names are not arranged in alphabetical order within the tables.* The names must be indexed before they can be alphabetized. The correct alphabetical order for the names in each table is shown in the margin.

Rule 1 Names of Individuals

sur'name

For names of individuals, each name or initial is a separate filing unit. The first filing unit is the *surname* (last name), followed by the *given* (first) name or initial and the middle name or initial. This rule is commonly referred to as "last name first."

	INDEXING ORDER		
Name	Unit 1	Unit 2	Unit 3
Ruth Sachs	Sachs	Ruth	
Calvin L. Beard	Beard	Calvin	L.
A. J. Reardon	Reardon	A.	J.
Mary Ann Bartolotti	Bartolotti	Mary	Ann

Bartolotti, Mary Ann
Beard, Calvin L.
Reardon, A. J.
Sachs, Ruth

Rule 2 Nicknames

Some individuals prefer to go by nicknames, and their records should show their preferences. For example, *Robert* may go by *Bob, Kathleen* by *Kathy* or *Kate,* and *Thomas* by *Tom.* When a person uses a nickname, treat it as the given name and make it the second filing unit. If the nickname is unusual or unrelated to the given name (for example, *Shorty, Sissy,* or *Bud*), cross-reference the names.

Exception: When an individual's nickname is not followed by a recognizable surname, index the name in the order written.

rec·og·niz'a·ble

Name	INDEXING ORDER Unit 1	Unit 2	Unit 3
Billy Overstreet	Overstreet	Billy	
Dee Denton (Mary Dolores)	Denton	Dee	
Mary Dolores Denton	Denton	Mary	Dolores
Wolfman Jack	Wolfman	Jack	

Denton, Dee
Denton, Mary Dolores
See: Denton, Dee
Overstreet, Billy
Wolfman Jack

Rule 3 Abbreviated First Names

ab·bre'vi·at·ed

When an individual's first or middle name is abbreviated, it is indexed and filed as if it were spelled out. Common abbreviations include *Chas.* (Charles), *Geo.* (George), *Robt.* (Robert), *Thos.* (Thomas), and *Wm.* (William).

Name	INDEXING ORDER Unit 1	Unit 2	Unit 3
G. Wm. Miller	Miller	G.	William
Robt. Banks	Banks	Robert	
Thos. P. Tillson	Tillson	Thomas	P.
Chas. Council	Council	Charles	

Banks, Robert
Council, Charles
Miller, G. William
Tillson, Thomas P.

Rule 4 Names with Prefixes

pre'fix

When the surname of an individual contains a prefix (as in *San Martin*), it is filed as one unit. This rule applies even when there is a space between the prefix and the name. Common prefixes include *d', Da, De, Du, La, Les, Mac, Mc, St., San, Van, von der*. As with other abbreviations, *St.* is filed as if it were spelled out in full *(Saint)*. The apostrophe found in prefixes *(D'Angelo)* is ignored in filing.

Name	INDEXING ORDER Unit 1	Unit 2	Unit 3
Kevin C. DeBruin	DeBruin	Kevin	C.
Carmen de la Parte	de la Parte	Carmen	
Edward B. St. John	Saint John	Edward	B.
Maureen M. O'Brien	O'Brien	Maureen	M.

DeBruin, Kevin C.
de la Parte, Carmen
O'Brien, Maureen M.
St. John, Edward B.

Rule 5 Hyphenated Names

hy'phen·at·ed

Hyphenated names, such as *Anders-Glanville,* are treated as a single filing unit. When computers are used, the hyphen is sometimes dropped and the two names are run together as one word. This treatment ensures that hyphenated names are filed as one unit.

Name	INDEXING ORDER		
	Unit 1	Unit 2	Unit 3
Janet Doan-Steele	Doan(-)Steele	Janet	
Jean-Luc Godard	Godard	Jean(-)Luc	
Louis Ryan-Walsh	Ryan(-)Walsh	Louis	
Harriet FisherMoore	FisherMoore	Harriet	

Doan-Steele, Janet
FisherMoore, Harriet
Godard, Jean-Luc
Ryan-Walsh, Louis

Rules 1–5 Review

To see how Rules 1–5 are applied to a list of names, study the following table. In the second column, the names are arranged in correct indexing order. Diagonal lines are used to divide the names into indexing units. The number of the rule that determines the indexing order is shown in the third column. The list of names is correctly alphabetized in the fourth column of the table that follows.

Name	Indexing Order	Indexing Rule	Alphabetical Order
Bob Norris	Norris/Bob	2	Cox(-)Pearlman, Ruth
Geo. Norris	Norris/George	3	d'Arcy, Michael J.
Ruth Cox(-)Pearlman	Cox(-)Pearlman/Ruth	5	Delmonte, Patricia Lane
G. W. Norris	Norris/G./W.	1	Norris, Bob
Patricia Lane Delmonte	Delmonte/Patricia/Lane	4	Norris, Bud (Norris, Wilbur)
Bud Norris	Norris/Bud (Norris,		Norris, G. W.
(Wilbur Norris)	Wilbur)	2	Norris, George
Michael J. d'Arcy	d'Arcy/Michael/J.	4	Norris, Wilbur (See: Norris, Bud)

For additional practice, index and alphabetize the names in Group 1 under Applying Office Skills, Activity 1.

Rule 6 Identical Names

i·den'ti·cal

When the names of two or more individuals are identical, look at the addresses to determine the correct filing order. Compare the parts of the addresses and arrange them in the following order:

1. alphabetically by city or town
2. alphabetically by state

3. alphabetically by street name
4. numerically by house or building number.

Name	INDEXING ORDER Unit 1	Unit 2	Unit 3	Unit 4	Unit 5
Karen Adams Reno, NV	Adams	Karen	Reno	Nevada	
Karen Adams Boise, ID	Adams	Karen	Boise	Idaho	
David Johnson 617 Blossom Lane Columbia, MD	Johnson	David	Columbia	Maryland	Blossom Lane
David Johnson 201 Moultrie Road Columbia, MD	Johnson	David	Columbia	Maryland	Moultrie Road

Adams, Karen, Boise, ID
Adams, Karen, Reno, NV
Johnson, David, Columbia, MD, Blossom Lane
Johnson, David, Columbia MD, Moultrie Road

Rule 7 Titles and Degrees

pro·fes'sion·al

Courtesy and professional titles and degrees are usually not considered in filing. However, they may be included in parentheses after the last filing unit and used to distinguish between or among individuals with identical names. When the courtesy titles *Mr., Mrs., Miss,* and *Ms.* are used to determine filing order, they are alphabetized in abbreviated form.

Religious or foreign titles followed by a first name only are filed in the order written.

Name	INDEXING ORDER Unit 1	Unit 2	Unit 3
Diane A. Dunlap, Ph.D.	Dunlap	Diane	A. (Ph.D.)
Miss Diane A. Dunlap	Dunlap	Diane	A. (Miss)
Major John Farber	Farber	John (Major)	
Princess Caroline	Princess	Caroline	

Dunlap, Diane A. (Miss)
Dunlap, Diane A. (Ph.D.)
Farber, John (Major)
Princess Caroline

Rule 8 Seniority Titles

sen·ior'i·ty

Titles that indicate seniority, such as Sr. (Senior), Jr. (Junior), II (Second), and III (Third), are treated as the last filing unit in a personal name. These titles are used to determine the filing order when two or more names are identical. When placing personal names in alphabetical order, the titles Jr. and Sr. are arranged in alphabetical order. The titles II and III are arranged in numeric order. The indexing table that appears at the top of the next page shows how titles of seniority are arranged in the correct indexing order.

Carmichael, Edwin D., Jr.
Carmichael, Edwin D., Sr.
Ryan, G. Daniel, II
Ryan, G. Daniel, III

Name	INDEXING ORDER			
	Unit 1	Unit 2	Unit 3	Unit 4
G. Daniel Ryan, III	Ryan	G.	Daniel	III
G. Daniel Ryan, II	Ryan	G.	Daniel	II
Edwin D. Carmichael, Sr.	Carmichael	Edwin	D.	Sr.
Edwin D. Carmichael, Jr.	Carmichael	Edwin	D.	Jr.

Rule 9 Married Women

A married woman's name is usually indexed in the following order: (1) her husband's surname, (2) her first name, and (3) her middle name or maiden surname. In some cases a woman may choose to add her husband's surname to her own with a hyphen. When this is the case, the rule for hyphenated surnames applies, and the name is treated as a single filing unit. For example, suppose Susan A. Harter marries Stuart C. Pierce. She may choose to change her name to *Susan A. Pierce, Susan Harter Pierce,* or *Susan A. Harter-Pierce.* (She may also decide to keep her own name, unchanged.) For legal and filing purposes, she does *not* become *Mrs. Stuart C. Pierce.* If it is necessary to note her husband's name, it can be shown in parentheses as part of the last unit.

Harter-Pierce, Susan A. (Stuart C. Pierce, husband)
Pierce, Susan A. (Stuart C. Pierce, husband)
Pierce, Susan Harter (Stuart C. Pierce, husband)

Name	INDEXING ORDER		
	Unit 1	Unit 2	Unit 3
Mrs. Stuart C. Pierce (Susan A.)	Pierce	Susan	A. (Stuart C. Pierce, husband)
Susan Harter Pierce	Pierce	Susan	Harter (Stuart C. Pierce, husband)
Susan A. Harter-Pierce	Harter(-) Pierce	Susan	A. (Stuart C. Pierce, husband)

Rule 10 Foreign and Unusual Names

ac'cents

When you cannot determine which part of a name is the surname, treat the last written name as the surname. Ignore accents in foreign names.

Daniel, Eric
Kuang, Lu Mei
Marquez, Gabriel Garcia
Rhys, Rybczyk

Name	INDEXING ORDER		
	Unit 1	Unit 2	Unit 3
Eric Daniel	Daniel	Eric	
Lu Mei Kuang	Kuang	Lu	Mei
Rybczyk Rhys	Rhys	Rybczyk	
Gabriel Garcia Marquez	Marquez	Gabriel	Garcia

Illustration 10–1
Arranging folders in alphabetical order

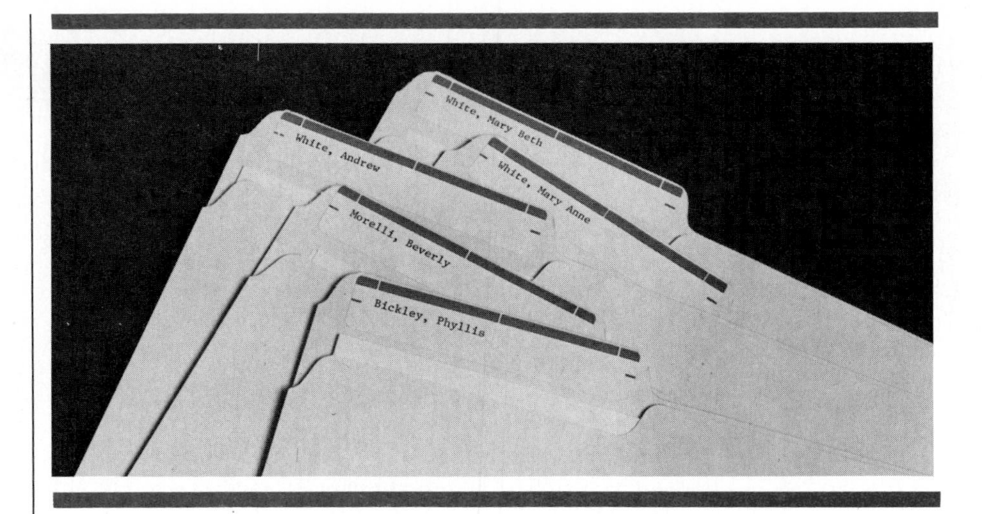

Rules 6–10 Review

The table below shows how Rules 6-10 are applied. It indicates the indexing and alphabetical order. It also gives the number of the rule that applies.

Name	Indexing Order	Indexing Rule	Alphabetical Order
Mrs. Peter Janeway (Melissa Stoner)	Janeway/Melissa/Stoner (Peter Janeway, husband)	9	Abdul(-)Kader, Abdullah
Jason Bearde, Salem, NH	Bearde/Jason/Salem/ New/Hampshire	6	Bearde, Jason (Salem, Massachusetts)
Abdullah Abdul-Kader	Abdul(-)Kader/Abdullah	10	Bearde, Jason (Salem, New Hampshire)
Melissa Stoner-Janeway	Stoner(-)Janeway/Melissa	9	Haufman, William T. II
Melissa Stoner Janeway D.D.S	Janeway/Melissa/Stoner (D.D.S.)	7	Haufman, William T. III Janeway, Melissa Stoner
William T. Haufman, III	Haufman/William/T./III	8	(Peter Janeway, husband)
Jason Bearde, Salem, MA	Bearde/Jason/Salem Massachusetts	6	Janeway, Melissa Stoner (D.D.S.)
Wm. T. Haufman II	Haufman/William/T./II	8, 3	Stoner(-)Janeway, Melissa

VARIATIONS IN INDEXING RULES

When you begin working, you may find that your supervisor or office follows slightly different rules for indexing. As with any office procedure, you should learn and apply the rules of the company in which you work. Because materials in the files must be easy to locate, it is especially important that everyone with filing responsibilities follow the same procedures.

var·i·a'tions

Here are some common variations in indexing and alphabetizing of personal names:

1. A nickname may be changed to the given name for filing. For example, *Bill* is changed to *William* and *Beth* to *Elizabeth.*
2. A hyphenated surname may be treated as two separate filing units, rather than one unit. For example, the first filing unit in *Linda Baker-Wright* would be *Baker;* the second would be *Wright.*
3. A married woman's records may be filed under her husband's name rather than her legal name.
4. Foreign names may be indexed in the order written.

REVIEWING KEY POINTS

1. Employees must follow a standard set of filing procedures so that files will be complete and records will be accessible.
2. Alphabetizing is arranging words in *A*-to-*Z* order. To alphabetize individual names, divide them into filing units and compare the units letter by letter.
3. Each word, initial, or abbreviation in a name is considered a separate filing unit when indexing.
4. Indexing is arranging the units of a name in correct order so that you can compare them for alphabetizing.
5. The usual indexing order for individual names is last name first, first name (or initial), and middle name (or initial).
6. When alphabetizing, remember that "nothing comes before something." That is, a name with a blank — no middle name or initial, for example — in a filing unit will be filed ahead of the identical name that contains a middle name or initial. For this reason, initials are filed ahead of names beginning with the same letter.
7. There are ten basic rules for indexing individual names. The best way to learn these rules is to study examples and practice applying the rules.
8. Some companies follow a slightly different set of indexing rules. Be sure to learn and apply the rules for *your* company.

DEVELOPING HUMAN RELATIONS SKILLS

1. Jose Garcia, a friend of yours from high school, has just been hired as a file clerk at your company. After a few days on the job, he tells you, "These

people don't know how to file right! I learned the rules for indexing, alphabetizing, and cross-referencing in school. Why can't I just use those rules here?"

a. What problems could result if everyone in your department were to follow Jose's suggestion?

b. What should you tell Jose?

2. Your friend, Carolyn DeLuz, usually goes by her nickname, Lyn. Yesterday afternoon when Lyn went to her dentist for a checkup, there was a new receptionist, and she asked Lyn to complete a new-patient form. Lyn insisted that she had been coming to this dentist for years and that her records were already on file.

   After searching for several minutes, the receptionist finally asked Lyn her full first name, since there were no records for Lyn DeLuz. When Lyn told you about this incident, she complained that "the dumb receptionist made me waste a lot of time because she couldn't find my records."

   a. How could Lyn have prevented this problem from developing?

   b. What could the receptionist do to make sure this kind of situation does not happen again?

IMPROVING COMMUNICATION SKILLS

Refer to Appendix A 1.38–1.40.

1. On a separate sheet of paper, keyboard the following sentences, inserting parentheses where needed.

   a. The tallest girl Emily was 6 feet tall.

   b. The lease states that the monthly rent will be three hundred dollars $300.

   c. The younger students 7 to 10 years old will be dismissed at noon.

   d. ARMA Association of Records Managers and Administrators has compiled a set of filing rules.

   e. Diane was late for her appointment at least 1 hour and the personnel director had left.

   f. Dale Goodman is he here? is the winner of the award.

   g. Mark bought the shirt for $15.

   h. The IRS Internal Revenue Service audits suspicious income tax returns.

   i. The hurricane winds are now 85 mph is in the Gulf of Mexico.

   j. Our new supervisor we met her last week assumes her new duties Monday.

2. Compose a letter to Mr. Jerrad Isock, 2345 14th Avenue W, Bradenton, FL 33529. Tell Mr. Isock that you have received the documents related to the sale of his property in Dallas, Texas. Also tell him that you will call to tell him

BU

1. Re
   wo
   a.
   b.
   c.

Name
A. Ma
T. Nel
B. Oak
K. Perc
T. Rake

Group 1
1. Frances Belvin-Cox
2. Barbara L. Cortese
3. Bob Koenigsberg
4. Chuck Morgan
5. Julie McAlhany
6. Robert C.
7. G. Wm
8. Lou

2. Refer tc
   questio
   a. Each
      avera
   b. What for all employees?

APPLYING OFFICE SKILLS

1. For this activity, you will need 50 index cards or sheets of paper approximately 3 x 5 inches. Arrange the names in each of the groups on page 388 in alphabetical order according to these instructions:
   - **a.** Keyboard each name in correct indexing order in the upper left corner of a card.
   - **b.** In the upper right corner, keyboard the number that appears before the name. (The numbers will help in checking the answers.)
   - **c.** Arrange the cards *for each group* in alphabetical order. (You should sort the cards by letter groups before you arrange them in alphabetical order.)
   - **d.** Record your answers for each group on the form provided in your workbook or on a separate sheet of paper.
   - **e.** Arrange all the cards from all three groups in one alphabetical sequence. Record your answers on the form you used in Step *d.*

olten

. Anderson

is C. LaBorde

9. Patricia L. Ferguson
10. Dana Banks-Higgins
11. Alice Dell-Brown
12. Maribeth Karandisevsky
13. Carolyn C. Dolecheck
14. Betsy Jackson
15. Chas. C. d'Haveland

oup 2

16. G. Jeff Lamb, CPA, Mountain Home, Idaho
17. Dr. Joan Anderson, San Juan, Puerto Rico
18. J. E. Hulbert, Jr., Newark, Delaware
19. Miss Piggy
20. Cynthia O. Hayes, Columbia, Maryland
21. Vu Huw Dang, Waco, Texas
22. Mrs. Vincent Hall (Doris), Monroe, Ohio
23. Cynthia O. Hayes, Columbia, South Carolina
24. Theresa Chan, Brockton, Massachusetts
25. Sr. Mary McManus, Fairbanks, Alaska
26. Luke B. Cassidy, III, Pueblo, Colorado
27. Gouma El-Ahrish, Jackson, Tennessee
28. John Chi-Jui, Grand Forks, North Dakota
29. J. E. Hulbert, Sr., Olympia, Washington
30. Countess Marie, London, England

Group 3

31. Ms. Carol LeBlanc
32. Rev. Kurt Munson
33. Henry Johnston, M.D.
34. Martha Morgan
35. Leroy Chaisson, Sr.
36. Dr. F. M. Busch, Jr.
37. M. R. Johnson, CPA
38. Big Jack
39. Hoang Ngoc Kim
40. E. G. Beyda-Lee
41. Mrs. Marlene Holmes-Durkey
42. Leroy Chaisson, II
43. Harriett C. Corbello
44. H. C. Corbello
45. Mrs. Miriam Gibbons (Walter)
46. Hoy Horahan
47. Dr. Ruth Bruner
48. Joyce L. Giglioni, LLB
49. Capt. K. L. Lee
50. E. P. Goza

2. **(Optional)** For this activity, you will need 10 index cards or sheets of paper approximately 3 x 5 inches. Keyboard the names in correct indexing order in the top left corner of each card; keyboard the number in the top right corner. Arrange the names in each group in correct alphabetical order.

   Group 1

   1. Ms. Angela O'Conner, 602 Sherwood Circle, Villa Park, CA 92667
   2. Obwa Osimbo, 224 Kainoa Place, Honolulu, HI 96821
   3. Ralph Ober, 929 Gaurley Drive, Boise, ID 83705
   4. Randy O'Berg, 609 Broadwell Street, Albion, MI 49224-8611
   5. Angela O'Conner, 436 Archer Street, Salinas, CA 93901

   Group 2

   1. Larry Fink, 3720 Loma Lane West, Phoenix, AZ 85201
   2. Mrs. Edna Finklin (Edward R. Jr.), 21 Mill Lane, Tacoma, WA 98444
   3. Edward R. Finklin, Jr., 8310 Cayuga Street, Buffalo, NY 14211
   4. Emma Fink-Lea, 401 Main Street, Buffalo, ND 58011-3210
   5. Larry Finke, 721 Ocotillo Circle, Phoenix, AZ 85016

CHAPTER 2

ALPHABETIC INDEXING FOR BUSINESS AND OTHER ORGANIZATIONS

In most businesses, correspondence and other records relate to other companies and organizations as well as to individuals. Thus, if you use an alphabetic filing system, you will be arranging many records by name of company or organization. Before you can alphabetize company names, you must index them, just as you must index names of individuals. Rules for indexing names of business, governmental, and other types of organizations are presented in this chapter.

As you study the rules and examples, you will notice that many of the indexing rules that apply to individual names also apply to company names. For example, in both company and individual names, a hyphenated word is treated as a single filing unit. Being aware of the similarities between the two sets of rules will help you remember these rules and apply them.

As you study this chapter, you will find answers to the following questions:

- What are the rules for indexing and alphabetizing company names?
- How do you index and alphabetize the names of government agencies and other organizations?
- What are some of the common variations in indexing and alphabetizing company names?
- What do the following terms mean: **compound geographic name, compass point?**

INDEXING RULES FOR COMPANY NAMES

As in the last chapter, the tables show the names arranged in indexing order and divided into indexing units. Correct alphabetical order of the names in each table is shown in the margin.

Rule 11 Company Names

A company name is indexed as written, unless it includes the complete name of an individual. This rule also applies to names of foreign businesses.

Banco Centroamericano
Central Office Supply
Central Radiology Laboratories
Coleman Marine Repairs

Name	INDEXING ORDER Unit 1	Unit 2	Unit 3
Coleman Marine Repairs	Coleman	Marine	Repairs
Central Office Supply	Central	Office	Supply
Central Radiology Laboratories	Central	Radiology	Laboratories
Banco Centroamericano	Banco	Centroamericano	

Rule 12 Companies Named After Individuals

re·main′der

When a company name includes the full name of an individual, it is indexed in the following order: (1) the individual's surname, (2) the first name or initial, (3) the middle name or initial, and (4) the remainder of the company name, in the order written.

There are two instances in which this rule is *not* followed:

1. when an individual's name makes up the name of a well-known company (such as *Howard Johnson* or *Ethan Allen Galleries*);
2. when a personal, professional, or religious title is followed by only one name (such as *Prince Edward Resorts* or *Mr. Radiator*) in a company name.

In both cases, changing the order of the name might be confusing. Instead, the name is indexed in the order written.

Adams, Tara Designs
Cort, John Management Consultants
Gulliver, Charles O. Miniatures
St. Joseph Aspirin
Taft, Smiley Used Cars

Name	INDEXING ORDER Unit 1	Unit 2	Unit 3	Unit 4
John Cort Management Consultants	Cort	John	Management	Consultants
Smiley Taft Used Cars	Taft	Smiley	Used	Cars
Charles O. Gulliver Miniatures	Gulliver	Charles	O.	Miniatures
Tara Adams Designs	Adams	Tara	Designs	
St. Joseph Aspirin	Saint	Joseph	Aspirin	

Illustration 10-2 Electronic equipment makes storing and retrieving files easier and more efficient

Rule 13 Articles, Conjunctions, and Prepositions

con·junc'tions

pa·ren'the·ses

Articles *(a, an, the)* and conjunctions *(and, or, &)* are not treated as separate filing units. Prepositions (such as *at, of, on, with,* and *for*) are also not treated as separate filing units, *except* when they are the first word in a company name *(At the Top Employment Agency).* To indicate that these words are not considered in filing, place them in parentheses immediately after the words they follow. However, when an article or conjunction is the first word in a company name, place it in parentheses as part of the first unit.

Federal Savings and Loan Association
In (the) Mood Disco
Jan (&) Joe (for) Flowers
(The) Last Chance Garage

Name	INDEXING ORDER Unit 1	Unit 2	Unit 3	Unit 4
Federal Savings and Loan Association	Federal	Savings (and)	Loan	Association
Jan & Joe for Flowers	Jan (&)	Joe (for)	Flowers	
The Last Chance Garage	(The) Last	Chance	Garage	
In the Mood Disco	In (the)	Mood	Disco	

Rule 14 Abbreviations and Single Letters

As in individual names, abbreviations in company names are indexed and filed as if they were spelled out. When single letters or initials appear in company names, each letter is treated as a separate filing unit. Single letters are filed ahead of words beginning with those letters, because of the rule "nothing before something." The table at the top of the next page shows abbreviations and single letters arranged in correct indexing order.

ABC Diaper Service
Miser (and) Co., Inc.
Public Media System
WNOE Radio

Name	INDEXING ORDER Unit 1	Unit 2	Unit 3	Unit 4	Unit 5
Miser and Co., Inc.	Miser (and)	Company	Incorporated		
ABC Diaper Service	A	B	C	Diaper	Service
WNOE Radio	W	N	O	E	Radio
PMS	Public	Media	System		

Rule 15 Hyphenated Words in Company Names

Hyphenated words in company names are treated as a single filing unit, just as they are in names of individuals.

Air(-)Flo Heating Systems
Mid(-)Town Bowling
U-Catch-Um Fish Ranch
Wright-Farnsworth Insurance Company

Name	INDEXING ORDER Unit 1	Unit 2	Unit 3
Mid-Town Bowling	Mid(-)Town	Bowling	
Wright-Farnsworth Insurance Co.	Wright(-)Farnsworth	Insurance	Company
Air-Flo Heating Systems	Air(-)Flo	Heating	Systems
U-Catch-Um Fish Ranch	U(-)Catch(-)Um	Fish	Ranch

Rules 11–15 Review

di·ag′o·nal

To see how Rules 11–15 are applied to a list of company names, study the table below. The names are divided into indexing units by diagonal lines and arranged in indexing order. The rule governing indexing order is shown in the third column. The names are listed in correct alphabetical order in the last column. If after you complete this practice you would like additional practice, index and alphabetize the names that you will find in Group 1 under Applying Office Skills, Activity 1.

Name	Indexing Order	Indexing Rule	Alphabetical Order
Ken Norton Sports Arena	Norton/Ken/Sports/Arena	12	N(&)R Advertising
N & R Advertising	N(&)/R/Advertising	13, 14	Northern Savings Bank
Queen Anne Reproductions	Queen/Anne/Reproductions	12	Norton, Ken Sports Arena
Quick Treat Incorporated	Quick/Treat/Incorporated	14	Queen Anne Reproductions
Northern Savings Bank	Northern/Savings/Bank	11	(The) Queen (of) Hearts
The Queen of Hearts	(The) Queen (of)/ Hearts	13	Quick Treat Incorporated
Quick-Kopy Printing	Quick(-)Kopy/Printing	15	Quick(-)Kopy Printing

Rule 16 Companies with Identical Names

When two or more companies have the same name, the addresses determine the correct filing order. Compare the parts of the addresses, as you would for individual names, in the following order: city or town, state, street, and building number.

First National Bank, Appleton
First National Bank, Denver
Greenhouse Cafe, Milford, MA
Greenhouse Cafe, Milford, OH Fall Street
Greenhouse, Cafe Milford, OH Winslow Street

	INDEXING ORDER				
Name	Unit 1	Unit 2	Unit 3	Unit 4	Unit 5
First National Bank 607 Tremont Street Denver, CO	First	National	Bank	Denver	
First National Bank 2809 Main Street Appleton, WI	First	National	Bank	Appleton	
Greenhouse Cafe 543 Meadow Avenue Milford, MA	Greenhouse	Cafe	Milford	Massachusetts	
Greenhouse Cafe 1261 Fall Street Milford, OH	Greenhouse	Cafe	Milford	Ohio	Fall
Greenhouse Cafe 800 Winslow Street Milford, OH	Greenhouse	Cafe	Milford	Ohio	Winslow

Rule 17 Compound Geographic Names

ge·o·graph'ic

Each word in a **compound geographic name** — a place name that includes a prefix such as *Los, San, New, Mt., St.* — is treated as a separate filing unit and indexed as written. As usual, abbreviations are filed as if they were spelled out. (Notice that *San* and *St.* are treated differently in business and individual names.)

Ann Arbor Cleaners
El Paso Poodle Pamperers
Mount Ida Inn
San Diego Car Rentals

	INDEXING ORDER			
Name	Unit 1	Unit 2	Unit 3	Unit 4
Ann Arbor Cleaners	Ann	Arbor	Cleaners	
San Diego Car Rentals	San	Diego	Car	Rentals
El Paso Poodle Pamperers	El	Paso	Poodle	Pamperers
Mt. Ida Inn	Mount	Ida	Inn	

Rule 18 Names with Compass Points

com'pass

When a **compass point** — a word indicating a direction such as *North* or *East* — is part of a business name, it is considered a separate filing unit. If the name contains more than one compass point, such as *South East,* each one is treated as a filing unit, even when the compass points are combined as one word, as in *Northeast* or *Southwest*. A permanent cross-reference in the files may be helpful.

Name	INDEXING ORDER Unit 1	Unit 2	Unit 3	Unit 4
North East Sales Center	North	East	Sales	Center
South Dakota Distributors, Incorporated	South	Dakota	Distributors	Incorporated
Northwestern Appliance Repair	North	western	Appliance	Repair
Southwestern	South	western		

North East Sales Center
Northwestern Appliance Repair
South Dakota Distributors Incorporated
Southwestern

Rule 19 Possessives and Contractions

pos·ses′sives

The apostrophe in possessives (as in *Robert's*) and contractions (as in *Can't*) in company names is ignored in filing. The word containing the apostrophe is treated as a single filing unit. The apostrophe is placed in parentheses as shown in the table below.

Name	INDEXING ORDER Unit 1	Unit 2	Unit 3	Unit 4
Robert's Refrigeration Service	Robert(')s	Refrigeration	Service	
Kids' Stuff Apparel	Kids(')	Stuff	Apparel	
It's Fresh Bake Shop	It(')s	Fresh	Bake	Shop

It(')s Fresh Bake Shop
Kids(') Stuff Apparel
Robert(')s Refrigeration Service

Rule 20 Numerical Names

nu′mer·als

or′di·nal

To file company names that begin with numerals, do *not* spell out the numeral. Arrange these names in numeric sequence and place them in front of the entire alphabetic file. If the name contains an ordinal numeral (such as *1st* or *6th*), ignore the *st, nd,* or *th* and place it in parentheses after the number. File names beginning with numbers that *are* spelled out (such as *Fifth Wheel Retreads*) in regular alphabetical sequence.

When a numeral appears in any position other than the first, file the company name in the alphabetical file immediately ahead of the same name without a numeral. For example, you would file *Andrew's 2nd Act* ahead of *Andrew's Answering Service.* The indexing table that appears at the top of page 396 shows how company names containing numerals are arranged in the correct indexing order.

20(th) Century Tours
24 Hour Developing
One Park Square Apartments
(The) Second Hand Clothier

Name	INDEXING ORDER Unit 1	Unit 2	Unit 3	Unit 4
24 Hour Developing	24	Hour	Developing	
20th Century Tours	20(th)	Century	Tours	
One Park Square Apartments	One	Park	Square	Apartments
The Second Hand Clothier	(The) Second	Hand	Clothier	

Rules 16–20 Review

To see how Rules 16–20 are applied to a list of company names, study the table below. The rules governing the indexing order are shown in the third column. The names are listed in correct alphabetical order in the last column.

Name	Indexing Order	Indexing Rule	Alphabetical Order
Northwest Freight Co.	North/west/Freight/Company	14, 18	7(th) Street Galleries
Seven Seas Restaurant	Seven/Seas/Restaurant	20	Mr. Steak Restaurant Tampa, Florida
Mr. Steak Restaurant Topeka, KS	Mr./Steak/Restaurant Topeka,/Kansas	20	Mr. Steak Restaurant Topeka, Kansas
The Surf and Sand	(The)Surf(and)/Sand	13	Northwest Freight Company
Surf's Up Rentals	Surf(')s/Up/Rentals	19	Northern Savings Bank
San Diego Realtors	San/Diego/Realtors	17	San Diego Realtors
7th Street Galleries	7(th)/Street/Galleries	20	Seven Seas Restaurant
Mr. Steak Restaurant Tampa, FL	Mr./Steak/Restaurant/Tampa,/Florida	12, 16	(The) Surf (and) Sand
Northern Savings Bank	Northern/Savings/Bank	11	Surf(')s Up Rentals

For additional practice in filing company names, index and alphabetize the names in Group 2 under Applying Office Skills, Activity 1.

INDEXING RULES FOR GOVERNMENT AGENCIES AND OTHER ORGANIZATIONS

ed·u·ca'tion·al

In many offices, the 20 indexing rules you have learned so far are all you need to file efficiently. However, in other offices you may be filing records related to government agencies, educational institutions, civic organizations, and other non-business organizations. There are special indexing rules that apply in these situations. The most common are presented here. You may learn other special rules on the job.

Rule 21 Government Agencies

bu'reau
in·stal·la'tions

gov·ern·ment'al

When filing names of federal government agencies, the first three filing units are the words *United States Government.* The remaining units contain (1) name of the department, (2) name of the bureau, (3) name of the division or subdivision, and (4) title of the official. Military installations are also filed under *United States Government,* followed by the installation's name.

State and local governmental agencies are filed with the name of the state, county, or city as the first filing unit. The second filing unit is the word *State, County,* or *City,* followed by the department, bureau, and title of the official. Terms such as *department, department of,* and *division of* are placed in parentheses and not considered in filing.

Name	Indexing Order
District Director, U.S. Dept. of Commerce	United/States/Government/ Commerce (Dept. of)/ District/Director
Fort Hood	United/States/Government/ Fort/Hood
Deputy Secretary, Florida Department of Community Affairs	Florida/State/Community/ Affairs (Dept. of)/ Deputy/Secretary
Suffolk County Sheriff's Department	Suffolk/County/ Sheriff's (Dept.)

Florida, State, Community Affairs (Dept. of), Deputy Secretary
Suffolk County, Sheriff's (Dept.)
United States Government, Commerce (Dept. of) District Director
United States Government, Fort Hood

Rule 22 Schools and Colleges

The name of an elementary, middle, or high school is indexed in the order written unless it contains the full name of an individual. When it does, the individual's name is indexed last name first. The city, state, street address, and building number are used to distinguish schools with identical names.

dis·tin'guish

Names of colleges and universities are transposed if necessary so that the most important part of the name is the first filing unit.

Name	INDEXING ORDER Unit 1	Unit 2	Unit 3	Unit 4	Unit 5
James High School	James	High	School		
Booker T. Washington High School	Washington	Booker	T.	High	School
Walsh College, Canton, OH	Walsh	College	Canton	Ohio	
Walsh College, Morristown, NJ	Walsh	College	Morristown	New	Jersey
University of Portland	Portland	Univer-sity(of)			

James High School
Portland, University of
Walsh College, Canton, OH
Walsh College, Morristown, NJ
Washington, Booker T. High School

Rule 23 Churches, Hospitals, and Organizations

The names of churches, synagogues, and hospitals are indexed in the order written. The names of labor unions and civic organizations are also indexed in the order written. Cross-references are used when the official name of the organization is not the one in common use.

	INDEXING ORDER			
Name	Unit 1	Unit 2	Unit 3	Unit 4
Temple Israel	Temple	Israel		
St. Paul's Episcopal Church	Saint	Paul(')s	Episcopal	Church
Taft Memorial Hospital	Taft	Memorial	Hospital	
Daughters of the American Revolution	Daughters (of the)	American	Revolution	
International Brotherhood of Welders	International	Brotherhood (of)	Welders	
Society of Jesus	Society (of) See: Jesuits	Jesus		

Daughters (of the) American Revolution
International Brotherhood (of) Welders
Jesuits
St. Paul(')s Episcopal Church
Society of Jesus (See: Jesuits)
Taft Memorial Hospital
Temple Israel

Rule 24 Magazines and Newspapers

The names of magazines and newspapers are filed in the order written. The city (or town) and state may be placed as the last filing units to distinguish between or among newspapers with identical names.

	INDEXING ORDER		
Name	Unit	Unit 2	Unit 3
Vacation Digest	Vacation	Digest	
Journal of Agribusiness	Journal (of)	Agribusiness	
The Daily Herald (Minneapolis)	(The) Daily	Herald	Minneapolis
The Daily Herald (Mobile)	(The) Daily	Herald	Mobile
The Orlando Sentinel	(The) Orlando	Sentinel	

(The) Daily Herald, Minneapolis
(The) Daily Herald, Mobile
Journal (of) Agribusiness
(The) Orlando Sentinel
Vacation Digest

Rule 25 Hotels and Motels

re·versed'

Names beginning with *Hotel* or *Motel* are transposed, or reversed, so that the most important word in the name is the first filing unit. In all other cases, hotel and motel names are indexed as written. The indexing table that appears at the top of the next page shows how hotel and motel names are arranged in the correct indexing order.

California, Hotel
Holt's Inn (and) Resort
Saint Gregory Hotel
Seacrest Motel

Name	INDEXING ORDER Unit 1	Unit 2	Unit 3
Hotel California	California	Hotel	
Hotel St. Gregory	Saint	Gregory	Hotel
Seacrest Motel	Seacrest	Motel	
Holt's Inn and Resort	Holt's	Inn (and)	Resort

Rules 21–25 Review

Review Rules 21–25 by studying how they are applied to a list of organizations' names. The rules governing the indexing order are shown in the third column. The names are listed in correct alphabetical order in the last column.

Name	Indexing Order	Indexing Rule	Alphabetical Order
Wm. T. Moore Elementary School	Moore/William/T. Elementary/School	22	6 Motel
League of Women Voters	League (of)/Women/Voters	23	Calhoun Baptist Church
Department of Highway Safety, Calhoun County	Calhoun/County/ Highway Safety (Dept. of)	21	Calhoun County Courier(-) Times
Motel 6	6/Motel	20, 25	Calhoun, County Highway Safety (Dept. of)
College of William and Mary	William (and)/Mary/ College (of)	22	League (of) Women Voters
Montana Dept. of Education, Teacher Certification Division	Montana/State/Education (Dept. of)/Teacher/Certification (Div. of)	21	Montana, State Education (Dept. of), Teacher Certification (Div. of)
Calhoun County Courier-Times	Calhoun/County/Courier(-)Times	24	Moore, William T. Elementary School
Williamsburg Inn	Williamsburg/Inn	25	William (and) Mary College (of)
Calhoun Baptist Church	Calhoun/Baptist/Church	23	Williamsburg Inn

For additional practice in filing names of governmental agencies and organizations, index and alphabetize the names in Group 3 under Applying Office Skills, Activity 1.

VARIATIONS IN INDEXING RULES

sim·plic'i·ty

The indexing rules presented in these chapters reflect the current trend toward simplicity in records management. Knowing these 25 rules, you can set up a well-organized alphabetic filing system. More important, though, with very little additional training you will be able to follow the filing procedures in companies all around the country.

If your job duties include filing, you may find some slight differences in the indexing rules used in your company. For example, in some filing systems, company names beginning with numerals *(21)* are filed as if the numerals were written in words *(twenty-one)* and arranged in alphabetical order. Compass points such as *Northeast* may be treated as one filing unit, not two. You may also come across different rules for indexing and filing hyphenated terms and possessive forms (such as *Banker's* or *Norman's*). These are minor differences that you can quickly learn. The important thing is to understand and follow the procedures for filing where you work.

REVIEWING KEY POINTS

1. Names of companies are usually indexed in the order written. Each word and initial is considered a separate filing unit.
2. When the name of an individual is included in a company name, the individual's name is indexed with the surname first.
3. Articles and conjunctions are not considered in filing, but they are written in parentheses to indicate the correct placement in the name. A preposition is considered only when it is the first word in the company name.
4. A term containing hyphens is treated as a single filing unit.
5. Each word in a compound geographic name is considered a separate filing unit. Each part of a compound compass point is also considered a separate unit, even when written as one word.
6. The apostrophe in possessives *(Bartlett's)* and contractions *(What's)* is ignored in filing.
7. Names containing numerals as the first unit are placed in front of the alphabetic section. When a numeral appears within a name, the name is filed ahead of the same name without numerals.
8. Governmental records are filed under the name of the governmental unit (such as *United States Government*), state name, county name, or city name.
9. Names of churches, civic organizations, labor unions, magazines, and newpapers are indexed in the order written.
10. The most important word in the name of a college, university, hotel, and motel is treated as the first filing unit.

DEVELOPING HUMAN RELATIONS SKILLS

1. In your department, you are responsible for retrieving all documents requested from the central files. You usually make four trips to the filing

department daily — at 8:30, 11, 2, and 4:30 — rather than going there each time a request is submitted. If there is an urgent request, however, you retrieve the file as soon as you receive the request. You have noticed that one person who was recently hired marks all requests "urgent."

   a. With whom should you discuss this problem?

   b. How would you explain the problems that might result?

2. There are four file clerks in your department, and one of them has been working there only one month. You have noticed that recently some of the folders have been filed incorrectly and that there are several folders missing. You suspect that the recently hired clerk is responsible for these mistakes.

   a. With whom should you discuss this problem?

   b. What steps can be taken to prevent these problems from developing in the future?

IMPROVING COMMUNICATION SKILLS

Refer to Appendix A 1.38–1.40.

1. On a separate sheet of paper, keyboard the following sentences, inserting the closing parentheses in the appropriate places.

   a. The borrower agrees to pay interest annually at the rate of ten percent (10%.

   b. File delivery service is provided to offices on all floors (except those on the 1st and 2nd floors.

   c. Helen Stieff (do you know her? was promoted to supervisor of the filing department.

   d. If you plan to attend the training program (on October 25, please send your reservation by Monday, October 21.

   e. Is the new training manual (have you received your copy? more accurate than the old manual?

   f. Raises this year are low (unusually low!

   g. The company will introduce two new products (in our computer line: the PC Traveler and integrated software.

   h. Complete the section of the application form that relates to your previous employment (page 2.

   i. The brightest student (Jason was accepted by all four colleges.

2. Compose a letter to Ms. Julie Anderson, 18 Lampton Drive, Charleston, SC 29407. Tell Ms. Anderson that an appointment has been scheduled with Mr. Atkins for 10:30 A.M. on Wednesday, January 23, 19 – – in Room 207 of the Conference Center in Charleston. Also tell Ms. Anderson that if this time is not convenient, she should contact you to arrange another appointment. Use the letterhead in your workbook or plain paper.

BUILDING PROBLEM-SOLVING SKILLS

1. The Gerber Company's policies state that all records will be returned within four working days. When should each of the following records be returned to central files?
   - **a.** A document borrowed on Monday, November 3
   - **b.** A folder borrowed Wednesday, November 5
   - **c.** A document borrowed Tuesday, November 11
   - **d.** A folder borrowed Friday, November 14
   - **e.** A folder borrowed Thursday, November 20
2. The circle graph shown here indicates the percentage of the Gerber Company's records that are classified as permanent, active, inactive, and to be destroyed. According to the Records Manager, the company has a total of 500,000 records. Refer to the graph; then, on a separate sheet of paper, answer the questions.

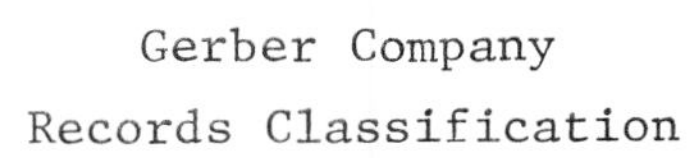

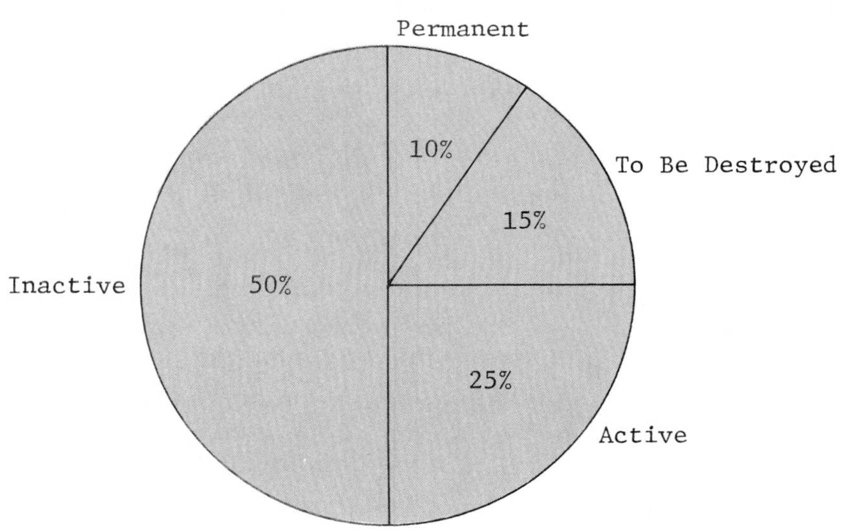

   - **a.** How many records are classified as active? inactive? permanent? to be destroyed?
   - **b.** If 4,000 records are stored in a file drawer, how many file drawers are needed for the active records?
   - **c.** How many drawers will become available after the records to be destroyed are removed?

APPLYING OFFICE SKILLS

1. For this activity, you will need 50 index cards or sheets of paper approximately 3 x 5 inches. Arrange the names in each of the following groups in alphabetical order according to these instructions:
   a. Keyboard each name in correct indexing order in the upper left corner of a card.
   b. In the upper right corner, keyboard the number that appears before the name. (The numbers will help in checking the answers.)
   c. Arrange the cards *for each group* in alphabetical order. (You should sort the cards by letter groups before you arrange them in alphabetical order.)
   d. Record your answers for each group on the form provided in your workbook or on a separate sheet of paper.
   e. Arrange the cards from all three groups in one alphabetical sequence. Record your answers on the form used in Step *d*.
   f. Keep these cards to be used in the activities at the end of the next chapter.

Group 1

1. Simmons Travel Service
2. M & O Auto Repairs
3. Paul Symes Jewelry Store
4. Carl St. Martin Insurance Agency
5. Top of the Town Lounge
6. Martin-Perrin Industries
7. WDSU Television
8. WOWO Radio
9. Mid-South Enterprises
10. R & S Pen Company
11. Oil Center Employment Agency
12. Ralston Construction Company
13. Miller Hardware
14. Picked-Fresh Vegetables, Inc.
15. The Towers

Group 2

16. Mt. Pleasant Insurance Company
17. Mountain View Estates, Fresno, CA
18. Southwest Travel Service
19. San Antonio Beverage Service
20. Vincent's Spa
21. Tenth Street Laundry
22. 6 Corners Grocery
23. Mountain View Estates, Charlottesville, VA
24. Southern Sounds Recording Studio
25. You're Tops Boutique
26. Vincent's 1-Hour Cleaners
27. 12th Street Barbers
28. Mother Nature's Greenhouse
29. Your Father's Moustache

Group 3

30. Taco-Tico, San Antonio, Texas
31. Muscatine Community School, Muscatine, Iowa
32. South East Scrap & Salvage
33. Polk County Law Enforcement Division, Des Moines, Iowa
34. The 8-Ball Lounge, Fayetteville, Arkansas
35. Southern Bank and Trust, Jackson, Mississippi
36. While-U-Wait Copies, Roswell, New Mexico
37. R. J. Reynolds High School, Winston-Salem, North Carolina
38. University of Wisconsin, Whitewater, Wisconsin
39. YMCA, Miami, Florida
40. Hotel Roanoke, Roanoke, Virginia
41. Tastee Bakery, Belmont, California
42. The Washington Post, Washington, D.C.
43. FBI
44. Surfside Resort Hotel, Myrtle Beach, South Carolina
45. Utah Business Machines, Ogden, Utah
46. South Dakota Industries, Aberdeen, South Dakota
47. Fort Benning, Columbus, Georgia
48. Southern Bank and Trust, Charlotte, North Carolina
49. Union of Soviet Socialist Republics (Russia)
50. Sam Houston State University, Huntsville, Texas

2. **(Optional)** Arrange the following names in correct alphabetical order. Keyboard or write your answers on a separate sheet of paper.

1. Anderson's Boutique
   340 Twelfth Street
   Huntington, WV 25701
2. Adler Child Care Center
   231 Shandon Place
   Columbia, SC 29205
3. G. A. Anderson
   412 Shannon Place
   Columbia, MO 65201-3110
4. Andy's Place
   721 Lester Drive
   Albuquerque, NM 87112
5. Adam's Sports Equipment
   727 Main Street
   Bloomington, IL 61701
6. Adam's Sports Equipment
   719 College Street
   Bloomington, IN 47401-7321
7. G. A. Andersen
   1902 Queen Maria Court
   Columbia, MD 21044
8. Anderson Box Company
   2319 Jackson Keller
   San Antonio, TX 78270
9. Dr. Arthur Andersen
   1839 University Avenue
   Monroe, LA 71201
10. Anders Book Store
    1309 DelSaird
    Monroe, LA 71201

CHAPTER 3

DOCUMENT FILING IN AN ALPHABETIC SYSTEM

In order to file letters, memorandums, and other types of business documents, you need to know how to index and alphabetize names of individuals and businesses. You also need to know how to identify which name in a document is the most important for filing. As you already know, most business letters contain at least three names: the name of the company in the letterhead, the name of the addressee, and the name of the sender. Under which of these names should you file a letter? There are standard guidelines for selecting the name, or caption, to be used for filing. Everyone in a company must follow these guidelines so that all related documents are filed together.

As you study this chapter, you will find answers to the following questions:

- What procedures should you follow to prepare documents for filing?
- How should you prepare cross-references, and why are they important?
- What are some common procedures for storing and retrieving records?
- What do the following terms mean: **incoming correspondence, outgoing correspondence, interoffice correspondence, release mark, caption, coding, miscellaneous folder, requisition form, follow-up system?**

PREPARING DOCUMENTS FOR FILING

in'com·ing

out'go·ing

Most documents fall into one of three categories. **Incoming correspondence** refers to documents that are addressed to your company or to individuals within your company. **Outgoing correspondence** includes documents written by individuals within your company and sent to other companies and individuals. **Interoffice correspondence** refers to the memorandums written by someone in your company to another employee of your company. Each type of document is filed by special procedures.

main·tain'

When you prepare documents for filing, you must first identify them as incoming, outgoing, or interoffice. Then, before you place documents in the files, you must inspect, read, index, code, cross-reference and sort them. To maintain an accurate filing system, you must complete each of these filing activities.

Inspecting

re·leased'

Before filing a document, you must be certain that it has been released for filing. You do not want to make the mistake of filing a document that has not been seen or processed yet. On incoming correspondence, check for the release mark, that indicates that the addressee is finished with the document. A **release mark** is a person's initials, a ''file'' stamp, or some other method of marking to indicate that a document is ready to be filed.

Identifying the Caption

ap·pro'pri·ate

Once you have determined that the document is ready to be filed, you must identify the appropriate caption. The **caption** is the name under which a document is filed. For filing purposes, the best caption is the name by which the document will be requested.

Incoming correspondence Incoming correspondence is usually filed by the company name appearing in the letterhead. In a few cases, the name of the sender is clearly more important than the name of the company, and the individual's name should be used. For example, it is quite common for people to write letters of a personal nature on company letterhead. The sender's name, as it appears in the signature, is also the correct name to use when the letter is written on plain stationery.

sta'tion·er·y

e'qual·ly

When the company name and the name in the signature seem to be equally important, file the document under the company name.

Outgoing correspondence The name of the addressee is usually the most important name for filing outgoing correspondence. If the inside address contains the name of a person and the name of a company, the company name is preferred for filing. The exception is personal correspondence mailed to a person's business address, which is filed under the person's name.

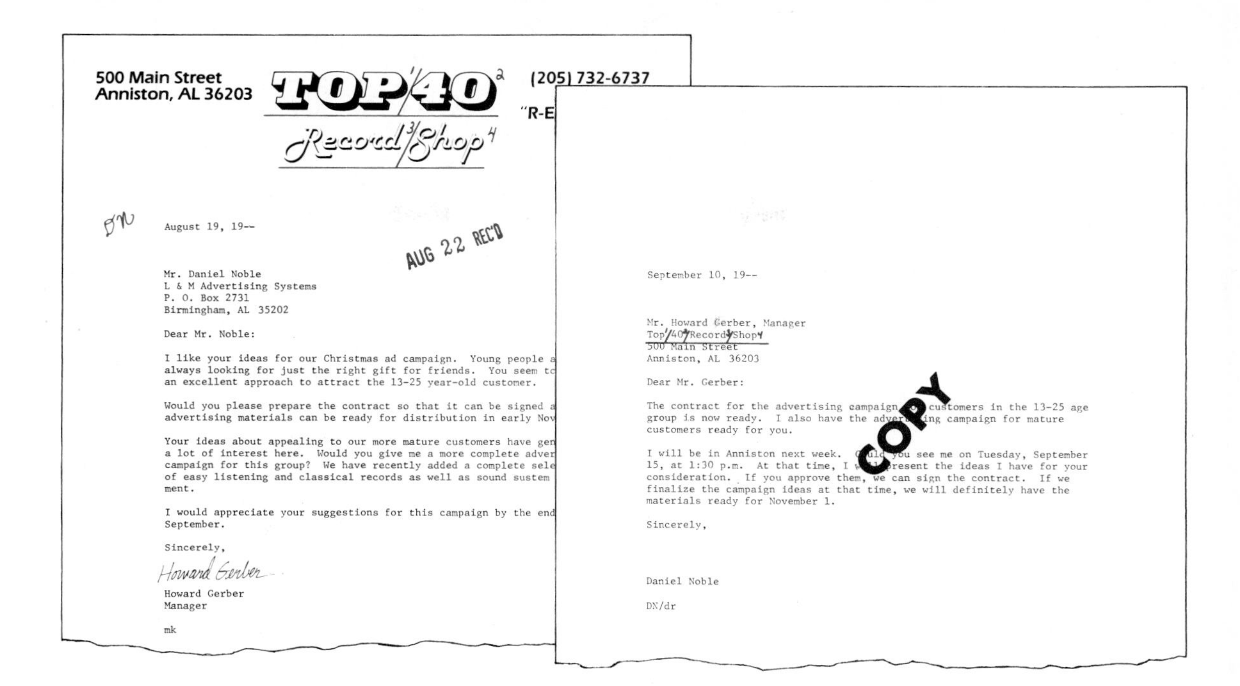

500 Main Street
Anniston, AL 36203

TOP 40 Record Shop

(205) 732-6737
"R-E

August 19, 19--

AUG 22 REC'D

Mr. Daniel Noble
L & M Advertising Systems
P. O. Box 2731
Birmingham, AL 35202

Dear Mr. Noble:

I like your ideas for our Christmas ad campaign. Young people a
always looking for just the right gift for friends. You seem tc
an excellent approach to attract the 13-25 year-old customer.

Would you please prepare the contract so that it can be signed a
advertising materials can be ready for distribution in early Nov

Your ideas about appealing to our more mature customers have gen
a lot of interest here. Would you give me a more complete adver
campaign for this group? We have recently added a complete sele
of easy listening and classical records as well as sound sustem
ment.

I would appreciate your suggestions for this campaign by the end
September.

Sincerely,

Howard Gerber

Howard Gerber
Manager

mk

September 10, 19--

Mr. Howard Gerber, Manager
Top/40/Record/Shop
500 Main Street
Anniston, AL 36203

Dear Mr. Gerber:

The contract for the advertising campaign [illegible] customers in the 13-25 age
group is now ready. I also have the adver[illegible]ing campaign for mature
customers ready for you.

I will be in Anniston next week. [illegible] you see me on Tuesday, September
15, at 1:30 p.m. At that time, I [illegible] present the ideas I have for your
consideration. If you approve them, we can sign the contract. If we
finalize the campaign ideas at that time, we will definitely have the
materials ready for November 1.

Sincerely,

Daniel Noble

DN/dr

COPY

Illustration 10–3
Incoming and outgoing letters coded for filing

Miscellaneous correspondence Interoffice correspondence (such as a memorandum) is frequently filed by subject. The subject is usually found in the subject line, but you may have to read the memorandum to find the subject.

Sometimes documents are filed by subject rather than by name. Subject filing is used when the topic of the document is more important than the name. For example, a letter about a person applying for a job may be filed in the subject section of the files under *Applications.* Generally, if a document is to be filed by subject, the person releasing it for filing notes the correct caption on the document. In some cases, however, you may have to select the appropriate caption yourself. If so, read the document carefully.

If several names or subjects seem to be equally important, select one name for filing and cross-reference the item under the other name. When in doubt, check your company filing manual or ask your supervisor.

man'u·al

Coding

Coding is the process of underlining or highlighting the name that is used for filing. In some companies, coding may also include marking the indexing order. Usually, coding is marked on the face of the document in colored pencil. Businesses vary in their coding procedures. One way to code is to use diagonal slash marks (/) to divide the underlined name into indexing units. Enclose in parentheses any words not considered in filing. Then number the units in indexing order, as shown in Illustration 10–3.

Illustration 10–4
Letter coded for cross-reference

SOUTHERN INDUSTRIES Inc.

203 Huger Street, Columbia, South Carolina 29201 (803) 235-9645

January 21, 19--

Miss Ann Kelly, Executive Secretary
Future Business Leaders of America
904 Rutledge Building
Columbia, SC 29201

Dear Miss Kelly:

SUBJECT: FBLA State Conference

I will be happy to judge the Clerk-Typist I competitive event at the South Carolina State Conference at Trident Tec in Charleston on April 20 at 8:30 a.m.

As you know, I am a strong supporter of student organizations in the high school. I am especially impressed with the students I have worked with at the conferences the last few years. It is nice to know we have such qualified people entering the business world.

If I can help in any way, please let me know.

Sincerely,

Mary C. Cassidy

Mary C. Cassidy
Personnel Manager

kc

Cross-Referencing

When a document may be requested by more than one name or subject, you should file it under the most appropriate caption and place cross-references in the other file locations. Cross-references save time by leading you directly to the location of the record you are looking for.

For example, if you were looking for the letter in Illustration 10–4, you might look in the files under Southern Industries, Inc., the name in the letterhead. If you didn't find the letter there, where would you look? Perhaps someone filed the letter under the sender's name, Mary C. Cassidy, or under the name in the subject line, FBLA State Conference. If you place a cross-reference sheet showing the filing location in each of the other possible positions, you avoid having to look through three separate files. Cross-reference sheets are shown in Illustration 10–5 on page 410. Notice how they are filled out.

To indicate that a document is cross-referenced, draw a wavy line beneath each name under which a cross-reference sheet is filed. Place an *X* in the margin alongside this name. In the example, if you decide to file the letter under *FBLA State Conference,* you can prepare cross-reference sheets and place them in the folders for Southern Industries, Inc., and Mary C. Cassidy. Notice how the caption and the cross-references are marked on the letter in Illustration 10–4.

Most company filing manuals identify those situations in which cross-references should be made. Because cross-reference sheets take time to complete and take up space in the files, it is important to follow your company's filing rules and avoid unnecessary cross-referencing. However, if a real chance for confusion exists, it is probably better to cross-reference.

con·fu'sion

As you saw in the last unit, a cross-reference can refer to an entire folder as well as to a single document within a folder. In this case, a cross-reference guide may be placed in the files. Cross-reference guides would usually be prepared in the following situations:

1. When an individual goes by an unusual nickname. For example, if Randolph Allen is better known as Buzzy, a cross-reference is made.

Allen, Randolph (See: Allen, Buzzy)

2. When a woman's name changes through marriage.

McCory, Janina (See: Symes, Janina McCory)

3. When a company name contains the names of two or more individuals. For a company called *Tanya Graham and Anthony DeCarlo, Caterers,* for example, a cross-reference would be prepared for the second name.

DeCarlo, Anthony
(See: Graham, Tanya and DeCarlo, Anthony, Caterers)

4. When a company is commonly referred to by its initials.

United Parcel Service (See: UPS)

sub·sid'i·ar·y

5. When a company is a subsidiary or affiliate of another company.

Fisher Price Toys (See: Quaker Company, Fisher Price Toys)

trus·tees'

6. When legal offices use the names of guardians, trustees, and receivers.

Rhodes, Doris, Trustee (See: Rhodes, Keith, Estate [of])

Some companies make photocopies of documents to store in these other locations. Such copies eliminate the need for cross-reference sheets. Making photocopies is sometimes more expensive than preparing cross-reference sheets, but it may save money in the long run by reducing the time spent looking for records.

CROSS-REFERENCE SHEET

Name or Subject Mary C. Cassidy

Date of Item January 21, 19--

Regarding Clerk-Typist Judge

Name or Subject FBLA State Conferen

CROSS-REFERENCE SHEET

Name or Subject Southern Industries, Inc.

Date of Item January 21, 19--

Regarding Clerk-Typist Judge

SEE

Illustration 10-5 Cross-reference sheets

Sorting

You can save filing time by sorting documents into groups. For instance, you can group documents to be stored in the *A* section of the files together, those to be stored in the *B* section together, and so on. If you sort the documents as you inspect and code them, you will save an extra step. You can save even more time by arranging the documents in each section in alphabetical order before going to the file cabinets. When you actually begin to file, you will move through the files without going back and forth.

As you read in the last unit, you can purchase sorting equipment. If you do not have many documents to sort at a time, though, you can simply sort them into five or six stacks on your desk.

STORING AND RETRIEVING RECORDS

Drawer labels and file guides are filing aids that help you to locate a particular folder in the files. For example, if you were looking for the folder for Tilley's Farm Supplies, you would go to the file drawer labeled *T*. The folder you want would be filed behind the guide *Tea–Tok*. The procedure for locating a folder is the same whether you are storing or retrieving one.

Records Storage

Placing items in folders within file drawers is what is generally thought of as filing. Once you have identified the caption for a document, you can easily locate the correct folder by using drawer labels, file guides, and folder captions. Place the document in the folder so that the top is to the left when the folder is placed in the file drawer. Since the most recent document is the most frequently used, you want it to be easy to find. For this reason, arrange documents in chronological order in the folder, with the most recent on top.

mis·cel·la′ne·ous

If you do not find a folder labeled with the caption you are looking for, check the miscellaneous folder. A **miscellaneous folder** is used to hold records when there are fewer than five documents related to an individual, company, or subject. There is a miscellaneous folder for every primary guide. The miscellaneous folder is usually the last folder in a section, just before the next primary guide. Records in miscellaneous folders are grouped by name or subject. The names (or subjects) are arranged in alphabetical order.

If you find other items in the miscellaneous folder related to the document you are filing, count the items. When there are five related items, remove them from the miscellaneous folder and prepare an individual folder. If there are fewer than five related items, file the most recent in front of all of the others.

la′beled

If you do not find any other documents labeled with the same caption, it *may* be a signal that you have selected the wrong caption for filing. Double-check the document and the files to determine whether other documents related to that name or subject are filed under another caption.

Records Retrieval

Just as drawer labels and file guides help you when you store records, they also help you when you retrieve records from the file.

The request for a record or file may come to you in person, over the telephone, or in writing. Companies with centralized filing departments often require employees to fill out requisition cards or sheets when they request records. When records are requested by telephone, the person answering the call in the filing department completes a requisition form. The **requisition form** identifies the record or records being requested, and it can be used to follow up on lost or misplaced records. Clerks in the filing department prepare *out forms* using information contained in the requisition forms. An out form is placed in the files when a record or folder is removed.

mis·placed′

In some companies, out forms serve the same purpose as requisition forms. Out forms are made available to each department so that employees can prepare an out form for each record they want from the files. This system saves time and money, since only one form is filled out, not two.

re·serve′

Although out forms may be used to requisition records, this is not their chief purpose. Out forms "reserve" space for a record (or folder) in the files until it is returned. Refiling of records is thus much easier. Out forms also provide proof that a record has been borrowed, not just filed incorrectly.

au·thor·i·za′tion

When you retrieve records for other employees' use, it is important that you check for proper authorization. Some files are confidential, and they can be released only to certain people in the company. These folders may be clearly marked or may be stored separately from the other files. Some information contained in the general files may also be confidential. So, to be safe, you should not discuss the contents of any folder.

Follow-Up Procedures

A **follow-up system** is a method of keeping track of records that have been borrowed from the company files. In most companies, the records management policies specify what records may be checked out, by whom, and for how long. Follow-up procedures usually reflect these policies.

re·mind′er

Requisitions are one way to keep track of borrowed records. In some companies, these forms are filed in chronological order according to the date the record is due back in the files. When a record is returned, the form is removed from the follow-up file. A reminder is sent if a record is not returned.

In other companies, a large calendar can be used. When a record is checked out, a note is made on the date the record is due. The note is crossed out when the record is returned. If the record is not returned by the due date, the person who has the record should be called or sent a reminder.

PRACTICING GOOD FILING TECHNIQUES

con·trib′ute

Filing is one of the major responsibilities of many office workers. If it is one of your job duties, take it seriously. Organized and up-to-date files are necessary for the success of a company. By developing good filing habits, you can contribute to your company's success. Many office workers recommend the following filing techniques:

1. Set aside a certain time each day for filing, and don't get behind. If filing is not done daily, it becomes a chore and the files are not up to date.
2. When a folder becomes full — when it contains more documents than can fit flat on the scored edge — prepare another folder. Date the folders to remind file workers to put new items in the new folder. The captions may read

   Continental Steelcorp (1984–85)
   Continental Steelcorp (Current)

   Place the most recent folder in front of the other folders with the same caption.
3. Prepare captions in indexing order, spelling out abbreviations when space allows.

4. Remove folders from the file drawer by grasping the sides. Pulling a folder by the tab will eventually cause it to tear.
5. When adding records to the files, pull the folder out of the drawer far enough so that you can insert the record without tearing or wrinkling it.
6. Keep a supply of out forms handy as a reminder to use them.

REVIEWING KEY POINTS

1. When filing, classify documents as incoming, outgoing, or interoffice.
2. Before filing a document, you must (a) inspect it for the release mark; (b) identify the caption; (c) code it; (d) prepare a cross-reference, if necessary; and (e) sort it.
3. In general, the caption for incoming correspondence is the company name appearing in the letterhead. For outgoing correspondence, it is the name of the addressee. For interoffice correspondence, the caption is the subject.
4. When coding, underline the caption and indicate the indexing order.
5. Prepare cross-references for documents that may be requested by more than one name or subject.
6. Use drawer labels, file guides, and folder captions to help you locate folders.
7. Store documents in chronological order within file folders.
8. File items in miscellaneous folders if there is not an individual folder labeled with that caption. When five documents accumulate in the miscellaneous folder, prepare an individual folder.
9. When you remove records from the files, replace them with out forms.

DEVELOPING HUMAN RELATIONS SKILLS

1. As you were looking for a folder for one of the department managers, you found an out form that showed that the document had been out for nearly two months. Company policy states that folders are to be checked out for only one week at a time and are not to be taken out of the office. When you called the person whose name is on the out form to ask her to return the folder, she replied, "I've been working on that material at home for the last few weeks. I'll bring the folder back tomorrow."
   a. How should you explain this problem to the department manager?
   b. What can be said to the file clerk who did not follow the policy?

IMPROVING COMMUNICATION SKILLS

Refer to Appendix A 1.38–1.40.

1. On a separate sheet of paper, keyboard the following paragraph. Make all necessary corrections in the placement and use of parentheses.

   Here is the proposal for correcting the environmental deficiencies that were identified by OSHA (Occupational Safety and Health Administration. Mr. Roger Ransom he visited our plant in July will review our proposal before we make any changes. Dwight Gibbs (did you meet him last week? will oversee the implementation of the proposal. If you have any questions, please send them to Dwight or me before Friday (September 6.

2. Compose a memo to Mr. Dwight Gibbs telling him you received the proposal and that the changes recommended seem to solve the problems noted by the OSHA visitation team. Also tell him that you will be happy to help set the standards for the furniture used with the terminal in the filing department. Use the memo form in your workbook or plain paper.

BUILDING PROBLEM-SOLVING SKILLS

1. Your department has 250,000 documents in its files. Each month 17 percent of the records are requested. On a separate sheet of paper, answer the following questions.
   a. How many records are requested each month?
   b. If 0.5 percent of the documents requested cannot be found, how many records cannot be found?
   c. If 82 percent of the documents requested are returned the same day, how many records must be refiled daily?
2. Your office has 90,000 cards to be filed alphabetically. The average rate of filing cards is 250 per hour. Answer the following questions.
   a. How many hours will it take to file these cards?
   b. How many 8-hour days will it take to complete the filing?

APPLYING OFFICE SKILLS

1. The items in this activity are to be filed in the miscellaneous folder in the "D" section of the files. In what order would you arrange them? On an index card, keyboard the caption you would use for each item and code it in indexing order. Group the items by captions. Then, arrange the items in the order in which you would place them in the folder.
   a. A letter dated November 19 from Derrick Manufacturing Company about a new piece of equipment.

b. A copy of a letter dated November 23 to Daniel Management Company asking for some information.

c. A letter dated October 29 from Charles Dunbar announcing a new consulting service.

d. A letter dated November 15 from Candy Dillingham asking for an appointment to discuss personnel management techniques.

e. A letter dated November 30 from Daniel Management Company enclosing some brochures.

f. A copy of a letter dated November 24 to Derrick Manufacturing Company asking for a price list and specifications of equipment.

g. A letter dated November 7 from Keith Dent recommending the new consulting service provided by Charles Dunbar.

h. A copy of a letter dated November 23 to Cathy Daniels sending some brochures.

i. A copy of a letter dated November 9 to Charles Dunbar asking for more information about his consulting service.

2. For this activity, you will need the cards you filed in Activity 1, Applying Office Skills, in the last chapter. Assume that the cards are files. You will also need out forms. Prepare out forms from 15 index cards or sheets of paper 3 x 5 inches. Mark the top edges with colored pen or pencil so the forms stand out.

Assume you are a file clerk and get the following requests for files. Prepare an out form for each file requested. Include the date of the request, the file requested, and the department requesting the file. Remove each folder in the order requested and put an out form in its place. When a file is returned, replace it and remove the out form. When you are finished, make a list of the departments that have not yet returned files and identify the missing files.

a. May 2, Sales Department requested WDSU Television file.

b. May 2, Finance Department requested Taco-Tico file.

c. May 3, Media Department requested Radio WOWO file.

d. May 3, WDSU Television file returned.

e. May 3, Finance Department requested Surfside Resort Hotel file.

f. May 6, Sales Department requested Taco-Tico file.

g. May 6, Radio WOWO file returned.

h. May 7, Finance Department requested Miller Hardware file.

i. May 7, Taco-Tico file returned.

j. May 7, Media Department requested Television WDSU file.

k. May 8, Purchasing Department requested R & S Pen Company file.

l. May 8, Finance Department requested Southern Bank, Charlotte, file.

CHAPTER 4

SPECIALIZED FILING METHODS

Almost 80 percent of the filing done in offices is alphabetic. There are many situations, though, in which the alphabetic system is not the most efficient one to use. Because records provide information for decision making, they must be stored so that they can be retrieved quickly when the information is requested. For example, a manufacturer may frequently need to know how well a product is selling in certain sections of the country. In this case, a geographic arrangement of sales records would be the most efficient. An office supply company, on the other hand, may want quick access to price information on various paper products. The most efficient system here might be subject filing, with records organized by use.

In some companies — and even in some offices within the same company — other filing systems may be more efficient to use. Geographic, subject, numeric, and chronological files can be used alone or in combination with alphabetic name files. When space is a problem, micrographic storage techniques can be used. The differences in these specialized systems and alphabetic filing procedures are discussed in this chapter.

As you study this chapter, you will find answers to the following questions:

- What are the procedures for geographic, subject, numeric, and chronological filing?
- What are the various types of micrographic storage systems?
- What do the following terms mean: **geographic filing, subject filing, numeric filing, alphabetic card file, alphabetic miscellaneous file, accession book, terminal digit filing, chronological files, reading file, tickler file, micrographics?**

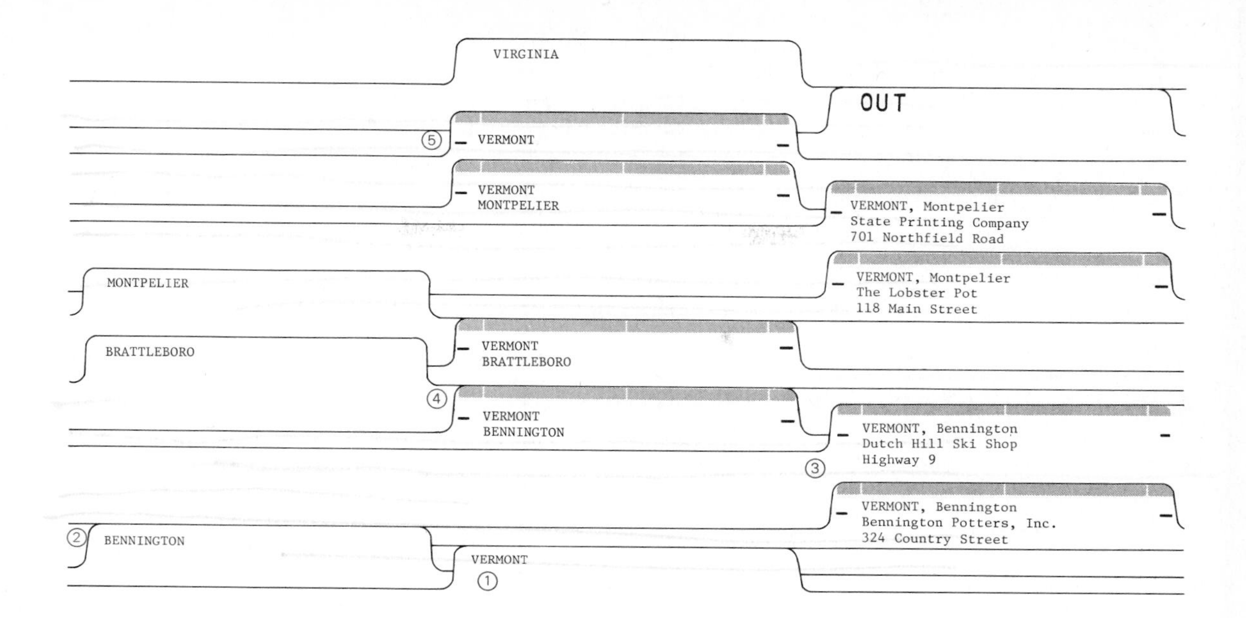

SPECIALIZED FILING SYSTEMS

Illustration 10–6
A section of geographic files

The procedures for filing correspondence and other business records depend on the filing system used: geographic, subject, numeric, or chronological.

Geographic Filing

Geographic filing is a method by which records are stored according to the geographic locations they refer to. For companies that need information about their business according to the geographic areas served, this filing system may be the most efficient to use.

In geographic files, records are arranged in alphabetical order by location. The caption that determines filing order in a geographic filing system is the name of the city, county, state, or region. For instance, a national company may set up its files with state names as the primary division and with counties or cities as the secondary or subdivisions. The division and subdivisions are arranged alphabetically in the files. Individual folders are stored alphabetically within each division and subdivision.

sub'di·vi·sions

Arrangement of geographic files Illustration 10–6 shows a section from a typical file drawer in a geographic filing system. The file guide labeled with the state name, Vermont (No. 1), indicates a major division. The files are subdivided by guides labeled with the names of cities in Vermont: Bennington, Brattleboro, and Montpelier (No. 2). Individual folders (No. 3) have been assigned to companies located in each city. These company names are arranged in alphabetical order according to the indexing rules presented in the last chapter.

Each city has a miscellaneous folder (No. 4) to hold records for companies in that city that have not accumulated at least five items. The last file folder in the Vermont section (No. 5) is the miscellaneous folder for the state. This folder contains records for companies located in cities that have not yet been assigned a folder. Records in the miscellaneous folder for Vermont are arranged in alphabetical order by city and by company, and in chronological order by date with the most recent date in front.

ac·cu'mu·lat·ed

Alphabetic name file What if you are looking for a letter written to Able Corporation, but you don't know where the company is located? In most offices where geographic filing is used, there is a card file of all correspondents arranged in alphabetical order by company name. The cards also list addresses of the correspondents. When you know the name of the company and not the location, the alphabetic name file gives you the information you need to find records in the file quickly.

cor·re·spon'dents

Coding procedures When preparing documents for filing in a geographic system, you follow the same basic steps you read about in the last chapter. After checking for a release mark, you identify the appropriate captions and code them on the document.

In geographic filing, there are two captions. The primary caption consists of the city and state name. The secondary caption is the company or individual name. As in alphabetic filing, the captions for an incoming letter are usually those in the letterhead. For an outgoing letter, the captions you use are those in the inside address. Circle the state and city and number them. Then underline the company or individual name used as the secondary caption. Identify the indexing units and number them.

Once the document is coded, it is ready to be filed. Prepare an address card for the alphabetic card file if you do not find any other documents related to that company in the files. When filing documents in a miscellaneous folder, mark an *M* on the index card (for *miscellaneous*).

Subject Filing

Subject filing is a method of storing records in alphabetical order by subject matter rather than by individual or company name. In an interior design firm, for example, information is often requested by product category, such as furniture, wall coverings, lamps, and draperies, rather than by the names of the companies that make or sell these products. If a customer wants to purchase draperies, the interior designer can find all the necessary information — fabric samples, styles, and price lists — in one section of the files, under "Draperies."

re·quest'ed

Illustration 10–7
A section of subject files

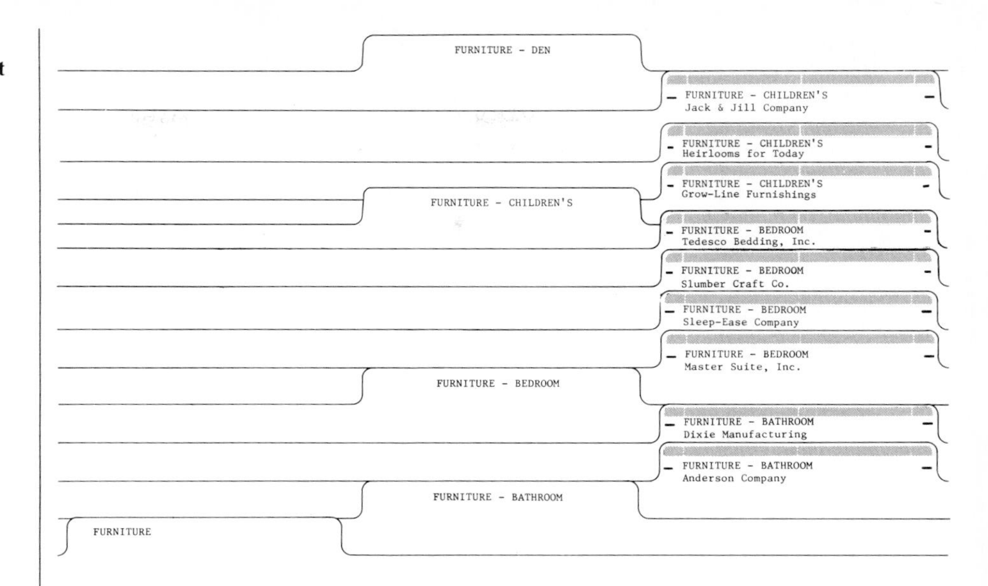

com·plex′

Arrangement of subject files Subject filing systems may be very simple or very complex, depending on the subject categories used. In Illustration 10–7, the subject categories are divided into subdivisions marked with secondary guides. The individual folders group records by company. This is not always the case, however. In some companies, it may be preferable to use subject captions on the individual folders. For example, behind the secondary guide for *Furniture — Bedroom* you may find folders for styles of bedroom furniture: Contemporary, Danish Modern, and so forth. One advantage of subject filing is that subject captions can be interfiled with name captions.

To prevent filing errors, use two captions on individual folders in subject files. The first caption should contain the subject category. The second caption should identify the individual folder.

Indexes to subject files Another way to avoid filing errors in subject filing systems is to prepare and use an index. There are two basic types of indexes. The first is similar to the table of contents of a book. It may simply list the captions of the primary and secondary guides in the same order that these subjects appear in the file. Such a list may be all that is necessary if you have a very simple filing arrangement and not many records.

The second type of index is an alphabetic card index. Just as the index at the back of a book tells you the page number of a particular topic, a card index tells you the location of a particular folder in a subject file. Cards are made for each individual folder and arranged in alphabetic order by subject or company name. The cards tell you where to find the folder, usually by referring you to the major subject category. Sample cards for an alphabetic index are shown in Illustration 10–8 on the next page.

Illustration 10–8
Index cards used in subject filing

```
Sleep-Ease Company
822 West Pinewood Street
Wilmington, DE 19808

See:  FURNITURE--BEDROOM
```

```
Barbeque Grills

See:  FURNITURE--PATIO
```

de·ter′mine

Coding procedures When documents are filed by subject, you frequently have to read them to determine the correct subject caption to use. You also need to be familiar with the subject categories used in your company. Print the captions neatly in the upper right-hand corner. The letter in Illustration 10–9, for example, is coded to show that it is filed behind the *Office Supplies* guide in the *Forms* folder. Note that the company name is also indexed and coded. Documents in each individual folder are arranged alphabetically by company name.

Numeric Filing Systems

In **numeric filing** systems, records are arranged in numerical order. This method of filing is very useful when the records are already numerically sequenced. Purchase orders, invoices, and requisitions, for example, are often printed with numbers. Even when records are not numbered, they can be filed numerically. Records are grouped by subject matter or name, and a number is assigned to them. For example, you might assign the number 110203 to the documents dealing with Micro Manufacturing Company. The caption on the file folders and guides would then be numbers rather than company names. Numeric filing is especially helpful when records are stored on a computer.

Organization of numeric files It is impossible to remember the number assigned to every folder in the file. So, in numeric filing, you need a system to help you keep track of records. There are generally four parts in a numeric filing system: (1) the alphabetic card file; (2) the alphabetic miscellaneous file; (3) the accession book; and, of course, (4) the numeric files themselves.

The **alphabetic card file** contains alphabetically arranged index cards showing the names or subject categories for and the numbers assigned to all records in a numeric file. When a record is requested, you look up the appropriate caption in the alphabetic card file to find the assigned number. Because all of the folders are arranged in numeric order within the files, you can easily locate any record that you are looking for once you have the number.

If you find the letter *M* instead of a number on the card, it means that documents related to that caption are filed in the alphabetic miscellaneous file. The **alphabetic miscellaneous file** consists of miscellaneous folders in which records are stored by name or subject matter until five related items accumulate. There is usually one miscellaneous folder for each letter of the alphabet. When five related items have accumulated in a miscellaneous folder, prepare an individual folder, assign it a number, and mark the number in the alphabetic card file. The accession book tells you what number to assign.

ac·ces'sion

Illustration 10–9 Letter coded for subject files

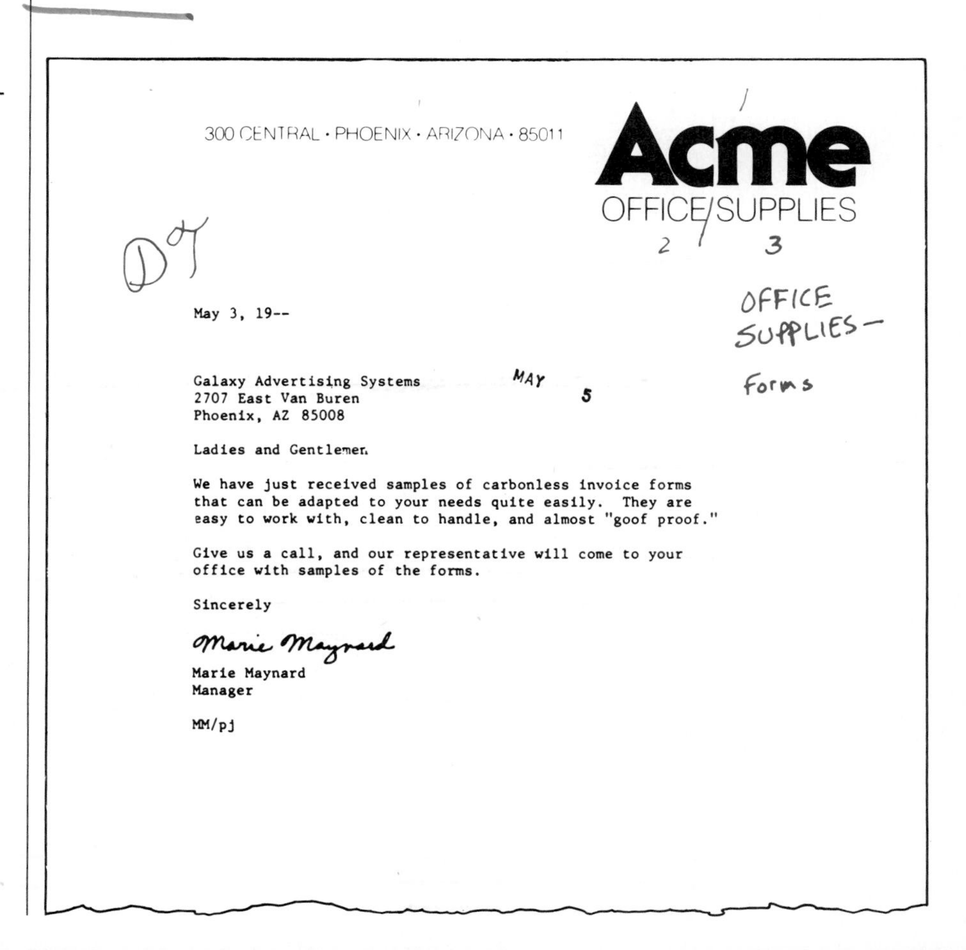

300 CENTRAL • PHOENIX • ARIZONA • 85011

Acme OFFICE/SUPPLIES

May 3, 19--

Galaxy Advertising Systems
2707 East Van Buren
Phoenix, AZ 85008

Ladies and Gentlemen

We have just received samples of carbonless invoice forms that can be adapted to your needs quite easily. They are easy to work with, clean to handle, and almost "goof proof."

Give us a call, and our representative will come to your office with samples of the forms.

Sincerely

Marie Maynard
Manager

MM/pj

Illustration 10–10
The accession book is arranged numerically

NUMBER	NAME	NUMBER	
1063	Phil's 500 Club	1083	
1064	Bob Gecke	1084	
1065	Benson's Spa	1085	
1066	Ann Arbor Cleaners	1086	
1067	Hampton Terrace Homes	1087	
1068	House of Glass	1088	
1069	Camden Travel Service	1089	
1070	Roberts Candy Company	1090	
1071	Cassidy Insurance	1091	
1072	Emma Bridges	1092	
1073	Andy's Place	1093	
1074	C & S Pen Company	1094	
1075	Bee's Grocery	1095	
1076	The Pampered Poodle	1096	
1077		1097	
1078		1098	
1079		1099	

The **accession book** is an index to the files arranged in numeric order. The accession book shows what numbers have already been assigned and the next number available. When it is used properly, the accession book can prevent someone from assigning the same number to more than one folder. As you can see in Illustration 10–10, if you know the number of a folder, the accession book identifies its contents. If you know what subject or name the contents relate to, the alphabetic card file will tell you its accession number. Both the accession book and the alphabetic card file are necessary for numeric files to work efficiently.

se·lect'ed

Coding procedures Proper indexing and coding are very important in numeric filing. The name or subject caption for a document must be selected with care. If the caption is an individual or company name, the name must be indexed correctly so that it can be found in the alphabetic card file. The name or subject matter is indexed and coded as in other filing systems. When you find the accession number for the caption in the alphabetic card file, mark it on the face of the document. This is the number of the folder in which the document will be filed.

con·ges'tion

e·lim'i·nate

dig'it

Terminal digit filing When filing in numeric order, you generally read numbers from left to right. So folders labeled 103705, 103706, and 103707 are filed one after another in the files. When a new folder is prepared, it is assigned the next available number in the accession book. Thus, the most recent folders are stored together in the files. Because recent folders tend to be used frequently, there may be congestion or crowding of file clerks around the drawer containing these folders. **Terminal digit filing** is a variation of numeric filing designed to eliminate file room congestion.

In terminal digit filing, accession numbers are assigned to folders in normal sequence: 103708, 103709, 103710, and so on. The difference is in how the numbers are read for filing purposes. Basically, the numbers are read as pairs of digits (numerals), and the pairs are read in reverse order. For example, if you were looking for folder 103709, you would divide the digits into three pairs: 10-37-09. Then you would read the number *from right to left* to find it in the files:

09 is the primary location
37 is the secondary location
10 is the individual folder.

First, you would locate the file drawer containing the records with numbers ending in 09. Next, you would find the guide for 37 and, behind it, the folder beginning with the number 10. The folders in this section of the file drawer would be:

13	37	09
12	37	09
11	37	09
10	37	09
09	37	09
08	37	09

The main advantage of terminal digit filing is that it spreads out the active files. For example, say that you assigned numbers to three new folders: 103711, 103712, 103713. These folders would be filed in three separate locations, not in the same drawer. The first would be filed with the other folders ending in 11; the second, with the folders ending in 12; and the third, with the folders ending in 13.

For ease of reading, leave spaces between the pairs of digits when you are keyboarding folder labels for numeric files.

Chronological Filing

Chronological files are arranged according to time sequence. The files are divided by month and then by day. Chronological filing is occasionally used as the basic system for storing records, but more frequently chronological filing is used with another system. The two most common examples of chronological files are reading files and tickler files.

tick'ler

Reading files A **reading file** is a temporary record of all outgoing correspondence. When documents are prepared, two copies are made. One copy goes into the regular document file. The extra copy is put into the reading file. Materials in the reading file are arranged in the order of completion; that is, by date. This file provides a quick reference to all recent documents.

Reading files are especially useful in a company with centralized files. An office worker can frequently locate records in the reading file in less time than it would take to requisition the records from the central filing department. As the file grows, though, it is not as convenient to use. So, after a few months, the materials in the reading file are disposed of.

Tickler files A **tickler file** is a chronological file used for future references, not for past actions as other files are. Materials in tickler files are stored by future dates. For example, suppose your supervisor tells you, "Call the Omaha office next Tuesday to see if they've received the report." Behind the guide for that date, you would put a reminder to make the call. Actions pending and reminders are frequently filed in a tickler file. The simplest tickler file is a calendar with notes written on it.

MICROGRAPHICS AND OTHER STORAGE SYSTEMS

al·ter′na·tive

As many companies are faced with growing storage and retrieval problems, they have begun to explore other methods of storage. Computer storage is one popular alternative. Records stored on computers take up very little space and can be retrieved quickly. As you will see in Units 12 and 14 (which discuss information processing and integrated office equipment), however, computers do not do away with paper records. Even when computers are used, traditional filing systems and equipment continue to be an important part of every office. So, a well-prepared employee needs to be familiar with all kinds of records storage systems.

mic·ro·graph′ics

Micrographics is another method of storing information in an efficient manner. Through micrographics, information is recorded in a reduced form on film (called *microfilm*) by means of a photographic process. *Micro* means *small,* and micrographic processes were developed to store information in a very small space. In fact, micrographic records can be stored in about $\frac{1}{50}$ of the space needed to store the original records.

To store records in micrographic systems, a company needs several pieces of special equipment: (1) a *camera* is used to photograph the original records; (2) equipment called a *reader* displays and enlarges the microfilm (the reader serves the same purpose as a slide projector); and (3) a *printer* makes a paper copy from the microfilm (just as a print is made from a slide or negative). Micrographic records can be produced in several forms, including microfilm, microfiche, aperture cards, and computer output microfilm (COM). A general name for these micrographic records is *microform.*

Microfilm

Microfilm, like regular camera film, is available in reels, cartridges, or cassettes. Records are photographed on the film, one page to a frame (picture). Microfilm is frequently used for storing records arranged in numeric or chronological order, such as checks, sales invoices, newspapers, and lengthy reports. Duplicates of the microfilm can be made if the information is needed at more than one location. Many companies make a microfilm copy of their vital records that can be stored in a separate location for safekeeping.

Microfiche

Microfiche (pronounced *mi cro feesh'*) is a clear film card that holds individual frames of microfilm. A single microfiche measuring 4 x 6 inches can hold up to 392 pages of information, depending on the amount of reduction. It is also available in other sizes, such as 3 x 5 inches and 5 x 8 inches. Microfiche is one of the most popular microforms because it is easy to file and retrieve. Microfiche records are usually stored in card files. Captions printed at the top of the microfiche describe the contents and permit filing in alphabetic, numeric, or chronological order.

Aperture Cards

ap'er·ture

An *aperture card* is a microform designed to be used with data processing equipment. These cards have an aperture, or window, that holds a frame of microfilm. The cards can be identified with a caption for easy sorting and retrieval by hand or by machine.

Computer Output Microfilm (COM)

Some computers are equipped with cameras so that they can record information directly on microfilm rather than on paper. This special method of recording information is known as computer output microfilm (COM). Just as you can think faster than you can keyboard, a computer can produce information faster than it can print it. By skipping the printing stage, a computer can produce microfilm copies of records in just a fraction of the time.

This method of recording represents an integration of two office components, the computer and micrographics. You will learn more about the integration of office components, such as the computer and micrographics, in Unit 14, Integrating Office Systems.

REVIEWING KEY POINTS

1. Alphabetic filing is the basic system used in most companies. However, there are instances in which a company may use geographic, subject, numeric, or chronological files along with or instead of alphabetic files.
2. Records in geographic files are arranged in alphabetical order by geographic location. An alphabetic name index contains the addresses of all correspondents so that their records can be quickly located in the files.
3. In subject files, records are grouped by subject category and arranged in alphabetical order.
4. Subject filing systems are most efficient when employees are familiar with the subject categories used. An index to subject categories and filing location is an important aid in subject filing systems.
5. Numeric filing systems usually have four parts: an alphabetic card file, an accession book, the alphabetic miscellaneous files, and the numeric files (which contain the folders and records).
6. In numeric filing, when you know the contents of a folder, you can find the number assigned to it by looking in the alphabetic card file. If you know the number, you can find the name or subject caption in the accession book.
7. Terminal digit filing is a variation of numeric filing. It is used to spread out the active files and reduce crowding in the file room.
8. Chronological files are arranged according to time sequence. Reading files and tickler files are two common examples of chronological files.
9. Records can be stored in a fraction of the space when they are photographed, reduced, and filed as microfilm, microfiche, aperture cards, or computer output microfilm.

DEVELOPING HUMAN RELATIONS SKILLS

1. As you are filing some materials, you notice that one of the file clerks is removing files without replacing the folders with out forms.
   - **a.** What problems could result from this practice?
   - **b.** What should you say to the file clerk?
2. Your supervisor has an urgent request for a file folder that is not in the file cabinet. Since there is no out form to indicate who has the folder, you cannot find the folder. Your supervisor is upset and says, "You are going to have to be more careful about what you are doing."

a. How should you explain this situation to your supervisor?

b. What, if anything, should you say to the other file clerks?

IMPROVING COMMUNICATION SKILLS

Refer to Appendix A 1.38–1.40.

1. On a separate sheet of paper, keyboard the following paragraph. Insert parentheses where needed.

   We have received the estimates for repairing the items damaged in the recent storm. The insurance company will pay $1,595.50 90% of the lowest estimated repair costs. Atlas, Inc. will begin repairing items on December 3 Monday. We can expect some inconvenience as the repairs are being made. If you have any major problems I hope not please call me.

2. Compose a memo to your supervisor requesting permission to attend a training seminar for file clerks on Wednesdáy of next week. Tell your supervisor why you think the training seminar will help you perform your job more efficiently. Use the memo form in your workbook or plain paper.

BUILDING PROBLEM-SOLVING SKILLS

1. A time-management specialist has determined that each of the five file clerks in your department is losing 35 minutes of work time each day because of inefficient techniques. On a separate sheet of paper, answer the following questions.
   a. What is the total time lost each day by all the file clerks combined?
   b. How much time is lost each week?
   c. If the average hourly wage is $4 for the file clerks, how much is the lost time costing the company each week?
2. Your company has determined that 60 percent of the cost of operating the filing department is for salaries, 20 percent is spent on rent, 15 percent on equipment and supplies, and 5 percent on overhead. On a separate sheet of paper, answer the following questions.
   a. If the annual budget is $65,500, what is the yearly costs for each of these items (salaries, rent, equipment and supplies, and overhead)?
   b. What are the monthly costs for each of these items?

APPLYING OFFICE SKILLS

1. Assume you work for a company that uses a numeric filing system. On the form in your workbook or plain paper, write the numbers of the folders in

Activity 2 can be done on information processing equipment.

which the following pieces of correspondence should be filed. (Miscellaneous folders labeled *A, B,* and *C* are available to hold records until five related items accumulate.) If you need to open new folders, assign a number from the accession book. Indicate where cards for the new names are in the alphabetic card file by writing the names that come before and after the new cards.

A-C Section of an Alphabetic Card Index		Accession Book	
Crosley & Sons	728	730	B & B Laundry
Crosby, Amy	734	731	Brown's Cleaners
Columbus Insurance	735	732	American Industries
Columbia Supplies	725	733	Bascom, Jane
Brown's Cleaners	731	734	Crosby, Amy
Bascom, Jane	733	735	Columbus Insurance
B & B Laundry	730	736	
Archer Sports Equipment	729	737	
American Industries	732	738	

a. A letter from Jane Bascom, 207 Main Street, Cranston, Rhode Island, dated April 7.

b. A letter from Crosley & Sons, 417 Power Street, Providence, Rhode Island, dated March 30.

c. A copy of a letter to Columbia Supplies, 603 Taft Street, Coventry, Rhode Island, dated April 6.

d. A letter from Hunter Cassidy, 2019 Hope Street, Bristol, Rhode Island, dated April 1.

e. A letter from Columbus Insurance, 207 Quaker Lane, Warwick, Rhode Island, dated April 13.

f. A copy of a letter to B & B Laundry, 7310 Bellevue Avenue, Newport, Rhode Island, dated April 13.

g. A copy of a letter to Hunter Cassidy, 2019 Hope Street, Bristol, Rhode Island, dated April 2.

h. A letter from Robyn Chamblee, 719 Meeting Street, Providence, Rhode Island, dated March 30.

i. A copy of a letter to Amy Crosby, Rt. 1, Box 213, Warwick, Rhode Island, dated April 1.

j. A copy of a letter to Brown's Cleaners, 217 Cranston Street, Pawtucket, Rhode Island, dated April 3.

k. A letter from Ted Brown, 207 S. Main Street, Coventry, Rhode Island, dated April 7.

l. A copy of a letter to Hunter Cassidy, 2019 Hope Street, Bristol, Rhode Island, dated April 7.

m. A letter from Hunter Cassidy, 2019 Hope Street, Bristol, Rhode Island, dated March 28.

n. A copy of a letter to Hunter Cassidy, 2019 Hope Street, Bristol, Rhode Island, dated March 30.

2. Assume that you work for a company that uses geographic filing. Individual folders are labeled with the state and city name on the first line and with the individual or company name on the second line. On the form provided in your workbook, keyboard folder labels for the correspondence in Activity 1. If you do not have a workbook, keyboard the information on a sheet of paper or on folder labels.

3. You work in the purchasing department of a firm that uses subject filing. The subject index contains these captions:

OFFICE EQUIPMENT	PAPER PRODUCTS
Calculators	Bond
Copiers	Business Forms
Dictation Equipment	Carbon Paper
Electronic Typewriters	Continuous-Form Paper
Microcomputers	Copier Paper
Transcribers	Letterhead Stationery

Prepare an index card for each company listed below to be filed in the alphabetic card index. You will need approximately ten index cards or pieces of paper approximately 3 x 5 inches. Keyboard the name and address of the company on the card, beginning on line 3 and indented three spaces from the left. Then keyboard the captions that the company's correspondence should be filed under. Use the categories in the subject index. When you have completed the cards, arrange them in correct alphabetical order by company name.

a. A letter from Anders Office Equipment, 207 N. Main Street, Bowling Green, Kentucky 42101, about the electronic calculators recently ordered.

b. A copy of a letter to State Office Supply Company, 2103 State Street, Louisville, Kentucky 40206, requesting information about transcribing equipment.

c. A copy of a yearly service contract from Anders Office Equipment, 207 N. Main Street, Bowling Green, Kentucky 42101, for the electronic typewriters in the office.

d. A letter from General Office Supply, 1207 Newton Road, Lexington, Kentucky 40511, giving information on microcomputers.

e. A letter from Anders Office Equipment, 207 N. Main Street, Bowling Green, Kentucky 42101, giving information for dictation machines.

f. A letter from State Office Supply Company, 2103 State Street, Louisville, Kentucky 40206, asking for an appointment to demonstrate the transcribing machines.

g. A copy of a letter to Office Equipment Manufacturers, Inc., 7117 University Avenue, Bowling Green, Kentucky 42101, requesting prices for copiers.

h. A copy of a letter to Anders Office Equipment, 207 N. Main Street, Bowling Green, Kentucky 42101, giving specifications for the letterhead paper and envelopes recently ordered.

i. A copy of a letter to State Office Supply Company, 2103 State Street, Louisville, Kentucky 40206, thanking them for the price information on invoice forms.

j. A letter from Office Equipment Manufacturers, Inc., 7117 University Avenue, Bowling Green, Kentucky 42101, giving the date of delivery of the copy paper.

k. A copy of a letter to General Office Supply, 1207 Newton Road, Lexington, Kentucky 40511, requesting demonstration of a microcomputer.

l. A letter from Modern Office Equipment, Inc., 2319 Main Street, Louisville, Kentucky 40206, giving information about carbon paper.

Saving Time and Money

1. Related papers that are stapled and filed as a unit are more easily identified and removed as a unit if they are stapled in the upper right corner rather than the left corner. For example, a letter, the accompanying enclosure, and a copy of the response may be stapled together.
2. Attach half-size and odd-size sheets to full sheets of paper to prevent them from being lost in the files.
3. Allow about 20 percent of a file drawer for expansion and working space. When a drawer is overcrowded, errors are more likely to occur. (You are also more likely to get paper cuts on your hands!)
4. When removing a file folder for a short period, pull the next folder up so that you have a marker to show where the folder belongs when you return it.
5. If your company stores documents on information processing equipment, always keep backup copies of the files on disks.
6. Label each disk in a disk file with the document numbers and names.

UNIT 11

REPROGRAPHIC SYSTEMS

- Reprographic Processes
- Reprographic Procedures

CHAPTER 1

REPROGRAPHIC PROCESSES

In the office, producing just one or two copies of each letter, report, notice, or other business document is often not enough. Everyone involved in a business transaction needs copies of the related documents. Reprographics is the term used for the various methods available for making copies. All businesses need fast and economical ways of making copies.

Reprographic equipment can be grouped into two categories: duplicators and copiers. Suppose your supervisor asks you to make copies of a report for the 14 regional sales managers. To make the copies on a duplicator, you must first prepare a special duplicating master. To make them on a copier, you set the control for the number of copies you want and simply insert the original.

Wherever you work, there are likely to be two or more types of reprographic equipment from which to choose. You will need to be familiar with the various reprographic processes and how and when to use each.

As you study this chapter, you will find answers to the following questions:

- How are duplicators used in business?
- How are copiers used in business?
- What are some of the special features of copiers?
- What do the following terms mean: **offset, photocopier, convenience copier, high-speed copier, collator, reduction, enlargement, intelligent copiers?**

DUPLICATORS

There are three commonly used duplicating processes: spirit, mimeograph, and offset.

Spirit Duplicators

du'pli·ca·tors

You may be familiar with the spirit duplicating process, also known as "ditto," because some teachers use it to prepare class handouts and tests. Although spirit duplicators are popular in schools and church offices, very few businesses use this method of making copies.

The *spirit master* consists of a white sheet of paper bound at the top to a sheet of special carbon paper. Pressure against the white master from typewriter keys, or a print wheel, or a pen causes carbon from the backing sheet to adhere, or stick, to the back of the master. This carbon combines with fluid from the spirit duplicator and is transferred to the copy paper.

Spirit duplicating is a fast, simple, and inexpensive method of making copies. Because the copies are not as clear as those produced by other duplication methods, however, a spirit duplicator is usually used when speed is more important than appearance. For instance, a small restaurant may use a spirit duplicator to prepare the list of daily specials to insert in menus. These inserts must be prepared quickly, because it is not certain what foods are available until the buyer returns from the market each day.

Mimeograph Duplicators

mim'e·o·graph

A mimeograph duplicator, sometimes called a stencil duplicator, produces fairly clear copies. Many schools use the mimeograph process to prepare attendance reports, announcements to parents, and programs for school functions. Businesses that have mimeograph duplicators use this process for interoffice communications, as well as for routine announcements, instructions, and reports.

For example, a business may use a mimeograph to prepare copies of price lists to insert in catalogues. These catalogues, which often contain color photographs of products, are expensive to print. If the prices are printed in the catalogue, the entire catalogue must be reprinted when prices change. When prices are listed on a separate insert, however, the company needs only to mimeograph copies of a new price list if there is a change in prices.

con·sists'

The *stencil* used to produce mimeograph copies consists of a waxy sheet attached to a white backing sheet. It may also contain a clear plastic cover and a cushion sheet, which separates the stencil and backing sheet. As you keyboard or write on the stencil, you cut impressions or holes in it. When the stencil is run on a mimeograph machine, ink flows through these impressions and prints on the duplicator paper. To produce quality copies on the

Illustration 11–1
Stencil for mimeograph duplicator

mimeograph, use paper with a porous finish that absorbs the ink. Copies made on a mimeograph are usually printed in black ink, although other colors may be used. If you clean the stencil after using it, you can store it for future use.

Offset Duplicators

An offset duplicator, sometimes called a multilith press, produces material that is very close in quality to a keyboard original. As Illustration 11–2 shows, an offset duplicator has three main drums or rollers that press against one another as they turn. One roller is coated with ink. The master is attached to the second. As the rollers turn, the ink from the first roller adheres to the print on the master. Then the ink on the master is transferred to a rubber mat on the third roller. The copy paper picks up the inked image from the mat as the paper passes through the duplicator. This process is called **offset** because the print is "offset," or transferred, from the master to the mat and from the mat to the copy paper.

ad·heres'

trans·ferred'

Offset equipment is commonly found in reprographic departments of businesses that make thousands of high-quality copies on a frequent basis. For instance, an insurance company may reproduce the forms for policies on an offset. The offset process is also used to print order forms, form letters, and office procedures manuals.

An offset master is a single sheet of specially coated paper or metal. Horizontal and vertical lines indicate the keyboarding area on the master.

Illustration 11–2
The inked image is "offset" from the master to the mat

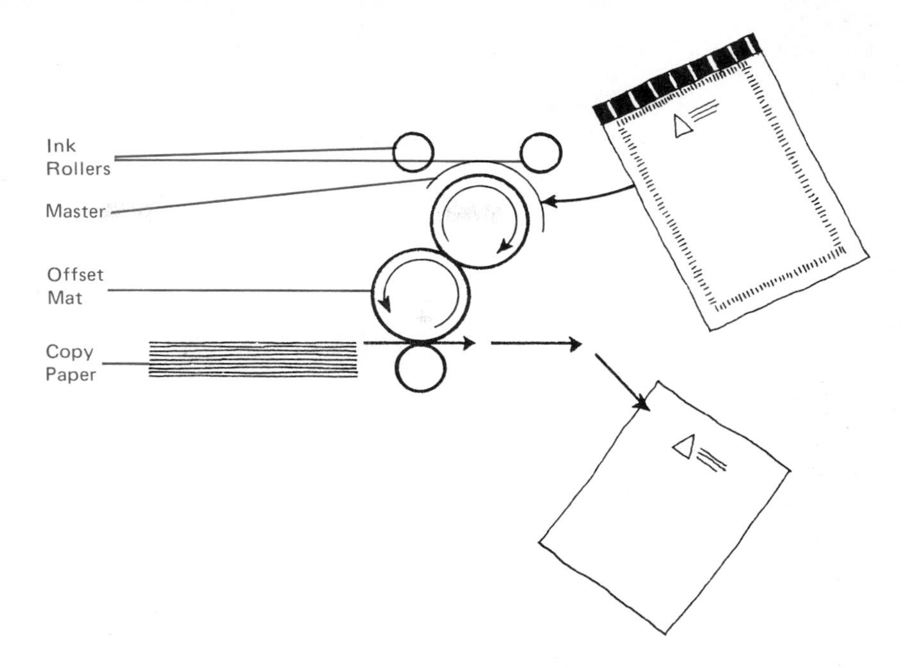

Paper masters To prepare a paper master, follow these steps:

1. Clean the typewriter keys or print wheel.
2. Check to see that the typewriter or printer has either a carbon ribbon or a special fabric ribbon.
3. Insert the master into the typewriter or printer so that the coated side is toward you. Move the rollers on the paper bail to the outside edges.
4. If you make an error, erase it lightly with an offset eraser or a soft pencil eraser. Then keyboard the correction.

Companies that prepare many offset masters may have special equipment that produces a master from a regular keyboarded page. Preparing a master on this special equipment is more expensive than keyboarding directly on the master. However, this process is much faster, especially when you need copies of something that is already in an acceptable format. By using this special equipment, you don't waste time rekeying the information on a master.

Metal masters When thousands of copies are needed, a metal offset master can be prepared. Metal masters last longer and can be stored for future use. However, they are more expensive than paper masters, and you need special equipment to prepare them. Companies that print their own forms usually use metal masters. When additional forms are needed, it is easy to remove the master from storage and print the copies requested.

Although office workers frequently prepare masters or originals for offset duplication, a company usually has employees specially trained to operate offset equipment. A trained offset operator can quickly produce very high-quality copies on paper of various colors and weights, including letterhead paper and even post cards. Although black ink is the most popular, offset ink is available in a variety of colors.

PHOTOCOPIERS

pho'to·cop·i·er

A **photocopier** is a type of reprographic equipment that makes copies directly from an original document. The original can be printed, keyboarded, handwritten, or drawn. Because they make copies quickly and are easy to operate, photocopiers are very popular with businesses.

Types of Photocopiers

sen'si·tized

There are two types of photocopying equipment available: equipment that uses plain paper and equipment that uses treated or *sensitized* paper.

Plain-paper copiers A plain-paper copier prints copies on any kind of paper — letterhead stationery, bond paper, duplicating paper, and other heavy papers. The print produced by plain-paper copiers is usually dark black, so it is easy to read even when colored paper is used. A copy of a letter printed on letterhead paper looks almost exactly like the original.

xer·o·graph'ic

Plain-paper copiers produce copies using a *xerographic* process. This process is similar to taking a picture with a camera. The most expensive plain-paper copiers even reproduce color photographs.

Treated-paper copiers Copying machines that print only on special paper are frequently referred to as treated-paper copiers. The paper is treated with special chemicals. When exposed to the bright lights inside the copier, these chemicals react by producing an image from the original. Copies made on treated paper do not have the same quality appearance as copies made on plain paper. Frequently they have a gray background and a slick finish. The slick finish is difficult to write on with some pens. The main advantage of treated-paper copiers is that they are generally less expensive than plain-paper copiers.

Thermographic copiers These are treated-paper copiers. They make copies directly from an original using an *infrared,* or heat, process and special treated-paper.

Photocopier Capabilities

ca·pa·bil'i·ties

In addition to classifying photocopiers according to the type of paper they use, manufacturers often identify their copying equipment by size, capabilities, and ease of operation. Terms such as *convenience copiers, high-speed*

rel'a·tive·ly

copiers, and *intelligent copiers* are relatively new and reflect some of the advancements in copier technology. These terms can be applied to both plain-paper and treated-paper copiers.

Convenience copiers A **convenience copier,** sometimes called a desk-top copier, is relatively inexpensive and simple to operate. This small copier is designed to be used when fewer than ten copies are needed. Many companies have convenience copiers located throughout their buildings, close to the workers who use them.

High-speed copiers A **high-speed copier** is designed to be used when more than ten copies are needed. This copier can make hundreds of copies in a matter of minutes. A company usually has only one high-speed copier in a building. Frequently, this equipment is located in a centralized reprographic department and must be run by a trained operator.

Most high-speed copiers, like the one shown in Illustration 11–3, have special features that enable you to do more than just make copies. For example, many have built-in collators. The **collator** separates the pages of a multiple-page document as the copies come out of the copier and arranges the pages in order. On a copier without this collating feature, all the copies are fed into a single stack, and the pages are not arranged. The operator must separate the copies and assemble the pages in order by hand.

as·sem'ble

re·duc'tion

Some high-speed copiers have a special **reduction** feature that decreases the print size. By reducing the print size of the copy, you can print more information on a sheet of paper. For example, you can reduce a legal-size document to fit on a letter-size sheet of paper. With an even greater reduction, you can fit two letter-size sheets side by side on a single sheet of

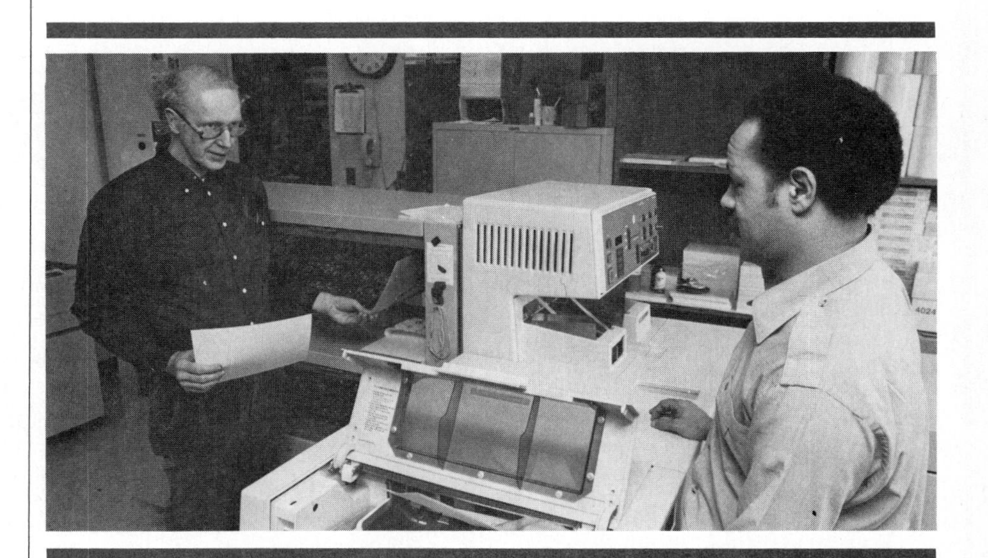

Illustration 11–3
A high-speed copier with a collator attached increases office efficiency

paper. Thus, the reduction feature can result in lower paper costs and in lower mailing costs if the copies are being mailed.

The instructions for operating the reduction feature are usually displayed on the copier. Usually, you simply choose the amount of reduction, such as 74 or 65 percent.

en·large'ment

An **enlargement** feature, available on some high-speed copiers, increases the print size of the copy. This feature is useful when the print on your original is difficult to read. Of course, when copies are enlarged, the print is enlarged, and less material will fit on a page.

Copiers that can print on both sides of a sheet of paper are called two-sided copiers. With this feature, you can print a ten-page document, for example, on the front and back of five sheets of copy paper. Because you use only half the paper, you cut your paper costs in half. You save on mailing costs too, because it costs less to mail five sheets of paper than to mail ten.

On some copiers you can make transparencies that are used with overhead projectors. Your teachers may use transparency masters to project the solutions to accounting or keyboarding problems. At business meetings, speakers frequently use transparencies to illustrate key points. These visual aids help the audience understand what is being said.

in·tel'li·gent

type'set·ting

Intelligent copiers **Intelligent copiers** are sophisticated machines that combine the features of copiers, computers, word processing equipment, and typesetting equipment. Some intelligent copiers can produce over 7,000 pages per hour with a minimum of attention from the operator. They can make copies of information stored on magnetic tapes or disks, so there is no need to keyboard an original. They can print copies in several different typefaces and type sizes, and in a variety of forms. For example, intelligent copiers can produce computer output microfilm (COM).

REVIEWING KEY POINTS

1. Companies make copies of documents and correspondence using various reprographic processes.
2. Duplicating processes — which include spirit, mimeograph, and offset — require the preparation of a master or stencil.
3. Spirit duplicators are used because they are inexpensive and easy to operate and the masters are easy to prepare.
4. The mimeograph duplicator is used in some businesses because it makes fairly clear copies at a reasonable cost. The mimeograph is used for interoffice communications and announcements, instructions, and reports.

5. The offset duplicator produces copies that look like printed copy.
6. A plain-paper copier produces a very good quality copy directly from the original. Copies can be made on inexpensive paper as well as on high-quality letterhead.
7. Copies made by treated-paper copiers are good for office use. However, the finish on the paper may be difficult to write on.
8. Convenience copiers are generally used for fewer than ten copies. When more than ten copies are needed, a high-speed copier is usually more economical.
9. Collating, reduction, enlargement, and two-sided copying are features found on many high-speed copiers. These features help you work more efficiently and help reduce the cost of copying.
10. Intelligent copiers combine the features of copiers, computers, word processing equipment, and typesetting equipment.

DEVELOPING HUMAN RELATIONS SKILLS

1. There is one convenience copier in your office. As a result, people generally have to wait in line to use it, and usually they talk and joke while waiting for their turns. Because your desk is located near the copier, you are frequently bothered by the noise and traffic.
   a. Whom would you talk to about the noise and traffic?
   b. What suggestions would you make for solving the problem?
2. Your company has a policy that restricts the use of copiers for personal copies. Janice is getting ready to go to Europe on a vacation with some friends who live in another state. This morning Janice asks you to make copies of some travel brochures so she can share them with her friends. Janice is a very good friend and has been saving her money for a long time to be able to take this vacation.
   a. What would you do?
   b. What would you say to Janice?

IMPROVING COMMUNICATION SKILLS

Refer to Appendix A 1.41–1.44.

1. On a separate sheet of paper, keyboard the following sentences, inserting quotation marks where needed.
   a. Kathy asked, Why do we make carbon copies of letters? Isn't it easier to use the copying machine?
   b. The supervisor gave each employee a copy of the article, How to Reduce Reprographic Costs.

c. Reprographics is defined as reproduction of records and information.

d. Lynn asked for help with making copies of the report.

e. Lynn's supervisor asked, Do you want a part-time assistant or help from someone in the office?

f. The title of the speaker's presentation is Planning for a Career as an Office Worker.

g. The speaker said that many young ladies think of work as a job, rather than a career.

h. The office manager said, Listen to the weather reports. If the rain turns to freezing rain, we will go home early.

2. On a separate sheet of paper, compose the first draft of a letter of transmittal to be sent with your company's quarterly report (see Chapter 1 of Unit 8 for a description of letters of transmittal). The title of the report is "Summary of Second Quarter Earnings," and its purpose is to provide sales representatives with updated sales figures on new products.

BUILDING PROBLEM-SOLVING SKILLS

1. On a separate sheet of paper, compute the cost of the following reprographic supplies.

   a. Stencils are packaged 24 to a box. If one box costs $3.60, how much does one master cost?

   b. The cost of one dozen bottles of correction fluid is $13.80. What is the cost of a single bottle?

   c. Offset masters cost 42 cents each. A box of masters sells for $21.00. How many masters are in a box?

   d. Based on the above what is the total cost of the following items:
   10 stencils
   3 bottles of correction fluid
   $\frac{1}{2}$ box of offset masters

2. The chart shown here records the number of copies made by each department for a week. Study the chart. Then, on a separate sheet of paper, answer the questions at the top of the next page.

Records of Copies Made

Department	Monday	Tuesday	Wednesday	Thursday	Friday
Accounting	145	217	381	120	110
Production	95	105	115	220	80
Marketing	200	175	225	90	75
Shipping	150	75	120	135	220

a. How many copies were made by each department for the entire week?
b. How many copies were made each day by all departments combined?
c. What percent of the weekly total is each of the department totals?
d. What percent of the weekly total is each of the daily totals?

APPLYING OFFICE SKILLS

Activities 1 and 2 can be done on information processing equipment.

1. On a plain sheet of paper, keyboard a neat copy of the following inventory list for the Reprographics Department. Arrange the equipment by purchase date with the newest equipment at the top of the list.

REPROGRAPHICS EQUIPMENT INVENTORY

Equipment	Model Number	Purchase Date
Duo Spirit Duplicator	250	January 15, 1975
A.D. Bach Mimeograph	750	September 20, 1979
ABS Copier	Copier II	February 1, 1984
Echo Copier	9200	November 1, 1984
Solo Copier	780	December 1, 1982
OM Multigraphics Offset	1250-N	February 1, 1985

2. Using the memorandum form in your workbook or plain paper, keyboard a copy of the following memorandum. Make any corrections carefully so that they will not show when copies are made on the photocopier.

To: all Employees   Date: (today's)

From: Dennis Farrow   Subject: Reprographic Equipment

Our new high-speed copier has ~~now~~ been installed. With the new copier, we can print copy two-sided and reduce or ~~expand~~ enlarge the size of copy. ¶ By printing on both sides of the paper, the costs of copying and mailing can be reduced significantly. Please rem ember these new features when you request copying service.

If you would like to see what the equipment can do, please ~~drop~~ come by the reprographics department. We have samples of work to show you. We will also demonstrate the equipment for you.

CHAPTER 2

REPROGRAPHIC PROCEDURES

As you read in Chapter 1, there are many types of reprographic methods available. How can you decide which of these processes to use? Obviously, no single process is best for all circumstances. You would not use the same method for making ten copies of an interoffice memorandum as you would for making 50 copies of a 30-page report. When choosing a copying method, you must consider not only the quantity of copies you need but also the desired quality and the average price per copy.

Most businesses have established guidelines regarding which copying method to use in various situations. However, you need to know what factors to consider when choosing a copying method. You should be prepared to choose the fastest and most economical method to fit each situation.

As you study this chapter, you will find answers to the following questions:

- What factors should you consider in order to choose the appropriate reprographic process?
- What can you do to control the costs of reprographic services?
- What steps do companies take to regulate the use of photocopying equipment?
- What do the following terms mean: **cost per copy, turnaround time, copyright laws, auditron?**

CHOOSING A REPROGRAPHIC PROCESS

Many companies have several kinds of reprographic equipment. When there is more than one reprographic process available, you must select the process that is most appropriate for the job. Factors that determine which process is most appropriate include the desired quality of the copy, the number of copies needed, the cost, and the preparation time. These factors are related to one another. For example, the highest quality copies usually cost the most to produce. Therefore, when choosing a process, you may need to make trade-offs. The table shown in Illustration 11–4 on page 445 compares the various reprographic processes to help you make your selection.

Quality of Copy

The quality of the copy produced by the various processes differs greatly. Of course, the quality of the paper on which the copies are made and the care with which the master or original is prepared also affect the appearance.

Copies made on an offset duplicator are sharp and clear. When the copies are printed in black ink on bond paper, they are very close in quality to the original. Mimeograph copies rank next in quality. If the stencil is prepared properly and mimeograph bond paper is used, the quality of the copies is suitable for many purposes.

suit'a·ble

Copies made on a spirit duplicator may be very clear and easy to read. The quality of such copies is not consistent, though. Usually the print on the last copies is lighter than on the first. In addition, the slick paper and the color of the print make it very obvious that the copy is not an original.

ob'vi·ous

Copies produced by plain-paper copiers vary in quality, depending on the paper used. When letters are copied on bond letterhead, it is difficult to tell the copy from the original. Because treated-paper copiers use paper treated with chemicals, copy quality is not as good as on plain-paper copiers.

When selecting a reprographic process, you need to consider whether the appearance of the copy is important. How will the copy be used? Who will see it? When you are trying to make a good impression on the reader, choose a process that produces high-quality copies. For example, if you are sending a notice to customers announcing new office hours, you should be concerned about the appearance of the copies. On the other hand, if you are preparing an interoffice memo announcing the opening of a new employee parking lot, you should select the least expensive process.

im·pres'sion

Quantity Needed

The number of copies needed also determines which reprographic process to use. A spirit duplicator usually makes 75 to 125 copies that are clear and readable. If you set the controls properly and use the recommended paper, you can produce up to 300 copies from some spirit masters.

On mimeograph and offset equipment, you can make hundreds or thousands of copies. Furthermore, the stencil or master can be stored and used again. A metal offset master produces the largest number of high-quality copies. The master is prepared from an original using a special machine. Because metal masters are expensive to make, you should use a paper master when you need only several hundred copies.

You can make any number of copies on a photocopier. However, when costs are considered, the photocopying process is usually the most efficient method to use when you need fewer than ten copies.

Cost

When selecting a reprographic process, choose the method that produces the quality you need at the lowest cost.

Duplicating processes The cost of making copies includes the cost of the master, the cost of the paper on which the copies are printed, and the cost of running the equipment. It also includes labor costs—the salary paid to the office worker for the time spent preparing the master and running the copies.

To determine the least expensive method, compare the costs per copy. The **cost per copy** is the total cost divided by the number of copies made. Look at how the cost of 100 copies made on a spirit duplicator is determined:

Cost of preparing and running the master (labor)	$2.25
Cost of the master	.17
Cost of paper (100 sheets)	.75
Cost of equipment	+.20
Total cost	$3.37

The cost per copy when 100 copies are made is a little more than three cents each: $3.37 ÷ 100 = $.0337.

Generally speaking, the spirit duplicator is the least expensive duplicating process when the costs of the equipment and masters are considered. Offset is the most expensive, with mimeograph falling in between.

Photocopying processes The cost of photocopying is determined by the type of copier used and the number of copies produced. On a convenience copier, the cost of each copy is the same — about five cents a copy. On a high-speed copier, the more copies you make, the lower the cost per copy is. For example, the first six copies made from an original cost seven cents each. But for each copy over six, the cost is only two cents apiece. You can compute the total for 15 copies like this:

com·pute′

Convenience Copier	High-Speed Copier
15 copies × $.05 = $.75	6 copies × $.07 = $.42
	+9 copies × $.02 = $.18
	15 copies $.60

The cost per copy is simply the total cost divided by the number of copies made. As the following chart shows, convenience copiers are more economical to use when only a few copies are needed. If you need ten or more copies, however high-speed copiers are usually the most economical copiers to use.

	CONVENIENCE COPIER		HIGH-SPEED COPIER	
Number of Copies	Total Cost	Cost Per Copy	Total Cost	Cost Per Copy
1	.05	.05	.07	.07
5	.25	.05	.35	.07
6	.30	.05	.42	.07
7	.35	.05	.44	.0628
8	.40	.05	.46	.0575
9	.45	.05	.48	.0533
10	.50	.05	.50	.05
15	.75	.05	.60	.04
20	1.00	.05	.70	.035

Preparation Time

When choosing a reprographic process, you need to consider the time needed to make copies. For example, your supervisor may be leaving on a business trip and may need copies of a report quickly. You may have to rush to get copies of the agenda prepared in time for a meeting. If you need copies immediately, you may have to use a fast but more expensive reprographic process, such as photocopying. When time is not an important factor, one of the other processes may be a better choice. As these examples show, the time it takes you to keyboard the information and set up and run the copies plays a big role in determining which reprographic process you will use.

Illustration 11–4

COMPARISON OF REPROGRAPHIC PROCESSES

Process	Equipment Cost	Average Cost Per Copy	Quality of Copies	Quantity of Copies for Economical Use
Spirit Duplicator	Inexpensive	Low to medium	Fair to medium	10–150
Mimeograph Duplicator	Medium	Low	Good	10–5,000
Offset Duplicator	Expensive	Low to medium	Excellent	10–10,000
Convenience Copier	Medium to expensive	Medium to expensive	Medium to excellent	1–10 1–10
High-Speed Copier	Very expensive	Medium	Excellent	Over 10
Thermographic Copier	Inexpensive	Expensive	Fair to medium	1–10

com'pli·cat·ed

Keyboarding and set-up time Because spirit masters, stencils, and offset masters are all prepared on a typewriter or information processor, they take approximately the same time to prepare. However, the time required to run the copies on various duplicating machines differs. Spirit duplicators and mimeograph machines are very simple to set up and operate. The offset press is more complicated, so it takes longer to set up and run copies.

The photocopying process is, of course, the fastest method of making copies. This is especially true when the document you want to reproduce is already in an acceptable format. When this is the case, rekeyboarding is not needed. In addition, most photocopiers are so easy to operate that you have your copies in seconds.

Turnaround time In addition to keyboarding and set-up time, you need to consider turnaround time. Some companies have centralized reprographics departments where all copies are made, regardless of the process used. When using the services of the reprographics department, you need to allow for the **turnaround time** — that is, the time required to prepare your copies.

Company policies usually state the minimum amount of time that you should allow for preparation of copies. For instance, if the turnaround time is four hours, copies needed by 3:00 P.M. should be delivered to the reprographics department no later than 11:00 A.M.

CONTROLLING COSTS FOR REPROGRAPHIC SERVICES

In many companies, reprographic equipment is conveniently placed in several locations. When copies are needed, you simply go to the nearest machine and make the number you need. Although this arrangement is convenient for employees, it can be expensive for the company. It is not unusual to find employees making photocopies instead of carbon copies of correspondence. Employees may use the machine located nearby instead of a piece of equipment that is less expensive to operate. Some employees use company equipment to make copies for their personal use. Not only does personal copying increase office costs, but it prevents other workers from using the equipment for business purposes. Because such practices increase costs, many companies have special policies for using reprographic services.

Centralization of Reprographic Services

Some companies find that centralized reprographic equipment helps provide better quality copies because the people preparing the copies are trained to operate the equipment. Having a centralized reprographics department also helps the company control the costs of reprographic services. For example, there are usually fewer equipment breakdowns when the equipment is run

Illustration 11–5
Copy order form used in centralized reprographics department

JOB NO._____

REQUEST FOR DUPLICATING SERVICES

NAME__________ DEPARTMENT__________

Date Received__________ Time Received__________

Date Needed__________ Time Needed (circle one) AM PM

Number of Originals__________ Number of Copies__________

Process (circle one) Mimeograph Offset Copier

Stock Specifications: _____White Bond _____Colored paper_______ (specify)

_____Letterhead _____Transparencies

_____Other__________ (specify)

Paper Size: _____8 1/2 x 11 _____8 1/2 x 14 _____Other_______ (specify)

Printing: _____1 side only _____ 2 sides

Reduction: _____Yes _____ No

Collate_____ Staple_____ Clip_____ 3-hole punch_____

INSTRUCTIONS TO OPERATOR__________

by trained operators. In addition, trained operators are more likely to select the most economical process for the quality and quantity of copies needed.

In a company with a centralized reprographics department, you will usually find a copy order form similar to the one in Illustration 11–5. When you need copies, you complete this sheet with specific instructions and attach it to your original. The employees in the reprographics department file this sheet when your work is completed. The filed records are used to determine the number of copies and charges for each department.

Company Policies

Companies reduce costs by setting policies that state what types of documents may be reproduced and which process should be used in a given situation. The following policy is typical:

Tim Richert works in the reprographics department of a large company that has an offset duplicator, a convenience copier, and a high-speed copier. The company recently developed these guidelines for Tim's use.

Number of Copies	***Machine to Be Used***
1–10	*Convenience Copier*
11–250	*High-Speed Copier*
Over 250	*Offset Duplicator*

Other policies state:

1. *No copies may be made for personal use.*
2. *Only one copy can be made of copyrighted material.*
3. *Any request that does not comply with the guidelines must be signed by the department supervisor.*

In addition, Tim's supervisor has told him that, whenever possible, materials should be copied on both sides of the paper to reduce costs.

cop′y·right·ed
per·mis′sion

In addition to controlling costs, a company must be concerned about using and copying copyrighted materials. **Copyright laws** prohibit making copies of copyrighted material without the written permission of the publisher of the material. A copyright statement is printed on all copyrighted books and periodicals. Look on the back of the title page of this textbook, and you will see a copyright statement.

cir′cum·stanc·es

Copyright laws do allow copyrighted materials to be reproduced without written permission in certain circumstances. For example, making a single copy is usually permitted. For this reason, most companies limit you to making only one copy of any copyrighted document on their equipment.

Special Controls on Photocopying Equipment

Some companies charge reprographic costs to each department requesting copies. In centralized reprographics departments, the copy order form serves as a record of the number of copies requested. When the reprographic equipment is not centralized, other types of controls are needed.

au′di·tron

One type of control used for convenience copiers is a device called a key or **auditron**. The person making copies inserts the key into the copier to unlock the controls; then copies can be made. Some control keys have a counter that records the total number of copies made. A separate key is assigned to each person or department. At the end of the month, the key holders are charged for the number of copies recorded on their keys.

Employees may also be asked to keep a record of the copies they make on a form such as the one in Illustration 11–6. When you make copies, record the total number of originals, the number of copies made of each original, and your initials or department name in the appropriate space on the form.

PRODUCING PROFESSIONAL-LOOKING COPIES

pro·fes′sion·al

You can ensure that the materials you prepare for copying look professional by carefully proofreading the content and by making sure the original or master is neat in format and appearance. Keyboard the original or master in an attractive format with even top and side margins.

Illustration 11-6 Auditron sign-out sheet

DATE	NAME OF USER	METER COUNT		NUMBER OF:		
		IN	OUT	ORIGINALS	COPIES EACH	TOTAL COPIES
11/3	Brenda Folsom	008265	008277	4	3	12
	Bill Warner	008277	008292	15	1	15
	Kathy Dern	008292	008337	9	5	45
	F.J. Roberts	008337	008349	6	2	12
	Adam Cochran	008349	008379	10	3	30
11/14	Rose Medvitz	008379	008419	28	5	140

Proofreading and Correcting Errors

Careful proofreading is very important for all work that you keyboard. But proofreading is even more important when copies are going to be made, because an error on the original will be multiplied by the number of the copies made. When you use the proper correction techniques, the errors will not be visible on the copies.

You can make corrections easily while preparing a document for photocopying. As you learned in Chapter 3 of Unit 7, you can use correction liquids, correction papers and tapes, and erasers to make corrections on the original. You can also use the cut-and-paste method. When cutting and pasting material, on a separate sheet of paper you rekey sections with corrections, cut the sections out, and paste or tape them in position on the original. In most cases, such corrections are not visible on copies. If the copier produces copies with lines at the edges of the cut-and-pasted sections, apply correction liquid to cover the lines on one copy. Then use that copy to make all other copies.

Binding and Trimming Methods

Most reprographics departments contain special equipment, such as hole punches, binding equipment, and paper cutters, that can be used to give reports, brochures, and booklets a more professional look. A hole punch is used to punch holes uniformly in pages that are to be inserted in a ring binder. When reports need to be bound permanently, binding equipment may be used. As you learned in Unit 8, documents can be either topbound or leftbound. Binding equipment punches holes in the pages and inserts a plastic-ring binder. A paper cutter is used to trim copies to the desired size. Pages trimmed with a paper cutter have neat, straight edges. Use the appropriate office supplies and equipment to give your copies a finished, professional look.

REVIEWING KEY POINTS

1. Reprographic processes vary in quality, quantity, and cost of copies produced; cost of equipment; and time required to prepare the master (or original) and make copies.
2. Select the reprographic process that will produce the quality you need.
3. Consider the number of copies you need when selecting a reprographic process. For a few copies, use a photocopier or spirit duplicator.
4. In general, when the appearance of the copy is not important, choose the reprographic process with the lowest cost per copy.
5. With most reprographic processes, the cost per copy decreases as you make more copies.
6. The cost of making copies includes labor, supplies (master and paper), and use of the reprographic equipment.
7. You should consider keyboarding, set-up, and turnaround time when you select a reprographic process.
8. Most companies have policies or guidelines to help employees select the most appropriate and efficient reprographic process to use.
9. Companies use keys, auditrons, and request forms to help control costs.
10. Pay attention to the accuracy and appearance of items being reproduced.

DEVELOPING HUMAN RELATIONS SKILLS

1. There are two copiers in the office — a convenience copier to be used for fewer than 10 copies and a high-speed copier to be used when more than 10 copies are needed. The high-speed copier prints very high-quality copies. Your supervisor needs 20 good copies of a three-page report as soon as possible. When you took the report to the copy center, you learned that the high-speed copier is not working properly and won't be repaired until tomorrow morning.

a. What would you do?

b. What would you say to your supervisor?

2. Your supervisor, Mr. Corley, frequently waits until the last minute to have copies made. Most of the time you know he is going to need copies, but you can't take the copy request to the reprographics department until Mr. Corley gives you the material. Twice in the last month the reprographics employees have reminded you that turnaround time is one-half day except in real emergencies.

   a. What problems is Mr. Corley causing, and who is affected by them?

   b. What can you do to help Mr. Corley get the copies he needs on time?

IMPROVING COMMUNICATION SKILLS

Refer to Appendix A 1.41–1.44.

1. On a separate sheet of paper, keyboard the following paragraphs. Insert quotation marks where needed.

   In the staff meeting Wednesday, Ms. Logan, the reprographics supervisor, said, The new reprographic equipment will be installed Friday. Beginning Monday, all equipment will be operated by employees in the reprographics center. The brochure, We'll Make Copies For You, was distributed to all office workers.

   Tamara asked, How long will the turnaround time be? Ms. Logan answered, Fewer than five copies will be made while you wait. More than five copies will be made on the high-speed copier and will take about two hours. Ms. Logan further explained that only emergency copies will be made on a rush basis. Each employee should allow at least two hours turnaround time in order that everyone's needs can be accommodated.

2. Your supervisor has asked you to compose a letter to Mr. Bruce Allen, 2027 Williams Boulevard, New Orleans, LA 70121. Your supervisor wants you to send Mr. Allen a copy of the brochure, "We'll Make Your Copies For You." Compose your draft on a separate sheet of paper, being sure to use correct spelling and punctuation.

BUILDING PROBLEM-SOLVING SKILLS

1. The chart shown on the next page lists the auditron readings for four departments. The readings are taken near the end of each month to determine how many copies each department has made. For example, the accounting department made 674 copies during the month of January (000859 − 000185 = 000674). Answer the questions that follow by referring to the chart. Show all of your work. Write your answers on a separate sheet of paper.

a. How many copies were made in each department in January?

b. How many copies were made in each department in February?

Date of Reading	Accounting Department	Personnel Department	Sales Department	Production Department
Dec. 27	000185	000798	002986	000356
Jan. 29	000859	001502	005231	000929
Feb. 26	001120	002030	008608	001687

2. Refer to the chart in Activity 1 to answer these questions.

a. What is the total copies made for all departments for January?

b. What is the total copies made for all departments for February?

c. Which department made the most copies in January and February?

Activities 1 and 2 can be done on information processing equipment.

APPLYING OFFICE SKILLS

1. Using the memo form in your workbook or plain paper, keyboard a final draft of the memo shown here, making all corrections necessary.

To: All Employees

From: Tommy Little, Reprographics Manager

Date: March 13th, 19--

Subject: Turn-around Time

During the last two weeks we have received several complaints about copying equipment and services. There are two main reasons for the recent problems:

1. Staples and paper clips dropped inside the copiers are jamming the machines.

2. The Reprographics Department is operating without two of its regular employees. As most of you know, Paul Weisberg has emergency surgery and Louise Gomez broke her leg in an automobile accident. Both Paul and Louise will be out for three or four weeks.

We are trying to give you the best possible service. You can help us by using extra care to remove all staples and paper clips away from the convenience copier. Also, check to see that the controls are set properly before making copies.

2. Use the cut-and-paste method to make the following changes on the memo that you prepared in Activity 1. (If you prepared the memo on information processing equipment, use the automatic features of the equipment to make these changes. Then print out a final copy of the memo.)

   a. In the first paragraph, change *Two* to *Three* both places it appears.

   b. Add the following as the new paragraph #2:

      2. The high-speed copier needs some major repairs. The parts have been ordered and the repairs should be made within the next week or so.

   c. Change the current paragraph #2 to #3 and change *three or four* to *several.*

Saving Time and Money

1. For clearer, better quality copies, use the type of paper and supplies recommended by the manufacturer.
2. Keep the rollers on the paper bail clean and outside the keyboarding area to prevent marks on your copies.
3. Copies will be clear and easy to read if you keep your typewriter keys or print wheel clean. If your typewriter or printer has a fabric ribbon, make sure that the keyboarded impressions are dark and clear.
4. Before running copies of materials that contain several corrections, run a test copy to see if the corrections show. If the corrections do show on the copy, make the necessary adjustments:
   - On photocopies, use correction liquid to cover smudges on the original. If the copier produces copies with lines at the edges of cut-and-pasted sections, apply correction liquid to cover the lines on one copy. Then use that copy to make all other copies.
   - Place transparent tape over errors and smudges on spirit masters.
   - Use correction liquid to cover errors and tears on mimeograph stencils.
5. Avoid making or requesting more copies than needed. Extra copies are wasteful and, if filed, take up valuable storage space.
6. If you find it difficult to make a transparency on a thermographic copier because the impressions on the original are faint, run the original through a photocopier. The new copy should be dark enough to reproduce well as a transparency.
7. Carbon copies are still the least expensive method of making copies. Carbon copies should be used for file copies. Copies to be sent to others may be made on a convenience copier because the print is usually clearer and easier to read.

ENERGETICS, INC.

Welcome back to Energetics, Inc. This is the second of four office simulations. Office Simulation No. 2 contains five jobs. These jobs will provide you with a variety of keyboarding experience. You will be asked to keyboard an announcement and name tags for the annual Branch Managers' Meeting. You will also be asked to keyboard a legal form and some routine correspondence. An introduction to Office Simulation No. 2 appears below.

Office Simulation No. 2

Ms. Clay has called and asked you to help out for a few days while the staff at Energetics, Inc., gets ready for the annual Branch Managers' Meeting next week. All employees in the Sales, Advertising, and Equipment Design Departments attend the meeting. This year it is going to be held at a hotel in Lafayette.

The purpose of the meeting is to give the branch managers and sales representatives a chance to learn about the new line of Energetics, Inc., exercise equipment. Members of the Equipment Design Department demonstrate new products, and the Sales Manager, Whit Jones, outlines the advertising and promotion campaign. An hour of "work out" time is set aside at the end of the conference so the sales representatives can try out the new equipment.

Most of the arrangements have already been made for the meeting, but there are still last-minute things to be done. For example, name tags have to be prepared for the people attending. Ms. Clay said she would like you to help ease the work load by attending to some of these last-minute details. In addition, you'll be covering the telephone and doing some light keyboarding.

Turn to Office Simulation No. 2 in your *Student Activities* (pages 127-136) to see what projects Ms. Clay has assigned to you.

UNIT 12

INFORMATION PROCESSING SYSTEMS

- Information Processing Concepts
- Information Processing Equipment and Systems
- Information Processing Procedures and Skills
- Dictation and Transcription Procedures

CHAPTER 1

INFORMATION PROCESSING CONCEPTS

The term information processing is new. However, the concepts of word and data processing have been around for many years. With the invention of equipment like the typewriter, dictation machines, and computers, businesses have been able to operate more efficiently. Not only are keyboarded communications easier to read, but they can be produced faster and at a lower cost. Today, businesses depend on sophisticated equipment. Its use increases productivity, improves the quality of work, and helps reduce the effort it takes to process information.

As you study this chapter, you will find answers to the following questions:

- What is information processing?
- How is information processing being used by businesses today?
- What is the purpose of software?
- What do the following terms mean: **information processing, integrate, word processing, data processing, document cycle, inputting, information, processing, central processing unit, main memory, soft copy, hard copy, floppy disk, outputting, software?**

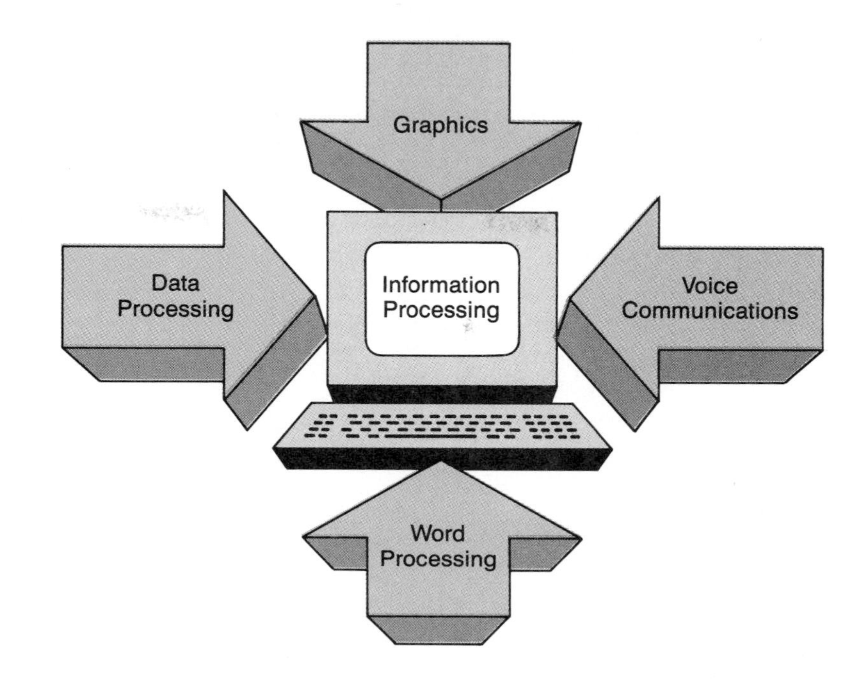

Illustration 12–1
An information processing system integrates basic office components

INFORMATION PROCESSING

The office is the communication center of business. Its size doesn't matter. Large or small, it is the place where information — words, data, voice, and graphics — is gathered, processed, and distributed to its users. The process of using electronic equipment to handle and move information through a company is called **information processing.**

In years past, office workers used items such as pencils and pens, typewriters, dictation equipment, telephones, and adding machines to prepare business documents. Office workers no longer have to depend only on this equipment. With the invention of electronic office equipment, such as electronic typewriters, word processors, and computers, office workers have increased their productivity. This equipment makes it possible to gather, process, store, and distribute more information in less time than ever before.

However, the use of this equipment alone is not enough. For a company's information processing system to be effective, it must **integrate,** or bring together, the office components needed to handle and process information. Illustration 12–1 shows that **word processing,** the handling of words and sentences, and **data processing,** the handling of numbers, are important components in an information processing system. For a company's information processing system to be effective, voice communications and graphics must also be present. The presence of these four basic components allows an information processing system to be productive. It also allows a system to function with the greatest efficiency.

com·po'nents

Illustration 12–2
The information processing system

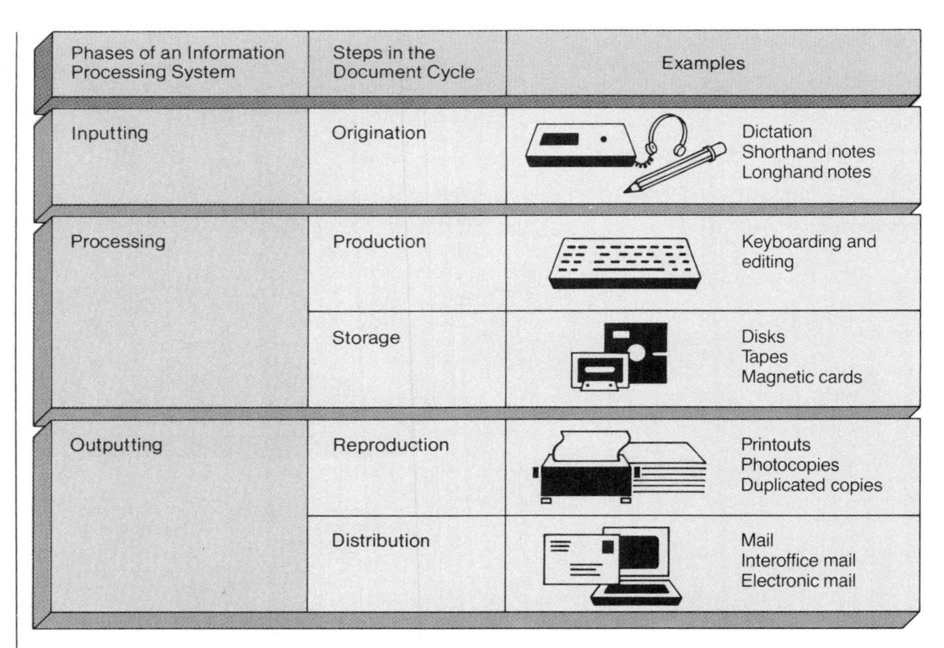

Phases of an Information Processing System	Steps in the Document Cycle	Examples
Inputting	Origination	Dictation Shorthand notes Longhand notes
Processing	Production	Keyboarding and editing
	Storage	Disks Tapes Magnetic cards
Outputting	Reproduction	Printouts Photocopies Duplicated copies
	Distribution	Mail Interoffice mail Electronic mail

THE INFORMATION PROCESSING SYSTEM

con'cept

The concept of information processing may be new to you. However, the office routine that it affects probably is not. Illustration 12–2 shows how the phases of the information processing system — inputting, processing, and outputting — relate to the five steps of the document cycle. The **document cycle** is the steps a document takes from the time of origination to distribution.

Electronic typewriters are considered "low-level" word processors. However, discussion in this chapter will be limited to word processors and computers that use word processing software.

Inputting

o·rig'i·na·tor

dic·ta'tion

The first phase in the information processing system is called **inputting.** At this phase **information** — words, data, voice, and graphics — is entered into the system by an originator. In Unit 7, you learned that the originator is the person who creates the document. As shown in Illustration 12–2, information for inputting is prepared during the origination step. Take a letter, for example. An originator may record the letter on dictation equipment. The originator may also dictate the letter to someone who records it using shorthand or write the letter in longhand. Dictated recordings, shorthand notes, and handwritten drafts are all forms of input.

Processing

Processing is the second phase. During this phase the production and temporary storage of the document take place. Production—the organizing and revising of the information—is controlled by the **central processing unit** (CPU). The CPU is the part of the computer containing the electronic circuits that allow processing to take place. During the processing phase, the information is stored internally in the **main memory**, the temporary storage device for all keyboarded material.

Production and revision During production, information is keyboarded into a word processor or a computer by an operator. The keyboarded material is shown on a video display terminal (VDT). This display is called **soft copy.** While the operator is working at the VDT, the soft copy can be edited and corrected, and insertions and deletions can be made. When the changes have been made, the operator can print a copy of the document on a draft, or dot-matrix, printer. This printed copy of the keyboarded material is called a **hard copy**.

dis·play′

Once a rough draft of the document has been printed, the originator reviews it for accuracy and format. If further changes are needed, the originator marks them on the document (often using proofreader's marks). The edited document is then returned to the word processing operator.

re·vi′sions

Revisions are very simple to make. Because only the changes are keyboarded, the operator can provide a final draft in minutes. The revised materials are sent to the originator again for approval or more editing.

Storage and retrieval The second step in the processing phase is the storage of the document. When information is entered in the word processor or computer, it is stored in the main memory. The main memory stores the information and the instructions for processing it. However, the main memory is not large enough to store all of this material for all of the documents processed in the office. Consequently, this material is usually "filed," or moved from the main memory to an external storage medium. External storage devices include floppy disks, magnetic cards, and magnetic tape. A **floppy disk** is a flexible plastic disk coated with magnetic material used to store information.

Outputting

The third phase of the information processing system is called **outputting.** When the originator approves the document, it is printed in final-draft form and reproduced through the most appropriate reprographic method. Then it is distributed to the proper individuals for use.

re·pro·duced′

Reproduction As you read in Unit 11, the number and quality of copies desired will help you determine which reprographic method to use.

Distribution and communication Once the document has been reproduced, it can be distributed to the proper individuals by several methods. When the document is being sent to another employee within the company, interoffice mail may be used. Communications to be distributed outside the company are usually sent by the U.S. Postal Service. Procedures for preparing communications for mailing are discussed in Unit 6.

A more recent development in sending communications is electronic mail. Many companies are now using electronic mail to send mail faster and at a lower cost. In addition to TWX/Telex, facsimile, and mailgram, which you read about in Unit 5, companies can send communications using computers linked by telephones.

THE IMPORTANCE OF SOFTWARE

pro′grams

The equipment in an information processing system is directed to perform through instructions called programs. Such programs, which spell out what is to be done and in what order, are referred to as **software.**

Generally, the information processing operator does not create the software. Instead, software is created by computer programmers.

Because the information processing needs of businesses are so similar, prepackaged software is available for use. Four such software packages include data base management, electronic spread sheet, word processing, and integrated software.

Data Base Management Software

re·lat′ed

re·trieve′

This software consists of one or more files of related data or information. For example, names and addresses of customers would be related data. This software allows the operator to organize, move around, retrieve, and file data contained in the data base. Using this software, an operator can arrange data in desired order, add or delete records, and perform other activities as needed.

Electronic Spreadsheet Software

An electronic spreadsheet allows the operator to perform calculations on data that is in the computer. The operator enters the data and formulas needed for the calculations. The software performs the calculations according to the data entered by the operator.

Word Processing Software

This software is used to prepare letters, memos, and reports. In keyboarding the information, errors may be corrected. If the software contains a spelling verification feature, for example, misspelled words are automatically located

Illustration 12–3
A variety of prepackaged software is available for use

by the computer. Word processing software also allows the operator to set margins and page lengths. It makes the addition, deletion, and movement of words, sentences, paragraphs, or pages an easy task.

Integrated Software

Integrated software combines tasks such as word processing and electronic spreadsheets into a single, easy-to-use package. This software allows the operator to perform more than one type of task at the same time.

REVIEWING KEY POINTS

1. Information processing saves time, money, and effort for office workers by eliminating, automating, or simplifying tasks.
2. Information processing is a combination of the following various office components: word processing, data processing, voice communication, and graphics.
3. Information includes all of the words and data entered into an information processing system.

4. Information moves through a document cycle that directly relates to the three phases of information processing. These phases are inputting, processing, and outputting.
5. Information processing operates through instructions called programs, which are commonly referred to as software.
6. Integrated software combines more than one task such as word processing and electronic spread-sheets into a single software package.

DEVELOPING HUMAN RELATIONS SKILLS

1. Jeremy Lyons and Marge Schott both work in the office of a fast growing company. Every year the company updates its information processing equipment with the purchase of new equipment. Like many others in the office, Jeremy and Marge have to attend training sessions after work or on Saturday morning. Jeremy complains to Marge about having to use his personal time for training on the new equipment. He believes that the company should provide training during the regular workday. With Jeremy's constant complaints about the training hours, Marge is getting to the point that she hates to be around Jeremy.
   a. Can a company expect its employees to train on their own personal time? Explain.
   b. If Jeremy is upset, how should he handle the situation?
   c. How should Marge handle Jeremy's constant complaints?
2. Your supervisor is studying the information processing activities of your office. This is being done to determine what type of computer to purchase. Everyone has been asked to keep a record of their information processing activities for the next thirty days. Ellie, a friend of yours, says that your supervisor must be kidding. She's not going to spend time recording her information processing activities. She says she's just going to take an hour or so one evening and make up her report. She doesn't feel that her made-up information will be that far off. Even if it is, it probably won't matter.
   a. Do you agree with Ellie? Explain.
   b. What could you say to Ellie?
   c. Should you report Ellie to your supervisor?

IMPROVING COMMUNICATION SKILLS

Refer to Appendix A 1.36–1.37.

1. On a separate sheet of paper, keyboard the following sentences, supplying underscores as needed.
   a. The Wall Street Journal provides up-to-date business articles.
   b. The Secretary is a magazine read by professional secretaries.

c. With all the frustrations in today's office, it's no wonder that the book Stress-Free Living is so popular.
d. Working 9 to 5 is a popular song around here.
e. We use Office Systems and Procedures in our office procedures class.
f. My boss reads every issue of Information Processing Monthly.
g. The title of the article is Information Processing and You.
h. How to Win a Promotion appeared in Management World last month.
i. Word processing software was bought for the computers, not integrated software.
j. The newspaper carried an article titled Manners Are Back in Style.

2. Compose a letter to Ms. Irene Lawrence, Marketing Representative, Business Computers, 434 Montgomery Square, Cincinnati, OH 45242-0210. The subject of your letter is "Down Payment on a PC." Tell Ms. Lawrence that you are sending a $500 down payment on the New Horizon Personal Computer that you viewed yesterday. Tell her you will pay the balance and make plans to attend the training program on Saturday. Ask her if the equipment can be delivered and installed within a week. Also tell Ms. Lawrence how much you appreciate her help and look forward to using your new equipment. Use plain paper for your letter.

BUILDING PROBLEM-SOLVING SKILLS

1. The 35 originators of Johnson Patterson Company are connected to the company's centralized dictating system by phone. By lifting the receiver and dialing 254, they can record dictation.
   a. The originators dictate a total of 10,000 lines a week. On an average, how many lines does each originator dictate each week?
   b. At a cost of 18 cents a line, what's the cost of each originator's dictation each week?
   c. If one originator dictates 20 percent fewer lines than the average, how many lines would that be?
2. The average cost of producing a business letter when the originator dictates to a secretary is $9.10. The cost of producing the same business letter when dictation equipment is used is $7.40.
   a. What is the difference in cost of producing the same letter using each of the two methods of dictation?
   b. If your employer had five letters to dictate, how much money would be saved by using the dictation equipment?
   c. The monthly office budget for producing correspondence is $750. How many letters can be produced using each method of dictation?

Activities 1 and 2 can be done on information processing equipment.

APPLYING OFFICE SKILLS

1. Read a magazine article about the use of information processing equipment in today's offices or about the impact of information processing on office career opportunities. On a sheet of plain paper, keyboard a summary of the article.
2. You have gathered the information shown here concerning the top-selling portable computers for your supervisor. Prepare this information in table format so that the vendors' names appear in alphabetical order. Use the title "Portable Computers."

Vendor	Weight	Memory	Features	Price
Paqcom	25 lbs.	128K	Suitcase Size, 9-inch Screen	$2,695
Prokay	25 lbs.	64K	Suitcase Size, 9-inch Screen, Word Processing Program	$1,295
MBI	30 lbs.	256K	Suitcase Size, 9-inch Screen	$2,795
SRT Model 100	4 lbs.	8K	Notebook Size	$ 799
Otrona Attache	20 lbs.	64K	Suitcase Size, 5 1/2-inch Screen	$2,395
Workslate	31 lbs.	16K	Briefcase Size	$ 899
GRID	10 lbs.	256K	Briefcase Size, 24-line Screen	$5,995

CHAPTER 2

INFORMATION PROCESSING EQUIPMENT AND SYSTEMS

The number of documents produced in businesses has been increasing at a tremendous rate. These documents are vital to the decision-making activities of management. Because there are so many documents to be processed, businesses are always looking for more efficient equipment to handle them. Electronic typewriters, word processing equipment, and computers are being used in more offices today. By using the latest equipment, businesses can to process more documents in less time than ever before.

As you study this chapter, you will find answers to the following questions:

- What equipment is needed for an information processing system to operate efficiently?
- How is recognition equipment used to input information?
- What is the difference between a stand-alone information processing system and a shared-logic information processing system?
- What do the following terms mean: **magnetic media, microprocessor chip, alphanumeric keyboard, impact printers, nonimpact printers, mainframes, minicomputers, microcomputers, memory, menu?**

INFORMATION PROCESSING EQUIPMENT

A variety of equipment is needed to process words and data. Generally, when you think about information processing, you think about word processors and computers. However, other equipment is also used for the processing of words and data. For example, electronic calculators are used to process orders in a manufacturing company's office. Dictation equipment, on the other hand, is used to process correspondence in many other offices. Let's take a look at some of the equipment used for processing words and data in an information processing system.

Electronic Calculators

ca·pa·bil'i·ty

When you are handling quantitative data, you probably will use an electronic calculator. Calculators are generally classified in terms of their computing capability, size, and type of display.

a·rith'me·tic

Computing capability The most inexpensive calculators contain ten number keys (including zero) and keys for the basic arithmetic operations: addition, subtraction, multiplication, and division. If your work requires more complex calculations — such as finding square roots $\sqrt{}$ or figuring percentages (%) — you will probably use a more expensive model that contains additional keys for these operations. Calculators designed for engineers, scientists, and business executives contain programs for the special mathematical formulas they use in their work.

for'mu·las

The most advanced electronic calculators can be programmed to perform a series of operations. The *programmable calculators,* as they are called, are actually small computers. Because they are relatively expensive, they are not found in most business offices where a simpler calculator is all that is needed.

Illustration 12–4
Electronic calculators with printed tape and lighted display

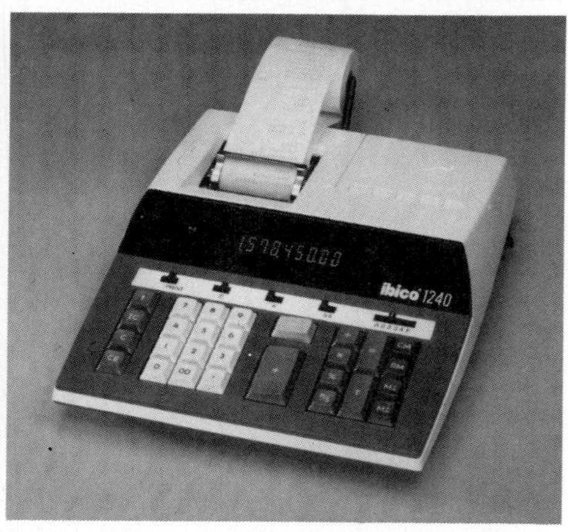

de·pend'ent

Size As people have become more dependent on their calculators, calculators have become smaller and more portable. They range in size from desk-top models, which are generally smaller than adding machines, to hand-held models that fit easily in a pocket or purse.

Type of display When electronic calculators were first introduced, the numbers keyed in and the answers to the problems were shown in lighted figures in the display window. Today, you can also purchase desk-top and hand-held printing calculators. These models produce a paper tape that records the operations. Some calculators offer both options — lighted display window and printed paper tape.

Dictation Equipment

Dictation equipment allows the originator to record spoken messages on magnetic media so that the message can be transcribed at a later time. The most common **magnetic media** are cassettes, belts, and disks.

cas·settes'

Dictation cassettes, belts, and disks can be corrected. The originator can correct or change the wording of the dictated message by one of three methods. On some dictation equipment, the originator simply backs up the tape and dictates the correct information. On other types of dictation equipment, the originator marks on an indicator slip the spots where changes occur. These marks tell the word processing secretary to listen ahead for a change in dictation. On still other types of dictation equipment, the originator presses a button when a change is made. This records a tone on the dictation tape. The tone tells the word processing secretary to listen ahead for a change in the dictation.

Dictation equipment can be a portable unit, a standard desk-top unit, or a remote-control unit. The type of equipment that a company chooses depends on the size of the business and the organization of the business.

Portable dictation units A wide variety of portable dictation equipment is available. Portable equipment, which is lightweight and easy to carry, enables the originator to dictate anywhere: at home, in a car, or on a plane.

Standard desk-top units Standard desk-top dictation equipment may consist of a single unit or separate recording and transcribing units. The recording unit is usually kept on the originator's desk while the transcribing unit is kept on the secretary's (or transcriber's) desk.

mi'cro·phone

Remote-control systems In a remote-control system, the originator and the dictating machine on which the message is recorded are not at the same location. The originator dictates into a special hand-held microphone or a telephone receiver. The microphone or receiver is hooked up to recording equipment located in the word processing center.

Electronic Typewriters

An electronic typewriter is an electric typewriter that contains a microprocessor chip. A **microprocessor chip** is a tiny piece, or chip, of silicon containing electrical circuits that carry out operating instructions. This chip allows the electronic typewriter to perform basic word processing functions such as centering, inserting, and deleting using a limited memory.

Electronic typewriters may be referred to as word processors because they have some word processing capabilities. However, they do not display text on a VDT. It is predicted that by the late 1980's the majority of typewriters sold will be electronic.

Several advantages for using electronic typewriters include:

1. Electronic typewriters are easy to operate.
2. They cost less than a word processor.
3. The storage capacity of electronic typewriters can be increased.
4. Electronic typewriters can automatically center, insert, and delete text. They can format columns and print in various pitch sizes.

Word Processing Equipment

Word processing equipment is automated equipment with memory and storage capabilities. These capabilities allow the operator to keyboard information with ease, move it with the least amount of rekeyboarding, and store it for retrieval.

All word processors have four basic components: an inputting device, a processing device, a memory and storage device, and an outputting device.

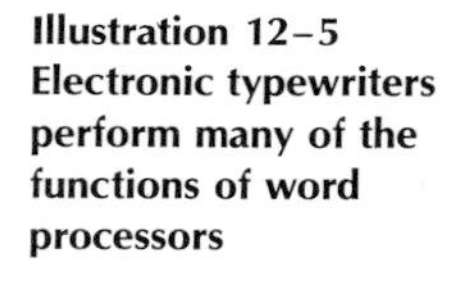

Illustration 12–5 Electronic typewriters perform many of the functions of word processors

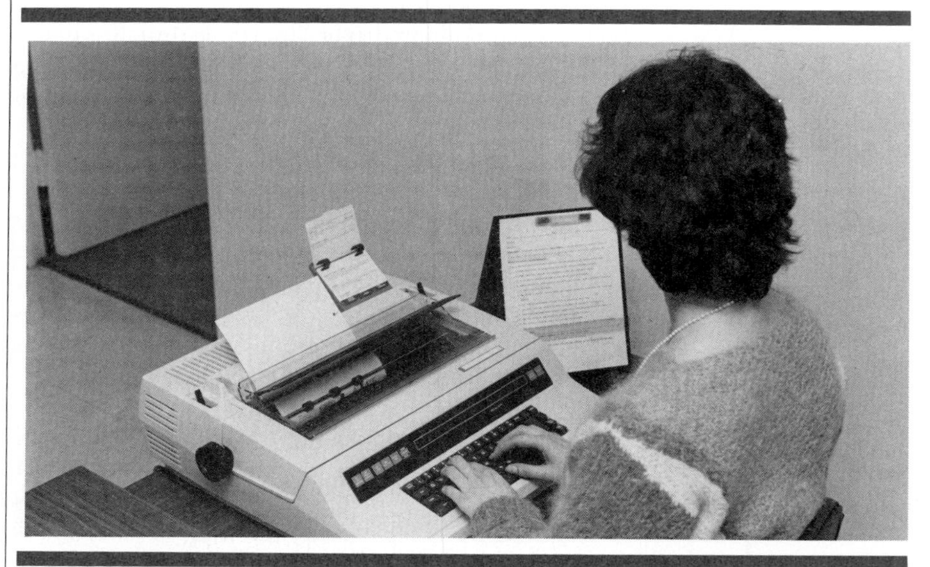

Inputting device The most common inputting device on a word processor is the keyboard. Most keyboards consist of an **alphanumeric keyboard** — that is, they have keys for the alphabet and for numbers — plus a series of function keys. For example, most word processors contain function keys to perform a variety of functions such as insert, delete, move, and replace information. Some keyboards also contain a ten-key numerical pad to the right of the alphanumeric keys, which permits fast calculations to be made.

Many word processors come with movable keyboards. This allows the operator to position the keyboard for easier use and less fatigue.

Processing device The disk drive unit on a word processor holds the floppy disk and is considered the processing device, or *brain,* of the word processor. Some disk drives are separate pieces of equipment, while others are part of the VDT unit. This device activates, by spinning, the disks that give the word processing system its operating instructions.

Storage and memory device The floppy disk is the storage medium for most word processors. The storage device holds the document when you have finished keyboarding it. If you want to work on the document again, you retrieve it from storage, work on it, and then send it back when you are done.

Outputting devices The printer is a common outputting device. It produces the copy on the paper. Printers are of two types: **impact printers** (those that strike the ribbon and then the paper) and **nonimpact printers** (those that use ink sprays or laser beams to create the characters).

char'ac·ters

Illustration 12–6
The printer is a common outputting device

ver'i·fy

Another form of output is provided by the VDT. The VDT allows the operator to verify text content and format before it is printed. The VDT may display full or partial pages of text. A common display has 20 lines of text with 80 characters per line. To exceed 20 lines, the operator may scroll (roll) the text.

Computers

lab'o·ra·to·ries

si·mul·ta'ne·ous·ly

In an information processing system, computers are used to process words and data. Computers come in many shapes, sizes, and price ranges. Full-size computers are called **mainframes.** They are used by large institutions such as government agencies, schools and colleges, scientific laboratories, and big business.

A step down from the large computers are **minicomputers.** Minicomputers have the same parts and work the same way as large computers. However, they cannot perform as many operations simultaneously — that is, at the same time.

The main advantage of minicomputers — and one reason for their increasing popularity — is that they are relatively simple to operate. Companies can buy ready-to-use programs to handle most of their data processing tasks, so they don't have to hire a large computer staff. And, because these programs are written in simple language, even a layperson can quickly understand and use them.

The smallest computers are **microcomputers.** These are usually desktop machines, a little larger than an office typewriter. Microcomputers are used by individuals — teachers, students, homeowners, doctors, accountants — and by small businesses, such as retail stores and real estate offices. Most of the discussion in this unit will deal with microcomputers. They are referred to as computers.

Like word processors, computers have four basic components: an inputting device, a processing device, a memory or storage device, and an outputting device.

Inputting device In information processing systems, the most common inputting device is the keyboard. Most computer keyboards are alphanumeric. Like the keyboards of many word processors, some computer keyboards are movable. Others are attached to the VDT.

Information can be entered into computers in several forms. Computers will accept data recorded on paper tape and magnetic disks. Each of these types of input must be used with special recording and reading equipment.

Processing device The movement of information takes place in the CPU according to the instructions contained on the software. It is the CPU, with the help of software, that allows the operator to move paragraphs around automatically. It is also the CPU that stores material in electronic files, hyphenates and justifies margins automatically, and checks the text for spelling errors.

de·scribed'

Memory or Storage Device The computer's **memory** stores information. Computers are often described in terms of their memory or storage capacities. Even the smallest computers store thousands of pieces of data.

What kind of information does the computer store? First, it stores the words and data that are fed in through the inputting devices. Second, it stores the program, or instructions, that tells the computer what to do with the information. Third, it stores the results of operations for later calculations.

in·tel'li·gent

Outputting devices The most common computer outputting devices are the printer and the VDT. Other outputting devices include intelligent copiers and facsimile machines. Intelligent copiers produce photocopies automatically. Facsimile machines transmit information originating in printed form.

Optional Information Processing Equipment

In addition to the basic information processing equipment just discussed, some companies purchase optional information processing equipment. Optical Character Recognition, Magnetic Ink Character Recognition, and Voice Recognition equipment are three types of optional equipment.

tech·nol'o·gy

Optical Character Recognition (OCR) The process of preparing information for inputting can be costly and time consuming. For that reason, machines have been developed that automatically "read" and record data in a form that is usable by machine. The technology of reading data on a source document is called Optical Character Recognition (OCR). OCR devices can read

Illustration 12–7
The keyboard is the most common inputting device on a computer

keyboarded, computer-generated, and in some cases handwritten information. As the OCR device scans the material, it records the information in magnetic form. For example, the operator can keyboard a rough draft of a lengthy report on any machine. The originator reviews the draft and marks the desired changes. The keyboarded rough draft is inserted in the OCR, which scans the information and records it on magnetic medium such as a disk. When the disk is inserted into a word processor or computer with a VDT, the operator can see where to make the changes requested by the originator. When all changes have been made, a corrected copy is printed.

Magnetic Ink Character Recognition Another method of inputting is Magnetic Ink Character Recognition (MICR). It is widely used in the banking industry to process checks. Before issuing checks to a customer, the bank prints identification information in magnetic ink at the bottom of each check. The magnetic characters speed the sorting and processing of checks.

i·den·ti·fi·ca'tion

Voice recognition equipment A voice recognition unit allows an originator to dictate a message directly to a computer. The computer matches the

Illustration 12–8
An Optical Character Recognition device saves time by scanning keyboarded information and recording it on a disk

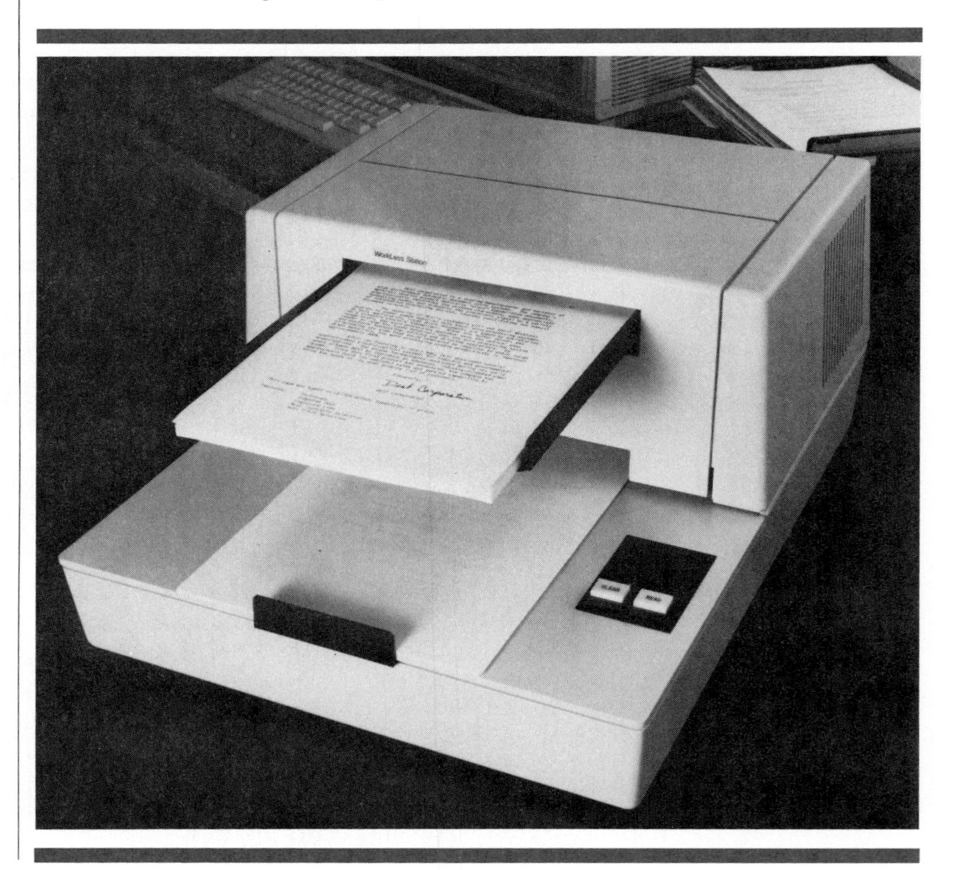

spoken word to the words stored in the computer memory and prints out the message. Of course, the originator must be careful when pronouncing words. Many words, such as *their* and *there; to, too,* and *two; council* and *counsel* sound similar, and voice recognition equipment cannot select the correct word. Strong accents and mispronounced words may also cause problems.

mis·pro·nounced'

pri·mar'i·ly

Currently, this equipment is being used primarily for inventory control. However, as improvements are made, more companies will be able to use voice recognition equipment to increase the efficiency of communications.

INFORMATION PROCESSING SYSTEMS

You have just read about the equipment needed for an information processing system to operate efficiently. For an information processing system to be the most productive, it must be arranged to suit the needs of the company and its workers. Equipment in an information processing system can be set up into four different arrangements: stand-alone, shared-logic, distributed-logic, and time-shared systems.

Stand-alone System

A stand-alone system contains a single station of equipment that is self-contained. It may be a word processor or a computer. It has its own processing power, memory, and printing capability.

A stand-alone unit may have a keyboard, screen, processor, and printer. These may be housed in one piece of equipment, or they may be four separate pieces of equipment connected by cables.

Many stand-alone units can be linked with other stand-alone word processors or computers. Linking these units allows them to communicate or send information from one location to another location.

ap·pro'pri·ate

ac'ti·vat·ed

Stand-alone units, with the appropriate software, can provide the user with everything necessary to create, edit, store, and print documents. This equipment and its software offer more automated features than the electronic typewriter. Such features may be activated by means of function keys or with the aid of a **menu** in the software. A menu is a list of tasks displayed on the VDT. The user can choose what task will be completed next from this list.

Shared-logic System

con·nects'

A shared-logic system connects two or more word processors to a mainframe computer. Because they are connected to a computer, word processors in a shared-logic system can store more information and process it faster than stand-alone machines can. Shared-logic systems are frequently found in larger companies where many people and departments need access to the same stored information. For example, addresses of customers may be stored and played out at any time by any department to print mailing labels or to address envelopes.

Distributed-logic System

A distributed-logic system is very similar to a shared-logic system. There is one difference, however. The word processors or computers are said to be *smart*. This is because memory from the CPU is distributed throughout the system, giving each word processor or computer its own memory. Consequently, if there is a failure in any one of the parts of the system, each individual word processor or computer can continue working.

Time-shared System

In a time-shared system, businesses rent processing time from large computer systems. The businesses pay by the minute for the time used. In a time-shared system, the only equipment needed is a word processor or a computer that connects to the time-shared computer by telephone lines.

REVIEWING KEY POINTS

1. A variety of equipment is needed to process information in an information processing system.
2. Electronic typewriters can perform basic word processing functions because they contain microprocessor chips. These functions include centering, inserting, and deleting text automatically.
3. All word processors have four basic components: an inputting device, a memory and storage device, a processing device, and an outputting device.
4. Computers with word processing software are used to process words and data in an information processing system.
5. Computers have the same four basic components as word processors. They have an inputting device, a processing device, a memory and storage device, and an outputting device.
6. Recognition equipment is optional information processing equipment. The use of recognition equipment such as OCR and MICR can reduce inputting costs.
7. Information processing equipment can be set up in four different system arrangements to provide for the utmost office productivity.
8. A stand-alone unit is a self-contained system. It does not need other equipment to operate.
9. Shared systems use equipment that is tied together and shares the memory of a mainframe computer.

DEVELOPING HUMAN RELATIONS SKILLS

1. Marcia Hesoun operates a word processor in the marketing department. All information to be processed comes to the Word Processing Supervisor, Mildred Jenkins. Mildred assigns the work to the operators.

   Marcia has been in the department for only a month. However, she is beginning to doubt her own capabilities as a word processing operator. Even when the corrections or changes to be made are the originator's changes, Mildred makes Marcia feel as though her work is not good. Just this morning when Mildred returned Marcia's edited work, she made the following comment: "Marcia, you've got errors to correct on just about every page of this report."

   a. Do you think Marcia is being too sensitive? Explain.

   b. Should Marcia say something to Mildred.?

   c. What should she say?

IMPROVING COMMUNICATION SKILLS

Refer to Appendix A 1.36–1.37.

1. An underscore is used to place emphasis on a word or phrase. Keyboard the following paragraph on a separate sheet of paper. Use double spacing. As you keyboard this copy, identify key words that might be emphasized by underscoring them.

   Procedures for taking the test are spelled out in detail. All participants are instructed to write their names at the top of every page. The date and section number should be written directly below the individual's name on every page. Answers are to be placed only on the answer sheets. All answers should be made with a #2 pencil. Every question must be answered; one unanswered question will cause your test to be eliminated from the scoring. At the completion of the test, give the test monitor three items: your pencil, test, and score sheet. When you leave the test facility, you are asked not to discuss any of the test information with anyone else. Test results will be available on Friday of this week. Do not call before Friday. Your test grade will be given only to you in the Business Education Department office.

2. Compose and keyboard a letter to a professional office journal to which you wish to subscribe. You can obtain the mailing address for the journal from the library. In your letter tell the publisher that you are an office procedures student interested in subscribing to the journal. Ask the publisher how much an annual subscription will cost. Include any other questions that you would like to ask about the journal or taking out a subscription.

BUILDING PROBLEM-SOLVING SKILLS

1. Study the monthly work record for information processing operators below. On a separate sheet of paper, calculate the following:
   a. the weekly subtotals
   b. break time for each week
   c. total productive hours for each week

Factor	Week 1	Week 2	Week 3	Week 4
Basic Hours (7 × 40)	280	280	280	280
Overtime	+ 40	+ 27	+ 12	+ 15
Subtotal	?	?	?	?
Nonproductive Hours	− 65	− 39	− 22	− 25
Subtotal	?	?	?	?
Break Time (15%)	− ?	− ?	− ?	− ?
Total Productive Hours	?	?	?	?

2. Refer to the work record chart in Activity 1. Then, on a separate sheet of paper, answer the following questions.
   a. What is the total number of overtime hours worked for the month?
   b. What is the weekly average of overtime hours worked?
   c. What is the weekly average of nonproductive hours?
   d. Nonproductive hours represent what percentage of the *total* hours worked (basic hours + overtime)?
   e. Productive hours represent what percentage of the total hours worked?

APPLYING OFFICE SKILLS

Activities 1 and 2 can be done on information processing equipment.

1. Your boss has requested a listing of the purchase orders received from the countries in Europe with whom your company does business. You collected the information shown here. Keyboard this information in an attractive double-spaced format. Title the information "Current Purchase Orders." Arrange the countries alphabetically. For the date received and the date shipped, insert the actual dates. Calculate these dates using today's date.

Country	Date Received	Order #	$ Value	Date Shipped
Italy	4 weeks ago	72118	3,761	Yesterday
Britain	3 weeks ago	43372	18,000	1 week from now
Germany	6 weeks ago	33782	16,915	2 weeks ago
Austria	Last Monday	23567	17,411	3 weeks from now
Hungary	1 week ago	23549	883	4 weeks from now
France	4 weeks ago	13011	20,867	1 week from now
Romania	2 weeks ago	34358	6,575	2 weeks from now
Spain	Today	67219	590	5 weeks from now
Portugal	5 weeks ago	37721	4,590	1 week ago
Greece	2 months ago	23314	15,600	1 month ago

2. A rock concert is to be held at your local sports arena at the beginning of the summer. Although posters have been put up around town announcing the concert, your office does not have all the ticket information yet. Therefore, a form letter has been written for those persons requesting ticket information. Prepare copies of the letter to be sent to the people listed here. The form letters are in your workbook. In the first line of the form letter, insert the word *rock concert* and *May 5*. Keyboard the inside address in approved style and use an appropriate salutation. If you do not have a workbook, keyboard the letters, inserting the correct names and information.

   a. Jon B. Barnes, Adams Rodeway Inn, Central Adams, Durango, CO 81301.

   b. Sue Noble, 1911 Lake View Avenue, Boulder, CO 80311.

   c. Allen Feore, 3500 Tenth Avenue, Peyton, CO 80831.

Colorado Springs, Colorado 80911 (303) 772-1919

Ticket information for the
will be available . Here at the Rocky Ridge Coliseum we are always trying to bring our patrons the best in family entertainment, music, and sports.

Enclosed is a list of area stores where tickets for Coliseum events may be purchased. You can also call our switchboard at the number shown in our letterhead for updated information of all Coliseum events.

Thank you for your interest in the Rocky Ridge Coliseum.

Sincerely yours

Thelma Lask
Director of Public Relations

TL/krd

Enclosures

CHAPTER 3

INFORMATION PROCESSING PROCEDURES AND SKILLS

Businesses in the United States spend more than $250 billion a year just to run their offices. In spite of this tremendous expense, productivity levels are often only 40 to 60 percent of what they could be. This is why most companies try so hard to cut costs and to increase productivity. In particular, they look for ways in which they can process information at a lower cost and at a faster rate.

Many companies have increased their productivity by changing to information processing systems. The newer equipment that you read about in the last chapter provides the technical support for workers who collect, process, and make available the information needed for decision making.

Companies can reduce their information processing costs, speed the processing, and increase the accuracy of their information. They can do this by using sound decision-making techniques, establishing efficient office procedures, and hiring qualified employees.

As you study this chapter, you will find answers to the following questions:

- What role does information processing play in a management information system?
- How do you properly set up a work station in an information processing system?
- How has the information processing movement affected office careers?
- What do the following terms mean: **management information system, standardized procedures, work requisition form, continuous-form, job, career?**

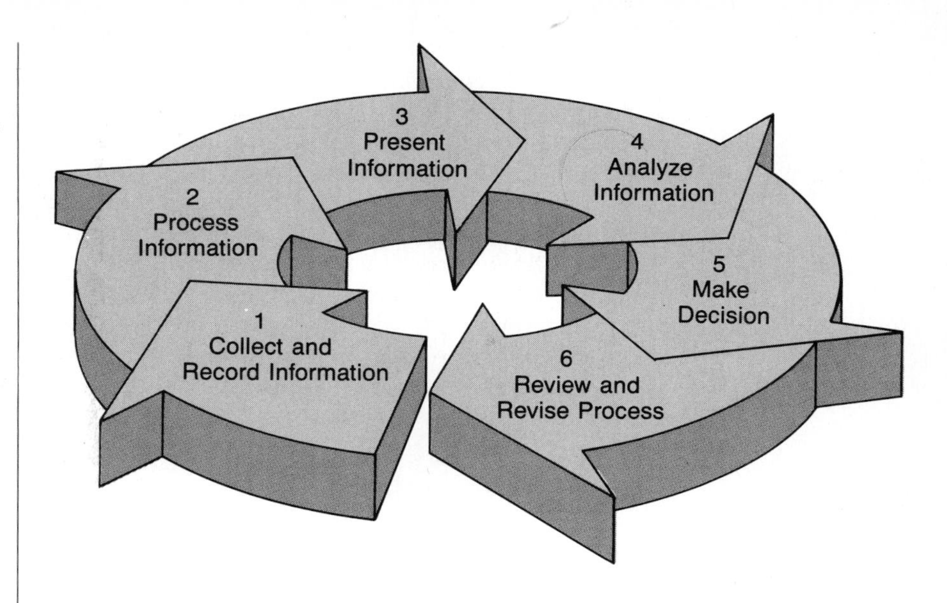

Illustration 12–9
The cycle of decision making in a management information system

MANAGEMENT INFORMATION SYSTEMS AND YOU

knowl'edge

Every business decision is based on the manager's knowledge of past events combined with new information. Information processing systems provide the information on which managers base their decisions. The decision-making process used by a management information system contains these five steps:

1. Collect and record the information.
2. Process the information.
3. Present the information.
4. Analyze the information.
5. Make the decisions.

The first three steps are information processing steps. These steps are usually performed by employees such as word processing operators, account clerks, order entry clerks, payroll clerks, and information processing specialists. The other activities are usually performed by managers and supervisory personnnel who are involved in decision making.

A **management information system,** also called an MIS, is a plan for effective decision making. It outlines what should be done at each step in the decision-making process. For example, at the first step — information collection and recording — an MIS might specify

- what information will be used
- how it will be obtained
- who will collect it
- what equipment will be used

re·view'

An MIS always includes a sixth step: review of the decision-making process. On a regular basis, companies using MIS look closely at the equipment and procedures their employees use in processing information. The purpose is to find the best way to produce accurate information at the lowest cost and in the shortest time. This review may show the need for better employee training programs, simpler information processing forms, or new equipment. When all changes are made, the cycle begins again.

stan'dard·ized

As an office worker, you may find yourself working for a company that is developing or making changes in its management information system. If you do, you may be asked to set up your own work station and to assume responsibility for the ordering and storing of information processing supplies. You may also be asked to follow standardized office procedures to help ensure uniformity in the work that you process.

Setting Up Your Work Station

in'te·grate

Information processing, like any other office system, requires the use of proper equipment to produce high-quality documents efficiently. Many information processing systems integrate the use of several pieces of office equipment. The goal of the operator, therefore, is to effectively use the equipment that is available in the system to complete each task. This should be done with the least amount of effort, the greatest degree of accuracy, and the lowest possible cost. This can only be achieved if the operator's work station is set up correctly.

For workers who spend several hours a day working with information processing equipment, it is important that their work stations contain the proper furniture and equipment. Use of proper furniture and equipment insures greater productivity and prevents health problems.

de·tach'a·ble

Furniture and equipment should fit the individual operator's needs. Designers have developed adjustable desks, chairs, keyboards, and screens so that operators can adapt their work stations to fit their own needs. For example, desks can be raised or lowered, while their work surfaces may be tilted slightly. Chairs, too, can be adjusted. Most chairs can be raised or lowered. In addition, the backs on many chairs are now being designed so that they support the lower back. On other chairs, the back rest is movable and should be placed so that it supports the lower back. Like desks and chairs, many word processors and computers can be adapted to the operator. They come with detachable keyboards and adjustable screens. These features provide greater flexibility by allowing the operator to position the keyboard and screen at different angles and varying distances.

Following Standardized Procedures

ver'sa·tile

The most versatile equipment and work stations will not increase productivity if all of the workers are following their own procedures. Productivity requires **standardized procedures** — that is, established guidelines that u'ni·form

are followed by everyone. Generally a company's procedures for performing office tasks are found in its office procedures manual. Manuals help ensure that all employees perform tasks in a uniform, consistent, and correct manner. They allow employees, especially newer employees, to locate answers to questions they may have without having to ask other employees for help.

Standardized procedures set out step-by-step instructions for the carrying out of certain office tasks — for example, the coding of documents. Illustration 12–10 shows how documents keyboarded at the Garland Company are coded. If you were to check the Garland office procedures manual, you would find the following instructions for coding documents:

1. Position your code in place of your reference initials, a double space below the originator's name and title and at the left of the margin.
2. Keyboard your initials in all caps, followed by a diagonal line. Then keyboard the number of the day of the week (1 = Monday, 2 = Tuesday, and so on), a hyphen, and the number of the document (1 = the first document keyboarded that day, 2 = the second document).

As you process information, keep your office procedures manual handy. Your manual lists the standardized procedures adopted by your company. When you are in doubt about the correct format or procedure to follow, refer to your office procedures manual.

If you work for a company that does not have a procedures manual, you can make your own. Begin by developing a file. In your file, keep a separate folder for each office task that is assigned to you. For example, you would have one folder for telephone procedures, another for keyboarding documents, and still another for filing procedures. In each of these folders, file your notes on the procedure you used for completing each task. Also see that samples of any documents needed for performing each task are filed in these folders. Then using these files as guides, you write the step-by-step procedures to be included in your office procedures manual.

Illustration 12–10
Coded document

In your letter you mentioned that you were going to follow up on the proposed contract with Western Industries. Perhaps our new products brochure can help you get this contract finalized.

Good luck on this contract. Your prospects list is challenging, and you should have an exciting year ahead.

Sincerely,

Roger Mercer

Roger Mercer
Sales Manager

FL/2-7

Illustration 12–11
Work requisition form

WORK REQUISITION

Originator *Hatsumi Masuda*

Department *Sales* Extension *3331*

Document Form: ✓ Letter / ___ Memo / ___ Contract / ___ Report / ___ Statistical / ___ Other ________

Stationery: ✓ Letterhead / ___ Printed form / ___ Bond paper / ___ Report size / ___ Legal size / ___ Other ________

Spacing: ✓ Single / ___ Double

No. of Copies: *1* Carbon / ___ Photocopy

Document Retention: *2* Weeks / ___ Permanent

Type of Document: ___ Revision / ___ Draft / ✓ Final

Special Instructions: ________________________________

Maintaining Efficiency

As you follow the procedures for processing information, you must be efficient. Because so much money is invested in equipment, supplies, and staff in an information processing system, many companies take measures to control the work flow. There are two ways of controlling the amount of work flow. One way is through the use of work control forms, such as work requisitions. The other way is through work measurement.

Work control forms The form most commonly used in offices to control the flow of work is the **work requisition form.** This form describes how the document is to be prepared. As you can see in Illustration 12–11, the originator has indicated on the requisition form the type of document being created and any keyboarding instructions.

Work measurement If you work for a company that is developing or making changes in its management information system, you may be asked to keep careful records of the work you perform. An activity log sheet, similar to the one in Illustration 12–12, is used to record the types of tasks you perform and the amount of time you spend on each one. At the end of the week or month, your supervisor or office manager will analyze the information on your daily activity log to see if any improvements can be made. A log of work productivity can help management answer these questions:

1. Is any of the work being performed unnecessarily?
2. Are the employees' special skills being used to the fullest extent?
3. Are work loads evenly distributed?
4. Is the office productive?

Illustration 12–12
Daily log sheet

DAILY LOG SHEET

Date March 23, 19-- Correspondence Secretary D. Bowes

Time In	Tape Number	Originator	Dept.	Type of Document LMRS	Input Form DHPR	Lines	Time Out	Total Time
8:30	2	J. Bishop	Acct.	R	H	137	9:10	40
9:11	2	J. Bishop	Acct.	M	D	11	9:17	6
9:18	5	B. Davis	Sales	L	P	24	9:25	7
9:26	6	M. Morrell	Prod.	R	R	187	10:17	51
10:32	12	C. Bogner	Cust. Rel	L	P	17	10:40	8
10:41	13	H. Masuda	Sales	L	P	23	10:50	9

Maintaining Office Supplies

In Unit 3, you read about the use and organization of supplies for office work. These same supplies are, of course, used in management information systems. However, you will need some additional supplies. Depending upon the type of equipment you are using, you may need to store and use supplies such as printer paper, magnetic disks, and software programs.

Printer paper Printer paper comes in single sheets and in **continuous-form** — that is, sheets with horizontal perforations for easy separation. Printer paper is available in different fiber contents just like other paper. It may be plain or printed with letterheads, form, or memo headings. Envelopes are available as single envelopes or, like paper, in continuous form.

Printer paper is purchased in cartons of 1,000 to 5,000 sheets. Generally it is stored in the carton. In the case of continuous-form paper, it may be fed directly to the printer from the open box or from printout storage racks. The printer paper should be kept neat. You will want to set up the paper so that it feeds easily into the printer and so that the output falls and stacks neatly.

den'si·ty

Magnetic disks Disks may be purchased by the single disk or in a box of ten. To order disks, you must identify the size ($5\frac{1}{4}$ inch or $3\frac{1}{2}$ inch) and the density (single or double). You must also specify whether you want single- or double-sided disks. Double-sided and double-density disks have increased storage capacity.

up'right

When you open a box of disks, you should format all disks so that they are ready for use. Take special care of your disks. Disks should be stored in an upright position in a file box, binder, or case. Always store your disks in a moderate temperature. Excessive heat can warp or melt the disks.

Disks must be labeled clearly so that you can file and retrieve them quickly and easily. Labels can be kept in one of your top desk drawers. Each label should contain the date, the name of the program, and the type of computer. Labels can be kept in one of your top desk drawers so that they are always handy.

back'up

Software programs Your company will purchase the appropriate software for your information processing equipment. Always make a backup copy of the software. Store the original software with its manual in its box or binder in an upright position on a shelf near your equipment.

car'tridge

Printer ribbons Just as you select and store ribbons for a typewriter, you must select and store ribbons for a printer. Ribbons for printers are usually purchased in a cartridge. They may be either film or fabric ribbons and are usually ordered by printer model number. Because ribbons are not changed very often, they may be stored in a central office location or in an out-of-the-way area of your desk.

Print wheels A print wheel is a plastic or metal wheel on which the typeface is arranged. Print wheels are available in a variety of different pitches and type styles. Plastic and metal print wheels are not usually interchangeable due to differences in weight and balance. Therefore, you will want to be sure you are specifying the right type when you order print wheels for your printer. Print wheels should be stored with the printer.

Cleaning kits Many different kinds of cleaning kits are available to help you keep your equipment in good working condition. You should know your equipment well enough that you can choose the correct cleaning equipment and supplies. Your supervisor can help you select the correct cleaning equipment and supplies. It is also important that you establish a regular cleaning schedule. Your supervisor can help you set up an appropriate cleaning schedule. Because cleaning materials will be used only periodically, they should be stored in a bottom desk drawer.

INFORMATION PROCESSING SKILLS

You have just read about management information systems, what they are, and your responsibilities as an information processing worker in such a system. To be successful as an information processing worker, you must have the following four traits:

- accuracy and attention to detail
- skill in using office equipment
- ability to organize work
- flexibility and a willingness to learn

Accuracy and Attention to Detail

If you work around people in information processing, you are bound to hear the phrase "Garbage in, garbage out." This phrase describes what happens when the information put into a computer is incorrect. When this happens, the output is also incorrect. How can this happen? Computers are supposed to be so accurate!

Computers *are* accurate, but they can't think or make judgments, as people can. Take this example: A computer can multiply 786,258 by 1,093,214 over and over a million times and always get the same correct answer. But it won't really be the correct answer if you *meant* to multiply 786,258 by 1,039,214. Because computers can't think or tell when a number looks incorrect, people who work with any information processing equipment must pay special attention to accuracy. They must be careful to record information correctly. This is important whether they are writing it down for someone else to enter or entering it into the computer themselves. They must also be careful to proofread and check their work for errors.

Handwriting Many errors in information processing are caused by poor handwriting. The data entry clerk who keyboards information from the invoice you wrote may not be able to tell if that curved line is a *5* or an *S*. The letter *O* and zero are easily confused when handwritten, as are the numbers *1* and *7*. To distinguish between or among similar characters, you may be asked to slash your zeros (Ø) or cross your 7s (7). This practice will vary from company to company.

When filling out any information processing form, make sure all letters and figures are readable. Remember that the person who keyboards the information has hundreds of forms to process. Fill out the forms neatly, completely, and accurately, so that there will be no questions about any of the information.

Keyboard accuracy Most information processing systems rely on the entry or recording of information through a device such as a keyboard. Care must be taken to enter information accurately. It is important not only to strike the correct key but also to position the information correctly. For example, the number 253 may be read 2,530, 253, 25.3, 2.53, or .253, depending on its position in the layout of information.

Proofreading When information is copied by hand, errors creep in. Modern information processing systems are designed to reduce the manual copying and recording of information, but they can't eliminate it entirely. Even in the most sophisticated systems, at some stage the input is copied, recorded, or keyboarded by hand. The only way to prevent errors from being introduced is to proofread carefully. Make sure you have copied the information correctly from the original. Be especially careful to check numbers to see that they are written in the right order.

Illustration 12–13 Attention to detail is a must in information processing)

Skill in Using Office Equipment

As you read in the last chapter, there are several kinds of equipment that can be used to speed the processing of information. Because most equipment is only as fast or as accurate as its operator, companies look for employees with good skills in operating information processing equipment. To use equipment effectively, you need accuracy, speed, and knowledge of your particular equipment's capabilities.

Employers expect beginning office workers to be skillful in operating the basic types of office equipment. The skills you develop in the classroom can be easily adapted to the specific models used in the office. Once you know the basics, you can find all the information you need to operate many machines in the operating manuals that come with them.

Companies that require skill in operating more specialized equipment generally provide on-the-job training for their employees. This training gives you an opportunity to ask questions as you develop skill in using the equipment. On-the-job training is valuable because you learn correct procedures for the equipment and forms actually used in your job.

Organization

A cluttered desk, poor arrangement of supplies in and on the desk, and awkward placement of equipment reduce a worker's accuracy and productivity. Organize your work area to meet the needs of your particular job activity. Before you begin, assemble the necessary supplies and equipment and position them for efficient use. When you finish, clear your desk of any unnecessary materials and return them to their proper storage place.

Flexibility

It is a fact of life that today's workers face a constantly changing work environment. Advances in technology produce better equipment — faster, more accurate, and easier to operate. Because of the benefits that can be gained from using information processing equipment, it is only natural that business will buy it. And it is also natural that employers will be expected to develop new skills and techniques in using equipment.

The prospect of change generally carries with it a fear of the unknown. Technological changes in your work can make you feel helpless or insecure. You may view the new equipment as a threat to your job because it can perform some work more efficiently than you can. You may resent having to spend more time with a machine and less time with sales representatives, customers, and coworkers.

How can you cope with such changes in your work environment? You can become more flexible by recognizing that automation and mechanization — the increased use of machines and equipment — will benefit you as an office worker. For example:

- New equipment gives you a chance to learn new skills.
- The equipment does boring, repetitive, and routine tasks for you.
- Since the equipment does the routine tasks, you are free to do more planning, preparing, and analyzing of information.
- The use of sophisticated information processing equipment may create new opportunities for advancement and open up new career paths.

Instead of resisting change, the successful office worker looks forward to the opportunities for new challenges in the area of information processing.

CAREER PATHS IN INFORMATION PROCESSING

New technology has created new career opportunities. Office personnel and procedures are being reorganized. Today there is a wide variety of job titles related to information processing systems. As a result of the new technology, there are also more advancement opportunities in a career path.

A worker with information processing skills enjoys a great flexibility of movement from one position to another in a company. This is because a worker can move *laterally* — that is, move across the company from one department to another — as well as up in a company. For example, Joseph Jackson, a high school graduate, is hired for an entry-level position as a clerk typist in the Marketing Department. As Illustration 12–14 shows, Joseph may move up in the company by being promoted to a position as a transcriber in the Marketing Department. A promotion like this may take some time. If, however, Joseph feels that his chance for promotion might come sooner in

Illustration 12–14
Career paths

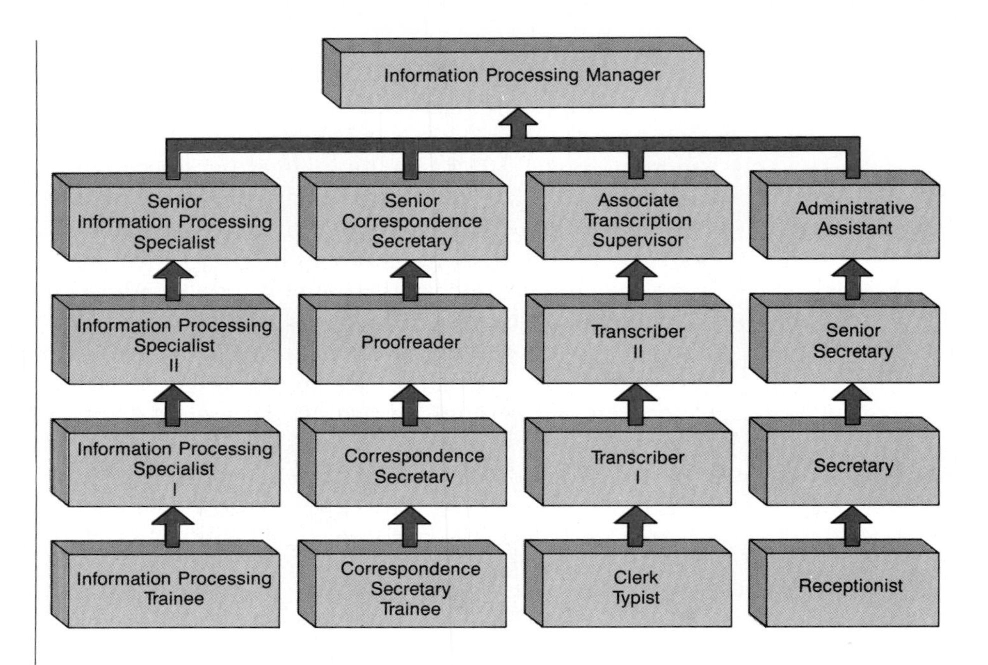

another department, he also has the option of moving laterally across the company. He can do this by accepting a position as a clerk typist with one of the other departments. From this position, he can then move up to other positions in the company.

The listing that follows shows how the information processing movement has increased the number of positions available in just the area of word processing alone. These are just some of the positions that are available in some companies today.

Clerical Specialist	Correspondence Technician
Clerk Typist	Transcriptionist
Proofreader	Technical Typist
Word Processing Operator	Word Processing Supervisor
Technical Writer	Word Processing Trainer
Word Processing Specialist	Word Processing Trainee
Staff Analyst	Secretary

With the number of job titles and job opportunities increasing as a result of the new technology, it is important to think and plan in terms of a career, not just a job. A **job** is just a series of tasks that an employee performs according to his or her position. A **career** is a series of jobs an employee performs in pursuit of his her career goals.

Illustration 12–14 shows career options — that is, a series of jobs leading to specific goals. In Unit 15, you will learn about the specific techniques you can use to plan and direct your career in today's automated offices.

REVIEWING KEY POINTS

1. A management information system is a plan for decision making.
2. The cycle of decision making includes collecting and recording information, processing it, presenting it, analyzing it, making a decision, and reviewing and revising the process.
3. When a work station is set up properly, it can increase productivity and foster good personal health.
4. Productivity at a work station is increased when procedures are standardized and detailed in an office procedures manual.
5. Set procedures for workflow and work measurement help make proper use of equipment and staff.
6. Additional supplies may be needed for MIS equipment; and they must be purchased, stored, and used in an efficient, cost-effective way.
7. Most people who work with information processing equipment share common traits such as attention to accuracy, equipment skill, organizational ability, and flexibility.
8. Information processing equipment and systems have created new job titles and new career paths for today's office workers.

DEVELOPING HUMAN RELATIONS SKILLS

1. Harry DelCupolo works as a word processing operator for the Baker Manufacturing Company. All operators have been advised to consult their supervisors when questions arise concerning work. If the supervisors cannot answer the operator's questions, the supervisors are suppose to contact the originators.

   Harry has been with the company for 10 years. His supervisor has been with the company for only a year. Because his supervisor is so new to the company, Harry feels that his supervisor can't answer his questions. So, Harry doesn't ask his supervisor for help; instead, he asks his coworkers or the originator. His coworkers wouldn't mind so much, but Harry interrupts their work to ask them questions.

   a. Why doesn't Harry want to follow the standardized procedures set out by the company?
   b. What would you say to Harry to convince him to follow the procedures that have been set up?
   c. Should you say something to your supervisor?

IMPROVING COMMUNICATION SKILLS

Refer to Appendix A 1.36–1.37.

1. On a separate sheet of paper, keyboard the sentences as they appear here, inserting underscores as needed.
   a. An article titled The Future of DOS appeared in the May issue of High-Tech World.
   b. She said no, and she meant it!
   c. Business Communication: An Administrative Approach is the title of the new book.
   d. The instructor told us never to touch the exposed area of the disk.
   e. The books we were asked to read are as follows: Job Burnout, Developing Ideas, and Internal Modems.
   f. Do it now!
2. Using plain paper, compose and keyboard a letter to the journal publisher you wrote to in Improving Your Communication Skills, Activity #2, in Chapter 2. Keyboard the letter in block format with open punctuation. Use the subject line: Subscription to (use name of journal). In your letter explain that after receiving three issues of the magazine, you find the magazine does not meet your information processing needs. Use a bad news format to tell the publisher to cancel your subscription and refund the unused portion of your subscription.

BUILDING PROBLEM-SOLVING SKILLS

1. Your supervisor compiled the following figures on the production of the information processing operators. For each operator, compute the lines per hour and the percentage of error.

IP PRODUCTION REPORT
March 22, 19 – –
Report # 32401-3

Operator	Lines	Hours Available	Lines with Errors
01 Dufour	8,190	39	8
02 Kraus	7,300	36.5	4
03 Riley	5,104	22	7
04 Ellis	5,781	23.5	0
05 Tisch	3,720	15	2

2. Using the daily log sheet for D. Bowes on page 483, answer the following questions:
   a. How many lines did D. Bowes keyboard?

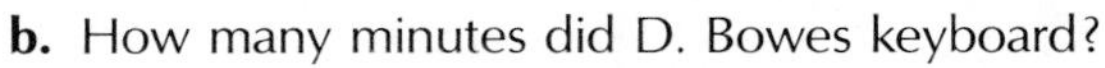

b. How many minutes did D. Bowes keyboard?

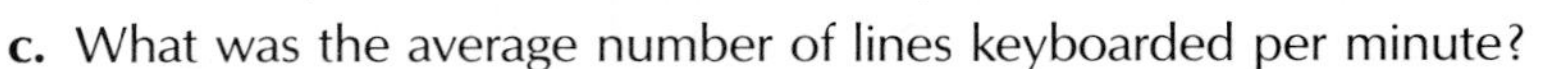

c. What was the average number of lines keyboarded per minute?

Activities 1 and 2 can be done on information processing equipment.

APPLYING OFFICE SKILLS

1. A position is open in the information processing center for an information processing trainee. Information about this position is to be posted on the bulletin board in your company. Keyboard the following job description in an attractive format. If you are using information processing equipment, print five copies. If you are using a typewriter, make four carbon copies. There must be a copy of the posting on each of the five bulletin boards in your company.

Information Processing Trainee

Entry-level position for the right person with 0-12 months' information processing experience. Trainee will perform routine transcription and manipulation of text from various types of source information (dictation, handwritten, etc.). Trainee will be required to proofread own work and perform light secretarial duties.

Typical Responsibilities

Keyboarding correspondence and reports
Transcribing dictated material
Proofreading all keyboarded work
Formatting correspondence and reports
Handling revisions of keyboarded work

2. Tony Garcia dictated a report to be keyboarded in final copy. As you transcribe the report, you find that many words are garbled and there is a lot of static on the tape. Your supervisor recommends that you keyboard the report as well as you can in rough-draft form. He also asks you to write a memo to Mr. Garcia explaining that there is something wrong with the tape, offering to rekeyboard it as soon as he proofreads the draft and makes the corrections. Keyboard your memo on the memo form in your workbook or on plain paper.

CHAPTER 4

DICTATION AND TRANSCRIPTION PROCEDURES

When it's your responsibility to process words in an information processing system, it is especially important to have good dictation and transcription techniques. The company for which you work will expect you to have the skills and work habits needed to produce documents with speed and accuracy. Of course, good keyboarding skills are necessary. But an understanding of the procedures used for developing and keyboarding office documents is also needed if you are to be a productive worker.

As you study this chapter, you will find answers to the following questions:

- Why are good dictation and transcription skills important to information processing workers?
- What dictation and transcription skills are needed for success?
- How can following standardized procedures for dictation and transcription make work easier in an information processing system?
- What do the following terms mean: **listening, transcription, dictation?**

USING DICTATION AND TRANSCRIPTION SKILLS

As you read earlier in this unit, the material you are asked to transcribe may come to you in a variety of forms. In many offices, the originator may dictate using dictation equipment. If you take shorthand, the originator may dictate while you record the dictation in shorthand.

Advantages of Using Dictation Equipment

Dictation is more efficient and less costly when dictation equipment is used. With dictation equipment, the originator is the only one involved in the dictation process. This frees the transcriber to perform other tasks within the office. Furthermore, the originator can dictate whenever time is available. If the dictation process is interrupted, it can be stopped and continued later. With a quick review of the material already dictated, the originator is ready to continue. And, if a portable or remote-control system is available, the originator can dictate anywhere, even at home after hours.

Advantages of Using Shorthand

The use of dictation equipment is encouraged in many companies with information processing systems. Even so, many companies still prefer to hire employees who are trained in one of the shorthand systems. There are many opportunities during the workday to use your shorthand skills. Shorthand is useful for recording minutes of meetings, telephone messages, and instructions. Shorthand is frequently more efficient than tape recording a discussion because only relevant information is recorded by the worker.

rel'e·vant

Furthermore, there are employers who want an employee with shorthand skills because they do not like to use dictation equipment. Instead, they prefer working with an individual who can assist them by supplying appropriate words or phrases. Other originators may dictate only key ideas and ask their employees to compose the document.

SKILLS NEEDED FOR SUCCESS

To be successful on the job, there are some basic dictation and transcription skills you should possess.

Skills Needed for Taking Dictation

If your job requires you to take shorthand, you should develop your shorthand skills to their fullest. In addition, you must be able to listen carefully and remain flexible to your supervisor's needs.

flex'i·ble

Listening Listening is an important skill that most people can develop or improve. You may have been told "you didn't listen!" when you know you have heard every word. We *hear* most noises and conversations around us — but we don't always listen. **Listening** involves not only hearing but *thinking* about what you hear.

eve'ry·day

Flexibility Learn to be flexible to the needs of the originators in your office. The originator and the information processing worker must work as a team to produce the work necessary to carry on everyday business. There will be times when you must be ready to take dictation at a moment's notice because documents must be prepared immediately. Employers value a worker who can remain calm and complete work accurately in such situations.

Skills Needed for Transcription

Transcription, the process of keyboarding documents from dictated material, requires more than simply keyboarding the originator's words. Whether you transcribe machine or shorthand dictation, you must have good language skills and pay close attention to details. When transcribing from a machine, you also need good listening skills and knowledge of the equipment.

Punctuation Very few originators dictate the punctuation marks used in documents. Listen carefully for a slight pause in dictation to determine the end of a sentence. A shorter pause may indicate that a comma or a semicolon is needed. Use punctuation marks correctly to give the intended meaning. See how the placement of a comma can change the meaning of a sentence.

Nancy used the computer software and printer.
Nancy used the computer, software, and printer.

In the first sentence Nancy used two items. In the second sentence Nancy used three items. As you can see, even a misplaced comma can change the meaning of a message.

Grammar Knowledge of grammar is necessary for anyone who works in an office, but especially for information processing workers. The originator may dictate *was* when the correct verb is *were,* or may dictate an incomplete sentence. You will be expected to make the necessary corrections as you transcribe. Most originators will appreciate your making minor changes to the dictation. Before you make any changes, though, be sure you are correct. A reference manual is useful for anyone who transcribes.

cap'i·tal·ize

Capitalization Very few originators tell you what words to capitalize as they dictate; you are expected to know and apply the rules of capitalization as you transcribe. Of course, you always capitalize the first word of a sentence, important words in a title, and all proper nouns. However, there are other rules of capitalization you must follow. For instance, compass points are capitalized when they refer to a specific section of the country (as in "back East"). However, they are not capitalized when they are used simply to indicate direction.

re·flect'

Spelling Good spelling skills are a must for the information processing worker. If you are unsure of the correct spelling of any word, look it up in a dictionary or word book. A word that is not spelled correctly detracts from the message being sent. Misspellings reflect poorly on you, the originator, and the company. If you are not naturally a good speller, make a special effort to improve your spelling skills.

Word choice When you are taking dictation or transcribing material, you must be able to select the correct word to use. Many words sound alike or very similar. A word written in shorthand may represent several similar-sounding words. You will be expected to choose the correct word for the intended message. When you are not sure which word should be used, refer to your dictionary. If the dictionary doesn't help you determine the correct word, ask the originator.

con'cen·trat·ing

Proofreading Always proofread keyboarded work carefully. Don't depend on "feeling" errors as you keyboard. If you are keyboarding and concentrating on the message, you may not realize that you have made an error. To proofread efficiently, begin by checking to see that all material is properly formatted on the page. Then proofread for keyboarding errors. Finally, read through the material for understanding. This step involves more than just reading each word. It involves reading for meaning.

Attention to details Learn to pay attention to details. While you are keyboarding, you may notice that the originator has called the addressee one name in the salutation and another in the body of the letter. The price quoted for an item may be wrong, or the arithmetic used to figure the total price may be incorrect. An alert employee will catch such errors and correct them. An employee who does not pay attention to details will probably not discover the errors until it is too late to correct them.

PROCEDURES FOR GIVING DICTATION

Most people speak faster than they write or keyboard. Unfortunately, it is difficult to speak and organize your thoughts at the same time. However, being able to organize your thoughts as you dictate a message is a valuable skill. The key to **dictation**, the process of giving material orally to another for transcription, is to plan what you want to say. This can be done by preparing a written outline. It is the most efficient way for an originator to transmit a message. Dictating to a shorthand writer or dictation equipment is must faster than preparing the document in longhand.

Machine Dictation

pro·mot'ed

As a beginning worker in an information processing center, you will probably not need dictation skill. As you gain experience, however, you may be promoted to a position that requires that you coordinate the work in the information processing center. Eventually, you may be promoted to the position of supervisor. People who work in supervisory positions in information processing frequently train the word originators to use the system. Training often includes correct techniques for giving dictation using dictation equipment. There is some basic information that should be given when dictating. This information includes:

1. The dictator's name, department, and date.
2. The type of document (such as letter or report, draft or final copy).
3. The number of copies needed.
4. Special mailing and handling instructions, such as *Registered Mail* and *Confidential.*
5. The addressee's name and address, as well as the spelling of any unusual names or technical terms.
6. The appropriate complimentary closing.
7. Correspondence relating to the dictation.

Shorthand Dictation

As a beginning employee, you probably will not have an opportunity to dictate to someone who records the dictation in shorthand. However, if you should become an administrative secretary, you may find that your responsibilities include handling routine documents. If your job includes dictating to a shorthand writer, you will find the following suggestions helpful:

1. Watch the shorthand writer. This helps you pace the dictation to the writer's speed. If the shorthand writer hesitates, this is a signal to slow down or perhaps spell a word that is confusing or technical.
2. Give the shorthand writer the material that relates to the dictation being given. The name, address, and other printed information can be copied rather than dictated.
3. Avoid reading paragraphs from related documents being answered. Instead, give the material to the shorthand writer. It is more efficient to keyboard directly from the original.
4. Speak in a natural tone. Pause to indicate the end of a sentence.
5. Give any specific instructions that will help in the transcribing process.
6. Give the shorthand writer an opportunity to ask questions about each item before starting to dictate the next item.

sched'ule

7. Try to schedule a certain time each day for dictation. The ideal dictation time is when there are the fewest interruptions so that time is not wasted. A regular dictation period helps the shorthand writer plan the day's work.

Illustration 12–15
Taking dictation in shorthand

PROCEDURES FOR TAKING DICTATION

Most employers who require shorthand skill expect you to be able to write at least 80 words a minute. Originators dictate at an average rate of 80 words a minute. However, there are times when dictation may be faster or slower. If your shorthand skill does not allow you to take dictation at 80 words a minute, you may have difficulty recording all of the dictation.

When your job responsibilities include taking dictation, you must be flexible enough to change your work schedule to fit the originator's schedule. Keep a shorthand notebook, pens, and a colored pencil ready at all times. Many people who take shorthand use a rubber band to keep all of their transcribed notes attached to the cover of the shorthand notebook. In this way, the notebook opens to clean pages. Most people prefer to use a pen for writing shorthand because ink flows smoothly. A colored pencil is useful for marking corrections and insertions because the marks are easy to see.

It is a good idea to date your shorthand notes either at the bottom of the first page or at the end of the dictation. If you need to refer to the notes in the future, you will know when the dictation was given. If you take dictation from more than one person, label the notes with the originator's name or use a different shorthand notebook for each person's dictation.

When you take dictation, select a place that allows you to write comfortably. You may prefer to sit by a desk or table so that you can rest your notebook and arm on a firm surface. However, you might be just as comfortable holding a shorthand notebook on your lap as you write. While the originator is dictating, pay close attention to what is being said. It is easier to transcribe your notes when you understand the intent of the message. If you fall behind in dictation or do not understand what is being said, politely tell the originator. It is better to ask the originator to speak more slowly or repeat a sentence than to miss parts of the dictation.

If the originator you work with usually makes a lot of changes, you may find it helpful to take dictation in the left column of your notebook. Use the right column for changes or special instructions. Avoid flipping the shorthand pad to write on both sides of the paper, because it takes time and makes your notes more difficult to transcribe. When you have written on the front side of all the pages, simply turn the book over and write on the clean side.

TRANSCRIPTION PROCEDURES

Transcription skills are essential whether you transcribe from a machine or from shorthand notes. However, the procedures differ slightly when transcribing from a machine and when transcribing from shorthand notes.

Machine Transcription

When you are ready to transcribe, check the indicator slip. This slip is placed in a special holder attached to the front of most dictating machines. As shown in Illustration 12–16, the indicator slip allows the dictator to indicate the length of each item dictated and all corrections that need to be made.

During dictation, the dictator indicates the length of each item by placing marks on the slip. A glance at these markings indicates the approximate length of each item. In many offices, margins are set for the standard six-inch line. Adjustments for length are then made in vertical placement. For example, when transcribing a short letter, you would keyboard the date line lower on the page.

stan'dard

Once you have set your margins, you are ready to load the tape into the machine. Then adjust the volume, speed, and tone controls to a comfortable level. Learn to work the foot pedal so that you can keyboard at a continuous pace. If you do not understand a word or phrase, use the reverse on the foot pedal to have the word or phrase repeated. Most transcribing machines have a control to determine how much dictation will be repeated when the reverse pedal is used. You can set the control so that only one or two words or sentences are repeated.

A good transcriber listens to all corrections before beginning to transcribe. This saves time and additional corrections. Special instructions such as the number of copies needed may also be given by the originator. These

Illustration 12–16
Transcription machine with indicator slip

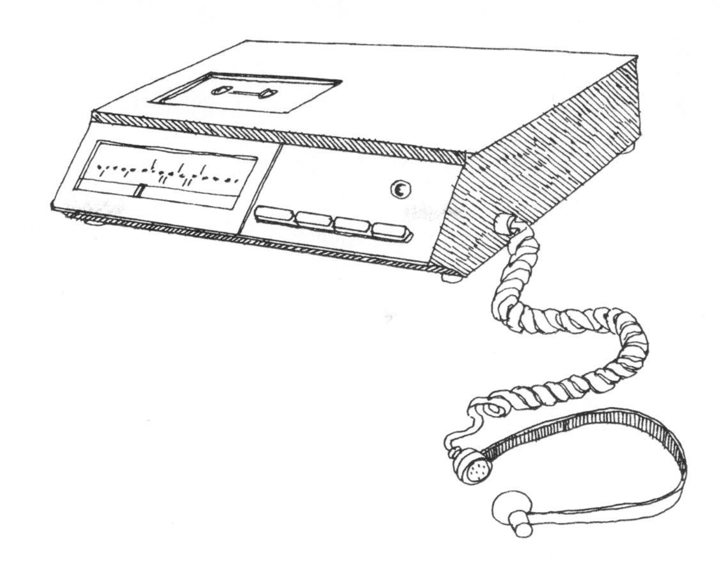

instructions are usually dictated at the beginning of the tape. As you gain practice using transcription equipment, you will learn to listen ahead so that you keyboard each item correctly the first time.

Shorthand Transcription

Before starting to transcribe your shorthand notes, review them carefully. Insert punctuation and check capitalization and spelling. Spell out unfamiliar words in your notes. When you begin keyboarding, you will be able to keyboard without hesitating. By reviewing your notes before keyboarding, you will also be reminded of special instructions on mailing, copies, and enclosures. If necessary, write out these special instructions as a reminder to yourself.

pri·or′i·ty

Determine the priority of your work. Those documents that are more important or need to be put into the mail early should be transcribed first.

Once you have set the order of keyboarding, you can determine placement and margins. It is important to arrange each document attractively on the page. Looking at the amount of space occupied by your shorthand notes will give you a clue to the length of the document. With practice, you will learn to be able to judge the margins for all documents.

After you have transcribed your notes, draw a line through them so that you know you have transcribed them. Some firms store full shorthand notebooks for future reference. If your company does file notebooks, write your name on the cover, along with the beginning and ending dates of the dictation recorded within the notebook. Shorthand notes of confidential information must be protected just as carefully as the transcribed notes. Keep them in a locked file cabinet or desk drawer — never on top of your desk.

REVIEWING KEY POINTS

1. It is less expensive to use dictation equipment than to use shorthand.
2. Dictation equipment frees the transcriber to perform other tasks during dictation and makes it possible for the originator to dictate any time or place.
3. Some originators prefer to dictate to a shorthand writer.
4. Very few originators dictate punctuation or capitalization.
5. Dictation is the process of giving material orally to another person for transcription.
6. A written outline is the best plan for dictation.
7. Before beginning to transcribe from either machine dictation or from shorthand notes, a transcriber listens to the tape or reads through the shorthand notes.
8. Keyboarding final draft copy from dictation is a good transcription habit.

DEVELOPING HUMAN RELATIONS SKILLS

1. Margie Harris was hired for an entry-level secretarial position. As her experience with the department increased, she was given the opportunity to use her shorthand skills. In her first dictation session, Margie was a little nervous, even though her shorthand skills were good. The originator talked rapidly, gave all punctuation marks, and spelled words that Margie knew. Margie got most of the dictation; she felt she could fill in the words she had missed. However, she was irritated at the dictation of all the punctuation marks and the spelling of words that she knew. Margie wonders whether she'll be able to continue to take dictation from this originator.
   - **a.** Should Margie have said anything to the originator about the speed of the dictation? Explain.
   - **b.** Should Margie indicate to her originator that giving all of the punctuation and spelling a lot of words is unnecessary? Explain.
2. Willard Olson is a correspondence specialist. He transcribes the dictation of several originators, usually in final-draft format. However, there is one originator that drives Willard crazy. Even though Willard transcribes this originator's dictation perfectly, the originator never fails to make a change in the dictation. Willard finally asked the originator if it would be more efficient for him to prepare a rough draft of the dictation since changes were made frequently in the transcribed material. The originator found this to be an

irritating suggestion. Final-draft copy was what the originator wanted. It's true Willard can make changes in the transcribed copy easily with the information processing equipment. However, Willard feels that the originator should listen to the dictation and make all changes before it is sent to the information processing center.

a. Is it Willard's responsibility to make suggestions to the originator? Explain.

b. What choices does Willard have now?

IMPROVING COMMUNICATION SKILLS

Refer to Appendix A 1.36–1.37.

1. Keyboard the following sentences on a separate sheet of paper. Insert underscores where needed.

   a. Your letter asking about Office Dynamics, the book by Dr. James, was sent to our office for response.

   b. You'll be glad to know that the musical composition is named Laura.

   c. If you had followed directions, your computer would work.

   d. We are proud to announce that the Daily Herald is 50 years old.

   e. So you won't miss an issue of Women in Business, check "Yes" on the subscription renewal card and mail it today.

   f. We want you to order now.

   g. The Professional Secretary's Handbook is so popular that we have had to reorder our stock.

   h. On the same day we receive your payment, we will mail your copy of the book on office procedures.

2. Using the letterhead stationery in your workbook or plain paper, compose and keyboard a letter to the Barker Office Supplies Company, 37 Brook Lane, Houston, TX 77089. In your letter, order the following transcription supplies. Ask that the items be shipped parcel post and that your company be billed for the full amount.

   12 electronic high-yield ribbons at $1.85 each (Catalogue # L40121)
   3 letter gothic print wheels at $20.00 each (Catalogue # L55756)
   4 flip files for disks at $17.95 each (Catalogue #L59153)

BUILDING PROBLEM-SOLVING SKILLS

1. There are seven transcribers in the information processing center. For each of the transcribers, the number of lines produced during a timed transcription are shown in the table on the next page. On plain paper, show your calculations and answers to the questions that follow.

a. What is the total number of minutes used for transcription by all operators?

b. What is the total number of lines transcribed?

c. What is the average number of lines produced?

d. What percenage of the total number of lines produced did Operator 3 keyboard?

e. What percentage of the total number of lines produced did Operator 6 keyboard?

MACHINE TRANSCRIPTION

Operator	Minutes	Lines
1	10	12
2	35	55
3	180	203
4	5	11
5	9	15
6	24	47
7	18	25

2. Transcribers must be skilled in following instructions. Copy the square shown here on a separate sheet of paper. Then test your problem-solving skills by placing numbers from 1 to 16 so that each vertical, horizontal, and one diagonal column equals 34. Use *all* the numbers from 1 to 16 (each only once). Four numbers have already been placed in the square to get you started.

		3	
5			
			12
	14		

APPLYING OFFICE SKILLS

Activities 1 and 2 can be done on information processing equipment.

1. To save reference time in transcription, prepare a listing of the two-letter state abbreviations that appear on the last page of this book. Use an appropriate format. Title your listing "State Abbreviations."

2. Using the letterhead in your workbook or plain paper, keyboard the following letter in block format. Set your margins for a six-inch line. Backspace and keyboard over any errors you make, just as you would on information processing equipment. Record your beginning and ending

times. Then count the lines in the body of the letter. Divide the total lines by your keyboarding time to compute your lines per minute.

Mrs. Emily Doran / 2133 Wilkes Boulevard / Seattle, WA 98168 / Dear Mrs. Doran / (¶) I will be happy to meet with you on Wednesday, May 12, at 2:00 P.M. at your office to demonstrate our new word processor. The new word processor can perform more functions than any other models presently on the market. (¶) If you would like, please schedule all of your operators to attend the demonstration. I will answer any questions you may have. I will also leave the word processor in your office for a week so that you can test it using your work. (¶) I'm looking forward to seeing you Tuesday afternoon. Sincerely / Lee Chin / Sales Representative.

Saving Time and Money

1. Keep samples of work produced on any dictation, transcription, or information processing equipment that is not working properly. These samples will help the service representative determine what is wrong with the equipment.
2. Make an alphabetical list of words that you find difficult to spell. You can find the correct spelling of a word faster in your own notebook list than you can in a dictionary or word book.
3. Make a written list of any special instructions your originator gives you at the beginning of dictation.
4. Transcribe machine dictation in rough-draft format if you make an error that cannot be corrected. Then keyboard a correct copy from your draft.
5. Develop your own shorthand abbreviations for frequently used terms. For instance, a legal secretary may use *C/C* for *Clerk of Court, C/R* for *County of Richland,* and so forth. A secretary in an insurance agency may use *d/c* or *dc* for *date of claim* and *cp* for *cancellation of policy.*
6. Use a standardized code to identify all documents processed in your office.
7. Prevent loss and speedup retrieval of documents by storing them in the electronic files of your computer.

PROFESSIONAL INSIGHTS

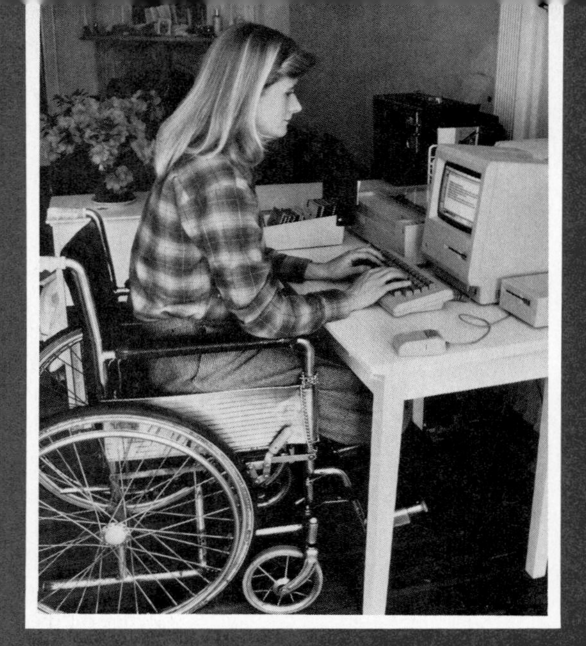

TELECOMMUTING

Today staying home from the office does not always mean the same thing as having a day off from work. There is a growing trend in business today to allow workers to spend at least part of the work week telecommuting—that is, using computers and telecommunications equipment to work at home. Some day many of us will be able to "go to work" without leaving home.

The technology that makes telecommuting possible is so new that commuting by computer is not yet a widespread practice. However, by the year 2000 up to 20 percent of the workforce will take advantage of various link-ups of personal computers, communication equipment, and facsimile transmitters to work at home full time or part time.

Telecommuting has advantages for both employers and employees. Employers can save on costs for office space, utilities, and lunch rooms. Employees can often get more done at home in less time. Also, when employees have flexibility as to when and where they work, they feel better, and employers have fewer worries about employee dissatisfaction.

Telecommuting is not without its problems, however. Staying at home eliminates the customary interaction and sharing of ideas with coworkers. We will probably never become a nation of "computer commuters." Interacting with others will remain an important part of working. However, telecommuting is here to stay, and the flexibility and opportunities that it creates are likely to have a positive effect on the work world.

1. What other advantages of telecommuting can you think of for employees?
2. Unions have opposed the trend toward working at home. Why do you think this is so? Should working at home be regulated by the government? Explain.

UNIT 13

FINANCIAL SYSTEMS

- Banking Services
- Order Processing and Inventory Control
- Payment Procedures
- Payroll Procedures

CHAPTER 1

BANKING SERVICES

All businesses keep cash on hand, either in cash registers or in petty cash funds. However, businesses keep most of their money in checking accounts at banks. When a company deposits cash in its checking account, the amount in that account increases. When the company writes checks against the account, the amount decreases. Deposit slips and checks are the records used to keep track of transactions affecting the amount of money in a checking account.

Your role in performing banking activities and keeping records will depend on the size of the company that you work for. If you work for a small company, you may be responsible for all or some of these activities. In a large company, you may not be involved in these activities at all, since they will be handled by the employees in the accounting department. However, because all businesses use the services of commercial banks, you will be expected to understand basic banking services and procedures even if you are not directly responsible for handling them.

As you study this chapter, you will find answers to the following questions:

- What procedures should you follow for opening, using, and making deposits in a checking account?
- What are the three types of check endorsements, and what does each mean?
- What is the procedure for reconciling a bank statement?
- What do the following terms mean: **signature card, checkbook register, payee, stop-payment request, blank endorsement, restrictive endorsement, full endorsement, bank statement, reconcile, Electronic Funds Transfer System (EFTS)?**

CHECKING ACCOUNTS

Most businesses and individuals pay their bills by check. Banks issue checks to customers who have accounts with them. The check serves as an order to the bank to pay a stated amount of money from the customer's account to the person or firm named on the check. A checking account is a safe, convenient, and accurate way to manage money. There are three main advantages to using a checking account instead of using cash:

in·sured'

- Safety — Cash can be lost, stolen, or destroyed. If a check is lost, stolen, or destroyed, it can be rewritten. Also, money kept in a checking account is insured by the federal government.
- Convenience — Checks can be sent through the mail safely, whereas cash cannot. Therefore, you can pay bills by mail instead of in person.
- Accuracy — Checks serve as accurate sources of information for recording payments in company books. Also, canceled checks provide proof of payment if questions arise later about whether bills have been paid.

can'celed

Banks usually charge a fee or service charge for checking account service. A bank may charge a monthly service fee that is based on the average amount of money kept in an account. It may charge a fee for each check written on the account during the month. Or it may charge a fixed monthly service charge. The type of service charge depends on the type of account that is opened with the bank. Some banks do not charge a service fee if a minimum balance is kept in an account.

Accounts are usually set up according to *who* can write checks against them. There are three basic types of checking accounts:

- Personal — only one person may write checks against the account
- Joint — two or more persons may write checks against the account; for example, husband and wife
- Business — one or more persons may write checks against the account of a company or organization

The banking procedures discussed in this chapter are used in all three types of checking accounts.

Opening an Account

ap·prov'al

Opening a checking account is easy. First the type of checking account must be selected. Then everyone who will be writing checks on the account must sign a signature card. The **signature card** gives the bank approval to cash checks that are signed by any person whose name and signature are on the card. Illustration 13–1 on the top of the next page shows a signature card. Notice it contains the information listed below the illustration.

Illustration 13–1 Signature card for a checking account

A/C NAME COM Consultants — A/C # 565-851

TYPE OF ACCOUNT: CHECKING ☐ SAVINGS ☐ SAVINGS PLUS ☐ C/D ☐

OWNERSHIP: PARTNERSHIP ☐ CORPORATION ☐ CLUB/ASSN. ☐ PROPRIETOR ☐ FIDUCIARY ☐

THE BANK IS HEREBY AUTHORIZED TO RECOGNIZE THE SIGNATURE(S) SUBSCRIBED BELOW IN THE PAYMENT OF FUNDS OR THE TRANSACTION OF ANY BUSINESS FOR THIS ACCOUNT. ALL TRANSACTIONS SHALL BE GOVERNED BY APPLICABLE LAWS AND THE BANK'S TERMS (COPY ACKNOWLEDGED AS RECEIVED HEREWITH) THAT PERTAIN TO THE TYPE OF ACCOUNT AND STYLE OF OWNERSHIP INDICATED ON THIS CARD. REFER TO RESOLUTION FILE FOR AUTHORIZATION OF SIGNATURES.

SIGNATURES REQUIRED 3

OFFICE:

OTHER SERVICES: CA ☐ CL ☐ PTD ☐ ICD ☐ SA ☐ CD ☐ SP ☐ SD ☐

TITLE

1 Kris Mallory
AND OR
2 James Stein
AND OR
3 Matthew Zorn
AND OR
4
AND OR
5
AND OR
6

500 SIG (11/72) —

DATE OPENED	INITIAL DEPOSIT	ACCOUNT OPENED BY	INCORPORATED IN	SIGNATURE AUTHORITY DATED
1/15/8–	550.00	K. Mallory		1/15/8–

ADDRESS Castlegate Professional Building — NO. YRS. 1 — PHONE 844-5000
100 Castle Drive — T/A #
Gainesville, FL — ZIP 32601 — HOLD ☐

BUSINESS COM Consultants
INTRODUCED BY

PREVIOUS ADDRESS — IF PRESENT LESS THAN 3 YRS.	CITY STATE	NO. YRS.
32 Dover House	Gainesville, FL	3

OTHER COMMENTS

BANK REFERENCES

NAME OF BANK	ADDRESS	TYPE ACCT.
Riverside Savings	43 River Road, Gainesville, FL	Savings

- name, address, and telephone number of the business or individual
- date account is opened and by whom
- references
- type of account
- authorized signatures for checks

au'thor·ized

Those who write checks against the account must sign the checks exactly the way they signed their names on the signature card.

Opening a business checking account requires that additional forms be completed in order to meet government information requirements. As an office worker, you may be asked to prepare these forms. Once you have completed these forms, have them signed by the person or persons authorized to write checks for the company. Keep copies of all forms in the office files.

check'book

Selecting the type of checkbook to be used and depositing an amount of money in the account are the last two steps in opening a checking account.

Illustration 13–2 Checkbook register for recording checks and deposits

DATE 19—	CHECK NO.	DESCRIPTION OF CHECK (OR DEPOSIT)	DEPOSITS (Add)	CHECKS (Subtract)	✓	BALANCE	CHECK FEE (IF ANY)
Balance Brought Forward →						550 —	
2/1	1	Florida Light & Power (utilities)		62 50		487 50	
2/1	2	Bennett Supply Co.		325 00		162 50	
2/10	3	UPS		12 90		149 60	
2/15		Deposit	300 00			449 60	

COM Consultants
100 Castle Drive
Gainesville, FL 32601
Phone 844-5000

No. 004

63-068
631

_____________ 19___

PAY TO THE ORDER OF _______________________ $ ________

_______________________________ DOLLARS

FIRST NATIONAL BANK

MEMO ______________ ______________

⑆0631⑆⑈0068⑆ 0100 565851⑈

Selecting a Checkbook

Checks usually come in a padded form with 25 or more checks to a pad. Numbers identifying the bank and the account number are printed on each check in magnetic ink. The magnetic ink permits electronic sorting and processing by MICR (Magnetic Ink Character Recognition) equipment. Some banks provide checks printed with the company's name and account number free of charge. If the company's address and telephone number are also to appear on the checks, then the bank usually charges the company for the printing. This charge is automatically deducted, or subtracted, from the account by the bank. Then, at the end of the month the company is notified of this charge by the bank.

de·duct'ed

Banks usually have many colors and styles of checks and checkbook covers to choose from. There are also several types of checkbook registers available. The **checkbook register** is a form used to record the date, amount, and purpose of each check written. Deposits are also recorded on the register. The checkbook register may be a separate booklet, which fits into the checkbook cover as shown in Illustration 13–2. Or, it may consist of stubs at the ends or tops of the checks.

Illustration 13–3
A correctly written check

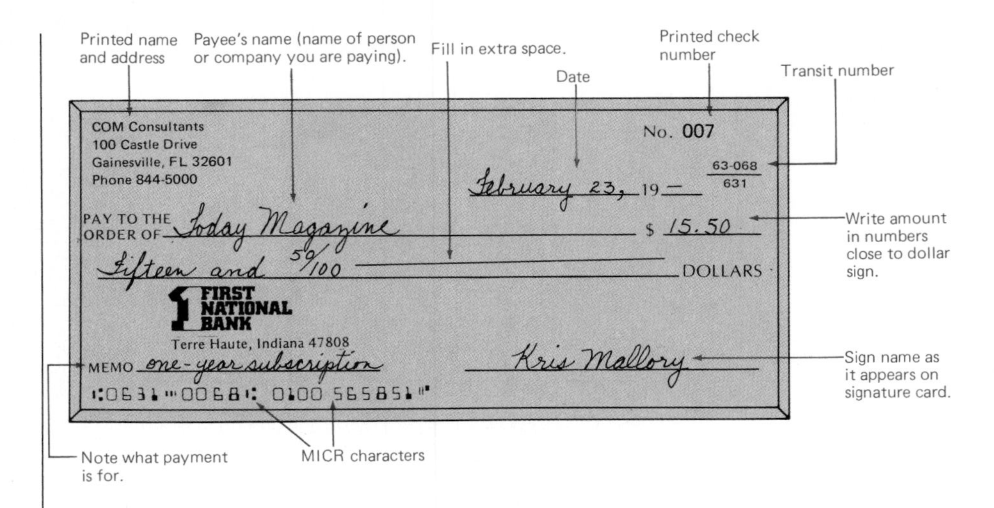

Writing a Check

Because checks are a form of payment, you need to treat them as carefully as you would cash. Always complete all of the information for which there is space on the check. Look at the check in Illustration 13–3 and notice how it is filled out. There are four safeguards to observe when writing a check:

1. Fill out the check register *before* you write the check to make sure you have a record of the transaction.
2. Always use ink, a typewriter, or a check writer to prevent anyone from changing what you write on the check.
3. Use a line to fill in any extra space after the name of the **payee** (the person or business to whom the check is written) and the amount of the check. Filling in this space prevents anyone from adding information.
4. Sign your name *after* you have filled in the rest of the information.

pay·ee'

If you make a mistake, do not erase or try to correct it. Instead, write *Void* across the front of the check, remove it from the checkbook, and file it.

Stopping Payment on Checks

On occasion, it may be necessary to ask the bank to stop payment on a check. A **stop-payment request** is a request that the bank not process a check after it has been written and submitted as payment to someone. A company might stop payment on a check if the check gets lost in the mail, for example. Payment might be stopped if the service or item paid for by check is faulty. For example, suppose your supervisor arranges to have a computer terminal installed in your office. If the terminal is not installed properly, or if the equipment turns out to be defective, the company that installed it should correct the problem immediately. If the computer company does not correct

fault'y

the problem, your supervisor may request that the bank stop payment on the check. Stopping payment on the check makes it possible for your company to withhold payment until the computer company gives your company satisfactory service.

If your supervisor tells you to make a stop-payment request, first call the bank and give a description of the check. Include the date it was written, the check number, the name of the person or company it was made out to, and the account number. If the check has not been processed at the time of the stop-payment call, the bank will start the necessary procedures. In addition, the bank usually requires that a form be filled out as a record of the stop-payment request. Most banks will charge a special fee for processing a stop-payment request.

Making Deposits

de·pos'it

en·dorse'

An addition of money to a bank account is called a *deposit*. To ensure that the bank records the deposit in the correct account, a depositor must fill out a deposit slip and endorse all checks.

Deposit slips Banks provide their customers with personalized deposit slips similar to the one shown in Illustration 13–4. These slips are usually printed with the customer's name and account number. Blank deposit slips are usually available in the bank lobby as well. Follow these steps to prepare a deposit slip:

1. If you are using a blank deposit slip, keyboard or write in ink the company name, the date, and your account number. On personalized deposit slips, you need keyboard or write only the date.

Illustration 13–4
Deposit slip for a checking account

DEPOSIT TICKET

COM Consultants

DATE *March 1,* 19 —

FIRST NATIONAL BANK
Terre Haute, Indiana 47808

CURRENCY		17	00
COIN		4	65
CHECKS	LIST SINGLY 63-420	16	20
TOTAL		37	85

⑆0631⑈00681⑆ 0100 565851⑈

ITEMS CREDITED SUBJECT TO VERIFICATION AND DEPOSIT AGREEMENT OF THIS BANK

2. Count all bills and coins; count them again to verify your total.

- Turn all bills face up and group like bills together — ones, fives, tens, twenties, etc.

de·nom·i·na'tion

- Put coins of the same denomination together and count them. If you are depositing large sums of coins, put them in the wrappers available from the bank. Wrappers are available for pennies, nickels, dimes, quarters, and half dollars. Write or stamp the company name or your name on each wrapper.

cur'ren·cy

- Write in ink the total amount of currency (bills and coins) in the appropriate spaces on the deposit slip.

3. List each check and its amount on the deposit slip.

- Be sure that each check is endorsed for deposit (endorsement is discussed in the next section).
- Identify each check on the deposit slip by transit number and by name (for local banks) or by city and state (for out-of-state banks).

4. Add the figures. Write them clearly and check all totals.

You can make deposits in person, by mail, through night deposit, or by automatic teller machines. Most banks provide special bank-by-mail envelopes as a customer convenience. You can safely deposit checks by mail, but *never send cash through the mail.* For a night deposit, place the deposit in a deposit bag, take the deposit to the bank, and put it in the night deposit opening. Banks usually provide customers with a special lock-bag for night deposits. To use most automatic teller machines, your company will have a magnetic card and code number. Insert the card, keyboard the code number and the amount of the deposit, and place the money bag or envelope in the deposit slot.

en·dorse'ment

Endorsement An *endorsement* is the signing of one's name or the company's name on the back of the check in order to get the amount shown on the face of the check. The endorsement gives the bank authority to process the check for payment. *Processing* can include either cashing the check or depositing it to an account. For example, if your company writes a check to a supplier in payment for purchases, then the supplier must endorse the check before depositing it in the bank.

Most banks prefer that the endorsement be made on the left side of the back of the check. If the endorsement is a person's name, then it should be a handwritten signature. Most companies use a rubber stamp to endorse checks with the company name. Using the stamp saves time.

There are three types of endorsements, as shown in Illustration 13–5.

1. A **blank endorsement** consists of only the payee's name (either handwritten or stamped) on the back of the check. With a blank endorsement, a check is just like cash. The bank is authorized to pay

Illustration 13–5
Three types of endorsements

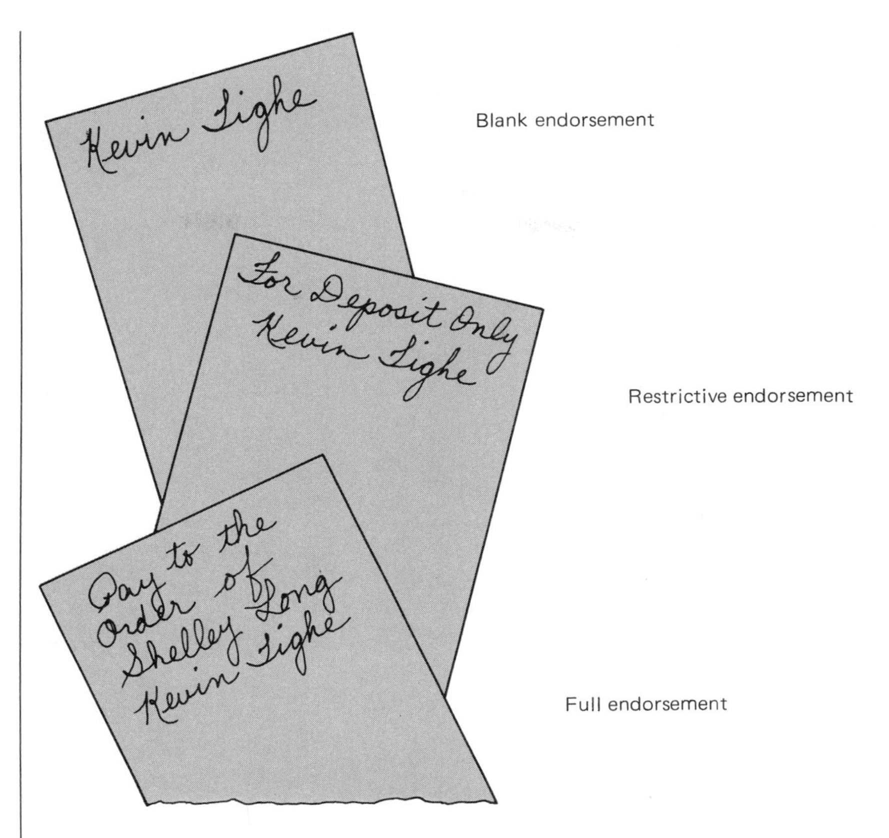

anyone who presents it to the bank. For safety, a blank endorsement should be written only at the time the check is presented for cashing.

re·stric'tive

2. A **restrictive endorsement** consists of the payee's name, either signed or stamped, along with the identification of the special purpose for which the check is to be used. Usually, the restriction is *For Deposit Only,* which means that the money is to be deposited in the person's or company's account.
3. A **full endorsement** is a signed or stamped name along with the phrase *Pay to the Order of* followed by the name of a particular person or company. Only the person or company named in the endorsement can cash the check.

mis·spelled'

The endorsement on the back of the check should match exactly the name as written on the front of the check. If the check is made out incorrectly — for example, if the name is misspelled — then the endorsement should be written in the same misspelled form. The correct spelling should be signed underneath it. In Illustration 13–6 on page 514, the check was made out to *Chris* Mallory, but she spells her name *Kris.* Kris endorses the check as it was made out; below that, she then endorses it with her signature as it appears on the signature card on file with the bank.

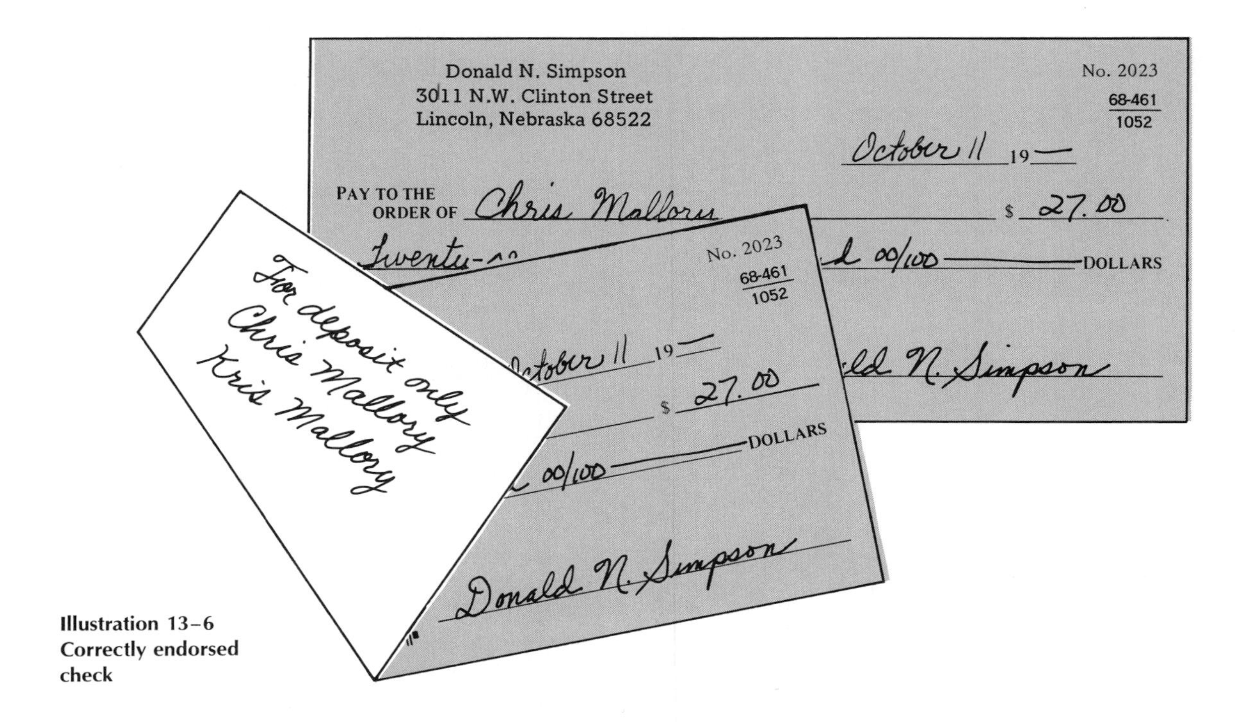

Illustration 13–6
Correctly endorsed check

Balancing the Checkbook

As you have seen, information about each check is recorded in the checkbook register before the check is written. The check amount is *subtracted* from the balance, or amount, in the checking account. When a deposit is made, the amount is also written in the checkbook register. Deposits are *added* to the checkbook balance.

At the end of each month, the bank sends a **bank statement** that shows all of the checking account transactions — service charges, deposits made, and checks processsed — for the month. Most banks also return all checks that have been processed for each account. These returned checks are called *canceled checks.* When the bank statement arrives, the statement figures and canceled checks must be compared with the checkbook register figures to check the accuracy of the balances.

The balance shown on the bank statement and the balance shown in the check register are usually *not* the same. Why? There are several reasons. First, some checks may not have been processed by the bank at the time the statement was prepared. These checks, called *outstanding* checks, are not included in the bank's figures. Second, the bank may have deducted a service charge, which has not been recorded in the checkbook register. Third, some deposits may not have been received by the bank at the time the statement was prepared.

out·stand'ing

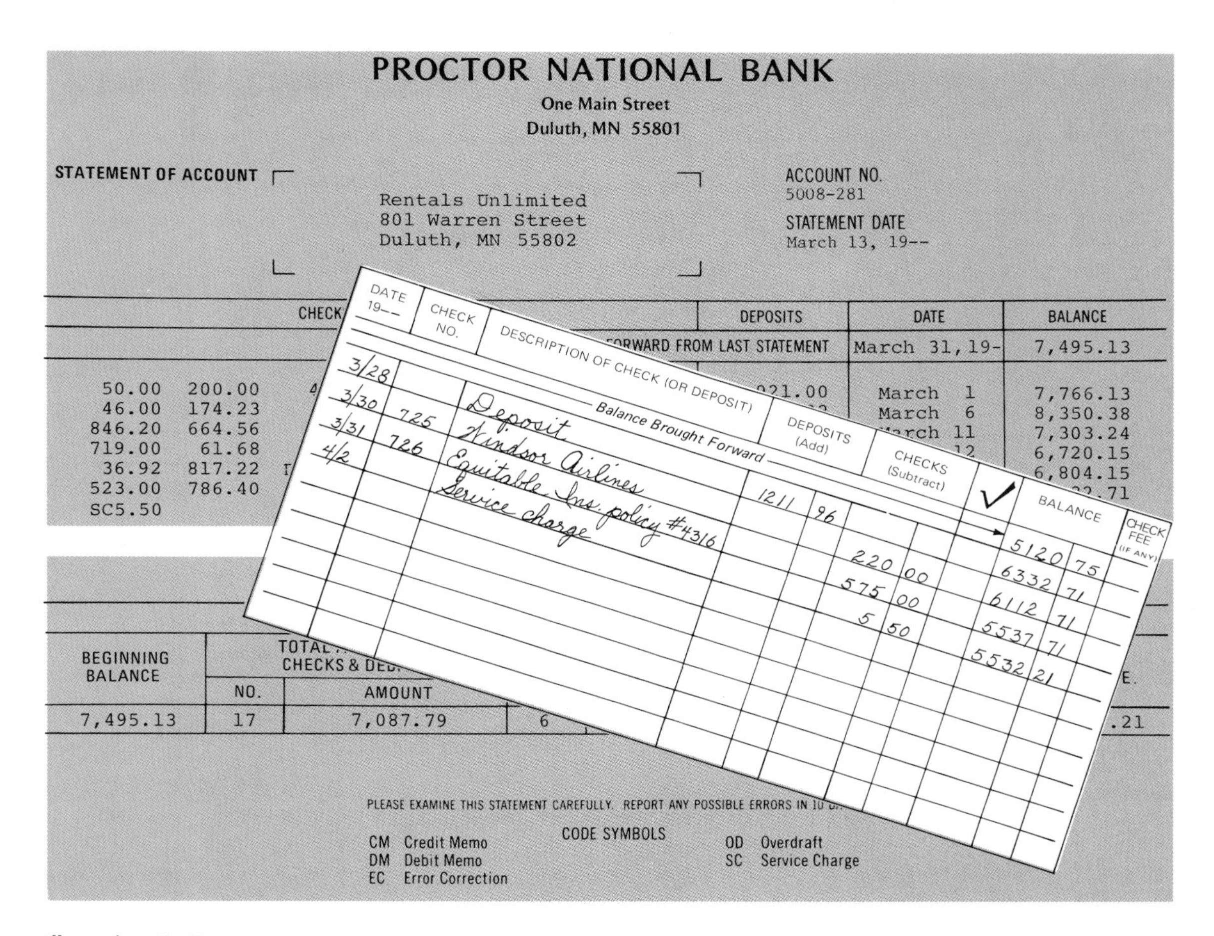
PROCTOR NATIONAL BANK
One Main Street
Duluth, MN 55801

STATEMENT OF ACCOUNT

Rentals Unlimited
801 Warren Street
Duluth, MN 55802

ACCOUNT NO.
5008-281
STATEMENT DATE
March 13, 19--

CHECK		DEPOSITS	DATE	BALANCE
		FORWARD FROM LAST STATEMENT	March 31, 19-	7,495.13
50.00	200.00	921.00	March 1	7,766.13
46.00	174.23		March 6	8,350.38
846.20	664.56		March 11	7,303.24
719.00	61.68			6,720.15
36.92	817.22			6,804.15
523.00	786.40			.71
SC5.50				

BEGINNING BALANCE	TOTAL CHECKS & DEB. NO.	AMOUNT		
7,495.13	17	7,087.79	6	.21

PLEASE EXAMINE THIS STATEMENT CAREFULLY. REPORT ANY POSSIBLE ERRORS IN 10 DA.

CODE SYMBOLS
CM Credit Memo
DM Debit Memo
EC Error Correction
OD Overdraft
SC Service Charge

DATE 19--	CHECK NO.	DESCRIPTION OF CHECK (OR DEPOSIT)	DEPOSITS (Add)	CHECKS (Subtract)	✓	BALANCE	CHECK FEE (IF ANY)
		Balance Brought Forward				5120 75	
3/28		Deposit	1211 96			6332 71	
3/30	725	Windsor Airlines		220 00		6112 71	
3/31	726	Equitable Ins. policy #4316		575 00		5537 71	
4/2		Service charge		5 50		5532 21	

Illustration 13–7
Record the service charge in the checkbook register

Because there is usually a difference between the balances shown on the bank statement and on the checkbook register, it is necessary to **reconcile** the bank statement — that is, to determine whether the bank records agree with the checkbook register. Reconciling the bank statement is also called *balancing* the checkbook.

When the bank statement is received, the service charges shown must be subtracted from the total in the checkbook register. The listing of these charges includes the date each charge was made to the account, the amount of the charge, and the code letters explaining the reason for the charge. A key to the meaning of the code letters appears at the bottom of the statement.

An example of the checkbook entry for service charges is shown in Illustration 13–7. This adjusted checkbook balance is the figure used for reconciling the bank statement.

rec·on·cil·i·a′tion

Many banks print a reconciliation form, similar to the one in Illustration 13–8, on the back of the monthly statement. To reconcile a statement, you can follow the instructions on that form or the ones given on the next page.

CHECKS OUTSTANDING		
NUMBER	AMOUNT	
563	23	40
564	119	95
566	50	00
568	61	25
Total of Checks Outstanding	254	60

TO BALANCE YOUR CHECKBOOK, PLEASE COMPARE YOUR CHECKBOOK RECORD WITH THE ENTRIES ON THIS STATEMENT.

1. Check off in your checkbook all the checks posted on this statement. Note that they are posted in number order so that there is no need to sort your checks.
2. List at the left any checks you wrote that are not recorded on this statement plus any checks outstanding from a prior statement period.
3. Add NOW interest, if any, to your checkbook record.
4. Subtract Service Charge, if any, from your checkbook record.
5. Enter in your checkbook any other transactions appearing on this statement that you have not yet recorded, and adjust your balance accordingly.

6. Enter statement balance (see New Balance on other side). →	2,385	11
7. Add deposits not credited on this statement. If any of these were made in a prior statement period, contact us immediately. →	250	00
SUB-TOTAL	2,635	11
8. Subtract total of checks outstanding. →	254	60
TOTAL should agree with your checkbook balance. →	2,380	51

IF IT DOES NOT:
- make sure all balances carried forward in your checkbook are correct
- be certain you have adjusted your checkbook balance for any NOW interest, service charges, Advance Account, or other transactions you had not previously recorded.
- double-check all your math both in your checkbook and on the form used here
- make certain all transaction amounts, including check amounts, listed on this statement are the same as those you entered in your checkbook

Illustration 13–8
Bank reconciliation form

1. Arrange canceled checks in numerical order. (The check number is usually printed on the check.)
2. In the checkbook register, put a check mark (√) beside the entry for each canceled check. As you mark off each check, compare the amount entered in the register to the amount written on the face of the check.
3. Put a check mark (√) in the checkbook register beside each deposit shown on the bank statement.
4. Subtract bank service charges listed on the statement, if any, from the total in the checkbook register.
5. List and total all deposits and checks that are *not* shown on the bank statement. (These outstanding deposits and checks do not have check marks next to them in the checkbook register.)
6. List the bank balance shown on the bank statement. Add outstanding deposits to that balance; then subtract outstanding checks.
7. The adjusted total from the statement should now equal the total shown in the checkbook register.

If the reconciled bank statement balance is not the same as that shown in the checkbook register, then there is an error. To be sure that the error is not in the checkbook register, first be sure that all figures entered in the register are correct. Then check your addition and subtraction. Check the listing of outstanding checks and the addition and subtraction of the amounts. Next check the listing of the outstanding deposits and be sure that your addition is correct.

If there is an error in the bank statement, report it immediately to your supervisor. The bank must be called immediately, since it assumes the statement is correct unless an error is reported within a few days after receipt of the statement. If you cannot find the error, the bank will gladly help you. Just call them and set up an appointment. Be sure to take the checkbook, bank statement, and canceled checks with you when you go for the appointment.

BANKING TRENDS

e·lec·tron′ic

The major trends in banking services today center on the use of electronic equipment. A major development in banking service is the **Electronic Funds Transfer System (EFTS).** EFTS is an automated system by which banks help customers manage their money. With a special identification card, a customer can (1) conduct routine banking transactions on an automatic teller, (2) transfer money from a personal checking account directly to store accounts using in-store terminals, and (3) withdraw money from a checking account or charge it to a Mastercard or Visa account.

Currently, many banks offer customers a bill-paying service that enables them to pay bills by phone — without the use of checks. This service is popular because it is so convenient.

As an office worker with responsibilities for banking activities, you need to keep up to date about banking procedures and services. This knowledge saves you time and money by enabling you to choose the right service.

REVIEWING KEY POINTS

1. A checkbook is used to keep track of money kept in a bank.
2. A check serves as an order to the bank to take money from a checking account and pay it to the person or business named on the check.
3. Checking accounts are set up according to who can write checks on them; they may be personal, joint, or business accounts.
4. To open a checking account, everyone who will be writing checks against the account must sign a signature card that is then kept on file by the bank. Signatures on checks must match the signatures on file.
5. The checkbook register is a form that is used to record the date, amount, and purpose of each check and the date and amount of each deposit.

6. Once a check has been written, the bank can be asked to stop payment on it. A stop-payment request involves calling the bank and completing an appropriate form.
7. Deposits to accounts may be made by mail, in person, by night deposit, or by automatic teller machines.
8. An endorsement authorizes the bank to process a check; the endorsement may be either blank, restrictive, or full.
9. Bank reconciliation is the process of making sure that the checkbook register agrees with the bank's records.

DEVELOPING HUMAN RELATIONS SKILLS

1. Barbara works in an office where she is the only secretary. In her position, she performs a variety of activities; and she never has a spare moment. On top of all her work, her supervisor regularly asks Barbara to reconcile his personal bank statement each month. Barbara thinks her supervisor should reconcile his own statement.
   a. What problems could result in the office if Barbara continues to handle her supervisor's personal banking?
   b. How should Barbara explain this problem to her supervisor?
2. Denise works in the accounting department, where she is responsible for mailing deposits to the bank. One afternoon she could not find the rubber stamp that is used for endorsements, so she wrote a blank endorsement on each check.
   a. Is the blank endorsement safe for mailed deposits? Why or why not?
   b. If the deposit were lost in the mail and someone else were to cash some of the checks, should Denise be held responsible? Why or why not?

IMPROVING COMMUNICATION SKILLS

Refer to Appendix B 3.1 — 3.10.

1. Keyboard the words here and at the top of the next page in a three-column format. Each word is hyphenated as if it were at the end of a line in keyboarded copy. If a word can be hyphenated as shown below, copy it as it is. If a word cannot be hyphenated as shown, correct the hyphenation.

accepta-ble	deduc-ting	ed-ited
accord-ance	de-ny	er-a
ad-s	develop-ing	essen-tial
a-ppoint	diss-imilar	etiquet-te
co-workers	do-ors	ex-it
dead-lines	dropp-ing	expres-sing

fel-low	involve-ment	un-dergo
find-ing	key-board	reg-ulate
handle-d	less-ons	returna-ble
harm-ful	mer-it	vi-sa

2. Find the mailing address for your local newspaper from an issue of the paper or from your telephone directory. On a separate sheet of letter-size paper, keyboard a letter in block format ordering a one-year subscription to the paper. State that you want the paper mailed to your home address and that you are enclosing a check for the full amount of the subscription.

BUILDING PROBLEM-SOLVING SKILLS

1. You are about to write checks to pay your monthly bills. Your current checkbook balance is $592.62. You plan to write checks for the following amounts: $26.78, $15.95, $49.50, $89.95, and $5.79. On a separate sheet of paper, answer the following questions.
   a. What is the new balance after you write each check?
   b. After you paid your bills, you deposited $185. What is the new balance after the deposit?
2. On a separate sheet of paper, determine the total amount of the deposit shown here:

Bills		**Coins**		**Checks**
42	$ 1 bills	40	quarters	$ 14.50
27	$ 5 bills	175	pennies	117.75
13	$10 bills	137	dimes	19.64
12	$20 bills	15	half dollars	45.56
				84.00

APPLYING OFFICE SKILLS

1. Write checks for the following transactions using the checkbook register and blank checks in your workbook. Sign your name and use today's date.

Pay to	**Purpose**	**Amount**
Stationery House	Carbon Paper	$ 35.85
Sporty's Tool Shop	Calculator	37.00
Armstrong Stationery Co.	File Cabinet	76.95
Dohrn Transfer, Inc.	Invoice #680	55.40
Able Offset Service, Inc.	Invoice #48	25.75
Office Skills Institute	Communication Seminar	250.00
Reardon Industries, Inc.	Insulation	300.00

2. The checkbook register for Gabriel Santos and the bank reconciliation form are in your workbook. Bring the checkbook register up to date and reconcile the following bank statement.

DATE 19--	CHECK NO.	DESCRIPTION OF CHECK (OR DEPOSIT)	DEPOSITS (ADD)		CHECKS (SUBTRACT)		✓	BALANCE		CHECK FEE (IF ANY)
							→	912	50	
7/1	114	Discount Mart			21	70		890	80	
7/2	115	Bank Charge I			140	00	✓	750	80	
7/2		Service Charge			4	50	✓	746	30	
7/3	116	Wayside Apts. - rent			295	50		450	80	
7/7		Deposit	750	80				1201	60	
7/9	117	Star Grocers			57	00		1144	60	
7/12	118	Commonwealth Life Ins.			330	00		814	60	
7/15	119	Federal Bank - car loan			275	25		539	35	
7/18		Deposit	435	00				974	35	
7/19	120	Star Grocers			55	25		919	10	
7/22		Deposit	750	80				1669	90	
7/28	121	Jiffy Mart Foods			22	12		1647	78	
7/30	122	Cecil's Salads			11	28		1636	50	

VALLEY BANK AND TRUST

Sepulveda at Broad
San Fernando, Ca. 94103

STATEMENT OF ACCOUNT

Gabriel Santos
524 Sutter Avenue Apt. 4-A
San Fernando, CA 94101

ACCOUNT NO.
3260-016

STATEMENT DATE
July 30, 19--

CHECKS AND OTHER DEBITS	DEPOSITS	DATE	BALANCE
BALANCE BROUGHT FORWARD FROM LAST STATEMENT		June 29, 19--	768.00
21.70		July 3	746.30
295.50		July 6	450.80
	750.80	July 8	1,201.60
57.00		July 11	1,144.60
330.00		July 14	814.60
275.25		July 17	539.35
	435.00	July 18	974.35
55.25	750.80	July 23	1,669.90
SC 4.20			1,665.70

CHECKING SUMMARY

BEGINNING BALANCE	TOTAL AMOUNT OF CHECKS & DEBITS NO.	TOTAL AMOUNT OF CHECKS & DEBITS AMOUNT	TOTAL AMOUNT OF DEPOSITS & CREDITS NO.	TOTAL AMOUNT OF DEPOSITS & CREDITS AMOUNT	SERVICE CHARGE AMOUNT	ENDING BALANCE
768.00	7	1038.90	3	1936.60	4.20	1,665.70

CHAPTER 2

ORDER PROCESSING AND INVENTORY CONTROL

A large part of the daily operations of most businesses involves receiving and recording payments for goods or services and making payments to cover utilities, supplies, and other operating costs. A company's financial success depends on the ability of its employees to process information, forms, and records related to making and receiving payments.

Processing orders for goods or services and keeping track of inventory are two of the most important functions in most businesses. As an office worker, you need to be familiar with the procedures and forms used to perform these activities, since they are the basis of all the other financial activities of the company.

As you study this chapter, you will find answers to the following questions:

- What are the procedures for placing and filling orders?
- What are the two most common inventory systems, and how do they operate?
- How are computers used in order processing and inventory control?
- What skills are required for the accurate and efficient processing of orders?
- What do the following terms mean: **purchase requisition, purchase order, purchase order register, stock requisition, invoice, bill of lading, inventory, perpetual inventory systems, periodic inventory system?**

Illustration 13–9
Purchase requisition form

Bean & Dow, Inc.
200 Ozark Street
Cedar Rapids, IA 52402

PURCHASE REQUISITION
No. C-623

Department Manufacturing — Date of Request July 2, 19--
Advise on delivery Mr. Jordan — Date Required Aug. 5, 19--

Quantity	Description
100	83C Wire Nut Connector
4	30P Side Wear Plate
2	42B Bottom Blade
10	14G Grounding Plug
4	01R Roller

Approved by Leona Gardner — Requested by C. P. Jordan

For Purchasing Dept. Use Only

Purchase Order No. 5346
Date July 5, 19--

Issued to: Gates, Inc.
2734 Brady Street
Des Moines, IA 52806

FORMS AND PAPERWORK FLOW

All businesses buy and sell products and services. So, each company is both a supplier *and* a buyer. It is a *supplier* in that it sells its products or services to other companies. It is a *buyer* in that it buys materials and services from other companies in order to produce its own products and services. Therefore, regardless of the type of company for which you work, you will find that it processes information and forms in placing, filling, receiving, stocking, and tracing orders.

Placing an Order

Order processing begins when an employee fills out a supplies requisition and sends it to the warehouse or supply room. The supplies requisition is an in-house order for raw materials and other supplies used in the factory or business offices. In the warehouse, the *stock clerk* checks the stock record to see if the item is carried in inventory. If the item is not in inventory, or if the supply is getting low, the stock clerk completes a **purchase requisition**, a form used to request the purchase of something that is needed. This form, shown in Illustration 13–9, authorizes (directs) the purchasing department to purchase the necessary materials.

au'thor·iz·es

Illustration 13–10
Purchase order sent to supplier

Bean & Dow, Inc.
200 Ozark Street Cedar Rapids, IA 52402 319-989-5839

Purchase Order

To: Gates, Inc.
2734 Brady Street
Des Moines, IA 52806

Date: July 5, 19--
Order No.: 5346
Ship Via: Truck

Quantity	Description	Unit Price	Total
100	83C Wire Nut Connector	.048	4.80
4	30P Side Wear Plate	6.95	27.80
2	42B Bottom Blade	9.95	19.90
10	14G Grounding Plug	3.00	30.00
4	01R Roller	34.65	138.60
			221.10

James Martin
Purchasing Agent

When the purchasing department receives the purchase requisition, the purchasing agent approves the purchase. A *purchasing clerk* then prepares the purchase order, the form sent to the supplier. A **purchase order**, as shown in Illustration 13–10, is a form that lists the quantity, description, unit price, and total price for each item being purchased. It is a legal contract and must be carefully prepared.

Most companies use printed forms for their purchase orders. Usually, multiple copies are prepared. One copy is kept in the purchasing department's files; one copy is sent to the receiving department; one copy is sent to the accounting department for bookkeeping purposes; and the original is sent to the supplier.

Filling an Order

When the supplier receives the purchase order, the *order clerk* there checks the accuracy and clearness of the order content. The clerk checks the prices on the order form against the company's current price list. If there are any questions about the order, or if the prices have changed, the order clerk contacts the buyer by mail or by phone.

reg'is·ter

The order clerk also enters each order as it is received in a **purchase order register,** shown in Illustration 13–11 on the next page. This register serves as a record in case an order form is accidentally lost or destroyed. In some companies, purchase order registers are stored on information processing equipment so that they can be updated easily.

Once the order has been recorded in the purchase order register, it is sent to the credit department. An *accounting clerk* checks the buyer's credit; that is, the ability to pay. If the buyer's credit is good, the purchase order is approved

Purchase Order Register

Entry Date	Name	Address	PO No.	PO Date	Qty.	Item	Unit Price
12/1/—	KDI Company	5721 Dragon Way	421	1/27/—	2	Teak Desks	258.50
		Atlanta, GA 30301					
	Electrodine	116 Clairmont Square	48	1/28/—	1	CRT Data	169.00
		Augusta, GA 33030				Desk	

Illustration 13–11
Purchase order register

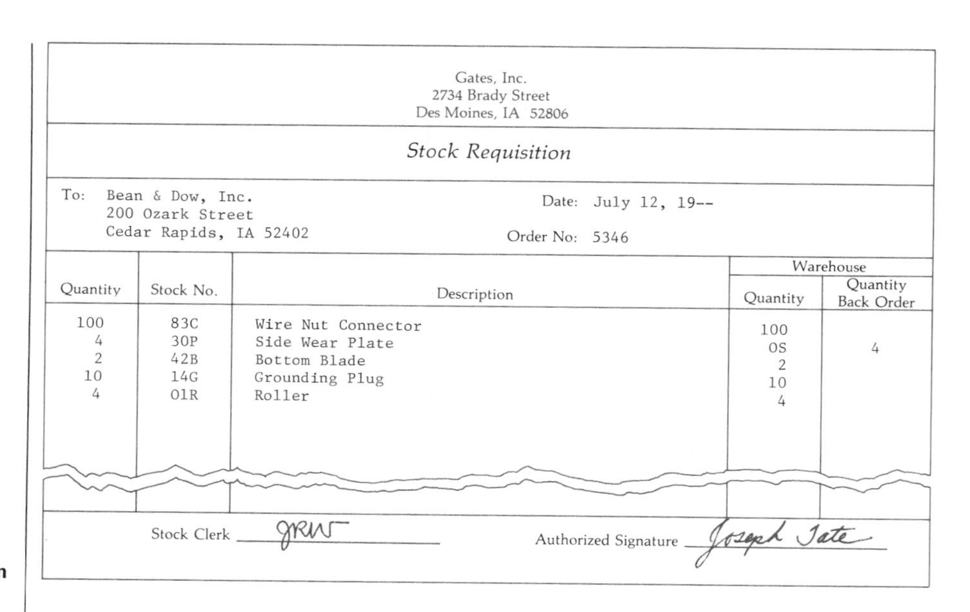

Gates, Inc.
2734 Brady Street
Des Moines, IA 52806

Stock Requisition

To: Bean & Dow, Inc.
200 Ozark Street
Cedar Rapids, IA 52402

Date: July 12, 19--

Order No: 5346

Quantity	Stock No.	Description	Warehouse Quantity	Warehouse Quantity Back Order
100	83C	Wire Nut Connector	100	
4	30P	Side Wear Plate	OS	4
2	42B	Bottom Blade	2	
10	14G	Grounding Plug	10	
4	01R	Roller	4	

Stock Clerk JRW

Authorized Signature Joseph Tate

Illustration 13–12
Stock requisition form

and sent to the warehouse for processing. If the buyer's credit is not good, the buyer will be asked to pay cash.

A *stock clerk* then prepares a stock requisition, shown in Illustration 13–12. (Notice that both the buyer and the supplier employ stock clerks.) A **stock requisition** is a form that tells the warehouse workers what goods to remove from inventory. In preparing the stock requisition, the clerk copies information from the purchase order. The clerk then checks the stock records to see whether all items requested are in stock. Any items not in stock are marked OS (for *out-of-stock*) on the stock requisition.

Illustration 13–13
Invoice sent to buyer

Invoice

Gates, Inc.
2734 Brady Street
Des Moines, IA 52806

To:

Bean & Dow, Inc.
200 Ozark Street
Cedar Rapids, IA 52402

Date: July 13, 19--
Invoice No.: 3810
Order No.: 5346
Shipped By: Truck
Terms: 2/10 net 30

Quantity	Description	Unit Price	Total
100	83C Wire Nut Connector	.048	4.80
2	42B Bottom Blade	9.95	19.90
10	14G Grounding Plug	3.00	30.00
4	01R Roller	34.65	138.60
			193.30

Partial shipment. Items on back order.

For each in-stock item, the clerk enters the stock number on the stock requisition form. Using the stock number as well as the descriptive name helps the warehouse workers find the items quickly.

The stock requisition is then sent to the warehouse, where workers pull the items on the requisition from stock. One copy of the stock requisition is kept in the warehouse as a record of the removal of stock from inventory. The other copies accompany the items to the shipping department, where they are used to prepare packing slips and customer invoices.

re·mov'al

When the items are received in the shipping department, a *billing clerk* prepares an invoice for the shipment. The **invoice** is the bill the supplier sends to the buyer. The invoice provides the supplier with a record of the shipment and presents the buyer with an official bill. The invoice also gives the shipping department authorization to pack and ship the items.

au·thor·i·za'tion

A completed invoice form is shown in Illustration 13–13. An invoice must be carefully prepared. Billing errors cost the company money and can result in the loss of customers. To be sure that the invoice is accurate, the *shipping clerk* makes a final inspection, checking the goods against the invoice.

in·spec'tion

Shipping clerk responsibilities vary from company to company. In some small companies, the shipping clerk may be responsible for selecting the method of transportation. In many large companies, however, there is also a *traffic clerk* who chooses the method of transportation and makes arrangements for shipping.

The shipping or traffic clerk is thoroughly familiar with the advantages and disadvantages of each method of transportation and knows the most efficient method for each type of shipment. The clerk arranges for the carrier to pick up the goods or for the shipment to be delivered to the carrier.

Straight Bill of Lading—Short Form
ORIGINAL — NOT NEGOTIABLE

Shipper's No. B-12649

Iowa Express Transport
(Name of Carrier)

Carrier's No. ______

RECEIVED, subject to the classifications and tariffs in effect on the date of the issue of this Bill of Lading.

at Des Moines, IA 7/13 19-- From Gates, Inc.

the property described below, in apparent good order, except as noted (contents and condition of contents of packages unknown), marked, consigned, and destined as indicated below, which said carrier (the word carrier being understood throughout this contract as meaning any person or corporation in possession of the property under the contract) agrees to carry to its usual place of delivery at said destination, if on its own route, otherwise to deliver to another carrier on the route to said destination. It is mutually agreed, as to each carrier of all or any of said property over all or any portion of said route to destination, and as to each party at any time interested in all or any of said property, that every service to be performed hereunder shall be subject to all the terms and conditions of the Uniform Domestic Straight Bill of Lading set forth (1) in Official, Southern, Western and Illinois Freight Classifications in effect on the date hereof, if this is a rail or a rail-water shipment, or (2) in the applicable motor carrier classification or tariff if this is a motor carrier shipment.

Shipper hereby certifies that he is familiar with all the terms and conditions of the said bill of lading, including those on the back thereof, set forth in the classification or tariff which governs the transportation of this shipment, and the said terms and conditions are hereby agreed to by the shipper and accepted for himself and his assigns.

Consigned to Bean & Dow, Inc. 200 Ozark Street
(Mail or street address of consignee—For purposes of notification only.)

Destination Cedar Rapids State Iowa ~~County~~ XXXXX 52402 Delivery Address★ ______
(★ To be filled in only when shipper desires and governing tariffs provide for delivery thereat.)

Route ______

Delivering Carrier Iowa Express Transport Car or Vehicle Initials CN No. 5346

No. Packages	Kind of Package, Description of Articles, Special Marks, and Exceptions	*Weight (Sub. to Cor.)	Class or Rate	Check Column
100	83C Wire Nut Connector	3#		
2	42B Bottom Blade	20#		
10	14G Grounding Plug	2#		
4	01R Roller	24#		

Subject to Section 7 of Conditions of applicable bill of lading, if this shipment is to be delivered to the consignee without recourse on the consignor, the consignor shall sign the following statement:
The carrier shall not make delivery of this shipment without payment of freight and all other lawful charges.

______
(Signature of Consignor)

If charges are to be prepaid, write or stamp here, "To be Prepaid."

Illustration 13–14
Bill of lading

Using the invoice and the purchase order information, the billing clerk prepares the bill of lading. The **bill of lading**, shown in Illustration 13–14, is the legal contract between the shipper and carrier. The company shipping the order keeps one copy of the bill of lading and the carrier keeps one. The original is sent along with the shipment to the buyer (also called the *consignee*).

Receiving an Order

When the buyer receives the shipment, the *receiving clerk* checks the bill of lading and the invoice against the purchase order. The receiving clerk also checks for damage and records receipt of the items on a receiving report.

re·ceipt'

If the shipment is complete and accepted by the receiving department, the items are sent to the purchasing agent, who processes it for payment. With that activity, the flow of forms is complete: goods have been ordered, transported, received, and stored.

Inspecting and Tracing Orders

Not all shipments are received on time and in acceptable condition. Upon checking the shipment, the receiving clerk may find damaged items. The shipment may be "short," or missing some of the items ordered. In these situations, the receiving clerk notifies the carrier, whose job it is to find out who is responsible for the missing or damaged items — the supplier or the carrier. For example, the items may not have been packed properly by the supplier, or the boxes may show signs of rough handling by the carrier.

If a shipment is lost or delayed, the carrier's tracer clerk is notified. The *tracer clerk* reviews the bill of lading and other shipping forms to check the route and contents of the shipment. Then a form known as a tracer is prepared, and the search for the missing shipment begins.

INVENTORY CONTROL

Once orders are received on time and in good condition, the goods are stored. This supply or stock of goods is called an **inventory.** In retail stores, the inventory is composed of the products customers want to buy: toothpaste, shoes, wallets, bicycles, and dry roasted peanuts, for example. A retailer also keeps a supply of cash register tapes, shopping bags, and employee time cards in inventory. In business offices, the inventory contains such things as letterhead paper, business forms, and correction products. These items are used in providing service to the company's customers.

com·posed'
re'tail·er

In manufacturing companies, there are two types of inventories: (1) the inventory of raw materials and parts used in the production process, and (2) the finished goods inventory of items to be sold. If there are items out of stock in the raw materials inventory, the production line shuts down and nothing can be produced. If there are items out of stock in the finished goods inventory, the company may lose the sale and the customer.

As you can see, all types of companies must have procedures for keeping track of the items they have in stock. When the number of items on hand drops below a certain point, called the *reorder point,* the item is reordered. If the company has planned properly, the order will be received before the last item is taken from stock.

Companies use several types of systems to keep track of their inventories. The most common are the *perpetual* and the *periodic* inventory systems. For both systems to work properly, employees must have good clerical skills and follow the procedures for taking inventory.

per·pet'u·al

Perpetual Inventory Systems

In **perpetual inventory systems,** there is always an exact count of the items on hand. Every time an item is taken from inventory — and every time a new shipment of items is received — the inventory records are adjusted. The inventory clerk may record the changes in inventory level on the stock record as shown in Illustration 13–15 on the next page. This record is filed numerically in a card file. Various businesses require different information on their stock records, but most include the facts listed on the next page.

ad·just'ed

Illustration 13–15 Stock record used in perpetual inventory systems

STOCK AND INVENTORY CONTROL									STOCK NO.		
Microfiche file cabinet (8-drawer)									SF-8		
SUPPLIER: Castro Manufacturing						UNIT: ea.			REORDER POINT: 15		
ADDRESS: Charlotte, N.C.						TELEPHONE: (704) 287-4081			REORDER QUANTITY: 30		
RECEIVED			ISSUED								
DATE	QUANTITY	BALANCE	DATE	QUANTITY	BALANCE	DATE	QUANTITY	BALANCE	DATE	QUANTITY	BALANCE
3/13	On hand	16									
3/16	30	46	3/18	3	43	3/27	5	38	4/7	7	31
			4/12	8	23	4/15	9	14			
5/2	30	44	5/2	5	39	5/3	1	38	5/8	2	36
			5/21	7	29	5/29	3	26	6/7	5	21
			6/11	4	17	6/19	6	11	6/23	4	7
6/27	30	37	7/2	3	34						

- stock number and descriptive name of item
- supplier (or source, if the item comes from another department within the company)
- number of items ordered and the date received
- number of items sold (or removed from inventory) daily
- current balance or quantity on hand.

trans·ac′tion

Perpetual inventory systems are often computerized. As items are removed from or added to inventory, an inventory clerk enters the transaction into the computer. To find out the quantity of an item in stock, the clerk simply enters the stock number of the item. In some computerized inventory systems, the computer can be programmed to print purchase orders when the number of items in inventory reaches the reorder point.

For a perpetual inventory system to work, the employees must keep careful daily records. Receiving slips provide records of items added to stock; stock requisitions provide records of items taken from stock. In addition, the inventory clerk must keep the supply room or warehouse locked and allow only authorized warehouse employees to enter.

Periodic Inventory Systems

pe·ri·od′ic

In a **periodic inventory system,** inventory workers take a physical count of the items in stock on a regular basis, such as every month or every two weeks. If the stock level is too low, the stock clerk prepares a purchase requisition. Periodic inventory systems are usually used when items can be counted easily and ordered quickly.

The Annual Inventory

Regardless of the type of inventory system they use during the year, most companies also take an annual count of the items in inventory for accounting purposes. In a department store, for example, all items in the warehouse and on the showroom floor are counted. When the inventory is large and must be counted quickly, employees from other departments may be asked to help.

dis·rupt'ed

Companies take their annual inventories on weekends or at other times when business will be least disrupted. Because an accurate count of the items is important, employees may work in teams, with one person counting the items and the other recording them. As the items are counted, they may be tagged or marked so they won't be counted twice.

COMPUTERS IN ORDER PROCESSING AND INVENTORY CONTROL

It costs a company about $25 to process one purchase order manually — that is, in the method described at the beginning of this chapter. Most of these costs arise out of paperwork, such as filling out forms, keyboarding them, and distributing them to the right departments.

Besides being costly, processing orders manually can be slow. If a customer's order is not filled quickly, the customer is likely to change suppliers. Therefore, a company must have efficient procedures for processing purchase orders and related forms.

Many companies are now using computers to speed the flow of paperwork and reduce the cost of filling orders. With a computer system that connects the sales, production, purchasing, billing, and shipping departments, the cost of processing a purchase order drops to about $3. Office and warehouse workers are freed to check the accuracy of records, solve problems, and provide customer service. Imagine how much money and time a company can save each year by changing to a computerized system!

Here is an example of how a computerized system might work:

When the supplier receives a purchase order from a customer, a clerk enters the order into the computer. The computer quickly checks the customer's credit against the accounting records. If the credit is approved, the computer checks the order against the inventory records. If the items are in stock, the computer automatically prints invoices and sends copies to the warehouse and the shipping department. (Printers or CRTs, located in the warehouse and shipping department, are connected to the main computer.) The invoice tells the warehouse workers to send the items to the shipping department; it also tells the shipping clerk to make arrangements for shipping. In addition to printing the invoice, the computer can figure extensions, discounts, and the total.

ex·ten'sions

While the computer is checking the inventory records and printing the invoice, it is also making records of the order and storing them in memory. One result is up-to-the-minute inventory records. If the number of items on hand falls below a certain level, the computer can print a reorder report as a reminder to the purchasing department.

SKILLS IN FORM PREPARATION

The success of any company depends on the skills and knowledge of its employees. There are skills that are especially essential in order and inventory work, since keeping track of materials, products, and orders requires so much paperwork. Processing an order usually requires the preparation of a variety of forms. Information processing equipment has reduced the amount of time office workers must spend keyboarding forms. But this equipment has not reduced the need for accuracy, neatness, and familiarity with forms and terminology.

Accuracy

Once you know what information to enter on the form, you must be careful to perform all calculations correctly and record the information accurately.

Keyboard accuracy Some forms are designed to be filled in neatly by hand, especially those that are used within the company only. However, forms that are sent to suppliers, shippers, or customers are usually prepared and printed on information processing equipment. Whether you are using a typewriter or a computer keyboard, you should not sacrifice accuracy for speed.

sac'ri·fice

trip'li·cate

Most forms used in order processing are prepared in duplicate or triplicate. If you have worked with carbon paper or NCR forms, you know how difficult it is to make corrections on the copies. Reducing your keyboarding speed, especially when you are keyboarding numbers, can reduce errors and save you time in the long run. Setting tabs when you keyboard information in columns can also help you avoid errors on forms.

Corrections are easier to make on a computer terminal hooked to a CRT screen. On most models, you simply move the cursor to the incorrect letter or word and enter the correct one. With this equipment, the problem is not correcting errors, but finding them. Once an error gets into the computer, it may not be noticed until it appears on the customer's invoice. Such "computer errors" are really employee errors. You can prevent them by carefully proofreading the information as it is displayed on the CRT screen.

Mathematical accuracy Many of the forms used in order processing contain dollar amounts and quantities that must be added, subtracted, multiplied, or divided. Workers who prepare these forms must develop good math skills and get into the habit of checking their work.

When preparing an invoice, for example, you need to compute extensions and various discounts. The *extension* is the total price of an item. To compute the extension, multiply the unit price of the item by the quantity purchased. (Notice that the invoice in Illustration 13–13 contains columns with these headings.) For example, if the customer buys four rollers that cost $34.65 each, the total price or extension is 4 × $34.65, or $138.60.

Some suppliers offer various discounts off the *list*, or published, price:

- **Quantity discounts** — for buying an item in large amounts, such as a ton (2,000 lbs.) or a gross (12 dozen).
- **Cash discounts** — for paying cash when the invoice is received.
- **Trade discounts** — for buying an item from a certain supplier.

Discounts, which are expressed as a percentage, may range from 1 or 2 percent for a cash discount to 25 percent or more for a trade discount. To compute the discount, first change the percent to a decimal, then multiply to find the amount of the discount.

$6.95	list price
× .20	20% discount
$1.39	discount

To find the *net price,* or actual price the buyer pays, subtract the discount from the list price:

$6.95	list price
− 1.39	discount
$5.56	net price

Cash discounts usually apply only if merchandise is paid for in full within a specified time, such as 10 days. For example, if a company offers credit terms of *2/10, n/30,* a buyer receives a 2 percent discount if the invoice is paid within 10 days of the purchase. No discount applies after 10 days. The *n/30* means that the total amount of the invoice must be paid within 30 days from the date that the invoice is received.

There are a few general tips you can follow to increase your accuracy when working with numbers:

a·lign'

re·verse'

1. Write legibly so that you and others can read the numbers.
2. Align decimal points when adding or subtracting numbers.
3. Learn to estimate. Estimating the answers before you figure them out manually or on the calculator will help you catch your errors.
4. Become familiar with your calculating equipment and use it properly.
5. Check your work! It takes only a few seconds to add a column of figures in reverse order to make sure your answer is correct.

222		339
143		143
+ 339		+ 222
704	=	704

Check subtraction by adding the difference to the amount that was subtracted. If you don't get your original amount, you've made an error.

$305.40	
− 104.60	
$200.80	difference
+ 104.60	
$305.40	original amount

o·mis'sions
de·tailed'
punc·tu·a'tion

Proofreading Always reread your completed forms. Check for keyboarding, spelling, and punctuation errors, and look for possible omissions (letters or material left out). To do a thorough job on lengthy or detailed material, ask another person to help you. In the teamwork approach, one person reads aloud from the original while the other proofreads the final draft. The reader should speak softly but clearly and alert the proofreader to punctuation, capitalization, and spacing. For example, the number 6.08 would be read: "Six point oh eight."

Neatness and Readability

Most forms are designed to allow enough space for the necessary information. If you realize that you are going to need more room than the form allows, adjust the size of your handwriting; or, if using 10-pitch type, change to 12-pitch. Keyboard above the line or within the space provided. Avoid keyboarding through the line, since the characters will be difficult to read. Use your tab key or decimal tab for neatly aligned columns and for faster keyboarding time.

Most companies require that one or more copies of every form be prepared. When making multiple copies, make sure that all of them can be read. If you try to make too many copies using NCR or carbon paper, the back copies will be light or smudged. You can normally make up to four good copies if you use a ballpoint pen on the original. A manual typewriter will give you about six readable copies; an electric typewriter, about twelve.

Standard Abbreviations

con·fu'sion

You can save space on most business forms by using abbreviations for frequently used words and phrases. Be sure to use standard abbreviations, or you will cause confusion. Refer to an office reference book for the following and other standard abbreviations.

Abbreviations used in mailing and shipping Forms that contain the mailing address of the customer or shipping instructions may also contain these abbreviations:

care of	c/o	express	exp.
cash on delivery	COD	freight	frt.

department	dept.	merchandise	mdse.
free on board	FOB	route	rte.

Amounts and quantities A few of the abbreviations used in manufacturing to express amount or quantity are:

barrel	bbl.	gross	gro.
box	bx.	kilogram	kg
100	C	liter	*l*
dozen	doz.	package	pkg.
each	ea.	pieces	pcs.
gallon	gal.	quart	qt.

Miscellaneous You will also see these abbreviations and symbols frequently used on forms for orders and inventory:

amount	amt.	numbers	nos.
at	@	order	ord.
cents	cts., ¢	quantity	qty.
each	ea.	total	tot., TL
minimum	min.	weight	wt.
maximum	max.	description	desc.

REVIEWING KEY POINTS

1. A purchase order is a legal contract to buy goods from a supplier.
2. A stock requisition authorizes removal of goods from inventory.
3. The invoice provides the supplier with a record of the shipment and presents the buyer with an official bill.
4. A supply or stock of goods is known as an inventory.
5. Companies keep track of inventory using one of two methods: perpetual or periodic. Many companies have computerized inventory systems.
6. At the end of the year, most companies take an actual inventory of goods in stock.
7. When a keyboard is used to complete forms, accuracy is usually more important than speed. All forms must be proofread for keyboarding, spelling, and punctuation errors.
8. Suppliers offer quantity, cash, or trade discounts to get larger orders, quick payments, or steady business from a buyer.

9. The extension is the total price of an item — the unit price multiplied by the quantity.
10. Standard abbreviations should be used on forms to save space and time.

DEVELOPING HUMAN RELATIONS SKILLS

1. Tina's company uses a perpetual inventory system for keeping track of office supplies. Employees must submit a signed requisition before Tina can issue the supplies they want. Everett Pell, who rides in Tina's carpool, telephoned her last week and asked her a favor. "Tina, we need a supply of V-395 to finish this payroll report. I'm in a real rush. Could you send up some, and I'll fill out the requisition slip later?" Tina sent the forms, but so far Everett has not sent her the requisition slip.
   a. Should Tina remind Everett about the requisition? How?
   b. What do you think might happen if the annual inventory count does not agree with the daily records?
   c. If you were Tina, would you do Everett any more favors like this? Why or why not?
2. Doug Looney and Harriett Weiskopf have been assigned the task of taking the annual inventory of departmental supplies. One person will count the items, and the other will write the information on the form. As they are taking the inventory, the following situations occur. If you were Harriett, what would you do in each situation?
   a. As they begin work, Doug says, "I'll do the counting, since I don't like to sit and write." Harriett doesn't like to sit and write either.
   b. Doug suggests estimating some items like the pens, file folders, and paper clips.

IMPROVING COMMUNICATION SKILLS

Refer to Appendix B 3.1–3.10.

1. The division of a word at the end of a line should be avoided whenever possible. However, sometimes such division is necessary. In the following sentences, the underlined word is one that must be divided at the end of a keyboarded line. Keyboard each sentence showing the correct division of the underlined word.
   a. Because of the increasing use of computers, people are beginning to look for better methods of data entry.
   b. Productivity and ergonomics are becoming central issues.
   c. Electronic keyboards eliminate the problem of keys jamming.
   d. It's not necessary for "speed limits" to be incorporated in keyboard designs.

e. Technological advancements mean that most keyboards can now be changed by putting caps on keys.

f. On the Dvorak keyboard, you can keyboard 3000 single words on the home row keys.

g. People tend to resist change, so Dvorak's innovative keyboard has been ignored for years.

h. Dvorak designed a keyboard that puts the most commonly used letters on home row.

i. Some studies show that Dvorak users are 40 percent more productive than users of the "QWERTY" keyboard.

2. Compose and keyboard a modified block letter on plain paper to order a copy of your class textbook as a gift for a friend. Address the letter to Houghton Mifflin Publishing Company, One Beacon Street, Boston, MA 02108. Request a copy of the text by name. Since you do not know the price of the book, direct them to ship the book C.O.D. (Collect on Delivery). You would like to have the text by three weeks from today.

BUILDING PROBLEM-SOLVING SKILLS

1. In the following portions of purchase orders, there are addition and/or multiplication errors. Find and correct the errors.

	Qt.	Description	Unit Price	Total
a.	3	Print/non-print calculator	$99.95	$298.89
	9	Personalized credit card calculator	35.95	322.65
		TOTAL		$521.50
b.	2	Automatic dial phone	$299.95	$579.18
	2	Ravaphone portable telephone—touch dial	379.95	759.90
	3	Muraphone	89.95	259.85
	3	Phone Mate	159.95	379.85
		TOTAL		$1,978.78
c.	2	Bio-clock calculator	$149.95	$298.90
	5	Bio-rhythm clock/calendar	79.95	399.75
		TOTAL		$688.65
d.	5	Jogging Suit	$59.95	$889.15
	12	Jogger's Watch	29.95	245.40
	18	Jogger's Calculator	59.95	1,169.10
	10	Jogging Platform	14.95	149.50
		TOTAL		$2,503.15

2. Name-Brand Distributors gives its best customers cash discounts ranging from 1 to 3 percent on invoices paid within 10 days. Study the table shown on the next page. Then, on a separate sheet of paper, answer the questions.

Invoice No.	Terms	Invoice Total	Discount	Net Price
4087	1/10 net 30	$ 683.95		
4088	3/10 net 30	459.11		
4089	2/10 net 30	2,096.23		
4090	2/10 net 30	788.50		
4091	3/10 net 30	281.71		
4092	1/10 net 30	98.32		
4093	3/10 net 30	118.65		

a. What is the net price each customer will pay if the discount is taken?
b. If every customer pays within 10 days, how much money will Name-Brand Distributors collect for these invoices?

3. Compute the extensions for the following items ordered from Devok Data Products. Write your answers on a separate sheet and show your work.
10 FileLoks @ $18.50/ea.
2 Hygrometers @ $98/ea.
25 Mag Tape Mailers @ $1.35/ea.
14 Printout Rulers @ $4.95/ea.
75 Floppy Storage Pages @ $.83/ea.
35 Diskette Mailers @ $1.05/ea.

APPLYING OFFICE SKILLS

Activities 2 and 3 can be done on information processing equipment.

1. You work in the Public Relations Department. Prepare a purchase requisition dated today using the following information. The information should be handwritten neatly and accurately on the form in your workbook. If you do not have a workbook, use a plain sheet of paper on which you have keyboarded the appropriate headings.

Requisition No. 7131/ Date needed: $1\frac{1}{2}$ months from today/ Order to be delivered to you/ 1 HPR721 Executive Desk/ 1 HP2011 Executive High Back Chair (Brown)/ 1 HP0113 Arm Chair (Gold)/ 3 HNB27 42" Steel Bookcases

2. Select two office supply companies from the telephone book and use them in preparing invoices for the following items. Use the addresses you find in the telephone book. Figure the extensions, total the invoices, and check your work. Use standard abbreviations. Keyboard the invoices on the forms provided in your workbook or on a sheet of paper with appropriate headings.

a. Invoice No. 1–226, Order No. 921, ship by truck, 2/10 net 30.

- Inventory Card Forms (BC–C–014) 2 Boxes, $5.20 per box
- Snap-Away Reply Forms (EC–44–146) 1 Box, $27.20 per box
- NCR Order Forms (D2–3720) 4 Packages, $4.20 per package
- Acknowledgment of Order Cards 5 Packages, $4.25 per package

b. Invoice No. 1–227, Order No. 8135, ship by truck, 2/10 net 30.

- Rotary Diskette Stands (RS–200) 10 @ $29.95 each
- Heavy Duty Data Binders (A9–16–811N) Blue 13 @ $9.70 each or five for $45.00
- Open Top Data Racks (A9–24–11T) 2 @ $87.90 each
- Punched-card Trays (A9–24–145T) 4 @ $16.10 each

3. Prepare a purchase order register using the information shown here and on the next page. Use the purchase order register in your workbook. If you do not have a workbook, use a sheet of paper that you have ruled to resemble a purchase order register.

The LINCOLN Company **PURCHASE ORDER**

9 Sparhawk Street
Anchorage, AK 99504
Phone (907) 388-9232

To: Natmar, Inc.
211 South Washington Street
South Bend, IN 46601

Date: March 12, 19--
Order Number: 339
Shipped by: Rail

Quantity	Item	Unit Price	Total
6	A-1 Temp gauges	$21.41	$128.46

HAUGEN & CATRON, Inc. **Purchase Order**

482 Commercial Street
Salem, OR 97301
(503) 865-3893

TO:
Natmar, Inc.
211 South Washington Street
South Bend, IN 46601

Date: March 11, 19--
Order No.: 921
Shipped By: Truck

QUANTITY	ITEM	UNIT PRICE	TOTAL
500	Steel ball knobs	$1.60	$800.00

SYSTEMS COMPANY 482 Brandon Road, Charleston, West Virginia 25704 304-889-9992

Joan Carroll, Owner

PURCHASE ORDER

Sold To:
Natmar, Inc.
211 South Washington Street
South Bend, IN 46601

DATE: March 11, 19--
Order No.: 057
Shipped By: Truck

Quantity	*Description*	*Unit Price*	*Total*
4	Dial indicator test sets	$97.80	$391.20

I. A. Hines, Ltd. 12 Ahlers Blvd., Ottawa, Ontario, Canada 613-290-6669

Purchase Order

To
Natmar, Inc.
211 South Washington Street
South Bend, IN 46601

Date: March 12, 19--
Order No.: 112
Ship Via: Railroad express

Quantity	Item	Unit Price	Total
3	Magnetic contour gauges	$19.50	$58.50

CHAPTER 3

PAYMENT PROCEDURES

When a company buys products and services, checks are the most frequently used form of payment. They can be safely sent through the mail, as you have read, so they are convenient to use. Using a checking account is also helpful in maintaining good records of payments. When kept up to date, the check register provides a record of payments from and deposits to the checking account. And canceled checks provide proof of payment.

Despite the popularity of checking accounts with businesses and individuals, there are times when other forms of payment are used. These other forms include petty cash, credit cards, and money orders. There are also various special types of checks, including certified checks, cashier's checks, and traveler's checks.

As you study this chapter, you will find answers to the following questions:

- What is the purpose of a petty cash fund?
- How do you set up, use, and replenish a petty cash fund?
- What are the five other forms of payment that are frequently used by businesses and individuals?
- What do the following terms mean: **petty cash fund, petty cash voucher, certified check, cashier's check, money order, traveler's check?**

Illustration 13–16
Petty cash book

	DATE		VOU. NO.	EXPLANATION	PETTY CASH RECEIVED	PETTY CASH PAID OUT
1	Apr.	1		Set up fund	50 00	
2		1	001	Postage		6 00
3		3	002	Calculator repair		21 40
4		5	003	Newspapers		75
5		10	004	Notary fee		1 00
6		15	005	Special delivery		5 50
7		20	006	Classified ad		6 50
8		20		Totals	50 00	41 15
9						
10				Balance in fund $8.85		
11		23		Replenish fund, Chk. No. 368	41 15	
12		26	007	Taxi fare		8 75
13						

PETTY CASH

e·mer'gen·cy

Most companies keep a certain amount of cash on hand in the office to pay for small business expenses. Small business expenses include items that cost less than fifty dollars, such as postage, notary fees, and emergency office supplies. These items are paid for with cash taken from the **petty cash fund,** a fund of money kept on hand for small purchases. If you work for a company that has a petty cash fund, part of your support responsibilities may include recording petty cash transactions.

Setting Up the Petty Cash Fund

re·plen'ish·ing

The amount of money kept in the petty cash fund is based on an estimate of the small purchases that are likely to be made during a short period, such as a month. The petty cash fund is set up by writing a check for this amount. For example, the company may estimate that it spends about one hundred dollars a month on small expenses. A check is cashed for this amount, and the money is turned over to the petty cash clerk or an office worker responsible for the fund. This person is responsible for keeping records, making payments, and replenishing the petty cash fund when it gets too low. The petty cash clerk generally has other office responsibilities as well, which may include keyboarding, filing, or receiving callers.

The petty cash clerk records the amount of money received in the petty cash book. All petty cash transactions are recorded in the book, along with explanations of the transactions. As Illustration 13–16 shows, when the fund is set up, the amount received is recorded in the Explanation column.

DISTRIBUTION OF EXPENSES					
OFFICE EXPENSE	DELIVERY EXPENSE	MISC. GEN. EXPENSE	OTHER EXPENSES		
			ACCOUNT	AMOUNT	
					1
		6 00			2
21 40					3
		75			4
		1 00			5
	5 50				6
			Advertising Exp.	6 50	7
21 40	5 50	7 75		6 50	8
					9
					10
					11
		8 75			12
					13

Recording Cash Payments

How does the petty cash fund work? Suppose you are preparing some contracts that are to be mailed. Your supervisor asks you to leave work a little early so you can stop by the post office and send the contracts by certified mail. You pay the postage fees out of your own money and keep a receipt for the amount paid. You will be reimbursed, or paid back, this amount out of petty cash.

re·im·bursed′

In order to get reimbursed, or whenever payment is made from petty cash, you need to do the following:

vouch′er

1. Prepare a **petty cash voucher** similar to the one shown in Illustration 13–17 on page 542. This form contains the date, your name, the amount of money desired, the reason for payment, and the type of expense.
2. Submit the petty cash voucher to your supervisor for approval.
3. Give the approved voucher to the petty cash clerk in exchange for the cash requested.

Whenever cash is taken from the petty cash fund, the petty cash clerk records information from the voucher in the petty cash book. As with other types of accounting records, the petty cash book must be kept in balance. Every payment transaction requires two entries: one entry in the Petty Cash Paid Out column and one entry in the Distribution of Expenses column.

dis·tri·bu′tion

Look at the second line in Illustration 13–16, which shows the entry for the postage. The date, voucher number, and explanation of the expense are entered. The amount of the expense, $6, is entered in the Distribution of

Illustration 13–17
Petty cash voucher

PETTY CASH VOUCHER

No. 001 Date April 1, 19–

Paid to U. S. Postal Service $ 6.00

For Certified Mail fees

Account Miscellaneous expense

Approved by G. Carpentier

Payment received by E. Jordan

clas·si·fi·ca′tion

Expenses column under the account titled Miscellaneous General Expense. The correct expense classification comes from the Account line on the petty cash voucher. Because two entries are required for each payment transaction, the same amount is entered in the Petty Cash Paid Out column.

Replenishing the Petty Cash Fund

At the end of a week, month, or quarter (depending on the number of cash payments), the paid-out vouchers are totaled and the cash left in petty cash is counted. The sum of the vouchers and of the cash on hand should equal the original amount of the petty cash fund. For example, suppose that the petty cash fund was started with $100. If the remaining balance at the end of the month or quarter is $20, then the paid-out vouchers should total $80.

When the amount of cash in the petty cash fund drops below a certain level — $20, for example — the petty cash clerk prepares a report to get enough cash to bring the petty cash fund back to its original total. This is called *replenishing* the petty cash fund. The procedures for replenishing the fund are as follows:

es·tab′lish

1. Draw a single line beneath all columns in the petty cash book and total each column.
2. Add the account totals of the Distribution of Expenses column to make sure they equal the total of the Paid Out column. Then draw a double rule across all columns containing amounts.
3. Subtract the Petty Cash Paid Out total from the amount of the check used to establish the petty cash fund. Write the difference in the Explanation column with the words *Balance in Fund.* (Check to be sure that this amount of cash is actually left in the fund.)
4. Complete a Petty Cash Report (shown in Illustration 13–18) to replenish the fund.

   - Sort the paid-out vouchers according to type of expense (account title) and total the amounts. Record the account titles and amounts on the Petty Cash Report.

Illustration 13–18
Petty cash report

Payments	
Account	Amount
Office expense	21.40
Delivery expense	5.50
Miscellaneous expense	7.75
Advertising expense	6.50
Total Requested	41.15

Date 4/20/-- Clerk Bob Fagin

Check No. 368 Date 4/21/--

By Harriet Goldstein

- Submit the form to the company accountant. The accountant writes a check for the amount needed to replenish the fund and completes the bottom of the Petty Cash Report. This information includes the check number, date, and accountant's name.

5. Enter the amount of the check in the petty cash book with the explanation *Replenish Fund;* include the check number.
6. File the paid-out vouchers and the petty cash report form in a folder or envelope labeled *Petty Cash Paid Out.*

ac'cu·rate

The petty cash clerk is responsible for replenishing the fund as necessary to ensure that there is enough cash on hand. For this reason, accurate records must be kept of every petty cash transaction. These records, and the fund itself, must be stored in a safe place. Frequently, a locked box is used to hold petty cash and related records.

OTHER FORMS OF PAYMENT

Petty cash is a convenient means of paying for small purchases. But writing checks on a business account is the preferred way to make most payments.

Illustration 13-19
Money order

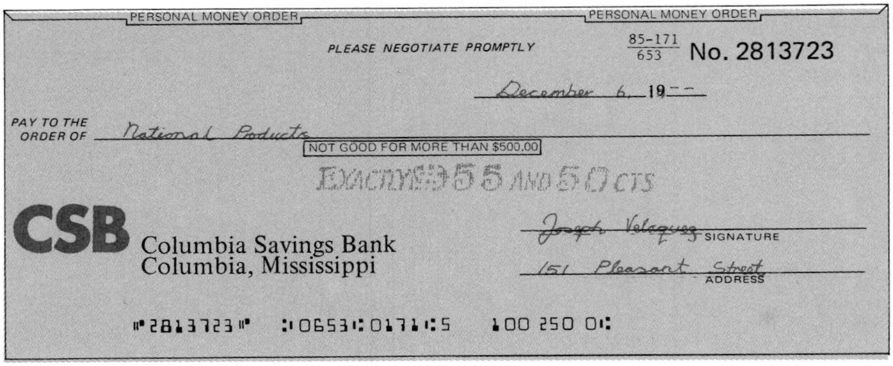

PERSONAL MONEY ORDER | PERSONAL MONEY ORDER

PLEASE NEGOTIATE PROMPTLY | 85-171/653 No. 2813723

December 6, 19--

PAY TO THE ORDER OF National Products

NOT GOOD FOR MORE THAN $500.00

EXACTLY $55 AND 50 CTS

CSB Columbia Savings Bank
Columbia, Mississippi

Joseph Velazquez SIGNATURE

151 Pleasant Street ADDRESS

2813723 0653 0171 5 100 250 0

However, there are times when a check is not acceptable and when carrying large amounts of cash is not wise. For example, some businesses do not accept out-of-town checks. So, business people who travel may find it hard to cash checks in other cities. Because checks are not always accepted, there are other methods of payment available through banks and other companies. These methods include credit cards, certified checks, cashier's checks, money orders, and traveler's checks.

Credit Cards

Many banks offer credit cards that are accepted by businesses nationwide. Visa and Mastercard are two examples. There are also companies that issue credit cards and provide other services to members who pay an annual fee. American Express, Carte Blanche, and Diner's Club are examples of such cards. Individuals and businesses can apply for these cards.

card'hold·er

When payment is made with a credit card, the cardholder gives the card to the cashier. The cashier completes a credit card form, which the cardholder signs. The store, the cardholder, and the credit card company each receive a copy of this form. At the end of the billing period, the cardholder receives a statement listing all purchases made with the credit card. If the statement is correct, the cardholder pays the credit card company part or all of the amount owed. Generally, the cardholder is required to pay only a portion of the total each billing period and is charged interest on the balance.

Certified Checks

cer'ti·fied

A **certified check** is a check guaranteed by a bank. The bank certifies — or guarantees — that the person has money in the account to cover the amount of the check. To purchase a certified check, you go to the bank and write a check for a particular amount. The bank sets aside that amount from your account and stamps *Certified* across the face of the check. Certified checks are frequently used for large cash purchases or for legal transactions.

Illustration 13–20
Traveler's check

Cashier's Checks

A **cashier's check** is a bank's own order to make payment out of bank funds. You can purchase a cashier's check by presenting a check or cash — plus a fee — to any bank. The bank then writes a check on its own account to the person or company that you specify. You receive a copy for your records.

Money Orders

A **money order** is similar to a cashier's check, but it can be purchased at post offices and some convenience stores, as well as at banks. A money order is made out to a specific person or company and for a specific amount. When the person named endorses the money order, it can be used just like cash.

Money orders can also be purchased from and sent by Western Union. The amount of the order is given to Western Union along with the name and address of the payee. There is a fee for the money order. If a message is to be sent with it, there is an additional charge. The money is sent by Western Union, and the payee is notified by a local Western Union office when the money arrives. To get the money, the payee must go to the Western Union office and provide identification.

Traveler's Checks

A **traveler's check** is a special payment device designed for people who travel. The checks are printed in various amounts, usually $10, $20, $50, and $100. You choose the total amount and the denominations in which you want that amount. For example, you may ask for five $10 traveler's checks. When you purchase the checks, you pay a small fee and sign your name on each check at the top. When you want to cash a traveler's check, you must *countersign* it — that is, sign your name a second time. If your checks are lost or stolen without this second signature, your money is refunded.

REVIEWING KEY POINTS

1. Petty cash is kept on hand for small business expenses.
2. Petty cash transactions are usually recorded in a petty cash book.
3. A petty cash voucher is prepared whenever money is taken from the petty cash fund.
4. When cash is paid out of petty cash, the payment is listed in both the Petty Cash Paid Out and Distribution of Expenses columns.
5. When money is added to the petty cash fund to bring it back to its original balance, the fund is said to be *replenished.*
6. Credit cards and traveler's checks are convenient methods of payment, particularly when you are out of town.
7. Certified checks, cashier's checks, and money orders are accepted almost anywhere because payment is guaranteed.

DEVELOPING HUMAN RELATIONS SKILLS

1. A friend of yours at the office manages the petty cash fund. A couple of times each month she borrows small amounts of money from the fund — usually when she has forgotten to cash a check or is running short of cash. She always leaves an IOU and always repays the amounts before the fund has to be replenished.
   a. In your opinion, is this honest? Explain.
   b. What do you think might happen to your friend if a supervisor found the petty cash fund "short"?
2. The clerk in the accounting department is irritated at Deann Mears. Deann is the office receptionist and petty cash clerk. At the end of every month, Deann submits a Petty Cash Report to replenish the fund. The amount of the fund is $50. Because few cash payments are made, the vouchers submitted to replenish the fund often add up to only $5 or $10. The accounting clerk resents the extra work of having to prepare a check for such small amounts.
   a. How frequently do you think the fund should be replenished?
   b. Whom should the clerk discuss the problem with — Deann or her supervisor? Why?
   c. If you were the clerk and you decided to say something to Deann, what would you say and how would you tactfully bring it up?

IMPROVING COMMUNICATION SKILLS

Refer to Appendix B 3.1–3.10.

1. Keyboard the following sentences on a separate sheet of paper. For each underlined word, show how it might be divided at the end of a line. After you have completed keyboarding all of the sentences, go back and proofread each sentence carefully.
   a. Try to maintain a positive attitude.
   b. Don't dwell too much on disappointments and setbacks.
   c. Be motivated. Set goals and take pride in reaching them.
   d. Try to keep your self-confidence high.
   e. Don't be thwarted by time wasters, procrastination, and lack of organization.
   f. Learn to appreciate the little treasures presented to you each day: a witty remark or a word of praise from a friend.
   g. Focus on the end result of a project, the creative solution to a problem, and the reward for a job well done.
   h. Be enthusiastic about routine tasks, such as stuffing envelopes.
   i. Adopting an enthusiastic attitude and being positive, motivated, and determined can make work less tedious.
2. From your telephone Yellow Pages, select the name of a bank and copy its complete address. Using the letterhead stationery in your workbook or plain paper, keyboard a letter to the bank requesting information about the services that it offers to businesses. Your subject line is to be "Banking Services for Businesses." Indicate that your company is new to your city and that you need to select a bank with which to do business. Ask for a list of the services offered to businesses. Request that a customer service representative call to set up an appointment to present information to your supervisor.

BUILDING PROBLEM-SOLVING SKILLS

1. The Tarnow Company plans to set up a petty cash fund. Records for the last twelve months show that the following amounts were spent on small cash purchases: $27.50, $41.22, $53.90, $23.55, $48.63, $52.12, $35.50, $24.80, $43.75, $45.25, $37.65, and $28.60.
   a. What is the total amount for small cash purchases?
   b. What is the average amount spent each month on cash purchases? Round your answer to the nearest cent.
   c. Which of the small cash purchases were over the average monthly amount?
   d. Which of the purchases were less than the average monthly amount?

e. What percent of the small cash purchases were over the average monthly amount?

f. What percent of the small cash purchases were less than the average monthly amount?

g. What amount do you recommend should be used to establish the petty cash fund?

2. Identify by name and address a bank in your area. On a separate sheet of paper, prepare detailed instructions, including a rough map, of how to get to that bank from your school.

APPLYING OFFICE SKILLS

Activity 2 can be done on information processing equipment.

1. The following list shows the petty cash transactions for two departments in your company. Each department has a separate petty cash fund. In your workbook, there are petty cash vouchers, a petty cash book, and a Petty Cash Report to be used for recording these transactions. Working with a partner, complete the following activities:

   a. Select the department for which you will write petty cash vouchers. Your partner will write the vouchers for the other department.

   b. Complete a petty cash voucher for each transaction. Have your partner record your vouchers in the petty cash book.

   c. When you receive your partner's vouchers, record them in your petty cash book.

April — Personnel
- 2 Cashed $50.00 check to start petty cash fund.
- 5 Paid $1.29 for bandages.
- 6 Paid $2.50 for telegram.
- 15 Purchased file folders for $5.35.
- 16 Paid $3.05 for delivery charges.
- 22 Paid $5.50 COD charges.
- 23 Paid $11.20 for local newspaper subscription.
- 30 Requested replenishing check.

April — Copy Center
- 1 Cashed a check for $30.00 to set up petty cash fund.
- 2 Paid $14.50 for business cards.
- 6 Paid $4.60 for express charges on purchase.
- 9 Requested replenishing check.
- 12 Paid $7.50 for flowers for hospitalized worker.
- 20 Paid $3.50 freight charges.
- 21 Purchased coffee supplies for $12.73.
- 23 Paid $5.25 for taxi fare.

2. Compose a memo to all company employees informing them that a petty cash fund has been set up. Julie Stinson, Room 306-C, will be responsible for the fund. Explain the purpose of the fund and describe the procedures for submitting vouchers to receive payment. Each voucher must be approved by a department supervisor. Keyboard the memo on the memo form in your workbook or plain paper using today's date and your name.

CHAPTER 4

PAYROLL PROCEDURES

Every company, regardless of its size, needs payroll procedures and records. Employees expect to get paid for the work they do for a company, and the government requires companies to keep on file certain payroll information about every employee.

Payroll procedures vary from company to company. However, there are certain features common to all payroll systems. Whether a company prepares its payroll manually or by computer, it must figure total salaries and wages, withhold certain deductions, and maintain accurate records of all payroll activities.

Payroll is one of the most important and detailed systems in office work. In a small company, your regular duties may include some responsibility for payroll records and procedures. In a large company, payroll responsibilities are usually handled by payroll clerks in the accounting department. Whether you work for a small or a large company, however, you should be informed about payroll procedures because they affect how you are paid — and how much you are paid.

As you study this chapter, you will find answers to the following questions:

- How do you calculate salaries for hourly wages, piece rates, and commissions?
- What are the various required and optional payroll deductions?
- What are the differences between manual and automated payroll systems?
- What do the following terms mean: **salary, gross pay, deductions, net pay, commission, payroll check voucher, direct deposit?**

NAME	MARITAL STATUS	NO. OF EXEMPT.	TOTAL HOURS	EARNINGS REGULAR	EARNINGS OVERTIME	EARNINGS TOTAL
Alan Campbell	M	2	42	285 00	21 38	306 38
Roberto Barragan	S	0	40	331 75	—	331 75
Julia Sugarman	M	1	43	370 04	41 63	411 67
Christine Zimmerman	S	1	37½	290 63	—	290 63

Illustration 13–21
Payroll register

HOW EARNINGS ARE COMPUTED

ac·com'plish·ment

For many people, work brings a feeling of personal satisfaction and accomplishment. But, no matter how much people like their jobs, they expect to be paid for doing their work.

Earnings can be computed in several ways. Employees may be paid by the week or the month, by the hour, or by the piece. In some occupations, they may be paid according to how much money they make for the company. There are different procedures for determining earnings in each of the above situations.

Salaries

A **salary** is a weekly or a monthly rate given in exchange for a certain number of hours worked. Typically, full-time employees on salary are expected to work 40 hours a week. If they work more than 40 hours, they usually do not receive any additional (or overtime) pay. In most companies, salaried workers are not required to keep daily records of the hours they work. Those employees who are on salary usually are in upper-level positions with supervisory or administrative duties.

su·per·vi'so·ry

Hourly Wages

Many job positions within business and industry are classified as nonadministrative. Employees in these positions — including many office positions — are paid according to the number of hours they work. The standard work week for full-time employees is usually 40 hours, but in some companies it may be only 35 hours. Under the 1938 Fair Labor Standards Act, employees who are paid according to the number of hours they work must receive $1\frac{1}{2}$ times their regular pay rate for every hour they work over the standard number of work hours. For this reason, employees must keep records of the number of hours they work each week.

DEDUCTIONS					PAID
FEDERAL INCOME TAX	FICA TAX	OTHER		TOTAL	NET AMOUNT
		CODE	AMOUNT		
39.00	20.37	04	7.40	66.77	239.61
70.00	22.06	02	12.50	104.56	227.19
70.40	27.38	03	4.50	102.28	309.39
52.10	19.32	02	12.50	83.92	206.71

Computing wages The wages of hourly employees may be expressed as a weekly, monthly, or annual rate. In order for wages to be computed for a pay period, however, this rate must be expressed as an hourly rate.

Edwina Fuller is an hourly employee who earns $200 for a 40-hour week, or $5 an hour. In one week, she works 48 hours. Her earnings for the week include her regular wages plus 8 hours of overtime pay:

$200	*$5.00 per hour for 40 hours*
+60	*$7.50 per hour ($1\frac{1}{2} \times$ $5.00) for 8 hours*
$260	*Total earnings for the week*

time'cards

Using timecards Most companies issue timecards or time sheets to their employees. These forms are used to record the number of hours worked each day. Timecards may be filled in by hand or by machines. Employees record the time they begin work, the time taken out for lunch or breaks, and the time they leave at the end of the workday.

de·duc'tions

In some companies, employees figure their total regular hours worked and total overtime hours. In other companies, employees simply sign their completed timecards and send them to the payroll department, where the hours are totaled. Payroll clerks figure **gross pay** (the total amount earned), **deductions** (amounts subtracted from earnings), and **net pay** (gross pay minus deductions). Net pay is also known as take-home pay. This information is usually recorded on a payroll register similar to the one shown in Illustration 13–21.

Many companies have automated time clocks to record the hours worked. When employees arrive at work or leave for lunch, breaks, or for home at the end of the day, they "punch" in or out. They insert their timecards in the clock, which automatically prints the time. A typical timecard is shown in Illustration 13–22 on page 552.

ac'ti·vat·ed

Some time clocks are activated by an employee identification card. When entering or leaving the office, the employee inserts the card in the time clock. A computer reads the employee information from the card, records the time, and stores the information in memory.

Illustration 13–22
Employee timecard

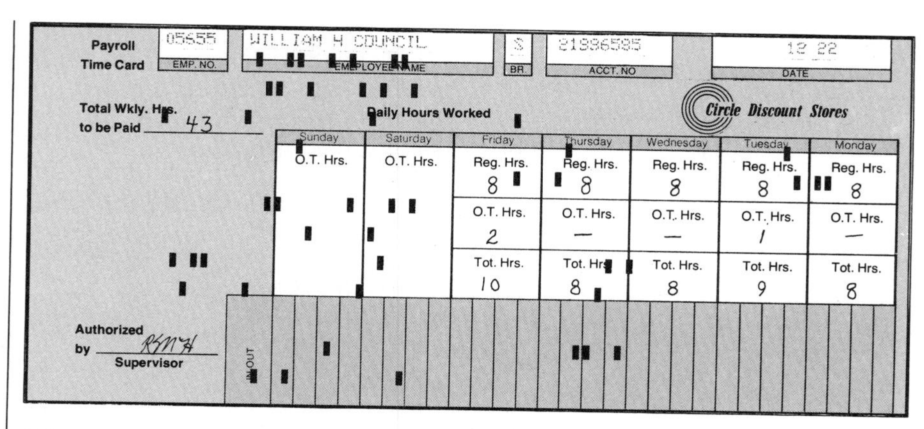
Payroll Time Card

EMP. NO.	EMPLOYEE NAME	BR	ACCT. NO	DATE
05655	WILLIAM H COUNCIL	S	21996585	12 22

Circle Discount Stores

Total Wkly. Hrs. to be Paid 43

Daily Hours Worked

	Sunday	Saturday	Friday	Thursday	Wednesday	Tuesday	Monday
Reg. Hrs.			8	8	8	8	8
O.T. Hrs.			2	—	—	1	—
Tot. Hrs.			10	8	8	9	8

Authorized by RSM Supervisor

IN OUT

Piece Rates

Employees who are paid by the piece receive a certain amount for each item produced. For example, a worker may recieve 15 cents for every electrical switch assembled. If the worker assembles 170 switches in a workday, then the pay for the day's work is $25.50, or 170 × $.15. With this system, accurate records must be kept of what each employee produces.

Commissions

com·mis'sion

In some businesses, all or part of a person's earnings are in the form of commissions. A **commission** is a percentage of money paid to a worker based on the performance of certain services. For example, a salesperson might be paid a base salary of $15,000 a year, plus a 10 percent commission on any sales above a certain dollar amount.

Bob Fagin sells men's shoes for a local department store. Bob receives $273 as a weekly salary. If he sells more than $1,000 worth of shoes a week, he also earns a commission of 10 percent on the amount over $1,000. In one week, Bob's sales totaled $1,350.50. His pay is figured as follows:

$ 1,350.50	*Week's sales*	*$273.00*	*Salary*
− 1,000.00	*Expected sales*	*35.05*	*Commission*
$ 350.50	*Base for commission*	*$308.05*	*Gross pay for week*
× .10	*Commission percentage*		
$ 35.0500	*Earned commission*		

TYPES OF PAYROLL DEDUCTIONS

No matter how much or how little an employee earns, in most instances, the employer takes certain deductions from the employee's total earnings. Deductions are of two types — required and optional.

Illustration 13–23 Employee's Withholding Allowance Certificate (W-4 form)

Form **W-4** | Department of the Treasury—Internal Revenue Service
Employee's Withholding Allowance Certificate

Print your full name ▶ Janet A. Conn | Your social security number ▶ 543 : 24 : 1680
Address (including ZIP code) 1582 North Pierce Street, Spokane, WA 99204
Marital status: ☐ Single ☒ Married ☐ Married, but withhold at higher Single rate
Note: *If married, but legally separated, or spouse is a nonresident alien, check the single block.*

1 Total number of allowances you are claiming (from line F of the worksheet on page 2) 1
2 Additional amount, if any, you want deducted from each pay (if your employer agrees) . . . . . $
3 I claim exemption from withholding because (see instructions and check boxes below that apply):
a ☐ Last year I did not owe any Federal income tax and had a right to a full refund of ALL income tax withheld, AND
b ☐ This year I do not expect to owe any Federal income tax and expect to have a right to a full refund of ALL income tax withheld. If both a and b apply, enter "EXEMPT" here . . . . ▶
c If you entered "EXEMPT" on line 3b, are you a full-time student? . . . . ☐ Yes ☐ No

Under the penalties of perjury, I certify that I am entitled to the number of withholding allowances claimed on this certificate, or if claiming exemption from withholding, that I am entitled to claim the exempt status.

Employee's signature ▶ Janet A. Conn Date ▶ February 1, 19—
Employer's name and address (including ZIP code) (FOR EMPLOYER'S USE ONLY) | Employer identification number

Required Deductions

com·pen·sa'tion

Required deductions include federal income tax, social security, workmen's compensation, and state income tax.

spon'sored

Federal income tax The U.S. Constitution gives Congress the power to impose and collect taxes on income earned in the United States. Therefore, every worker pays federal income taxes. These taxes are used to pay for government expenses and for programs sponsored by the government.

with·hold'

al·low'anc·es

ex·emp'tion

The federal government requires workers to complete an Employee's Withholding Allowance Certificate when they are hired. This form, shown in Illustration 13–23, is also known as a W-4 Form. Based on information supplied on this form, an employer is required by law to withhold (deduct) a specific amount from the employee's paycheck each pay period. Tax tables supplied by the government show the employer how much to withhold. The amount of income tax to be withheld is determined by the employee's total earnings, the employee's marital status, and the number of allowances (or exemptions) claimed. For example:

> *Janet Conn is married and earns $267 a week. On her W-4 Form, she claimed only one exemption — herself. The federal income tax table in Illustration 13–24 shows that married people earning between $260 and $270 weekly with one exemption must pay $34.60 in federal taxes. Each week, Janet's employer deducts that amount from her paycheck toward payment of that tax.*

dis·a'bled

Social security In 1935, the Federal Insurance Contribution Act (FICA), better known as social security, was passed to provide a minimum income for the elderly and for disabled workers and their dependents. Social security also provides funds for hospital care for the retired. All workers are required to have a social security number, assigned by the federal government, to aid in the required record keeping.

Illustration 13–24
Federal income tax table

WEEKLY Payroll Period—Employee MARRIED

And the wages are—		And the number of withholding allowances claimed is—										
At least	But less than	0	1	2	3	4	5	6	7	8	9	10 or more
		The amount of income tax to be withheld shall be—										
70	72	3.70	.80	0	0	0	0	0	0	0	0	0
72	74	4.00	1.10	0	0	0	0	0	0	0	0	0
74	76	4.30	1.40	0	0	0	0	0	0	0	0	0
76	78	4.60	1.70	0	0	0	0	[illegible]	0	0	0	0
130	135	13.10	[illegible]	[illegible]	[illegible]	[illegible]	[illegible]	[illegible]	[illegible]	[illegible]	[illegible]	[illegible]
135	140	14.00	10.80	7.90	5.00	2.20	0	0	0	0	0	0
140	145	14.90	11.60	8.70	5.80	2.90	0	0	0	0	0	0
145	150	15.80	12.40	9.40	6.50	3.70	.80	0	0	0	0	0
150	160	17.20	13.70	10.60	7.70	4.80	1.90	0	0	0	0	0
160	170	19.00	15.50	12.10	9.20	6.30	3.40	.50	0	0	0	0
170	180	20.80	17.30	13.80	10.70	7.80	4.90	2.00	0	0	0	0
180	190	22.60	19.10	15.60	12.20	9.30	6.40	3.50	.60	0	0	0
190	200	24.40	20.90	17.40	14.00	10.80	7.90	5.00	2.10	0	0	0
200	210	26.20	22.70	19.20	15.80	12.30	9.40	6.50	3.60	.80	0	0
210	220	28.10	24.50	21.00	17.60	14.10	10.90	8.00	5.10	2.30	0	0
220	230	30.20	26.30	22.80	19.40	15.90	12.50	9.50	6.60	3.80	.90	0
230	240	32.30	28.30	24.60	21.20	17.70	14.30	11.00	8.10	5.30	2.40	0
240	250	34.40	30.40	26.40	23.00	19.50	16.10	12.60	9.60	6.80	3.90	1.00
250	260	36.50	32.50	28.50	24.80	21.30	17.90	14.40	11.10	8.30	5.40	2.50
260	270	38.60	34.60	30.60	26.60	23.10	19.70	16.20	12.70	9.80	6.90	4.00
270	280	40.70	36.70	32.70	28.60	24.90	21.50	18.00	14.50	11.30	8.40	5.50
280	290	42.80	38.80	34.80	30.70	26.70	23.30	19.80	16.30	12.90	9.90	7.00
290	300	45.10	40.90	36.90	32.80	28.80	25.10	21.60	18.10	14.70	11.40	8.50

Social security is paid for by a tax placed on the earnings of the employee. The employer also pays FICA tax, matching the amount paid by the employee. All people are taxed equally for social security up to a certain amount of their earnings. When their earnings reach this amount, which is determined by Congress, no additional social security tax is deducted from their earnings.

Today, a worker has 7.15 percent deducted on the first $43,200 of earnings. The maximum that can be deducted is $3,088.80. Additional income over $43,200 is not taxed for social security. Because the employee and the employer contribute equally, the maximum social security tax on a worker's gross income for one year amounts to $6,177.60 — $3,088.80 doubled. Each pay period, the employer deducts from the worker's salary a portion of the amount toward payment of the tax. The maximum amount of earnings to be taxed and the percentage are set by Congress and changed as the need arises.

con·trib'ute

Workmen's compensation Workmen's compensation insures the employee against loss of pay resulting from accidents on the job or from job-related illnesses. It pays some or all of the worker's medical expenses and pays a portion of the wages while the employee is unable to work. Both the employer and the employee pay for this insurance. The employer pays an amount depending on (1) the danger of the job and (2) the safety record of the company. For example, a construction company might pay $20 per $200 paid in salaries to construction workers for workmen's compensation. A company employing office workers may pay only 50 cents per $100 in salaries, since the work is much less dangerous than construction work. The employee also contributes a small amount to workmen's compensation.

State income tax Most states (and some cities) require a tax on personal income. State income taxes provide the state with the money it needs to finance government programs such as education, highway construction, welfare, and public transportation.

State income tax may be a flat rate (such as 5 percent) or — like federal income tax — a rate that increases as the taxpayer's income goes up. For example, a person earning between $8,000 and $9,999 may pay 3 percent in state income tax. A person earning between $14,000 and $15,999, on the other hand, may pay 6 percent.

Optional Deductions

op'tion·al

Other payroll deductions are optional and are made at the request of the employee or the employer. Many of these optional deductions are considered benefits of employment.

cov'er·age

Group health or life insurance Some companies offer insurance programs to employees at a reduced rate. Employees pay for their coverage through payroll deductions.

re·tire'ment

Retirement programs Many companies provide retirement or pension programs as a fringe benefit of employment. In some companies, the employee pays all or part of the cost of the retirement program through regular payroll deductions.

Credit union A credit union is an employee organization that provides loans and savings programs to its members. A credit union usually makes arrangements with the payroll department to allow its members to make payments on loans or make deposits to savings accounts through payroll deductions.

char'i·ties

Charitable donations Some companies make it easier for employees to make donations to certain charities through payroll deductions.

Union and association dues When membership in a union is required for employment with a company, union dues are automatically deducted from the employee's paycheck. When union membership is not required, employees may still request that union dues be deducted from their paychecks.

The kinds of optional deductions that can be made from an employee's paycheck are determined by the managers of the company in keeping with federal and state laws.

PAYROLL RECORDS

Each business develops its own forms for payroll and personnel administration. If you are responsible for payroll or personnel records, study the necessary forms carefully before completing them. Although accuracy is always important in office work, you should take extra care when handling any forms that may affect another employee's earnings. And remember that many payroll and personnel records are confidential. Never discuss them with people outside the payroll department.

af·fect'

PAYROLL ACCOUNTING SYSTEMS

bi·week'ly

Weekly, biweekly, or monthly, companies issue paychecks to their employees. Computing the payroll and preparing the paychecks for payday require an efficient payroll accounting system. A payroll accounting system involves all of the forms, policies, and procedures having to do with paying employees. It includes the following activities:

- recording of hours worked, salaries, piece rates, and commissions
- computing gross pay, deductions, and net pay
- preparing employee earning records
- issuing paychecks
- recording payroll expenses in the company's books
- preparing reports for employees, government agencies, labor unions, and management

is'su·ing

Most payroll systems used today in businesses are either manual or computerized systems.

Manual Payroll Systems

In many small companies, the payroll is prepared by hand. The name of every employee is listed on a payroll register or record sheet. The employee's earnings and deductions are also recorded in the appropriate columns of the register. The payroll clerk uses these figures to prepare the paycheck (or cash, in some cases) for each employee.

stream'lined

This manual procedure has been streamlined in some businesses through the use of *folding bookkeeping systems,* also called *pegboard systems.* These systems consist of payroll forms with holes punched along the edge so that they can be bound together in a book-type fashion. These holes align the various payroll forms so that, in one writing, you can record information on several forms at once. For example, as you write a paycheck, carbon entries go onto the earning records and the payroll journal. Folding bookkeeping systems reduce the chance that copying and recording errors will be made.

In most instances, the employee's paycheck has a stub attached, called a voucher. The **payroll check voucher** lists the employee's gross earnings, deductions, and net pay. If employees are paid in cash, an employee in the payroll department usually prepares one check for the total amount of cash needed for payroll. After the check is cashed, a payroll clerk counts out each employee's earnings and puts them in individual pay envelopes. On the pay envelope, or on a slip of paper that is put in the envelope, the payroll clerk lists the amount of gross earnings, deductions, and net income.

Computerized Payroll Systems

Most companies today prepare their payrolls using information processing equipment.

Master payroll information — employees' names, social security numbers, deductions, and exemptions — is stored in the computer. At the end of a pay period, a payroll clerk inputs the number of hours worked by each employee. If a time clock is used, employee hours can be entered directly into the computer as the employees punch in and out. Based on information stored in the computer, the computer calculates gross earnings, subtracts deductions, and determines net pay.

The computer is used to print the payroll register, paychecks, and check stubs with earnings information. Financial reports can also be prepared easily with the computer, since the information is stored in memory and can be easily manipulated.

As a result of today's technology, many companies are offering their employees the option of direct deposit of their paychecks. With **direct deposit,** an employee's net pay is deposited directly, by means of Electronic Funds Transfer, to his or her personal checking account. The employee gets the voucher for the check; the bank gets a computer tape or card showing the earnings that are to be added to the employee's account. The bank then runs the tape or card through the bank's computer system.

REVIEWING KEY POINTS

1. An employee's earnings may be based on a weekly or monthly salary, an hourly wage, a piece rate, or a commission.
2. Hourly workers receive overtime pay of $1\frac{1}{2}$ times their regular wages for each hour of work over a certain standard, usually 40 hours.
3. Timecards or time sheets are used to record the hours an employee works.
4. A commission is a percentage of money paid to a worker based on the performance of certain services.
5. An employee's net pay, also called take-home pay, is the gross pay minus any deductions.
6. The two types of deductions are required and optional.

7. Required deductions include federal income tax, social security, workmen's compensation, and state income tax.
8. Optional deductions may be made for group health and life insurance, retirement programs, credit union, donations to charities, and union and association dues.
9. All employees must complete an Employee's Withholding Allowance Certificate and have a social security number.
10. A payroll accounting system involves all of the forms, policies, and procedures related to paying employees. Both manual and computerized payroll systems are used in business.

DEVELOPING HUMAN RELATIONS SKILLS

1. Ken Fitts and Lisa Beatty are good friends, and they work for the same company. Ken is a technical secretary in the engineering department; Lisa is a payroll clerk in the accounting department. Ken and Lisa frequently take coffee breaks together and sometimes have lunch together.

   At lunch one day, Ken tells Lisa about his career path plans. He is very interested in his supervisor's job responsibilities and salary rate. Ken knows that Lisa handles the payroll information for his department, and he is hoping that she will volunteer this information. But Lisa doesn't. Finally, Ken's curiosity gets the best of him. He asks Lisa what salary his supervisor is paid.
   - **a.** How do you think Lisa should respond to Ken's question? Why?
   - **b.** What types of information do you believe should remain confidential in the office? Why?
2. A friend of yours gives you a copy of the payroll register printout for the workers in your office. She got someone in payroll to run an extra copy. She points to your salary and the salary of another person in the office. There is a $75 difference in pay. That person has the same credentials as you but is earning more.
   - **a.** What problems could result if everyone in the office had copies of the payroll register?
   - **b.** What would you do now that you know you are earning less than a coworker who has the same qualifications as you?

IMPROVING COMMUNICATION SKILLS

Refer to Appendix B 3.1–3.10.

1. On a separate sheet of paper, keyboard the correct syllabication of the following words. Use the same three-column format that is shown here.

a. transportation	**c.** report	**e.** through
b. cancellation	**d.** repetition	**f.** bulletin

g. organize
h. reimbursement
i. business
j. budget
k. internal
l. accept

2. Compose and keyboard an order letter for two books that will help you with your tax information. Use block format and a subject line of "Order for Books." The books are published by Williams Publishing Company, 1230 Avenue of the Americas, New York, NY 10020-0045. Direct the order to the Tax Department. You are interested in purchasing STEIN'S INCOME TAX GUIDE by J. D. Stein and THE COMPLETE PERSONAL TAX RECORD BOOK by Darlene Hesoun. Stein's book is $19.95; Hesoun's book is $6.95. You are enclosing a check for the full amount.

BUILDING PROBLEM-SOLVING SKILLS

1. Using a separate sheet of paper and showing all your calculations, figure the amount of commission and gross salary for the following people.
   a. Deborah Chalk — salary of $360 plus a commission of 3.5% on sales of $6,000.
   b. Mindy Bork — salary of $425 plus a commission of 5% on $2,000.
   c. Steven Boyde — 6% commission on sales of $8,550.
   d. Homer DeWald — salary of $308 plus a commission of 4.5% on $1,500.
   e. Tripta Desai — $475 salary with a 2% commission on sales of $1,000.
2. Using plain paper, show your work to convert the minutes shown here to hours. Convert any parts of hours to decimals. For example, 135 minutes = 2.25 hours (2 hours and 15 minutes).

a. 90′ =	d. 145′ =	g. 45′ =	j. 150′ =
b. 285′ =	e. 30′ =	h. 375′ =	k. 175′ =
c. 192′ =	f. 140′ =	i. 470′ =	l. 125′ =

APPLYING OFFICE SKILLS

1. Complete the timecards in your workbook for the following employees:

Joy Haynes
Hourly Rate $4.10

M	7:30–11:31	12:01–4:04
Tu	7:30–11:33	12:03–6:00
W	7:30–11:30	12:00–4:02
Th	7:30–11:30	12:02–4:13
F	7:28–11:28	11:59–4:01

Charlie Lim
Hourly Rate $4.00

M	7:28–11:30	12:00–4:59	
Tu	7:31–11:31	12:02–4:01	
W	7:27–11:29	11:58–4:03	
Th	7:31–11:33	12:29–4:00	4:31–7:30
F	7:30–11:30	12:00–4:01	8:00–10:55

Ed Martin Hourly Rate $5.05		
M	8:00–11:59	12:59–4:02
Tu	7:59–12:00	12:58–3:59
W	8:03–12:05	1:03–4:59
Th	7:57–12:01	12:59–4:05
F	7:00–12:01	1:03–3:55

Judith Stevens Hourly Rate $4.90			
M	8:00–11:55	12:59–4:07	4:30–6:00
Tu	7:01–12:00	1:00–5:01	
W	7:30–12:01	1:01–4:59	
Th	8:01–11:59	12:58–4:04	6:00–6:30
F	7:01–12:00	1:01–4:09	

2. Using the information in Activity 1 and the tax table on page 554, complete the payroll register. A copy is provided in your workbook.

PAYROLL FOR WEEK ENDING

NAME	MARITAL STATUS	NO. OF EXEMPT	TOTAL HOURS	EARNINGS REGULAR	EARNINGS OVERTIME	EARNINGS TOTAL
Phelps, Irene	S	0	40	210 00		210 00
Voyles, Jude	S	1	40	290 50		290 50
Hill, June	M	3	42	250 00	18 75	268 75
Martin, Ed	M	2				
Belcher, Gary	S	1	45	180 00	33 75	213 75
Sebbe, Nancy	S	1	40	350 00		350 00
Haynes, Joy	M	1				
Lim, Charlie	M	1				
Hatch, Eric	S	0	44½	340 00	57 38	397 38
Stevens, Judith	M	2				

Saving Time and Money

1. Check monthly statements for accuracy as soon as you receive them. Notify the bank at once if you find an error.
2. Keep blank checks in a safe place. If any numbered checks are lost or stolen, notify the bank at once.
3. Protect canceled checks. They are your proof of payment. Also, a forger could use them to copy your signature.
4. Stop payment on lost checks or checks that have not been cashed within a few months.
5. Cash or deposit checks you receive from others as soon as possible.
6. Don't accept a check that is more than six months old without first checking with the bank on which it is drawn.

UNIT 14

INTEGRATING OFFICE SYSTEMS

The Electronic Office •

Integrated Office Systems at Compuchips, Inc. •

CHAPTER 1

THE ELECTRONIC OFFICE

You have learned about the procedures and systems used by the departments in a company to process information. You have also learned how information processing systems are used to process information in its various forms — words, data, voice, and graphics. Now you will learn how information processing systems can be integrated so information becomes more accessible to all of its users. Office systems that are integrated are also called automated office systems or electronic office systems. In this unit, we will refer to these systems as integrated office systems.

As you study this chapter, you will find answers to the following questions:

- What is an integrated office system?
- How do various office workers use integrated systems?
- How can productivity be improved with an integrated office system?
- What do the following terms mean: **integrated office system, integrated software, local area network (LAN), data base, electronic mail?**

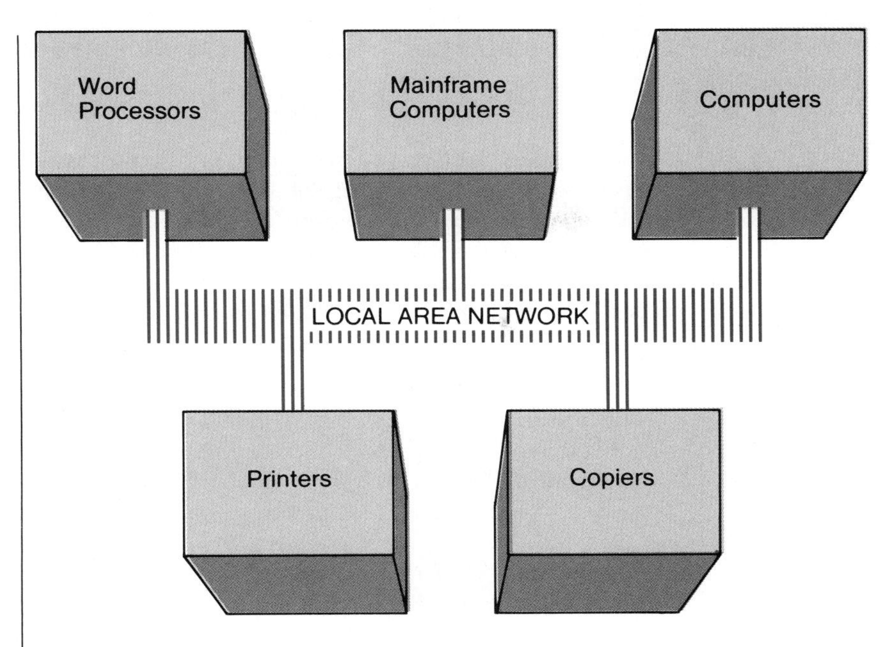

Illustration 14–1
A local area network (LAN) links equipment in an integrated office system

INTEGRATED OFFICE SYSTEMS

so·phis'ti·cat·ed

The office of today is an exciting place. It contains sophisticated electronic equipment that permits the daily office functions, such as keyboarding and filing, to be automated. As you read in Unit 12, many companies now have their own information processing systems in which all of their information is processed. In addition, many companies are linking their office functions and equipment to create integrated office systems. Companies are doing this in order to make the fullest use of their equipment and the information that is being processed on it.

You may be wondering just what an integrated office system is. The answer to this question is simple. An **integrated office system** is a system in which office functions and equipment are linked. For example, a company can integrate its office functions, such as word processing and data processing, through the use of **integrated software.** Integrated software combines both of these functions into a single easy-to-use package.

com·bines'

That same company can also integrate its equipment through the use of a **local area network (LAN).** As Illustration 14–1 shows, a LAN allows different types of equipment to be linked so that users can share information. A LAN can be used to link the equipment found in a single office building. It can also be used to link the equipment in the main office with the equipment in the branch offices several miles away.

PROCESSING WORDS IN AN INTEGRATED OFFICE SYSTEM

In an integrated office system, words may be processed on computers with the use of integrated software. The software provides the instructions needed for the processing of the words. In addition, the software includes the instructions needed for other functions, such as the creation of graphs and charts. You may also find, as in the example that follows, that word processors linked to a LAN are used to process words.

Let's look at how a sales report is processed in an integrated office.

On Monday morning, Norman Miller, the assistant sales manager at the New Jersey branch office of Systems, Inc., dictates the company's annual sales report. Monday afternoon, Karen Ames, Norman's secretary, keyboards the document on her computer. Her computer is linked to the integrated office system. On Tuesday, Norman calls up the document on his computer. As he reads the document, he wants to check some of the sales figures for the California area. By accessing the system's ***data base,*** *Norman can call up the sales figures. A data base is a collection of related data that is stored in the computer. This information can be accessed, updated, and retrieved easily by many users for many different applications. When Norman has gained access to the data base, the figures appear on his VDT. Norman verifies the figures. Then he decides to add a bar graph comparing the sales in the six sales regions. Using the same integrated software, Norman indicates what information is to be included in the graph. Then he selects the type of graph he wants. The computer constructs the graph and adds it to the report at the point that Norman selects.*

ac'cess·ing

ver'i·fies

On Thursday, Lois Standish, the sales manager in the New Jersey branch office, calls up the sales report on her computer. As she reads through the report, she adds some information she has just received.

On Friday, when the document is completed, Karen sends it to the copier. When the copies have been made, the report is ready for distribution within the company.

PROCESSING DATA IN AN INTEGRATED SYSTEM

Like words, data can be processed in an integrated office system with the use of integrated software. Electronic spreadsheets are usually considered part of an integrated software package, as you will see in the next example. As with the processing of words, integrated office equipment plays an important role in the processing of data in an integrated office system.

Let's see how data is processed in the integrated system at Systems, Inc.

Systems, Inc., uses electronic cash registers in its retail shops. Katie Sullivan, a customer, purchases word processing software and charges it to her account. As the salesclerk enters the sale into the cash register, several things happen. First, the sale is posted to Katie's account. Then the inventory records are adjusted to show that the software was sold. Finally, the sale is recorded on the salesclerk's record. At the end of the day, a sales report is processed showing the sales information that was entered in the registers that day. These same sales figures are also transferred electronically to the computers at the main office in California.

Once a month Arthur Thornley, executive sales manager, prepares a company sales report on his computer. When the report is completed, Arthur has his administrative assistant, Joanne Feige, distribute the report to each branch office location via **electronic mail.** *An electronic mail system allows an office worker to transfer documents from one office to another, using electronic machinery. With this type of mail system, there is no actual movement of paper.*

vi'a

Systems, Inc., plans to expand its operations. So when Jon Michaels, regional manager, receives his report, he uses the electronic spreadsheet of the integrated software to make some predictions. Spreadsheets are frequently used by managers to forecast business conditions. Managers can ask "what if?" questions of the computer. For example, Jon could ask the computer, "What will happen if we open a new branch office in Texas?" Using the spreadsheet function of the integrated software, the computer will perform the calculations needed to answer Jon's question. The answers to questions like this help managers make decisions. These decisions are usually communicated to the manager through some form of document such as a letter, memo, or report.

fore'cast

PROCESSING VOICE COMMUNICATIONS IN AN INTEGRATED OFFICE SYSTEM

Speaking is the fastest method of transmitting information. At the present time there are two types of equipment used for processing voice communications — voice messaging and voice recognition equipment.

Voice Messaging

Voice messaging, also known as voice mail or voice store-and-forward, allows a caller to leave a message on a computer linked to a Touch-Tone telephone. When an individual is ready to receive telephone messages, the voice mailbox number is dialed, a code is entered, and any messages are played out. In an integrated system, these messages can be recalled, rerouted to another person, or erased.

re·rout'ed

Voice messaging is especially useful for reaching individuals in other time zones — even in foreign countries. This is because voice messaging

for'eign

Illustration 14–2
Voice messaging equipment allows a caller to leave a message on a computer

equipment receives and stores messages electronically, without the help of a telephone operator. With the use of this equipment, individuals being called decide when they want to receive their telephone messages. As a result, these individuals can work without interruptions. Voice messaging eliminates "telephone tag." This is a situation in which two people who are trying to contact one another leave messages for the other because they are never available at the same time. Voice messaging differs from electronic mail in that the message is spoken and heard rather than keyboarded and read. It is also different from a traditional telephone call because the conversation is one-way. A traditional telephone call involves two-way conversation.

e·lim′i·nates

Voice Recognition

com·mands′

Voice recognition equipment allows an individual to give commands to a computer orally. These verbal commands are usually single words such as *yes* or *no.* At the present time, voice recognition is used primarily in data processing. Because word processing involves so many similar-sounding words, the use of voice recognition equipment is more often found with the processing of data rather than words.

con·fi·den·ti·al′i·ty

One type of voice recognition equipment is called speaker verification. This system is used when security and confidentiality are needed. For instance, some security systems use spoken codes to determine whether the individual speaking is authorized to gain access to information.

Let's take a look at how voice processing is used at Systems, Inc.

Every morning, William Perez, the branch manager, transmits the previous day's reports to Emily Amalfi in the home office. Since the San

Diego office does not open until noon New Jersey time, William calls the home office's voice mail system and leaves any messages. When Emily arrives at the office, she dials her voice mailbox and receives her messages. If at the end of the day, Emily has a message for William that he should have early the next morning, she calls William's voice mailbox and leaves the message. The message will be waiting for him in the morning when he arrives at work. Systems, Inc., also has a voice recognition security system instead of conventional locks. When employees arrive at the office building each morning, instead of using keys to unlock the door, they give a verbal code. When the correct code is given, the door opens.

PROCESSING GRAPHICS IN AN INTEGRATED OFFICE SYSTEM

Integrated software often includes a graphics function. As the name implies, graphics software permits the development of charts, graphs, and diagrams. Some software packages have color capability. This permits the graphics to be displayed and printed in color. Other systems simply use different types of shading to add emphasis to the graphics. When a graphic aid is needed, the information is entered into the computer. The computer uses this information to develop the graphic aid.

Let's take a look at how graphics are used at Systems, Inc.

Bill Hotasumi decides to develop a line graph to show the number of printers sold during the years 1984, 1985, 1986, and 1987. To do this, he instructs the computer that he wants to make a line graph. Then he accesses the data base for each of the four years. The computer takes the figures and sets up the graph in the correct proportions. Because graphics are included in the integrated software package, this graph can be added to the report Bill prepared using the word processing function.

pro·por'tions

THE INTEGRATED OFFICE SYSTEM OFFERS MANY ADVANTAGES

The integrated office is no longer a novelty. It has become a reality. For many companies, the use of electronic equipment to form an office system is an accepted way of life. For many other companies, the use of an information processing system will become commonplace in the years ahead.

As you have read, an integrated office system integrates electronic equipment, office workers, and standardized procedures to increase its productivity. But an increase in the number of documents a company processes is not the only advantage gained when an office system is integrated. Other advantages may include those given on the next page.

Illustration 14–3 Charts and graphs can be included in documents if integrated software is being used

1. An integrated office system is designed to meet a company's individual needs. For example, in a doctor's office, the accurate recording of patients' appointments on the office calendar is essential. With the use of calendaring software, the doctor's need for maintaining an accurate schedule can be met.
2. An integrated office system makes it possible to keep an office's information up to date. This same information is easily accessible for use by one worker or several workers simultaneously. For example, as a car is being serviced, the mechanic at the garage enters information into the computer about the repairs being made. In the office, at the same garage, a service clerk answers a customer's telephone call about the cost of her car's repairs. A quick check with the computer provides the information that is needed. At the same time, a billing clerk uses information stored in the computer to prepare another customer's bill.
3. An integrated office system provides a safe storage place for an office's documents. All documents entered in the electronic files are coded. These documents can be retrieved and transferred from one piece of equipment to another. All of this can be done without any loss of documents. For example, a worker at an office supply company needs to refer to a new price list from one of its suppliers. An office worker enters the document's code into the computer and the document appears on the VDT. If the worker wants a copy of the price list, a hard copy can be made on the intelligent copier. And, of course, all of this is accomplished without the loss of any documents.

4. An integrated office system allows workers to assume greater responsibility on the job. For example, a manager of a computer store is trying to determine whether or not it is profitable to carry an additional line of software. Using the spreadsheet function of his computer's software, he can ask the computer if it will be profitable. The computer does most of the work and gives the manager an answer. This software has saved the manager a great deal of time — time that can be much better spent doing other company tasks.

These are just some of the advantages of using an integrated office system. With advantages like these, there is no doubt that the integrated office system is the trend of the future.

REVIEWING KEY POINTS

1. Many companies are linking their office functions and equipment to create integrated office systems.
2. Office functions can be integrated through the use of integrated software.
3. Office equipment can be linked through the use of a local area network (LAN) in an integrated office system.
4. A data base is a collection of related data that is stored in a computer. This information can be accessed, updated, and retrieved easily by many workers for many different uses.
5. Electronic mail is the transfer of documents through the use of electronic equipment in the office.
6. Spreadsheets are used to forecast business conditions by allowing managers to ask the computer "What if?" questions.
7. There are two types of equipment for processing voice communications. Voice messaging allows a caller to leave a message on a computer. Voice recognition equipment allows an individual to give oral commands to a computer.
8. Graphics software allows the user to develop graphic aids that can be integrated into other documents.

DEVELOPING HUMAN RELATIONS SKILLS

1. You have been given a report to keyboard right away. While you are keyboarding the report, you notice that some of the calculations are wrong.

Your supervisor is at a meeting that is expected to last several hours, but the working papers are on her desk.

   a. What can you do to complete the work correctly?

   b. Would you discuss this with your supervisor when she returns? Explain your answer.

2. Amy Lissman has worked for Brighton Products for ten years. Her company has grown to the point that it can now afford to begin integrating its equipment. Amy does not know much about electronic equipment, but she is definitely against it. Even though she has been told that she will not lose her job, Amy thinks she will. She has heard that the company will train employees to work with the equipment, but she thinks it will be too hard for her to learn. Every time something is said about the company's plans for integrating its equipment, Amy lets it be known that she doesn't like the idea at all.

   a. What are some of Amy's fears about the new integrated equipment?

   b. Do you think most people might have the same fears in this situation? Why or why not?

   c. What can Amy do to overcome her fears about the company's decision to integrate its equipment?

IMPROVING COMMUNICATION SKILLS

Refer to Appendix B 4.1 – 4.13.

1. A number can be written as a figure or as a word depending on its use. Decide whether each number in the following sentences should be written as a figure or as a word. Keyboard the sentences on a separate sheet of plain paper.

   a. The computer is about 8 years old.

   b. 85 people process information in our company system.

   c. There are 4 managers, 12 supervisors, and 69 workers in our company.

   d. The company just purchased 2 more minicomputers.

   e. The 64 work stations are in full use.

   f. We process 1 billion documents annually.

   g. Emily mailed 1500 form letters yesterday.

   h. The order contained 5 8-inch disks.

   i. The report was keyboarded on July 18.

   j. All orders should be sent to 1 Paradise Lane.

2. Write a letter of thanks to the Brockton Office Systems Company for information it sent to you about integrated office systems. Its address is 11358 Norton Road, Muncie, IN 47301. Be sure to thank the company for its quick response to your inquiry. Also thank the company for sending you several interesting articles and photographs on integrated office systems. Keyboard your letter on the form in your workbook or plain paper.

BUILDING PROBLEM-SOLVING SKILLS

1. The Welton Company has been experimenting with a flexible work schedule that allows some workers to telecommute (work at home) two days a week. The chart shown here lists the number of telecommuting employees in each department and the estimated increase in productivity resulting from telecommuting. Study the chart, then on a separate sheet of paper, answer the questions that follow.

Department	Total No. of Employees	Total No. of Telecommuters	Percentage Increase in Productivity
Public Relations	12	2	8
Word Processing	15	5	15
Editorial	22	8	5
Customer Service	10	6	20

   a. How many Welton Company employees are not telecommuters?

   b. Which department has the largest percentage of telecommuters?

   c. Which department has the smallest percentage of telecommuters?

   d. What percentage of the total number of employees are telecommuters?

2. Refer to the chart in Activity 1. On a separate sheet of paper, answer the following questions.

   a. Which department had the highest estimated increase in productivity? the lowest?

   b. If the word processing employees were processing an average of 40 documents a day before the new schedule was put into effect, how many *more* documents should they be able to process each day under the new telecommuting schedule?

Activities 1 and 2 can be done on information processing equipment.

APPLYING OFFICE SKILLS

1. Read a magazine article about integrated office systems or electronic office equipment. On a sheet of plain paper, keyboard a summary of the article.
2. The form letter shown on the next page is being sent to new charge customers. Prepare a copy of the letter for each person whose name and

address is listed. The form letters are in your workbook. Fill in the blanks with the information given. Keyboard the inside address in approved format and use an appropriate salutation. If you do not have a workbook, keyboard the letters, inserting the correct names and information.

Dear (name):

We are happy to welcome you as a new charge customer. Your credit limit has been set at (credit limit). Your account number is (account number).

You can use your charge card at any of our stores in the state. Your statement will be sent to you on the (date) of each month. Payment is due within two weeks of the date of the statement.

As a charge customer, you will be notified of our special sales. Since special sales items are available only to our regular charge customers, you must use your charge card when making these purchases. Of course, you are welcome to use your charge card for all of your purchases at Ruskin's.

Our regular summer sale starts next Wednesday, July 5. Be sure to come in and take advantage of the sale on clothing for the whole family.

Sincerely,

a. Mrs. Molly Kapar
203 Scottsville Road
Greensboro, NC 27410
Credit limit $300
Account number 158 421
Statement date 15th

b. Mr. Ralph Gerhardt
427 Main Street
Harrisburg, NC 28075
Credit limit $500
Account number 130 111
Statement date 20th

CHAPTER 2

INTEGRATED OFFICE SYSTEMS AT COMPUCHIPS, INC.

You have learned how information processing systems help office workers process work more efficiently. In the last chapter, you learned that information processing systems can be integrated. This is done so that information is processed without needless duplication of work. An integrated office system also makes all information more accessible to all of the departments in a company.

In this chapter, you will have the opportunity to visit a company with an integrated office system. Compuchips, Inc., the company that you will be visiting, has recently noticed a sizable increase in its productivity. The president of Compuchips, Inc., Andre Kelly, feels that this increase is a result of the company's careful integration of its office employees, its electronic equipment, and its standardized office procedures. Read through the next few pages to see just how Compuchips' new integrated office operates.

As you study this chapter, you will find answers to the following questions:

- How did Compuchips, Inc., integrate its office system?
- What advantages did Compuchips, Inc., gain by integrating its office systems?
- What do the following terms mean: **calendaring, electronic files?**

LOOKING AT COMPUCHIPS, INC.

To see how an integrated office system is used to process information, let's look at Compuchips, Inc., located in San Francisco, California. Compuchips manufactures microchips for computers. As its sales increased and customers started asking for more software and other related computer accessories, Compuchips began expanding its product line.

Compuchips has five divisions:

1. The Administrative Services Division handles correspondence for the entire company. Records management, telecommunications and mail services, and reprographics are also handled by the Administrative Services Division.
2. The Finance Division handles the payroll, accounting, purchasing, resource planning, and budget development.
3. The Manufacturing Division has responsibility for research and development of new products.
4. The Marketing Division conducts market research and develops advertising materials. This division is also responsible for the sale of products, product warranties, and customer inquiries and complaints.
5. The Personnel Division is responsible for hiring employees for the entire organization. It maintains all of the personnel records. The Personnel Division also handles employee benefits, training programs, and public relations programs.

war'ran·ties

Each division must know about the information processed and the decisions made by other divisions within Compuchips, Inc. As you know, a decision made in any one of the divisions within an organization affects all divisions. Therefore, all decisions and information must be communicated quickly and accurately.

MAKING PREPARATIONS FOR THE REPORT

One Monday morning Andre Kelly, president of Compuchips, Inc., asked Carolyn Dole, manager of the Administrative Services Division, to prepare a report on the status of Compuchips, Inc. Andre was leaving town the same day to visit the Geneva Branch Office. However, he wanted to see the report as soon as it was available. Andre needed to know the current inventory figures. He also needed to know the number of units produced and sold in the last six months and the advertising cost for that same period.

stat'us

One year ago, Carolyn would have spent days contacting the managers of the other divisions to get the information Andre needed. Since Compuchips, Inc., has integrated its information processing system, all of the information Carolyn needed was stored in the data base of the computer. With all of the information processing equipment linked to a local area network, Carolyn used her computer to obtain the information she needed for the report. Since the report was of high priority, Carolyn asked her secretary, Tony Kao, to direct telephone calls to the voice messaging system. She also asked her secretary to cancel her appointments for Monday afternoon and all day Tuesday. Tony used the **calendaring** function of the system's software, which allows the computer to store Carolyn's appointment calendar, making it simple for Tony to find whom Carolyn had appointments with. Tony did not have to ask Carolyn for the names of people with appointments. All of that information was available on Carolyn's computerized calendar.

PROCESSING THE REPORT

Carolyn started by retrieving the information about inventory by accessing the inventory control records. There she found out exactly how many units of each product were available at the end of the previous day. She also accessed the sales records for each product to determine the total sales for each product for the last six months. Carolyn then checked to determine the number of units manufactured during the last six months.

As Carolyn collected the information, she was also keyboarding the report using the word processing function of her computer. When all of the information was collected and a draft of the report was completed, Carolyn had the computer check for misspelled words in the report. This was done by using a spelling verifier. When she knew that all of the words were correctly spelled, she edited the report. As she edited it, she decided that some of the

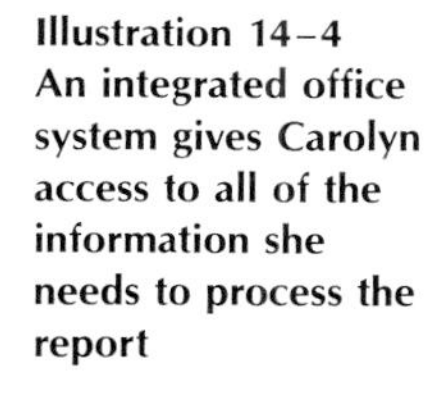
Illustration 14–4
An integrated office system gives Carolyn access to all of the information she needs to process the report

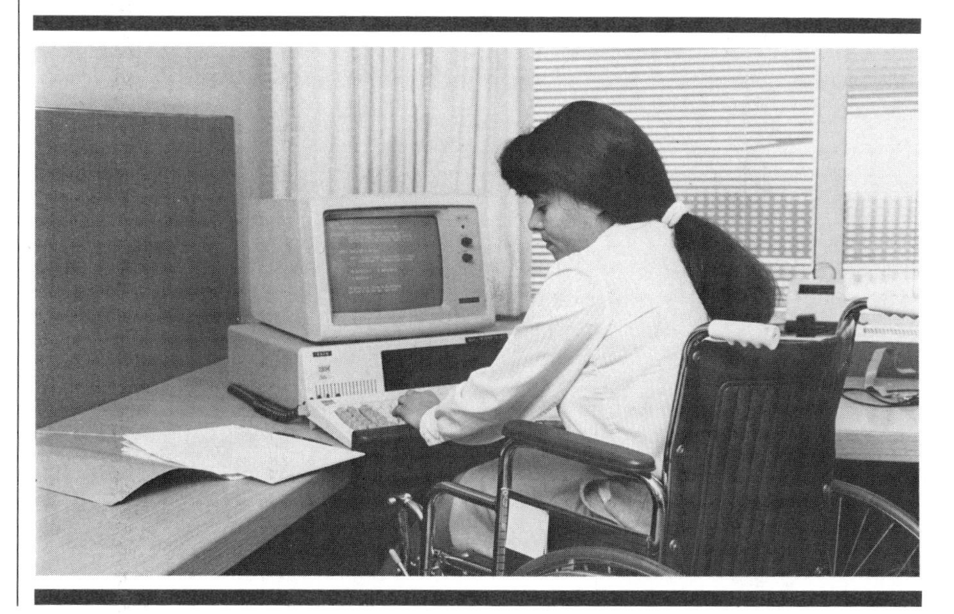

Illustration 14–5
With the use of integrated software Carolyn is able to include a graph in the report

material on the first page should be moved to the second page. As she was keyboarding the report on her computer, she merely pressed the correct function key to move the material. There was no need to rekeyboard the report.

While Carolyn was editing the report, she noticed an interesting trend in the sales figures for the last six months. The sales figures for one of the products had a steady increase each month. She also noticed that the sales for other products had either remained the same or decreased. Carolyn decided to insert a graph to compare the monthly sales of each product. To do this, she keyboarded the sales figures and used the graphics function to produce the graph.

TRANSMITTING THE REPORT

When Carolyn finished the report Tuesday afternoon, she checked Andre's schedule on his electronic calendar. She learned that Andre would still be in the Geneva office the next day. Using the electronic mail function, she sent the report to Andre in Geneva.

When Andre arrived at the Geneva office at 8:30 A.M. Wednesday morning, he read the report. As he was reading the report, Andre used the computer in the Geneva office to retrieve some additional information that was entered at the home office. This was possible because the information he needed was stored in the computer's **electronic files.** These files are similar to traditional office files, with one exception. The documents are stored on magnetic media in the computer rather than on paper. Even though it was only 6:30 A.M. in San Francisco, Andre was able to obtain the information

re·trieve′

Illustration 14–6 Andre uses the system's voice messaging equipment to leave a message for Carolyn

because the computers were linked by telephone lines. He dialed the telephone number of the computer in San Francisco and entered the codes.

Andre finished reading the report. Then he left a voice message for Carolyn to have ten copies of the report printed. Carolyn also sent messages to each of the division managers. She asked them to study carefully the report, which was stored in the computer. She also asked them to be ready to discuss cost-saving measures at a meeting on Friday afternoon at 3:30. Carolyn chose this time because the managers' calendars stored in the computer showed that all of the managers were available then.

meas'ures

The managers of the Finance and Marketing Divisions were out of the San Francisco office on Wednesday. However, as they were in branch offices, they could use the computers in the branches to obtain copies of the report.

As the manager of the Finance Division read the report, he realized that some cost analysis was necessary. Since he did not have time to do the cost analysis himself, he left a message with his assistant to use the electronic spreadsheet to perform the cost analysis. By Thursday afternoon at 1:30, each of the managers had copies of the cost analysis to read and study.

a·nal'y·sis

TRANSMITTING OTHER DOCUMENTS

While Carolyn was working on the report, her secretary, Tony, was busy processing other information that Carolyn needed for another assignment. Carolyn had asked Tony to send letters to all customers who had purchased a system during the past year. Carolyn wanted to tell each customer about new features that could be added to the system.

ex·ist'ing

Tony knew the products Compuchips, Inc., produced and how each feature could be integrated into an existing system. First, Tony used his computer to access the electronic files. He did this to develop a list of Compuchip's customers and their systems. Next, Tony keyboarded a variety of paragraphs to be used in the letters. Each paragraph described a feature that could be added to a system purchased by a customer. Since many customers had purchased similar systems, form paragraphs could be used to describe the features. However, not all paragraphs were appropriate for all customers. Tony had to select which paragraphs should be used in each customer's letter. After the paragraphs were stored, Tony used the mailing list to obtain the correct mailing addresses. Once Tony had the list of customers and the information about their systems, he coded the computer to develop each letter. Using the system's printer, Tony printed the letters error free.

SCHEDULING A MEETING

con·ven'ient

trans·mit'ted

Tony's next assignment was to set up a meeting with all of the supervisors in the Administrative Services Division. Carolyn had asked Tony to find a convenient time when everyone was available. Tony used his computer to access each supervisor's calendar stored in the computer. He also checked the schedule for the conference room to make certain that it was available. He found that the supervisors and the room were available at 10 A.M. on Friday morning. Tony accessed each supervisor's calendar again and recorded the meeting on their calendars. He then composed a memo to be sent to all supervisors telling them about the meeting. When the memo was completed, he transmitted it to each supervisor's electronic mailbox. Tony likes working with the computer. He knows that since the computer has been used to record and schedule appointments, he has not had to make as many telephone calls. Tony thinks this feature saves many hours.

RETRIEVING OTHER DOCUMENTS

Carolyn also asked Tony to retrieve several contracts from the electronic files. She wanted to take them home with her to work on that evening. When Tony located the documents in the electronic files, he had the documents sent to the printer to have a hard copy printed for Carolyn to take home.

LEAVING MESSAGES

During this busy day at Compuchips, Inc., Tony used the computer to record messages left by telephone callers. The messages were automatically transmitted to each worker's electronic mailbox.

After the day's work was completed, Tony thought about the integrated office system and how it had helped him become more efficient. He was even somewhat amused. He was one of the secretaries who was not happy when he found out that he would have to learn to process information on a new system. Now, Tony wouldn't trade his computer for anything!

REVIEWING KEY POINTS

1. It is important that information processed and decisions made be communicated quickly and accurately.
2. Some software contains a calendaring function, which allows a computer to store the workers' appointment calendars.
3. A computer can check for misspelled words in a keyboarded document by using a spelling verifier.
4. Figures can be accessed from the data base to create a graph using the graphics function of the software.
5. The system's electronic files store documents on magnetic media. When magnetic media is used, no paper is needed.
6. An electronic spreadsheet function allows the user to compare data.
7. Form letters can be quickly developed using form paragraphs stored in the computer.
8. Special functions of computer software such as calendaring, electronic files, and electronic mailbox increase office efficiency and productivity.

DEVELOPING HUMAN RELATIONS SKILLS

1. At your weekly staff meeting, your supervisor announces that the company is sending two people from each department to a workshop on integrating office equipment. You are very interested in learning about integrated offices, and you think that what you learn at the workshop will help you on the job.
   a. Describe how you would convince your supervisor that you should be one of the people chosen to attend the workshop.
   b. Explain how you would share the information you gain from the workshop with your coworkers.
2. You are sitting in a small conference room with several people from your department. All of you are participating in a training program to learn

procedures for the company's new integrated office system. You suddenly find that you do not understand what you are to do and why. However, everyone else seems to understand what the instructor is saying. In fact, practically no one is asking questions.

a. What should you do?

b. Give the reasons for your answer.

IMPROVING COMMUNICATION SKILLS

Refer to Appendix B 4.1 – 4.13.

1. Keyboard the following sentences, expressing all numbers in the correct format.
   a. The workshop will begin around 9 o'clock.
   b. Office Systems, Inc., is located on 2nd Street in East Milton Square.
   c. The system operates with 100 percent accuracy.
   d. The report contained 5 10-page chapters.
   e. There will be 1235 people at the Office Systems Conference.
   f. You have 21 days to process the publication.
   g. The company purchased 12 computers, 5 printers, and 2 copiers for its system.
   h. 2 representatives from each department were sent to the meeting.
   i. The integrated office system has been in use for about 2 years.
   j. We began processing the report on Monday, November 17.
   k. The electronic calendar schedules appointments for 231 employees.
   l. 75 terminals and 9 printers were installed today.
   m. The meeting is scheduled to be held on March 29 at 2:30 p.m.
2. Melanie Delorey, a consultant for the Apex Integration Company, spoke to you and your coworkers at a seminar on integrated office systems. You have been asked to write a thank you letter to Melanie. In your letter, thank Melanie for taking the time to come to speak to you and your coworkers. Also thank her for sharing information about processing systems and guidelines for their use. Melanie's address is Apex Integration Company, 86 Elliott Way, Portland OR 97231. Keyboard your letter on the form provided in your workbook or on a plain sheet of paper.

BUILDING PROBLEM-SOLVING SKILLS

1. The Nimbus Company recently integrated its office systems. The chart shown on the next page compares document preparation times before and after the integration of the company's office systems. Study the chart, then on a separate sheet of paper, answer the questions that follow.

Document Type	Old Preparation Time	New Preparation Time	Total Number of Documents Produced per Month
Short reports	4 hours	2 hours	25
Long reports	15 days	10 days	2
Sales letters	2 hours	30 minutes	85
Response letters	$2\frac{1}{2}$ hours	45 minutes	60
Sales summaries	8 hours	5 hours	8

a. How much time was spent each month under the old system in preparing each type of document?

b. How much time is spent each month under the integrated system in preparing each type of document?

c. What is the total amount of time saved in document preparation each month under the integrated system?

2. Refer to the chart in Activity 1. On a separate sheet of paper, answer the following questions.

a. What percentage of the old preparation time is the new preparation time for each of the document types?

b. What percentage of the total old preparation time is the total new preparation time for all documents?

APPLYING OFFICE SKILLS

Activities 1, 2, and 3 can be done on information processing equipment.

1. Your supervisor, Berniece Davis, would like to purchase four new electric typewriters to replace the old ones in your department. She asks you to find out what equipment is available. You find the names of three office equipment suppliers in the Yellow Pages of your telephone directory. When you call them, all three suppliers tell you that they do not advise you to purchase electric typewriters. They suggest that you consider purchasing electronic typewriters or computers instead.

   Keyboard a memo to your supervisor. In your memo, give the names of the three suppliers you called (use your local Yellow Pages to find names of equipment suppliers in your area). Then present what you have learned from your telephone calls. Briefly explain the differences in these types of equipment in case Berniece is not familiar with them. Keyboard the memo on the form provided in your workbook or on plain paper.

2. Your supervisor, Jordan Marshall, asked you to gather information about integrated software packages. The information you gathered is shown at the top of the next page. Prepare this information in table format so that the manufacturers' names appear in alphabetical order. Use the title "Integrated Software Packages" and the column headings "Manufacturer," "Functions," and "Cost."

Manufacturer	Functions	Cost
Micro-Systems, Inc.	Word Processing Data Base Spreadsheet	$369.00
Com-Tech	Word Processing Data Base Graphics	$339.00
Cable Associates	Word Processing Data Base Spreadsheet Graphics	$435.00
Data-Mate, Inc.	Word Processing Data Base	$189.00
Graphics Unlimited	Data Base Spreadsheet Graphics	$290.00

3. Use the following instructions to keyboard and make copies of a one-page report for the Computech Company.

a. Keyboard a rough draft of the following report, making all corrections in spelling, grammar, and punctuation that are needed. Use the title "Computech Announces New Location."

(P) Computech, a local firm for more than thirty years, anounces thta it is moving its corporate hedquarters on May 1 to 35 Comercial Plaza in the newly constructed Northshore Center. (P) Conputech will ocupy the entire third floore. Individual depratments will be located as follows:

Sales	Suite 300
Personel and Reception Area	Suite 301
Executive Ofices	Suite 302
Purchasing	Suit 303
Office Services	Suite 304
Resaerch and Development	Suite 305
Accounting	Suit 306

(P) In adition Computech continues its commitment to the finest in customer service by the addition of an Infornation Processing Center. When the center is fully operational all customer inquiries should be answered within 24 hours. (P) The new site si planed to be a model of energy conservation for both heating and cooling. Teh unique system was designed and installed by Putnam Associates of Waverly, who also developed the acclaimed solar energy system for the Empire Complex in the down town Executive Plaza. (P) An open house and tour of the new facilities will be held on May 15 from one oclock until eihgt o'clock. The public is cordialy invited to attend.

b. When your rough draft has been keyboarded, proofread it, marking any additional corrections needed in proofreader's symbols. Then keyboard a final draft of this unbound report on plain paper. If necessary, review the guidelines for keyboarding reports in Unit 8.

c. When you have completed your final-draft copy of the report, use the cut-and-paste method of correction you learned in Unit 11 to make the following changes in it. If you have information processing equipment, use the automatic features to make these changes.

- In paragraph 1, change the moving date to July 1. In paragraph 5, change the date of the open house to July 15.
- Change the third floor in paragraph 2 to the fifth floor. Also change the suite number in the listing to correspond.

d. When you have made all of the changes above, use your photocoping equipment or printer to make 5 copies of the report.

Saving Time and Money

The advantages gained through the use of an integrated office system are of little value if the system does not function efficiently. To increase the efficiency of your company's system, follow these guidelines:

1. Learn how to operate all of the equipment you will be using in your company's system. Do this by reading the operation manuals before you begin using any of the equipment.
2. Keep the telephone number of the equipment repair person in your personal telephone directory. Call this person immediately if a piece of equipment breaks down.
3. Become familiar with your company's standardized procedures. You will find these procedures in your company's procedures manual.
4. Attend workshops on the integrated office. Keep notes of techniques that will increase the efficiency of your system.
5. Make use of all of your system's equipment. An integrated office system in which only part of the system's equipment is used is not operating efficiently.
6. Read magazine articles about the integrated office and its equipment to obtain information about new techniques and equipment.
7. Talk with people who also work in integrated offices to discover new techniques for processing information.

ENERGETICS, INC.

It's nice to see you again. Welcome back to Energetics, Inc. This is the third of four office simulations. In this simulation, you will be completing five jobs. As in the past, your work will include a variety of keyboarding tasks. You will be asked to keyboard routine correspondence. You will also be asked to keyboard an order/invoice form and a travel expense report. In addition to your keyboarding tasks, you will verify price increases and update a petty cash book. An introduction to Office Simulation No. 3 follows.

Office Simulation No. 3

Every year manufacturers of health and physical fitness equipment are invited to display their line of products at an Equipment Fair in New York. Buyers from health and physical fitness centers across the country attend the fair to see products and buy new equipment.

Doug Shelton, head of the Equipment Department, and Denise D'Angelo, a staff member in that department, will be attending the Equipment Fair. Doug Shelton asked Ms. Clay to have you work with Mark Dolcheck while Mr. Shelton and Ms. D'Angelo are in New York. Ms. Clay explained that you will be answering telephones and preparing forms for the Equipment Department. Mr. Dolcheck will give you the information you need to answer questions. When you are not busy on the phone, you may have other short projects to do.

Turn to Office Simulation No. 3 in your *Student Activities* (pages 137–147) to find your complete assignments.

UNIT 15

A PROFESSIONAL OFFICE CAREER

- Procedures for Employment
- Interview Techniques
- Procedures for Advancement

CHAPTER 1

PROCEDURES FOR EMPLOYMENT

No matter what office knowledge and skills you possess, no matter what professional qualities or career goals you hold, all are of little value to you unless you can find a position where you can use them. To find the right position, you must have a plan of action.

As you will learn in this chapter, career power can help you achieve all of the things you include in your plan of action. Career power will help you find and evaluate job opportunities. It will help you apply for a particular position once you have made your evaluation. It will also help you obtain an interview and ultimately a job offer.

As you study this chapter, you will find answers to the following questions:

- How can I organize a plan of action?
- What is career power?
- How do I prepare a résumé?
- How do I apply for a position?
- What do the following terms mean: **career power, professional expertise, confidence, selling ability, self-inventory, résumé, letter of application, application form?**

Illustration 15–1 Personal characteristics leading to employment and career advancement

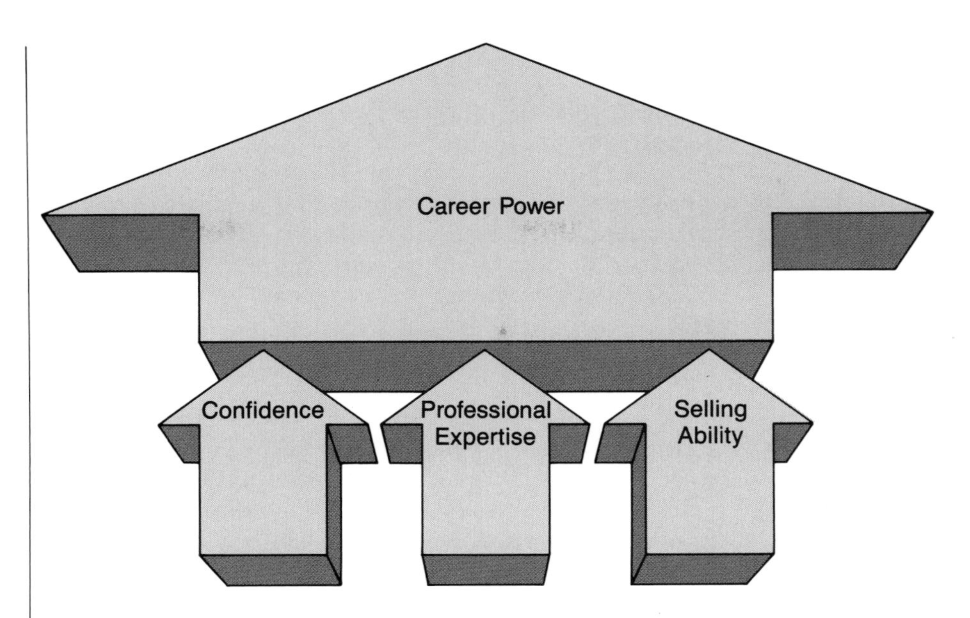

BUILDING CAREER POWER

ex·per·tise′

Career power is the ability to direct your career toward the career goal you want to achieve. To do this, you must have professional expertise, confidence, and selling ability. This chapter describes each of these career qualities. It tells you how to analyze your present career power. It also explains how to organize a plan of action in order to improve your career power.

Acquiring Professional Expertise

cre·den′tials

Professional expertise is the ability to be good at what you do. It is having the necessary credentials to prove what you can do. Your high school diploma, skills certificates in typing and shorthand, test scores, and letters of recommendation are examples of credentials that prove you have the skills and ability to do the job.

Possessing Confidence in Yourself

Confidence is having a positive outlook about yourself and about your abilities. Confidence is the feeling that you can succeed in whatever you try to do. This does not mean to say that you are perfect. It does mean, however, that you are able to recognize any weaknesses that you have. It also means that through the use of the human relations techniques you studied in Unit 2 and have developed throughout this course, you not only recognize your weaknesses but strive to overcome them.

Having Selling Ability

con·vince'

Selling ability is the ability to sell your knowledge and skills to others. It's the ability to convince others that they want and need to have you work for them. This means being able to communicate information about yourself to other people. Through your studies in this course, you have developed the communication skills necessary to convey this information. These skills include reading, writing, speaking, and listening as well as skills needed when applying human relations techniques.

ANALYZING YOUR CAREER POWER

Before you can begin your career planning, you need to take a look at your career power as it presently exists. Then you must decide what needs to be done to improve your career power so that you can accomplish the goals that you set for yourself. Begin by evaluating yourself. The easiest way to evaluate yourself is to take a look at your professional expertise, confidence, and selling ability. You can use a **self-inventory** to evaluate your knowledge, skills, and abilities in the areas of the three career powers. Illustration 15–2 shows a sample self-inventory form. When preparing a self-inventory for yourself, you may find the questions on the next page helpful.

Illustration 15–2
Self-inventory form

Self-Inventory

Name Lois Yarish Address 1642 Hollywood Drive Leesburg, FL 32748

Age 17 Health Excellent Marital Status Single

Physical Limitations none

Dependents none

Hobbies Reading, tennis, jogging, ceramics

Personal Characteristics: Rate yourself on each characteristic.

Character	Usually	Sometimes	Seldom
Cheerful	✓		
Courteous	✓		
Enthusiastic	✓		
Patient	✓		
Positive	✓		
Respectful	✓		
Sense of Humor	✓		
Sympathetic	✓		
Tactful	✓		

Grooming	Usually	Sometimes	Seldom
Clean Body	✓		
Clean Clothes	✓		
Coordinated Clothes	✓		
Clothes Appropriate for Occasion	✓		
Hair Clean	✓		
Hands and Nails Clean	✓		
Teeth and Breath Clean	✓		

Appearance	Usually	Sometimes	Seldom
Flattering Clothes	✓		
Body Weight Appropriate for Height	✓		
Posture Good	✓		
Appropriate Cosmetics	✓		

Voice	Usually	Sometimes	Seldom
Emphasis	✓		
Rate not too fast or slow		✓	
Interesting and Varied Pitch	✓		
Pleasant Volume	✓		
Good Pronunciation	✓		

Work Habits	Usually	Sometimes	Seldom
Accept Criticism		✓	
Accurate	✓		
Dependable	✓		
Neat	✓		
Organized	✓		
Shows Initiative		✓	
Good Time Management	✓		

Communication Skills	Usually	Sometimes	Seldom
Builds Vocabulary		✓	
Reads Rapidly		✓	
Easily Comprehends	✓		
Listens Carefully	✓		
Avoids Slang	✓		
Aware of Nonverbal Communication		✓	

Things I Value

Money ✓ Creativity ___ Power ___

Approval of Others ___ Challenge ___ Status ___

Social Contacts ✓ Professional Recognition ✓

Other: Travel

Educational Information

High School: Leesburg High School
High School Address: 38 Main Street, Leesburg, Florida 32748
Career Courses: Accounting, Typewriting, Shorthand, Secretarial Procedures, General Business, Data Processing
Skills: 80 wpm Gregg Shorthand; 70 wpm Typing; 20 wpm Transcription
Office Machines Operated: Electronic Calculators, Ditto, Mimeograph, Keypunch
School Activities: Basketball (Captain), Future Business Leaders of America, Student Government Council (Secretary, Vice President)

Work Experience	Dates	Business	Position
Part-Time Paid Jobs:	9/80–present	QuickServe, 114 Wilson Avenue, Leesburg	Cashier
Full-Time Paid Jobs:	Summer–1980	Johnson's Med. Clinic, Leesburg	Receptionist
Volunteer Positions:	9/80–present	Hoyt Hosp., Leesburg, FL	

Community and Church Activities

Group Name	Activities and Responsibilities
United Methodist Church	Active in youth group

Professional Expertise
Ask yourself:

- What are the names and addresses of schools I have attended?
- In what subjects did I do well?
- What skills did I develop? What level of skill did I attain?
- In what organizations or activities have I held leadership roles?
- What diplomas or certificates have I received?

lead'er·ship

Confidence
Ask yourself:

- What are my physical attributes — age, height, weight, and health?
- Do I have a positive self-concept?
- Am I highly motivated?
- Can I make decisions?
- Do I enjoy new challenges?

Selling Ability
Ask yourself:

- Do I work well with others?
- Can I communicate effectively on the telephone?
- Am I a good listener?
- Are my reading techniques effective and efficient?
- Can I organize my ideas and present them in clear, correct sentences?

When answering the self-inventory questions, be honest with yourself about what you have done and what you are capable of doing. Being clear and honest about yourself and your abilities will help you set realistic goals.

ORGANIZING YOUR PLAN OF ACTION

The first step in any plan of action is to decide on the steps you want to follow in your plan. Then you need to organize these steps into a sequence. As you work through this sequence, it is helpful to keep notes and organize them into an employment file. Illustration 15–3 on the next page shows a sample employment file. Notice there is one division for prospective employers, one for employment preparation, and one for career information. Each of these divisions has also been subdivided into several sections.

The sequence of steps you follow in your plan of action will influence the outcome. To be successful, your plan should include these steps:

1. Investigate career demands and opportunities.
2. Locate companies with career openings.

Illustration 15–3
Organize your job search by keeping an employment file

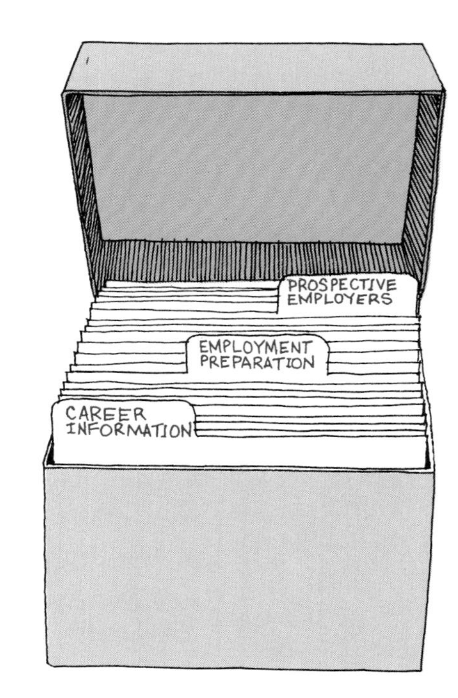

Career Information
  Office Market
  Typist
  Word Processing

Employment Preparation
  Application Forms
  Application Letters
  Résumé
  Self-Inventory

Prospective Employers
  A & E Design Associates
  Hixson Inc.
  Ross Enterprises
  Wright Partnership

3. Develop a résumé.
4. Apply for particular openings.
5. Interview for an opening.
6. Write a follow-up letter.
7. Enter a new job.

Exploring Career Demands and Opportunities

coun'sel·or

In order to make a choice about the type of job you want, you need to gather information about career demands and opportunities. You can obtain information from your guidance counselor, your state employment agency, professional organizations, and your school or public library. Information is also available in publications such as *The Occupational Outlook Handbook,* published by the U.S. Department of Labor, and professional, trade, and vocational magazines.

Finding Job Openings

Once you have decided on the type of position that you want, the next step is to find out which companies have job openings within that job area.

Several sources of job opening information are available. Friends, relatives, teachers, and school counselors can lead you to job openings. These people can let you know when a position becomes available. They can give you accurate information about the skills and previous work experience required. They can also provide you with the names of people who can be contacted for information about specific positions.

Many people contact employment agencies for employment information about possible openings. Employment agencies try to match qualified people with available jobs. There are public as well as private employment agencies. Public employment agencies do not charge a fee for their job placement services. Most private employment agencies, however, charge a fee. In some cases, this fee is paid by the applicant; in others, it is paid by the employer.

Newspaper ads are another source of job information. They give the position available, the qualifications needed, and a telephone number that you can call or an address where you can write to inquire about the position. Most good jobs are taken quickly; and when good jobs are advertised in the newspaper, there is usually a lot of competition for them.

ad'ver·tised

When you locate a job lead, find out what you can about the company. What services or products does it provide? Where is it located? What is the company's reputation within the local business community? Is the company considered a good company to work for? The answers to questions like these may be found in the company's annual report, in city directories, and from people who work for the company. After reviewing such information, you can decide if you are interested in working there.

rep·u·ta'tion

Preparing Your Résumé

When you have selected a company that you feel meets your needs, prepare your **résumé**. This document summarizes your knowledge and skills in an easy-to-read format. The purpose of a résumé is to sell these qualities to a prospective employer. Usually, information in the résumé is arranged into categories such as education, work experience, activities, and references. Illustration 15–4 on the next page shows a sample résumé.

The information presented in your résumé is taken from your self-inventory. The résumé is prepared with several guidelines in mind.

con·sis'tent

- Use a format that presents your information attractively. Margin headings should be balanced and keyboarded in a consistent style.
- Use tabulations when possible to save time in keyboarding and reading.
- Present your name, address, and telephone number first. Center this information or keyboard it at the left margin.
- Give the most important information first. If you have more education than work experience, present your education first. However, if you have more work experience than education, present your work experience first.
- List the most recent information first. Employers are more interested in your strengths at the present time, so begin with the most recent facts about your education and work experience.

Illustration 15–4
A neatly keyboarded résumé makes a good impression

Lynda Yang
107 Rockton Drive
Cleveland, OH 44106
Telephone (216) 443-6709

EDUCATION

September 1984 to present — Highland College, Cleveland, OH 44115. Will receive Associate of Arts degree in Secretarial Science on May 22, 19--, with 3.0 average in all course work.

September 1980 to June 1984 — Cleveland Central High School, Cleveland, OH 44119. Courses in business, English, mathematics, and social science. Graduated with honor.

EXPERIENCE

December 1985 to May 1986 — Harmon, Little, and White, Attorneys-at-Law, 401 Central Boulevard, Cleveland, OH 44111. Served as legal secretary in Highland College intern program.

September 1985 to November 1985 — Highland College Registrar's Office, 3003 College Drive, Cleveland, OH 44115. Part-time secretary to the Registrar while attending school.

June 1984 to August 1984 — Dirham Construction Company, 741 Mill Street, Cleveland, OH 44102. Clerk-typist in the Contract Procurement Department.

ACTIVITIES

President, Highland College Business Club
Member of Highland College Student Senate
Placed fourth in state typewriting contest while attending Central High School

REFERENCES

Dr. Elaine Thompson, Professor, Business Education Department, Highland College, 3003 College Drive, Cleveland, OH 44115, (216) 422-6600

Miss Wanda Brill, Dirham Construction Company, 741 Mill Street, Cleveland, OH 44102, (216) 427-1632

Reverend Dru Wilson, First Baptist Church, 702 Main Street, Cleveland, OH 44106, (216) 435-8945

- Provide complete educational information, including the names and addresses of schools, dates of attendance, and diploma or degree received or expected. List any courses or job-related skills.
- Provide complete work experience information. Include dates, the name and location of the business, and the position that you held. You may also include the name of your supervisor.
- List the professional organizations you belong to and the professional activities in which you are involved. Be sure to include any accomplishments that emphasize qualities of leadership and scholarship.
- List appropriate references. Give the names of at least three people who can verify your education or experience qualifications. Include their names, titles, addresses, and telephone numbers. You should have written or oral permission from every person you list as a reference on your résumé.

per·mis′sion

Illustration 15–5
Letter of application

107 Rockton Drive
Cleveland, OH 44106
May 12, 19--

Mrs. Ellen Rider
Personnel Director
Tele-Vac Corporation
1406 Dow Circle
Cleveland, OH 44111

Dear Mrs. Rider

Mr. Thomas Delaney, Placement Director of Highland College, has told me of your need for a competent secretary in the legal department of Tele-Vac Corporation. Please consider me an applicant for the position.

On May 22, I will complete the secretarial program at Highland College and will receive an Associate of Arts degree in Secretarial Science. As indicated by the enclosed resume, I have the training and the experience needed to make a real contribution to your firm. In addition to the basic secretarial program, my training included special emphasis on legal secretarial skills. I served as an intern in the legal office of Harmon, Little, and White for a period of six months. In addition, I plan to enroll in the paralegal program at South Cuyahoga College in the fall to further my education.

May I have the opportunity to discuss my qualifications with you and the extent to which I could contribute to the success of Tele-Vac Corporation. You may telephone me at 443-6709.

Sincerely

Lynda Yang

Lynda Yang

Enclosure

- Proofread your résumé several times for content, layout, and neatness. It represents *you* to prospective employers, and you don't want to appear careless or sloppy.

Applying for a Job

Once you have located an appropriate job opening and prepared a résumé, you are ready to apply for a job.

in'ter·view
stress'es

Letter of application You can show interest in a position by writing a **letter of application.** In this letter, you apply for a specific position and request an interview. Notice that the letter in Illustration 15–5 mentions the specific position the applicant is interested in. It stresses at least one major point of educational preparation. It also points out what the applicant can do for the company. And, the letter closes by asking for an interview.

The main purpose of the letter of application is to obtain an interview. To do this, the application letter must create a favorable impression of you. It needs to help the prospective employer picture just what you can do for the company. Send along a copy of your résumé to give the employer an even clearer picture of your abilities.

As you look at the letter, check to see that it is keyboarded neatly and accurately in an attractive format. Whenever possible, it should be written to a specific person. You may need to call the company to obtain the name of the person to whom the letter should be addressed.

Employment application When you apply for a position, you may be asked to complete an **application form** before the interview. The application form provides the employer with information that may not be provided in your letter of application or résumé.

Carefully read the application and complete every blank neatly and accurately. You should read through the application form completely before you begin filling in the information requested. Be sure that you follow directions carefully. For items on the form that do not pertain to you or for which you do not have an answer, draw a short line (or write *NA* for *not applicable*) in the blank to show that you have not skipped the item. If there is a blank for your expected salary figure, you might want to write in the word

Illustration 15–6
A neatly completed application for employment

Application for Employment
An Equal Opportunity Employer

TELE-VAC CORPORATION
Cleveland, OH 44111

PERSONAL INFORMATION

Name: Yang (Last) Lynda (First) ___ (Initial) Date: May 28, 19--
Present Address: 107 Rockton Drive (Street) Cleveland (Town or City) OH (State) 44106 (ZIP)
Phone Number: 443-6709 Social Security No: 427-54-7403
Citizen of U.S.? Yes
Position Desired: Secretary, Legal Department Salary Desired: Open
In Case of Emergency, Notify: Mr. and Mrs. C. W. Yang
107 Rockton Drive, Cleveland, OH 44106

EDUCATION

School	Name and Location	Dates Attended		Did You Graduate?	Course
		From	To		
Elementary	Hillsdale Elementary School Cleveland, OH 44119	Sept. 1966	June 1974		
High School	Cleveland Central High School Cleveland, OH 44119	Sept. 1974	June 1978	Yes	Bus., Eng., Math., Soc. Science
College or University	Highland College Cleveland, OH 44115	Sept. 1978	Present	In June	
Other					

Check Business Courses Taken in School:

x Accounting
___ Business Law
x Business Math
___ Consumer Economics
x General Business
x Office Machines
x Office Practice
___ Record Keeping
x Shorthand
x Typewriting
Other: Legal Secretarial

Typewriting Speed 70 WPM Shorthand Speed 120 WPM

List Extracurricular Activities and/or Scholastic Honors:
President, Highland College Business Club; Graduated with honor from Cleveland Central High School; Member of Highland College Student Senate; Member BSU; Placed fourth in State Typing Contest

EMPLOYMENT

Employed		Company Name and Address	Position	Reason for Leaving
From	To			
Dec. 1979	May 1980	Harmon, Little, and White 401 Central Boulevard Cleveland, OH 44111	Legal Secretary	Concluded Intern Program
Sept. 1979	Nov. 1979	Highland College 3003 College Drive Cleveland, OH 44115	Registrar's Secretary	Started Intern Program
June 1978	Aug. 1978	Dirham Construction Company 741 Mill Street Cleveland, OH 44102	Clerk-typist	Started School

REFERENCES
Do not list relatives or former employers.

Name	Address	Phone No	Occupation
Dr. Elaine Thompson	Highland College Cleveland, OH 44115	442-6600	Professor
Miss Wanda Brill	Dirham Construction Co. 741 Mill St., Cleveland, OH	427-1632	Off. Mgr.
Rev. Dru Wilson	First Baptist Church, 702 Main, Cleveland, OH 44106	435-8945	Minister

Are You Currently Employed? No Date Available for Work: June 15, 19--

To the best of my knowledge all of the foregoing information is true and is given voluntarily.

I hereby give permission to contact my references, including previous employers, and to confirm my credentials.

Signature: Lynda Yang

TO BE COMPLETED BY INTERVIEWER

Interviewed By ___ Date Interviewed ___
Remarks ___
Date Employed ___ Position ___
Department ___ Salary ___

Open or *Discuss.* Be sure to ask for clarification about any questions that you do not understand. Your care in filling out the application form neatly, completely, and accurately could result in an interview with the company. It may even result in a job offer!

REVIEWING KEY POINTS

1. Having career power means that you have professional expertise, confidence, and selling ability.
2. A high school diploma, skill certificates, test scores, and letters of recommendation prove your professional expertise.
3. Confidence is the feeling that you can succeed in whatever you do.
4. Selling ability is the ability to present your knowledge and skills to others so that they will want you to work for and with them.
5. A self-inventory helps you decide what your career goals are and helps you prepare information to present to prospective employers.
6. Your guidance counselor, state employment agencies, professional organizations, and your school or public library can provide you with information about career demands and opportunities.
7. A résumé summarizes your knowledge and skills.
8. A letter of application should name the position you want, present your education and experience, and state that you want an interview.
9. An application form should be filled out neatly, completely, and accurately.

DEVELOPING HUMAN RELATIONS SKILLS

1. Barry Thorney is just graduating from high school. He prepared his résumé for a position in information processing. However, he was concerned because his résumé looked so short. He decided to solve the problem by adding false information to make the résumé longer. Barry has heard that prospective employers do not always check all résumé information.
   a. Do you agree with Barry's approach? Why or why not?
   b. What problems may Barry encounter by giving false information?
2. Nancy Carroll is applying for an office position. Her letter of application is shown on the next page. Read through her letter carefully. Then, on a separate sheet of paper, answer the questions that follow.

254 Evelyn Lane
Quincy, MA 02171
November 15, 19 – –

Spencer & Norton, Inc.
1180 Beacon Avenue
Boston, MA 02108

Gentlemen

I am just graduating from high school and want to get an office position with a good company. I think I can handle any kind of office work.

I can keyboard, write, work office machines, and do simple bookkeeping. I like people and am willing to work hard. I've not had any work experience, but I have very good grades in high school. I feel sure I can do accurate work, though, and I am really interested in getting a job.

If you want additional information about me, I will be glad to give it to you.

Sincerely yours
Nancy Carroll

a. What are the weak points in Nancy's letter? How would you point out those weaknesses to her?

b. What suggestions would you make to Nancy for improving her letter?

IMPROVING COMMUNICATION SKILLS

Refer to Appendix B 4.14–4.25.

1. A number can be written as a figure or as a word depending on its use. Decide whether each number in the following sentences should be written as a figure or as a word. Use a separate sheet of paper.

- **a.** The average age in the office is 27.5 years.
- **b.** The average number of years of employment for a clerk is 4 years.
- **c.** The cleaning fluid must contain $1\frac{1}{2}$ cups of ammonia.
- **d.** A $\frac{2}{3}$ majority voted for the DAX Equipment.
- **e.** Everyone will have a $\frac{1}{2}$-day holiday.
- **f.** Elaine has 5 percent of her salary deducted for savings.
- **g.** 75% of all people terminated lose their jobs because of poor human relations skills.

2. Select a person whom you would like to use as a reference. Using plain paper and block format, keyboard a letter to this person. Tell this person when you will be graduating. Ask to use this person's name as a reference. Be sure to explain how you know this person. Close your letter by asking if there are any questions concerning your use of this person's name.

BUILDING PROBLEM-SOLVING SKILLS

1. The table below shows average weekly salaries for several positions. Using these figures, compute answers to the following questions:

Position	SALARY	
	Current	Last Year
Word Processing Operator	$342.00	$316.00
Accounting Clerk	394.00	361.00
File Clerk	284.00	274.00
Purchasing Clerk	375.00	349.00
Payroll Clerk	358.00	338.00
Secretary	379.00	357.00
Executive Secretary	407.00	392.00
Clerk Typist	300.00	271.00

   a. What is the difference in pay between the highest paying position and the lowest one?

   b. For each position, what is the percentage of increase from last year's salary to the current salary?

   c. Which position has had the greatest percentage of increase?

2. Office work often requires the worker to look for simple solutions rather than complex ones. Test your ability to identify the simple rather than the complex solutions by solving the following problems:

   a. There are, of course, 12 one-cent stamps in a dozen. How many two-cent stamps are there in a dozen?

   b. One month has 28 days. Of the remaining 11 months in the year, how many have 30 days?

   c. How many times can you subtract the number 2 from 24?

   d. Take 5 floppy disks from 7 floppy disks, and what have you got?

APPLYING OFFICE SKILLS

Activities 1 and 2 can be done on information processing equipment.

1. Prepare a résumé for yourself. Your résumé should be one keyboarded page. Refer to Illustration 15–4 on page 592 as you keyboard.
2. Select a Help-Wanted Ad for a position that interests you. Keyboard a letter of application in which you apply for this position. Use Illustration 15–5 on page 593 as a guide.
3. **(Optional)** Prepare a self-inventory by completing the form provided in your workbook.

CHAPTER 2

INTERVIEW TECHNIQUES

After reading through all the applications for a position, the hiring company schedules employment interviews with those applicants who have the desired qualifications. If you are well qualified for the position, you may succeed in getting an interview. Generally, the employment interview is the only chance the company has to make a first-hand evaluation of a prospective employee.

The employment interview is as important to the hiring company as it is to you. The interview allows the company to gather information about you that does not appear on your résumé or the application form. This information includes such things as your career plans, appearance, personality, poise, and attitudes. At the same time, the interview allows you an opportunity to gather information about the company's policies, working conditions, and benefits. It also gives you an opportunity to meet with some company employees and obtain an impression of the company.

A successful interview can be the deciding factor in whether or not you receive a job offer. However, a successful interview doesn't just happen. There are many things that you must keep in mind. This chapter discusses the interview process and what you can do to prepare for it.

As you study this chapter, you will find answers to the following questions:

- What questions should I ask during an interview?
- How can I demonstrate my abilities?
- What follow-up activities are necessary after my interview?
- What do the following terms mean: **interviewer, role-playing, employment test, follow-up letter?**

PREPARING YOURSELF FOR A JOB INTERVIEW

nerv'ous
un·known'

Most people are frightened and nervous at the thought of a job interview. These feelings are often the result of a fear of the unknown. Many job applicants go to an interview not knowing what questions they will be asked.

Experience has shown, however, that the more prepared applicants are for interviews, the less fearful they are. When preparing for an interview, you will find it helpful to ask yourself certain questions.

- Why should this company hire me?
- What questions should I ask?
- What questions will I be asked?
- How should I dress for the interview?
- How can I make a good impression during the interview?

Why Should This Company Hire Me?

spe·cif'ic

be·liev'ing

Throughout this book you have read about the various office positions available and their specific responsibilities. In the last chapter, you also read about the importance of evaluating your career power and matching your knowledge and skills to those positions in demand. Therefore, when you apply for a particular position, you do so knowing the responsibilities and believing that you can handle them.

During the interview, you must sell yourself to the hiring company. It is up to you to make the **interviewer**, the person who is interviewing you, aware that you have the knowledge and skills that fit the job responsibilities of the advertised position. It is your responsibility to present your abilities in terms of the company's needs. With a little planning, this can be easily done. For example, suppose you are applying for a word processing position with a large and rapidly expanding engineering company. During the interview your comments might show that you are aware of and willing to meet the many urgent deadlines that the company has. Within a large company, flexibility and cooperativeness are important.

dead'lines
co·op'er·a·tive·ness

What Questions Should I Ask?

You should gather information about the company with which you will be interviewing. Based on this information, prepare a keyboarded or neatly written list of facts that you want to review just before your interview. On this same sheet, also make a list of questions that you want to ask about the company's operations, products, and so on. With the fear and nervousness that often accompanies interviewing, you may forget questions that are not written down. You can place this sheet in a folder and carry it into the interview with you.

nerv'ous·ness

Illustration 15-7 Prepare a list of questions to ask the interviewer

Dravo Products Company
502 Spring Grove Avenue
Cleveland, OH 44106

Facts

1. Produces cleansers (drain, glass, copper, silver, and toilet bowl), furniture polish, rust remover, scouring pads, and air fresheners
2. Established in 1910
3. Employs 48 people
4. Owned by Dravo, Inc.
5. President is Arthur Nolan

Questions

1. Why is there an opening in this position?
2. What advancement opportunities are available to people who begin in this entry-level position?
3. Will I be trained in to understand any special manufacturing terminology that is used?
4. Does the company encourage its workers to join professional organizations?

At some time during the interview, most interviewers ask applicants if they have any questions. At this time, it is appropriate to tell the interviewer that you have prepared a list of questions. Taking your sheet from the folder, glance down the list and look for questions that have not been answered. At this point, feel free to ask any questions that you may have. Preparing a list of questions shows the interviewer not only that you have taken time to prepare for the interview but also that you are interested in a position with the company. Examples of questions you might want to ask during an interview include the following:

- How will my work contribute to the advancement of this company?
- What new products does this company plan to produce?
- What duties will this job involve?
- Does this company have a training program for this position?
- Does this position provide opportunities for advancement?

Applicants are always concerned about the question of salary. Asking questions about salary may indicate to the interviewer that you are more interested in money than in the job. The interviewer will bring up salary information at an appropriate point in the discussion. If salary has not been mentioned by the close of the interview, then you may inquire, "May I ask the starting salary for this position?"

crit'i·cisms

One of the biggest criticisms of young people is that they do not ask enough questions. The above suggestions make it easy to ask appropriate questions and to show that you have prepared for your interview.

What Questions Will I Be Asked?

As mentioned earlier, the interview allows the company to gather information about you that does not appear on your résumé or the application form. This additional information can be obtained by questioning you during the interview. You will find that most questions asked concern your career goals, knowledge, skills, and character.

Most interviews have much in common. You will find that certain questions are frequently asked. Some of the most commonly asked questions include:

- What can you tell me about yourself?
- What subjects did you like best in school? Why?
- What do you know about this company?
- Why do you want this particular job?
- Do you prefer working with others or by yourself?

Because these questions are so frequently asked, it is to your advantage to plan answers to them and to similar questions. Your answers should clearly show an employer why you are the right person for the job.

dis·crim'i·nate

Just as some questions can be expected during the interview, there are some questions that the interviewer may not legally ask during an interview. These questions deal with sex, age, race, religion, national origin, and disabilities. Any questions requiring answers that could be used to discriminate against an applicant are illegal. Question guidelines are set and enforced by the Equal Employment Opportunity Commission. Examples of questions that should not be asked during an interview include the following:

- What is your age or date of birth?
- What is your race?
- Are you married, divorced, separated, widowed, single?
- Do you have children?
- What church do you attend?
- Have you ever been arrested?

If you are asked an unlawful question, you may, of course, answer it. You may also refuse to answer it. If you want the job, though, and realize that you are being asked an unlawful question, ask the reason for the question. If the

Illustration 15–8
Dress appropriately for the interview

jus'ti·fies

reason justifies an answer, respond appropriately. For example, if you are asked, "Do you have plans to marry in the immediate future?" you might respond by asking, "Is marital status important for the position?" Remember that the way you handle questions tells the interviewer as much about you as what you say.

How Should I Dress for the Interview?

com'pli·ment

con·ser'va·tive·ly

When you go to an interview, appearance and dress are very important. Your appearance makes a lasting impression. Most companies prefer to hire neat, appropriately dressed applicants. The applicant who pays the company a compliment by dressing appropriately for the interview is usually well received. But just what is meant by "appropriate" dress? Most often it is a matching or coordinated suit, shirt, and tie for men and a suit and blouse or dress for women. If you are not sure what to wear, try to dress conservatively. Even though a company allows casual dress, you do not want to be too casual in appearance when applying for a job. For instance, blue jeans are not appropriate dress for an interview. This comment is often heard: "Even if you wear them at work, I don't like to see you wearing them to an interview."

Whatever you choose to wear to the interview, be sure that you have worn the outfit before and that it is comfortable. You have enough to think about when interviewing without worrying about what you are wearing.

Also keep in mind that a clean, healthy look is a winning look. Your hair should be an appropriate length, and your fingernails clean and trim. Only when you look your best can you be yourself during an interview.

How Can I Make a Good Impression?

re·spon′ses

Once you have gathered information for your interview, you can practice your responses by **role-playing** the interview. In role-playing, you practice your responses to questions you might be asked and to situations you are likely to find yourself in. Then you plan how you will handle such questions and situations. Through role-playing, you increase your confidence by reducing your uncertainty about the interview.

When preparing for the interview, keep these points in mind:

- Be on time. If you are unsure of the location, check the address on a city map. Allow yourself extra time for possible delays.
- Go to the interview by yourself.
- Introduce yourself to the receptionist. State who you are, why you are there, and whom you want to see.
- Use good eye contact. Look at the interviewer as you listen to and answer questions.
- Stand as you greet the interviewer. If a hand is extended, shake hands with a firm grasp.
- During the interview, maintain good posture. Avoid putting your hands together, because this indicates nervousness.
- Think ahead of time where and how you will hold your file folder and reference materials. Women should plan where to place their purses.
- Speak up loudly and clearly. Be aware of the volume and pace of your speaking.
- Show that you have initiative and flexibility by stressing the work experience you have had. Even if you are young, you probably have had a part-time job or done some useful volunteer work. Babysitting, life guarding, yard work, and other part-time job experience indicate that you want to be useful and that you have worked with people in various situations.
- If you are handicapped, stress your abilities — not your disabilities.
- Sense the end of the interview. Thank the interviewer and express a positive interest in the job.

Before you leave the interview, find out when the interviewer expects to make a decision and when you should expect to hear about the job.

DEMONSTRATING YOUR ABILITIES

During the interview process, you may be asked to take an **employment test** — a test on the skills and knowledge that are required for the position. Various types of tests can be given. The type of test depends upon the position you are applying for. For instance, when applying for a secretarial position, you might be asked to take keyboarding and transcription tests. You might also be asked to take vocabulary, reading comprehension, and spelling tests. Usually, you will be given an opportunity to warm up on the keyboard and to take practice dictation before actual testing begins.

Illustration 15–9
A follow-up letter confirms your interest in the position

107 Rockton Drive
Cleveland, OH 44106
May 29, 19--

Mrs. Ellen Rider
Personnel Director
Tele-Vac Corporation
1406 Dow Circle
Cleveland, OH 44111

Dear Mrs. Rider

Thank you for the opportunity to discuss with you yesterday my qualifications for the secretarial position with your firm. I was impressed with your description of the position and with the opportunities that exist. I am certain that the work would be challenging and interesting.

I am very much interested in the job and hope that you feel, as I do, that my training and skills would be useful to your firm. The potential growth of the company and the many opportunities to make a contribution certainly appeal to me.

Please do not hesitate to call me if you need additional information. I hope to hear from you soon regarding your decision.

Sincerely

Lynda Yang

Lynda Yang

On the other hand, if you are applying for a position as a recordkeeping clerk, you may be asked to take a series of arithmetic tests. The purpose of these tests is to check your basic math skills. Other tests include aptitude tests that measure your ability to do specific types of jobs. Personality tests may be given to determine whether your personality is suited to the type of position you are applying for.

FOLLOWING UP YOUR INTERVIEW

After the interview, spend a few minutes making notes about the interview. Put these notes on a sheet of paper and add them to your employment file. Think back about what went right or wrong during the interview, and make notes of DOs and DON'Ts that may be of help to you in another interview. For example, what questions could you have answered more completely, more clearly, or differently? What points did you forget to make? It is also a good idea to mark on your calendar the date you or the company is supposed to take specific action.

On the same or the next day, write a **follow-up letter** to the interviewer to reinforce what you achieved in your interview. In this letter, as shown in Illustration 15–9, you should thank the interviewer for talking with you. The follow-up letter serves the following purposes:

- It strengthens the good impression you made during the interview.
- It reminds the employer of your interest in the job.
- It keeps your name in the employer's mind.
- It shows the employer that you complete tasks.
- It is evidence of good manners.

ev'i·dence

Composing and keyboarding a follow-up letter takes only a few minutes. Yet those few minutes may be your last chance to convince the interviewer that you are the person for the job.

REVIEWING KEY POINTS

1. The more prepared you are for an interview, the less fearful and nervous you will be.
2. You can influence a company to hire you by presenting your abilities in terms of the company's needs.
3. You should take to the interview a list of important facts about the company and a list of questions that you would like answered.
4. Planning your answers to those questions that interviewers frequently ask will help you be better prepared for an interview.
5. You should dress appropriately and neatly for the interview.
6. Role-playing will help you feel more confident about the interview.
7. Employment tests may be given to test your abilities.
8. Making notes for your employment file after every interview will give you useful information for future interviews.
9. A follow-up letter can help your chances of success.

DEVELOPING HUMAN RELATIONS SKILLS

1. You and a friend are practicing for upcoming interviews. It's your turn to interview your friend. During the interview your friend makes the following statements. Help your friend by rewording these statements so that they are more positive. Keyboard your statements on a separate sheet of paper.
   - **a.** That's about all I have to say about myself.
   - **b.** I've worked for only one company.
   - **c.** Yes, I was just a file clerk.
   - **d.** I liked the job, but the supervisor was really a turkey; so I just quit.

e. I won't graduate until the first week in June.
f. I was in a lot of school activities so I never worked any.
g. My grades were not so great, but they were okay.
h. No, I don't have any questions.

2. Kerry Sutter uses a wheelchair. She is interviewing for a position as a recordkeeping clerk. She has the skills for the position and the ability to do the work. Despite her physical disability, she is in excellent health. How can Kerry communicate her ability to do the job and avoid any doubts about her physical limitations?

IMPROVING COMMUNICATION SKILLS

Refer to Appendix B 4.14–4.25.

1. Keyboard the following sentences, expressing all numbers in the correct format.
   a. She bought a $10.00 chair cushion and a $15.00 glare shield.
   b. Denise earned $525.50 last week; Jon earned $595.00.
   c. The contract stated that the payee would receive $3,000 (Three Thousand Dollars) for services rendered.
   d. The committee was divided into 3 groups of 4.
   e. On the training review test, there were 8 95s.
   f. Chapter 1 of the Procedures Manual presented suggestions for disk care on pages 9 and 10.
   g. Scottie had to drive 40 miles one way to get to work.
   h. The office temperature should be about 68 degrees.
   i. Her office is 13 feet by 20 feet.
   j. 5 people were laid off from our office.
2. You are going to apply for an office position with the largest employer in your area. To obtain information about this company, compose a letter to the director of personnel requesting a copy of this year's annual report. Indicate a date by which you would like to have the report and express your appreciation for the director's assistance. Keyboard your letter on plain paper. Use block format. Be sure to include your complete return address.

BUILDING PROBLEM-SOLVING SKILLS

1. The weekly salaries for all of the office workers in your company follow. The company has just announced a 3 percent cost-of-living increase for all workers. On a separate sheet, compute the new salary for each worker.

a. M. Morgan, $360
b. T. Herrick, $407
c. S. Dove, $512
d. J. Kres, $387
e. D. Morse, $490
f. E. Itri, $473
g. S. Greer, $308
h. R. Freitag, $452
i. R. Isbart, $284
j. B. Craft, $325

2. Employment tests frequently test your ability to read and understand data. Test your reading comprehension by using the information in the following table to answer the questions listed here:

Department	Number of Employees	Letterhead Stationery		Plain Stationery	
		In Stock	Requisitioned	In Stock	Requisitioned
A	24	188	500	175	300
F	15	176	250	202	175
H	12	167	200	133	150
K	11	194	200	271	175
L	29	216	600	179	800
N	10	189	150	138	200
P	10	139	105	165	240
S	25	324	450	313	450
U	21	277	850	290	150
Z	13	112	280	109	225

a. Which department has the greatest amount of letterhead stationery in stock?
b. Which department is requisitioning the greatest amount of plain stationery?
c. Which department is requisitioning the smallest amount of letterhead stationery?
d. Which departments have the same amount of plain stationery in stock?
e. Which department employs the largest number of people?

APPLYING OFFICE SKILLS

Activities 1 and 2 can be done on information processing equipment.

1. Compose and keyboard a follow-up letter to Mrs. Mabel Wagner, Personnel Director of the Schneider Cornelius Company, 312 North 45th Street, Pomeroy, WA 99347. You interviewed with her yesterday for a position as a word processing operator, and you are very interested in getting the job.
2. Using the Help Wanted section of your local newspaper, locate a Help Wanted Ad for a position that you would like to apply for. Compose a list of ten questions you would ask during an interview for this position.
3. **(Optional)** In your best handwriting, complete the application form in your workbook.

CHAPTER 3

PROCEDURES FOR ADVANCEMENT

Your career as an office worker begins when you locate your first office position. Success in your career depends on the job opportunities in your field, on your knowledge and skill development, and on your needs and wants. There is no magic formula for success in a career. However, there are procedures that you can follow to increase the likelihood of success and advancement. Procedures for career growth and advancement focus on four main points: getting a successful start, planning for the future, achieving professional growth, and participating in professional organizations.

As you study this chapter, you will find answers to the following questions:

- How can I learn about company policies, procedures, and regulations in a new job?
- What steps can I take to ensure that I will get along with my coworkers in a new job?
- How can I prepare for career advancement?
- What are the advantages of participating in professional organizations?
- What do the following terms mean: **orientation meeting, office procedures manual, professional business organizations, professional certification?**

Illustration 15–10
Asking questions is one way to learn about your job and company

GETTING A SUCCESSFUL START

It is important for you to make a successful start beginning with your first day on the job. Having a pleasant personality, being intelligent, and possessing the necessary skills aren't enough. You must also possess the good work habits discussed in Unit 1. It is especially important that you work to develop habits such as efficient use of time from your first day on the job. You are hired to perform a particular job during certain hours. If you are to complete your work on schedule, you must arrive and leave work on time and observe time limits for breaks and lunch.

You will find that most offices have rules relating to talking, the assignment of certain responsibilities, the use of the telephone for personal business, and so on. You are expected to follow these rules as are all of the other employees. Many of these rules will be explained to you on the first day. You will hear about other regulations during your **orientation meeting**, in which you will receive an introduction to company policies and procedures, employee benefits, and other information related to your new position. You can obtain additional information about company regulations from the office procedures manual or by observing other workers.

o·ri·en·ta′tion

Learning About Your New Job

During the first few weeks on the job, you will have much to learn. You cannot expect to learn everything at once. It will take time for you to become familiar with the procedures that need to be followed and the order in which work must be completed. As you progress through the first few weeks, you will find an attitude of willingness and a desire to learn very helpful.

In a new job, there will be times when you need help or must ask questions. Do not hesitate to ask for any help you need to complete your assigned work. Your employer will prefer that you ask questions so that you can do your job accurately the first time.

Although it takes time to become accustomed to the company's practices, it is to your advantage to learn the procedures of the company as quickly as possible. The **office procedures manual** explains these procedures and the organization of the company. It also sets out the general rules that affect all employees. Your own department may have job description sheets for the positions in the department. You should study these descriptions. They list the responsibilities of your position and of all other positions in the department. The more you know about your job, the more valuable you will be to your company.

Getting Along with Your New Coworkers

With a new job come many new people and many new names. As you meet new people, try to learn their names and office titles. You might practice mentally recalling their names and titles whenever you have a few moments.

men'tal·ly

During the first few weeks, it is a good idea to observe how people greet each other and how titles are used. Pay attention to how visitors are greeted. These procedures help you fit into the organization. They can help you win the acceptance and cooperation of other employees. If you have doubts about the practice that is used, check with your supervisor. For example, if everyone in your department seems to be on a first-name basis, you might ask if this practice is followed all of the time.

thor'ough

You can get a successful start by being thorough, positive, and professional in your approach to work responsibilities. A job is never made just for you. Every job requires some adjustment and effort on your part. This effort is needed to meet the challenge of the position and the challenge of working with other people.

PLANNING FOR THE FUTURE

If you choose your job carefully, there's a good chance you will find it challenging, interesting, and worth your effort. However, it is unlikely that this will always be true. As time passes, your needs, desires, wants, and goals may change.

Being successful in your career depends on your ability to recognize changes in your needs. It also depends on your ability to develop new goals to fulfill these needs. For example, you may at sometime decide to go back to school or to buy a house. As a result, your need for money will be greater.

ful·fill'

Illustration 15–11
A job change may be necessary if your career goals change

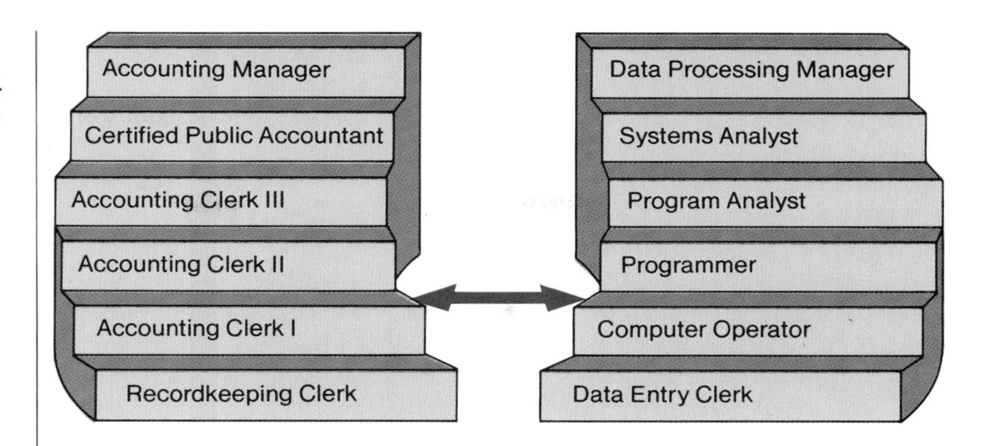

Your present job may not hold the salary potential that makes it possible for you to meet this need. If you stay in this job, you will probably become very dissatisfied because your need for a higher salary is not being fulfilled.

Setting Goals for Advancement

You can set new goals by planning to advance through your career path. For instance, you may decide to meet your need for a more challenging position or for a higher salary by advancing from a position as a data entry clerk to a position as a computer operator. In addition, it may be possible to change career paths within the company for which you work. For example, a recordingkeeping clerk following the career path for accounting may decide to change to the computer career path by accepting a company position as a programmer. Depending on how much your needs change, of course, it may even be necessary to look for a job with another company.

Career planning must also take into account changes within your position and your company. The effect that information processing has had on office jobs illustrates the change that can occur within a particular field. As a result of the rapid growth of information processing, new jobs have been created and new career paths have been established. If a person is up to date on such trends, career advancement and challenge are sure to occur.

ad·vance′ment

Rating Your Job Performance

In your work, you will be evaluated by your supervisor periodically. Your supervisor will complete a written evaluation form as a rating of your job performance. After reading through the form, you should discuss your evaluation with your supervisor. The evaluation should point out your job strengths as well as areas that need improvement. Once you know what areas you need to improve, you can start making the changes needed.

ACHIEVING PROFESSIONAL GROWTH

As you know, office work is constantly changing. For instance, think about how much the use of computers and electronics has changed information processing. As an office worker, you are responsible for updating your knowledge and skills as changes take place.

sem'in·ars

To update your professional knowledge, read articles in newspapers and professional journals that relate to your career and the business office. You should also take advantage of courses and seminars offered by your company, vocational schools, and colleges as a means of developing and improving your knowledge and skills. Joining professional organizations such as Professional Secretaries International also promotes professional growth.

Suggestions from coworkers and supervisors can be helpful to you. You can show your desire for improvement by your willingness to accept and use such suggestions.

PARTICIPATING IN PROFESSIONAL ORGANIZATIONS

There are many **professional business organizations.** These organizations have been established to promote professional growth within certain professions. They do this by setting goals for their professions. They also influence changes in standards and practices within the profession. Organizations such

Illustration 15–12 Many companies offer training seminars to keep workers up to date

spon'sor·ing

as these promote professions by sponsoring special programs. They also publish articles in newspapers and journals to help keep their members up to date on developments within the profession.

Certain standards are set for membership in these organizations. Standards, of course, differ with each organization. Some organizations require a certain number of years of experience, while others require a certain level of education. Still others require only that you be a member of a certain profession. To join a professional organization, you may be asked to complete an application form, which may later require the approval of the other members or a special membership committee.

The Function of Professional Organizations

Professional business organizations perform a wide variety of worthwhile functions. For example, they often conduct salary and job description surveys. These surveys help standardize salaries and job responsibilities for given positions throughout the nation.

Leadership skills are often developed through participation as an officer or a committee member in a professional organization. These leadership skills are important not only in the organization, but also on the job. Being a leader rather than a follower sets you apart from other workers and increases your chances for advancement.

cer·ti·fi·ca'tion

Still another function of a professional organization is to help its members achieve **professional certification** — that is, some form of recognition for passing an examination in their field. Certifying examinations are available for many positions, such as the Certified Professional Secretary (CPS) and the Certified Administrative Manager (CAM). Certification is one way of proving you are a professional. It proves that you have passed a qualifying examination showing that you have the knowledge and skills necessary to be certified within a particular area. Many professional organizations post announcements of coming examinations and provide review sessions to motivate their members to take certifying examinations.

mo'ti·vate

Choosing the Right Professional Organizations

There are many professional business organizations to which you can belong. When selecting an organization, study it carefully to make sure it suits your needs. In making your selection, you may want to ask some of the following questions:

- What are the purposes and objectives of this organization?
- What types of professional activities does this organization engage in?
- What are its standards for membership?
- How many members does this organization have?
- What are the membership dues?
- What is the reputation of this organization?

If you are an office worker, you may be interested in becoming a member of any of the following professional organizations:

- American Medical Records Association
- Association of Administrative Assistants
- Executive Secretaries, Inc.
- National Association of Educational Secretaries
- National Association of Legal Secretaries
- Professional Secretaries International
- National Federation of Business and Professional Women's Clubs
- Association of Information Processing Professionals

Include your membership in these professional organizations on your résumé. Your participation shows your interest in keeping up to date in your career and indicates a professional attitude about yourself and your work. When combined with good job performance and interpersonal skills, membership in professional organizations spells success!

REVIEWING KEY POINTS

1. Professional growth and advancement come as a result of getting a successful start, planning for the future, achieving professional growth, and participating in professional organizations.
2. "Getting a successful start" depends on learning and following company regulations and procedures.
3. When you start a new job, take time to ask questions and observe how others do their work.
4. Planning for career advancement involves thinking about your needs, your present job responsibilities and opportunities, career trends, and your future desires.
5. Career advancement depends a great deal on success in your present job.
6. Professional growth through reading, studying, and updating your skills and knowledge is necessary because the business office is changing so rapidly.

DEVELOPING HUMAN RELATIONS SKILLS

1. You have worked at Bradwell & Bowin for six months. Recently you have thought that you would like to join the local chapter of the Professional Secretaries International. During a break, you ask your coworkers if they

belong. Your coworkers react by laughing at you. One makes this comment, "You'll have to see Emily about that. She is the only one trying to make points by joining a professional organization. Most of us don't have time to go to meetings. Besides, if you join one of those groups, you'll have to do work for them."

a. What would be your response to such comments?

b. Do you think such a philosophy will serve your coworkers well?

c. Would you expect to work for an organization that you joined? Why?

2. If you were new to the job, how would you handle the following situations?

a. Some people in the office are on a first-name basis; others are not.

b. One of your coworkers constantly criticizes your immediate supervisor.

c. One of your new friends in the office takes advantage of break time. Instead of taking 20 minutes, she takes 30. She frequently invites you to join her.

d. Several of the people in the office dress very casually for work even though the company encourages appropriate business dress. It is tempting to wear casual clothes on some days, and you think you could probably get away with it since some of the others do.

e. You have been hired for a newly formed word processing department. Some older established workers have been transferred to the department. These workers are very negative about the whole idea.

IMPROVING COMMUNICATION SKILLS

Refer to Appendix B 4.14–4.25.

1. Keyboard the following sentences, expressing all numbers in the correct format.

a. 13 people attended the meeting.

b. The order is for 2 boxes of correction fluid.

c. The committee is composed of 2 people from the department.

d. His supervisor gave him a 5 pound box of candy for Secretary's Day.

e. The Dow Jones Industrial Average increased $15\frac{1}{2}$ points.

f. Jeremy got a $7\frac{1}{2}$% increase in salary.

g. The company was founded 25 years ago.

h. The average response rate of our new computer is 30 seconds.

i. He took 4 dollars from petty cash to pay the postage.

j. The conference leader expected about 400 people.

2. Assume that you work as an administrative assistant for Breckenridge, the sportswear manufacturer, where your duties include answering correspondence, collecting information for reports, and supervising other office workers. Compose and keyboard a letter to the director of admissions at a local vocational school or college. Ask about courses or seminars being offered that will help you update your knowledge and skills. Request the director send you a copy of the latest catalogue. Explain to the director what duties your job involves and ask for course or seminar recommendations.

BUILDING PROBLEM-SOLVING SKILLS

1. The office workers at Nolan Industries receive merit pay increases every April. The chart below shows the percentage of merit pay each office worker will receive. Compute the dollar amount of merit pay for each worker. Then use that amount to compute each worker's new salary. Write your answers on a separate sheet of paper.

Employee	Current Salary	% Merit Pay Increase
K. McLafferty	$442	2%
F. Mossar	494	4
L. Noyd	431	3
L. Olason	497	5
J. Paolucci	416	3
A. Pinelo	452	2
B. Barrie	384	5
L. Renz	359	3
A. Rini	458	4
K. Rosenthal	476	2

2. Using the amounts you computed in Activity 1, answer the following questions. Write your answers on a separate sheet of paper.

a. Which worker received the largest dollar amount of merit pay?

b. Which worker received the smallest dollar amount of merit pay?

c. After the increase, which office worker will receive the highest salary?

d. After the increase, which office worker will receive the lowest salary?

e. What is the difference between the highest and lowest salary paid?

f. What was the average amount of merit pay received by the workers?

g. What is the difference between the highest and lowest amount of merit pay received?

h. What percentage of workers received merit pay of 4% or above?

i. What percentage of workers received merit pay of 3% or below?

j. What is the total dollar amount of all merit pay awarded the workers?

APPLYING OFFICE SKILLS

1. Using the library, telephone directories, information from the Chamber of Commerce, and articles from newspapers, make a list of professional

Activity 1 can be done on information processing equipment.

organizations within your local community. Keyboard your list in an attractive format.

2. On a separate sheet of paper, draw a diagram of the career path that you plan to follow. Below your diagram explain:
   a. Where you would begin on the path given the skills and experience you currently have.
   b. What steps you can take for advancement.
   c. What responsibilities you would have at each step.

Saving Time and Money

Get organized and save time in seeking a job by preparing an employment checklist. Begin by making a list of things you need to do before you can apply for positions. For example, if this is your first job, you may need to obtain a social security card, prepare a résumé, and identify people who agree to serve as your references.

During each step of your job application process, you should prepare a list of reminders for yourself. The night before your interview, for example, you should review the list of things on your interview checklist. It might contain the following reminders:

1. Prepare a list of questions to ask during the interview.
2. Go over the key points you plan to make in the interview.
3. Choose and lay out clothes so that you will be neatly dressed.
4. Get a good night's rest.
5. Take a pen or pencil to the interview to complete the job application or take tests.
6. Take several copies of your résumé with you.
7. Review the exact location of the company and the nearest parking or public transportation facilities.

ENERGETICS, INC.

We're so glad to see you back at Energetics. This simulation is the last of the four Energetics, Inc., office simulations. As with the other three simulations, you will be completing five office jobs. In addition to the routine keyboarding tasks, you will be asked to keyboard a quarterly activity report about the use of the company's information processing equipment. In this simulation, you will also be asked to complete the payroll register for the company's office staff. An introduction to Office Simulation No. 4 follows.

Office Simulation No. 4

In every company, there are periods of heavy work loads that occur on a regular basis. At Energetics, Inc., work overloads occur at the end of each quarter, when sales, equipment design, and financial reports are due.

The managers' meeting, which is held quarterly, places additional demands on the office support staff. Although only people from within Energetics, Inc., attend this meeting, there are still announcements to be sent and the agenda to be prepared. This quarter, the managers of the Sales and Advertising Departments, Whit Jones and Lyn Ann Knudsen, will be using visual aids in their presentations. All of these arrangements for the meeting are in addition to regular work responsibilities.

Ms. Clay has called to see whether you will be available for a few afternoons to help meet these end-of-quarter deadlines. Because all of the departments at Energetics, Inc., are affected, you will be counted on to help wherever you are needed. "We probably have some new assignments for you this time," Ms. Clay tells you. "Are you ready to try something new?"

Turn to Office Simulation No. 4 in your *Student Activities* (pages 147-158) to see what you'll be doing this week at Energetics, Inc.

APPENDIX A
PUNCTUATION AND GRAMMAR REVIEW

1 PUNCTUATION RULES

This brief review is intended to provide you with a ready answer to some of the most common punctuation questions. It is by no means complete and should not be considered your final authority. For a fuller and more authoritative guide, consult one of the publications listed in Appendix D, Reference Sources.

Period

1.1 Use a period after declarative sentences, after commands, and after polite requests.

These files are to be placed in the in basket. [Declarative sentence]
Place these files in the in basket. [Command]
Would you please place these files in the in basket. [Polite request]

1.2 Use a period after initials, academic degrees, and most abbreviations.

Robert L. Stevenson	Jan. 17, 1903
Mercedes Solano, D.D.S.	6 a.m.

1.3 See also Rule 1.40 under Parentheses and Rule 1.44a under Quotation Marks.

Question Mark

1.4 Use a question mark after a direct question.

Have you processed the purchase invoice? [Direct question]
She asked if you had processed the purchase invoice. [Indirect question does not take question mark]

1.5 See also Rule 1.40 under Parentheses and Rule 1.44c under Quotation Marks.

Exclamation Point

1.6 Use an exclamation point to express strong feelings or to emphasize a command.

Great! This design is really good. [Strong feeling]
Don't move! Your sweater is caught on the chair. [Emphatic command]

1.7 See also Rule 1.40 under Parentheses and Rule 1.44c under Quotation Marks.

Comma

1.8 A comma is used to separate the items in a series.

Clear your desk of unnecessary pencils, books, and papers. [Words]
We ordered seven of size 8, six of size 10, and a dozen of size 14. [Phrases]
Peggy chose the dull gray, Elizabeth picked the loud purple, and I selected the tasteful beige. [Short independent clauses]

1.9 A comma is used to separate independent clauses of a compound sentence when they are joined by a coordinating conjunction *(and, but, or, nor, yet, for, so)*.

Karen joined the team, and Mike was benched.
Paul didn't do his share, so we all had extra work.

1.10 A comma is used to separate adjectives that precede and modify the same noun.

A tall, friendly person waited on me. [Both *tall* and *friendly* modify *person*.]
The Historical Society bought the old grist mill in the town of Lexington. [*Old* modifies *grist mill*.]

1.11 A comma is used to separate the parts in dates and addresses.

On February 18, 1962, our first branch store was opened.
The store nearest you is at 370 Elm Court Street, Tyler, Texas.

1.12 A comma is used to set off the names of individuals in direct address.

I realize, Mr. Moreno, that you may not be able to meet with us then.

1.13 A comma is used to set off an appositive; that is, a word or phrase that explains or describes the noun or pronoun it follows.

Mrs. Olin, our vice president for marketing, will be out of the office until the middle of next week.
Our stockroom supervisor, Hal Rubin, says that our supply of that item is low.

1.14 A comma is used to set off parenthetical expressions. Parenthetical expressions are words, phrases, or clauses that interrupt a sentence and could easily be omitted with no effect on the sentence's meaning.

Alma's work, I must say, continues to be outstanding.
This method, for example, can also be used on larger animals.

1.15 A comma is used to set off nonrestrictive phrases or clauses. A nonrestrictive phrase or clause is one that provides additional but unnecessary information. A restrictive phrase or clause, on the other hand, is one that contains information essential to the meaning of the sentence.

Nora's book, which I left on the hall table, is full of statistics. [Nonrestrictive. The clause provides some information, but it is not essential.]
Bring me the book that I left on the hall table. [Restrictive. The clause provides information that is essential to the meaning of the sentence.]

1.16 A comma is used to set off introductory words, phrases, and dependent clauses in sentences.

No, I cannot have that completed by noon. [Word]
Before leaving, I will have it proofread and photocopied. [Phrase]
After I have finished keyboarding the report, I can give it to you. [Clause]

1.17 A comma is used to set off direct quotations.

The purchase order is correct. She clearly said, "I want thirty cases."

1.18 See also Rule 1.40 under Parentheses and Rule 1.44a under Quotation Marks.

Semicolon

1.19 A semicolon is used to separate the items in a series if one or more of the items contains a comma.

Send six copies to Mr. Reed, Dallas office; two copies to Ms. Bellagio, Chicago office; and one copy to Mrs. Cermak, San Francisco office.

1.20 A semicolon is used to separate independent clauses of a compound sentence when they are *not* joined by a coordinating conjunction (*and, but, or,* etc.) or when they are joined by a conjunctive adverb (*however, therefore, accordingly, nevertheless, thus,* etc.).

Nathan will keyboard the inside addresses; Ellen will prepare the envelopes. [No coordinating conjunction]
You can leave early tonight; however, you'll have to make up the time tomorrow. [Conjunctive adverb]

1.21 See also Rule 1.40 under Parentheses and Rule 1.44b under Quotation Marks.

Apostrophe

1.22 An apostrophe is used to show possession.

a. For singular or plural nouns that do not end in *s*, show possession by adding an apostrophe and *s* ('s).

I left it on Tina's desk. [Singular]
It disappeared in the children's bedroom. [Plural]

b. For singular or plural nouns that end in *s*, show possession by adding only an apostrophe.

Dickens' novels are just as popular today as they were fifty years ago. [Singular]
This equals three hours' work. [Plural]

c. For joint possession, add an apostrophe and *s* ('s) to the last name.

The party was held at Sara and Karl's house. [Joint ownership of one house]

d. For individual possession by two or more persons, add an apostrophe and *s* ('s) to each person's name.

Harry's and Nita's bikes are brand new. [Individual ownership of two bikes]

1.23 An apostrophe is used to show the omission of letters or numbers in contractions.

It's only make believe, isn't it? [Letters]
They still talk about the blizzard of '78. [Numbers]

1.24 An apostrophe is generally used to form the plural of words used as words, numbers, letters, and abbreviations with periods.

You have to go. There are no *if's, and's,* or *but's* about that. [Words as words]
Many Europeans cross their 7's when writing that number. [Numbers]
Mind your p's and q's. [Letters]
Three of our employees have their M.A.'s. [Abbreviations]

Colon

1.25 A colon is used to introduce a list, an explanation, or a quotation that follows.

The following items are now available: index cards, file folders, and plastic guides. [List]
I don't like Mr. Abrams: He always tries to make fun of me. [Explanation]
Remember what Polonius said in Hamlet: "This above all, to thine own self be true." [Quotation]

1.26 A colon is used to separate hours and minutes in expressions of time.

The meeting will begin at 8:30 a.m.

1.27 See also Rule 1.40 under Parentheses and Rule 1.44b under Quotation Marks.

Hyphen

1.28 A hyphen is used to join the words of a compound adjective when it appears before the noun it modifies.

Use the heavy-duty stapler for this report.

1.29 A hyphen is used in spelling out compound numbers from 21 to 99.

There are thirty-seven workers participating in this program.

1.30 A hyphen is used in spelling out fractions used as adjectives.

The company achieved a one-third increase in productivity.

1.31 A hyphen is used to divide a word at the end of a line. See also Appendix B, Word Division Rules.

In the next three years, we fully expect to implement a new profit-
sharing plan.

1.32 A hyphen is used to separate certain prefixes from main words. These prefixes include *all-*, *ex-*, *great-*, *half-*, and *self-*.

Carmen has a high degree of self-regard.

Dash

1.33 Use a dash to add emphasis to a parenthetical expression.

Electronic filing—a new trend in filing—saves time.

1.34 Use a dash to indicate a sudden change in a sentence.

Check the Brown file—no, the Braun file.

1.35 Use a dash before an author's name that follows a quotation.

A penny saved is a penny earned.—Franklin

Underscore

1.36 An underscore is used to indicate the title of a book, magazine, newspaper, play, or musical composition.

For additional information, consult <u>The Reference Guide</u>. [Book]
Her short story first appeared in <u>Collier's</u>. [Magazine]
He read <u>The New York Sun</u> regularly until it ceased publication. [Newspaper]
<u>Madame Butterfly</u> has always been a favorite of mine. [Musical composition]

1.37 An underscore is used to place emphasis on a word or phrase.

The newspaper only indicated those who did <u>not</u> pass the examination.

Parentheses

1.38 Parentheses are used to set off words, phrases, or clauses that may clarify or further explain a part of a sentence but that are not necessary to the meaning of the sentence.

The brightest color (scarlet) was rejected immediately. [Word]
The smaller offices (ten feet by ten feet) are not enclosed. [Phrase]
The carton arrived damaged (in fact, all cartons in that shipment were damaged), and we refused to accept it. [Clause]

1.39 Parentheses are used to repeat for clarification dollar amounts in legal and business documents.

The undersigned agrees to pay the bearer Twenty-five Dollars ($25).

1.40 Parentheses are used with other punctuation marks as follows:

a. When the other punctuation mark applies only to the material enclosed in the parentheses, place the punctuation mark *inside* the right parenthesis.

Anna Marantz (is she still in school?) was one of the successful applicants.

b. When the other punctuation mark applies either to the part of the sentence in which the material enclosed in parentheses appears or to the whole sentence, place the punctuation mark *outside* the right parenthesis.

The following supplies are now available in all stockrooms (except those on the 26th and 30th floor): carbon packs, carbon ribbons, correction fluid, and No. 3H pencils. [Punctuation applies to part of sentence]

Answer the questions that concern your place of residence (page 63). [Punctuation applies to the whole sentence]

Quotation Marks

1.41 Quotation marks are used to enclose *direct* quotations.

Keith said, "Why do I have to do the laundry and the shopping?" [Direct quotation]

Sarah said that she would leave for Topeka on Thursday instead. [Indirect quotation]

1.42 Quotation marks are used to set off titles of articles, speeches, book chapters, short stories, songs, poems, and movies.

Please read the article "How to Reduce Photocopying Costs" in this month's <u>Modern Office Management Systems</u>.

1.43 Quotation marks are used to set off definitions, slang words, and words or expressions intended to show irony.

Economics is defined as the "allocation of scarce resources." [Definition]

The project delays are starting to "bug" the supervisor. [Slang]

Because it's supposed to be a "glamour" industry, publishing tends to pay less than many other careers. [Irony]

1.44 Quotation marks are used with other forms of punctuation as follows:

a. Periods and commas are always placed inside the closing quotation mark.

"Your plane takes off at noon," she said.

This is the tenth time that I've seen "Gone with the Wind."

b. Colons and semicolons are placed outside the closing quotation mark.

This should be "our song": "The One I Love Belongs to Somebody Else."

No, we haven't uncovered the class "spy"; however, we'll keep searching.

c. Question marks and exclamation points go either inside or outside the closing quotation mark depending on whether they are part of the quoted material or of the whole sentence.

Alice asked, "When do we eat lunch?" [Question is part of quoted material only]

Did Alice say, "I don't know when we should eat lunch"? [Whole sentence is question]

2 GRAMMAR GUIDE

Agreement

2.1 A verb should agree with its subject.

a. When the subject is singular, the verb should be singular.

The *secretary is* in his office.

b. When the subject is plural, the verb should be plural.

The *secretaries are* in their offices.

c. When there are two subjects joined by *either/or, neither/nor,* or *not only/but also,* the verb should agree with the closer subject.

Either *Tom* or his *assistants are* completing the report.
Neither *you* nor *I am* ready to begin the project.

d. When plural words come between a singular subject and its verb, the verb should still be singular.

One of the best secretaries of all those who work in the main office and its branches *was* honored today.

e. When certain singular pronouns (*anybody, anyone, anything, another, each, either, everybody, everyone, nobody, no one, somebody, someone*) are used, the verb should be singular.

Everyone is doing what's expected.

f. When a subject has a plural form but singular meaning, the verb should be singular.

Economics is the dismal science.
Four dollars is a lot to pay for one movie.

g. When words preceded by certain phrases (*as well as, except, in addition to, no less than, together with,* and *with*) are added to a singular subject, the verb should be singular.

Our marketing *manager,* together with her assistant, *is* presenting the new product.

2.2 A pronoun should agree with the word or words to which it refers.

a. A pronoun and the word or words to which it refers should agree in number.

Each *woman* displayed *her* handiwork. [Singular]
The *women* displayed *their* handiwork. [Plural]
Santos and *Bill* supported *their* school team. [Plural]

b. A pronoun and the word or words to which it refers should agree in gender.

Tanya went to *her* home, and *Martin* went to *his.*
She lifted the *car* by *its* fender.

c. A pronoun and the word or words to which it refers should agree in person.

Martin and I think *we* deserve to win. [First person]
Take this, *Beverly*: I want *you* to have it. [Second person]
Send a letter to *Mario* and tell *him* the news. [Third person]

Capitalization

2.3 Capitalize the first word of a sentence.

Exercise is good for your health, they say.

2.4 Capitalize proper nouns and adjectives, geographical names, and government or political units.

The office manager is Carol Chung. [Proper noun]
Carol is Chinese. [Proper adjective]
She came to us from Springfield, Illinois. [Geographical name]
She used to work for the Illinois Senate. [Government unit]

2.5 Capitalize all important words in business names.

Marketing and Information Services, Inc.
Top of the Mark
The Bank for Savings

2.6 Capitalize points of the compass when referring to specific locations. Do not capitalize when referring to direction.

Our main competitor is moving to the Southwest. [Specific location]
Do we have a branch in West Orange? [Specific location]
They live in the eastern part of the state. [Direction]

2.7 Capitalize days of the week, months of the year, and holidays.

The normal work week is from Monday through Friday. [Days of the week]
Your order was shipped on March 15. [Months of the year]
Passover and Easter do not fall at the same time this year. [Holidays]

2.8 Capitalize a noun that appears before a number or letter.

They are expected to arrive on Flight 187.
I think you'll find Mr. Esterhazy in Room 812.
Our best selling style is Model C.

2.9 Capitalize the main words in the titles of published materials.

Everytime I read Pride and Prejudice, I find something new to enjoy.
Although she no longer lives in Denver, she still subscribes to the Rocky Mountain News.

2.10 Capitalize the first word of an independent clause that follows a colon if the material preceding the colon is introductory.

The question is this: Can we raise the money?

APPENDIX B
WORD DIVISION AND NUMBERS

3 WORD DIVISION RULES

Avoid dividing a word at the end of a line whenever possible. When division is necessary, however, follow these basic rules. Always be sure to check a dictionary for correct syllabication of a word.

3.1 Divide a word only between syllables; never divide a one-syllable word, regardless of its length.

ac-com-mo-date
fringe
key-board
es-tab-lish
thought
doc-u-ment
ap-pro-pri-ate
turned
com-pu-ter

3.2 Never divide a word of five or fewer letters.

label *not* la-bel
asset *not* as-set
cycle *not* cy-cle
office *not* of-fice

3.3 If a word contains a single-letter syllable, divide the word after this syllable.

docu-ment *not* doc-ument
credi-tor *not* cred-itor
regu-late *not* reg-ulate
sepa-rate *not* sep-arate

3.4 Divide a word ending in *-ily, -able, -ible, -uble, -ably, -ibly, -acle, -icle,* or *-ical* before one of these suffixes.

chrono-log-ical *not* chrono-logi-cal
re-turn-able *not* returna-ble
read-ily *not* readi-ly
manage-able *not* managea-ble

3.5 Divide a word between two single-letter syllables that appear together.

vari-ation *not* var-iation
continu-ation *not* contin-uation
idi-omatic *not* id-iomatic
mime-ograph *not* mimeo-graph

3.6 Include two or more letters with the first part of a divided word and three or more with the last part.

iden-ti-cal *not* i-dentical
amend-ment *not* a-mendment
rever-ently *not* reverent-ly
diver-sity *not* diversi-ty

3.7 If a root word ends in a double consonant before a suffix is added, divide *after* the double consonant.

call-ing *not* cal-ling
assess-ment *not* asses-sment
trespass-ing *not* trespas-sing
express-ing *not* expres-sing

3.8 If the final letter in a root word is doubled before a suffix is added, divide between the doubled letters.

acquit-ting *not* acquitt-ing
ship-ping *not* shipp-ing
prefer-ring *not* preferr-ing
excel-ing *not* excell-ing

3.9 If at all possible, divide a compound word between the compound elements.

photo-copy *not* pho-tocopy
paper-work *not* pa-perwork
letter-head *not* let-terhead
under-go *not* un-dergo

3.10 If a compound word is hyphenated, divide at the point of the hyphen.

self-confident *not* self-confi-dent
court-martial *not* court-mar-tial

4 NUMBER RULES

A number can be written as a figure or a word depending on its use. The following rules for the expression of numbers will help you in deciding how to express a number in your work. When in doubt as to the correct use of a number, review these rules or refer to an appropriate source in Appendix D, Reference Sources.

4.1 Spell out numbers up to ten. Use figures for numbers over ten.

The company sent one manager, seven consultants, and three secretaries to the meeting.
The company has 1,127 employees in 21 locations.

4.2 Hyphenate spelled-out numbers between 21 and 99.

There are thirty-one days in January and twenty-nine in February this year.

4.3 Within a short section of text, treat all numbers consistently. If the largest number is written in figures, use figures for all.

There are 2 managers, 10 supervisors, and 27 workers.

4.4 Always spell out a number that begins a sentence. If spelling the number is awkward, rewrite the sentence.

Seventeen people attended the meeting.
The votes totaled 299. *not* Two hundred ninety-nine votes were counted.

4.5 Spell out approximate numbers and even hundreds, thousands, and millions.

The house is about fifty years old.
It is estimated that about three hundred thousand secretaries are needed in the United States.

4.6 Use figures to express very large *round* numbers and units of millions or billions.

1.75 million residents
2 billion particles

4.7 Always use figures with abbreviations or symbols.

35 mph	71%	13°C
12 yds.	7 − 4 = 3	1.61 Km

4.8 Use a comma in numbers of four or more digits.

3,173	1,132,210

However, when using the metric system, do not use the comma to separate groups of numbers. Instead, leave one space between groups of three numbers.

1 073 kg	3 072 191 Km

4.9 When two related numbers appear together, spell out the smaller of the two.

They ordered three 20-pound packages.
The package contains 20 three-ounce servings.

4.10 Spell out names of numbered streets up to and including ten. Use ordinal figures (figures with st, th, rd, or nd) for numbered streets over ten.

Third Street	56th Street
East 42nd Avenue	First Avenue

4.11 Use figures for house and building numbers, with the exception of *One*, and for ZIP Codes (separated from the state name by one space).

127 Chimney Hill Road	Provo, UT 84601
One Lakeshore Boulevard	Orlando, FL 32807

4.12 In correspondence, use figures for the day of the month and the year.

February 16, 1987	27 February 1987
The letter arrived on March 2.	

In legal documents, dates may be spelled out or expressed in figures with ordinals.

Witnesseth this third day of May, nineteen hundred eighty-seven.
Witnesseth this 3rd day of May, 1987.

4.13 In general, spell out the time of day except when stating the exact time. Always spell out the time when using *o'clock*. Always use figures with *a.m.* or *p.m.*

It gets dark around seven.
The bell rings at 2:30 p.m. every day.
We will begin at seven o'clock.

4.14 Always use figures for numbers containing decimals.

The average age of the workers is 32.3 years.
Most word processing operators keyboard 4.5 documents an hour.

4.15 Use figures for mixed numbers.

The recipe called for 3¼ cups of sugar and 1⅓ cups of pecans.

4.16 Hyphenate spelled-out fractions used as adjectives. When they are used as nouns, write the fractions as two words without hyphens.

The vote was a two-thirds majority for the motion.
She will work one half of the day and go to school in the afternoons.

4.17 Use figures for percentages, with either the percent symbol (%) or the word *percent*.

The interest rates for the special savings accounts are 6.5%, 7%, and 7.5%.
She invested 20 percent of her earnings.

4.18 When the percent number begins a sentence, spell it out and always use the word *percent*.

Fifty percent of the students from that school attend college.

4.19 Use figures for sums of money (with a dollar sign).

Her check was written for $279.34.

4.20 For sums of money less than $1, use figures and the word *cents*. Do not use the dollar sign or decimal point.

The card cost 65 cents.

4.21 Do not use a decimal point or ciphers (.00) with whole dollar amounts unless they appear with sums that include both dollars and cents.

The record cost $10, but it was advertised incorrectly.
Jane earned $50.00 while Bill only earned $33.75.

4.22 In legal documents, amounts of money are expressed in both words and figures.

The payee will receive Three Thousand Dollars ($3,000) in three installments.

4.23 For plurals of numbers written in figures, add *'s*. However, current usage favors the addition of an *s* only.

The class was divided into groups of 3's.
There were many 98s scored on the test.

4.24 Use figures for numbers of pages, chapters, volumes, etc.

The answers are in Volume 1, Unit 6, Chapter 3, pages 117–135.

4.25 Use figures for measurements—distances, length, area, volume, pressure, temperature, etc.

13 cm	150 pounds	78°F
3 grams	13′ x 20′	13°C
4 quarts	24 miles	

MATH SKILL REVIEW

5 WORKING WITH NUMBERS

5.1 Rounding

Whole Numbers

If the digit to the right of the desired rounding place is 5 or higher, add 1 to the digit in the desired rounding place and replace all succeeding digits with zeros. If the digit to the right of the desired rounding place is 4 or lower, leave the digit in the desired rounding place as it is.

Round to the nearest ten:

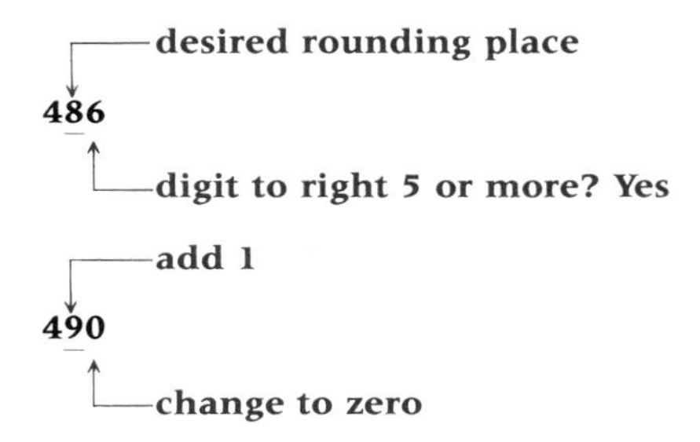

Decimals

If the digit to the right of the desired rounding place is 5 or higher, add 1 to the digit in the desired rounding place and drop all of the succeeding digits. If the digit to the right of the desired rounding place is 4 or lower, leave the digit in the desired rounding place as it is and drop all of the succeeding digits. See the example below. Compare it to the example above.

Round to the nearest hundredth:

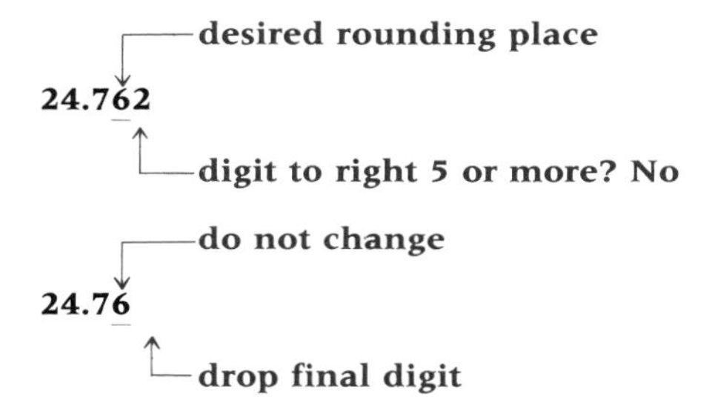

5.2 Estimating Results

Estimating an answer gives a guide to the correct answer. Round the numbers in the problem and calculate mentally. Compare your estimate with the answer.

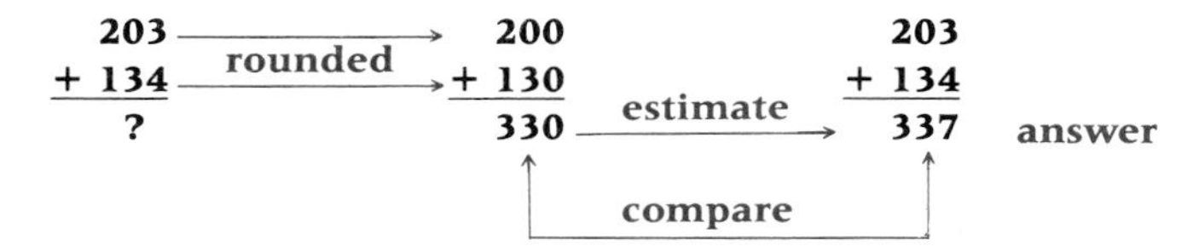

5.3 Finding Factors

A factor is any number that can be divided into another number a whole number of times with no remainder.

Find the factors of 12:

	1	**(12 ÷ 1 = 12)**
	2	**(12 ÷ 2 = 6)**
	3	**(12 ÷ 3 = 4)**
	4	**(12 ÷ 4 = 3)**
Not a factor of 12 →	**5**	**(12 ÷ 5 = 2, with 2 remaining)**
	6	**(12 ÷ 6 = 2)**
Not a factor of 12 →	**7**	**(12 ÷ 7 = 1, with 5 remaining)**
	12	**(12 ÷ 12 = 1)**

Factors of 12 are: 1, 2, 3, 4, 6, and 12.

6 WHOLE NUMBERS

6.1 Addition

In addition, two or more numbers are combined into one number called the *sum.* If the digits in a column total more than 9, carry a digit over to the column to the left.

```
  1 1 1    ← carry                 2   1 2    ← carry
  8 6 7 9                            7 3 5 7
+ 9 7 4 8                            9 2 8 9
                                 +   5 3 1 8
 18 4 2 7 ←—— sum ——→              2 1 9 6 4
```

6.2 Subtraction

Subtraction is the process of finding the *difference* between numbers. When one digit in the column is too large to be subtracted from the other, borrow from the column to the left.

```
  6       ← borrow              8 ¹2 ¹4      ← borrow
  7 ¹6                          9  3  5 ¹2
– 4  9    ← too large         – 4  6  9  4   ← too large
  2  7    ← difference          4  6  5  8   ← difference
```

6.3 Multiplication

Multiplication is the process of finding the product of two or more numbers.

```
      342
    × 211
      342 →1 × 342 = 342
    3 420 →10 × 342 = 3420
 + 68 400 →200 × 342 = 68,400
   72,162 →342 × 211 = 72,162 ← product
```

6.4 Multiplication by Multiples of 10

When multiplying by 10, simply add a zero to the right of the number being multiplied. When multiplying by 100, add two zeros. When multiplying by 1000, add three zeros, and so on.

$$\begin{array}{r}135\\ \times\ 10\\ \hline\end{array} = 1350 \qquad \begin{array}{r}265\\ \times\ 100\\ \hline\end{array} = 26{,}500 \qquad \begin{array}{r}978\\ \times\ 1000\\ \hline\end{array} = 978{,}000$$

6.5 Division without Remainder

In division, one number (a dividend) is divided by another (a divisor) to get the answer (the quotient).

```
divisor
  ↓                  1               18               183 ← quotient
 27)4941  →  27)4941  →  27)4941  →  27)4941
    ↑           −27          −27          −27
 dividend        22           224          224
                             −216         −216
                                8           81
                                           −81
```

6.6 Division with Fractional Remainder

The remainder of a quotient may be shown as a fraction.

```
       1                  14 12/48  = 14 1/4
  48)684  ———→  48)684
    −48            −48        reduce to
     20            204        lowest term
                  −192
remainder ———→      12
```

7 DECIMALS

7.1 Addition of Decimals

In addition with decimals, the decimal points must be aligned. If necessary, rewrite the numbers in vertical form. Align decimal points. Supply zeros as placeholders where needed. See the top of the next page for an example.

$$1.5 + 0.33 + 94 \qquad \begin{array}{r} 1.5 \\ 0.33 \\ +\ 94. \\ \hline \end{array} \qquad \begin{array}{r} 1.50 \leftarrow \\ 0.33 \\ +\ 94.00 \leftarrow \\ \hline 95.83 \end{array} \text{ placeholders}$$

7.2 Subtraction of Decimals

If necessary, rewrite the numbers in vertical form. Align decimals. Supply zeros as placeholders where needed.

$$882.163 - 32.1 \rightarrow \begin{array}{r} 882.163 \\ -\ 32.1 \\ \hline \end{array} \rightarrow \begin{array}{r} 882.163 \\ -\ 32.100 \leftarrow \\ \hline 850.063 \end{array} \text{ placeholders}$$

7.3 Multiplication of Decimals

The number of decimal places in the product is equal to the total number of decimal places in the numbers being multiplied.

$$\begin{array}{r} 6.24 \\ \times\ 2.1 \\ \hline \end{array} \rightarrow \begin{array}{rl} 6.24 & \leftarrow 2 \text{ decimal places} \\ \times\ 2.1 & \leftarrow 1 \text{ decimal place} \\ \hline 13.104 & \leftarrow 3 \text{ decimal places in product} \end{array}$$

$$\begin{array}{r} 0.06 \\ \times\ 0.03 \\ \hline \end{array} \rightarrow \begin{array}{rl} 0.06 & \leftarrow 2 \text{ decimal places} \\ \times\ 0.03 & \leftarrow 2 \text{ decimal places} \\ \hline .0018 & \leftarrow 4 \text{ decimal places in product} \end{array}$$

7.4 Division with Decimals

Division with Whole Number Divisors

When dividing by a whole number, maintain the position of the decimal in the dividend.

maintain decimal point

$$46\overline{)55.2} \rightarrow \begin{array}{r} 1.2 \\ 46\overline{)55.2} \\ -46 \\ \hline 9\ 2 \\ -9\ 2 \\ \hline \end{array}$$

Division with Decimal Divisors

Move the decimal point in the divisor and in the dividend the same number of places to the right.

$$6.6\overline{)27.72} \longrightarrow 6.6.\overline{)27.7.2} \longrightarrow \begin{array}{r} 4.2 \\ 66\overline{)277.2} \\ -264 \\ \hline 13\ 2 \\ -13\ 2 \\ \hline \end{array}$$

move one decimal place

$$0.032\overline{)14.4} \longrightarrow 0.032.\overline{)14.400.} \longrightarrow 32\overline{)14400}$$

move three decimal places

$$\begin{array}{r} 450 \\ 32\overline{)14400} \\ -128 \\ 160 \\ -160 \\ 00 \\ -00 \end{array}$$

Division with Remainder

Add zeros to the right of the decimal point in the dividend. Carry the division to one place beyond the desired rounding place in the quotient. Then round.

Round to nearest hundredth.

$$78\overline{)463.} \rightarrow \begin{array}{r} 5.935 \\ 78\overline{)463.000} \\ -390 \\ 73\,0 \\ -70\,2 \\ 2\,80 \\ -2\,34 \\ 460 \\ -390 \\ 70 \end{array}$$

5.935 → 5.935 rounded to the nearest hundredth is 5.94

8 FRACTIONS

8.1 Changing a Fraction to a Decimal

To change a fraction to a decimal, divide the numerator by the denominator. Round as indicated.

Write $\frac{1}{4}$ as a decimal.

$$\frac{1}{4} \rightarrow \begin{array}{r} 0.25 \\ 4\overline{)1.00} \end{array}$$

$$\frac{1}{4} = 0.25$$

Write $\frac{2}{3}$ as a decimal.

$$\frac{2}{3} \rightarrow \begin{array}{r} 0.6666 \\ 3\overline{)2.0000} \end{array}$$ ← **carry quotient to 4 decimal places**

$$\frac{2}{3} = 0.667$$ ← **round to 3 decimal places**

8.2 Expressing Equivalent Fractions

$$\frac{2}{3} = \frac{?}{15} \qquad \frac{6}{9} = \frac{?}{3} \qquad \frac{3}{4} = \frac{?}{16}$$

$$\frac{2}{3} \;(\times 5)\; \frac{10}{15} \qquad \frac{6}{9} = \;(\div 3)\; \frac{2}{3} \qquad \frac{3}{4} = \;(\times 4)\; \frac{12}{16}$$

8.3 Determining the Least Common Multiple (LCM)

A *common multiple* of two or more whole numbers is any whole number that is a multiple of the given numbers. The *least common multiple* (LCM) of two or more whole numbers is the least nonzero multiple that is common to all of the numbers that are given.

Find the least common multiple of 2 and 3.

Multiples of 2 are: 2, 4, (6), 8, 10, (12), 14, 16, (18), 20, 22, and so on

Multiples of 3 are: 3, (6), 9, (12), 15, (18), 21, and so on

Common multiples are: 6, 12, 18.

The least common multiple is: 6.

8.4 Determining the Greatest Common Factor (GCF)

The greatest common factor (GCF) of two or more numbers is the largest whole number that can be divided evenly, with no remainder, into each of the numbers. (See also 5.3)

Find the greatest common factor of 6 and 18.

Factors of 6 are: (1), (2), (3), (6)

Factors of 18 are: (1), (2), (3), (6), 9, 18

Common factors are: 1, 2, 3, 6.

Greatest common factor is 6.

8.5 Reducing Fractions to Lowest Terms

To reduce fractions to lowest terms, divide the numerator and the denominator by the greatest common factor.

$\frac{6}{18}$ ← **greatest common factor of 6 and 18 is 6** → $\frac{6 \div 6}{18 \div 6} = \frac{1}{3}$

8.6 Writing Mixed Numbers as Improper Fractions

An improper fraction is a fraction with a numerator equal to or greater than its denominator.

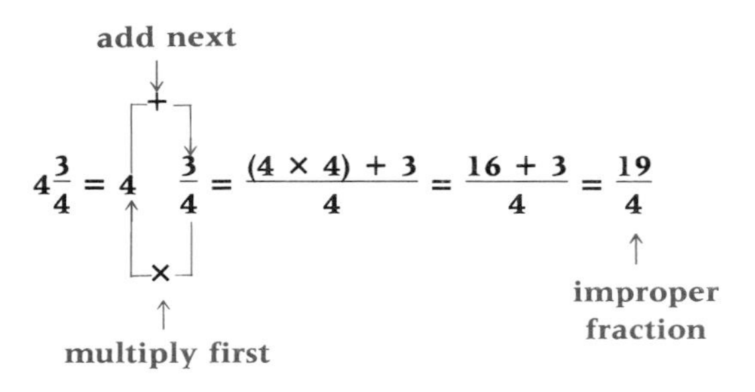

9 PERCENTS

9.1 Changing a Decimal to a Percent

To change a decimal to a percent, move the decimal point two places to the right and write a percent sign.

0.73 = ?%
0.73 → 0 . 7 3.

move decimal point 2 places right

0.73 = 73%

write percent sign

0.055 = ?%
0.055 → 0 . 0 5.5

move decimal point 2 places right

0.055 = 5.5%

write percent sign

9.2 Changing a Percent to a Decimal

To change a percent to a decimal, move the decimal point two places to the left and drop the percent sign.

11.75% → .1 1 . 7 5

move decimal point 2 places left and drop percent sign

11.75% = 0.1175

0.75% → .0 0 . 7 5

move decimal point 2 places left and drop percent sign

0.75% = 0.0075

9.3 Finding a Percentage of a Number

To find the percentage of a number, multiply the percent times the base.

percentage ↓ percent ↓ base ↓

What is 25% of $750?
25% of $750 = ?
0.25 × 750 = ?
0.25 × 750 = 187.50
25% of $750 = $187.50

percentage ↓ percent ↓ base ↓

What is $16\frac{3}{4}$**% of 800?**

$16\frac{3}{4}$**% of 800 = ?**
0.1675 × 800 = ?
0.1675 × 800 = 134
$16\frac{3}{4}$**% of 800 = 134**

9.4 Finding the Percent One Number Is of Another

To find the percent one number is of another, divide the percentage by the base.

percent ↓ base ↓ percentage ↓

What % of 10 is 2?

?% of 10 = 2

(Continued)

(Continued)

$$?\% = \frac{2}{10} \rightarrow 10\overline{)2.0}\;\; 0.2 \qquad .20. = 20\%$$

move decimal point 2 places right and write percent sign

20% of 10 is 2

10 METRIC MEASUREMENT

10.1 Metric Length

In the metric system of measurement, the common units of length are the millimeter, centimeter, meter, and the kilometer.

A millimeter (mm) is about equal to the thickness of a dime.
A centimeter (cm) is about equal to the width of a sugar cube.
A meter (m) is about equal to the length of a baseball bat.
A kilometer (km) is 1000 m and is used to measure long distances.

10.2 Metric Weight and Volume

The common units of weight and volume in the metric system are the gram, kilogram, metric ton, liter, and kiloliter.

A gram (g) is about the weight of a paper clip.
A kilogram (kg) is about the weight of a hammer.
A metric ton (t) is 1000 kg and is used to measure very heavy objects.
A liter (L) is about the same amount of liquid as in a can of motor oil.
A kiloliter (kL) is 1000 L and is used to measure large volumes.

APPENDIX D
REFERENCE SOURCES

As an office worker, you may be asked to supply information such as the population of a city, a specific word to express an idea, or a quotation to fit a special occasion. You can help your supervisor if you know where to look for such information. The reference room of your public library is a very valuable source of information. In addition, you should keep frequently used reference books in your office.

11 GRAMMAR, PUNCTUATION, AND STYLE

Every office reference shelf should contain a sampling of reference materials from each of the following categories.

11.1 Dictionaries

Dictionaries show the syllabication, part of speech, pronunciation, synonyms, and definition of words arranged in alphabetical order. The majority of dictionaries contain only the most commonly used words. A number of specialized dictionaries are available containing terminology for specific professions—legal, medical, and so forth.

The American Heritage Dictionary of the English Language. New College Edition. Boston: Houghton Mifflin Company, 1981.

Funk & Wagnalls Standard Desk Dictionary. Rev. ed. Scranton, PA: Funk & Wagnalls Co., distributed by Harper & Row Publishers, 1980, paper 1984.

Webster's Third New International Dictionary. Springfield, MA: Merriam-Webster Inc., 1981.

11.2 Spelling Guides

Spelling guides are lists of the most frequently used words arranged in alphabetical order. These guides show the correct spelling and syllabication in a convenient format.

Leslie, Louis A. *20,000 Words.* 7th ed. New York: Gregg Division, McGraw-Hill Book Company, 1977.

Silverthorn, J. E., and Perry, Devern J. *Word Division Manual.* 2nd ed. Cincinnati: South-Western Publishing Company, 1984.

The Word Book II. 2d ed. Boston: Houghton Mifflin Company, 1983.

11.3 Thesaurus

A thesaurus classifies words by ideas, showing words that have similar meanings. In a dictionary you start with a word and find the definition, whereas in a thesaurus you start with an idea and find the word to fit. Words are arranged alphabetically and words of a similar meaning are listed.

The Right Word. Rev. ed. Boston: Houghton Mifflin Company, 1983.

Roget, Peter M. *Roget's International Thesaurus.* 4th ed. Scranton, PA: Thomas Y. Crowell Company, distributed by Harper & Row Publishers, 1977.

11.4 Office Reference Handbooks

These reference manuals usually contain guides for correct punctuation, capitalization, expression of numbers, grammar, word division, spelling, typing techniques, and letter styles, as well as information relating to postal and telecommunication services. Special handbooks are available for medical, legal, and other professions.

Holmes, Ralph M. *The Reference Guide: A Handbook for Office Personnel.* Boston: Houghton Mifflin Company, 1980.

House, Clifford R., and Sigler, Kathy. *Reference Manual for Office Personnel.* 6th ed. Cincinnati: South-Western Publishing Company, 1981.

Whalen, Doris H. *Handbook of Business English.* New York: Harcourt Brace Jovanovich, Inc., 1980.

11.5 Style Books

A style book is very helpful when you are keyboarding reports and manuscripts. The correct format is shown for the various parts of the report, such as the table of contents, footnotes, and bibliography. If you keyboard reports and/or manuscripts, you should have a style manual so that the keyboarding format will be consistent.

Campbell, William, et al. *Form and Style: Theses, Reports, Term Papers.* 6th ed. Boston: Houghton Mifflin Company, 1981.

Keithley, Erwin M., and Schreiner, Philip J. *A Manual of Style for the Preparation of Papers and Reports.* 3rd ed. Cincinnati: South-Western Publishing Company, 1980.

12 GENERAL INFORMATION

In many offices, it is necessary to locate facts of a general nature to include in letters and reports. You may want to purchase some of the books listed here. They may be worthwhile additions to your professional library.

12.1 Atlases

Atlases contain maps of various countries. Some atlases also contain information about the climate and special features of the various regions shown in them.

Britannica Atlas. Chicago: Encyclopaedia Britannica, Inc. 1984.

Rand McNally Cosmopolitan World Atlases: New Census Edition. Chicago: Rand McNally & Company, 1981.

12.2 Almanacs

Almanacs are reference sources that are updated and published annually. They contain information and facts about important events, geography, history, politics, statistics, and sports.

Information Please Almanac. Atlas and Yearbook. Boston: Houghton Mifflin Company.

World Almanac and Book of Facts. New York: Newspaper Enterprise Association, Inc.

12.3 Biographical Publications

General information about notable individuals is included in biographical reference sources. The information generally includes personal background and information, education, profession, honors, and accomplishments. Some of these publications give information about individuals who are deceased; others contain information about living individuals. These publications are updated frequently, especially those listing living individuals.

Who's Who in America. Chicago: Marquis Who's Who, Inc. Annual.

Who's Who in Finance and Industry. Chicago: Marquis Who's Who, Inc. Annual.

12.4 Directories

Directories are used to locate the names and addresses of people, companies, products, or services. Many directories also include information about company officers and products.

City directories. These directories usually provide the names, addresses, and occupations of residents in the city.

Congressional Directory. Washington, DC: Superintendent of Documents, U.S. Government Printing Office. Annual. This directory lists the members of Congress and people in the executive branch of government.

Dun & Bradstreet Ratings and Reports. New York: Dun & Bradstreet, Inc. This publication lists credit ratings of firms.

Standard & Poor's Register of Directors and Executives. Annual. New York: Standard & Poor's Corp. This directory gives information about the executives of corporations in America and Canada.

12.5 Encyclopedias

Encyclopedias provide general information on many topics such as arts, sciences, technology, cities, countries, and so forth.

Encyclopedia Americana. 30 vols. New York: Grolier Educational Corporation, 1983.

The New Encyclopaedia Britannica. 15th ed. 32 vols. Chicago: Encyclopaedia Britannica, Inc. 1985.

12.6 Indexes

Indexes list the contents of books and articles that appear in periodicals. Items are usually listed alphabetically by subject and author. Information given includes the date of publication, source, and publisher.

Books in Print, U.S.A. New York: R.R. Bowker Company. Annual.

Reader's Guide to Periodical Literature, 1900 to date. New York: The H.W. Wilson Company.

12.7 Quotations

Dictionaries of quotations list familiar quotations by author or by subject of the quotation. You may be asked to help your employer by finding the author of a specific quotation to include in a speech or report.

Bartlett's Familiar Quotations. 15th ed. Boston: Little, Brown and Company, 1980.

International Encyclopedia of Quotations. Rev. ed. Garden City, New York: Doubleday & Company, Inc., 1978.

Stevenson, Burton E. *Home Book of Quotations: Classical and Modern.* 10th ed. New York: Dodd, Mead & Comapny, 1984.

12.8 Travel Information

It is easier to plan travel and make arrangements if you can refer to the following directories.

Hotel and Motel Red Book. Annual. New York: American Hotel Association Directory Corporation. This publication lists hotels and motels alphabetically by state and city. Information such as address, telephone number, room information, and rates is provided.

Official Airline Guide. Monthly. Oak Brook, IL: Official Airline Guides, Inc. Lists flight information for commercial airlines.

12.9 ZIP Code Information

Every office should have a copy of a current ZIP Code directory to ensure prompt handling and delivery of outgoing mail. This directory lists ZIP Codes by post office, street, town, city, and state.

National ZIP Code Directory. Annual. Washington, DC: Superintendent of Documents, U.S. Government Printing Office.

GLOSSARY

A

accession book an index to files arranged in numeric order (p. 422)
active files records that are frequently used (p. 353)
addressee the person to whom a letter is sent (p. 249)
advice another's opinion (p. 103)
agenda a list of items to be discussed at a meeting (p. 329)
alphabetic an A-to-Z arrangement of records (p. 349)
alphabetic card file a card file in which index cards are arranged in alphabetic order (p. 421)
alphabetic miscellaneous file a file in which records are stored alphabetically until five related records accumulate (p. 421)
alphabetize to arrange in A-to-Z order (p. 377)
alphanumeric keyboard an input device that contains both alphabet keys and number keys (p. 469)
AMS-Simplified format a letter style in which all letter parts begin at the left margin; a subject line is used, but the salutation and complimentary close are omitted (p. 257)
announcement a notice announcing a meeting or other event (p. 328)
application form a form that a job applicant completes when applying for a job (p. 594)
appointment calendar a calendar in which the workdays are divided into half-hour or 15-minute time periods (p. 126)
assets resources (p. 332)
attitude a person's outlook, disposition, or frame of mind (p. 30)
auditron a key for a photocopier that unlocks the controls and records the total number of copies made (p. 448)
automatic pagination an information processing function that divides a document into pages of a set number of lines (p. 322)

B

backing sheet a keyboarded cover for a legal document (p. 339)
Balance Sheet a record of a company's assets, liabilities, and owner's equity (p. 332)

Bank-By-Phone service a telephone service that permits banking to be done using a Touch-Tone telephone (p. 187)

bank statement the bank's record of checking account transactions for the month (p. 514)

baronial office stationery measuring 5½" by 8½" used for short messages (p. 280)

bibliography a listing of the sources used in preparing a report (p. 321)

bill of lading a legal contract between the shipper and the carrier (p. 526)

blank endorsement a check endorsement consisting of only the payee's signature (p. 512)

block format a letter style in which all letter parts begin at the left margin (p. 257)

body language nonverbal communication by means of speech patterns, posture, gestures, and facial expressions. (p. 50)

bond letter-quality paper with a dull, smooth finish (p. 281)

bulk mail mail sorted by ZIP Codes and put in bundles of at least 10 pieces each (p. 240)

C

cable a message in any language or code sent to a foreign country (p. 194)

calendaring a software function that allows storage of appointment calendars (p. 575)

Call Director a small desk-size telephone unit that permits up to 30 telephone lines to be answered from one location (p. 180)

caption a name, number, or short phrase on a file label, identifying the records stored in the folder (p. 361, 406)

career a series of jobs performed in pursuit of employment (p. 488)

career power the ability to direct your career toward a specific goal (p. 587)

cashier's check a bank's order to make payment out of bank funds (p. 545)

central processing unit the computer part containing the electronic circuits that allow processing to take place (p. 459)

centralized files records stored in a central company location (p. 350)

Centrex Telephone System a system that allows incoming calls to be answered at the extension dialed or at the switchboard (p. 181)

certified check a check guaranteed by a bank (p. 544)

channel the method used to send a message (p. 45)

checkbook register a form used to record the date, amount, and purpose of checks written and deposits made (p. 509)

chronological an arrangement of records by day, month, or year (p. 349)

chronological files records arranged in time sequence (p. 423)

COD (Collect on delivery) a mail service that allows the purchaser to pay the mail carrier the cost of merchandise when it is delivered (p. 211)

coding the process of underlining or highlighting the name used for filing a document (p. 407)

collator a copier device that arranges the pages of a multi-page document in order as copies are made (p. 437)

commission a percentage of money paid to a worker based on performance (p. 552)

common carrier a company that offers telecommunication services for a fee (p. 168)

communication the exchange of information through speech, writing, or signals (p. 45)

communication satellites a form of electronic mail that involves relaying keyboarded information by satellite to distant locations (p. 198)

compass point a word indicating direction such as *North* or *East* (p. 394)

compound geographic name a place name that includes a prefix such as *Los, San, New, Mt., St.* (p. 394)

confidence having a positive outlook about yourself and about your abilities (p. 587)

confidential information not meant to be repeated (p. 158)

constructive criticism criticism that is intended to improve behavior (p. 73)

continuation sheets plain stationery used for the second and additional pages of letters (p. 253)

continuous-form printer paper with horizontal perforations for easy separation (p. 483)

convenience copier a small, relatively inexpensive, and simple-to-operate copier used when fewer than ten copies are needed (p. 437)

copyright laws regulations that prohibit the copying of printed and other materials without written permission of the publisher (p. 448)

cost per copy the total cost of copying divided by the number of copies made (p. 444)

cross-reference sheet a form filed when a record may be requested by two captions (p. 363)

cut the width of a file folder tab, ranging from full width to one fifth width (p. 360)

cut-and-paste function an information processing function allowing an operator to move text from one place to another within a document without rekeyboarding (p. 322)

D

data base a collection of related data stored in the computer (p. 564)

Data-phone telephone equipment that links computers so stored information can be sent directly from one computer to another computer (p. 187)

data processing the handling and processing of numbers (p. 457)

decentralized files records stored in many locations throughout a company (p. 350)

decode to determine a message's meaning (p. 46)

deductions amounts subtracted from gross earnings (p. 551)

desk organizer a vertical or horizontal storage device with compartments for storing papers or other materials (p. 81)

dial-direct service (or station-to-station calls) telephone calls placed without operator assistance (p. 168)

dictation the process of giving material orally to another individual for transcription at a later time (p. 495)

direct deposit Electronic Funds Transfer that allows employees' net pay to be deposited directly to their checking account, eliminating the need for separate trips to the bank so that employees can personally cash their own paychecks (p. 557)

discretion using good judgment in speaking and acting (p. 36)

document cycle the five steps a document takes from origination to distribution, which include origination, production, storage, reproduction, and distribution (p. 458)

domestic mail mail sent within the United States, its territories, and its possessions; to military post offices; and to the United Nations (p. 207)

E

electronic files documents that are stored on magnetic media in computers (p. 576)

Electronic Funds Transfer System (EFTS) an electronic system through which bank customers can transfer their money (p. 517)

electronic mail a system that allows the electronic transfer of documents from one office to another (p. 197, 565)

employment test a test of the skills and knowledge required for a position (p. 603)

endnotes notes presented on a separate page at the end of a report that indicate the source of quotations, facts, or statistical material or provide additional informtion or details for the reader (p. 320)

endorsement the information that appears on the cover for a legal document (p. 339)

enlargement a feature on some photocopiers that increases, in varying degrees, the print size of the copy (p. 438)

essential records records that are classified as vital, important, or useful to the operation of the business or company (p. 352)

executive office stationery measuring 7¼″ by 10½″ used by executives for their personal and business letters (p. 280)

express mail a mail service that provides next-day delivery of letters, packages, or bundles if these items are received at the post office before 5:00 p.m. (p. 209)

F

facsimile equipment that can send and receive exact reproductions of pages (p. 198)
feedback the verbal or nonverbal response to a message (p. 46, 72)
file folders folded sheets of heavy paper used to hold, identify, and protect records (p. 359)
file sorters devices used to arrange records in filing order prior to filing (p. 369)
filing the arranging and storing of documents in an orderly manner so they can be found quickly and easily (p. 21, 349)
filing system a set of rules that determines how records will be organized (p. 349)
filing units the words, initials, or abbreviations that determine alphabetical filing order (p. 377)
financial statements summaries of accounting information (p. 331)
first-class mail mail, such as letters and post cards, weighing less than 12 ounces (p. 207)
first-class service the most expensive class of air travel that provides the best service (p. 138)
flexibility the ability to adapt to change (p. 18)
floppy disk a flexible plastic disk coated with magnetic material for storing information (p. 459)
follow-up letter a letter sent to the interviewer after the job interview (p. 604)
follow-up system a method of keeping track of records borrowed from a company's files (p. 412)
footnotes notes placed at the foot of a page (p. 320)
form letters standardized responses used to answer a variety of similar requests (p. 274)
form paragraphs/boilerplate copy standard paragraphs from which appropriate paragraphs can be arranged to create a unique letter (p. 274)
format the arrangement of letter parts according to accepted procedures (p. 256)
fourth-class mail (or parcel post) all mail that is not first-, second-, or third-class and that weighs 1 to 70 pounds (p. 207)
full endorsement a check endorsement consisting of the check writer's signature, the phrase *Pay to the Order of,* and the name of the payee (p. 513)
full-rate telegram a telegraphic message that is delivered by telephone within two hours (or by messenger within five hours) of its arrival at the Western Union office nearest the receiver (p. 192)

G

geographic filing a method by which records are stored according to the geographic locations (p. 417)
goodwill a feeling of friendliness (p. 115)
government office stationery measuring 8″ by 10½″ (p. 280)
graphs visual aids that replace numbers with lines, bars, or sections of circles (p. 317)
gratuity tax added to the cost of meals (p. 146)
gross pay the total amount of money earned (p. 551)
guides rigid pieces of cardboard that divide a file drawer into sections, serve as markers to help locate records quickly, and provide support for folders (p. 362)

H

hard copy the printed copy of keyboarded material (p. 459)
header and footer instructions an information processing function that prints standard information at the top or bottom of a page (p. 322)
high-speed copier a copier used when more than ten copies are needed (p. 437)
hold button (or key) a button, or key, on a telephone that is pressed to place a call on hold (p. 160, 180)

homonyms words pronounced exactly alike but with different meanings and with different spellings (p. 60)

horizontal placement the location of a letter on a page as determined by the position of the side margins (p. 256)

I

impact printers a type of printer that strikes the ribbon and then the paper (p. 469)

implementing carrying out a decision or choice (p. 104)

impression the image of or feeling about a person, place, or thing that is retained by the mind (p. 113)

inactive files records no longer used (p. 353)

incoming correspondence documents addressed to individuals in your company (p. 406)

indexing the arrangement of the parts of a name so that the name can be alphabetized (p. 377)

information words, data, voice, and graphics entered into a system for processing (p. 458)

information processing the process of using electronic equipment to handle and move information through a company (p. 457)

initiative the ability to begin or follow through with a task without being told to do so (p. 32)

inputting the first phase in information processing in which information is entered into a system for processing (p. 458)

integrate to bring together the components needed to handle and process information (p. 457)

integrated office system a system in which office functions and equipment are linked (p. 563)

integrated software a software package that combines functions, such as word processing and data processing, into one package (p. 563)

intelligent copiers copiers that combine the features of copiers, computers, word processing equipment, and typesetting equipment (p. 438)

INTELPOST (International Electronic Post) a method of transmitting documents by facsimile equipment and international satellite (p. 212)

interdependent the quality whereby the success of one department or employee is dependent on the success of others (p. 30)

interoffice correspondence correspondence sent from one employee to another employee in the same company (p. 406)

interoffice memorandums correspondence sent from one employee to another in the same company (p. 262)

interpersonal communication using communication skills to interact with others (p. 68)

interpersonal skill the ability to get along with others (p. 8)

interviewer the person who interviews a job applicant (p. 599)

intuition a subconcious feeling of what should be done or of what is right or wrong (p. 103)

inventory a company's stock of goods (p. 527)

invoice the bill that the supplier sends to the buyer (p. 525)

itinerary a list of travel plans for a business trip (p. 143)

J/K

job a series of tasks an employee performs according to his or her position (p. 488)

key line the combination of the longest item in each column and the spaces between columns in a table to be centered (p. 316)

Key Telephone System a telephone system that provides 6 to 18 telephone lines with a key for each line (p. 179)

kraft envelopes mailing envelopes made of strong, unbleached paper (p. 284)

L

labels gummed or adhesive-backed tags placed on file tabs on which captions are written to identify the folder (p. 361)

lateral files file cabinets in which file folders are arranged from side to side (p. 366)

legal office stationery measuring 8½″ by 13″ that is used for keyboarding legal documents or large charts (p. 280)

legal document a keyboarded or printed record, usually drawn up by a lawyer, that contains details agreed to by the individuals who sign it (p. 334)

letter format a report style containing standard letter parts, margins, and spacing (p. 297)

letter of application a letter in which a specific job is applied for and a request for an interview is made (p. 593)

liabilities debts owed by a business (p. 332)

listening the process of not only hearing but thinking about what is heard (p. 494)

Local Access and Transport Areas (LATAs) divisions of a telephone company's service area (p. 168)

local area network (LAN) a system that allows different types of electronic equipment to be linked so that users can share information (p. 563)

M

magnetic media cassettes, belts, and disks that are used to record and store information (p. 467)

mailgram a message transmitted by Western Union to a post office near the destination and then delivered with the regular mail (p. 194)

main memory the temporary storage device on electronic equipment for all keyboarded material (p. 459)

mainframes full-size computers (p. 470)

management information system (MIS) a plan for effective decision making (p. 479)

manuscript format a report style consisting of paragraphs with headings that divide the report into sections (p. 299)

memorandum format a report style that uses the same format, margins, and spacing as an interoffice memorandum (p. 298)

memory the part of electronic equipment that stores information (p. 470)

menu a list of tasks displayed on the VDT of a computer to guide the user with selection procedures (p. 473)

message form a printed form used to record information about telephone calls (p. 159)

microcomputers the smallest computers (p. 470)

micrographics a method of storing information in reduced form on film (p. 424)

microprocessor chip a tiny piece of silicon containing electrical circuits that carry out operating instructions (p. 468)

minicomputers computers that are generally smaller than a mainframe computer and larger than microcomputers (p. 470)

minutes the official record of what takes place at a meeting (p. 330)

miscellaneous folder a folder that is used for records when there are fewer than five documents related to a particular individual, company, or subject (p. 411)

mixed punctuation a punctuation style in which the salutation is followed by a colon and the complimentary close is followed by a comma (p. 252)

modified-block format a letter style in which the date, the complimentary close, and the signature and title lines always begin at the center of the paper (p. 257)

money order a type of check that is available from a post office, or a bank, that orders payment from the funds of the organization that issues it (p. 545)

move an information processing function allowing an operator to move text without rekeyboarding (p. 322)

N

net pay gross pay minus deductions (p. 551)

nonessential records documents that may provide useful information but are not of lasting interest to a company (p. 348)

nonimpact printers a type of printer that uses ink sprays or laser beams to create the characters (p. 469)

nonverbal communication through facial expressions and gestures (p. 45)

numeric an arrangement of records in 1-2-3 order (p. 349)

numeric filing a method of storing records in numerical order (p. 420)

O

OCR format the style in which the address on an envelope is keyboarded in capital letters without punctuation so it can be scanned by Optical Character Recognition equipment (p. 260)

office interrupters activities that disrupt the normal office schedule and waste time (p. 94)

office procedures manual a manual explaining the procedures and organization of a company and the general rules that affect all employees (p. 610)

office support workers workers who support or assist in the work done in all departments of a company (p. 7)

offset a printing process in which the print is transferred from the master to the mat and from the mat to the copy paper (p. 434)

open punctuation punctuation style in which no punctuation follows the salutation or the complimentary close (p. 252)

operator-assisted calls long distance calls that require an operator to complete (p. 169)

Optical Character Recognition (OCR) electronic equipment used by the post office for sorting and processing mail (p. 232)

orientation meeting a briefing for new employees on company policies and procudures, employee benefits, and other information of importance (p. 609)

originator the person who wrote a business letter (p. 254)

out forms forms used to identify and hold the place of records that have been removed from the files (p. 365)

outgoing correspondence documents written by individuals within your company and sent to other companies and individuals outside your company (p. 406)

outline a written plan that sets out material in the order in which it will be presented (p. 59, 295)

outputting the third phase of the information processing system in which the document is reproduced, and distributed (p. 459)

overnight telegram telegraphic message transmitted during the night and delivered by 2:00 p.m. the next day (p. 193)

owner's equity the amount of money invested in a business by its owners (p. 332)

P

payee the person to whom a check is written (p. 510)

payroll check voucher a stub on an employee's paycheck that lists gross earnings, deductions, and net pay (p. 556)

periodic inventory system a system in which workers take a physical count of stock (p. 528)

perpetual inventory system a system in which inventory workers keep an ongoing record of merchandise in stock (p. 527)

petty cash fund a fund of money that is kept on hand in many offices for small purchases that need to be made (p. 540)

petty cash voucher a form that contains the date, name, amount of money desired, reason for payment, and type of expense for a petty cash payment (p. 541)

photocopier reprographic equipment that makes copies directly from an original document (p. 436)

Picturephone meeting service a telephone service that provides visual as well as voice communication (p. 184)
planning setting out the details of activities to take advantage of the most efficient use of time (p. 90)
poise the ability to appear calm, composed, and confident even though the situation is tense (p. 32)
position the location of the tab on a file folder (p. 360)
positive words words that suggest good instead of bad (p. 62)
postage meter a machine that prints a postmark and the amount of postage selected on each piece of mail (p. 237)
predicting forecasting what will happen under given conditions (p. 104)
preferences one's choices (p. 125)
presort first-class mail volume mail of at least 500 pieces that is sorted and bundled by ZIP Code (p. 240)
priority mail any first-class mail weighing more than 12 ounces (p. 208)
Private Business Exchange (PBX) System a telephone system that allows incoming calls to be directed either to individual extensions or to the switchboard and outgoing calls to be dialed directly from any extension (p. 181)
procedures guidelines for the efficient and systematic completion of office tasks (p. 5)
process a series of actions or operations that leads to a result (p. 45)
processing the second phase of the information processing system during which the production and temporary storage of a document take place (p. 459)
professional business organizations groups established to promote professional growth of certain professions (p. 612)
professional certification recognition for passing an examination in a certain field (p. 613)
professional expertise the ability to be good at what you do (p. 587)
Profit and Loss Statement the financial statement that presents a company's income and expenses for a particular period (p. 332)
proofreader's symbols a kind of shorthand, with recognized meanings, used to mark changes or corrections in a rough draft (p. 274)
purchase order a form that lists the quantity, description, unit price, and total price of each item being purchased (p. 523)
purchase order register the record showing each order as it is received (p. 523)
purchase requisition a form used to request the purchase of an item (p. 522)

R

reading file a temporary record of all outgoing correspondence (p. 424)
reconcile the process of checking to determine whether the bank records agree with the checkbook register (p. 515)
records management the activities involved in organizing, storing, and protecting company records (p. 347)
reduction a feature on some high-speed copiers that decreases the print size of the copy that is being made (p. 437)
release mark a person's initials, a "file" stamp, a check mark, or other method of marking to indicate a doucment is ready to be filed (p. 406)
requisition form a form used to request a record or file (p. 364, 411)
restrictive endorsement a check endorsement consisting of the payee's name along with the purpose for which the check is to be used (p. 513)
résumé a document that summarizes your knowledge and skills in an easy-to-read format (p. 591)
retention schedule guidelines specifying how long each type of record should be kept and how to dispense of each (p. 352)
retrieve to find and remove a record from a file (p. 352)
role-playing practicing responses to questions that might be asked or situations that might occur during a job interview (p. 603)
routing slips slips attached to documents indicating names or departments to which the documents should be sent (p. 221)

S

salary a weekly or a monthly amount given for a certain number of hours worked (p. 550)

screen (or screening) the process of determining the purpose and importance of office visitors, incoming telephone calls, and incoming mail (p. 115, 157, 224)

second-class mail mail such as newspapers, magazines, and other regularly published periodicals (p. 207)

self-inventory an evaluation of your knowledge, skills, and abilities (p. 588)

selling ability the ability to sell your knowledge and skills to others (p. 588)

sentence outline a written plan in which material is presented in complete sentences (p. 296)

setting priorities deciding which of several tasks you should complete first (p. 31)

setting work priorities evaluating duties and responsibilities to determine which tasks should be done first (p. 90)

signature card a form that gives a bank approval to cash checks that are signed by any person whose name and signature is on the card (p. 507)

soft copy the keyboarded material that is shown on a (VDT) (p. 459)

software programs that spell out what has to be done and in what order (p. 460)

Speakerphone telephone equipment that allows you to talk and listen to telephone conversations without picking up the receiver (p. 182)

special delivery special handling at the destination post office to ensure prompt delivery, even on Sundays and holidays (p. 211)

special services register a register in which receipt of incoming mail requiring special handling, such as certified mail or special delivery mail, is recorded (p. 222)

standardized procedures established guidelines that are followed by everyone who works for a particular business (p. 480)

station-to-station calls (or dial-direct service) telephone calls for which charges begin as soon as the telephone is answered (p. 168)

stationery separator a device that provides for the storage of several types of stationery in the same drawer (p. 83)

stock requisition a form that tells warehouse workers what goods to remove from inventory (p. 524)

stop-payment request a request that the bank not process a check after it has been written and submitted as payment (p. 510)

subject filing a method of storing records in alphabetical order by subject matter rather than by individual or company name (p. 418)

switchboard operator an employee who answers all incoming calls at a central switchboard (p. 181)

synonyms words are similar in meaning (p. 60)

T

tact the ability to do or say the appropriate thing at the appropriate time (p. 116)

terminal digit filing a variation of numeric filing where the numbers are read in pairs and the pairs are read in reverse order (p. 423)

text editor a typewriter that can store information as it is keyboarded (p. 198)

The Five C's the qualities of effective business writing: completeness, clarity, correctness, conciseness, and courtesy (p. 59)

third-class mail mail such as circulars, books, or catalogues weighing less than 16 ounces (p. 207)

tickler file a chronological file in which future references are kept (p. 424)

topic outline a written plan in which a word or short phrase identifies the content to be presented (p. 296)

Touch-Tone telephone a telephone with twelve buttons instead of a rotary dial (p. 179)

tourist-class service an economical class of air travel service that does not provide the special features available in first-class service (p. 138)

transcription the process of keyboarding documents from dictated material (p. 494)

transposition error the accidental reversing of written or keyboarded numbers (p. 334)
travel agency business that arranges transportation and accommodations for travelers (p. 138)
travel authorization form a form that an employee submits for reimbursement when a personal car is used for business purposes (p. 141)
traveler's check a special payment device, available in various denominations, designed for people who travel (p. 545)
turnaround time the time required to prepare copies (p. 446)
TWX and Telex teletypewriter exchange services offered by Western Union (p. 197)

V

variable an element such as a name or an invoice number that varies from one form letter to the next (p. 274)
verbal written or spoken communication (p. 45)
vertical files standard file cabinets in which file folders are stored on the scored edges and arranged from front to back in long drawers (p. 366)
vertical placement the location of a letter on a page as determined by the letter's length (p. 256)
visualize the process of forming a mental picture of your telephone listener so you can relate what you are saying to the listener's point of view (p. 156)
vital records all of those documents that are so important to a company that a company absolutely cannot operate without having them on file (p. 348)

W

WATS line (Wide Area Telecommunications Service) a special telephone service that permits long-distance calling within a selected area for a set monthly rate (p. 173)
word processing the handling and processing of words and sentences (p. 457)
work requisition form A form used to request work be done (p. 482)

INDEX

D

E

F

G

H

I

J

K

L

M

P

Q

R

S

T

U

V

W

Y

Z

Art and Photo Credits

Design by Vanessa Piñero.

Logo for Office Simulations and Applying Office Skills sections by Graphics Etcetera.

All technical art by ANCO/Boston, Inc.

Charts by David Hannum, pages: 7, 45, 101, 487, 458, 479, 488, 563, 587, 611.

Line drawings by George Ulrich, pages: 80, 81, 123, 208, 219, 236, 237, 241, 283, 433, 499, 590.

Photos by Mike Malyszko, pages: 22, 33, 61, 68, 70, 111, 162, 180, 196, 197, 221, 224, 281, 284, 360, 366, 368, 382, 432.

Photos by Mark Lennihan, pages: 3, 43, 79, 93, 145, 183, 205, 280, 281, 349, 431, 435, 468, 486, 575, 576.

i Bill Gallery/Stock, Boston
i Steve Stone/The Picture Cube
i Werner Keidel/The Stock Shop
i Milton and Joan Mann/Marylin Gartman Agency
iii Chuck Keeler, Jr./After-Image
iii Frank Siteman/Marylin Gartman Agency
iv Michael Philip Manhiem/Marylin Gartman Agency
v Dario Perla/After-Image
1 Hewlett Packard, Inc.
4 Ellis Herwig/Stock, Boston
5 Haworth, Inc.
6 Michael Heron/Woodfin Camp & Associates
17 Robert Schoen
18 Liquid Paper Company
21 Hewlett Packard, Inc.
23 Rhoda Sidney/Monkmeyer Press Photo Service
31 Charles Gupton/Stock, Boston
42 Leane Enkellis/Stock, Boston
47 Bohdan Hrynewych
49 Dictaphone Corporation
58 Christopher Morrow/Stock, Boston
71 Christopher Morrow/Stock, Boston
74 Milton and Joan Mann/Marylin Gartman Agency
84 I.B.M.
102 Freda Leinwand/Monkmeyer Press Photo Service
110 Haworth Inc.
113 Ellis Herwig/Stock, Boston
114 Frank Fisher/After-Image
116 A. T. &T.
153 Lawrence Migdale
155 Bell Laboratories
169 D. Aronson/Stock, Boston
180 Siemens
181 Pat Berrett
185 Richard Sobol/Stock, Boston
186 A. T. &T.
238 Pitney Bowes
240 Hewlett Packard, Inc.
247 Bohdan Hrynewych/Stock, Boston
291 D. Aronson/Stock, Boston
343 Elizabeth Hamlin/Stock, Boston
390 John McGrail
455 Lawrence Migdale
461 Robert Schoen
466 Houghton Mifflin Company
469 Robert Schoen
471 Honeywell, Inc.
472 Dest Corporation
497 Gill Garner/After-Image
504 Dan McCoy/Rainbow
505 Bohdan Hrynewych/Stock, Boston
561 Russell Lappa
566 Russell Lappa
568 Hewlett Packard, Inc.
577 Christopher Morrow/Stock, Boston
585 Michael Kagan/Monkmeyer Press Photo Service
609 Ellis Herwig/The Picture Cube
612 Margarite Bradly/Positive Images

Two-Letter Abbreviations

U.S. State, District, Possession, or Territory	Two-letter Abbreviation
Alabama	AL
Alaska	AK
Arizona	AZ
Arkansas	AR
California	CA
Canal Zone	CZ
Colorado	CO
Connecticut	CT
Delaware	DE
District of Columbia	DC
Florida	FL
Georgia	GA
Guam	GU
Hawaii	HI
Idaho	ID
Illinois	IL
Indiana	IN
Iowa	IA
Kansas	KS
Kentucky	KY
Louisiana	LA
Maine	ME
Maryland	MD
Massachusetts	MA
Michigan	MI
Minnesota	MN
Mississippi	MS
Missouri	MO
Montana	MT
Nebraska	NE
Nevada	NV
New Hampshire	NH
New Jersey	NJ
New Mexico	NM
New York	NY
North Carolina	NC
North Dakota	ND
Ohio	OH
Oklahoma	OK
Oregon	OR
Pennsylvania	PA
Puerto Rico	PR
Rhode Island	RI
South Carolina	SC
South Dakota	SD
Tennessee	TN
Texas	TX
Utah	UT
Vermont	VT
Virgin Islands	VI
Virginia	VA
Washington	WA
West Virginia	WV
Wisconsin	WI
Wyoming	WY

Canadian Province	Two-letter Abbreviation
Alberta	AB
British Columbia	BC
Labrador	LB
Manitoba	MB
New Brunswick	NB
Newfoundland	NF
Northwest Territories	NT
Nova Scotia	NS
Ontario	ON
Prince Edward Island	PE
Quebec	PQ
Saskatchewan	SK
Yukon Territory	YT